T0323567

"This is a first-rate book on how to understand China's new 'Foreign Investment Law.' In this volume, Professor Shen reassesses a collection of key issues that shape China's complex regime on foreign investment, such as the major changes in Foreign Investment Law 2019, the rise of negative list, national security review, and the interactions between domestic and international rules. The analysis is comprehensive and thoughtful which makes this book a most valuable and important contribution to foreign investment literature."

Julien Chaisse, *Professor of Law, City University of Hong Kong and President, Asia Pacific FDI Network, Twitter: @jchaisse*

"China has presented excellent opportunities for investment in recent decades and appears poised to continue this trend. However, language barriers, misinformation and political polemic can obscure judgement about investing in China. This authoritative new book by Professor Shen offers very welcome insight and clarity in this difficult context. I am confident that Professor Shen's study of China's foreign investment law will both guide the uninitiated and enlighten China specialists for years to come."

David Donald, *Professor Emeritus of Law, Chinese University of Hong Kong*

"This book provides a timely and comprehensive analysis of China's new Foreign Investment Law of 2019, examining a variety of relevant issues, such as negative list, unreliable entity list, intellectual property protection, bilateral investment treaties and national security review. It should be compulsory reading for anyone interested in the development and regulation of foreign investment in China."

Robin Hui Huang, *Professor of Law, Chinese University of Hong Kong*

"In this timely book, Professor Shen makes an essential contribution to our understanding of China's foreign investment law landscape. Professor Shen situates China's 'new' investment reforms in their proper historical context, and carefully distinguishes substantive novelty from rebranded continuity. In clear and analytical language, Professor Shen thoughtfully dissects key elements of China's foreign investment law framework, making this book a treasure-laden resource for academics and practitioners involved in navigating the Chinese investment regime."

Mark McLaughlin, *Global Visiting Assistant Professor, Singapore Management University*

"As an integral component of China's opening-up and economic reforms, its foreign investment regime has undergone waves of remarkable changes. Professor Shen's book provides not only a comprehensive review of the regime's evolution but also sophisticated analysis of some of its most important elements which are under-studied and not widely understood. This book further offers detailed discussions of China's latest regulatory developments in response to mounting challenges posed by foreign sanctions, which have considerable and far-reaching implications for the future development of China's foreign investment regime. Faced with the pressing need to stabilize and enhance the international economic legal order, this book provides a timely and valuable source for academics, policymakers, practitioners, and other stakeholders."

Associate Professor Weihuan Zhou, *Member of the Herbert Smith Freehills China International Business and Economic Law (CIBEL) Centre, Faculty of Law & Justice, UNSW Sydney*

CHINA'S FOREIGN INVESTMENT LAW IN THE NEW NORMAL

This book analyzes China's new foreign investment law which came into force in January 2020. The new law implemented sweeping changes and overhauled China's foreign investment law regime of the last four decades. The foreign investment law aims to make the business environment more investor-friendly and address some of the contentious issues between US and China in the ongoing trade war.

The book explains how the law enhances regulatory transparency. It also outlines the new approval process, that is the pre-establishment negative list system which has replaced the former approval system for foreign investment projects. The book also analyzes China's series of anti-sanction laws.

This book will help give readers a better understanding of major changes and benefits under the new law and will be the first of its kind looking at the implications of this important law.

Shen Wei is the KoGuan Distinguished Professor of Law at Shanghai Jiao Tong University Law School. He is also the Global Professor of Law at New York University School of Law and L. Bates Lea Visiting Professor of Law at Michigan Law School.

CHINA'S FOREIGN INVESTMENT LAW IN THE NEW NORMAL

Framing the Trajectory and Dynamics

Shen Wei

With contributions by Dr. Zhang Beibei

LONDON AND NEW YORK

Designed cover image: @Getty Images

First published 2023
by Routledge
4 Park Square, Milton Park, Abingdon, Oxon OX14 4RN

and by Routledge
605 Third Avenue, New York, NY 10158

Routledge is an imprint of the Taylor & Francis Group, an informa business

British Library Cataloguing-in-Publication Data
A catalogue record for this book is available from the British Library

ISBN: 978-0-367-67256-0 (hbk)
ISBN: 978-0-367-67257-7 (pbk)
ISBN: 978-1-003-13049-9 (ebk)

DOI: 10.4324/9781003130499

Typeset in Bembo
by Apex CoVantage, LLC

In deep memory of my parents
Shen Guanqun and *Qian Meifang*

CONTENTS

ACKNOWLEDGEMENTS

I planned to write a short book in 2019 about the newly passed Foreign Investment Law, which was a natural follow-up after I started to look into the ongoing US–China trade war. When I started writing the book, there were more new developments and China passed several anti-sanction regulations and laws in response to the escalated trade war. This added a new layer to the Foreign Investment Law. Then the writing got harder than planned. Fortunately, I had grateful help from Dr Zhang Beibei who generously crafted the chapters on the blocking statutes and anti-sanction law and allowed me to use our co-authored non-performing loan article, Dr Li Xingxing who gave me the chance to expand her article on security review with updated materials, and Dr Carrie Shu Shang who agreed our co-authored article on US–China IP bilateralism to be included. This book will not be possible without their generosity and contribution.

I owe great debt to Justice Anselmo Reyes who was kind to read the monograph and write the foreword, which clearly outlined the key theme of the book.

I greatly benefited from many fruitful discussions and exchanges about various topics and issues covered in this book with – in alphabetical order – Douglas W. Arner, Emilios Avgouleas, Robert P. Bartlett III, Omri Ben-shahar, Sir William Blair, Ross P. Buckley, Congyan Cai, Julien Chaisse, Yun-chien Chang, Lei Chen, Li Chen, Weitseng Chen, Iris H.Y. Chiu, Jacques deLisle, David Donald, Ming Du, Hualing Fu, Tom Ginsburg, Say Goo, Andrew Gorwin, Mitu Gulati, Li Guo, Paul H. Haagen, M. Todd Henderson, Nicholas C. Howson, Robin Hui Huang, Gloria Xin Jin, Qingjiang Kong, Rainer Kulms, Saul Levmore, Yuwen Li, Chien-chung Lin, Feng Lin, Ulla Liukkunen, Dora Neo, Matti Nojonen, Michael Palmer, Yue Peng, Eric Posner, Adam Prichard, Tong Qi, Albert Romano, Roberta Romano, Steven Schwarz, Wenhua Shan, Carrie Shu Shang, Zen Shishido, Mathias Siems, Thomas Stanton, Robert Chang-hsien Tsai, Dicky Tsang, Frank Upham, Matthias Vanhullebusch, Jiangyu Wang, Wen

Yeu Wang, Casey Watters, Samuel Wong, Chao Xi, Qingkun Xu, Dali Yang, Simon Young, Kenny Yu, Tao Yu, Sheng Zhang, Wei Zhang, and Yun Zhao.

I warmly thank all the colleagues at Routledge including Cynthia Harasty for her professional editing input. Five autonomous reviewers gave very constructive comments on the book proposal, and later they all agreed to write endorsements for the book, showing their great support.

This book also benefits from a grant from China's Naitonal Social Sciences Foundation (Major Project: 21&ZD208).

Above all, I am most grateful to my parents for their unconditional support and love throughout my life. My lovely daughter Yixi brings great joy (and challenges) to me. My wife Jin Xin supports my efforts and time on writing and research though she may not support all my decisions. My parents-in-law often offer their kind support while I am occupied by other tasks. This book is dedicated to them.

ABBREVIATIONS

AMC	asset management company
ASEAN	Association of Southeast Asian Nations
AUD	Australian dollar, the lawful currency of Australia
BIT	bilateral investment treaty
BRI	Belt and Road Initiative
CCP	Chinese Communist Party
CFIUS	the Committee on Foreign Investment in the United States
CJV	contractual joint venture (or cooperative joint venture)
CSM	complaint and settlement mechanism
EJV	equity joint venture
FDI	foreign direct investment
FET	fair and equitable treatment
FIE	foreign-invested enterprise
FTA	free trade agreement
FTT	forced technology transfer
IIA	international investment agreement
IPR	intellectual property rights
ISA	investor-state arbitration
ISDS	investor-state dispute settlement
LLC	limited liability company
M&A	merger and acquisition
MFN	most favoured nation
MNC	multinational corporation
MOFCOM	Ministry of Commerce (previously the Ministry of Foreign Trade and Economic Cooperation)
NDRC	National Development and Reform Commission
NPC	National People's Congress of China

NPL	non-performing loan
OBOR	One Belt One Road Initiative
OFDI	outward foreign direct investment
PRC	People's Republic of China or China, for the purpose of this book, excluding the Special Administrative Region of Hong Kong, the Special Administrative Region of Macau, and the territory of Taiwan
RMB	the lawful currency of China (renminbi or yuan)
SAFE	State Administration of Foreign Exchange
SAMR	State Administration for Market Regulation (the successor of the State Administration of Industry and Commerce, SAIC)
SOE	state-owned enterprise
SPV	special purpose vehicle
TTIP	EU–US Transatlantic Trade and Investment Partnership
TIPs	treaties with investment provisions
TIT	trilateral investment treaty
TPP	Trans-Pacific Partnership, now CPTPP
US$	US dollar, the lawful currency of the United States of America
USMCA	United States–Mexico–Canada Agreement
VCLT	Vienna Convention on the Law of Treaties
VIE	variable interest entity
WFOE	wholly foreign-owned enterprise

ILLUSTRATIONS

Figures

Tables

FOREWORD

At the heart of this book is a paradox which Professor Shen Wei identifies early on in his riveting narrative. That is the "uneasy tension" between the Chinese government's espousal of a "corporatist state" approach to the economy and the acknowledgement that sustained growth and the retention of political power also calls for "reformist efforts not only to modernize [the] national economy but also to upgrade its law, legal infrastructure, and legal system." For Professor Shen, this paradox is the key to China's phenomenal economic growth from the late 20th century onwards. Thus, modern China's economic history can be characterized as a series of initiatives seeking, on a trial-and-error basis, to reconcile the imperative of state control with the need for free market measures. An initiative is adjudged successful insofar as it leads to an increase of foreign investment and thereby fuels China's transformation into a regional and global power.

It would be wrong, however, to think that this book is a mere historical retrospective. Having covered the chronology of China's economic growth in his first chapter and introduced China's Foreign Investment Law 2019 in his second chapter, Professor Shen takes a deep dive into the challenges facing China today in the wake of the COVID-19 pandemic and increasingly anti-globalist sentiments. In lucid and clinical fashion, Professor Shen dissects China's approaches to intellectual property (IP) protection, the non-performing loans market, the regulation of telecommunications, the negotiation of bilateral investment treaties (BITs), national security issues, US trade sanctions, and recent counter-sanction legislation. While noting the strengths of specific measures, Professor Shen does not hold back from criticizing weaknesses and suggesting how initiatives might be modified to tackle the "new normal" in which the whole world currently finds itself. An interesting sub-theme is Professor Shen's comparison of the difficulties facing foreign investors in China with those facing Chinese investors abroad. The challenges which would-be investors in Belt and Road countries must overcome mirror the hurdles currently faced by foreign investors in China. Ironically, to the extent that they have been cushioned by the state-controlled regime at home, Chinese investors have found themselves ill-prepared to respond effectively to competition in foreign markets.

In a final chapter, Professor Shen pulls together the many threads explored in his individual chapters. He reflects on how the paradox that he has spotlighted is likely to play out in years to come. He foreshadows an inevitable clash between the two mindsets that have emerged out of the still ongoing US–China trade war. While foreign investors are demanding greater liberalization of the economy, China is embarking on a policy of greater state control with the objective of developing self-sufficiency in technological and other strategic sectors. The reader must decide for oneself whether Professor Shen's tentative prognosis is an optimistic or gloomy one, or possibly something in between.

Enough has been said to indicate that this is not just an ambitious book. It is an important one. It is required reading for anyone wishing to get up to speed on what has been, is, and will likely be happening to foreign investment in China. I have learned much from it, and I commend it to all.

Anselmo Reyes
Kyoto
1 July 2022

1

WHEN FOREIGN INVESTMENT MEETS CHINA

Legal Development and Legal Landscape (1978–2018)

1. Introduction

1.1 Foreign Investment Law in China – History and Background

The history of foreign investment into the People's Republic of China (the "PRC" or "China")[1] is brief indeed. The PRC's first three decades witnessed the "self-reliance" policy, a forced choice due to the expedient birth of China and its isolation from both the United States and the Soviet Union. The failure of the "self-reliance" policy in Maoist China, an alternative to the capitalist and Stalinist approaches to economic growth,[2] triggered the dramatic or logical change to the "open door" policy in 1978, which demonstrated the Chinese leadership's recognition of the importance of foreign investment in pursuit of economic growth and its commitment to a more pragmatic, other than a pure independent or isolated, path towards development. Starting from 1978, China began transforming its economic and political structures with the goal of promoting international trade and utilizing foreign investments.[3]

A major impetus for economic reform was the urgent need to improve living standards.[4] The switch from the "self-reliance" policy to "open door" policy has not been smooth largely because of the sharp contrast between dependency and neoclassical approaches to economic development and their ideological and philosophical foundations.[5] The "open door" policy together with the economic reform signalled China's determination to utilize market mechanisms and foreign resources to accelerate the modernization and growth of the economy. This uneasy move has been evidenced by the tension between encouraging foreign investment to achieve favourable economic outcomes and maintaining state control over foreign business activities, which in turn influenced the structure and implementation of foreign investment law and policy in the PRC. Albeit the heavy criticism by

DOI: 10.4324/9781003130499-1

critical theorists of law and development, the course of China's economic development and modernization entails ongoing tensions among the state, law, and foreign investment and domestic commercial elites, a combination of state control and rampant free market capitalism.[6]

Of all the legal institutions that were rebuilt or created in the past four decades, those related to foreign investment have developed the fastest. The urgency of attracting foreign investment and satisfying foreign investors' needs to have their investments well protected triggered the tremendous effort to create and grow a foreign investment regime. Against this background, it is not surprising to see the first piece of legislation enacted right after the adoption of the "opening door" policy was the law on joint ventures in 1979.[7] This piece of law was intended to encourage foreign participation in China's modernization programme. Other primary legislation and secondary implementation regulations in subsequent years allowed foreign companies to set up representative offices,[8] wholly foreign-owned enterprises (WFOEs),[9] and contractual joint ventures[10] in China. The fourth Constitution revised in 1982 contains a critical provision offering the promise to protect "the lawful rights and interests of foreign investors."[11] These laws represented a break with both the rhetoric and the practices of China's first 30 years when China often condemned foreign investment as expropriation of developing countries. A large body of laws centring on the encouragement and protection of foreign investments were promulgated later on. Tax rules, foreign exchange controls, customs regulations, and intellectual property laws were drafted and promulgated. Nonetheless, the foreign investment policy at the early stage was primitive and inconsistent, moving between two extremes of openness to restriction. A widespread lack of uniformity, consistency, and self-contradiction occasionally endangered the foreign investment community's confidence on China. Although the legal institutions and infrastructure rebuilt after the Cultural Revolution cannot fulfil their supposed role, function, and goal of defining and helping to vindicate legal rights, they have already contributed considerably to the economic and societal development in the past four decades.

A unique Chinese characteristic or regulatory ethic of the foreign investment law regime in China is the centrality of the state's role as the primary agent for economic and social development. The fundamental role of the state in Chinese society and economy is articulated in the PRC Constitution 1982.[12] The subsequent amendments to the Constitution in 1993, while replacing the state planned economy with a socialist market economy, did not dilute the state-centric function in the economic development. The state's critical role for development appeared to be positive and constructive in the East Asia economies,[13] with the state playing multifaceted functions ranging from being the catalyst for development,[14] the force transforming national industrial structures[15] to mediating relations between foreign capital and local entrepreneurship.[16] Notwithstanding its sharp contrast with critical approaches in most Western nations that tend to view the state as the source of problems, inefficiencies, and dysfunctions, the state-centric model of economic growth and development well explains the key features of the foreign investment law regime in China that pursue policies of import substitution, export-led growth, technology transfer, and other development strategies such as encouraging foreign investment into infrastructure, high-tech, and environment friendly sectors and channelling foreign investment towards the achievement of long-term social development goals. The state-centric theme of China's economic development, or more specifically, its foreign investment regime also well explains the success of the labour-intensive and export-oriented industries during the past four decades.

While the theories of dependency may be flawed in overlooking local political and policy causes for underdevelopment,[17] they have offered useful approaches to understanding the relationship between the state and foreign capital in developing economies.[18] The dependency perspectives are able to reveal the partnering relationship between the state and foreign investment in that the state acts as a corporatist ally of foreign capital by offering policy, economic, and tax incentives to foreign investors whereas the foreign investors provide capitals, managerial skills, and technologies to the host state which facilitates substituting short-term parochial goals for the long-term development priorities of building the infrastructural and technological foundations for long-term economic growth.[19]

Unlike some jurisdictions where the so-called corporatist states used formalistic and authoritarian legal systems to retain power,[20] the Chinese government has been making reformist efforts not only to modernize its national economy but also to upgrade its law, legal infrastructure, and legal system. One line of critique of law and development claimed that liberal economic policies may be the source of underdevelopment.[21] This fortunately is not the case in China where liberal economic policies effectively limit or reduce state involvement and intervention in economic and commercial activities aimed at developing a free market system supported by private law rules and institutions. Nonetheless, neither the "open door" policy nor the liberal economic policies truly undermine the state's regulation of foreign investment albeit the inhibitive effect on the state's control given the transnational character of foreign business. Different from the critical studies perspectives and dependency theories,[22] the use and growth of the liberal private law system in China does not seem to contribute to weakening the state's capacity to control economic activities, which evolves into a development model opposite to the US free market model. The multilayers of China's economic success remind us of the difficulty and complexity in understanding and justifying China's development efforts, strategy, and model (if any). In this sense, the foreign investment regime in the PRC demonstrates both prospects and dilemmas, which are complexly and paradoxically related to the state.[23]

The growth and overall trend in foreign investment in China is positive. The first decade starting from 1979 witnessed an uneven but steady growth. In the first half of the period, an annual average of foreign investment was over US$2 billion. The figure jumped to US$6.3 billion in 1985. There was a decline in 1989 and 1990 due to the Tiananmen accident. The volume of foreign investment soon resumed and was nearly US$12 billion for 1991.[24] It climbed up very quickly and the contracted foreign investment reached US$57.2 billion and US$122.7 billion in 1992[25] and 1993[26] respectively.[27] Foreign direct investment (FDI) declined again in 1997–1999 largely due to the Asian financial crisis. FDI inflows increased in the new millennium: the utilized FDI amounts were US$40.72 billion, US$46.88 billion, and US$52.74 billion in 2000, 2001, and 2002 respectively. FDI inflows were in the explosive growth after China's accession to the WTO and the utilized amounts reached US$53.51 billion, US$60.63 billion, US$60.33 billion, US$69.47 billion, and US$82.66 billion in 2003, 2004, 2005, 2006, and 2007 respectively.[28] FDI to China was US$92.4 billion in 2008, an increase of 23.6% from 2007.[29] These statistics indicated that China became an attractive target for foreign capital in the past three decades. The foreign investment projects played a constructive and positive role in China's economic development: the foreign-invested enterprises (FIEs) accounted for 52% of China's total exports in 2002 and 57% in 2007.[30] The surge of FDI has made China the world's largest capital-importing country.[31] FIEs represented 16% of the total economy and 48% of exports.[32] China's limitless consumer market, impressive production capacity, and rich natural resources make it an indispensable market for multinational companies and foreign investors.

1.2 Government's Policy Towards Foreign Investment: A Chronological Review

The foreign investment regime in China has evolved significantly since its inception immediately after the adoption of the "open door" policy in 1978.[33] Policy plays a very critically important role in this regime. Unlike other jurisdictions, policy in China not only affects the content and application of laws but also the day-to-day life of individuals and corporates. Another feature of policy in China is its constant (and somehow unpredictable) change. The underlying rationale of these features is that policy as well as law are regarded and used as an instrument to accomplish long- or short-term objectives and reflect the ideology of the Chinese Communist Party (CCP) in ruling the country. The Chinese government repeatedly stressed the importance of attracting foreign investment into China and the necessity to change orientation from self-reliance and economic restrictiveness to economic openness. However, during the economic opening process, the way of attracting and using foreign investment has always been a hot issue in the policy-making process. Gradually, the government becomes more concerned with guiding investment flows and influencing foreign investment projects to match the state economic or developmental needs.

1.2.1 First Ten Years: 1978–1988

From 1978 to 1988, the overall objective was to attract foreign investment while limiting the scale and scope of foreign investment. The Chinese government made a great effort to establish legal and institutional infrastructure to welcome foreign investment. To this end, it enacted the Regulations on Encouraging Foreign Investment in 1986 which created a favourable environment to foreign investment and established special economic zones and coastal economic opening regions where more preferential and flexible economic and legal policies were offered to attract foreign investment. The first government organ, the Ministry of Foreign Trade and Economic Cooperation (MOFTEC), was formed within the government structure with the specifically designated duties to approve and supervise foreign-invested projects. Subsequently, an approval hierarchy was established to facilitate the approval of joint ventures. The first piece of legislation governing foreign investment was the PRC Equity Joint Venture Law in 1979,[34] which was no more than a statement of general principles governing equity joint ventures (EJVs). Later on implementing rules were passed to provide additional detail to the general law.[35] The government gradually approved other forms of foreign investment including contractual (or cooperative) joint ventures, and WFOEs. Basic laws were also enacted on contract,[36] taxation,[37] foreign exchange,[38] employment,[39] and others. As a result, the foreign exchange system was reformed very early and, consequently, the dual currency system was eliminated.[40]

During this period, the Chinese government sent a strong signal to foreign investors indicating its strong willingness to attract foreign investment. It renewed attention to induce foreign investment by offering more regulation and tax incentive packages. Although some initial progresses were made during this period, policy inefficiencies and shortcomings were also obvious. In particular, the Chinese government imposed controls and restrictions over foreign investment and tried to separate foreign investment from the local economy.[41] The overall policy over foreign investment was still very restrictive. As a result, greenfield foreign invested projects were less significant compared to foreign loans. For instance from 1979 to 1982, 85.82% of foreign capital was raised in the form of foreign loans, and in 1985 foreign loans accounted for 57.84% of the total amount of actually utilized foreign capital.[42] Overall, the first few years after the adoption of the "open door" policy witnessed a growing enthusiasm of the foreign investment community.

1.2.2 Second Ten Years: 1989–1999

The decade of 1990s was a complicated period in terms of the Chinese policies towards foreign investment. China's "open door" policy towards foreign investment has shifted back and forth in the spectrum from the extreme of restriction to the extreme of openness[43] largely due to the Tiananmen accident in 1989. The State Council's effort in the first decade to boost the foreign investment was soon doomed by the Tiananmen accident and the subsequent economic downturn. The domestic politics became a source of influence: the government and CCP feared corruption from abroad which may erode the CCP's ruling in China. The retrenchment policies caused the disappointment of foreign investors.[44] Deng Xiaoping's southern tour in 1992 played a critical driving role engineering China to a socialist market economy. While the foreign business community resumed optimism thereafter, they also experienced frustration due to the lack of the functioning legal system and judiciary, and a multitude of practical obstacles.[45]

The entire 1990s witnessed differential liberalization dominance as well as a departure from the conventional state planning system of the old days to a more market-oriented macroeconomic regulation and control.[46] The conceptual approach drove the Chinese government to rely on industrial policies in regulating and directing foreign investment. The then State Planning Commission issued the Foreign Investment Industrial Guidance Catalogue in June 1995. The Catalogue is a list of investment guidelines that classified foreign-invested projects into four categories: "encouraged," "permitted," "restricted," and "prohibited." The "restricted" category limited the equity share that foreign firms could have in certain industries. The Catalogue signalled the state policies in attracting (or distracting) foreign investment. The State Council approved a revised Guidance Catalogue on 9 December 1997 and the new Catalogue came into force on 1 January 1998. The 1997 Catalogue removed barriers to foreign participation in some restricted sectors such as distribution, infrastructure, energy, and power generation. The Catalogue also favoured those enterprises that were willing and able to bring high technology to China or promote exports and offered tax exemptions and other benefits to FIEs. In the category of "encouraged" investments, an emphasis was placed on high technology and some industries were moved to the "restricted" category. This differential liberalization policy de facto disfavoured SOEs and domestic private enterprises, which effectively gave FIEs a super-national treatment. Against this background, China's openness became a dominant theme again. By 1994, for instance, FDI comprised 78.14% of China's total actually utilized foreign capital.[47] Greenfield FIEs were the major mode of foreign invested projects. Among others, the first batch of foreign mergers and acquisitions also appeared in the Chinese market, which, however, only occupied a very small portion of total foreign investments.[48] At this period, some doubts over the concessions made to FIEs appeared in the policy and law marking circles. The enactment of the Company Law in 1993 heralds a partial effort to unify the corporate law regime hosting both foreign and domestic businesses.[49]

1.2.3 Third Ten Years: 2000–2010

China's accession to the WTO on 11 December 2001 marked a new chapter of foreign investment in China. The significance of this event was to outline a legally binding road map for China to further liberalize and modernize the economy and foreign investment regime per se. As a result, many remaining restrictions on foreign investment were removed, the principle of national treatment was more expansively implemented, and the regulation and supervision of foreign investment activities were more subject to legal rather than administrative means. Other significant changes to foreign investment policies included repealing the requirements for foreign exchange balance and nationalization of foreign investment, eliminating non-tariff barriers, improving market access to foreign goods and services, offering more protections to intellectual property rights, improving transparency, and establishing a legal framework more compatible with the requirements and principles of

WTO. China's accession to the WTO brought positive impacts on FDI activities in China. For instance American exports to China shot up by 118% from 2001 to 2005.[50] More fundamentally, China's accession to the WTO has been deepening China's integration into the world investment and trading system and facilitating China's institutional reform along with its economic reform. China's accession to the WTO also transformed China's governance or regulatory system. It has made laws and policies more transparent and publicly available. It has revised laws to reflect the principle of national treatment. It has reduced tariffs and quotas. It has increased market access in key industries. Overall, China has by and large lived up to its WTO commitments. The WTO Director General gave China an "A+" for fulfilling its WTO undertakings in September 2006.[51]

During the first decade of the 21st century, other economic and governance infrastructure has also been reformed, that is the foreign exchange regulatory regime towards internal convertibility of the renminbi. As a result, the foreign investment regime departed from the previous route placing more emphasis on export and foreign exchange generation and focused on the importation of technology and managerial skills. The Guidance Catalogue was further amended in 2002 to solidify China's WTO commitments, which reflected a liberalizing trend.[52] As far as the FIEs are concerned, the approval, capitalization, market access, and financing have been reformed as well. The State Council further reformed the investment system, which raised the threshold on local government approvals of investment projects from US$30 million to US$100 million for projects failing within the "encouraged" and "permitted" categories in the Catalogue.[53] Foreign investment projects that did not utilize state funds only need to be verified rather than examined or approved. A wide range of foreign investment related matters have been addressed by new or revised legislation such as taxation, labour, customs, bank lending and guaranties, import and export licenses, intellectual property protection, and environmental protection. Some Western types of business models have been introduced into and utilized in the Chinese market. Recent years have seen a surge of mergers and acquisitions activities, which fostered the need for a regulatory structure dealing with the transfer of corporate control. The 2006 Provisions on Acquisitions of Domestic Enterprises by Foreign Investors, issued by the MOFCOM, SAIC, and other four ministries, superseded earlier scattered regulations and constituted a concrete legislative development in the field of foreign investment.[54] A new takeover code, the Acquisition of Listed Companies Administrative Procedures, was issued by the China Securities Regulatory Commission in 2006 and repealed the old one of 2002. The new takeover code aimed to boost domestic and cross-border mergers and acquisitions activities involving PRC-listed companies. The regulatory framework facilitated cross-border mergers and acquisitions transactions. During the period from 2000 to 2007, there were over 1,500 reported deals with a total disclosed value of over US$200 billion.[55] Given the size of its domestic market, vast human resources and capacity for low-cost manufacturing, and its economic potential, China has become and will continue to be the magnet of foreign investment and global economic growth. With US$90.03 billion of foreign direct investment (FDI) inflows in 2009,[56] China has become the largest capital absorbing country in the world.

1.2.4 Some Recent Trends in Aftermath of China's Accession to the WTO

It appears that there is a retrenchment in China placing a greater emphasis on industrial policy and regulatory regime to review the impact of foreign investment projects on national economic and security interests, which coincided with a notable trend towards a rising nationalism seeking to push back globalization[57] as well as a switch from fast economic growth to a new harmonious society policy.[58] This trend was evidenced by several rounds of revisions to the Guidance Catalogue,[59] and more recently, the Anti-Monopoly Law. The 2007 Catalogue demonstrated the new policy switch. For instance the Catalogue places more emphases on environmental protection, trade imbalances, and high-technology. Accordingly, the Catalogue decreases support for export-oriented industries, promotes foreign investment in high-tech and environment-friendly sectors, and restricts foreign investment in manufacturing and mining industries which were once welcomed foreign investment. These policy changes have been viewed as a new round of attempts to disadvantage foreign investors,[60] on the one hand, limiting market access by non-Chinese origin goods, and on the other hand, offering more resources and protections to domestic players that are less competitive in the marketplace.[61] The role of law is ambiguous in balancing control of foreign investment against facilitating the activities of FIEs.

China's policy-making process and environment in the field of foreign investment is complex and dynamic. Commentators were of the opinion that the Chinese foreign investment policy has been a product of bargaining dynamics,[62] personalities and clientelism,[63] and bureaucratic processes.[64] This process is now more contested than before among various domestic and foreign interest groups and constituencies as well as champions of global capitalism, notwithstanding the CCP's reliance upon a continuous growth for legitimacy, new goal of realizing a harmonious society and urgent needs to protect socially and economically vulnerable groups. The debate in China, that is economic nationalism vs. liberal treatment towards foreign investment, has been ongoing for decades[65] which may explain, if not rationalize, the policy change wavering. In contrast to the growing liberalization, a Chinese economic nationalism appeared in recent years. The legislation, that is the Provisions on Acquisitions of Domestic Enterprises by Foreign Investors, which block foreign purchases of Chinese companies involving "key industries" described as those whose operations influence or might influence "state economic security,"[66] gradually shows concerns that foreign interests are acquiring domestic assets at undervalue,[67] seizing control of strategic industrial sectors[68] and market share in China without adequate oversight and control.[69] The debate of liberalism vs. economic nationalism also mirrors the objective and direction of reform itself in a larger context. The foreign investment policy has also been an ad hoc and incremental response to continuous changes in the global and domestic economy. For instance the intensity of the negotiation for the 1989 and 1992 intellectual property agreements and the 1992 market access agreement, and later, the China's WTO accession agreement, between the US and PRC governments shows the extent of the business interests at stake in foreign commercial community's constant efforts to bring about reform of China's foreign economic law and legal protection regime. As a matter of fact, the content of these agreements closely mirrors the demands put forward by American business executives with commercial activities in China.[70] Given these dynamic factors, it is difficult to maintain regulatory consistency in the sense of Western governance or regulatory model. Although there have been policy changes along the economic reform, it might be optimistic to anticipate the general trend in a long term, that is a movement towards more openness and an increasingly competitive market economy with some "Chinese socialist characteristics."[71]

As long as China continues to regulate foreign investment comprehensively and closely, policy may remain and dominate the laws in regulating foreign investment and businesses. Meanwhile, the economic reforms that have significantly transformed China have made necessary development of the legal framework for foreign trade and investment. The three-decade reform witnessed the revival of some legal institutions such as the (still underdeveloped) judicial system, the emergence of some new legal institutions such as private lawyers, and, most fundamentally, the explosion of legislation. However, the past four decades did not see a success in creating a well-functioning legal order with a strong rights-consciousness[72] in a civil society.[73] The evolution of law, legal institutions, and legal infrastructure remains slow and uneven. The great concern often raised by the community of foreign investors was and continues to be the lack of laws and regulations and dysfunction of legal institutions and judiciary that offered insufficient protections to foreign investors and even Chinese citizens. While the level of predictability, functioning, and rights-consciousness cannot be and should not be assessed and measured exclusively in terms of Western ideals,[74] a fair evaluation is that the legal system in China is still in the institutional flux and has a long way to go. Although the totalitarian grip of the CCP has weakened since the late 1970s, the bureaucracy, official arbitrariness, spreading corruption, a more chaotic social order, and a crisis of social values need even more urgently and desperately the rule of law composed of strong legal institutions and a vibrant legal culture.

Along with the decentralization is the increased local autonomy and local protectionism which undermine the state's ability to manage foreign investment and the efficacy of the foreign investment regime. Guangdong, for example emerged to be the "fifth dragon" due to its strong labour force, convenient transport, easy access to technology and managerial skills, and most importantly, probably the close connection with Hong Kong and longtime commitment to establishing and implementing a consistent pro-investment policy.[75] The growth of local economies made the implementation of central economic policies more challenging than before. The most high-profile case was the central government's difficulty in implementing a two-tier tax system separating local and central tax revenues and outlays.[76] The gradual decline of the central state may result in the emergence of local autonomy which can manage foreign investment to reach local development targets. However, the decentralization also reveals "some of the worst disadvantages of the federal legal systems without the appropriate legal and political machinery even to resolve the resulting conflicts and tensions, far less to unify the law."[77]

While the laws and regulations are more available than before, the law enforcement remains the key hurdle to the rule of law in a Western sense. The administrative organs and officials, even if not granted, are used to exercising their discretionary power to interpret and enforce laws, which create more uncertainty, inconsistency, and complexity in enforcement. Without a functioning judiciary and rule of law tradition, the interpretation and enforcement of law and the exercise of discretion, uncontrolled by external agencies, are also parochial and inconsistent. Inconsistent regulatory and enforcement behaviours are a natural product of the "broad and indeterminate language-based" legislative techniques, and the gaming between different bureaucracies and local protectionism. This in turn undermines the effectiveness or legality of laws and regulations as institutional and systematic mechanisms for macroeconomic management and law enforcement. Although the 1990s saw some initiatives and attempts to build legal institutions to control administrative action and discretion, progress in reality is still slow.

It is worth noting that some new amendments to the 2013 Company Law have already been implemented in the Shanghai (China) Free Trade Zone and applied to both domestic enterprises and FIEs registered in the zone. In August 2013, the State Council officially approved the establishment of the Free Trade Zone in Shanghai. The new pilot free trade zone has been touted as the successor to the special economic zone set up in Shenzhen in the 1980s by Deng Xiaoping when he embarked on a series of market experiments. The free trade zone spans 28.78 square kilometres in Waigaoqiao, Yangshan port, and Pudong districts in Shanghai. The Chinese government is trying to introduce its own ambitious reforms. The new free trade zone is viewed by the business community and analysts as the Chinese government's most important policy move for economic reform in more than a decade. This zone will be used as a controlled laboratory to experiment with loosened regulations on key economic reform initiatives ranging from interest rates to foreign investment approvals. If the desired result can be achieved, the zone will spark wider market reforms.

The State Council in September 2013 outlined the policies for the Free Trade Zone in the Framework Plan for China (Shanghai) Pilot Free Trade Zone. The Shanghai Municipality Government promulgated the Administrative Measures for the China (Shanghai) Pilot Free Trade Zone (the "Administrative Measures"), effective as of 1 October 2013 as well as five pieces of administrative measures related to the establishment of the Free Trade Zone.[78] The Free Trade Zone formally started to accept applications for the filing of enterprises. According to the Administrative Measures, and the Several Opinions of the SAIC on Supporting the Development of the China (Shanghai) Pilot Free Trade Zone (Gong Shang Wai Qi Zi No. [2013] No.147), a company registration system is adopted, on a pilot basis, in the Free Trade Zone. This was effectively a stepping stone for the capitalization system reform for the Company Law, which was amended further in late 2014.

Unless the actual payment of registered capital of certain companies is otherwise prescribed by laws or administrative regulations, the SAIC office in the Free Trade Zone only registers the amount of registered capital or total equity capital subscribed for by all the shareholders (promoters) of a company instead of the paid-in capital. The shareholders are free to agree with each other on their respective amount of subscribed capital contributions, the method of payment, and the period of capital contribution and record these agreements in the company's articles of association.

The shareholders are responsible for the authenticity and legality of their payments of capital contributions. A company shall make public the amount of capital contribution subscribed for each of its shareholders, or the number of shares subscribed for, by each of its promoters, the method and period of capital contribution, as well as the actual payment of capital contribution through the market player credit information disclosure system. The disclosure system is put in place to strengthen the supervision of companies within the Free Trade Zone. The Free Trade Zone's SAIC office can make public the information of enterprise registration, filing, and supervision, and companies can make public their annual reports and approval certificates procured in connection with specific qualifications.

Except for the prior licensing matters for enterprise registration as prescribed by laws, administrative regulations or the decisions of the State Council, companies incorporated within the Free Trade Zone may engage in general production and business activities after applying for registration and obtaining a business license from the relevant SAIC. This is a significantly relaxed approach compared to the business scope rule (or the traditional objective rule in some common law jurisdictions) adopted in the Company Law, under which every business entity must act within its business scope as set out in its business license. FIEs, like all other legal entities in China, have a limited scope of approved operation as set out in the business license to be issued by the SAIC or one of its competent lower-level branches. It is generally not possible to obtain a general scope of business for an FIE in China.[79] Where the company wishes to engage in business activities involving prior licensing matters, it may then apply with the competent authorities for relevant licenses or approval documents within the Free Trade Zone.[80]

One of the key reforms in the Free Trade Zone is changing the existing pre-approval system for foreign investment to a filing system with the administrative committee in the Free Trade Zone, for an FIE to be established in the Zone (except for the industrial sectors in the negative list).[81] The filing system saves transaction costs involved in the investors' interaction with the local authority. Where special licenses or approvals are still required, foreign investors are not allowed to engage in full-fledged businesses until special permits/licenses are obtained.[82]

2. Admission of Foreign Investment

2.1 General Policy Concerning Admission

Despite the dominance of the labour-intensive manufacturing sector, the economic sectors in which foreign investment has been targeted also gradually extended to technology-based production. The Chinese government made a great effort to steer foreign investment to the export and technology sectors. As a result, special preferences were also given to enterprises denoted as "export oriented enterprises" and "advanced technology enterprises."[83] The Joint Venture Law and its Implementing Rules specifically encouraged joint ventures to export their products. The acquisition and importation of technology was encouraged by rules allowing intellectual property rights and know-how to be contributed as capital by foreign investors. Approval of joint ventures was to be contingent on the satisfaction of the criterion, either being an export-oriented enterprise or an importer of technology.[84] Preferential treatments in the form of tax holidays were also offered to those foreign investment projects which were able to satisfy these requirements. Accordingly, joint ventures were to receive tax holidays for the first two profit-making years and reductions in subsequent years.[85] Similarly, approval of WFOEs would be also conditioned on their use of advanced technology or exporting products.[86] Other tax incentives were provided to FIEs engaged in export activities and advanced technology production. For instance FIEs whose export production value was 70% of total production value were to be considered "export oriented enterprises" eligible for a 50% reduction in enterprise income tax, with additional reductions possible.[87] FIEs being designated as a "technologically advanced enterprise" were entitled to extend their initial three-year tax holiday by an additional three years.[88] Withholding taxes on profits remitted outside China could be exempted to technologically advanced enterprises and export enterprises, which meanwhile were entitled to exemption from the payment of state subsidies for enterprise staff and workers, priority in obtaining short-term loans, limits on certain site use fees, and extension of priority status for utility supply and infrastructural requirements.

In early attempts to attract more foreign investment, the Chinese government adopted various inducement measures emphasizing substantive operating conditions as the bases for preferences and location. The emphasis on location was obvious in the establishment of special economic zones in the early 1980s,[89] the establishment of Pudong New Area in the early 1990s, and the establishment of Tianjin Binghai Zone in the early 2000s.[90] The special economic zones were established to provide a platform for foreign investors. These zones and areas offer lower tax rates, streamlined and simplified approval procedures for setting up foreign-invested enterprises, and special customs treatment for import and export of goods. Goods produced in these zones could be exported absent special permission or approval.[91] Subsequent designation of 14 municipalities as open coastal cities and the establishment of economic and technology development zones in 12 of them centred primarily on the attraction of foreign technology, know-how, and intellectual property rights. Tax incentives were also offered to businesses located in special economic zones and economic and technology development zones. For instance all FIEs located in these zones for more than ten years would be entitled to a five-year tax holiday previously only extended to EJVs.[92] Withholding taxes were also reduced or waived, and exemptions and reductions from payments due under industrial and commercial consolidated tax were available.[93] The reduction of the tax liability was a great driver for foreign investment.

The investment incentive regime indicated that the primary emphasis had been placed on the promotion of export-oriented industries and technology acquisition. The role of the state has been strong in steering the direction of foreign investment and national economic development. Despite the reform of developing greater ties with the international systems of commerce and finance, state control over foreign investment has been a singular norm of the regulatory regime. The approval and/or registration procedures are prerequisite to foreign investment at almost all the stages of the project. For instance a contract which needs to be approved by the government authority comes into effect only after the receipt of the approval. The continued modernization of the Chinese legal system, infrastructure, and institutions is moving towards a hybrid configuration of strengthening the state's managerial role and liberating a closed society to be a liberal and open one.

Prior to China's accession to the WTO, one critical defect of the Chinese regulatory system is the lack of transparency and predictability in Chinese laws and regulations and in the policies and mechanisms. Chinese government authorities had a poor record of timely and properly informing the public of any changes to the policies. There was wide use of "internal documents" (or "red head" documents) other than publicly published laws and regulations which have significant bearing on the approval process and regulatory regime of foreign investment activities. The "internal documents" remained an invisible component of the regulatory system for a long time and jeopardized the foreign investment community's confidence on the regulatory regime in China. The use of "internal documents" increased transactional costs and liaison difficulties to foreign investors. In addition, the Chinese legislature and government did not have tradition to involve the general public in the law-making process through consultations. Under China's WTO Agreement, China agreed to "apply and administer in a uniform, impartial and reasonable manner" all its trade-related laws and to establish a mechanism "under which individuals and enterprises can bring to the attention of the national authorities cases of non-uniform application of the trade regime."[94] China's accession to the WTO eventually forced China to remove the "internal documents" from its regulatory system. According to China's WTO commitments, there seems to be less frequent use of "internal documents" other than laws and regulations, which are now all publicly available.

2.2 Regulation of Admission

The extent of state control is best evidenced by the approval regime in the admission of foreign investment. The government authorities are involved in all the stages of foreign investment projects, from the formation, operation to termination. Challenges of securing administrative licenses and business approvals and navigating China's licensing and regulatory procedures have been in existence since the inception of foreign investment. The area of law and practice is deeply problematic.

Unreasonable delays take place too often. The licensing and approval procedure may take much longer. Confusion arises very often when various authorities interpret and apply laws differently. Discretionary administrative powers and local standards often make it difficult for applicants to do preparation and paperwork and predict the results. Most foreign investors may have to devote much more management time and workforce to handling approvals and licensing issues.[95]

As far as the EJVs, CJVs, and WFOEs are concerned, preliminary approval is required for the feasibility study even before the negotiation and conclusion of the actual foreign investment contract (either in the form of the Sino–foreign joint venture agreement or the foreign investment agreement). Chinese parties to the joint ventures may need to obtain approval for a project proposal, the purpose of which is to list the project in the local economic planning. Without the approval for this project proposal, the Chinese party may even not be able to commence formal negotiation with the foreign party for the project. The articles of association and joint venture contract (or the foreign investment agreement for the WFOE) are also subject to the approval by the Ministry of Commerce or its local branch. The FIE's size of total investment decides the approval level for the project in the government hierarchy as indicated in Table 1.1. Until these documents are registered with the State Administration of Industry and Commerce, the company registry in China, and the business license is issued, the EJV, CJV, or WFOE is formally established. This whole process may take three to six months depending on the size and location of the project.

The actual business activities of the EJV, CJV, or WFOE are limited by the business scope specified in the articles of association and business license. Unlike some common law jurisdictions, the objects clause in the articles, together with the principle of *ultra vires*, is no longer restricted and the company is basically able to conduct any commercial activities it wants to. However, this is not the case in China. The parties to the joint ventures or WFOEs need to specify the business scope explicitly in the project proposal, feasibility study report, joint venture contract, articles of association, and finally business license. The scope of business in the business license will not only affect the scope of business activities the EJV, CJV, or WFOE is about to conduct but also influence the treatment the project

TABLE 1.1 Approval Levels for Foreign Investment Projects

Authority Level	Industries in Encouraged/ Permitted Category	Industries in Restricted Category
State Council	US$500 million or above	US$100 million or above
NDRC and MOFCOM	US$300 million or above	US$50 million or above
Provincial MOFCOM	Between US$30 million and US$300 million	Below US$50 million
Municipal MOFCOM	US$30 million or below	N/A

may receive from competent government authorities in terms of tax and other incentives. For instance the availability of import/export licenses, customs duties, investment incentives, preferential tax rates, market access, and other treatments largely depends on the scope of business set out in the business license. The business scope may also affect the way the company operates the business in terms of environment protection and labour management.[96] Like the operation of object clauses in a common law jurisdiction, the conduct of business activities outside the scope of business does not necessarily void to a bona fide third party. However, the conduct of legally prohibited or restricted business may be void from the very early beginning.

After its accession to the WTO, China is obligated to open to foreign investment sectors of its economy that were previously closed. Financial services and telecommunications are two areas that were closed to but must be opened to foreign investment under China's WTO commitments. In fulfilling its commitment to open the banking sector to foreign investment, China introduced regulations on the activities of foreign-invested banks that permitted them (through their PRC-incorporated subsidiaries in China) to engage in renminbi business in China.[97] The regulations also reduced the differences between the requirements for domestic banks and those for foreign-funded banks. By September 2006, 73 foreign-funded banks had 199 branches, 111 foreign-funded banks had representative offices in China, and foreign-funded banks in total had over US$100 billion worth of assets in China.[98] The capital markets were also opened to foreign investment banks in late 2007. Certain "qualified foreign investors" were allowed in 2002 to gain access to the A-share market, which was historically restricted to domestic investors. The concept of "foreign strategic investors" was introduced in 2005.[99] Accordingly, they were allowed to acquire tradable A-shares of China-listed companies.[100] Nevertheless, various conditions were attached to the opening of the capital markets, such as the limits on the scope of underwriting by Sino–foreign joint ventures and the size of the stakes that foreign investor is allowed to hold in new securities joint ventures. The foreign investment community has not been satisfied with the progress made by China in opening its financial sector, and the US government has continuously pressed China to accelerate the pace.[101]

Previously, foreign investment in operating networks was not allowed. Later on, China's State Council introduced regulations on the administration of foreign-invested telecommunications enterprises allowing foreign-invested joint ventures to invest and conduct activities in a broad range of areas which are to be phased in over a period of years. Nevertheless, in practice, it has been extremely difficult for FIEs to obtain telecommunications operating license. This may be attributable to the Chinese government's fear of foreign participation in the media and publishing industries, which may make the control and censorship of information more difficult,[102] and eventually make the CCP ruling less manageable. To have a bite of the profitable telecoms business in China, foreign investors worked out an artful business model to avoid the prohibition on foreign participation in telecommunications enterprises.[103]

The retail sector is another industry that is open to foreign investment according to China's WTO commitments. Previously, foreign investors had to reach agreements on foreign-owned retail operations that may have violated national legislation. According to the WTO Agreement, China has allowed foreign investors to participate in the distribution activities covering commission agents, wholesaling, retail sales, and franchising, as well as related services such as delivery, storage, sales promotion, installation, and maintenance and repair.

3. Restrictions on Foreign Investment

3.1 Fiscal Legislation

China's currency, yuan or renminbi, is not freely convertible. All earnings in the domestic Chinese market must be denominated in renminbi.[104] Prior to the foreign exchange reform in 1994, China adopted a dual currency system in which both renminbi and foreign exchange certificates were both in existence.[105] Foreign exchange transactions were required to comply with the foreign exchange plan, which was prepared by the State Administration of Foreign Exchange (SAFE) and supervised by the Bank of China.[106] All the transactions creating a liability to pay in foreign exchange are strictly controlled and must be approved by or registered with the SAFE. Foreign exchange accounts were closely monitored, and foreign exchange balancing required government approvals. Foreign investment projects were encouraged to adjust foreign exchange surpluses and deficits through currency adjustments with each other.[107] The foreign exchange monitoring regime effectively enabled the state to participate in and monitor the financial activities by foreign investors. The later use of an inter-bank foreign exchange market was a move towards a market-oriented mechanism, which, however, did not eliminate the state control and monitoring.

Due to the tight control over foreign exchange, one of the most significant problems for foreign investors in China was to meet the requirement to balance foreign exchange expenditures and revenues. Foreign exchange controls affect most accounting activities and should be factored into all financial planning. As discussed earlier, this includes how registered capital will be used, how foreign exchange financing will be obtained and on what repayment terms, how RMB financing will be obtained and secured, as well as routine foreign exchange accounting, such as the payment of imports, salaries, royalties, license fees, and dividends. However, the lack of free convertibility is not a serious problem for JVs which generate sufficient foreign exchange to meet their needs, but projects which do not generate enough foreign currency must obtain foreign exchange by other means. Foreign exchange risk can be managed well with adequate planning.

China's unified and controlled floating rate system was established in 1994. Beginning in 1996, the system for settlement, sale, and payment of foreign exchange was applied to FIEs.[108] Foreign investors can also retain a certain amount of foreign exchange with the approval of foreign exchange authorities in their foreign exchange bank accounts.[109] "Current international payment and transfers" were no longer restricted effective as of 1 December 1998.[110] Later on, the Chinese government abolished the system whereby FIEs had to swap their foreign exchange at designated foreign exchange adjustment centres. Since then, the FIEs may purchase and sell foreign exchange in the commercial bank's foreign exchange purchase and sale system. These reforms substantially facilitated foreign investment activities.

The level of control over inbound or outbound foreign exchange depends on whether the nature of the transaction involves the transfer of capital or ordinary expenditures. Accordingly, a distinction has been made between "capital account" and "current account" items. Current account items, such as trade payments, payments of interest (but not repayment of principal), and repatriation of dividends from a JV, which are classified as cross-border expenditure in the ordinary course of business, are able to flow freely and convertible without prior approval for each payment. FIEs may borrow foreign exchange loans without approval of the SAFE. FIEs are merely required to register such foreign exchange debts with the SAFE, which is a perfunctory matter.[111] Chinese banks remitting foreign exchange even for the current account purpose are required to confirm the authenticity of the remittance and the underlying transactions. For instance the proper customs clearance documents and technology licenses need to be presented to the bank for the purposes of sales price and royalties payments respectively. Given its purpose of creating capital, capital account items, such as equity investment (into a JV), loans (including repayment of principal), securities investments, guarantees benefitting a foreign entity, fixed assets, and working capital, are subject to strict movement control in the PRC currency market, that is such item has to be placed in a controlled bank account and cannot be converted into foreign exchange without the SAFE approval for each payment.

Balancing foreign exchange income and expenditure often requires satisfying two needs. First, the JV needs foreign exchange to pay for the imports of equipment and raw materials. While establishing a JV, a foreign investor should estimate foreign exchange needs, most common of which are raw materials, components, servicing foreign exchange loans, royalties for the use of technology, and intellectual property rights. The JV also needs foreign exchange to pay the salaries of senior management personnel in China. This problem may be solved by reducing foreign exchange needs, for example by contributing equipment or machinery as part of the JV's capital and sourcing raw materials locally. Other solutions involve generating foreign exchange, for example by exporting products or investing RMB profits in export sidelines, or by making and selling one product in RMB and then investing RMB profits in making another product which can be exported. When JVs remit foreign exchange for these purposes, Chinese banks will confirm the authenticity of the remittance and the underlying transaction by reviewing the SAFE documentation and other documents. For example remittances of payments for imported goods may be made only if proper customs clearance documents are presented to the bank and other anti-fraud and anti-money laundering requirements are satisfied. Similarly, remittances of royalties under a cross-border technology license contract are subject to presentation of registration certificates for the license contract. Second, the JV needs foreign exchange to repatriate dividends to its parent. Foreign investors may repatriate profits from an FIE without restriction subject to compliance with certain procedural requirements such as prior PRC accounting to determine profits, payment of income tax, allocation of after-tax profits to a reserve fund, an employee bonus and welfare fund, and an enterprise expansion fund, and obtaining SAFE approval which is routinely granted.

China's WTO accession has furthered liberalization with the abolishment of the long-standing foreign exchange balancing requirements. Nonetheless, the trend of relaxing the foreign exchange control is maxed by the measures to tighten foreign exchange rules from time to time, to maintain a stable renminbi exchange rate, which is the key policy driver in foreign exchange control.

The foreign exchange rate between renminbi, the Chinese currency, and other major currencies is probably the most high-profile economic dispute between China and its major trading partners such as the United States, European Union, and Japan. It is always claimed by the US, EU, and Japan that China is manipulating renminbi to the extent that it is undervalued by at least 20%, and China's competitive undervaluation is inflecting the entire global economy.[112] The US and other major economies are trying both unilateral[113] and multilateral[114] means to press China to appreciate its renminbi. Regardless of the possible currency war and the trade tensions, the foreign exchange was one of the areas that the Chinese government exerted its financial controls over foreign investment.

3.2 Labour Legislation

Under Chinese law, the JV (as well as WFOEs) is required to enter into collective or individual labour contracts. In JV companies, workers are represented by workers' unions. Collective labour contracts are made with the JV's trade unions and specify collective terms for the whole workforce. In practice, individual labour contracts are now replacing collective contracts as the norm. Chinese law also requires wages for domestic employees to be approximately 120–150% of those in SOEs. The JV company is required under Chinese law to pay unemployment insurance and medical and employee subsidies which are calculated in accordance with national and local regulations. The Chinese Labor Law and Labor Contract Law regulate many aspects of employment by setting, among other things, working hours limits, holiday and leave requirements, and termination policies.

A JV (as well as a WFOE), under the labour regulations, can be justified in discharging an employee because of the employee's

- Failure to meet the recruitment conditions in the probationary period;
- Disobedience to disciplines and company rules;
- Misconduct or malpractice;

- Criminal liability; or
- Incompetence.

Apart from these reasons, the employers generally have the right to lay off employees because of economic conditions, including a lack of work. The JV must make severance payments to an employee. Generally, severance payment is calculated as one month's actual wage for every 12 months or part thereof served in continuous employment with the JV, provided that such severance payment shall not exceed 12 months' salary. The Labor Contract Law, the purpose of which, as claimed, is to fight exploitation at work, may make layoff much more expensive than before and may cost multinational companies millions of dollars.[115] The Labor Contract Law has already had unexpected consequences including a sharp rise in overtime disputes.[116]

Generally, a JV may include non-competition and confidentiality clauses in the labour contract. However, non-compete clauses are not widely recognized in Chinese labour laws. A non-competition provision may be enforceable after the termination of employment if the employee is paid a severance package in consideration of a "cooling-off" period during which the employee agrees not to take employment with a competitor. With regard to the confidentiality clause, the Labor Law permits the parties to have special provisions in the contract. Also, the employer is entitled to claim the economic losses suffered from the breach of confidentiality provisions by the employee and the remedy of compensation is more acceptable. The employees of JVs have the right to establish grassroots labour unions.

The rise of local autonomy and the decline of central power undermine enforcement of central policies. As a result, the local governments have more resources to ally themselves with capital by sacrificing the benefits and interests of labourers. The declining labour conditions is one obvious example as a result of the emergency of local autonomy. From time to time, local authorities may add extra requirements to this autonomy.[117] For instance in some localities, local labour union approval may be necessary for the hiring and firing decisions.[118] Laws on foreign investment paid tremendous attention to labour conditions and benefits and pressured foreign investors to provide worker safety equipment, hygiene conditions, regular cash bonuses, social insurance, and benefits. JVs are also required to pay the same rate to Chinese managerial personnel as foreign managers. The primary purpose of these requirements is to channel foreign investment to local communities, workers, and staff. It was not a surprise to see the dismay expressed by the JV managers to the subordination of the commercial interests of foreign investment to the parochial interests of local workers.[119] Along with the deepening of the economic reform, stability and production took precedence over other matters and labour activism encountered the state discouragement or deterrence to the emergence of independent labour unions.[120]

The central government has been taking meaningful actions to the worsening labour conditions and benefits. The Labor Contract Law can be seen as a critical attempt to address the deteriorating employment relationship in the marketplace. The main aim of the Labor Contract Law seems to reduce management exploitation of labour, promote a certain level of worker rights, and strengthen the employee protection regime. As the practitioner pointed out,

> the law imposes new and greater liability on employers, grants some new rights and protections for workers, places some hard-to-miss enforcement requirements on the government, grants increased self-help remedies to the labor unions and the workers, and authorizes actions against negligent government enforcers of the new labor law.[121]

Another piece of labour legislation is the Labor Disputes Mediation and Arbitration Law, under which mediation ranks first as the favoured approach for resolution of labour controversies, and arbitration as the final step in certain disputes, subject to the right of appeal to the courts by employees protesting adverse arbitration outcomes. To encourage the use of mediation and arbitration is to reduce chances of worker protest, which may give rise to unrest, strikes, or even chaos. Both the Labour Contract Law and the Labour Disputes Mediation and Arbitration Law may help create a genuine collective bargaining system.[122]

3.3 Requirements of Local Collaboration

Under China's WTO commitments, China committed to eliminating local content for FIEs. However, in practice, local authorities still show their preference to consider local content in approving foreign-invested projects. The most well-known dispute in relation to the local content requirement was probably concerning Chinese tariffs on imported automobile parts that equal to the tariff on a complete automobile at the rate of 28% if the final assembled vehicle failed to meet certain local content requirements. This was an increase of the previously lower tariff at the rate of 10% to 14%. The US and EU brought the dispute to the WTO for settlement.[123]

The commitments to removing local content in the China's WTO accession agreement generally do not limit Chinese law or policy makers from guiding investment to selected industries.[124] Besides, China is still able to restrict some industries and sectors to foreign investors. In these sectors, foreign investors may have to work with Chinese partners and are subject to the equity cap listed in the Foreign Investment Industrial Guidance Catalogue. Requirements for local sourcing and commitments to exports that applied to WFOEs but not to joint ventures were eliminated. As a result, the number of WFOEs grows faster than that of joint ventures (including both equity and cooperative joint ventures).[125]

When purchasing necessary machinery, equipment, raw material, fuel, parts, means of transport and items for office use, a JV shall have the right to decide whether to purchase them in China or from abroad. Where conditions are equal, the purchase of materials abroad shall be subject to priority on and availability of domestic purchases. Given the cumbersome purchase and remittance procedure of foreign exchange and complicated import process, many JVs prefer to "buy local" whenever possible in order to pay for goods and services in RMB. It is recommended that a production and operating plan be prepared for approval by the board of directors.

3.4 Capitalization, Registered Capital, and Total Investment Under FIE Laws

The registered capital of an FIE (including EJVs, CJVs, or WFOEs) refers to the aggregate amount of capital contributed by the joint venture partners.[126] An EJV's profits and losses are shared by the parties on a pro rata basis in accordance with each party's contributed registered capital.[127] The parties to the EJV cannot reduce or withdraw their portion of the registered capital in the term of the joint venture unless specially approved by the competent authority.[128] In other words, capital contributions cannot be repatriated until the operating term has expired. The joint venture party's liability is limited to its pro rata share of the registered capital.

The term of "total investment" refers to the total sum of registered capital plus working capital and construction funds which may be injected into the venture as debt.[129] The total investment is the amount required to finance the enterprise. Minimum capitalization is determined by law based on a ratio between the registered capital and total investment to ensure the project is adequately capitalized.[130] It can be seen from Table 1.2 that there must be some registered capital into the venture. In other words, the joint venture project funded principally by debt will be viewed by the Chinese government as an abuse of government policy and law. In many cases, the approved capitalization of an FIE will be evaluated to determine whether it would match the capital investment, working capital, and business operation requirements indicated in the feasibility study report. If the business scope or investment size is expanded, the approval authority may request the investor's commitments for additional capital funding. Chinese law does not distinguish between paid-up and unpaid capital. Capital contributions must be fully paid in within statutory time limits but can be in cash or in kind.

The statutory ratios of registered capital to total investment are set forth in Table 1.2.[131]

TABLE 1.2 Statutory Ratios of Registered Capital to Total Investment

Total Investment	Ratio of Registered Capital/Total Investment[132]	Percentage of Registered Capital/Total Investment (or minimum registered capital requirement)
≤ US$3 million	at least 7:10	70% or US$0
> US$3 million but ≤ US$10 million	at least 1:2	50% or US$2.1 million (whichever is higher)
> US$10 million but ≤ US$30 million	at least 2:5	40% or US$5 million (whichever is higher)
≥ US$30 million	at least 1:3	33% or US$12 million (whichever is higher)

When an FIE increases its total investment amount, the ratio between the registered capital and the amount added to the total investment should be consistent with the ratio set out in Table 1.2.[133] This may suggest that the final ratio between the registered capital and total investment may differ from the original one applicable to the same entity after the total investment is increased.

The term "paid-in capital" refers to the capital contributions actually paid-in in accordance with the amount specified in the joint venture contract (for an EJV or CJV) or foreign investment agreement (for the WFOE), which is one of the application documents the investors need to submit to the competent authority for approval. Capital contributions can be in the form of (i) cash (of which the foreign party's contributions can be in a foreign currency while the Chinese party's contributions are in renminbi); (ii) tangible assets, such as buildings, factories, plant and machinery, and raw materials; (iii) intangible assets such as patents, trademarks, copyrights, know-how); and (iv) land use rights which are the main assets contributed by the Chinese party.[134]

Foreign currency contributed by a foreign party generally may be kept in a foreign currency account when it is sent to the JV's bank account. Plant, machinery, equipment, construction in progress, materials, and supplies contributed to the FIE should be entered into the accounts at the assessed value agreed upon in the joint venture contract. Land use rights, proprietary technology, patent rights, royalty rights, and other intangible assets contributed by one party should be transferred to the FIE. Foreign exchange regulations, however, are frequently updated and require close monitoring. A foreign party can even use the assets obtained by way of early recoupment of investment, liquidation, share transferring, capital reduction from FIEs it has previously invested in. An FIE should account for capital contributions in accordance with the actual contributions made by the respective parties.

There are certain regulations on in-kind contribution. For instance the technology contributed as registered capital by the foreign parties generally should not exceed 20% of the total registered capital.[135] Foreign investors may contribute technology valued in excess of the 20% limit (but in any event within the 35% registered capital cap) with special approval from the provincial or higher science and technology department.[136] Since the U.S. Tax Act removed the punitive tax on the outward bound transfer of technology in 1997, it is possible for US investors to contribute technology as part of their capital investment.[137] However, it may still be preferable for American investors to license technology and know-how to the JV company in a separate contract in return for a stream of fair market royalty payments. Under a licence structure, the foreign investor will be able to maintain greater control over its technology and know-how. The Chinese partner, however, will most likely prefer that technology and know-how be contributed as capital or otherwise be transferred permanently to the JV. Therefore, references to contributions of technology and know-how should be avoided even at the letter of intent stage. Alternatively, a foreign investor will contribute or sell to the JV certain assets of a personal or proprietary nature that such party wishes to retain upon the termination and dissolution of the JV. The articles of association can be properly drafted to provide for its priority rights of repurchase. Equipment contributed by the foreign investor generally should be indispensable to the JV's production and not readily available from Chinese domestic sources. It should be noted that Chinese tariff exemptions on contributions of equipment have largely been phased out in China.

Once the JV is approved, each party to the JV must inject its subscribed registered capital amount within the time limit set out in the articles of association. If paid in one lump sum, the registered capital contribution must be made within six months of the issuance of the business licence of the JV.[138] If capital will be contributed in instalments, at least 15% of the total capital must be contributed within three months after the JV is established. Chinese law also regulates a three-year period during which all capital contribution instalments must be made.[139] The time period varies depending on the size of the investment. The time limits are set out in Table 1.3.[140]

The time limit is also applicable to the purchase of assets or equity by a foreign investor in a domestic company. The foreign investor must pay the total purchase price within three months from the date on which the FIE's business license was issued. An extension of the payment period may be granted with the approval of the examination and approval authority. Even with approval, at least 60% of the price must be paid within six months of issuance of the business licence, and the balance must be contributed within one year from the same date. The profits will be distributed in proportion to the amount of the capital contribution actually paid.[141]

RMB financing is available for both working capital and fixed assets. As FIEs, JVs usually find it easier to access RMB financing by providing foreign exchange security to the Chinese banks. Such foreign exchange security may be either guarantees given by overseas banks or the Chinese branches of overseas banks, or foreign exchange cash collateral given by the JV itself, for example, unused registered capital in the JV's foreign exchange account. However, it should be noted that RMB financing secured by foreign exchange may not exceed a term of five years. Shareholders loans from the foreign parties are also permitted. All such loans should be registered with the SAFE and should not exceed the difference between the registered capital amount and the total investment amount.

TABLE 1.3 Capital Contribution Instalments Set by Chinese Law

Amount of Registered Capital	Time Limit for Contributing the Entire Interest After Issuance of Business Licence
Up to US$500,000	1 year
Up to US$1 million	1.5 years
Up to US$3 million	2 years
Up to US$10 million	3 years
More than US$10 million	determined by the approval authority case by case

One of the principal components of a typical venture capital or private equity transaction is that investors expect to be issued with preferred shares[142] together with an enhanced degree of control over the investee company as compared to ordinary shareholders as well as protection against various downside scenarios. However, the enforceability of preferred shares is questionable under Chinese law. Unlike the US or English law which allows multiple classes of preferred shares, each with a unique bundle of rights, the JV under the PRC Company Law can only have one class of shares (in the form of a certain percentage of registered capital or equity) according to the basic principle of "same share same interest."[143] There has been no equivalent concept of "preferred shares" which attach preferred rights in a common law jurisdiction. The parties to a JV often want to include preferred rights provisions in a JV contract and/or articles of association which are unlikely to be recognized by MOFCOM or its local branch. Practically speaking, the risk of being rejected by MOFCOM seems immaterial as the transaction can be unwound before the investment is made. To avoid transaction costs being wasted, the pre-approval review by MOFCOM to get feedback on the documents is feasible. If the JV contract and articles of association containing preferred rights provisions pass the scrutiny of MOFCOM or its local branch, the next question is whether such documentation would be recognized by the PRC courts if any dispute arises from these documents. Non-enforcement of preferred share rights is a real risk because enforcement ultimately requires assistance from the courts in China. Arguably, the PRC courts may recognize the preferred rights provisions as the approval authority has given a nod to the relevant provisions. Nevertheless, the test of PRC courts' attitudes may be costly and problematic.[144] Accordingly, the JV contract and articles of association may subject any potential dispute to overseas arbitration in a neutral third party, ideally a member to the New York Convention.[145] An offshore arbitral tribunal would be more familiar with the concept of preferred rights and the international practice in this regard and would be more likely to recognize the preferred rights.[146] As long as a foreign arbitral award recognizing the preferred rights provisions is issued, it may be slightly more difficult for a PRC court to refuse enforcement of such award giving prima facie effect to preferred rights provisions.[147]

3.5 Requirements of Environmental Protection

China's impressive economic growth has come at the cost of environmental degradation, including the alarming increase of severe pollutions, which is at the forefront of global concern.[148] This also triggers a rethink of China's growth model[149] with more focus on a higher rate of growth and less attention to social justice and legal institutions, which is not sustainable in a long run.[150] Due to the weak law enforcement at the local level, the black letters in the well-written environmental protection law do not deter the deteriorating environmental conditions. The local governments are actually more willing to overlook or even tolerate environmental non-compliance.

Environmental protection, in principle, is one of the priority requirements imposed by the Chinese government on the foreign investment projects. In principle, the Chinese government supports international efforts to protect the environment and has acceded to international conventions including but not limited to the World Heritage Convention, the Convention on International Trade in Endangered Species, the Montreal Protocol on Ozone Protection, and accords to realize the goal. In implementing its international treaty obligations, China often tries to keep a distance from developed countries on a differentiated basis allowing herself to comply with international environmental agreements in a different way corresponding to her unique cultural, political, economic, and historical features.

The Chinese government established an administrative agency at the ministry level in charge of environmental protection. The Ministry of Environmental Protection is staffed with trained and experienced personnel and is provided with funds for the operations. Although China has made great bona fide efforts to live up to its international environmental legal obligations, local legislation in China is a patchwork of inconsistent and piecemealed laws and regulations which leads to a less unified legal regime. Another difficulty is the lack of meaningful supervision of environmental legislation and its implementation.

3.6 Requirements Concerning Export Targets

A key objective of the Chinese government in adopting the JV law is to increase exports. This is also related to the objective to balance foreign exchange income and expenditure. Although there is no minimum legal requirement to export, JV regulations require the proportion of domestic and export sales to be approved, and the local government authorities often implement the investment policy to promote export. The foreign party may receive pressure from the Chinese party to commit to as high a percentage of export business as possible. However, if the foreign investor does not intend to export a large portion of the JV's products, it should resist agreeing to unrealistic export percentages because doing so may create difficulties in obtaining foreign exchange if such export targets are not met. Moreover, the foreign investor should consider this when designing its foreign exchange scheme.

In reality, the foreign party may be pressured by the Chinese party to commit to as high a percentage of export business as possible.

A 50% export quota requirement was once imposed on the WFOEs. In practice, the approval authority often showed their strict stance in implementing this requirement. For some high-tech enterprises, local approval authorities may also want to impose an export quota even though these enterprises are set up on the basis of the high-tech requirement and an export quota is not relevant. Partly due to the surging foreign exchange reserves, foreign investors nowadays feel less pressure from the approval authorities to set specific export quota. Even if the WFOEs fail to meet the export targets, they may not suffer adverse consequences.

Under China's WTO Agreement, China committed to eliminating export performance for FIEs. The foreign exchange control has been relaxed so that FIEs need not worry about exports to comply with foreign exchange balancing requirements. Nevertheless, some legislation, in particular, local rules, continue to "encourage" exportation. In practice, local authorities still prefer to consider the export factor in approving the foreign invested projects.[151]

3.7 Restrictions Based on Public Policy or Public Health

The expansion and modernization of the Chinese legal system and institutions in the 1990s somehow strengthened the state's managerial role.[152] The conduct of foreign investment is subject to a vast number of laws and regulations of general application. The principle of party autonomy or contractual freedom often surrendered to the administrative interference. The early Foreign Economic Contract Law, for example set the legal foundation for state intrusion in almost all foreign commercial transactions in China. Public policy is probably the last resort available to the Chinese government or Chinese judiciary in supervising or interfering with the foreign investment. Foreign-related contracts and activities were thus subject to Chinese public and social interests.[153]

To reinforce the state control, a sophisticated state approval mechanism is put in place. The wide range of approval processes contemplated by the vast number of laws and regulations allow various regulatory authorities to retroactively or prospectively review the substance and process of the commercial transactions to ensure compliance with law and social interest.

4. Investment Incentives

4.1 Income Tax and Profit Tax Relief

The provision of tax incentives to foreign investors has been a longtime tool to attract foreign investment into China. Until 2008, FIEs, including EJVs, CJVs, and WFOEs, and purely domestic enterprises were subject to two parallel and separate income tax regimes. The worldwide net income of FIEs[154] was taxed at a national rate of 30% plus a local rate of 3%.[155] The actual rate imposed on FIEs could be as low as 15% given a variety of tax holidays, tax deductions, and tax exemptions were available.[156] For instance preferential rates were available in special economic zones (15% for all FIEs), economic and technological development zones (15% for "production-orientated" FIEs), and coastal open economic zones (24% for "production-orientated" FIEs). By contrast, if FIEs are established in the old urban area of the city where the special economic zone or the economic and technological development zone is located, or in a coastal open city, the tax rate is reduced to 24% only.[157] The application of these taxes is further subject to adjustment by various bilateral tax treaties. FIEs were also offered a general two-year exemption from income tax, starting with the first profit-making year, and for a 50% reduction for the subsequent three years for "production-orientated" FIEs.[158] Technologically advanced enterprises additionally receive a three-year extension of their 50% tax reduction while exporting enterprises receive the same reduction for each year in which they export 70% or more of their output.[159]

In contrast, Chinese enterprises without FIE status including pure Chinese enterprises and FIEs in which foreign investors hold less than 25% of equity were subject to a different regime with average income tax rate of 25%,[160] with the highest rate of 55%. Thus, in terms of tax treatment, foreign investors indeed enjoy a super national treatment in China. Efforts had been made to remove disparities in the tax treatment of foreign and Chinese businesses. Proposals to harmonize the two parallel tax regimes had been under discussion since early 1990s. The purpose of the abolishment of foreign investment incentives was to level the playing field between foreign and domestic investors.[161] Although Chinese officials had repeatedly stressed the urgent need for unification, foreign investors and some Chinese government authorities lobbied against such a movement. The counter-argument against the unification of tax rates to foreign and domestic investors was its possible negative and blocking effects to foreign investors. As a result, China and Chinese labourers may suffer from the slow and small foreign investment. While the movement towards a uniform enterprise income tax regime is slow,[162] other taxes had been enacted which strive to tax foreign and Chinese businesses alike on turnover proceeds.[163]

The National People's Congress enacted the Enterprise Income Tax Law which came into force on 1 January 2008. This law consolidated the two separate tax regimes previously applicable to FIEs and domestic enterprises respectively. Under the new Enterprise Income Tax Law, all the enterprises in China must pay tax at the same rate of 25%. Incentives may be still offered to encourage foreign investors to invest in certain types of industries rather than locating in certain geographical areas.

The role of state control is heavily evidenced in the tax enforcement system. FIEs are subject to a regular tax reporting requirement which required them to produce accounting and bank statements as supporting evidence.[164] Repatriation of profits is only possible with proof that all applicable taxes had been paid.[165] The documentation indicating the clearance of tax liabilities must be submitted for the incentive adjustments.[166] The tax enforcement mechanism allows the state to access some financial information of foreign investment activities and serve the state control in the financial field.

4.2 Depreciation Allowance

Based on the nature and utilization method of fixed assets, an enterprise may determine a reasonable expected useful life and expected residual value for each asset and select a reasonable depreciation method after considering environmental, technological development, and other factors. A number of depreciation methods are available: the straight-line method, operation capacity method, sum-of-years' digits method, double-rate declining balance method, etc. The depreciation policy should be approved by the shareholders' meeting, board of directors, and management before it is submitted to and registered with the competent government authorities. Any changes to the approved depreciation policy should be registered with the government authorities and disclosed in the financial statements.

Expenses related to the acquisition of fixed assets are depreciated over time for tax purposes, with depreciation periods ranging from 20 years for buildings and premises and ten years for means of transport and other production-related equipment, to five years for electronic equipment. Intangible assets can also be depreciated according to the validity term of the license agreement.

4.3 Customs Duties Relief

Customs duties relief was once one of the most often used policy tools to attract foreign investment. For instance in the mid-1990s, the treatment of exemptions from import duty on capital equipment imported by FIEs was offered to FIEs for a decade. The exemption was revoked by the State Council in 1996 due to the resistance from the foreign investment community. To soften the resistance and impact of the policy change, the State Council in 1997 partially restored the duty exemption for certain classes of "encouraged" investment projects and extended it to purchases of domestically manufactured equipment. Another example is the reduction of a value-added tax rebate for exports from 17% to 9% in 1996. The purpose of this change was reportedly to deter the formation of export-processing ventures.[167]

In accordance with its WTO commitments, China has reduced tariffs and quotas as required. Its average tariff rate is 10%, which is much lower than that of other big developing countries such as India (50%), Indonesia (37%), Argentina (32%), and Brazil (31%). With respect to tariff reductions, China's commitments have been largely satisfied.[168]

4.4 Valuation of Assets

The Chinese valuation system is still evolving. Same as appraisals in the United States that must withstand the scrutiny of the Internal Revenue Service and the Securities and Exchange Commission (where the company is publicly held), valuations involving state-owned property in China and assets contributed by the foreign investors are also subject to scrutiny. For instance when an entity holding state-owned assets and a foreign investor form an EJV or a CJV, the transaction must be backed by valuation.[169] Valuation must be conducted for the sale of a Chinese party's equity in an FIE.[170] Assets contributed by foreign investors to FIEs may be appraised with the permission of the foreign investors when necessary.[171] In practice, when a foreign investor contributes assets in kind and intangible assets to the FIE, such assets must be valued under PRC law to determine the current value of the assets in question. Appraisal of foreign-contributed imported assets (as in-kind contributions) is subject to approval by the State Administration of Inspection for Import and Export Commodities or its local counterparts in the PRC.[172]

The value of assets contributed by the Chinese party must be approved by a Chinese-registered accountant. This usually takes place as part of the preparation of the feasibility study report. Valuations are not binding and the contract valuation may be negotiated by the parties. A Chinese-registered accountant must verify all contributions made to the JV. Under Chinese law, the value of foreign property contributed to the JV also will be subject to appraisal and assessment by Chinese authorities after its arrival in China. If the foreign party is contributing in-kind assets to the JV, it should be prepared to present adequate proof of the value of these assets for purposes of having that value credited as capital contribution. The issue of the appropriate valuation of in-kind contribution may be critical in the JV approval and registration process. Chinese authorities have been known to dispute in-kind property valuations, especially in the case of technology and refurbished equipment where standard invoices may not be available. If the value of a foreign party's capital contribution is being disputed, the Chinese party may likewise refuse to put in the full value of its agreed contribution until the dispute is resolved.

The valuation procedure is straightforward: the foreign investor applies for a verification. The application needs to describe the purpose for verification, the subjects, and requirements, and include a list of properties, customs clearance forms, contracts, invoices, inventory books, insurance policies, and technical documents. Thereafter, the value verification institution will examine the application, draft a verification plan, conduct a site inspection, and check documents and information; conduct domestic and foreign market research and collect information on similar subjects and properties; select applicable verification methods and undertake the verification; and finally issue a value verification report.[173]

The value verification methods include the replacement cost method, the market comparison method, and the present income value method. These methods are used in different scenarios. The replacement cost method is used in verifying the value of a piece of property that can be separated from other assets. The market comparison method is used when a comparable market price for subjects or properties similar to the property in question is available in either domestic or international market. The present income value method is used to value the future income and risks in the form of cash for bulk assets. In valuing land and buildings, there are three commonly accepted approaches: the market approach, the income approach, and the cost approach. The income approach is mainly applied to the valuation of tangible assets. The cost approach is the most often used in the valuation of plant and machinery. There are two methods used to implement: cost of new replacement and cost of new reproduction. The market approach is of little relevance to the valuation industry in China because of the lack of an active market for used plant and machinery.

For the purpose of setting up a joint venture, the Chinese party holding state-owned assets must apply to its department in charge or the relevant state-owned assets administration bureau for the approval to retain asset valuation agencies to perform valuation on relevant state-owned assets and property.[174] The department in charge will issue an opinion (or an approval notice) within ten days.[175] A domestic, Sino–foreign, or foreign assets valuation firm, with an asset valuation qualification certificate issued by the government, can be engaged to conduct the asset valuation. The selection of a valuation firm is a contested issue between the Chinese and foreign parties. The Chinese party often prefers to retain a certified PRC valuation firm while the foreign party may distrust the Chinese firm and shows preference over a foreign firm. The compromise is that the appraisal can be conducted by a foreign valuation firm jointly with a Chinese firm. Nevertheless, the foreign valuation firm is usually engaged to look after the foreign investor's interests. The asset valuation is usually conducted after the joint venture proposal is approved but before the approval of the feasibility study report. In some cases, the valuation can be conducted before the approval of the project proposal.

The first step in the appraisal process is a site inspection of the assets. The valuation firm will check the number and conditions of the assets. The valuation firm will also use the information supplied by the assets owner to perform the inspection. The valuation firm will choose an appropriate valuation method after the inspection is completed. When both Chinese and foreign valuation firms are appointed, the Chinese valuation firm will lead the inspection and the foreign valuation firm will make a trip to the factory for an on-site inspection of the assets and meet with the Chinese valuation firm. The valuation methodologies vary between two valuation firms. Prior to the inspection, it is more advisable for both valuation firms to meet and establish a mutually agreed upon approach and methodology with which to proceed. Two valuation firms also need to check the information from the asset owner and communicate often with each other, which is helpful to eliminate or mitigate potential points of conflicts.

The valuation result is supposed to be submitted to the state-owned assets administration bureau for examination and confirmation. This review process only applies to the Chinese valuation firm's report. The valuation result should not be submitted until the Chinese and foreign partners to the joint venture agree with it. If two partners disagree with the result, the negotiation should be carried out to reduce any discrepancies before the submission of the result. The state-owned assets administration bureau will verify whether the valuation firm is qualified to work; whether the valuation is in compliance with Chinese laws; and whether the scope of valuation is correct, the valuation method is appropriate, data and information are reliable and sufficient, all the factors are considered, and the conclusion is reasonable and unbiased, so on so forth. If the state-owned assets administration bureau is satisfied with the result, a confirmation notice will be issued granting the applicants to use the report as a basis for changes in ownership rights for the appraised assets. The valuation report will be used by the planning department and MOFCOM or their local branches in approving the feasibility study report and the joint venture contract. The valuation report is only valid for one year starting on the valuation baseline date unless there is significant change in the state's economic policy or if the involved parties modify their agreement.

4.5 Remittance of Profits

The JV or WFOE needs foreign exchange to repatriate dividends to its parent. Foreign investors may repatriate profits from an FIE without restriction subject to compliance with certain procedural requirements such as prior PRC accounting to determine profits, payment of income tax, allocation of after-tax profits to a reserve fund, an employee bonus and welfare fund, and an enterprise expansion fund, and obtaining SAFE approval which is routinely granted.

5. Exclusions to Foreign Investors' Market Entry

5.1 National Security

The Anti-Monopoly Law also gave rise to deep concerns largely due to, as some observers argued, the lack of an ideological commitment to a market economy. Against this background, the law may be "selectively or mendaciously employed as a trade weapon to protect domestic markets or domestic procedures" by those in authority who see competition law "as part of an overarching industrial policy to promote national champions by mercantilist means."[176] For instance the foreign commercial community is afraid of an arbitrary utilization of a national security review to rule out a foreign company's merger or acquisition deal in China. The concern of this national security review[177] may be further fuelled as SOEs are provided with some exemptions in key industries.[178] The enforcement of the Anti-Monopoly Law largely depends on how the law is interpreted and implemented by the Anti-Monopoly Committee (in charge of formulating competition policy and anti-monopoly guidelines policy, assessing the state of overall market competition) and the Anti-Monopoly Enforcement Authority (primarily handling coordinating enforcement work).[179] The implementation of the Anti-Monopoly Law and the basic free competition concepts will largely depend on the public choice of a variety of conflicting goals and factors such as economic growth, general well-being, consumer protection, economic efficiency, protection of infant industries and SOEs, employment protection, urban–rural inequality, and social stability.

5.2 Sectors Reserved for the State's Nationals

PRC regulations and policies prohibit the establishment of WFOEs in a number of industries. In these industries, joint ventures may be the only choice.

6. Foreign Investment Treatments

6.1 Standard of Treatment

China has revised its laws to make them consistent with the principle of national treatment in most areas.

6.2 Regulations on FIEs' Establishment and Operation

6.2.1 Approval and Registration Procedures

Although China has increasingly de-emphasized macroeconomic controls of its economy, foreign investment is still approved in much the same manner as it was under China's centrally planned economy 40 years ago. As all foreign investments must be approved, it is not yet possible to incorporate an off-the-shelf company in China. However, with the introduction of investment categories and expanded local investment approval authority, an encouraged investment can now be approved locally in weeks rather than months. Of course, the whole process of establishing an FIE, from the preparation of the feasibility study report ("FSR") to acquiring a site and business licence may take from three to six months or even longer depending on the location and complexity of the transaction. It was hoped that China's accession to the WTO would usher in a fresh spirit of transparency and openness in regulatory and governance environments and further trickle down to the local protectionism. Nevertheless, the business and investment relations at the local level have not become more uniform and less vulnerable to the vagaries of local intervention and protection. The approval process for setting up a JV or WFOE is a best example to show the main national challenge in implementing China's commitments to the WTO membership due to a structural asymmetry between national and local economic interests.[180]

The level of approval authority for JVs among various Chinese government authorities depends on the expected size of the project in terms of total investment as well as the classification of the project. There are two types of basic approval requirements for a foreign investment projects like JVs: (i) the project approval by the National Development and Reform Commission (the "NDRC") or its local counterparts; and (ii) the foreign investment approval by the Ministry of Commerce (the "MOFCOM") or its local counterparts. For foreign investment in the "encouraged" or "permitted" industries, if the total investment amount is US$100 million or more, the project must obtain approval from the central NDRC and MOFCOM with the attendant requirement that any project of US$500 million or more shall be submitted to the State Council for verification. For any project with a total investment of less than US$100 million, approval by the NDRC and MOFCOM counterparts at the provincial level or below (US$30 million) will be sufficient. By contrast, for foreign investment projects in the "restricted" industries, no approvals may be obtained below the provincial level, the threshold for national approval is lowered to US$50 million in total investment, and the threshold for verification by the State Council is lowered to US$100 million.[181] The general approval jurisdiction is outlined in Figure 1.1.

These approval limits have been liberalized somewhat in respect of encouraged foreign investment projects based on the classification in the Catalogue, but only for projects which do not require overall state balancing.[182] Encouraged foreign investment projects that are not deemed to require overall state balancing may be

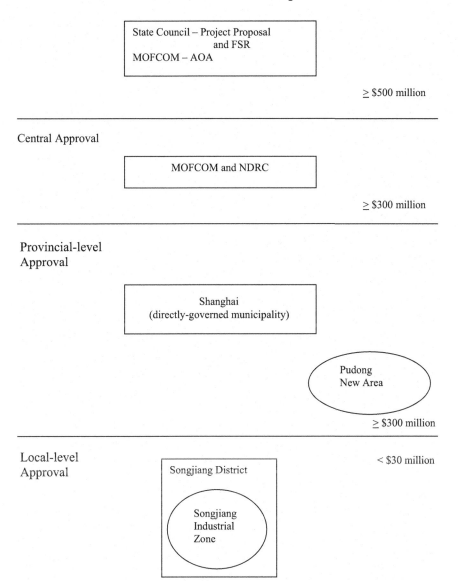

FIGURE 1.1 Approval Jurisdiction in General (e.g., Shanghai)

approved at the provincial level regardless of the total investment amount. Approval at a lower government level is generally preferred as it entails simplified procedures which can be less time-consuming, less expensive, but more flexible. While the approval process is well established, and the foreign investment vehicles in China are considered stable, MOFCOM and its local branches do exercise some discretion from time to time in certain aspects of the JV approval process.

The consequences of invalid approval are not clearly defined by Chinese law. However, relevant law requires inferior-level project approvals to be filed with superior-level approval authorities which then have 30 days to revoke the approval if they are of the opinion that it is defective.

6.2.2 Approval Procedure and Documentation

Usually, it is the Chinese/foreign investor who shall perform the approval process. However, it should be noted that there might be differences in approval procedure from place to place.

Letter of Intent

The initial step in the establishment of a Chinese EJV is the signing of a letter of intent, which is typically in the form of a non-binding document with the possible exception of provisions addressing confidentiality and responsibility for expenses.

Preliminary Project Proposal (or Report)

The next step in the establishment of a JV is for the Chinese partner to prepare a project proposal, which is typically in the form of a non-binding document.[183] The principal purpose of these documents is for the Chinese party to "list" the project in local economic plans and obtain the approval from the "responsible department" to proceed with the transaction and its submission to the relevant authorities for approval, that is MOFCOM or its local branch. Sometimes this project proposal is call a "Report." Although the relevant legislation distinguishes between a project proposal and a "Report," in practice they serve the same purpose.

The main contents of a project proposal (or Report) are preliminary assessments and proposals concerning matters such as the source of capital, conditions of construction and production, scale of production or business, technical levels, the domestic and overseas markets, economic effect, and the balance of foreign exchange of the proposed project.[184] A written reply must be issued within 30 days of its submission to the relevant government authorities at the county level or above. Upon receiving the approval of the project proposal from the approval authorities, the investors may embark on the FSR.

Feasibility Study Report ("FSR")

In China the preparation of the feasibility study is a very important process in the establishment of JV. FSR is a key document upon which the approval authority bases its consideration and approval of the project. The approved FSR is also the primary basis on which the JV or WFOE documentation is drafted, and for the JV or WFOE to plan and organize its production and operation. The feasibility study may have implications for a wide variety of issues, such as foreign exchange approval, obtaining raw materials, and tax treatment.

The FSR must be submitted to Chinese government authorities for approval as part of the approval process for JVs. In smaller investments, the FSR is often submitted at the same time as the submission of the signed JV Contract and Articles of association, although a preliminary FSR also may be submitted by the Chinese party to the Chinese department in charge of that party (which is similar to a parent company) early in negotiation of the transaction in order to obtain the approval of that department to allow the Chinese party to proceed with the transaction. In major investments, the FSR will be submitted before the other JV documentation because its approval is a condition of further negotiations. The FSR and JV documentation should be consistent. Where there are differences between a FSR and the JV documentation, the consent of the original examination and approval authorities shall be obtained.

The FSR is drafted jointly by the JV parties and sets forth the economic and technical assumptions under which the JV will operate. The JV parties should consider agreeing early in negotiations on the methodology and timetable for the preparation of the FSR and to the division of responsibility between the parties in preparing the Report. It may be necessary for the foreign party to dedicate substantial personnel, time, and other resources to the preparation of a quality FSR, including stationing its FSR team in China for days or weeks at a time to fully research feasibility issues.

The foreign party should be aware, however, that it may encounter resistance if it desires to perform a full due diligence investigation of the Chinese party's business. The Chinese party generally is not familiar with Western style due diligence investigations and may consider certain information requests to be intrusive. Despite resistance, the foreign party obviously will be in a better position to truly evaluate the feasibility of the proposed JV project and to effectively negotiate JV terms if it can access accurate information regarding the Chinese party and the Chinese business environment. The foreign investor should pay close attention to requests by the other party to delete information from the FSR or to modify information. Such requests may indirectly identify potentially significant issues relating to liability, supply, labour, or other operational matters.

Although the FSR is technically not considered binding on the parties like the JV contract, it is a critical JV document, and many of its provisions may be viewed by the Chinese as firm commitments by both sides as well as by the Chinese economic planning authorities. In some places, for example Shanghai, local approval authorities may provide standard FSR forms. Foreign investors should pay close attention to some items (e.g. the employment and export requirements) and modify them based on its own operation plan.

The FSR is expected to conduct comprehensive investigations and detailed surveys, calculations, and analyses of all the essential elements of the projects based on the approved project proposal. It should also comment specifically on the economic necessity, rationality, and practicality of the establishment of the projects; the advanced level, applicability, and reliability of the technology and equipment; financial profitability (including the balancing of foreign currency receipts and payments of the projects); and legitimacy.

As a minimum, the FSR should cover the following topics:

- Introduction to the proposed project;
- Description of the proposed JV and the industry in general;
- Market demand for products to be manufactured;
- Production capacity;
- Sales plan of the products;
- Financing;
- Sources of supply of principal raw materials;
- Proposed foreign exchange balancing methods;
- Export;
- Description of plant, property, and equipment;
- Technical engineering information;
- Utilities and natural resources requirements and environmental protection programmes;
- Organization and management of the JV and labour requirements;
- Plan and timetable for completing the project; and
- Financial and economic benefit analysis for the JV.

Joint Venture Contract ("JV Contract")

The JV Contract is one of the most important documentation in forming a JV. A JV Contract serves at least four important functions:

- It is a guide to the parties' business intentions and plans;
- It can provide safeguards for the parties and outline some degree of corporate governance;
- It regulates matters clearly in advance to avoid or minimize problems arising later between the JV partners. Vague terms in the JV Contract can lead to grey areas of uncertainty, which could cause disputes between the JV partners; and
- It can provide at least a sound and clear legal basis for legal action if the dispute really arises and cannot be resolved by the parties to the JV via mediation or friendly consultation.

A JV Contract, no matter how skillfully drafted, may not save the JV from a failure. However, it should be able to ensure that the parties have sufficient protective measures and an exit strategy. It should provide sufficient safeguards or leverage to the parties in case of problems at a later stage. The JV Contract also needs to put the corporate governance mechanism in place to secure the success of the JV.

Articles of Association

Articles of Association ("AOA") is also a constituent document for the formation of the JV. In nature, it is a key constitutional document for the JV. It is analogous to the Articles of Incorporation and by-laws of a Western company. Generally, the AOA should cover such matters as:

- The purpose and business scope of operations;
- The total investment and registered capital;
- The organizational framework and the powers and duties of its officers; and
- Principles governing finance, accounting, foreign exchange, labour management, duration, termination, liquidation, and amendment of the AOA.

The aforementioned key JV documents are prepared, submitted, and approved in the various stages of the formation of the JV (or WFOE) as indicated in Figure 1.2.

6.2.3 Issuance of Entry and Stay Visas

A foreigner, in general, must complete four steps in obtaining or completing all the requisite approvals and formalities to take up an employment and live in China. First, the employer applies for a foreigner employment permit (even if the employee is from Hong Kong, Macau, or Taiwan). Thereafter, the employee applies for the necessary visa for entry into China, the foreigner employment certificate, and the residence permit. A valid visa is required for a foreigner (excluding residents from Hong Kong, Macau, or Taiwan) to be employed, for entry into and exit from the country. An employment visa is normally valid for entry for 90 days from the date of issue. Accompanying family members of the expatriate should apply for valid visas under the category Z. However, the family members cannot take up employment in China unless they have obtained the foreigner employment permit and change their status from accompanying family members to foreign employees.

The foreigner must apply to the labour authority for an employment certificate within 15 days of entering China. The expatriate should go to the local health and quarantine bureau after arriving in China for a medical examination. The employment certificate is valid in the place specified by the issuing authority for a specified period of time (i.e. the term of employment).

The foreigner must apply for the residence permit to the public security bureau in the area where he intends to work and reside within 30 days of entering China. The accompanying family member also needs to apply for the same permit. The duration of residence is usually same as the validity period of the employment certificate. The residence permit is equivalent to the identity card to be carried by all Chinese nationals. The foreigner employment certificate is subject to compulsory annual renewal. The employer and expatriate need to apply to the labour bureau for the renewal of the foreign employment certificate within 30 days from the anniversary of the issuance of the certificate.

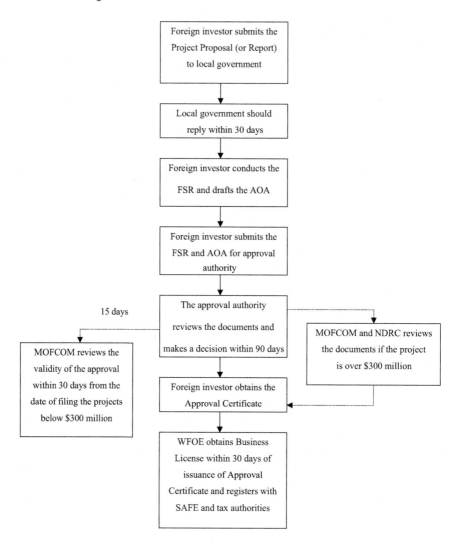

FIGURE 1.2 Approval Procedure and Key Documents

6.3 Transfer of Funds

6.3.1 Salaries and Wages of Foreign Personnel

The individual tax burden of a foreign employee is determined on the basis of factors such as the domicile in China, residence status (i.e. the duration of residence within a given year), and source of income (i.e. whether the salary is borne by a permanent establishment or fixed base in China).

If an employee has a domicile in China, or is resident for a full year, the individual's entire income (arising both inside and outside China) is subject to Chinese tax.[185]

This rule will apply to expatriates posted full time to China. The duration of residence (or length of stay) becomes relevant if an employee splits his or her time each year between China and other locations. The length of stay is calculated by reference to the number of days an individual actually stays in China (including holidays) in a tax year, which runs from 1 January to 31 December in a calendar year.

If the length of stay is less than 90 days, only income derived in China and paid by an employer in China will be taxable.[186] Income deriving from China and paid by an employer outside China will not be taxable. If the employee resides in China for 90 days or less, Chinese tax will not apply to income paid by a foreign employer and not attributable to the employer's places of business in China. Without a tax treaty, an individual who resides in China for a period of more than 90 days cumulatively but less than a full year will ordinarily be taxed under Chinese law on income earned in China.[187] Income derived from outside China is not taxable. A longer 183-day threshold[188] for residence applies before the individual's income is subject to Chinese tax where there is a tax treaty between China and the employee's home country.[189]

Attribution of individual income tax is critical for determining the applicability of Chinese tax. In the absence of a tax treaty, individual salary that is attributable to a foreign employer's institutions or facilities in China will be taxable under Chinese law even if the employee resides in China for 90 days or less. With a tax treaty containing provisions analogous to the US–China Tax Treaty, residence for less than the 183-day threshold period will not avoid application of Chinese tax if the employee's salary is paid by an entity resident in China or borne by a permanent establishment or fixed base in China. This suggests that the 90/183-day grace periods do not apply and tax liability will start on day one if the individual's salary is paid by a joint venture or a foreign representative office. The source of salary, that is salaries from the headquarters overseas, does not avoid imposition of Chinese tax since the salaries may be deemed borne by the joint venture or representative office and therefore taxable under Chinese law.[190] According to these rules, the effective strategy to avoid imposition of Chinese tax is to exceed the 183/90-day thresholds. For instance the expatriates may work in a regional office more than 183 or 90 days. The expatriate also needs to pay attention to the five-year threshold. Residence in China longer than five years may make the expatriate bear tax liability for his worldwide income.[191] If the stay is between one and five years, subject to the tax authority's approval, he or she may be allowed to pay tax only on income derived from China and paid by a company in China.[192] This suggests that income derived outside China or within China but paid outside China is exempted from tax.

Chinese tax is imposed on the salary and wage income (including bonuses, year-end extra dividends, profit sharing, allowance, subsidies, and other remuneration from the individual's job or other income related to the individual's employment); production or business income of individual industrial and commercial proprietorships; business income from contracted operation or leasing of enterprises and institutions; income from remuneration for personal services; income from publications; income from fees for the use of proprietary rights; interest, dividend, and bonus dividend income; property rental income; property transfer income;

incidental income; and other income. Depending on the residence or domicile status of the taxpayer, tax on these categories of income is imposed based on the source. For example income from labour services, leasing of property, assignment of buildings or land-use rights, franchise income, and interest dividends of bonuses from sources outside China will be taxable regardless of whether payment was made outside China.[193]

6.3.2 Net Revenues Realized From the Investment

Net revenues of the FIE is taxable income, that is gross income minus costs, expenses, and losses. The gross income includes income from manufacturing and business operation, non-operating income, and capital gains. Expenses related to manufacturing and business operation are deductible. However, capital expenditures, penalties, fines, and income tax payments are not deductible. Expenses related to the acquisition of assets can be depreciated over time for tax purposes. Losses can be carried over for five years but cannot be carried back.

6.3.3 Transfer of Funds

The Chinese currency, renminbi, is not freely convertible. Therefore, the remittance of funds in renminbi is not permissible unless renminbi is first converted into foreign currency. However, the remittance and use of foreign currency is subject to foreign exchange control, which is a heavily regulated area in Chinese regulatory system.

Under Chinese law, the Chinese government held out the promise that foreign exchange deficiencies experienced by joint ventures would be remedied.[194] In practice, this promise was hardly realized. The government's attempt to remedy foreign exchange problems was not always successful[195] and may likely create more chaotic problems.

6.3.4 Sale of Investment

Right of First Refusal Under the Company Law

The concern to investors is whether shares and equity can be freely transferred. For instance private equity investors will be keen to know what statutory rights apply to prevent or pre-empt transfers of shares and equity. The Company Law contains a provision regulating transfers of equity in a limited liability company that amplifies the previous provision. A shareholder wishing to transfer equity to a non-shareholder must obtain the consent of a majority of the other shareholders. If they do not respond within 30 days, they are deemed to have consented.[196] If a majority of the shareholders do not consent, those who withheld consent must purchase the equity proposed to be transferred. If an objecting shareholder fails to complete the purchase, he or she will be deemed to have consented to the transfer.[197] In addition, the other shareholders shall have a right of pre-emption over the equity to be transferred. Where more than one shareholder exercises his or her right of pre-emption, the shareholders can discuss how to allocate the equity between themselves. If they cannot agree, the equity will be allocated pro rata to their existing equity interests. These rules do not apply to transfers between existing shareholders. In practice, the articles of association should spell out clearly how rights of pre-emption should work. There are no similar restrictions for a company limited by shares.

The three-year restriction against the transfer of promoter shares has been reduced to one year. This is an important amendment for private equity investors that often invest in companies where the PRC management and investors hold promoter shares. Although the amendment will add liquidity to the private equity market, it also means that the statutory freeze is likely to have expired by the time a deal is done.

The Company Law creates for the first time a right of first refusal to subscribe for new equity. Shareholders of a limited liability company have a right to make further capital contributions pro rata to their paid-in contributions where the company proposes to increase its registered capital. It is assumed that this right would apply even after shareholders at a general meeting have approved the increase in registered capital, that is shareholders at a general meeting cannot override an individual shareholder's statutory right of first refusal. The shareholders can, however, agree to disapply the rule, for example in a shareholders' agreement to allow employees or certain shareholders to make additional capital contributions. It is interesting to note that there is no right of first refusal in the case of a company limited by shares.

The Company Law also outlines the rules as to the transfer of shares in judicial proceedings. Once shares of a limited liability company should be sold to satisfy the creditors' claims in judicial enforcement procedure, the court should first give the notice to the existing shareholders to exercise their pre-emptive rights within 20 days.[198]

The Company Law also confers on shareholders significant rights relating to the repurchase of shares or equity. Previously, a company could not repurchase shares except to reduce its registered capital or to merge with a company that holds its shares. These continue to apply to companies limited by shares, which can repurchase shares to grant them to employees as an incentive. Under the Company Law, a shareholder in a limited liability company can request the company to repurchase his or her equity at a reasonable price if he or she votes against a resolution at a general meeting that relates to any of the following matters: where the company has not distributed profits for five consecutive years and the company has been profitable during that period and meets the conditions for making distributions; a merger or division of the company; a transfer by the company of its principal assets; the company's term of operations has expired (or other grounds for dissolution as stated in the articles of association have arisen) and the shareholders have resolved at general meeting to extend the term of the company.[199] If no agreement is reached within 60 days of the shareholders' meeting at which the resolution was passed, the shareholder can institute proceedings in the court within a further period of 30 days. This is a very significant provision as it means that a shareholder can be asked to be bought out from a company if a company carries out an asset sale of its business. In the case of a company limited by shares, a shareholder can request a repurchase of shares where he or she opposes a resolution to approve the merger or division of the company. A repurchase of shares or equity would involve a reduction in capital. The Company Law provides for the first time a procedure for the reduction in capital.

Transfer of Equity Under FIE Regulations

As an alternative to the establishment of a new JV, it is possible to acquire the registered capital in an existing JV held by a domestic or foreign investor, a private enterprise or a state-owned enterprise.[200] A foreign investor may directly acquire an equity interest in an existing domestic enterprise (equity acquisition), and if the resulting foreign ownership of equity interest is more than 25% and the investment complies with the other laws, rules, and regulations applicable to FIEs, then the target domestic company can be converted into a new JV.[201] Alternatively, the foreign investor can form a new JV by doing an asset deal. In substance, the foreign investor can acquire assets of a domestic enterprise and inject these into an existing FIE or use such assets to form a new JV.

Under the JV law, the other party(ies) to a JV have a pre-emptive right to acquire the equity share of the proposed transferor and have absolute consent rights to any transfer generally. No assignment or transfer of an interest in the JV (including transfers of interests between the JV parties) can be made without the other party's consent,[202] an amendment to the AOA, unanimous approval of the board, and approval of the original approval authority. In the case of mergers, divisions, or significant transfers of registered capital, a Chinese registered accountant must be engaged to examine the details of the transaction and issue a capital inspection report. As a result, the transfer of registered capital in a JV is more complex than a simple transfer of shares in an offshore corporate entity generally as it invites a possible renegotiation of the AOA as a condition to the transfer. Gain on the sale of equity interests in a JV is taxable under PRC law at a rate of 20%, or at a rate of 10% pursuant to certain double taxation treaties between the Chinese and a foreign government. If the equity interest of a foreign investor is purchased by a domestic party, including an existing Chinese partner, then the Chinese purchaser needs to withhold such tax from the purchase price. To remit such purchase price offshore, the approval documents from MOFCOM and SAFE are required to be presented to the remitting bank.

Due to the restrictions on transfer of registered capital in a JV, "put" and "call" rights do not operate in the same manner as in other jurisdictions with respect to fully transferable shares. It is still possible for the parties to agree to such "put" and "call" rights subject to certain restrictions and requirements under applicable law and the provisions in the articles of association to address relevant issues. Nevertheless, it is not possible to eliminate all uncertainty in the exercise of such sights as a practical matter. If there is an offshore special purpose vehicle ("SPV") to act as the investing company of the JV, the assignment or transfer as well as the "put" and "call" rights may then be handled and realized at the SPV level, without Chinese government's approval,[203] rather than at the JV level. Although a sale of an indirect interest in an FIE via sale of shares in an offshore SPA can be simpler, tacit approval of remaining partners is still necessary as a practical matter.

6.3.5 Liquidation of Investment

The JV may be terminated upon the occurrence of specific events, such as a breach of the JV contract or ancillary contract, force majeure with adverse effect on the JV's business, inability of the JV to operate due to heavy losses, inability to access foreign exchange jeopardizing operations, insolvency of a party to the JV, or other expressly stated conditions. These events are generally left to the negotiation of the parties to the JVs and set out in the AOA. In the case of most termination events, the unanimous approval of the board meeting is usually required. If the parties cannot agree on dissolution, they may submit their dispute to an arbitration commission which may issue an award ordering termination. However, termination must still be approved by the original examination and approval authority.

Upon the termination of the JV, the JV Contract should provide for a valuation of the business. As an alternative to the liquidation of the JV upon termination, one party could have the right to buy out the other party at a fair market value price in order to keep the business intact. If the parties cannot agree on who should succeed to the business of the JV in such a buy-out situation, potential compromise approaches should be considered and documented so that liquidation or succession issues are not left unresolved until termination of the JV. Upon liquidation, the assets of the JV are distributed to the parties in proportion to their equity contribution. The parties may wish to consider the appropriate distribution of assets upon a dissolution of the JV (absent a buyout as described earlier), including the inclusion of a provision providing for allocation of certain specified assets to one party.

Termination is followed by liquidation and dissolution of the JV. Liquidation can be standard or special.[204] The board unanimously appoints a liquidation committee in a standard liquidation, and this committee follows the regulatory procedures and the JV's articles of association to liquidate the JV. A creditors' meeting is not required. A special liquidation applies in the cases that the board of a JV cannot reach a consensus on the dissolution, and the liquidation must be triggered by an application to the original approval authority. The difference between the standard and special liquidations is that the liquidation procedure is no longer in the hands of the JV parties in a special liquidation. Instead, the approval authority will appoint a liquidation committee to exercise the powers of the board and to report directly to the approval authority. In addition, a creditors' meeting will be called. Upon liquidation, the JV is to complete dissolution by filing the liquidation report with the approval authority. The JV ceases to exist, however, only after the completion of the de-registration of the JV with the tax, customs, and company registration authorities, and a public announcement of de-registration in a national and local newspaper. As termination, liquidation, and dissolution can be expensive and time-consuming, the parties to the JV usually prefer a buy-out instead.

6.3.6 Reinvestment of Funds

A foreign investor is entitled to a refund of 40% of the income tax paid if it uses its profits to increase the registered capital of its existing investment or uses that income to invest in a new or existing enterprise with an operating period of at least five years. This rule, however, does not apply to an equity purchase.[205] A foreign investor may be even entitled to a full refund if the direct reinvestment is made by establishing or expanding a technologically advanced or export-orientated enterprise.[206] A refund is not available if the profits have already been distributed to the foreign investor who then uses such profits to reinvest in China. The refund is also not available where the foreign investor uses the liquidation proceeds of one FIE to invest into another FIE.[207]

The refund rules do not apply to a foreign investor who contributes additional funds to an existing FIE, which may, however, benefit from the two-exemption-plus-three-half-deduction rule (that will be only triggered upon the establishment of a new FIE). Several conditions must be satisfied to be eligible for this benefit. First, the FIE must fall in the "encouraged" category. Second, the newly added capital must not be less than US$60 million or it must constitute at least 50% of the original registered capital and be at least US$15 million.[208]

7. Unfair Business Practices

Corruption has been a serious problem with the Chinese regulatory regime due to the lack of freedom of speech and effective checks and balances from the public. The Chinese government and judiciary openly admitted the seriousness of the problem. In 1992, for instance 101,000 cases of corruption were reportedly handled by the courts.[209] The situation has not improved since then. Transparency International's Corruption Perceptions Index, for example ranked China as 72.[210] The World Economic Forum's Global Competitiveness Report (2008–2009) features corruption as the sixth largest constraint for doing business in China.[211] A Carnegie Endowment for International Peace Policy Brief estimates that 10% of government spending, contracts, and transactions are misused as kickbacks and bribes or simply stolen.[212] It was reported that China investigated 7,450 commercial and industrial bribery cases involving US$303 million in 2007.[213] These assessments seem to suggest that corruption penetrated every level of society and substantially weakened the state power.

The Chinese government acknowledges public corruption as a threat to the country's economic development and political stability and launched a vigorous anti-corruption campaign. In 2008, for example 4,960 officials above the county level were penalized nationwide for corruption, commercial bribery, harming public interest, and other disciplinary action, and of those, 801 were prosecuted.[214] There is also an international dimension to the corruption problem in China. Multinational companies, inter alia, the US companies, doing business in China face increasing scrutiny under the US Foreign Corrupt Practices Act. Statistics indicate that the number of FCPA enforcement actions involving China pursued by the US authorities such as the US Department of Justice and the US Securities and Exchange Commission has increased along with a corresponding rise in penalties. It appears that multinational companies may have to pay substantial fines for FCPA violations in their China operations.

China's anti-corruption law primarily comprises two parallel systems: (i) the Criminal Law and (ii) the Anti-Unfair Competition Law. The Criminal Law mainly governs crimes as to official bribery and commercial bribery. The Anti-Unfair Competition Law, on the other hand, regulates unfair competition practices by businesses, including but not limited to the prohibition against offering and taking bribes in the process of selling and purchasing goods and services. In addition, some administrative regulations, judicial interpretations, and the Party's disciplinary rules also crack down on bribery in China.[215]

China's Competition Law requires business organizations, foreign or domestic, to adhere to principles of voluntariness, equality, fairness, honesty, and credibility when conducting businesses in the market.[216] Business organizations are not allowed to practice bribery by offering money, property, or by any other means to sell or buy goods.[217] The SAIC has jurisdiction with respect to commercial bribery violations under the Competition Law.[218] The concept of "commercial bribery" under the Competition Law is broader than that in the Criminal Law as it not only covers money and property but also "other means" to secure businesses.[219] "Other means" here refers to offerings other than money and property, such as domestic and overseas travel or study. The term "property" is further defined as cash and material objects including property paid in the name of fees for promoting sales, publicity expenses, support fees, research costs, service fees, consulting fees, commissions, and reimbursements in order to sell or purchase goods.[220] Paying "kickbacks" by one business entity to the other is explicitly disallowed.[221] "Kickbacks" are defined as the practice of secretly returning money, property, or other means to an entity or individual without entering them into the entity's accounts.[222] Omitting account entries, creating false accounts, or transferring payments to other accounts are all recognized as "kickbacks." In doing business, the business operators are not allowed to give cash or property to its business partners subject to some exceptional rules. For instance, the business operators may give discounts[223] or pay a commission[224] to others (such as the government officials or employees of the SOEs), and others may accept these discounts or commissions if these discounts or commissions are recorded in their financial accounts.[225] The payment of a small amount of "advertising gifts" is also allowed.[226]

Business operators committing commercial bribery may face a criminal charge for bribes if the value is a "relatively large amount."[227] However, any violation for bribery under the Competition Law does not trigger a criminal liability but administrative fines.[228] Business operators may be subject to a fine between renminbi 10,000 and renminbi 200,000 for offering a bribe and any illegal income will be confiscated.[229] Individuals or entities accepting bribes when purchasing or selling goods are subject to the same penalty as the business operators offering the bribes between renminbi 10,000 and 200,000 and the illegal income will be confiscated.[230]

8. Protection of Foreign Investment: State Responsibility for Injuries to Aliens

Under the international investment jurisprudence, host states to foreign investment often prefer foreign investors to exhaust local remedies before the disputes are brought to the international tribunals for settlement.

Prior to the passage of the PRC Administrative Litigation Law, some administrative decisions in the fields of taxation and customs could be appealed to the courts, and the Administrative Litigation Law extended this principle to a wider range of administrative decisions. Accordingly, foreign investors were able to challenge the validity or legality of administrative decisions made by various administrative organs in Chinese courts. Foreign investment projects may likely be better off with the Administrative Litigation Law as most administrative bureaucratic decisions that would have a significant impact on foreign investment are now subject to judicial review. These regulatory decisions include but are not limited to administrative decisions imposing fines, restricting or infringing on property rights, intervening in business operations, and denying approvals or licences. Through the Administrative Litigation Law, the foreign investors were able to challenge and avoid the abuse of administrative power and misconduct by individual officials, which can improve transparency and efficacy of the administrative law regime.[231] In addition to the restoration of the administrative appeal principle, the Administrative Litigation Law also outlined the procedural rules for appeals.

Together with other administrative laws such as the PRC Administrative Penalty Law, Administrative Permission Law, Administrative Review Law, and State Compensation Law, the PRC Administrative Litigation Law was at least part of the larger effort to make Chinese administrative bureaucracy more accountable, and it provides a platform. Nevertheless, the constraining function of the administrative law in China may be limited as the judicial review is not extended to discretionary decisions. Moreover, prior to judicial review, the foreign investor may have to exhaust administrative remedies by submitting the administrative decision to a higher level of government authority for administrative review, which may shield some administrative decisions from judicial review.[232] Therefore, it must be recognized that the administrative law may necessarily decrease the level of state intrusion.

Notes

1 For the purpose of this book, the PRC or China refers to the People's Republic of China, excluding Hong Kong Special Administrative Region, Macau Special Administrative Region, and the territory of Taiwan.
2 Alexander Eckstein, *China's Economic Revolution* (Cambridge: Cambridge University Press 1977), p. 123ff.
3 T.K. Ramsey, "China: Socialism Embraces Capitalism? An Oxymoron for the Turn of the Century: A Study of the Restructuring of the Securities Markets and Banking Industry in the People's Republic of China in an Effort to Increase Investment Capital" (1998) *Houston Journal of International Law* 20, 451, 477.
4 The Communique of the 1978 Third Plenum of the Eleventh Communist Party Congress of December 1978, p. 21.

5   This contrast also appeared in the economic development in other East Asian countries. See generally Stephan Haggard, *Pathways from the Periphery: The Politics of Growth in the Newly Industrializing Countries* (Ithaca & London: Cornell University Press 1990); Anis Chowdhury and Iyanatul Islam, *The Newly Industrializing Economies of East Asia* (London & New York: Routledge 1993).

6   John Gapper, "China's Business Elite Is Free Enough," *Financial Times*, 21 October 2010, p. 13 (arguing that the young generation of Chinese entrepreneurs have the acceptable level of freedom and the state is able to continue to grow while the state remains totalitarian).

7   The PRC Equity Joint Venture Law 1979.

8   Interim Regulations of the People's Republic of China Concerning the Control of Resident Offices of Foreign Enterprises (promulgated on 30 October 1980).

9   The Law on Enterprises with Sole Foreign Investment (adopted on 11 April 1986).

10 The Law on Sino-Foreign Co-operative Enterprises (adopted on 13 April 1988).

11 PRC Constitution 1982, Article 18 (adopted on 4 December 1982).

12 PRC Constitution 1982, Article 18.

13 Chalmers Johnson, *MITI and the Japanese Miracle: The Growth of Japanese Industrial Policy 1925–1975* (Stanford: Stanford University Press 1982); David Friedman, *The Misunderstood Miracle: Industrial Development and Political Change in Japan* (Ithaca & London: Cornell University Press 1988), Ch 5; Robert A. Scalapino, Seizaburo Sato and Jusuf Wanandi (eds), *Asian Economic Development: Past and Future* (Berkeley: Institute of East Asian Studies 1985).

14 Stephan Haggard, *Pathways from the Periphery: The Politics of Growth in the Newly Industrializing Countries* (Ithaca & London: Cornell University Press 1990), Ch 2; Lee Soo Ann, *Industrialization in Singapore* (Melbourne: Longman's 1973); Lim Chong Yah, *Economic Restructuring in Singapore* (Singapore: Federal Publication 1984).

15 Jung-en Woo, *Race to the Swift: State and Finance in Korean Industrialization* (New York: Columbia University Press 1991) (offering considerable evidence of the central role of the state in developing South Korea's industrialized economy).

16 Thomas B. Gold, "Entrepreneurs, Multinationals and the State" in Edwin A. Winckler and Susan Greenhalgh (eds), *Contending Approaches to the Political Economy of Taiwan* (Armonk, NY: M.E. Sharpe 1990), pp. 175–205.

17 Haggard, *supra* note 5, pp. 19–22.

18 Robert A. Packenham, *The Dependency Movement: Scholarship and Politics in Development Studies* (Cambridge, MA: Harvard University Press 1992); Paul A. Baran, *The Political Economy of Growth* (New York: Monthly Review Press 1968); Celso Furtado, *Development and Underdevelopment: A Structural View of the Problems of Developed and Underdeveloped Countries* (Berkeley: University of California Press 1964); Charles K. Wilber (ed), *The Political Economy of Development and Underdevelopment*, 2nd ed. (New York: Random House 1979).

19 Mark Singer, *Weak States in a World of Power: The Dynamics of International Relationships* (New York: Free Press 1972).

20 James A. Gardner, *Legal Imperialism: American Lawyers and Foreign Aid in Latin America* (Madison: University of Wisconsin Press 1980), p. 187ff.

21 Francis G. Snyder, "Law and Development in the Light of Dependency Theory" (1980) 14 *Law and Society Review* 722.

22 Richard W. Bauman, "Liberalism and Canadian Corporate Law" in Richard F. Devlin (ed), *Canadian Perspectives on Legal Theory* (Toronto: Emond Montgomery 1991), pp. 75–97; Mark Kelman, *A Guide to Critical Legal Studies* (Cambridge, MA: Harvard University Press), p. 249; Alan Stone, "The Place of Law in the Marxian Structure-Superstructure Archetype" (1985) 19(1) *Law & Society Review* 40–67.

23 Edward Friedman, "Theorizing the Democratization of China's Leninist State" in Arif Dirlik and Maurice Meisner (eds), *Marxism and the Chinese Experience* (M.E. Sharpe 1989), p. 179 (discussing the difficulties facing China in cloning the East Asian development experience).

24 "China Data" *China Business Review*, May–June 1992, p. 19.

25 "China Data" *China Business Review*, May–June 1993, p. 57.

26 "Statistical Communique of the State Statistical Bureau of the PRC on the 1993 National Economic and Social Development," *China Economic News*, Supplement No. 3, 14 March 1994, p. 5.

27 It must be pointed out that there was a gap between contract value and actually used amounts. For instance, US$57.2 billion foreign investment was contracted but only US$10.1 billion was used in 1991, and US$122.7 billion was contracted but only US$36.77 billion was used. See "Analysis of China's Use of Foreign Funds for 1992" *China Economic News*, 24 May 1993, p. 11; 1993 Statistical Communique, *supra* note 26, p. 5.

28 China Trade Performance, *US-China Business Council*, available at www.uschina.org

29 US-China Business Council, *Foreign Direct Investment in China*, available at www. uschina.org/statistics/fdi_cumulative.html

30 Ibid. https://www.statista.com/statistics/1288326/china-foreign-invested-companies-share-in-total-import-and-export/

31 "China to Draw US$50 Billion FDI, to be World's No.1 Recipient" *People's Daily*, 5 December 2002.

32 J.R. Woetzel, *Capitalist China: Strategies for a Revolutionized Economy* (Singapore: John Wiley & Sons (Asia) 2003), p. 2.

33 The Third Plenum of the 11th Central Committee of the Chinese Communist Party formally, though scantly, introduced the "open door" policy.

34 PRC Law on Joint Ventures Using Chinese and Foreign Investment (1979), as amended 1990).

35 Implementation Regulations for the Law on Joint Ventures Using Chinese and Foreign Investment (1983, as amended 1986).

36 PRC Economic Contract Law (1981) and PRC Foreign Economic Law (1985), which were later unified under the Contract Law 1998.

37 PRC Income Tax Law Concerning Joint Ventures with Chinese and Foreign Investment (1980); Detailed Rules for the Implementation of the PRC Income Tax Law Concerning Joint Ventures with Chinese and Foreign Investment; PRC Foreign Enterprise Income Tax Law (1980).

38 Provisional Regulations of the PRC Governing Foreign Exchange Control (1980); Rules for the Implementation of Foreign Exchange Controls Relating to Enterprises with Overseas Chinese Capital and Chinese-Foreign Equity Joint Ventures (1983).

39 The Notice Concerning Strengthening and Improving the Administration of Contributions Relating to Chinese Employees' Interests Made by Foreign Invested Enterprises; the Notice Concerning the Financial Issues Relating to the Residential Housing Reform for Chinese Employees in Foreign Invested Enterprises; Supplemental Provisions on Implementation of the New Enterprises Financial System in Foreign-invested Enterprises.

40 The Announcement of the People's Bank of China on Further Reforming the Foreign Exchange Management System (28 December 1993).

41 Pitman Potter, *Foreign Business Law in China: Past Progress and Future Challenges* (San Francisco: The 1990 Institute 1995), p. 35.

42 Guo Xinjun, *China's WTO Accession and New Strategies for Foreign Capital Utilization* (Beijing: Economic Daily Publishing House 2002), p. 153.

43 Jerome A. Cohen and Stuart J. Valentine, "China Business – Progress and Prospects" in William P. Streng and Allen D. Wilcox (eds), *Doing Business in China* (New York: Matthew Bender 1990), Introduction.

44 Martin Weil, "The Business Climate in China: Half Empty or Half Full?" in Joint Economic Committee, Congress of the United States (eds), *China's Economic Dilemmas in the 1990s: The Problems of Reforms, Modernization, and Interdependence* (Armonk, NY: M.E. Sharpe 1991), pp. 770–784.

45 Lynn Chu, "The Chimera of the China Market" *The Atlantic Monthly*, October 1990, pp. 56–78.

46 Final Version of the 14th CPC National Congress Report, FBIS Daily Report – China, 21 October 1992.

47 Guo Xinjun, *supra* note 42, p. 153.

48 UNCTAD, "Promoting Linkages" (2001) *World Investment Report* 341.

49 The corporate law regimes for FIEs and domestic enterprises remain parallel. Only when the FIEs' laws and regulations are silent or contradictory to the Company Law do the provisions in the Company Law apply. Otherwise, in most cases, the formation, operation, and termination of an FIE need to comply with the FIEs' laws and regulations.

50 Kenneth Lieberthal, "Completing WTO Reforms" *China Business Review*, September/ October 2006.

51 "Lamy: China Fulfilling WTO Commitments Well" *China Daily*, available at http:// www.chinadaily.com.cn/business/2006-09/06/content_682529_2.htm

52 The liberalizing trend was not extended to most publishing activities. Also, genetically modified organisms were also moved to the "prohibited" category.

53 The Decision of the State Council on Reforming the Investment System, issued by the State Council on 16 July 2004, available at http://en.ndrc.gov.cn/policyrelease/t20060207_58851.htm.

54 The regulations also addressed "round-tripping" investment activities, forbade the hiding of affiliations, legislated protection of key industries, and introduced the umbrella concept of "national security" to supervisor foreign investment.

55 Monique Ho and Molly Qin, "Important Legal and Strategic Considerations When Investing in China," *McDermott Will & Emery Newsletter*, Inside M&A (March/April 2008).

56 See www.mofcom.gov.cn/aarticle/tongjiziliao/v/201002/20100206785656.html.

57 Peter Hays Gries, *China's New Nationalism: Pride, Politics, and Diplomacy* (Berkeley: University of California Press 2004); Suisheng Zhao, "We Are Patriots First and Democrats Second: The Rise of Chinese Nationalism in the 1990s" in Edward Friedman, Edward McCormick and Barrett McCormick (eds), *What If China Doesn't Democratize? Implications for War and Peace* (New York: ME Sharpe 2000).

58 See generally, http://en.wikipedia.org/wiki/Harmonious_society, and Maureen Fan, "China's Party Leadership Declares New Priority: 'Harmonious Society'," *The Washington Post*, 12 October 2006. A harmonious society is of higher standards, not only trying to fill in the gap between the wealthy and poor but also providing an opportunity to the people for the self-fulfilment, which is akin to the capabilities approach advocated by Martha C. Nussbaum, *Frontiers of Justice: Disability, Nationality and Species Membership* (Cambridge, MA: Belknap Press Harvard University Press 2007) Chs 3, 5 and 7; Amartya Sen, *Developments as Freedom* (Oxford: Oxford University Press 1999).

59 Guidance Catalogue (amended in 2007), available at http://www.gov.cn/gongbao/content/2008/content_1018951.htm

60 China Market Intelligence, *China's 2007 Foreign Investment Guide*, https://www.uschina.org/cmi/mofcom-issues-2007-guidelines-attracting-foreign-investment-march-28-2007

61 United States Trade Representative, *Report to Congress on China's WTO Compliance* 6 (2005), www.ustr.gov/assets/Document_Library/Reports_Publications/2005/asset_upload_file293_8580.pdf.

62 Susan L. Shirk, *The Political Logic of Economic Reform in China* (Berkeley: University of California Press 1993).

63 Lucian Pye, *The Mandarin and the Cadre* (Ann Arbor: University of Michigan 1988).

64 Kenneth Lieberthal and Michel Oksenberg, *Policy Making in China: Leaders, Structures, and Processes* (Princeton: Princeton University Press 1988).

65 Yong Wang, "China's Domestic WTO Debate" (January/February 2000) 27(54) *China Business Review* 54.

66 To be more detailed, these industries refer to machinery, automobiles, telecommunications, construction, iron and steel, and non-ferrous metals. "Control Over Key

Industries, 'Crucial'" *China Daily*, 19 December 2006, available at http://english.people.com.cn/200612/19/eng20061219_333839.html.

67 For details, Shen Wei, "Is SAFE Safe Now? – Foreign Exchange Regulatory Control over Chinese Outbound and Inbound Investment and a Political Economy Analysis of Policies" (2010) 11(2) *Journal of World Investment and Trade* 227, 245–250.

68 Mure Dickie, "Chinese Takeover Fears Grow," *Financial Times*, 4 August 2006, p. 6; Geoff Dyer, Sundeep Tucker and Tom Mitchell, "Forbidden Country? How Foreign Deals in China are Hitting Renewed Resistance," *Financial Times*, 8 August 2006, p. 11.

69 The most high-profile and lasting battle was Carlyle's bid to take stake in Xugong, China's leading machinery maker, which was finally defeated. Sundeep Tucker, "Carlyle Concedes Defeat in Battle to Take Stake in China's Xugong," *Financial Times*, 23 July 2008.

70 This could be evidenced by comparing "The PRC and US Memorandum of Understanding Concerning Market Access" (1992) 31 *International Legal Materials* 1274 with statements of concerns of executives in "The Council's Investment Initiative" *China Business Review*, September–October 1992, pp. 6–8. Also compare the "Memorandum of Understanding between the government of PRC and the government of US on the Protection of Intellectual Property" (1992) with US–China Business Council, "Recommendation on Amendment of the China Patent Law (1988) and the 1989 IP Agreement, in Pitman B. Potter, "Bettering Protection for Intellectual Property" *China Business Review*, July–August 1989, pp. 27–29.

71 Constitution defines the model as a "socialist" market economy.

72 Some foreign scholars suggest that the Chinese notion of legal rights is "softer" than in the West. See Donald C. Clarke, "The Execution of Civil Judgments in China" in Stanley B. Lubman (ed), *China's Legal Reforms* (Oxford: Oxford University Press 1996), pp. 65, 69.

73 Martin King Whyte, "Urban China: A Civil Society in the Making?" in Arthur Lewis Rosenbaum (ed), *State and Society in China: The Consequences of Reform* (Boulder, CO: Westview Press 1992), pp. 77–101 (claiming that the essence of civil society involves "the idea of the existence of institutionalized autonomy for social relationships and association life, autonomy vis-a-vis the state . . . a well-formed civil society implies a degree of separation in the relationship between state and society, such that much social life goes on without reference to state dictates and policies.")

74 Law is the most overtly culture-bound of all the disciplines. Comparative legal study has not been successful in developing culturally neutral legal concepts. Therefore, the assumption of the universality of Western legal forms and legal ideals or a complete ignorance of cultural bias may not be a good technique to comparative legal study. See Gunter Frankenberg, "Critical Comparisons: Re-thinking Comparative Law" (1985) 26 *Harvard Journal of International Law* 434–440.

75 Lee A. Brudvig, "The Fifth Dragon" *The China Business Review*, July–August 1993, pp. 114–123.

76 "Zhu Rongji's Crackdown on Banks Reportedly 'Failed'" *Hong Kong Standard*, 14 March 1994.

77 Anthony R. Dicks, "Compartmentalized Law and Judicial Restraint: An Inductive View of Some Jurisdictional Barriers to Reform" in Stanley B. Lubman (ed), *China's Legal Reform* (Oxford: Oxford University Press 1996), pp. 82, 84.

78 Administrative Measures for Filing of Foreign Investment Projects of China (Shanghai) Pilot Free Trade Zone (Hu Fu Fa [2013] No.71); Administrative Measures for Filing of Outbound Investment Projects of China (Shanghai) Pilot Free Trade Zone (Hu Fu Fa [2013] No.72); Administrative Measures for Filing of Foreign-invested Enterprises of China (Shanghai) Pilot Free Trade Zone (Hu Fu Fa [2013] No.73); Administrative Measures for Filing of Outbound Investment in Setting Up of Overseas Enterprises of China (Shanghai) Pilot Free Trade Zone (Hu Fu Fa [2013] No.74); and Special Administrative Measures (Negative List) on Foreign Investment Access to the China (Shanghai) Pilot Free Trade Zone (2013) (Hu Fu Fa [2013] No.75).

79 The approved business scope is typically restricted to a specific category of manufacturing or service based on the contents of the feasibility study report. FIEs are still typically

manufacturing operations. FIEs intended primarily to import products for resale were prohibited until recently and now are permitted in certain jurisdictions only after heavy scrutiny and under stricter regulation. A large number of FIEs are restricted to be a re-investment vehicle for other China investments.

80 Reply on Approving the Trial Application of New Business License in the China (Shanghai) Pilot Free Trade Zone (gong Shang Wai Qi Zi [2013] No. 148) (26 September 2013); Provisions of the Shanghai AIC on the Administration of Registration of Enterprises in the China (Shanghai) Pilot Free Trade Zone (Hu Gong Shang Wai (2013) No. 329), promulgated on 21 October 2003 and implemented on 1 October 2013.

81 The negative list is similar in concept to the US' mooted Trans-Pacific Partnership Agreement, which places more than 200 restrictions on investments in 18 industries, including media and publishing, real estate, and telecommunications. It is apparent that the negative list should be shortened. Regulators encourage business players to offer ideas and solutions to revise the negative list.

82 Decision of the Standing Committee of the National People's Congress on Authorizing the State Council to Temporarily Adjust the Administrative Examinations and Approvals of Relevant Legal Provisions in the China (Shanghai) Pilot Free Trade Zone (promulgated on 30 August 2013 and implemented on 1 October 2013); Notice on Authorizing the China (Shanghai) Pilot Free Trade Zone Branch of Shanghai Administration for Industry and Commerce the Administrative Authority for Registration of Foreign-invested Enterprises (24 September 2013).

83 Provisions of the State Council for the Encouragement of Foreign Investment (1986).

84 Equity Joint Venture Law, Articles 5 and 9; Equity Joint Venture Law Implementing Rules, Articles 4, 28 and 62. Cooperative Joint Venture Law, Article 8.

85 Equity Joint Venture Law, Article 7; Joint Venture Income Tax Law, Article 5.

86 WFOE Law, Article 3.

87 Provisions of the State Council for the Encouragement of Foreign Investment.

88 Ibid.

89 Originally, there were four zones, that is Shenzhen, Zhuhai, Shantou, and Xiamen. Hainan Island was added as the fifth one in 1987.

90 For example the Decision of the Standing Committee of the National People's Congress Authorizing the People's Congress of Guangdong and Fujian Provinces and Their Standing Committees to Enact Various Specific Laws and Regulations for the Special Economic Zones under Their Jurisdiction (1981); Regulations of Guangdong Province for Special Economic Zones (1985).

91 For example Regulations on Special Economic Zones in Guangdong Province (1980), Article 9.

92 Provisional Regulations on the Reduction and Exemption of Enterprise Income Tax and Consolidated Industrial and Commercial Tax in Special Economic Zones and 14 Coastal Cities (1984), Articles I(1)(a) and II(1).

93 Regulations on Special Economic Zones in Guangdong Province, Articles 12–18.

94 Part I(A) of the Protocol on the Accession of the People's Republic of China, in WTO Ministerial Conference, Report of the Working Party on the Accession of China, WT/MIN/(01)3, at 75, available at www.wto.org/english/thewto_e/completeacc_e.htm

95 The US-China Business Council, Administrative Licensing and Business Approvals, USCBC 2007 Member Priorities Survey Executive Summary: US Companies' China Outlook: Continuing Optimism Tempered by Operating Challenges, *Protectionist Threats*, www.uschina.org/public/documents/2007/10/uscbc-member-survey-2007.pdf

96 PRC Environment Protection Law; Joint Venture Labour Regulations; Provisional Regulations on Environmental Control for Economic Zones Open to Foreigners.

97 PRC Regulations for the Administration of Foreign-invested Banks, effective as of 11 December 2006, and its implementing rules.

98 Michael G. DeSombre, *et al.*, "Landmark Regulations Expand China's Banking Sector" *China Law & Practice*, December 2006.

99 Matters Relevant to the Administration of Foreign Capital Involved in the Reform of the Division of Equity Interests of Listed Companies Circular (jointly issued by MOFCOM and CSRC, effective as of 26 October 2005).

100 Measures for the Administration of Strategic Investment in Listed Companies by Foreign Investors (2006).

101 US Treasury Department Office of Public Affairs, Financial Sector Reform, US Fact Sheet: Fourth Cabinet-Level Meeting of the US-China Strategic Economic Dialogue, 18 June 2008.

102 China's long-established policies in the publishing industry are to limit the scope of players and eventually to control the expression of ideas. Similarly, there have been restrictions on advertising content. Political sensitiveness also affects the monitoring model of market research players, which were required to register with the State Statistical Bureau and submit all surveys for prior approval and share their research products with security forces. There is no surprise that China failed to implement its trading rights commitments insofar as they relate to the importation of books, newspapers, periodicals, electronic publications, and audio and video products, and continued to reserve the right to import these products to state trading enterprises. United States Trade Representative, 2007 Report on China's WTO Compliance, 11 December 2007.

103 Notice on Strengthening the Administration of Foreign Investment in the Operation of Value Added Telecoms Services (issued by the PRC Ministry of Information Industry in 2006).

104 Certain qualifying products may be sold in the domestic market for foreign exchange with the appropriate approval from the SAFE. Provisions for Using Foreign Exchange for Settling Payments to Foreign Invested Enterprises (promulgated by the SAFE on 1 March 1989).

105 Announcement of the People's Bank of China on Further Reforming the Foreign Exchange Management System (28 December 1993).

106 Provisional Foreign Exchange Regulations 1980.

107 State Council Provisions on Encouraging Foreign Investment.

108 Provisions for the Administration of the Settlement, Sale and Payment of Foreign Exchange (promulgated by the People's Bank of China on 20 June 1996 and effective as of 1 July 1996).

109 Provisions for the Administration of the Settlement, Sale and Payment of Foreign Exchange, Article 10.

110 Foreign Exchange Control Regulations (14 January 1997).

111 The registration process includes authentication by SAFE under certain circumstances. In contrast, domestic enterprises are required to obtain SAFE approval for foreign exchange debts, and such SAFE approval is often very difficult to obtain.

112 Fred Bergsten, "We Can Fight Fire with Fire on the Renminbi" *Financial Times*, 4 October 2010, p. 13.

113 James Politi, "House to Hit Back on Renminbi" *Financial Times*, 30 September 2010, p. 2 (reporting that the US House of Representatives is set to pass legislation and to punish China for undervaluing its currency, which is damaging the competitiveness of US economy).

114 Arvind Subramanian, "America Cannot Win the Currency Wars Alone" *Financial Times*, 21 October 2010, p. 13 (suggesting the US take a multilateral action to induce Chinese cooperation such as mobilizing a broader coalition in the G20 summit).

115 Patti Waldmeir, "Labor Law Leads to 'Huge Payouts'" *Financial Times*, 1 June 2010, p. 3.

116 Ibid.

117 State Council, Measures for the Encouragement of Foreign Investment.

118 Shanghai Municipality Sino–Foreign Equity Joint Venture Labour Union Regulations, Articles 6 and 8.

119 Bill Purves, *Barefoot in the Boardroom: Venture and Misadventure in the People's Republic of China* (Toronto: NC Press 1991), pp. 35–62.

120 Ann Kent, *Between Freedom and Subsistence: China and Human Rights* (Hong Kong: Oxford University Press 1993), p. 240.

121 Ronald C. Brown, "China's New Labor Contract Law" (July 2007) 3(4) *China Law Reporter*.

122 Dongfang Fan, "Labor Contract Law Strengthens Chinese Union" (January 2008) VIII(1) *China Brief* at 7, available at https://jamestown.org/program/labor-contract-law-strengthens-chinese-union/

123 Request for the establishment of a panel by the United States, China – Measures Affecting Imports of Automobile Parts, WT/DS340/8 (30 March 2006).

124 United States General Accounting Office, World Trade Organization: Analysis of China's Commitments to Other Members (October 22) 69.

125 Donald C. Clarke, "Legislating for a Market Economy in China" (September 2007) 191 *China Quarterly* at 567, 575.

126 EJV Law, Article 21.

127 EJV Law, Article 4.

128 EJV Law, Article 22.

129 EJV Law, Article 20.

130 PRC regulations contemplate that an enterprise will have foreign investment enterprise status so long as the foreign ownership percentage is not less than 25% of the total registered capital. Foreign investors can invest less than 25% of the equity in a Chinese-registered company, but such investment vehicles do not qualify as FIEs or for the favourable tax and foreign exchange treatment.

131 See Provisional Regulations on the Ratio between the Registered Capital and Total Investment of Sino-Foreign Equity Joint Ventures, issued by the SAIC in 1987.

132 Exceptions to these ratios would require special approval.

133 Tentative Provisions on the Ratio of Registered Capital to Total Investment in Sino-Foreign Joint Ventures (promulgated by SAIC on 1 March 1987) Article 5.

134 EJV Law Implementation Regulations 2001, Article 22.

135 This can be increased with approval for certain encouraged projects.

136 Provisions on Several Issues Concerning Using High and New Technology Results as Capital Contributions (jointly promulgated by the State Science and Technology Commission and the State Administration of Industry and Commerce on 9 July 1997).

137 Contributions by an American investor of equipment, component parts, and other tangible items which will be sent from the United States to China or which otherwise contain American technology are subject to US export controls. The American investor should inquire early whether its contributions to the Chinese JV will be permitted under US export rules and whether it will need a general or validated export license in order to export the items.

138 Several Provisions on Capital Contribution by Parties to Sino-Foreign Equity Joint Ventures (approved by the State Council on 30 December 1987, promulgated by MOFERT and SAIC on 1 January 1988 and effective as of 1 March 1988), Article 4.

139 Several Provisions on Capital Contribution by Parties to Sino-Foreign Equity Joint Ventures, Article 4.

140 *See* The Notice on Certain Issues concerning the Further Strengthening of the Administration of the Examination, Approval and Registration of Foreign Investment Enterprises, issued by MOFTEC and SAIC in 1994.

141 Supplementary Provisions for Several Provisions on Capital Contribution by Parties to Sino-Foreign Equity Joint Ventures (promulgated by the SAIC and MOFTEC on 1 November 1997).

142 The term "preference shares" or "preferred shares" usually refers to a separate class of shares possessing unique rights and privileges. These rights usually go well beyond the rights enjoyed by ordinary shareholders.

143 The PRC Securities Law, PRC Contract Law, and the FIE-specific laws and regulations make no mention of preferred shares. FIEs do not even issue dividend shares, but only undivided "equity interests," which refer to the ownership of a specified percentage of the registered capital. However, it has been also argued that the principle of

"same share same interests" does not preclude the existence of multiple classes of shares as long as each class of shares is treated equally within its class.

144 China is not a common law jurisdiction where the doctrine of precedent applies even though decided cases may provide some guidance as to how certain PRC courts view the validity and enforceability of preferred rights provisions in legal documentation.

145 This is permitted by the PRC law as the contract is foreign-related.

146 Of course, it is open to the other side to dispute the validity of the preferred rights as a matter of Chinese law before the tribunal. However, it is still far more advantageous in an offshore arbitration compared to before a Chinese court or a Chinese arbitration tribunal.

147 Theoretically, the PRC courts still can refuse enforcement on public policy grounds of a New York Convention arbitral award, though the chances are low as the Chinese law does not expressly ban the adoption of preferred rights. The public policy argument would be of little relevance if the Chinese party has assets which can be enforced against in another jurisdiction.

148 Environment Directorate of the OECD, *Environmental Performance Review of China* (Paris: OECD 2007).

149 For a comparative account, Jagdish Bhagwati, "India's Reform and Growth Have Lifted All Boats" *Financial Times*, 1 December 2010, p. 13; James Lamont, "Sen Warns that India's Growth Must Not Come at Price of Food" *Financial Times*, 22 December 2010, p. 1.

150 David Pilling, "Nature Will Constrain China's Growth" *Financial Times*, 4 October 2010, p. 12 (holding the opinion that the Earth cannot sustain 1.3 billion Chinese adopting a Western lifestyle and reckless consumption).

151 United States Trade Representative, *2007 Report to Congress on China's WTO Compliance*, 11 December 2007, available at https://ustr.gov/sites/default/files/asset_upload_file625_13692.pdf.

152 James V. Feinerman, "Chinese Law Relating to Foreign Investment and Trade: The Decade of Reform in Retrospect" in Joint Economic Committee, Congress of the United States (eds), *China's Economic Dilemmas in the 1990s: The Problems of Reforms, Modernization, and Interdependence* (Armonk, NY: M.E. Sharpe 1991), p. 828.

153 For example Foreign Economic Contract Law, Articles 4 and 9.

154 The worldwide income includes all income from domestic and foreign branches. Income sources include dividends, interest, royalties, and rental income. Tax credits for foreign taxes paid were available. PRC Joint Venture Income Tax Law, Article 2.

155 PRC Foreign-invested Enterprises and Foreign Enterprises Income Tax Law (effective from 1 July 1991 to 31 December 2007); Implementing Rules of PRC Foreign-invested Enterprises and Foreign Enterprises Income Tax Law (effective from 1 July 1991 to 31 December 2007).

156 Prior to the passing of the unified Foreign Enterprise Tax Law, foreign enterprises without establishment in China were taxed at a flat 20% rate on income derived from domestic sources in the form of dividends, royalties, rentals, and other sources determined by the Ministry of Finance. All foreign businesses in China other than joint ventures were taxed under the Foreign Enterprise Tax Law and its Implementation Regulations at progressive rates ranging from 20 to 40% plus a local 10% surcharge.

157 Foreign-Invested Enterprise and Foreign Enterprise Tax Law (promulgated by the National People's Congress on 13 December 1981, and effective as of 1 January 1982), Article 7.

158 Foreign-Invested Enterprise and Foreign Enterprise Tax Law, Article 8.

159 Provisions of the PRC State Council for the Encouragement of Foreign Investment (promulgated by the State Council on 11 October 1986).

160 PRC Provisional Regulations on Enterprise Income Tax and its Implementing Rules (both effective from 1 January 1994).

161 "Foreigners May Lose Investment Privileges" *Hong Kong Standard*, 6 June 1994.

162 An evidence of this slow speed was that the delay of the legislative process for the proposed uniform enterprise income tax law was not tabled at the annual assembly of the National People's Congress in 2006 but was shelved for another year till 2007.

163 Decision on the Use of Interim Regulations Concerning Value-added Taxes, Consumption Taxes and Business Taxes on FFEs and Foreign Enterprises (1993).

164 PRC Law to Administer the Levying and Collection of Taxes (1992); Detailed Rules for the Implementation of the PRC Law to Administer the Levying and Collection of Taxes (1993).

165 Joint Venture Law, Article 10; Joint Venture Implementing Rules, Article 87.

166 Tax Administration Law and its Implementation Regulations.

167 Kimberley Silver, "Removing the Rose-Colored Glasses" (May/June 1997) 24(11) *China Business Review* 10–11.

168 Kenneth Lieberthal, "Completing WTO Reforms" *China Business Review*, September/October 2006.

169 Implementing Rules of the Measures for the Administration of State-owned Asset Valuation 1992.

170 Certain Regulations on Changes to Shareholders' Rights in FIEs 1997.

171 EJV Law Implementation Regulations, Article 43.

172 Procedures for the Administration of the Appraisal of Assets Invested by Foreign Investors (Promulgated by the State Administration for the Inspection of Import and Export Commodities and the Ministry of Finance on 18 March 1994 and effective as of 1 May 1994).

173 The value verification report is the basis for CPA firms to verify the paid-in contribution by the foreign investors to the registered capital.

174 The application usually includes information such as the name of the unit, affiliations and locations, the aim of the valuation, the type of assets to be valued, the scope and book values of the assets, and the relevant documents for approval of the change in ownership rights. An asset inventory and a financial report also need to be submitted together with the application.

175 The authority will examine whether the unit making the application has the right to use the state-owned assets; whether the change of ownership rights is in compliance with national laws, regulations, and policies; and whether the application information is complete and clear.

176 Mark Williams, "Competition Policy and Law" in Randall Peerenboom (ed), *Regulating Enterprises: The Regulatory Impact on Doing Business in China* (Oxford: Oxford Foundation for Law, Justice and Society 2007). https://www.fljs.org/sites/default/files/migrated/publications/Peerenboom_intro%25233%2523.pdf

177 The national security review is also adopted by other Western countries such as the United States in scrutinizing PRC investments in the US for their impact on national security. Some high-profile transactions like the failed bid for UNOCAL by CNOOC did not go smoothly. For details, Shen Wei, "Is SAFE Safe Now? – Foreign Exchange Regulatory Control over Chinese Outbound and Inbound Investment and a Political Economy Analysis of Policies" (2010) 11(2) *Journal of World Investment and Trade* 227, 230.

178 Anti-Monopoly Law, Article 7 (providing that the state shall protect the legitimate business activities of undertakings in "industries that are dominated by the state-owned economy and that have a direct bearing on national economic wellbeing and national security, as well as industries that conduct exclusive and monopolistic sales in accordance with law.")

179 Although the scope of duties of these two authorities are specified in the Anti-Monopoly Law, the administrative rank was not specified in the law, which may add a new layer of difficulty in implementing the law.

180 WTO commitments may make no economic sense for local governments to implement, as they are keen on protecting their revenue streams and view market liberalization as a distinct threat to their existing economic interests. To attract foreign investments or protect local industries, local governments often offer more tax and economic incentives. Foreign investors must deal with local rules and policies and shop around China to enjoy

the most favourable investment incentives. Two-year tax exemptions and three-year 50% reductions in tax are legal and widely used methods to attract foreign investment. However, most local governments may offer extended tax-free periods, for example rebates of local portions of value-added tax, or five years at 50% off the tax rate, or giving expatriate managers lower individual income tax rates, or rebates for individual income tax that is paid, all of which are unlawful investment subsidies and are contrary to WTO principles. The national unified enterprise income tax law is intended to end preferential tax laws, but the enforcement remains the key challenge.

181 See Articles 3 and 4 of the Interim Measures for the Administration of Examination and Approval of Foreign Investment Projects, promulgated by the NDRC on 9 October 2004.

182 A project is deemed to require overall state balancing if it involves investment or loans from the central government, specified infrastructure projects, and industrial projects and other foreign investment projects specified by the central government.

183 In early 2000, a new regulation was issued by the Shanghai government for the purpose of streamlining the approval process. Under this new regulation, it may be possible for foreign investors, depending on the merits of their project, to directly enter into the FSR stage, with the step relating to Preliminary Project Proposal being waived.

184 For example WFOE Rules, Article 10.

185 "Individuals who have residence in China" refers to these individuals who, by reason of their household registration, family, or economic interests, normally reside in China. Individual Income Tax Law Implementation Regulations, Article 2.

186 Individual Income Tax Law Implementation Regulations, Article 7.

187 Individual Income Tax Law, Article 1.

188 In calculating the number of days of stay in China, days for making temporary trips (not more than 30 days during a single journey or not more than 90 days accumulated over a number of journeys in the same tax year) out of China should not be deducted. Individual Income Tax Law Implementation Regulations, Article 3.

189 China has entered into double taxation treaties with around 40 countries including Australia, Austria, Belgium, Brazil, Canada, Denmark, France, Germany, India, Italy, Japan, Korea, Malaysia, Netherlands, Singapore, Spain, Sweden, Switzerland, Thailand, United Kingdom, and the United States.

190 Notice of the State Administration of Taxation on Certain Issues Concerning the Payment of Individual Income Tax by Individuals Without Residence Within the Territory of China Involving Tax Agreements (1995).

191 Notice of the Ministry of Finance and the State Administration of Taxation on Issues Concerning the Calculation of the Five-Year Residency Period for Individuals Without Residency in China (1995).

192 Individual Income Tax Law Implementation Regulations, Article 6.

193 Provisional Administrative Measures on the Levy and Collection of Individual Income Tax on Overseas Income (1998).

194 Article 75 of the Regulations for the Implementation of the Law on Joint Ventures Using Chinese and Foreign Investment states that "the unbalance [of foreign exchange] shall be solved by the people's government of a relevant province, an autonomous region or a municipality directly under the central government or the department in charge under the State Council from their own foreign exchange reserves."

195 Regulations of the State Council Concerning the Balance of Foreign Exchange Income and Expenditure by Sino-Foreign Equity Joint Ventures (promulgated on 15 January 1986).

196 Company Law, Article 72.

197 Company Law, Article 72.

198 Company Law, Article 73.

199 Company Law, Articles 138, 139, and 145.

200 Many foreign investors have been reluctant to take on the liabilities of existing state-owned enterprises. As a result, most FIE deals involving SOEs have taken the form of

asset acquisitions in which selected SOE assets have been contributed to or acquired by a new EJV (or CJV).

201 The tentative M&A rules jointly issued by MOFCOM and other authorities in March 2003.

202 Such consent would include a waiver to the pre-emptive rights.

203 In the case of transfer of WFOE's assets, a Chinese registered accountant must be engaged to examine the details of the transaction and issue a capital inspection report.

204 The FIE Liquidation Procedures. Also, see the PRC Enterprise Bankruptcy Law promulgated on 27 August 2006 and effective as of 1 June 2007.

205 Foreign-Invested Enterprises and Foreign Enterprises Income Tax Law, Article 10; Notice of the State Administration of Taxation Related to Enterprise Income Tax Refund for Reinvestment by Foreign Investors (17 July 2002).

206 Foreign-Invested Enterprises and Foreign Enterprises Income Tax Law, Article 81.

207 Notice on Relevant Questions Concerning Withholding Tax on Reinvestment by Foreign Investors in Their Foreign-Invested Enterprises (issued by the State Administration of Taxation on 5 June 1993), Item 3.

208 Notice of the Ministry of Finance and State Administration of Taxation, Articles 1(1) and (2).

209 PRC Supreme People's Court President Ren Jianxin's Report to the First Session of the Eighth National People's Congress, 22 March 1993.

210 www.transparency.org/policy_research/surveys_indices/cip/2008.

211 World Economic Forum, Global Competitiveness Report 2008–2009, at 135, available at www/weforum.org/en/initiatives/gcp/Global%20Competitiveness%20Report/index/htm

212 Minxin Pei, Carnegie Endowment for International Peace, Corruption Threatens China's Future, Policy Brief No.55 (October 2007) at 2.

213 www.chinadaily.com.cn/bizchina/2008-02/24/content_6479369.htm

214 The Chinese government website, "The Supervision Department of the Central Commission for Discipline Inspection Has Notified the Work of the Discipline Inspection and Supervision Organs in Investigating and Handling Cases Since the 17th National Congress of the Communist Party of China", 26 December 2008, http://www.gov.cn/jrzg/2008-12/26/content_1188673.htm.

215 For example the Regulation on Prohibiting State Functionaries from Giving or Receiving Gifts Whilst Undertaking Domestic Duties; the Regulations on Giving or Receiving of Gifts at Official Functions Involving Foreigners; the Interim Provisions Regarding Enhancing the Administration of Overseas Official Trip of Party's and Administrative Cadre.

216 Competition Law, Article 2.

217 Interim Regulations on the Prohibition of Commercial Bribery (promulgated by the SAIC on 15 November 1996), Articles 2 and 4.

218 Commercial Bribery Regulations, Article 10.

219 Competition Law, Article 8.

220 Commercial Bribery Regulations, Article 2.

221 Competition Law, Article 8.

222 Commercial Bribery Regulations, Article 5.

223 "Discounts" are defined in the Commercial Bribery Regulations as favourable prices given to the other party by a business operator, including when business operators deduct a portion of money immediately to the other party when selling commodities or returning a portion of money after the total payment.

224 "Commission" is defined in the Commercial Bribery Regulations as remuneration given by business operators to qualified intermediaries who provide services to the business operators during a business transaction.

225 Competition Law, Article 8; Commercial Bribery Regulations, Articles 6 and 7.

226 Commercial Bribery Regulations, Article 8.

227 Commercial Bribery Regulations, Article 9.
228 Competition Law, Article 22; Commercial Bribery Regulations, Article 9.
229 Competition Law, Article 22; Commercial Bribery Regulations, Article 9.
230 Commercial Bribery Regulations, Article 9.
231 The judicial review is, however, not extended to the lawfulness of the underlying regulations upon which the administrative decisions are made.
232 As a matter of fact, the CCP policies are not subject to judicial review, which makes judicial scrutiny infeasible to the most fundamental source of state intrusion.

2

NEW BOTTLE OR OLD WINE? – MAJOR CHANGES IN FOREIGN INVESTMENT LAW 2019

On 15 March 2019, the Second Session of the 13th National People's Congress approved the Foreign Investment Law of the People's Republic of China, which went into effect on 1 January 2020. With it, China's legal framework covering foreign investment enters a new era.[1] On 26 December 2019, the State Council issued the Regulation for Implementation of the FIL (FIL Implementation Regulation), coming into force on 1 January 2020.[2]

This chapter outlines some key changes made in the FIL and discusses some uncertainties surrounding the implementation of the FIL.

1. Shifting Purpose of FIL

The FIL is a result of legislative efforts taken by the Chinese government over the past several years. The Ministry of Commerce issued two drafts of the Foreign Investment Law for public consultation in 2015 and 2018 respectively. There were 170 clauses in the 2015 draft containing certain controversial provisions (such as those rules in relation to the variable interest entity structure or the VIE structure) as well as the national security review system. But the 2018 draft significantly shortened and simplified the provisions. The final draft of the FIL passed in March 2019 adopts the same approach as the 2018 draft.[3]

The FIL brings far-reaching changes to the regulatory framework that has governed foreign investment in China for the past 40 years.[4]

Both the FIL and its Implementation Regulations, aiming to further open China's market, encourages foreign investment flows, enhances investment protection, and regulates the administration of foreign investments.[5] The FIL replaces the so-called three FIE Laws: the Law of the PRC on Chinese-Foreign Equity Joint Ventures (EJV Law), the Law of the PRC on Chinese-Foreign Contractual Joint Ventures (CJV Law), and the Law of the PRC on Wholly Foreign-Owned Enterprises (WFOE Law).[6]

DOI: 10.4324/9781003130499-2

Compared with the three FIE Laws, the FIL pays more attention to promoting and protecting foreign investment. FIL no longer regulates the organizational behaviour of FIEs. Rather, the FIL contains a large number of provisions regulating the Chinese government's activities of delegation, supervision, and services, which will help create a better investment environment for foreign investors.[7] The organizational forms and corporate governance of FIEs would fall in the scope of the laws and regulations applicable to different types of market entities including but not limited to the Company Law.[8] Therefore, the inconsistencies between the three laws of FIEs as a whole would be eliminated.[9]

When the FIL enters into force, FIEs shall be established in the forms of limited liability companies, companies limited by shares, partnerships, and other enterprises in accordance with the Company Law, the Partnership Enterprise Law, and other relevant laws. The corporate governance structure and organizational behaviours of FIEs shall be operated in accordance with these laws.[10]

2. Simplifying the Procedure to Setting Up FIEs

As one essential component of the dualist system that regulated domestic and foreign investments separately,[11] the previous Chinese regulations on foreign investments served the purpose of attracting foreign investments, stimulating economic cooperation and technology exchange[12] in the early period of opening up and reforming the domestic market. However, they no longer suit the changing circumstances and rather constitute obstacles to the development goals mainly for two reasons: (i) they subject foreign investments to non-national (de facto discriminative) treatment and insufficient protection; and (ii) they create a defective system of post-entry supervision and management.

Although the recent reform has made some positive progress towards a better business environment, some shortcomings in China's foreign investment regulatory system still can be identified. This section assesses these problems in turn. Some issues that might have hindered the implementation of the approval regime in the past are solved in the recent reform. For instance the legal grounds based on which the authorities can find a violation are now more defined. The most notable issues in this regard are the risk of fragmented implementation triggered by multi-tiered regulatory oversights by various authorities under the new regime, the unstable regulatory and institutional environment, as well as the unreliability of the available remedies.[13]

The focus of previous FIE laws was placed more on enterprise regulation than foreign investment regulation. Accordingly, the FIE Laws stipulated various rules and norms regarding the establishment, organization, management, operation, and termination of FIEs,[14] which vary from one to the other depending on the type of the enterprise. FIE Laws granted investors less autonomy than those regulating domestically invested enterprises.

Under the FIE Laws, the establishment of foreign investment in China, whether through formation of a new FIE or by acquiring an existing Chinese company, must follow a three-step process: application, approval, and filing. The government approval as a device to control foreign investment is mandatory basically in relation to all the activities of an FIE as indicated in Table 2.1, while the filing is required as the post-approval procedural step which includes business registration and all other logistic matters relevant to an FIE's business operation including but not limited to tax filing.

The approval procedure previously in force was conducted by the Ministry of Commerce (MOFCOM) or its local counterparts depending on the total investment of the FIE as indicated in Table 2.2. It applied to all foreign investments and covered all essential stages of their life cycle including but not limited to their establishment, operation, extension, and dissolution. The aim was to ensure that the structure, operation, and transaction of FIEs complied with the pertinent rules. All investors were required to submit documents including contracts, articles of association, certificates of foreign investors, and creditworthiness letter, among others.[15] Depending on the circumstances, the procedure – which still applies to investments in the sectors covered by the negative lists – normally took one to three months[16] or even longer if the project is large or in a strategically important sector.

Together with other approval procedures – such as the project review conducted by the National Development and Reform Commission (NDRC) on investments covered by the Catalogue of Investment Projects Subject to Government Confirmation[17] – the approval procedure to authorize investments'

TABLE 2.1 Administrative Approvals for FDI Activities

	WFOE	EJV	CJV
Establishment	✓	✓	✓
Division, merger, or other major alteration	✓	✓	✓
Term of business	✓	✓	✓
Extension of term of business	✓	✓	✓
Dissolution	✓	✓	✓
Major amendments to the agreements, contracts, articles of association	✓	✓	✓
Entrustment given to others to carry out operations and management	✓	✓	✓

TABLE 2.2 Approval Levels for M&A Transactions With Foreign Investment

Authority Level	Industries in Encouraged/ Permitted Category	Industries in Restricted Category
State Council	US$500 million or above	US$100 million or above
NDRC and MOFCOM	US$300 million or above	US$50 million or above
Provincial MOFCOM	Between US$30 million and US$300 million	Below US$50 million
Municipal MOFCOM	US$30 million or below	N/A

entry and alteration has led foreign investments to fulfil China's needs. However, as both the macro economy and foreign investment are becoming more complicated, the usefulness of the approval procedure in controlling and guiding foreign investments has been in a decline.[18] For instance despite constant encouragement and priority policies, foreign investment remains relatively low in high-tech industries.[19] Moreover, restrictions in the approval procedure might be immaterial to, or even in tension with, China's new normal.[20]

One important feature of the approval procedure is the significant room for discretion – and thus arbitrariness – left to the approval authority, caused by the opacity and vagueness of the applicable rules. This feature cuts against the goal of further opening up the Chinese market and encouraging more foreign investment flows.[21] Explicit details, such as precise content requirements in the application documents, are missing from some of the procedures,[22] hence authorities can delay the entry of foreign investments with excuses. The conditions for approval or rejection are broadly defined and thus subject to the interpretation of approval authorities and to the application of other unwritten or unpublished rules. These may include the refusal to grant permits to foreign investment in some industrial sectors where China has committed to market access.[23] Approval authorities may attach further conditions for market admission – which can be investment-specific and discriminatory in nature – beyond written rules. For CJVs, Chinese partners are required to act as applicants in the approval procedure on behalf of the prospective venture.[24] This requirement hinders the communication between foreign investors and the competent authorities and allows the approval authority to favour Chinese partners in a non-transparent way, possibly leading to the imposition of favourable commercial terms for the Chinese entities at the expense of the foreign partners.[25] In reality, the approval process has become an administrative barrier to the entry of foreign investment into the Chinese market.[26]

To obtain necessary government approvals, it is estimated that foreign investors normally need to go through a total of seven steps. More specifically, the government authorities involved in the FIE regulatory process include the central and local level MOFCOM (for project filing and anti-monopoly review), the Administration of Industry and Commerce (for business name approval and registration), the Land and Resources Department (for approval of land-use rights), central and local environmental protection bureaus (for environmental impact assessment), the provincial planning department (for zoning opinion on planned location), the State-Owned Assets Supervision and Administration Commission (for acquisition and use of state-owned assets), the Development and Reform Commission (for project approval), and various industrial regulators (for business activities licences such as food and drug production, telecommunications, pesticide manufacturing, mining, among others).[27]

Despite the tremendous contribution, the FIE Laws have gradually fallen behind the dynamic market reality and could hardly address the emerging challenges with respect to foreign investment. For example, the three FDI Laws mainly focus on greenfield investment projects (i.e. foreign direct investment),

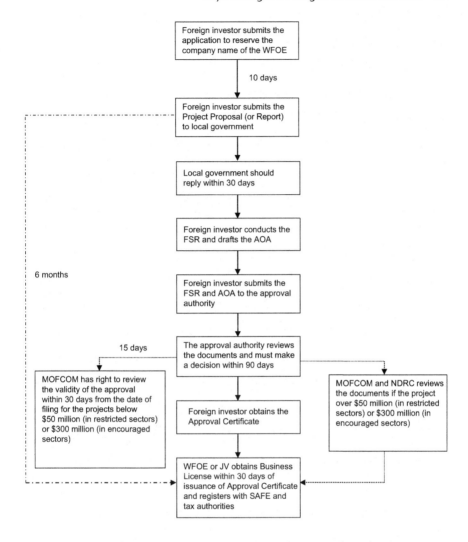

FIGURE 2.1   Approval Procedure in General

while other forms of investment, such as M&A and capital increase or subscription, are not well covered. In addition, the inconsistency between the three FIE Laws and the Company Law becomes apparent over the years, especially the rigidity of corporate governance rules under the EJV Law or CJV Law has tied over millions of joint ventures in China.[28]

The promulgation of the FIL creates a uniform mechanism regulating foreign investment and ends the tripartite system of laws that had governed foreign investments for decades in China.[29] Intended to address the common concerns from foreign businesses and governments and further boost foreign investment in

China, the FIL has been hailed as a landmark law to help build a uniform, stable, transparent, predictable, and fair market environment.[30]

The FIL is the basic law of unified management and the promotion of foreign investment. It no longer takes the organizational form of enterprises as its normative content or objective.

The State Council's Opinions on Further Improving the Use of Foreign Capital require local governments to promote foreign investment and serve FIEs better, by, for example delegating more approval powers and streamlining the local approval process. Addressing the obstacles to China's development goals in the pre-entry stage requires the simplification of administrative procedure.[31] Therefore, in 2016, an interim filing regime was established by the Interim Measures for the Recordation Administration of the Formation and Modification of FIEs (amended in 2018 and repealed) to replace the approval procedures described previously for foreign investments not included in the negative list, which was much streamlined, with a significantly shorter time frame, fewer required documents, and less room for the discretion of the authorities.[32]

However, it still allowed the authorities to either accept or reject the filing application[33] and thus to decide whether the FIEs could continue their operation. Accordingly, foreign investors still needed to endure more uncertainty and burden than domestic investors.[34]

The procedure for forming FIEs in China will be radically simplified according to the FIL. It currently takes many months to form a WFOE or a JV. The processes vary from one locality to the other. It is nothing like forming a company in the United States or Hong Kong. On the other hand, forming a domestic company is simple, fast, and inexpensive and very much like forming a company in the United States or Hong Kong. It is more or less a filing system. In many Chinese cities, forming a domestic company can take as little as one week and the costs of doing so are relatively trivial especially after the registered capital rule is abolished. Under the FIL, this simplified system should apply to all forms of FIEs: both wholly foreign-owned enterprises and joint ventures. Costs and time frames should radically decrease.[35] This is a substantial step to extend and apply the national treatment to foreign investors.

The Implementation Regulations have also now adopted a new approach by providing that "relevant administrative departments in charge" will not issue licences, but only process company establishment registration and others or grant fixed assets investment approvals if the relevant foreign investment is not in compliance with the negative list. In other words, the review on whether the foreign investment is in compliance with the negative list will be conducted in conjunction with the examination of the relevant application for industry-specific licences, company establishment registration, or fixed assets investment approvals.

With regard to foreign investment falling outside the negative list, previously a filing still needed to be made with MOFCOM before or after registering the establishment or any change of an FIE with AMR. Under the new FIL regime, a filing with MOFCOM is no longer required. As such, foreign investors can register the establishment and changes of their FIEs with AMR directly without the need to obtain an approval (for FIEs falling under the negative list) or a filing record (for FIEs falling outside the negative list) from MOFCOM.[36]

At the same time, the FIL has also formally done away with the prior systems that required approval by the Ministry of Commerce and registration with the Administration of Industry and Commerce before a foreign investment would be permitted into China.[37] If an investment was classified under the negative list, foreign investors could only register their companies with the relevant Market Supervision Administration after obtaining the MOFCOM's approval. However, this MOFCOM approval power was generally abolished on 1 January 2020.

3. Specific Issues on Corporate Governance

After the Company Law was revised in 2005, the relevant government authorities issued executive opinions to coordinate their efforts and require JVs, WFOEs, and foreign-invested joint-stock companies to establish shareholder meetings as their governing authorities (while the authority of a WOE is its shareholder) and install a board of directors (or executive director) in accordance with the provisions of the Company Law.[38]

Since the three FIE Laws were promulgated in 1979, decades of development and foreign investment have resulted in complicated laws, regulations, and rules, and judicial interpretations including the Provisions of the Ministry of Commerce on the Establishment of Foreign-Invested Investment Companies, the Provisions on Merger and Acquisition of Domestic Enterprises by Foreign Investors, and the Administrative Provisions on Foreign-Invested Telecommunications Enterprises. In conjunction with the promulgation of the FIL, the relevant authorities are expected to summarize, amend, and update current foreign investment rules in accordance with the requirements of the FIL, and successively promulgate laws, regulations, and regulatory documents that implement and enforce rules that accord with the FIL.[39]

3.1 Highest Governing Body

The FIL will have a major impact on the existing joint ventures. The main reason is that the organizational form and corporate structure under the JV Laws are radically different from those set out under the Company Law. The FIE Laws constrain the freedom of contract and absence of agreement will normally lead to gridlock and an inability of the investors to move forward.

Before the FIL and under the EJV Law, the highest decision-making organ of an EJV was the board of directors appointed by the shareholders according to their respective shareholding percentages. The following matters were subject to unanimous consent by all directors attending the board meeting or in the case of a written resolution in lieu of a meeting, the consent and signatures by all the directors: (i) amendment to the AOA of the EJV, (ii) suspension or dissolution of the EJV, (i) increase or decrease of the registered capital of the EJV, and (iv) merger or split of the EJV. While this consensus rule is supposed to protect the minority shareholders in a better way, the director is likely to end up in a dilemma – either vote in the best interest of the company or in the interest of the shareholder who appoints her. When the interests of the company and the shareholder are not aligned, voting in the interest of the appointing shareholder may lead the director to a breach of her fiduciary duty.

With the repeal of the three FIE Laws, these provisions have become history. The Company Law applies to the EJV's corporate governance whereby the shareholders' meeting is now the highest decision-making organ of an EJV. Under the Company Law, the previously listed matters as well as the conversion of the corporate form of an EJV (e.g. from a limited liability company to a company limited by shares) must be approved by shareholder(s) representing at least two-thirds (2/3) of the "voting rights." This means that if the AOA of an EJV does not provide otherwise, a shareholder who holds two-thirds (2/3) of the equity interest in an EJV may make unilateral decisions on the previously mentioned important matters that previously required unanimous consent of all the board directors appointed by all the shareholders.

The coming changes will allow existing joint ventures to be restructured (subject to the caveats outlined here) to models that better allow for the majority shareholder to take decisive action.[40] In conjunction with the promulgation of the FIL, relevant authorities are expected to summarize, amend, and update current foreign investment rules in accordance with the requirements of the new law and successively promulgate laws, regulations, and regulatory documents that implement and enforce rules that accord with the FIL.[41]

Existing EJVs may choose a more conservative approach to keep the voting rights of each shareholder the same as in the previous arrangement designed in accordance with the EJV Law so that important matters (which previously required unanimous consent by the board members) will be required under the amended AOA to be approved by all the shareholders to be effective. This approach is especially important for minority shareholders who have less than one-third of the voting rights.

However, in practice, the shareholders' meeting can consider using the AOA to delegate to the Board the power to initiate the discussions and propose a board resolution related to the previously mentioned matters for the final verification and confirmation in the shareholders' meeting.

The three FIE Laws and the Company Law also have inconsistencies regarding the number of board members, the term of office, the quorum required for board meetings, and appointment of directors. The Company Law provisions shall govern the FIEs after the FIL comes into effect.

3.2 Equity Transfer to Third Parties

Under the EJV Law, unanimous consent of all other shareholders was required if a shareholder wants to transfer its equity interest in the EJV to a third party. The other shareholders had the right of first refusal to purchase the equity interest to be transferred to the third party. The terms and conditions of the proposed transfer to the third party could not be more preferential than those of the proposed transfer to the other shareholders.

The Company Law provides for more flexible conditions on equity transfer to third parties. Based on Article 71, consent of more than half of the other shareholders is required if a shareholder wants to transfer its equity interest to a third party unless otherwise provided by the AOA. The term "half" refers to the number of shareholders rather than the capital contribution percentage of the shareholders. For example if an EJV has five shareholders and one shareholder wants to transfer its equity interest to a third party, consent from at least three of the other four shareholders is required absent any provisions to the contrary in the AOA. The shareholder that wants to transfer shall notify the other shareholders in writing for their consent. Failure to reply by any of the other shareholders within 30 days upon receipt of the written notice shall be deemed as consent to the transfer. Where at least half of the other shareholders do not consent to the transfer, such non-consenting shareholders shall purchase the equity interest to be transferred. Failure to purchase the equity interest shall be deemed as consent to the transfer.

3.3 Dividend Distribution

Under the EJV Law, the profit distribution among shareholders must be in proportion to their respective contribution to the registered capital of the joint venture and there is no room for the shareholders to agree otherwise. The CJV Law provides very flexible dividend distribution mechanism allowing the investors to share profit based on the joint venture contract.

According to the Company Law, shareholders may agree on the proportion and mode of profit distribution separately without consideration of the proportion of capital contribution so as to realize the contract-based "recovery of investment in advance" by some shareholders.[42] The inconsistency might cause problems after the expiration of the transition period of the FIL.[43] There needs clear guidance to this inconsistency.[44]

The FIL will have very limited impact on WFOEs' corporate governance as the organizational form and corporate structure of WFOEs largely followed the Company Law, including that the highest authority of a WFOE should be the shareholders meetings rather than the board of directors.

In accordance with the three FIE Laws and their implementation regulations, if agreed in a CJV contract that all fixed assets will be owned by the Chinese partners at the expiration of the cooperative period, then the foreign partners can recover the investment in advance during this period. Moreover, EJV or CJV parties shall be allowed to distribute the residual assets of the JV according to the agreement.[45]

3.4 Total Investment and Foreign Debt

In the current foreign investment legal system, FIEs have certain special features in accordance with provisions of the three FIE Laws. For example FIEs have "total investment," and they can borrow foreign debts within the amount of the difference between the total investment and the registered capital without obtaining additional approval from relevant PRC authorities. When establishing EJVs, joint ventures partners need to sign joint venture contracts. After the three FIE Laws were abolished, further clarification will be necessary as to whether the previously mentioned concepts and corresponding practices will continue to exist.

The foreign debt quota for FIEs is the difference of its registered capital and total investment. After the effectiveness of the FIL, it is uncertain whether the concept of "total investment" will still exist and whether the foreign debt quota will be different for an FIE.[46]

The FIL expressly contemplates FIEs using various financing methods on the same basis as domestic companies, such as the public issue of stocks, bonds, and other securities. Historically, no law prohibited an FIE from undertaking a public offering in China, but it was rare in practice. The FIL may facilitate the FIEs' use of the debt and equity markets in China for fundraising.[47]

3.5 Minimum Shareholding Requirement

Under the EJV Law and its Implementation Regulations, the shareholding held by a foreign investor in a joint venture shall generally not be lower than 25%.[48] In case the shareholding of the foreign investors in a joint venture is lower than 25%, the foreign investors may not be able to enjoy preferential tax treatment as the joint venture will be viewed as a domestic enterprise.[49] The tax preferential treatment has been substantially dwindled since 2008, and FIEs are subject to the same enterprise income tax as domestic companies at 25%.

3.6 Appointment of Directors, Legal Representative, and Senior Management

The three FIE Laws require that the directors must be appointed by the parties in proportion to their equity ratio and the chairman and vice chairman must be appointed by different parties. After the implementation of the FIL, the parties will only need to follow the Company Law, which will give the parties much more room to decide how to appoint board members and senior management in accordance with the AOA, without being subject to extra mandatory requirements.

Therefore, after FIL coming into force, the existing FIEs will need to revise the joint venture contracts and the AOA as soon as possible. The adjustments may include (i) adjusting the highest authority of the company from the board of directors to the shareholders meeting; (ii) adding relevant provisions regarding the power of the shareholders, the voting methods; and (iii) adjusting relevant provisions regarding the duties and responsibilities of the board of director, the election method of directors, the voting mechanism, and the quorum of board meetings.

Due to the difference between the three FIE Laws and the Company Law on corporate governance, it is foreseeable that the investors will start a new round of negotiations on the corporate governance and the business terms associated therewith, when adjusting the joint venture contracts and articles of associations of their EJVs and CJVs in accordance with the Company Law.[50] This change offers investors new flexibility in the structuring and operation of FIEs.[51] In contrast to the method of differentiating supervision measures according to different organizational forms in the FIE Laws, the FIL unifies the organizational form and organization structures with the Company Law and the Partnership Enterprise Law.[52] On the one hand, the unification implements the national treatment for foreign investors. On the other hand, it avoids conflicts with the Company Law, Partnership Enterprise Law, and their subsequent amendments.[53] This is also good for a more functioning legal system regulating foreign investment.

In practice, FIEs will need to agree on the transfer rules of equity, profit distribution, and other important matters of the company.[54] There would be a new game between Chinese and foreign shareholders on the adjustment of corporate governance structure and related rules.[55] If there are disputes or even deadlocks between the parties, how should the law be applied to handle these problems? Relevant provisions should be thus adopted shortly. With the abolition of the three FIE Laws, the contractual joint venture contracts and equity joint venture contracts will lose their original position as controversial documents and return to the role of shareholder agreements.[56,57]

4. Protection and Promotion of Investment

The investment environment is further improved by the inclusion of two chapters – Chapter 2 "Promotion of Foreign Investment," and Chapter 3 "Protection of Foreign Investment" – regarding investment protection and promotion. Beyond the generic statements that China encourages, protects, and promotes foreign investments,[58] these two chapters also stipulate detailed measures, which can be divided into the following categories. First, certain major recurring concerns of foreign investors regarding investment protection are addressed. Since outright expropriation is the worst case scenario for foreign investors,[59] the FIL affirms that China will only expropriate foreign investments under special circumstances, for the purpose of public interest, in a non-discriminatory manner, under legal procedures, and with fair and reasonable compensation based on the market value and paid in a timely manner.[60] These requirements reiterate those regulating the expropriation of property,[61] and the standard of compensation is clearer than those regarding expropriation of other assets.[62] The protection against direct expropriation is strengthened.

Addressing the issue of investment promotion, the FIL introduces another prominent measure that could quell concerns relating to administrative system governing foreign investment in China. The FIL mandates soliciting of opinions and suggestions of FIEs in the process of formulating domestic norms relating to foreign investment.[63] Some of the other notable investment promotion measures introduced by the FIL includes application of enterprise development policies equally to FIEs, establishment of a foreign investment service system to provide counselling and services about relevant laws, policy measures, participation of FIEs in formulation of standards and in government procurement activities, and granting of freedom to local governments to formulate foreign investment promotion policy measures in accordance with laws and administrative regulations.[64] Many of these investment promotion provisions, though abstract, could have positive impacts on foreign investments.[65]

Underlying the rules is the general principle of active promotion and protection of foreign investment.[66] In addition, as provided in the FIL, the State establishes multilateral and bilateral investment promotion cooperation mechanisms with other countries, regions, and international organization and strengthens international exchange and cooperation in the field of investment.[67] Internally, the FIL requires government authorities at all levels, under the axiom of facilitation, efficiency, and transparency, to simplify bureaucratic procedures, enhance work efficiency, optimize government services, and improve the level of foreign investment services.[68,69]

To further promote foreign investment in China, the FIL (Article 9) and the Implementation Regulations (Article 6) stipulate that foreign investors shall be treated equally with domestic companies regarding access to government funds, land supply, tax exemptions, licensing, project applications, and so on.[70]

Chapter 2 (Articles 9–19) of the FIL stipulates the investment promotion, mainly from five aspects.[71]

This chapter clarifies that all policies of the state to support the development of domestic enterprises shall be equally applicable to FIEs.[72] Article 9 shows that China will offer a fairer and equal investment environment to the foreign investors. Further, under the FIL, foreign investors may enjoy preferential policies in certain sectors and regions as designated by the Chinese authorities (Article 14).[73]

When formulating laws, regulations, and rules relating to foreign investment, Chinese legislatures shall listen to opinions and suggestions from FIEs. Normative and adjudicative documents related to foreign investment shall, according to law, be made public in a timely manner.[74] FIL includes that the state establishes and improves the service system for foreign investment, and it provides consultation and services on laws, regulations, policies, and measures on investment projects for foreign investors and FIEs.[75]

FIEs can participate in government procurement activities on an equal footing with domestic enterprises. Products and services provided by FIEs within the territory of China are treated equally in government procurement in accordance with the law.[76] FIEs may participate in government procurement through fair competition (FIL, Article 16), and must not be discriminated against in such procurement processes with respect to their products manufactured, and services provided, in China (Implementation Regulations, Article 15).[77] According to these articles, foreign investors can participate in the competition of government procurement as fairly as domestic investors.

FIL specifically allows FIEs to raise funds through public offerings of equity and debt securities (Article 17).[78] FIEs may, in accordance with the law, finance through the public offering of stocks, corporate bonds, and other securities.[79]

The government at all levels and relevant departments shall, in accordance with the principles of facilitation, efficiency, and transparency, simplify procedures, improve efficiency, optimize government services, and further improve the quality of foreign investment services.[80] FIEs may comment on new legislation and administrative rules concerning foreign investment (FIL, Article 10), and only published documents may form the basis for the exercise of administrative authority (Implementation Regulations, Article 7).[81] Clearly, such new provisions aim to encourage more foreign investment into China by constraining the government's discretionary power.[82]

Above all, the FIL provides that China will continue with the national policy of opening up and sets out a number of rules that are designed to promote and protect foreign investment in China, including:

- All national policies for supporting the development of enterprises shall apply equally to FIEs in accordance with law.
- When formulating laws, regulations, and rules relating to foreign investment, appropriate methods shall be used to seek the views of FIEs.
- FIEs shall be permitted to participate in government procurement projects through fair competition.
- FIEs may raise financing in China through the public offering of shares or issuance of corporate bonds.
- Foreign investors may freely remit profits, capital gains, royalties from intellectual property rights, lawfully obtained compensation and the proceeds of liquidation, out of China.
- The State protects the intellectual property rights of foreign investors and FIEs.
- The State respects the commercial agreement reached between foreign investors and Chinese partners on technology cooperation and prohibits government authorities or officials from mandating technology transfer by administrative means.
- An FIE or foreign investor which is of the view that its legitimate rights and interests have been infringed by a government authority or official may submit its complaint to a central system for handling complaints from FIEs. In addition, an FIE or foreign investor may apply for administrative review or commence administrative litigation in accordance with law.
- If an FIE needs certain operating permits, its application for such permits will be handled according to the same criteria and procedures applicable to a domestic company. Local governments should abide by any policy-related

undertakings made to foreign investors or FIEs and honour any contracts lawfully entered into with foreign investors or FIEs.[83] Investment facilitation is the first step towards improving the investment environment.

The FIL provides for a transparent law- and standard-setting process, entitling the participation of foreign investors; mandates a system enabling consultations regarding all investment law and policy matters; simplifies administrative procedures for FDI (e.g. permissions, licensing); and provides for the establishment of bilateral or multilateral cooperative institutions to enhance the international exchange of best practices for FDI, all of which reflect the principles of the WTO's Joint Ministerial Statement on Investment Facilitation for Development. This is supported by China's general policy to streamline administrative procedures, delegate powers, and improve regulations and services. As investment facilitation does not address market access, treatment standards, and dispute settlement, it does not impinge on the country's sovereignty and is therefore a rather low-hanging fruit for enhancing the doing-business environment.

5. Reporting Procedure

A new reporting mechanism is established by the FIL[84] to implement the pre-entry national treatment granted to foreign investments in sectors not covered by the negative list.[85] Detailed rules regarding the reporting mechanism are stipulated in the Measures for the Reporting of Foreign Investment Information (the Reporting Measures). All foreign investors are required to submit an initial or modified report when they establish or make material changes to their FIEs. Foreign investors or FIEs must submit investment information to the competent authority (i.e. the commerce department) through the enterprise registration system and the enterprise social credit information publicity system. The aim of the reporting procedure is to inform the competent authority rather than to obtain administrative approval or confirmation after a substantive or formal review. Under the previous system, information about FIEs was mainly collected by the State Administration for Market Regulation (SAMR, the successor to the State Administration of Industry and Commerce) and MOFCOM individually through their respective systems (Foreign Investment Comprehensive Management System managed by MOFCOM and Enterprise Registration System and Enterprise Credibility Information Publication System managed by the SAMR). Hence, the reporting procedure has become more streamlined than the previous approval and filing regime.[86]

In contrast to the approval system, the reporting procedure is not a prerequisite for the establishment or alteration of foreign investment. Instead, foreign investors only need to submit the report together with the registration procedure with the SAMR for the business licence (i.e. obtaining a business licence to confirm the formal establishment of the enterprise) or within 20 working days after material alteration is made.[87] Consequently, bureaucratic barriers to the establishment and alteration of foreign investment are significantly reduced.[88]

Fewer documents are needed for the report than they were previously for the approval and filing procedure. In the approval procedure, the authorities needed to conduct substantial examination and to exert tight control over the establishment and operation of FIEs. Therefore, investors were required to submit documents relating to every aspect of corporate structure, governance, and operation, with the list of required documents varying according to the matter for which approval was sought.[89] Compliance with the approval procedure was, accordingly, difficult for foreign investors. As to the filing procedure, investors were required to submit documents evidencing some basic information of the FIEs for a formal examination conducted by the authorities, which barely involved references to their substantive features.[90] The reporting procedure is a step away from this merit-based review system. There is no requirement for the submission of any proof materials, while investors are only required to fill in the report form with basic information of the FIEs.[91] There is a qualification that the content and scope of investment information to be reported will be determined based on the principle of "genuine necessity." The FIL provides that the state should establish a foreign investment information reporting system. The content and scope of the information reporting should be determined in accordance with the principles of necessity and strict control.[92] Foreign investors or FIEs should submit investment information to the relevant commerce departments through the enterprise registration system and the enterprise credit information publicity system.[93] The investment information, which can be obtained through the information sharing of different departments, shall not be required to report repeatedly.[94]

Unlike other administrative procedures, there is no need to obtain any approval or receipt from the authorities in the reporting procedure, which is not a prerequisite for any trading or business operation. The authorities will notify the investors if any error or omission is spotted, which must then be corrected within 20 working days.[95]

The FIL omits the details of the process[96] because Article 34 or other provisions of the FIL do not provide any guidance as to the information that will be required under a foreign investment information reporting system; it is not yet clear how the registration process and the reporting system will intersect.[97] The reporting procedure only requires the submission of an electronic report through an online system (i.e. Enterprise Registration System).[98] No paper document is required like in the approval procedure. This change not only reduces the cost of document submission but also contributes to the goal of environmental protection.[99]

The change has built a convenient, efficient, and low-cost reporting procedure for the market entry of most foreign investment in China,[100] and thus significantly relaxed administrative control. It will increase the ease of doing business for foreign investors and will presumably attract more foreign investment,[101] hence contributing to the development goals that depend on China's ability to attract more investment inflows.

It is unclear how the foreign investment information reporting system differs from or connects with existing systems.[102] To be specific, it is currently unclear as to whether the foreign investment information reporting system under the FIL fits in with the existing "enterprise credit information publicity system" operated by the State Administration for Market Regulation (which applies to both domestic companies and FIEs) and the foreign investment information reporting system managed by MOFCOM.[103]

6. Supervision Scheme

The FIL establishes the framework of the post-establishment supervision regime, which consists of two main components: supervisory inspection by competent authorities,[104] and a duty for foreign investors to submit information annually online (via the National Enterprise Credit Information Publicity System) after their establishment.[105] Although the latter only intends to collect information rather than establish an independent supervision regime, it can increase the efficiency of the inspection, through allowing the authorities to track the dynamic of FIEs and help to identify investments that need special attention. Investors failing to cooperate with the inspection or to fulfil the reporting obligation will incur legal liabilities and face the negative consequences of being recorded in the credit information system.[106] Therefore, the regime is likely to promote legal compliance.

To ensure effective operation of the report mechanism, the commerce departments are required to inspect the authenticity of the reports in the following ways: the random inspection, the inspection according to tip-offs, the inspection according to the suggestions of or information provided by relevant departments or the judiciary organs, and the inspection ex officio.[107] These conditions can ensure that the enterprises singled out for examination are chiefly those that require particular attention and improve inspecting efficiency.[108]

To facilitate the post-establishment management on foreign investments, information regarding the FIE's effective controller is required in the reports.[109] The inquiry provides the authorities with complete background data on FIEs. It can thus arguably help the authorities to prevent Chinese nationals from making illegal "round trip" investments under the disguise of foreign investments in order to obtain more preferential treatments (compared to pure domestic investments).[110] Since these investments make little contribution to China's development goals but occupy the resources for the needed foreign investments, the new obligation can effectively hinder this practice.[111]

The achievement of sustainable economic growth goals relies heavily on post-establishment supervision, especially the goals of protecting national security and participating in global economic governance. The inspection of the reports can ensure effective operation of the FDI regulatory mechanism, through which the authorities are able to effectively manage foreign investments after their entry into the market.[112]

Some new rules in the recent change are ambiguous or incomplete. Therefore, such rules will fail to guide adequately both the competent authorities' enforcement and foreign investors' performance and expectations. Consequently, this ambiguity may weaken the reform's objective to ensure compliance with the pertinent regulations and the alignment of China's investment policy to its development goals. The vaguest and most imperfect rules that urgently need detailed regulations or further clarifications are the rules governing the inspection regime, the rules regarding other procedures that foreign investors may need to undergo, and the special management measures imposed on restricted investments stipulated on the negative lists.[113]

The rules governing the supervision regime in both the FIL and the Reporting Measures are either vague or problematic. One provision stipulated in the FIL requires foreign investors to accept the supervisory inspection legally conducted by the competent authorities,[114] without specifying how to conduct the supervision, what to inspect, and where there might be potential liabilities. Such uncertainty can impede the achievement of the goals, as foreign investors may thus refrain from entering China's market; simultaneously, authorities can hardly conduct efficient supervision without the guidance of unified rules.[115]

The supervision regime in the Reporting Measures is inherited from the one in the filing regime. There are some problems. The first one relates to the lack of detailed rules regulating the random check. The only guideline provided is the so-called double random, one open principle to randomly assign inspectors and select enterprises for inspection, and to publish the issues being inspected along with the results.[116] These rules are insufficient to guarantee a unified and transparent approach, as authorities are free to establish a specific selection process in an unpredictable way. Therefore, a standardized selection approach is necessary to guarantee proper implementation of the random check and to increase the willingness of examinees to cooperate with the check, hence benefitting the functioning of the supervision regime and the achievement of the goals.[117]

Like the inspection in the filing regime, there are no rules regulating the frequency of the random check. So far, except for some results of inspection undertaken under the reporting mechanism, most of the published results after the entry into force of the Reporting Measures came from inspections conducted under the previous filing regime, including those uploaded in November 2020, while for the rest there is no relevant information.[118] Accordingly, it is uncertain whether the apparently robust rules can be a problem in practice. However, the random check conducted in the filing regime implies that the lack of detailed rules could trigger considerable variation in practice between different regions. From 12 July 2017 to 30 August 2019, there were 459 published positive results of the random check,[119] from only 33 cities (including both prefecture and county-level);[120] Suzhou alone contributed around 37% of the records, while Fuzhou and Huzhou counted for more than 15% and 9% respectively. Conversely, some major host cities of FIEs, like Guangzhou and Shenzhen,[121] had published no results of supervision.[122]

In addition, the number of FIEs being checked indicates that the authorities generally failed to supervise foreign investments properly.[123] To effectively conduct the random check, it is advisable to regulate the frequency in two respects. One is to regulate the frequency of an examination authority conducting random checks to guarantee reasonable and effective supervision. The other is to limit the frequency of a single examinee being examined so as to avoid meaningless and repeated review within a short period of time.[124]

The rules regulating the publication of the results are either incomplete or imperfect in the following aspects. One is the lack of rules specifying the timing and format of the publication. The same problem in the filing regime resulted in the publication of some results after more than six months of the examination with various contents. There were three categories of results in the publication platform: positive and negative credit information of FIEs, as well as negative credit information of foreign investors. However, except for two results published in the negative credit information of FIEs, all other results were published in the positive category, including those reporting the failure of conducting the filing procedure after altering the FIEs and their correction after the random check. The inclusion of such results in the positive category was misleading. Meanwhile, some records only reported the date and the form of the check without specifying the results, and some other records even left the results of the check blank. Such inconsistency can only be sorted through unified and detailed implementation rules.[125]

Unlike random checks that are required to publish all results, other inspections are only required to publish negative outcomes.[126] These publication requirements are not transparent enough to allow investors and stakeholders to assess the implementation of the examination process and to monitor the activities of registered enterprises and their investors. Conversely, to publish all results – including the positive ones of inspection according to tip-offs, inspection according to the suggestions of reports, and inspection ex-officio would considerably improve the transparency of the inspection procedures. Meanwhile, the publication of positive outcomes could serve as vindication for examinees of examination excluding random check, since they are selected to some extent upon a suspicion of illegality, which might encourage other investors to comply with the law. All results can be published together without indicating the category of inspection, as examinees other than those of random checks may prefer not to reveal it.[127]

The publication of the results is an important component of the post-entry inspection regime, as it can strengthen the deterrence of the inspection, promote compliance with the law, and enable public supervision of the management process. Therefore, proper design of publication rules can ensure the effectiveness of the post-entry inspection and thus contribute to the economic growth goals.[128]

The other issue that needs clarification is the regime governing national security review and anti-monopoly review. Even foreign investments in sectors not included on the negative lists may still be required to undergo these control mechanisms if they raise security or antitrust concerns.[129] The lack of clarity mainly derives from the following aspects. First, the scope, content, and criteria of the review are not specified. Although the Measures for Security Review of Foreign Investments were issued according to the FIL in December 2020, key issues of national security review remain under-defined. The factors for consideration are not provided, and the scope of review[130] is broad enough to cover transactions that have little nexus with national security, narrowly defined, like value-added telecommunication services.[131] Meanwhile, the ambiguous wording allows the government authority to target any transactions at their discretion and thus fails to address the concern that the process can be used as retaliation against foreign investors.[132] The obscurity is further exacerbated by the lack of transparency. There are no rules requiring the publication of decisions or reports; therefore, any insight into the operation of the mechanism is hard to come by. The anti-monopoly review suffers from similar problems. Foreign investors have already complained about the unequal application of the procedure under the existing mechanism,[133] as most of the conditional clearance and prohibition decisions relate to foreign investors, raising the suspicion that administrative powers may be misused to distort the competition between domestic and foreign investments.[134] Moreover, the interpretation of substantive rules is unclear in spite of several years of implementation, while the limited scope of the decisions being disclosed also provides little help to their understanding.[135] Unfortunately, the vague wording of the FIL and its Implementation Regulations does not address these problems. Accordingly, the lack of clarity of the review procedures can countervail the positive effect of the recent reform in encouraging investment flows.[136]

The connections between different procedures are also unclear. In addition to national security review and anti-monopoly review, investors may need to obtain permits from certain industrial sectors.[137] However, there is no indication regarding the sequencing of the procedures, nor are there any rules regarding the influence of the result of one procedure on another. These review procedures serve the function of protecting security and governing the economy. Without clear rules, however, foreign investors may fail to apply for the pertinent approval. Errors of this kind might result in undermining the protection of national security, or in unreasonable delays for the investment's entry into China, thus nullifying the positive step towards easing administrative procedures entailed by the recent reform. Therefore, detailed guidelines for handling and coordinating the different procedures are necessary for the fulfilment of China's development goals through reformed management of foreign investment flows.[138]

7. Regulating the Government Itself

7.1 Lack of Transparency and Standard

One of the fundamental concerns of foreign investors pertains to the lack of full transparency in the administrative and judicial appeal process amid legislative improvements introduced in the 80s and 90s. The perception of lack of effectiveness of the appeal or review mechanism will prove harder to address as this may require more fundamental reforms involving the broader judicial or legal systems.

Lack of clear criteria for administrative approval of foreign investments is a long-standing concern. Approval typically involves the exercise of discretionary powers and the discretion to evaluate investment proposals based on broader economic or development policies, which may not be easily defined.

Concerns have also been expressed about the differences in approval process for domestic and foreign investments, raising the issue of national treatment. The differences result in a more onerous treatment for foreign investment because of more approval requirements imposed on FIEs.[139] The potential causes for such differential treatment are attributed to China's industrial policies favouring domestic players, in particular, SOEs, the lack of transparency in FDI approval process, as well as the absence of effective means to challenge administrative acts that could violate relevant regulations or even China's WTO obligations.[140]

Although the availability of various administrative or judicial reviews is generally acknowledged, the use of these mechanisms has been rare. This may be attributed to various factors such as the broadly defined grounds for denying investment applications, the challenges in producing enough evidence to prove infringing administrative acts, the lack of judicial or administrative independence, and the general public's overall reluctance to challenge administrative acts.[141]

7.2 Regulatory Overlap

In China, foreign investments are subject to concurrent supervision by multiple regulatory agencies, which include but are not limited to the MOFCOM and the NDRC and their local counterparts. Along with the supervision scheme, various regulations, rules, orders, and guidelines have been issued, which are expansive and change constantly.[142] Such regulatory overlap not only increases compliance costs for foreign investors and significantly delays administrative processes, but also impedes the efficiency of regulatory framework due to unclear division of responsibility and the lack of cooperation between the authorities.[143] Moreover, the entanglement of multiple competences can undermine the effort of recent change to simplify the administrative procedures, as new approval requirements can be imposed by other authorities despite the removal of the MOFCOM approval.[144] Unfortunately, besides the mere requirement that authorities should act in accordance with their conferred duties,[145] the new law makes no dedicated effort to improve the situation.

The picture is further complicated because local authorities can enact detailed implementation rules provided that they are not against higher level laws and regulations.[146] They can also issue normative documents (circulars, notices, and others) to further specify applicable laws and regulations. These regulatory powers of local authorities inevitably cause inconsistent implementation of national laws, through the application of different detailed regulations adopted locally,[147] some of which imposed more (or less) restrictions on foreign investments than national laws under the previous foreign investment legal regime.[148] Although the latter problem is addressed in the FIL in the manner discussed earlier, the issue of inconsistent implementation can worsen with the provisions in the FIL that have intentionally vague wording, which enable local authorities to interpret and adapt laws according to their needs and conditions.[149] Such inconsistency may then cause two further problems. One is that authorities may fail to properly implement pertinent laws or even act against the object and purpose of recent reform, like selective enforcement of rules to the detriment of foreign investor interests; the other is the impact on the transparency of the applicable rules, which can hinder business confidence and generate confusion for foreign investors.[150] Therefore, inconsistent implementation is always an obstacle to market access and thus frustrates the effort of the recent reform.[151]

First, rules regulating the issuance of normative documents should be adopted. Although the FIL Implementation Regulations require that legitimacy examination of regulatory documents relating to foreign investment should be conducted,[152] there are no rules regulating the procedure and the competent authorities. Moreover, issues like the supervision of issuing authorities, the procedure to issue normative documents, and the competence of authorities should also be specified. These documents are considered quasi-regulations and play an essential role in governance. Therefore, to guarantee the effectiveness of the FIL, it is advisable to enact a comprehensive law regulating all pertinent issues.[153]

Second, the coordination between various regulatory authorities should be enhanced. Regarding the departments at the national level, centralized coordination should be strengthened in two ways. One is to delegate authority to the agencies through narrower statutory mandates and more careful definition of roles and responsibilities. The other is to authorize central institutions to act as centralized coordinators and monitor the performance of various departments to ensure that they act in line with the regulatory goals. Conversely, the coordination between local authorities can be realized through agreements entered between different regions.[154] This practice would effectively mediate legal conflicts and achieve coherence within the coordinating area, hence reducing the barriers for investment and trade flows.[155]

Third, more channels should be available for citizens and foreign investors to challenge the rules implemented locally. Currently, courts can only review the normative documents when they are the basis of a specific administrative act being challenged.[156] However, in 2018, only about 0.28% of administrative claims involved such review.[157] Administrative reconsideration is also available, but two further limitations are imposed on the competence of the administrative reviewing bodies: one is similar to that of administrative litigation, as the rules must be the basis of a challenged specific administrative act; the other is that the rules are not enacted by the departments or commissions under the State Council and local governments.[158]

Fourth, the supervision of rulemaking by the authorities should be strengthened. Although both the NPC and its specialized committee or Standing Committee have the authorization to review rules enacted by administrative authorities,[159] due to the lack of specific procedures or regulations and the vast number of various rules, such review is ineffective and needs to be improved through both legal and institutional change. One solution could be the establishment of a professional legal review authority,[160] which has been advocated for years.

7.3 Rule on Administrative and Governmental Actions

The FIL has some striking features that confer explicit duties on various administrative organs both at national and provincial levels to promote, protect, and manage foreign investments in different contexts.[161]

The FIL provides a positive improvement that mandates the competent administrative authorities to review licence applications of foreign investors using similar conditions and procedures applied to domestic investment, unless otherwise provided by laws or administrative regulations.[162] However, some of the provisions like the establishment of a foreign investment information reporting system mandating foreign investors to submit foreign-investment information reports and the establishment of a security review system for foreign investments could cause anxiety among foreign investors.[163,164]

In addition to the bans on the forced FTT and unauthorized disclosure of business secrets, the FIL contains two particular rules that govern government actions, especially at local levels. The first rule deals with local policies and measures that may affect the FIEs and foreign investors. Article 24 of the FIL requires that the governments at all levels and their relevant departments be in compliance with the laws and regulations in formulating normative documents concerning foreign investment.[165]

It is specifically provided in Article 24 that without being duly authorized by the laws or administrative regulations, the government at all levels may not (i) derogate from the legitimate rights or interests of the FIEs or increase their obligations; (ii) set conditions for market access and exit; or (iii) interfere with the normal production and operation of the FIEs.[166] The main theme of Article 24 of the FIL is to maintain the uniformity of the application of the law pertaining to the FIEs and to prevent local government interference with FIEs in their own jurisdiction.

The Implementation Regulations provide a compliance review mechanism for the regulatory or normative documents involving foreign investments adopted by the governments, central or local alike. In accordance with Article 26 of the Implementation Regulations, the regulatory documents made by the government and its relevant departments concerning foreign investment shall be subject to the State Council's review of their legality.[167] In addition, pursuant to Article 26, if a foreign investor or an FIE believes that a regulatory document made by a central government department or a local government and its departments based on which an administrative action is taken does not comply with the law or regulations, it may request for a compliance review while applying for administrative review or conducting an administrative lawsuit.[168]

Under Article 25 of the FIL, local governments and their departments shall honour their policy commitment made to foreign investments or FIEs under the law and shall fulfil various types of contracts legally concluded.[169] The purpose of Article 25 is to ensure the continuity of local policies made in favour of foreign investment and fulfilment of contractual obligations regardless of change of government structure and personnel. The Implementation Regulations define the "policy commitment" as the written commitment made by local governments at all levels and their relevant departments within the legal authority regarding the support policies, preferential treatment, and convenience conditions applicable to foreign investors and the FIEs' investment in the region.[170]

In case, however, the local governments have a need to change the policy commitments or contract terms, the change may take place if it meets the conditions provided in Article 25. First, the change must be made for the State or public interests; second, the statutory limits and procedures must be followed; and third, a compensation must be made to the foreign investors and FIEs for the losses they suffered as a result of the change.[171] Article 25 does not specify how the compensation should be made. But rather, it is provided in the Implementation Regulations.

Article 28 of the Implementation Regulations restates Article 25 of the FIL in a more specific way. On the one hand, Article 28 requires local governments to fulfil the policy commitments made to foreign investors and the FIEs and perform various types of contracts concluded thereby. Under Article 28, no breach or recession of contract shall be allowed on the grounds of administrative division adjustment, government change, institutional or functional adjustment, and replacement of relevant responsible persons.[172]

On the other hand, Article 28 of the Implementation Regulations clarifies the compensation standards. Under Article 28, if policy commitments or contractual agreements need to be changed due to national or social public interests, the change should be made in accordance with statutory authority and procedures.[173] It is required in Article 28 that foreign investors and FIEs be compensated for the losses resulting from the change promptly in a fair and reasonable manner in accordance with law.[174]

Finally, certain powers recognized under the FIL could trigger further concerns.[175] For example specific powers conferred upon administrative authorities, like the power to order the ceasing of foreign investment activities in prohibited areas, the power to confiscate the illegal proceeds, and the power to impose fines when foreign investors fail to submit investment information reports, are some of the areas that could trigger additional concerns for foreign investors. The government may be brought by the foreign investor to international investment arbitration if the exercise of such powers constitutes illegal expropriation under the Chinese BITs. Similarly, an explicit recognition of the power of the state to introduce corresponding measures against investments from a specific foreign country that imposes prohibitive or restrictive investment measures relating to Chinese investments could cause unease among foreign investors. The recognition of the possibility to impose legal sanctions and even criminal responsibility upon administrative officials who abuse their administrative authority or neglect their duties or misuse the power for personal benefit or unlawfully disclose trade secrets could be seen as a strong deterrent against administrative excesses.[176,177]

8. Dispute Settlement Mechanism

8.1 New Mechanism: CSM

Another striking feature pertinent to administrative law is the establishment of working mechanisms to receive and promptly resolve complaints from FIEs, especially when they perceive administrative acts as an infringement of their lawful rights and interests[178,179] Also, it is to facilitate communication with foreign investors in terms of policy coordination or public bodies' tortious acts. Although the new mechanism is designed to be an exclusive channel for foreign investors, it does not preclude them from seeking redressal through the administrative review process or administrative suits.[180] Moreover, enforceable procedures are absent, as well as explanations about the relationship between the complaint mechanism and existing administrative procedures. The FIL touches upon issues outside its scope and lacks enforceable mechanisms. This may arouse suspicion rather than boost the trust of foreign investors.[181]

A new feature in the FIL is the establishment of a grievance-redressing vehicle called Complaint and Settlement Mechanism (CSM). As a part of the effort to protect foreign investment, the CSM under the FIL is designed to provide a handy process for the FIEs and foreign investors to express their concerns and report their complaints.[182] Article 26 stipulates that the state should establish a complaint mechanism for FIEs, coordinate and improve major policies and measures in the complaint of FIEs, and promptly solve problems. If a FIE or its investors believe the administrative acts of the administrative organs and their staff infringe on its legitimate rights and interests, they may apply for administrative reconsideration and bring administrative proceedings in accordance with the law, in addition to applying for coordinated settlement through the complaint mechanism of the FIE.[183] Foreign investors and FIEs can establish and voluntarily participate in chambers of commerce and associations to safeguard their legitimate rights and interests.[184,185] In accordance with Article 26 of the FIL, the State shall establish a CSM for the FIEs to promptly handle the issues that are raised by the FIEs or foreign investors and to coordinate and improve relevant policies and measures involving foreign investment.[186] Article 26 further provides that if an FIE or its investors believe that the administrative action of an administrative agency or its staff infringes upon their legitimate rights or interests, they may apply to the CSM for a coordinated solution.[187,188]

Under Article 26, the CSM has two basic functions: (i) to handle and provide solutions to the concerns of foreign investment and (ii) to coordinate on the policy issues and foreign investment management measures. However, it is unclear in the FIL what the CSM looks like and how it is organized and operated. There is also a question about how the CSM will differ from the existing rules and procedures. The underlying concern is whether the CSM may offer any realistic and practical recourse to foreign investors that receive unfair treatment by the governmental authorities.[189]

To deal with these questions and concerns, the Implementation Regulations provide a two-faceted CSM to handle complaints filed by foreign investors or FIEs: central joint conference and local designated authority. According to Article 29 of the Implementation Regulations, an inter-ministry joint conference system established by the State Council is responsible for (i) coordinating and promoting the work of handing the complaints made by FIEs to the central government, and (ii) guiding and supervising the work concerning complaints made by the FIEs to the local government. At the local level, the government of a county or above level is required to designate an authority to accept complaints filed by the FIEs or their investors within the local area.[190]

Moreover, under Article 30 of the Implementation Regulations, where an FIE or its investor believes that its lawful rights and interests are infringed upon by an administrative agency and its staff, and applies for a coordinated resolution through the CSM, the relevant authority may make factual inquiries to the administrative agency and its staff against whom the complaint is made, and the latter shall be cooperative. The applicant shall be notified in writing of the result of coordination.[191] In addition, Article 31 of the Implementation Regulations forbids any entity or individual from suppressing or retaliating against the FIE or foreign investor who files the complaint or seeks for a coordinated solution through the CSM.[192]

8.2 Other Channels

In addition to the CSM, there are other channels available to the FIEs and foreign investors for legal remedies or reliefs. First, Article 31 of the Implementation Regulations allows an FIE or its investor to report problems or concerns to the government and relevant departments through other lawful means other than CSM.[193] Pursuant to Article 26, the FIE or its investors may also apply for administrative reconsideration or file an administrative lawsuit whenever their legitimate rights or interests are harmed.[194] Article 30 of the Implementation Regulations also provides that when an FIE or its investor seeks a coordinated solution for certain matters through the CSM, its option to apply for administrative review or to initiate an administrative litigation shall not be affected.[195,196]

Administrative review is a process in which an administrative organ at the same or a higher level, at the request of an individual or unit, conducts a review on the act of an administrative agency that is alleged to have infringed upon the legitimate rights or interests of such individual or unit. According to the

Administrative Reconsideration Law (ARL),[197] any citizen, legal person, or any other organization who considers that his or her or its lawful rights and interests have been infringed upon by a specific administrative act may apply for administrative reconsideration to an administrative organ which accepts the application for administrative reconsideration and makes a decision.[198] The ARL equally applies to foreigners, stateless persons, or foreign organizations that request an administrative reconsideration in China.[199,200]

Administrative litigation is governed by the Administrative Litigation Law (ALL).[201] It is a litigation brought by a citizen, legal person, or other organization believing that its lawful rights and interests have been infringed upon by an administrative act of an administrative agency or its staff.[202] Under the ALL, the court at trial level has a general jurisdiction over administrative cases in the first instance.[203] An administrative case shall be filed with the court of the place where the administrative agency that first took the administrative act is located. But for a case involving administrative reconsideration, the court at the location of the reconsidering agency has the jurisdiction.[204,205]

Unless the administrative reconsideration is required, a party may directly file an administrative case with a court. Alternatively, the party may first apply to the administrative agency for reconsideration and then bring the case to a people's court if not satisfied with the reconsideration decision.[206] If an administrative reconsideration shall first be requested, a court proceeding may be sought after the administrative reconsideration is complete if the party is not satisfied with the reconsideration decision.[207,208]

When an application for administrative reconsideration is submitted and accepted, or if an administrative reconsideration is required prior to an administrative suit, no administrative litigation may take place during the statutory period of time for administrative reconsideration.[209] On the other hand, if an administrative case is brought before a court, and the people's court takes the case, no administrative reconsideration may be conducted.[210,211]

An interesting part in the FIL is Article 27, which allows the FIEs to establish or join the chambers of commerce or associations. Under Article 27, the FIEs may establish or voluntarily join the chambers of commerce or associations according to the law. It is required that the chamber of commerce and association conduct their relevant activities in accordance with the laws, regulations, and its articles of association to safeguard the legitimate rights and interests of its members.[212] But it remains to be seen how the chamber of commerce or association so established or joined may serve as a safeguard of the interests of the FIEs.[213]

Under Article 7 of the Implementation Regulations, the chambers of commerce or associations should be consulted for comments or suggestions during the process of drafting the law, regulations, or local rules concerning foreign investments.[214] In accordance with Article 32 of the Implementation Regulations, an FIE may decide on its own to join in or withdraw from a chamber of commerce or an association, unless otherwise provided by the law or regulation, and nobody may interfere.[215, 216]

Foreign investors can resort to either administrative reconsideration or administrative litigation if they consider that specific administrative acts violate the law and infringe upon their lawful interests.[217] Moreover, administrative litigation can also be brought if investors are unsatisfied with the administrative reconsideration decision.[218] However, there are three main problems with these remedies. The first problem is the considerable length of the procedure. It may take 90 days to obtain an administrative reconsideration decision[219] or six months to receive an administrative judgement.[220] Therefore, foreign investors may choose to endure some violations by the authorities, like the requirements to conduct approval procedures for foreign investments not covered by the negative lists, in order to save time and loss. To address this problem, a speedy channel to handle complaints regarding minor or manifest violations of authorities can be established, which allows investigation and decision within a short period of time.

The success rate of remedies is low. According to the data collected by the Ministry of Justice, in 2018 only about 15.11% of China's administrative reconsideration applications succeeded, while about 62.86% of them were rejected and about 20.7% of them were terminated due to mediation or other reasons. As far as administrative lawsuits are concerned, only 28,403 claims were granted or partially granted, while 100,651 were rejected. Additionally, 50,722 cases did not enter the stage of substantial hearing due to dismissal of the complaint, *nolle prosequi*, termination of proceedings, and mediation. Perhaps most cases failed because the contentious administrative act is lawful. However, the low success rate still casts doubt on the effectiveness of the remedial regime and the capability of judicial organs to ensure proper implementation of the law when facing the powerful governments.[221]

In addition, the FIL allows foreign investors to seek remedies bringing complaints under a working mechanism or through a chamber of commerce or association.[222] However, their procedures, timelines, competent agencies, and possible results are not clear. Accordingly, some commentators are worried that the new procedures will become unattractive, or even a burden, to foreign investors.[223]

There are two solutions to this problem. One is to increase the transparency of the relief channels. Currently, judgements of administrative lawsuits are published online,[224] but court verdicts on cases in preliminary court proceedings are not available. There is also no unified statutory requirement for the publication of administrative reconsideration decisions.[225] The lack of transparency blocks public knowledge about the outcome of the remedy-seeking processes and thus triggers the doubt that both judicial and administrative authorities may operate in relative obscurity. Accordingly, the publication of all the verdicts and decisions may not only promote public understanding of the remedial channels and defeat the doubt but also improve the effectiveness of the procedure through the strengthening of public supervision. The other solution is to deepen the standard of review employed in the remedial procedures. Both administrative reconsideration organs and courts are required to respect the discretion of the authority being challenged and be prudent with its administrative acts and decisions; hence, they mainly review the legality of the procedural matters in the acts and will only change the administrative decisions when they are manifestly improper.[226] This is an important reason for the low success rate of remedy-seeking. Therefore, appropriate deepening of the standard of review will plausibly increase the success rate and the effectiveness of the remedial channels, which can help to build the trust of foreign investors in the implementation of the recent reform and thus fulfil the goal of encouraging foreign investments.

Therefore, it is essential to provide pertinent information in the FIL or the implementing measures, to allow foreign investors to fully assess each avenue of redress and make their choices.[227]

9. Five-Year Transitional Period

The FIL provides that the FIEs established under the previous FIE Laws will be "grandfathered" (i.e. without any need for change) for a period of five years as a Transitional Period. However, the FIL does not specify how FIEs established under the previous FIE Laws should be transformed so as to be in compliance with the FIL during such five-year period, nor does it specify the consequences for failure to do so at the end of such period.[228] The FIL generally provides that detailed regulations will be promulgated by the State Council. The Implementation Regulations only specify that the registration authority will not allow FIEs failing to complete corporate changes required under the FIL by the end of the six-month grace period after the five-year period (i.e. by 30 June 2025) to register any other changes and the registration authority will report companies that have failed to do so in the national enterprise information publication system.

For existing FIEs, they may keep their corporate structure unchanged for five years starting from the effectiveness of the FIL, that is January 1, 2020.[229] Given the partnership is barely adopted in practice for joint ventures, most FIEs will need to follow the Company Law.[230]

The Implementation Regulations further clarify that existing joint ventures established under the previous regime can retain the following specific arrangements previously agreed upon after the Transitional Period, which means the Articles of Association that contain the previously negotiated terms may still apply, even where they are inconsistent with the Company Law, for example early investment recoupment clauses in a CJV agreement and asset distribution arrangements in case of liquidation.[231]

FIEs established earlier should pay attention to the timely adjustment of their organizational forms in accordance with the provisions of the Company Law or the Partnership Enterprise Law. For example, EJVs should establish the shareholder meeting, board of directors, and board of supervisors (which is no longer compulsorily required) in accordance with the provisions of the Company Law.[232] In addition, the following content should be clarified in future implementation measures formulated by the State Council: (i) specific ways to adjust the organizational form, organizational structure, and activity criteria of the FIEs established under the three FIE Laws in accordance with the Company Law and the Partnership Enterprise Law, such as the establishment of two boards and the transfer of equity rights pursuant to the FIE Laws; and (ii) how to deal with non-timely adjustment after the expiration of the five-year transitional period.[233,234]

Foreign investors who have existing joint ventures in China will need to understand what this will mean for the corporate governance structure of their joint ventures. This may require the joint venture partners to come back to the negotiation table and potentially reopen the discussion over corporate governance terms and potentially other terms for the joint venture.

Foreign investors in this predicament will be well advised to discuss upfront with their partners the impending changes to the corporate governance structure that would be brought about by the implementation of the FIL.[235]

In this case, those FIEs established before the implementation of the FIL can retain their original organizational form for five years after the FIL is implemented.[236] The FIL focuses on foreign investment access and other important matters.

The first issue is the corporate structure of the FIEs. The FIEs under the FIE Laws take the business form of EJV, CJV, or WFOE. Since the FIL requires FIEs to be subject to the Company Law or the Partnership Law in their formation and operation, the CJV will not be an option anymore. A practical question is how the existing CJVs are to be dissolved. In addition, there has been another foreign investment known as Sino-Foreign Joint Exploration and Development of Natural Resources (JED). The JED commonly operates on a contractual basis. It is unclear if the JED is also included in the transitional period.[237]

During the five-year transitional period, how should those FIEs willing to retain their original organizational forms, corporate governance structures, and rules of activities solve the problem of applying laws?[238] Should they apply the current FIL or the three FIE Laws that will have been repealed? For those FIEs that cannot reach a consensus during the transitional period and cannot adjust their organizational form, corporate governance structure and rules of activities in accordance with the FIL, or cannot complete the adjustment within the transitional period, what should be done to regulate or solve the problems?[239] Similar issues need to be clarified in the implementation regulations. The bottom line is that the corporate organizational structures stipulated by the previous FIE Laws (especially EJVs) will gradually be phased out.[240]

10. Implementation, Prospects, and Uncertainties

The FIL marks a milestone in a 40-year foreign investment policy process, through which China has opened up to the outside world, while incrementally adopting international standards to drive domestic economic and governance reform. On face at least, FIL is to uplift China to a higher level of investment liberalization and facilitation. It will be recorded in history as a milestone of China's reform and opening-up process.[241]

The FIL and the State Council Opinions demonstrate China's intention to develop a more transparent, open, and investor-friendly business environment enabling China to remain competitive and attractive to foreign investors.

There will be challenges for investors and regulators alike given the lack of detailed guidance on implementation. The FIL stipulates only the broad principles to govern foreign investment. In spite of the fact that the laws and regulations in China are by-and-large very good (or well-written), the implementation differs across regions and different levels and hence whether the law will have the desired impact will depend on the implementation in practice.[242] Practical impacts – including the effect of the FIL on cross-border M&A and on corporate governance in Chinese subsidiaries of foreign companies – depend on implementing rules.[243] Until China takes the concrete step to implement the FIL and to open the market, the FIL will change little.[244] The real issue with China's treatment of foreign investors is that China continues to protect its domestic economy against foreign investors. That level of protection was perhaps appropriate for China before 2000, but it is not appropriate for a China that is now the second-largest economy in the world and that claims a market economy. It appears that the Chinese government has no plans to reduce its stronghold over China's economy which is evidenced by its unwillingness to enhance the state-owned sectors in recent years. The opening-up measures will remain constrained by China's fundamentally closed economy. Foreign investors are consigned to an increasingly small playing field within the Chinese economy. The rights that appear to open under the FIL may be largely illusory in reality. Put simply, for sectors of the Chinese economy prohibited to foreign investment, foreign investors will not have any of the new rights under the new Foreign Investment Law.[245] It is likely that China will continue to be selective about what investment in which area it wishes to encourage, and more detailed industry and sector-specific policies are expected. If China does not open its economy wider to foreign investment (which is exceedingly unlikely to occur), all the changes outlined in the FIL will be little more than putting lipstick on a pig.[246] In this sense, the FIL may be old wine in a new bottle.

For the benefits of foreign investors, areas of uncertainty need to be resolved in the coming years, and practical steps foreign investors need to take to adapt.[247]

Even though the FIL has been well received by the international business community, skepticism remains about its wording and definitions as well as its further implementation locally. Other vagueness includes the lack of specification of what kind of trade secret disclosures will be prohibited and what terms such as "national interest" and "social public interests" exactly entail.

Unfortunately, the FIL does not help much to improve confidence in this regard with its lack of details and clarity on implementation. Article 25 of the FIL states vaguely that "the various levels of local people's governments and their relevant department shall fulfill the policy commitments made to foreign investors or foreign-invested enterprises and the various types of contracts concluded in accordance with law," and where it is necessary that they change policy commitments or contractual agreements for the national or public interest, they shall proceed in accordance with legally prescribed authorities and procedures and compensate the foreign investors or foreign-invested enterprises for any loss sustained as a result in accordance with law.

However, these rules are hard to be implemented[248] and may even increase transaction costs due to their vagueness.

The Chairman of AmCham expressed the disappointment that "a lot of the implementing detail has been chopped out. . . . How are they going to be implemented in practice, that is what we cannot tell."

According to the survey undertaken by the Economist Intelligence Unit, the ease of doing business and strong rule of law are among the two most important factors affecting investment decision-making, while arbitrary or discriminatory treatment by the host state government is the second most frequently cited issue relating to the rule of law.[249] Most respondents have experienced the most significant rule of law issues in China.[250] Foreign firms also experienced the difficulties caused by government intervention in business operations and investment decisions,[251] or frustration over the limited access to China's market and the government policies discriminating against them.[252] The World Bank ranked China as 78th in the ease of doing business category due to the length of the procedure required to start a business.[253] These surveys suggest that a reform is needed to establish a clear, transparent, predictable, and equal investment climate for foreign investment, which can significantly improve the efficiency and quality of investment management and thus contribute to the development goals.[254]

From a high-level perspective, the FIL embodies China's resolve to continue to modernize its laws to reflect the changing global economy. At the same time, the FIL, as currently passed, is more high-level than the FIL proposed in 2015 and 2018 respectively, which contained more specific provisions but still left questions regarding its viability in implementation.

The FIL is positioned as the foundational law in the field of foreign investment.[255] It will apply uniformly across all foreign investment projects in China. It is expected that the relevant authorities will take this opportunity to systematically evaluate and revise the current foreign investment system and rules in order to form a unified legal system for foreign investment.

FIL also signals a new stage of increasingly difficult and substantive reforms. Notwithstanding the current criticism of globalization, the integration of global value chains has significant implications for the international economic order.

Based on the new "double circulation" strategy, "China is set to become the world's largest national market," and the focus of outer circulation is foreign investment, particularly in respect of industries that are internet-based, relating to "information technology" and "artificial intelligence" where China's innovation capability is fast expanding. Such a macro-background may allow for China's market opening up to continue at a rapid pace, with the current negative lists to be further trimmed, especially during the periods of tailwinds. Foreign investors and entrepreneurs continue to encourage the Chinese authorities to roll out a new programme of market liberalization. Nevertheless, Chinese authorities are not reluctant to air their concerns about "security, standards, consistency with international norms" when facing the pressure of enabling foreign investment to enjoy greater market access, especially in those fields strategically important for China's national well-being and safety.[256]

The FIL indicates that China is maintaining its commitment to further open up its market and boost inbound foreign investment. Several key changes under the FIL (such as national treatment of foreign investment subject to the Negative List, protection of foreign IP rights and trade secrets, and equal treatment of domestic and foreign companies in government procurement) address some of the "asks" from the US side under its trade negotiations with China, some of which have been further reflected in the phase one trade agreement recently concluded between the United States and China. While the FIL is encouraging, foreign investors should understand the major changes and benefits under the FIL, consider where further enforcement measures and concrete steps are required, and consider ways to take advantage of new investment opportunities in China.[257]

The FIL is more than China's response to a looming trade war coupled with deglobalization (i.e. a retreat from globalization). In a world that is increasingly erecting barriers, the FIL is a welcome message from the Chinese government that China is open for foreign businesses and globalization. After over 40 years of China's open-up and reform, it signals China as a, perhaps unlikely, champion of trade and investment liberalization.[258]

Notes

1 McDermott Will & Emery, "China's New Foreign Investment Law: What's New and What's Next" (*McDermott Will & Emery*, 9 April 2019) <https://www.mwe.com/insights/chinas-new-foreign-investment-law-whats-new-and-whats-next/> accessed 21 September 2022.
2 2019 Foreign Investment Law (adopted 15 March 2019, entered into force 1 January 2020) (2019 FIL) Article 42; 2019 FIL Implementation Regulations (adopted December 26, 2019, entered into force 1 January 2020) Article 49.
3 Barbara Li, "Great Expectations: China's New Foreign Investment Law Unpicked" (2019) 3 *International Financial Law Review* 48.
4 Morrison Foerster, "China's Foreign Investment Law: Are You Ready for It?" (*Morrison Foerster*, 3 January 2020) <https://www.mofo.com/resources/insights/200102-chinas-investment-foreign-law> accessed 25 April 2022.
5 FIL, Article 1.
6 FIL, Article 42.
7 "Delegation, supervision and service" refers to simplifying government control, decentralizing power, and optimizing service. 'Delegation' means simplifying administration, decentralizing power, and lowering access threshold. 'Management' means fair supervision and promotion of fair competition. 'Service' means efficient service to create a convenient environment of business.

8 *See* the answer to reporters' request by Gao Feng, Spokesman of the Ministry of Commerce, Regular Press Conference (27 December 2018) <www.mofcom.gov.cn/xwfbh/20181227.shtml>

9 Min Zhao, "Analysis and Interpretation of the New Foreign Investment Law of the People's Republic of China" (2019) 02 *China and WTO Review* 351.

10 Ibid.

11 Shu-Xue Jia, "On the Improvement of China's Legal System of Foreign Direct Investment" (2015) 8(4) *Journal of Politics and Law* 293.

12 Danling Yu, *Chinese Business Law* (Palgrave Macmillan 2018) 43.

13 Yawen Zheng, "China's New Foreign Investment Law and Its Contribution Towards the Country's Development Goals" (2021) 22 *Journal of World Investment & Trade* 388, 410.

14 Yumei Wang, *On China's Legal System Governing Foreign Direct Investment* (Law Press 2003) 35.

15 2016 Law of the PRC on Chinese-Foreign Equity Joint Ventures (adopted 3 September, entered into force 1 October 2016) (EJV Law) Article 3; 2017 Law of the PRC on Chinese-Foreign Contractual Joint Ventures (adopted 4 November, entered into force 5 November 2017) (CJV Law) Article 5; 2014 Detailed Rules for the Implementation of the Law of the PRC on Wholly Foreign-Owned Enterprises (adopted 19 February, entered into force 1 March 2014) (WFOE Law) Article 10.

16 EJV Law Articles 3, 13–14; CJV Law Articles 5, 7, 10, 12, and 24; WFOE Law Articles 6 and 20.

17 2017 Measures for the Administration of the Confirmation and Recordation of Enterprise Investment Projects (effective 4 August 2017) Articles 4–5; see also 2016 Catalogue of Investment Projects Subject to Government Confirmation (effective 12 December 2016) and 2017 Notice of the NDRC on Effectively Conducting the Relevant Foreign Investment Work Concerning the Implementation of the Catalogue of Investment Projects Subject to Government Confirmation (effective 14 January 2017).

18 China's GDP growth has been on average 10% a year in the last four decades, while more than 500 million people have been lifted out of poverty. World Bank and Development Research Centre of the State Council of the People's Republic of China (PRC), *China 2030: Building a Modern, Harmonious, and Creative Society* (World Bank 2013) 3–4.

19 See Ministry of Commerce of the People's Republic of China (MOFCOM), "Statistical Bulletin of FDI in China 2019" <http://images.mofcom.gov.cn/wzs/201912/20191226103003602.pdf> accessed 4 June 2020.

20 Yawen Zheng, "China's New Foreign Investment Law and Its Contribution Towards the Country's Development Goals" (2021) 22 *Journal of World Investment & Trade* 391.

21 Ibid.

22 For example according to 2014 Administrative Measures for the Confirmation and Recordation of Foreign-Funded Projects (effective 17 June 2014) Article 14, if the project may have substantial impact on public interest, the approval authority may solicit public opinion or consult experts. However, there is no rule concerning this consultation period.

23 For example see 2019 Implementation Regulations of EJV Law (effective 2 March 2019) Article 4(3), in which one of the conditions for rejection is the failure to satisfy the requirement of China's economic development. However, there is no further published clarification of such requirements. For instances of foreign investments subject to unwritten rules, see the US Chamber of Commerce, "China's Approval Process for Inbound Foreign Direct Investment: Impact on Market Access, National Treatment and Transparency" (2012) <http://www.uschamber.com/assets/archived/images/documents/files/020021_China_InboundInvestment.Cvr.pdf> accessed 28 October 2020.

24 2017 Implementation Regulations of CJV Law (effective 17 November 2017) act 7.

25 US Chamber of Commerce, "China's Approval Process for Inbound Foreign Direct Investment: Impact on Market Access, National Treatment and Transparency" (2012) <http://www.uschamber.com/assets/archived/images/documents/files/020021_China_InboundInvestment.Cvr.pdf> accessed 28 October 2020.

26 Yawen Zheng, "China's New Foreign Investment Law and Its Contribution Towards the Country's Development Goals" (2021) 22 *Journal of World Investment & Trade* 393.

27 Xiaojun Li, "Durability of China's Lawmaking Process under Xi Jinping: A Tale of the Two Foreign Investment Laws" <www.researchgate.net/publication/343949563> accessed 28 August 2020.

28 Mark Schaub, Atticus Zhao, Dai Xueyun and Zheng Wei, *China Foreign Investment Law: How Will It Impact the Existing FIEs?* (3 June 2019) para 2.

29 Mo Zhang, "Change of Regulatory Scheme: China's New Foreign Investment Law and Reshaped Legal Landscape" (2020) 37 *Pacific Basin Law Journal* 179, 181.

30 See Xin Hua, "Commentary: A Landmark Law in China's Opening Up" *NPC&CPPCC Annual Sessions 2019* (11 March 2019), www.xinhuanet.com/english/2019-03/11/c 137885467htm.

31 The procedure is applicable to both establishment and post-establishment material changes of foreign investments.

32 See the Interim Measures for the Recordation Administration of the Formation and Modification of FIEs (first issued in 2016, last modified in 2018) (2018 Interim Measures).

33 FIL, Article 11.

34 Ian K. Lewis, Mirror Zhou and Elfie J.Y. Wang, "China Investment Policy – Ensuring the Mice Will Be Caught" (2021) 22 *Journal of Investment Compliance* 53.

35 Dan Harris, "China's New Foreign Investment Law: Tain't No Big Thing" (*Harris Bricken*, 29 December 2019) <https://harrisbricken.com/chinalawblog/chinas-new-foreign-investment-law-taint-no-big-thing/> accessed 25 April 2022.

36 PriceWaterhouse Coopers, "China Welcomes Investors with New Foreign Investment Law" (*News Flash*, 13 February 2020) <https://thesuite.pwc.com/media/10831/china-foreign-investment-law-feb2020-en.pdf> accessed 25 April 2022.

37 Z. Alex Zhang and Vivian Tsoi, "China Adopts New Foreign Investment Law" (*White & Case*, 29 March 2019) <www.whitecase.com/publications/alert/china-adopts-new-foreign-investment-law> accessed 25 April 2022.

38 McDermott Will & Emery, "China's New Foreign Investment Law: What's New and What's Next" (*McDermott Will & Emery*, 9 April 2019) <https://www.mwe.com/insights/chinas-new-foreign-investment-law-whats-new-and-whats-next/> accessed 25 April 2022.

39 Ibid.

40 Mark Schaub, Atticus Zhao, Dai Xueyun and Zheng Wei, "China Foreign Investment Law: How Will It Impact the Existing FIEs?" (*King & Wood Mallesons*, 3 June 2019) <www.chinalawinsight.com/2019/06/articles/foreign-investment/china-foreign-investment-law>

41 McDermott Will & Emery, "China's New Foreign Investment Law: What's New and What's Next" (*McDermott Will & Emery*, 9 April 2019) <https://www.mwe.com/insights/chinas-new-foreign-investment-law-whats-new-and-whats-next/> accessed 25 April 2022.

42 According to Article 81 of the Company Law, the profit distribution of a company should be stipulated in its articles of association; that is to say, it is not necessary to distribute profits according to the proportion of capital contribution.

43 Nicolette Butler and Surya Subedi, "The Future of International Investment Regulation: Towards a World Investment Organisation?" (2017) 64 *Netherlands International Law Review* 43–72.

44 Min Zhao, "Analysis and Interpretation of the New Foreign Investment Law of the People's Republic of China" (2019) 02 *China and WTO Review* 351.

45 Ibid.

46 Mark Schaub, Atticus Zhao, Dai Xueyun and Zheng Wei, "China Foreign Investment Law: How Will It Impact the Existing FIEs?" (*King & Wood Mallesons*, 3 June 2019) <www.chinalawinsight.com/2019/06/articles/foreign-investment/china-foreign-investment-law>

47 Jones Day, "China Further Opens its Market with New 'Foreign Investment Law'" (*Jones Day*, February 2020) <www.jonesday.com/en/insights/2020/02/chinas-new-foreign-investment-law> accessed 25 April 2022.

48 Article 4 of the EJV Law, and the Notice on Issues relating to Strengthening Administration of Approval, Registration, Foreign Exchange and Tax Collection for Foreign Investment Enterprises.

49 The Notice on Issues relating to Strengthening Administration of Approval, Registration, Foreign Exchange and Tax Collection for Foreign Investment Enterprises.

50 Jindu Research Institute Public Account, "Foreign Investment Law: Highlights and Challenges" <https://mp.weixin.qq.com/s/3RcPjm4YKUA71wrcWpU-zw> accessed 17 March 2019.

51 Morrison Foerster, "China's Foreign Investment Law: Are You Ready for It?" (*Morrison Foerster*, 3 January 2020) <https://www.mofo.com/resources/insights/200102-chinas-investment-foreign-law> accessed 25 April 2022.

52 Before the implementation of the Foreign Investment Law, a large number of provisions of the three laws on foreign-invested enterprises focused on the form of organization and the code of conduct. In recent years, with the development of the modern enterprise system in China, the Company Law and Partnership Enterprise Law have been promulgated for the organization and behaviour of enterprises. In view of the norms of enterprise organization and behaviour, the three laws on foreign-invested enterprises have formed a dual-track system with the Company Law and the Partnership Enterprise Law inside and outside. After the implementation of the Foreign Investment Law, the supervision measures for the foreign-invested enterprises will be unified with the Company Law and the Partnership Enterprise Law because the three laws on foreign-invested enterprises will be repealed.

53 Xiaoxia Zhang, "The Conflict and Integration between the Foreign Investment Law and the Company Law" (2012) 12 *Rule by L. & Soc'y* 27.

54 Company Law Ch. 5.

55 Xiuping Yang, *A Comparative Analysis of the Protection Measures of Shareholders' Rights and Interests in Chinese and Foreign Management*, H.L.J. Foreign Econ. Rel. & Trade, 61 (2005).

56 For example Article 3 of the Law on Sino–Foreign Equity Joint Ventures stipulates that "the equity joint venture agreement, contract, and articles of association signed by the parties to the venture shall be submitted to the state's competent department," which means that the contract mentioned here has the same position as the articles of association. But after the law's being abolished, the contract will lose this position.

57 Min Zhao, "Analysis and Interpretation of the New Foreign Investment Law of the People's Republic of China" (2019) 02 *China and WTO Review* 351.

58 FIL, Articles 3, 5, and 7.

59 Pat K. Chew, "Political Risk and US Investments in China: Chimera of Protection and Predictability?" (1994) 34 *Virginia Journal of International Law* 615.

60 FIL, Article 20; FIL Implementation Regulation, Article 21.

61 2011 Regulation on the Expropriation of Property on State-Owned Land and Compensation (effective 21 January 2011) Articles 2–3, 19.

62 2007 Property Law of the PRC (adopted 16 March, entered into force 1 October 2007) Articles 42, 44, and 121.

63 FIL, Article 10.

64 FIL, Articles 9–19.

65 Muruga P. Ramaswamy, "The Impact of the New Chinese Foreign Investment Law 2019 on the Administrative Legal System Governing Foreign Investments and Implications for the Investment Relations with Lusophone Markets" (2019) 9(2) *Juridical Tribune* 330.

66 FIL, Article 1.

67 FIL, Article 12.

68 FIL, Article 19.

69 Mo Zhang, "Change of Regulatory Scheme: China's New Foreign Investment Law and Reshaped Legal Landscape" (2020) 37 *UCLA Pacific Basin Law Journal* 179.

70 Jones Day, "China Further Opens its Market with New 'Foreign Investment Law'" (*Jones Day*, February 2020) <www.jonesday.com/en/insights/2020/02/chinas-new-foreign-investment-law> accessed 25 April 2022.

71 Min Zhao, "Analysis and Interpretation of the New Foreign Investment Law of the People's Republic of China" (2019) 02 *China and WTO Review* 351.

72 FIL, Article 9.

73 Jones Day, "China Further Opens its Market with New 'Foreign Investment Law'" (*Jones Day*, February 2020) <www.jonesday.com/en/insights/2020/02/chinas-new-foreign-investment-law> accessed 25 April 2022.

74 *Id*. Article 10.

75 *Id*. Article 11.

76 *Id*. Article 16.

77 Jones Day, "China Further Opens its Market with New 'Foreign Investment Law'" (*Jones Day*, February 2020) <www.jonesday.com/en/insights/2020/02/chinas-new-foreign-investment-law> accessed 25 April 2022.

78 ibid.

79 FIL, Article 17.

80 FIL, Article 19.

81 Jones Day, "China Further Opens its Market with New 'Foreign Investment Law'" (*Jones Day*, February 2020) <www.jonesday.com/en/insights/2020/02/chinas-new-foreign-investment-law> accessed 25 April 2022.

82 Ibid.

83 Terence Foo, "China's New Foreign Investment Law – What Does This Mean for Foreign Investors In China?" (*Clifford Chance*, 22 March, 2019) <www.cliffordchance.com/briefings/2019/03/china_s_new_foreigninvestmentlawwhatdoe.html> accessed 25 April.

84 FIL, Article 34.

85 FIL, Article 4.

86 Yawen Zheng, "China's New Foreign Investment Law and Its Contribution Towards the Country's Development Goals" (2021) 22 *Journal of World Investment & Trade* 397.

87 FIL, Article 4.

88 Yawen Zheng, "China's New Foreign Investment Law and Its Contribution Towards the Country's Development Goals" (2021) 22 *Journal of World Investment & Trade* 398.

89 See 2015 MOFCOM Service Guide of Approval Items for Foreign Investment (effective 22 July 2015).

90 See 2018 Interim Measures, Article 8.

91 See Announcement No 62 [2019] of the MOFCOM -Announcement on Issues Concerning Information Report of FIEs (effective 1 January 2020).

92 FIL, Article 34.

93 FIL, Article 34.

94 FIL, Article 34.

95 2019 Measures for the Reporting of Foreign Investment Information (effective 1 January 2020) (Reporting Measures) Article 11.

96 Morrison Foerster, "China's Foreign Investment Law: Are You Ready for It?" (*Morrison Foerster*, 3 January 2020) <https://www.mofo.com/resources/insights/200102-chinas-investment-foreign-law> accessed 25 April 2022.

97 Z. Alex Zhang and Vivian Tsoi, "China Adopts New Foreign Investment Law" 29 March 2019 <www.whitecase.com/publications/alert/china-adopts-new-foreign-investment-law> accessed 25 April 2022.

98 FIL, Article 34; MOFCOM announcement, Article 1.

99 Yawen Zheng, "China's New Foreign Investment Law and Its Contribution Towards the Country's Development Goals" (2021) 22 *Journal of World Investment & Trade* 398.

100 According to the MOFCOM, 96% of foreign investments are exempted from the approval procedure. See MOFCOM Regular Press Conference of the Ministry of

Commerce (29 September 2017) <www.mofcom.gov.cn/xwfbh/20170929.shtml> accessed 23 October 2020.

101 After the entry into force of the FIL in 2020, China had received USD 163 billion in new foreign direct investment, overtaking the United States as the world's largest host State of new foreign investments. "China Takes New Foreign Investment Top Spot from US" (*BBC*, 25 January 2021) <www.bbc.co.uk/news/business-55791634> accessed 26 February 2021.

102 Z. Alex Zhang and Vivian Tsoi, "China Adopts New Foreign Investment Law" 29 March 2019 <www.whitecase.com/publications/alert/china-adopts-new-foreign-investment-law> accessed 25 April 2022.

103 Terence Foo, "China's New Foreign Investment Law - What Does This Mean for Foreign Investors in China?" (*Clifford Chance*, March 2019) para 3. <https://www.cliffordchance.com/content/dam/cliffordchance/briefings/2019/03/chinas-new-foreign-investment-law-what-does-this-mean-for-foreign-investors-in-china.pdf> accessed 22 September 2022.

104 FIL, Article 32.

105 FIL, Article 34; FIL Implementation Regulations, Article 14; MOFCOM announcement (n 16).

106 FIL, Articles 37–38.

107 FIL Implementation Regulation, Article 20.

108 Yawen Zheng, "China's New Foreign Investment Law and Its Contribution Towards the Country's Development Goals" (2021) 22 *Journal of World Investment & Trade* 408.

109 See MOFCOM announcement.

110 Alan Xu, "From Approval to Filing: A New Era for Foreign Investment in China" *Hong Kong Lawyer*, 26 January 2017 <www.hk-lawyer.org/content/approval-filing-new-era-foreign-investment-china> accessed 20 October 2020.

111 Yawen Zheng, "China's New Foreign Investment Law and Its Contribution Towards the Country's Development Goals" (2021) 22 *Journal of World Investment & Trade* 408.

112 Ibid.

113 Ibid., 410.

114 FIL, Articles 41–43.

115 Yawen Zheng, "China's New Foreign Investment Law and Its Contribution Towards the Country's Development Goals" (2021) 22 *Journal of World Investment & Trade* 410–411.

116 FIL, Article 21.

117 Yawen Zheng, "China's New Foreign Investment Law and Its Contribution Towards the Country's Development Goals" (2021) 22 *Journal of World Investment & Trade* 410–411.

118 The results of the inspection are available at MOFCOM United Platform of Service System, "Disclosure of Credit Information of Foreign Investments" <https://wzxxbg.mofcom.gov.cn/WebProBA/app/infoPub/creditPos> accessed 28 February 2021.

119 The records did not specify the types of investigation. However, since other types of investigations were required to publish only negative results (the 2018 Interim Measures (n 44) Article 22), they should be the results of the random check.

120 The numbers of China's prefecture-level cities and county-level cities are 294 and 363 respectively, in 2017, and 293 and 375 respectively, in 2018. Twelve more county-level cities were added in 2019. National Bureau of Statistics (NBS), "National Data" <http://data.stats.gov.cn/adv.htm?m=advqueryandcn=C01> accessed 15 August 2020.

121 "Guangzhou and Shenzhen Most Favored Investment Destinations in China" (*Newsgd*, 2 March 2018) <www.newsgd.com/news/2018-03/02/content_180969262.htm> accessed 25 October 2020.

122 See MOFCOM United Platform of Service System.

123 For comparison, there have been 456,578 records of establishment and alteration filed up until 27 August 2019. The records are available at MOFCOM United Platform of Service System, "Publicity of Filings of Foreign Investments" <http://wzzxbs.mofcom.gov.cn/WebProSP/app/infoPub/entpRecord> accessed 27 August 2019.

124 Yawen Zheng, "China's New Foreign Investment Law and Its Contribution Towards the Country's Development Goals" (2021) 22 *Journal of World Investment & Trade* 412.
125 Ibid.
126 2018 Interim Measures, Article 26.
127 Yawen Zheng, "China's New Foreign Investment Law and Its Contribution Towards the Country's Development Goals" (2021) 22 *Journal of World Investment & Trade* 412–413.
128 Ibid., 413.
129 FIL, Articles 33 and 35.
130 FIL, Article 4.
131 "China Enacts New Foreign Investment Security Review Measures" (*Baker & McKenzie*, 4 January 2021) <www.bakermckenzie.com/en/insight/publications/2021/01/china-enacts-new-foreign-investment-security> accessed 25 February 2021.
132 Amanda Lee, "China Tightens 'National Security' Review for Foreign Investments, Sparking Fears of Trade War Retaliation" (*South China Morning Post*, 13 May 2019) <www.scmp.com/economy/global-economy/article/3010002/china-tightens-national-security-review-foreign-investments?exp_signup=opt-ggl-sign-in> accessed 15 October 2020.
133 Guochen Wang, "The Possible Influence of Mainland China's 'Foreign Investment Law'" (2019) 183 *Economic Outlook Bimonthly* 68.
134 Sidney Leng, "China's Updated Anti-Monopoly Law Aimed at Further Protecting Foreign Firms Criticised for Not Doing Enough" (*South China Morning Post*, 9 January 2020) <www.scmp.com/economy/china-economy/article/3045224/chinas-updated-anti-monopoly-law-aimed-further-protecting> accessed 15 October 2020.
135 Markus Masseli, "The Application of Chinese Competition Law to Foreign Mergers: Lessons from the Draft New Guidelines" (2012) 3(1) *Journal of European Competition Law* 102.
136 Yawen Zheng, "China's New Foreign Investment Law and Its Contribution Towards the Country's Development Goals" (2021) 22 *Journal of World Investment & Trade* 414.
137 FIL, Article 30.
138 Yawen Zheng, "China's New Foreign Investment Law and Its Contribution Towards the Country's Development Goals" (2021) 22 *Journal of World Investment & Trade* 415.
139 Muruga P. Ramaswamy, "The impact of the New Chinese Foreign Investment Law 2019 on the Administrative Legal System Governing Foreign Investments and Implications for the Investment Relations with Lusophone Markets" (2019) 9 *Juridical Tribune* 330, 338–339.
140 The differential treatment has given rise to questions about China's compliance with national treatment obligations particularly arising out of the WTO General Agreement on Trade in Services. See US Chamber of Commerce, "China's Approval Process for Inbound Foreign Direct Investment: Impact on Market Access, National Treatment and Transparency" (2012) 34 <https://www.uschamber.com/assets/archived/images/documents/files/020021_China_InboundInvestment_Cvr.pdf> accessed 23 September 2022.
141 Ibid.
142 Ibid.
143 Xingxing Li, "An Economic Analysis of Regulatory Overlap and Regulatory Competition: The Experience of Interagency Regulatory Competition in China's Regulation of Inbound Foreign Investment" (2015) 67(4) *Administrative Law Review* 685.
144 Ibid.
145 FIL, Article 7.
146 2015 Legislation Law of the PRC (entered into force 15 March 2015) art 73.
147 For instance starting a business needs to follow different procedures in different cities of China, while the time frames of these procedures vary from 28 days to 55 days in the 30 cities under investigation. World Bank, "Doing Business: Starting a Business – China" <www.doingbusiness.org/en/data/exploretopics/starting-a-business/china> accessed 16 August 2020.

148 For example art 14 of the Regulations of Shanghai Regarding Application and Approval of Equity Joint Ventures, Chinese-Foreign Contractual Joint Ventures and Wholly Foreign-Owned Enterprises (effective 1 August 1986) required foreign investors to entrust an agent permitted by the approval authority to apply for approval, whereas the Implementation Regulation of EJVL allowed investors to apply directly.

149 Alexander Chipman Koty, 'China's New Foreign Investment Law' *China Briefing*, 20 March 2019 <www.china-briefing.com/news/chinas-new-foreign-investment-law/> accessed 18 August 2019.

150 US Department of State, "2019 Investment Climate Statements: China" (2019) <www.state.gov/reports/2019-investment-climate-statements/china/> accessed 19 August 2019.

151 Yawen Zheng, "China's New Foreign Investment Law and Its Contribution Towards the Country's Development Goals" (2021) 22 *Journal of World Investment & Trade* 417.

152 FIL, Article 26.

153 Yawen Zheng, "China's New Foreign Investment Law and Its Contribution Towards the Country's Development Goals" (2021) 22 *Journal of World Investment & Trade* 418.

154 For example 2016 Framework Agreement on Legislative Cooperation Between the Three North-Eastern Provinces (signed July 2006). See Ministry of Justice of the PRC, "Legislative Cooperation Between the Three North-Eastern Provinces Has Completed 22 Legislation Projects" 5 September 2012, <www.moj.gov.cn/news/content/2012-09/05/660_148383.html> accessed 10 June 2021.

155 Rao Chang-lin, "Legislative Cooperation Among Local Governments and its Realization" (2012) 3 *Journal of China University of Mining and Technology (Social Sciences)* 53.

156 2017 Administrative Litigation Law of the PRC (adopted 27 June, entered into force 1 July 2017) Article 53.

157 Ministry of Justice of the PRC, "2018 Statistics of Nationwide Administrative Reconsideration and Administrative Lawsuit Cases" (2019) <www.moj.gov.cn/organization/content/2019-05/09/560_234638.html> accessed 19 August 2019.

158 2017 Administrative Reconsideration Law of the PRC (adopted 1 September 2017, entered into force 1 January 2018) Article 7.

159 Legislation Law, Article 99.

160 Jiayu Chen, "On the Effective Supervision of Local Legislation in China" (2017) 38(9) *Journal of Chifeng University (Soc. Sci)* 68.

161 FIL, Article 7.

162 FIL, Article 30.

163 FIL, Articles 34 and 35.

164 Muruga P. Ramaswamy, "The Impact of the New Chinese Foreign Investment Law 2019 on the Administrative Legal System Governing Foreign Investments and Implications for the Investment Relations with Lusophone Markets" (2019) 9(2) *Juridical Tribune* 330.

165 FIL, Article 24.

166 Ibid.

167 *See* the Implementation Regulations, Article 26.

168 Id.

169 FIL, Article 25.

170 Implementation Regulations, Article 27.

171 FIL, Article 25.

172 Implementation Regulations, Article 28.

173 Id.

174 Id.

175 FIL, Articles 36, 37, and 40.

176 FIL, Article 39.

177 Muruga P. Ramaswamy, "The Impact of the New Chinese Foreign Investment Law 2019 on the Administrative Legal System Governing Foreign Investments and Implications for the Investment Relations with Lusophone Markets" (2019) 9(2) *Juridical Tribune* 330.

178 FIL, Article 26.
179 Muruga P. Ramaswamy, "The Impact of the New Chinese Foreign Investment Law 2019 on the Administrative Legal System Governing Foreign Investments and Implications for the Investment Relations with Lusophone Markets" (2019) 09(2) *Juridical Tribune* 330.
180 Yun Zheng, "China's New Foreign Investment Law: Deeper Reform and More Trust Are Needed" (*Columbia Centre on Sustainable Investment*, 4 November 2019) <https://ccsi.columbia.edu/sites/default/files/content/docs/publications/No-264-Zheng-FINAL.pdf>
181 Ibid.
182 Mo Zhang, "Change of Regulatory Scheme: China's New Foreign Investment Law and Reshaped Legal Landscape" (2020) 37 *UCLA Pacific Basin Law Journal* 179.
183 FIL, Article 26.
184 FIL, Article 27.
185 Min Zhao, "Analysis and Interpretation of the New Foreign Investment Law of the People's Republic of China" (2019) 02 *China and WTO Review* 351.
186 FIL, Article 26.
187 Id.
188 Mo Zhang, "Change of Regulatory Scheme: China's New Foreign Investment Law and Reshaped Legal Landscape" (2020) 37 *UCLA Pacific Basin Law Journal* 179.
189 Bao Zhi, et al., "China Issues a New Consolidated Law on Foreign Investment" (Global Compliance News, 9 May 2019) <https://globalcompliancenews.com/china-issues-new-consolidated-law-foreign-investment-20190318>
190 Implementation Regulations, Article 29.
191 FIL, Article 30.
192 FIL, Article 31.
193 Id.
194 FIL, Article 26.
195 Implementation Regulations, Article 30.
196 Mo Zhang, "Change of Regulatory Scheme: China's New Foreign Investment Law and Reshaped Legal Landscape" (2020) 37 *UCLA Pacific Basin Law Journal* 179.
197 Administrative Reconsideration Law (promulgated by the Standing Comm. Nat'l People's Cong., 29 April 1999, effective 1 October 1999), <www.cecc.gov/resources/legal-provisions/administrative-reconsideration-law-chinese-and-english-text>
198 FIL, Article 2.
199 FIL, Article 41.
200 Mo Zhang, "Change of Regulatory Scheme: China's New Foreign Investment Law and Reshaped Legal Landscape" (2020) 37 *UCLA Pacific Basin Law Journal* 179.
201 Administrative Litigation Law (2015 amended version) (promulgated by the Standing Comm. Nat'l People's Cong., 1 November 2014, effective 1 May 2015) <www.chinafile.com/ngo/laws-regulations/administrative-litigation-law-of-peoples-republic-of-china-2015-amended-version>.
202 FIL, Article 2.
203 FIL, Article 14. In China, first instance refers to trial, while the second in stance means appeal. Under the ALL, there are certain cases over which the Intermediate People's Court (Article 15), the High People's Court (Article 16), or even the SPC (Article 17) may conduct the trial at the first instance.
204 FIL, Article 18. Also upon an approval from the SPC, High People's Courts may, on the basis of the actual situation of their work, designate several intermediate courts with jurisdiction areas for administrative cases crossing administrative regions.
205 Mo Zhang, "Change of Regulatory Scheme: China's New Foreign Investment Law and Reshaped Legal Landscape" (2020) 37 *UCLA Pacific Basin Law Journal* 179.
206 FIL, Article 44.
207 Id.

208 Mo Zhang, "Change of Regulatory Scheme: China's New Foreign Investment Law and Reshaped Legal Landscape" (2020) 37 *UCLA Pacific Basin Law Journal* 179.

209 ARL, Article 16.

210 Id.

211 Mo Zhang, "Change of Regulatory Scheme: China's New Foreign Investment Law and Reshaped Legal Landscape" (2020) 37 *UCLA Pacific Basin Law Journal* 179.

212 FIL, Article 27.

213 Mo Zhang, "Change of Regulatory Scheme: China's New Foreign Investment Law and Reshaped Legal Landscape" (2020) 37 *UCLA Pacific Basin Law Journal* 179.

214 Implementation Regulations, Article 4.

215 Id., Article 32.

216 Mo Zhang, "Change of Regulatory Scheme: China's New Foreign Investment Law and Reshaped Legal Landscape" (2020) 37 *UCLA Pacific Basin Law Journal* 179.

217 FIL, Article 26.

218 Administrative Reconsideration Law, Article 5.

219 Ibid., Article 31.

220 Administrative Litigation Law, Article 81.

221 Some commentators believe that China's judiciary is too weak to get in the way of the powerful Chinese government. Judicial independence is also questioned considering the close relationship between courts and governments. Shi Han and Lei Zhang, "China's Environmental Governance of Rapid Industrialization" (2006) 15(2) *Environmental Politics* 271–292.

222 FIL, Articles 26 and 27.

223 Keith Bradsher, "China Law Responds to US Investment Demands: Critics Say It's Not Enough" (*New York Times*, 4 March 2019) <www.nytimes.com/2019/03/04/business/china-foreign-investment.html?_ga=2.183131183.805398511.1566855958-1761277219.15668 55957> accessed 22 July 2019.

224 Judgements are published on Supreme People's Court, "China Judgements Online" <http://wenshu.court.gov.cn/> accessed 20 August 2019.

225 The only requirement regarding transparency of administrative reconsideration is stipulated in art 4 of the Administrative Reconsideration Law (n 66), which requires administrative reconsideration authorities to follow the principles of openness. However, there are no further detailed rules about what should be published and how to do it.

226 FIL, Article 28(3)e; Administrative Litigation Law, Article 70(6).

227 Yawen Zheng, "China's New Foreign Investment Law and Its Contribution Towards the Country's Development Goals" (2021) 22 *Journal of World Investment & Trade* 424.

228 Clifford Chance, "China's New Foreign Investment Law – What Does This Mean for Foreign Investors in China?" (*Clifford Chance*, 22 March 2019) <www.cliffordchance.com/briefings/2019/03/china_s_new_foreigninvestmentlawwhatdoe.html> accessed 25 April.

229 Article 42 of the FIL.

230 Mark Schaub, Atticus Zhao, Dai Xueyun and Zheng Wei, "China Foreign Investment Law: How Will It Impact the Existing FIEs?" (*King & Wood Mallesons*, 3 June 2019) <www.chinalawinsight.com/2019/06/articles/foreign-investment/china-foreign-investment-law>

231 PriceWaterhouse Coopers, "China Welcomes Investors with New Foreign Investment Law" (*News Flash*, 13 February 2020) <https://www.tiangandpartners.com/en/news-and-activity/china-foreign-investment-law-feb2020.pdf> accessed 25 April 2022.

232 According to the three laws on foreign-invested enterprises, the highest authority of Sino–foreign equity joint ventures is the board of directors; the highest authority of Sino–foreign contractual joint ventures is the joint management committee; and the highest authority of foreign-funded ventures is the shareholder meeting or capital holders. After the implementation of the Foreign Investment Law, they need to change the highest authority to the shareholder meeting.

233 The Foreign Investment Law stipulates a five-year transition period, but there are no provisions about the measures for the delay in the adjustment and transition. *See* Foreign Investment Law Article 42.

234 Min Zhao, "Analysis and Interpretation of the New Foreign Investment Law of the People's Republic of China" (2019) 2 *China and WTO Review* 351.

235 Clifford Chance, "China's New Foreign Investment Law – What Does This Mean for Foreign Investors in China?" (*Clifford Chance*, 22 March 2019). <www.cliffordchance. com/briefings/2019/03/china_s_new_foreigninvestmentlawwhatdoe.html> accessed 25 April.

236 Ibid.

237 Ibid.

238 Min Zhao, "Analysis and Interpretation of the New Foreign Investment Law of the People's Republic of China" (2019) 2 *China and WTO Review* 351.

239 The Foreign Investment Law stipulates the five-year transition period but does not mention how the transition period should be regulated or what will happen if those enterprises cannot complete the transition within the given period. Detailed implementation measures shall be prescribed by the State Council in the near future.

240 Z. Alex Zhang and Vivian Tsoi, "China Adopts New Foreign Investment Law" (*White & Case*, 29 March 2019) <www.whitecase.com/publications/alert/china-adopts-new-foreign-investment-law> accessed 25 April 2022.

241 Kong Qingjiang, "New Foreign Investment Law Is Milestone in China's Opening-up Process" <https://news.cgtn.com/news/3d3d414e32597a4d33457a6333566d54/index.html?from=timeline&isappinstalled=0>, accessed 15 March 2019.

242 Moore Stephens Consulting Company Limited, "China's New Foreign Investment Law: Changes and Implications for Foreign Invested Enterprises" (*Moore MS Advisory*, 19 December 2019) <https://www.msadvisory.com/china-new-foreign-investment-law>

243 Morrison Foerster, "China's Foreign Investment Law: Are You Ready for It?" (*Morrison Foerster*, 3 January 2020) <https://www.mofo.com/resources/insights/200102-chinas-investment-foreign-law> accessed 25 April 2022.

244 Ibid.

245 Dan Harris, "China's New Foreign Investment Law: Tain't No Big Thing" (*Harris Bricken*, 29 December 2019) <https://harrisbricken.com/chinalawblog/chinas-new-foreign-investment-law-taint-no-big-thing/> accessed 25 April 2022.

246 Ibid.

247 Ibid.

248 Xiaojun Li, "Durability of China's Lawmaking Process under Xi Jinping: A Tale of the Two Foreign Investment Laws" (2020) *Issues and Studies* 1.

249 Yawen Zheng, "China's New Foreign Investment Law and Its Contribution Towards the Country's Development Goals" (2021) 22 *Journal of World Investment & Trade* 395–396.

250 N. Jansen Calamita and Jeffrey Jowell, "Risk and Return – Foreign Direct Investment and the Rule of Law" (2015) <https://papers.ssrn.com/sol3/papers.cfm?abstract_id=2946685> accessed 6 December 2019.

251 George Chen, "China Probe May Curb Foreign Deals: Sources" (*Reuters*, 31 October 2008) <https://www.reuters.com/article/china-foreigninvestment-approvals-idUKN31 35958220081031> accessed 4 October 2020.

252 Wendy Wu, "China Orders Ministries to Open up More of Economy to Foreign Investors" (*South China Morning Post*, 17 August 2017) <www.scmp.com/news/china/economy/article/2107190/china-orders-ministries-open-more-economy-foreign-investors> accessed 4 October 2020; see also Sylvia Schwaag Serger and Magnus Breidne, "China's Fifteen-Year Plan for Science and Technology: An Assessment" (2007) 4(1) *Asia Policy* 135–164.

253 World Bank, "Doing Business 2020: China's Strong Reform Agenda Places It in the Top 10 Improver List for the Second Consecutive Year" <https://www.worldbank.org/en/news/press-release/2019/10/24/doing-business-2020-chinas-strong-reform-agenda-places-it-in-the-top-10-improver-list-for-the-second-consecutive-year> accessed 23 September 2022.

254 Yawen Zheng, "China's New Foreign Investment Law and Its Contribution Towards the Country's Development Goals" (2021) 22 *Journal of World Investment & Trade* 396.

255 Jones Day, "China Further Opens its Market with New 'Foreign Investment Law'" (*Jones Day*, February 2020) <www.jonesday.com/en/insights/2020/02/chinas-new-foreign-investment-law> accessed 25 April 2022.

256 FIL, Article 35; FIL Implementation Regulation, Article 40.

257 Jones Day, "China Further Opens its Market with New 'Foreign Investment Law'" (*Jones Day*, February 2020) <www.jonesday.com/en/insights/2020/02/chinas-new-foreign-investment-law> accessed 25 April 2022.

258 Mark Schaub, Atticus Zhao, Dai Xueyun and Zheng Wei, "China Foreign Investment Law: How Will It Impact the Existing FIEs?" (3 June 2019) para 11.

3

NEGATIVE LIST

A Changing Governance Model

The modern international investment law regime is primarily an institutional structure in which international investment protection rules and the dispute settlement mechanism distribute and coordinate the interests of concerned subjects at a specific stage.[1] The dynamics among the stakeholders in global FDI activities have affected the long-term development and evolution of international investment law. The pursuit of investment interests by all states in the world has contributed to the shaping of a modern international investment law regime, and changes along with the development of FDI.[2]

The host state's surrender of sovereignty in the form of less regulatory power over foreign investment, a shorthand being the "leaving of the state," has achieved a balance between state sovereignty and protection of investors' rights and interests and pushed forward the shaping of a modern international investment law regime. In recent years, the "return of the state" by retreating from its liberal stance to foreign investment to a more conservative one has redistributed the balance between state sovereignty and foreign investors' rights in international investment protection rules, thereby pushing forward the reform of the modern international investment law regime to a new point.

China's participation in the construction of the international investment legal system has two important dimensions, namely the construction of the domestic legal system and the construction of bilateral investment treaties.[3] China's political, economic, legal, and bureaucratic dynamics have pulled its evolutionary engagement with the ISDS system, and more importantly, its possible role in pushing for a restructuring of international investment law in the years to come.[4] This chapter traces China's past and present and draws a matrix in which China's legal system and its development of FDI regime are evaluated. While the FDI regulatory landscape has been moving towards systemic efficiency with the aim of promoting economic growth, the complex metrics and underlying logics may change from time to time.

DOI: 10.4324/9781003130499-3

1. China's FDI Law in the Past Four Decades

FDI in China is the clearest and most dramatic manifestation of China's open-door and economic reform policy. FDI also exposed China to the outside world.[5] China's success in attracting FDI has made it a great example to other developing states.[6] China's national investment policy making offers some learning experiences to others which are about to boost their economy through attracting FDI. There is also a confirmed impact of Chinese BITs on China's inbound FDI.[7]

The history of foreign investment in China is brief indeed. The first three decades after China's founding witnessed the implementation of a self-reliance policy, the failure of which, however, triggered the dramatic and logical change to the "open door" and economic reform policy in 1978.[8]

The "open door" policy together with the economic reform signalled China's determination to utilize market mechanisms and foreign resources to accelerate economic growth and modernization. The uneasy process of implementing the "open door" and economic reform policy went hand in hand with the tension between encouraging foreign investment to achieve favourable economic outcomes and maintaining state control over foreign business activities to mitigate potential risks,[9] which in turn influenced the foreign investment law and economic structure as a whole.[10]

1.1 Attracting Inbound FDI as the Key Economic Development Strategy

In the past 40 years of reform and opening up, the basic tendency towards liberalization of China's foreign investment law has promoted the development of the country's economy through the continuous introduction of foreign capital, technology, and managerial skills. Relevant legislation also revolved around changes in the circumstances of China's attraction of foreign investment. As shown in Figure 3.1, since 1979, the introduction of foreign investment in China has shown a rapid growth in absolute terms. In relative terms, FDI share in total investment peaked at 14.3% of gross capital formation and 11.8% of fixed asset investment in the 1990s but now dropped to under 3% or 1% depending on the measure, indicating a diminishing role of FDI and an increasing size of China's entire economy.[11] Nevertheless, FDI has a strong spillover effect on the supply chains, research and development, and employment, accounting for between 11% and 29% of China's employment from 1995 to 2013.[12] From the trend and fluctuation of China's foreign capital inflow in the past 40 years, the four decades can be roughly divided into three stages in the 1980s, 1990s, and the new century. China's foreign investment law also has its own characteristics in each of the three stages.

Of all the legal institutions that were rebuilt or created in the past three decades, those related to foreign investment have developed the earliest and the fastest. The Sino-foreign Equity Joint Venture Law (the EJV Law) promulgated

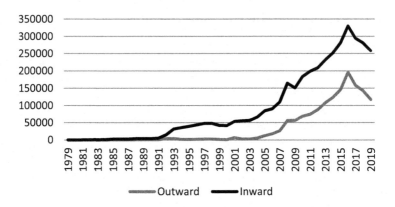

FIGURE 3.1 China's FDI Flows (1979–2019)[13] (USD Millions)
Source: Compiled by the author

in 1979 was the first law formulated by China for foreign investment since the reform and opening up. The law for the first time affirmed that foreign investors enjoy rights governed under civil law in China,[14] allowing foreign investors to enter China and to partner with Chinese companies to joint ventures, and through the law to clear the tax, exchange, and other issues facing foreign investors who invest in China.[15] At the same time, the law also requires that the relevant contracts must be filed with or approved by the Chinese government and that production materials should also be purchased in China.[16] The operating mode of the joint venture company should also conform to the economic system of China at that time. Meanwhile, the investment dispute should be settled in principle by the arbitration institution designated by the Chinese government, but the parties may agree that other arbitration institutions may also resolve such matters.[17] In the following year, China followed up with legislation on taxation and contracts and further refined and guaranteed the implementation of the EJV Law. In 1982, China revised the Constitution in all major aspects according to the new situation of reform and opening up. For the first time, it became clear from the language of the Constitution that foreign investors have the right to invest in China and protect their legitimate rights and interests in China.[18] With the continuous enhancement of China's ability to attract foreign investment and the deepening of economic system reform, the Wholly Foreign-owned Enterprise Law (the WFOE Law) promulgated in 1986 began to allow foreign investors to set up wholly foreign-owned enterprises in China.[19]

Similar to the EJV Law, the WFOE Law clearly stipulates tax incentives and exchanges for foreign investors but still emphasizes that investors should conduct investment activities in accordance with Chinese laws and accept the supervision of the Chinese government. The government has the right to seize investor property in the public interest. The promulgation of the Sino-Foreign Cooperative Joint Venture Law (the CJV Law) in 1988 was generally consistent with the previous two laws, emphasizing that foreign investors should be subject to the supervision of the Chinese government in terms of finance, taxation, and labour when cooperating with Chinese enterprises.[20] Without doubt, the law also shows restrictions on government power. For example, the disputing parties are allowed to choose other arbitration institutions or Chinese courts to resolve their disputes.[21] Although China's investment-related domestic legislation was still rough in the late 1980s and highly emphasized the government's regulatory power over foreign investment, it is undeniable that it has made tremendous progress over the collection of compensation, national treatment, most-favoured-nation (MFN) status, among others. China has extensively absorbed the legislative experience and international practices of other countries and outlined the basic framework of China's foreign investment legislation. China's regulatory framework for foreign investment has taken an initial shape.

It is not surprising to see the first piece of legislation enacted right after the adoption of the "open door" policy was the EJV Law in 1979. The urgency of attracting foreign investment and satisfying foreign investors' needs to have their investments well protected entailed tremendous efforts to create a foreign investment law regime from scratch. The key purpose of this EJV Law was to encourage foreign investors' participation in China's economic development and modernization programme.[22] Other primary legislation and implementation regulations in subsequent years allowed foreign companies to set up representative offices, wholly foreign-owned enterprises, and contractual joint ventures in China. The Constitution revised in 1982 contains a critical provision offering the promise to protect "the lawful rights and interests of foreign investors." The course of China's economic development through foreign investment entails ongoing tensions among the state, law, and market players. The best illustration is that these laws and other regulations centred on the encouragement and protection of foreign investments, with no exception, had Chinese characteristics, mostly in the form of some compromises between the legal rights protection, the Party-state censorship, and parental monitoring.[23] The foreign investment policy at this stage was primitive and inconsistent and was often moving back and forth between two extremes of openness and restriction. Although the legal institutions rebuilt after the Cultural Revolution cannot fulfil their supposed role, function, and goal of rights protection, they contributed considerably to the economic and societal development in the past four decades.

A unique Chinese characteristic or regulatory feature of the foreign investment law regime in China is the centrality of the state as the primary agent for economic and social development. The regulators are everywhere from the collection of taxes, exchange controls, customs regulation, intellectual property, protection from seizure of land, allocation of natural resources, and dispatch of employees. The fundamental role of the state in Chinese society and economy was articulated in the Constitution of 1982. The subsequent amendments to the Constitution in 1993, while replacing the state-centred planning economy with the socialist market economy,[24] did not dilute the state-centric function in economic development. In foreign investment laws, some commitments were made by the government not to expropriate foreign investment without public interest or compensation. While joint ventures set up by foreign and domestic investors were subject to government approval and monitoring,[25] FIEs were given the freedom to submit their disputes with their local partners to arbitration.[26] Nondiscriminatory standards such as national treatment and MFN treatment,[27] albeit post-establishment only, were codified in foreign investment law giving foreign investors confidence in China's overall legal system.

In the 1990s, as China's market economy reform continued to deepen, China had been gradually in a transition to a market economy system.[28] The entire 1990s witnessed differential liberalization dominance as well as a departure from the conventional state planning system of the old days to a more market-oriented macroeconomic regulation and control.[29] In 1990, China took the lead in opening the amendments to the EJV Law. Compared with the 1979 legislation, the amendments stipulated that the expropriation of joint ventures should be compensated.[30] Meanwhile, the approval items of some joint venture projects were adjusted and the government's approval authority and time limits are further specified. In the late 1990s, China further revised the WFOE Law and the EJV Law. The revision of these two laws is highlighted by the elimination of the restriction that raw materials could only be purchased in China. The production plan of the enterprise does not need to be reported to the government for approval, and the related products are allowed to be sold domestically.

The conceptual approach drove the Chinese government to rely on industrial policies, either sector-based or geography-based ones,[31] in regulating and directing foreign investment. In addition to the legislative amendments to the law, the then state planning authority, then State Planning Commission, the predecessor of the National Reform and Development Commission, issued the *Catalogue of Industries for Guiding Foreign Investment* (the Catalogue) in June 1995, which clarified the segmentation of industrial sectors into the categories of encouraging, permitting, restricting, and prohibiting foreign investment access to different industries, thereby improving the predictability of foreign investment. The "restricted" category limited the equity share that foreign investors could have in certain industries. The Catalogue signalled the state policies in attracting foreign investment.[32]

The State Council approved a revised Catalogue in December 1997, which removed barriers to foreign participation in some restricted sectors, such as distribution, infrastructure, energy, and power generation. The Catalogue also favoured those enterprises that were willing and able to bring advanced technology into China or promote exports and offered tax exemptions and other benefits to foreign-invested enterprises laws (FIEs laws). In the category of "encouraged" investments, an emphasis was placed on high technology, and some industries were moved to the "restricted" category. This differential liberalization policy *de facto* disfavoured SOEs and domestic private enterprises, which effectively gave FIEs a super-national treatment.[33] Against this background, China's openness became a dominant theme. However, the dominance of the state and the lack of an indigenous private sector also means the uniqueness of China's legal, regulatory, and administrative regime in guiding and overseeing FIEs.

Given the changing sector-based industrial policies reflected in the Catalogue, the economic sectors to which foreign investment has been targeted gradually extended from the labour-intensive manufacturing sectors to technology-based production. The Chinese government made a great effort to steer foreign investment to the export and technology sectors. As a result, particular preferences were given to FIEs denoted as "export-oriented enterprises" and "advanced technology enterprises."[34] The EJV Law and its Implementing Rules specifically encouraged joint ventures to export their products. The acquisition and importation of technology were encouraged by rules allowing intellectual property rights and know-how to be contributed as capital by foreign investors. Approval of joint ventures was to be contingent on the satisfaction of the criterion, either being an export-oriented enterprise or an importer of technology.[35]

Preferential treatments in the form of tax holidays were also offered to those foreign investment projects that were able to satisfy these requirements. These more preferential treatment is often labelled as the supra-national (or super-national) treatment which is not in line with the national treatment under the WTO.[36] Accordingly, joint ventures were to receive tax holidays for the first two profit-making years and reductions in subsequent years.[37] FIEs whose export production value was 70% of total production value were to be considered "export-oriented enterprises" eligible for a 50% reduction in enterprise income tax, with additional reductions possible.[38] FIEs being designated as a "technologically advanced enterprise" were entitled to extend their initial three-year tax holiday by an additional three years.[39] Similarly, the approval of WFOEs would also be conditional on their use of advanced technology or exporting products.[40] Withholding taxes on profits remitted outside China could be exempted for technologically advanced enterprises and export enterprises, which meanwhile were entitled to exemption from the payment of state subsidies for enterprise staff and workers, priority in obtaining short-term loans, limits on certain site use fees, and extension of priority status for utility supply and infrastructural requirements.

The legislation, that is the Provisions on Acquisitions of Domestic Enterprises by Foreign Investors, which block foreign purchases of Chinese companies involving "key industries," described as those whose operations influence or might influence "state economic security,"[41] gradually shows concerns that foreign interests are acquiring domestic assets below their value,[42] seizing control of strategic industrial sectors[43] and market share in China without adequate oversight and control.[44] The debate of liberalism versus economic nationalism also mirrors the objective and direction of reform itself in a broader context. Therefore, the foreign investment policy has been an ad hoc and incremental response to continuous changes in the global and domestic economy.

In general, the main direction of China's foreign investment legislation from 1979 to the mid-1990s was to attract foreign investment through continuous opening up and to promote the development of the country's economy. The growth and overall trend of foreign investment in China was positive in the first decade starting from 1979. During this period, the annual average of foreign investment was over US$2 billion. There was a decline in 1989–1990. But the volume of foreign investment resumed and was nearly US$12 billion for 1991. It then climbed up very rapidly and contractual foreign investment reached US$57.2 billion and US$122.7 billion in 1992 and 1993. FDI declined again in 1997–1999 due to the Asian financial crisis but reached a higher level in the new millennium. On the one hand, this phase has changed the attitude of vigilance and even hostility towards foreign investment that existed in the past. Through comprehensive legislation from the constitution to the law, the position of protecting the rights of foreign investors has been clarified and "reassured." On the other hand, China has increasingly attached importance to restrictions on government power. Before the reform and opening up, due to China's planned economic system and the imperfect legal system, the government's power was far-reaching. Investment as an economic activity rooted in the host country is closely related to the exercise of government power. Therefore, to truly protect the interests of investors, the government must limit its administrative power from both substantive and procedural perspectives. In this phase, China's investment legislation changed its position from its absolute intervention in investment and showcased the trend of China's intention to restrain its government power.

1.2 Joining the WTO and Conforming to the WTO Rules

China's accession to the WTO in 2002 marked a new chapter of foreign investment. The significance of this event was to outline a road map for China to further liberalize and modernize the economy and the foreign investment regime per se. China's entry into the WTO opened up a large-scale revision to legislation on various aspects including investment. The principle of national treatment was more expansively implemented, and regulation and supervision of foreign investment activities became more subject to legal rather than administrative means. Other significant changes to foreign investment policies included repealing the requirements for nationalization of foreign investment and establishing a legal framework more compatible with the requirements and principles of WTO.

The Catalogue was further amended in 2002 to solidify China's WTO commitments, which reflected an increasingly liberalizing trend.[45] As far as the FIEs are concerned, the approval system, capitalization, market access, and financing have been reformed as well. The State Council reformed the investment system, which raised the threshold on local government approvals of investment projects from US$30 million to US$100 million for projects falling within the "encouraged" and "permitted" categories in the Catalogue.[46]

As to foreign capital, relevant research shows that compared with political factors, a country's economic vitality and potential have a far-reaching impact on the country's ability to attract foreign investment.[47] Therefore, the key to enhancing China's foreign investment attraction is to further improve the market economy system. Since the new century, China's capital import has been increasing, and the call for revision of three FIEs laws has become increasingly greater. In 2001, China first revised the EJV Law. In addition to allowing joint ventures to purchase raw materials in the international market and providing foreign investors the right to resolve disputes in Chinese courts, the main emphasis is on the joint ventures to strictly abide by Chinese laws in terms of labour treatment and insurance.

The Catalogue (2007) demonstrated the new policy switch. For instance the Catalogue places more emphasis on environmental protection, trade imbalances, and high technology. Accordingly, the Catalogue decreases support for export-oriented industries, promotes foreign investment in high-tech and environmentally friendly sectors, and restricts foreign investment in manufacturing and mining industries that once welcomed foreign investment. These policy changes were viewed as a new round of attempts to disadvantage foreign investors,[48] on the one hand, limiting market access by non-Chinese origin goods and, on the other hand, offering more resources and protections to domestic players that are less competitive in the marketplace.[49] The role of law is ambiguous in balancing control of foreign investment against facilitating the activities of foreign-invested enterprises.

In 2016, the Chinese legislature revised the FIEs Laws in a unified manner. The main content is that in a field that does not involve the implementation of special management measures for entry into the country, the government will change from the past approval system to a filing system, thus relaxing supervision over foreign investment.[50]

In 2017, the legislature once again revised the CJV Law, mainly removing the partial approval power of the government authorities for CJVs. Therefore, judging from the existing legislation, China's foreign investment legislation on FIEs as its main link with the foreign investment community is still in the initial stage of "leaving," and the state government role is still heavy. For example, on the issue of expropriation, both the EJV Law and the WFOE Law stipulate that "the state does not implement nationalization and expropriation of foreign-funded enterprises; in special circumstances, according to the needs of social public interests, foreign-funded enterprises may be expropriated according to legal procedures and compensated accordingly."[51] The provision, on the one hand, shows the reference to the "Hull Standard." On the other hand, it is still essentially a Calvoism provision in the sense that expropriation and compensation are carried on according to domestic laws, and it does not involve the intervention of other countries. China's foreign investment legislation is always on the road to liberalization,[52] by restricting government power and respecting the rights of the expropriated people in China's relevant legislation.

The state-centric model of economic growth and development explains the key features of the foreign investment law regime in China that pursues policies of import substitution, export-led growth, and development strategies through specially designed state-driven industrial policies and grand plans.[53] These institutional arrangements have ensured the success of the labour-intensive and export-oriented industries in the past four decades. Heavy reliance upon foreign capital in Chinese foreign investment policy also justifies the Chinese government's willingness to offer policy, economic, tax, and legal incentives to foreign investors while foreign investors offer capitals, managerial skills, and technologies to China, shaping a unique bonding relationship between the two. This may explain the Chinese government's efforts to formalize, upgrade, and modernize its law, legal infrastructure, and legal system, though they are authoritarian in nature. The foreign investment law, together with other laws and norms, has not undermined the state's regulation of foreign investment and recognized the transnational character of cross-border foreign investment.

China's economic success consistently reminds us of the difficulty and complexity in understanding, justifying, and theorizing China's development model. The foreign investment regime in China demonstrates both prospects and dilemmas, which are complexly and paradoxically related to the state or the sovereignty. It appears that there is a retrenchment in China placing a greater emphasis on industrial policy and regulatory regime to review the impact of foreign investment projects on national economic and security interests, which coincided with a notable trend towards rising nationalism, seeking to push back globalization, as well as a switch from fast economic growth to a new harmonious society policy (or sustainable development). The debate in China, that is, economic nationalism versus liberal treatment towards foreign investment, has been ongoing for decades, underpinning the wavering policy change.[54]

China's policy-making process and legal environment in the arena of foreign investment is complex and dynamic. It is believed that the Chinese foreign investment policy had been a product of bargaining dynamics,[55] personalities and clientelism,[56] and bureaucratic processes.[57] This process is now more contested than before among various domestic and foreign interest groups and constituencies as well as champions of global capitalism, notwithstanding the CCP's reliance upon a continuous growth for legitimacy, a new goal of realizing a harmonious society, and urgent needs to protect socially and economically vulnerable groups. The debate in China, that is, economic nationalism versus liberal treatment towards foreign investment, has been ongoing and zigzag for decades[58] and that may well explain, if not rationalize, the wavering policy change. In contrast to the growing liberalization, Chinese economic nationalism has appeared in recent years. This may diffuse the difficulty of precisely identifying and predicting China's position in the BIT-making.

The great concern often raised by the community of foreign investors was and continues to be the lack of laws and regulations and the dysfunction of legal institutions and judiciary that are supposed to offer sufficient protections to foreign investors and even Chinese citizens. While the level of predictability, functioning, and rights-consciousness cannot be and should not be assessed and measured exclusively in terms of Western ideals,[59] a fair evaluation is that the legal system in China is still in institutional flux and has a long way to go. Although the totalitarian grip of the CCP has weakened since the late 1970s, the bureaucracy, official arbitrariness, spreading corruption, a more chaotic social order, and a crisis of social values need even more urgently and desperately the rule of law composed of strong legal institutions and a vibrant legal culture.

1.3 Encouraging Outbound FDI as a New Strategy

With the continuous strengthening of China's economy since the reform and opening up and the formal establishment of the socialist market-oriented economic system through the Constitution in 1993, China's opening up to the outside world has undergone new rapid changes.

As shown in Figure 3.1, China's inbound FDI since the turn of the millennium has continued to expand. In particular, the outbreak of the Asian financial crisis in 1997 highlighted a potential risk of excessive dependence on foreign investment. Besides, orderly capital outflow is not only conducive to domestic economic development but also to reduction of financial risks and economic stability. Therefore, in light of China's rising strength in investment and other fields, at the National Foreign Investment Conference held in December 1997, the then President Jiang Zemin proposed a new strategy of reform and opening up that combines "attracting foreign investment" and "going out," emphasizing the need to encourage Chinese enterprises, especially SOEs, to invest in Africa and other overseas markets while promoting the rational use of foreign capital. Investment in other countries and regions, making full use of the market and resources of the relevant countries to promote joint ventures and cooperation projects,[60] can give play to China's comparative advantages and better utilize both domestic and overseas markets and resources in both local and foreign markets.[61] The "go globally" strategy drove China to attach greater importance to outbound investment by unswervingly promoting outbound investment of Chinese enterprises. With the clear push of government policies,[62] the amount of Chinese outbound investment has gradually increased. Until 2014, China's FDI output exceeded input for the first time, marking China's transition from a traditional capital-importing country to a hybrid country with equal capital outflow and inflow. At the same time, China started new domestic reforms aiming at enhancing its economic reform and open door policy.

As early as 2013, President Xi Jinping proposed the "Belt and Road" Initiative for the first time during an overseas visit. After that, the Chinese government further promulgated relevant documents and clarified the development direction of the "Belt and Road" Initiative. As far as investment is concerned, first, China targets to eliminate barriers in investment and trade by promoting measures of investment facilitation and free trade. Second, China plans to expand the scope of foreign investment and the breadth and depth of cooperation in the field of investment along the Belt and Road. Third, China has initiated the establishment of the Asian Infrastructure Investment Bank[63] to focus on investment cooperation in various areas such as infrastructure and construction projects along the Belt and Road.[64] As shown in Figure 3.2, China's investment in countries along the Belt and Road has been on the rise since 2013, especially during the period from 2013 to 2015. Although the investment in 2016–2017 has declined, it has rebounded again in 2018 and has basically recovered to the level of 2016. In 2017, China's outbound investment projects in Belt and Road countries accounted for 12.7% of China's total outbound investment.[65] From the

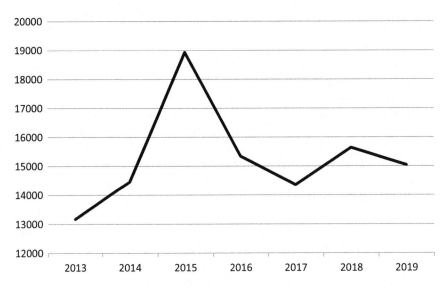

FIGURE 3.2 China's Outbound FDI Along Belt and Road Initiative Countries[66] (USD Million)

Source: Compiled by the author

characteristics of investment activities under the Belt and Road Initiative over the past five years, unlike the traditional rule-oriented investment framework based on IIAs, the cross-border investment activities under the Belt and Road Initiative are mainly project-based.

Chinese companies are the key business elites in China's transnational networks, not only presenting China's global posture but also channelling the Chinese government's outbound investment policies to the globalized market. Chinese companies play multiple roles such as enhancing the bonding between China and the Western capitalism, piggybacking offshore jurisdictions to experiment transnational rules, adapting to the liberal modes of networking, and integrating Chinese supply and technology chains with the world.

Chinese SOEs occupy a dominant position in China's outbound investment projects, and the investment areas are mainly concentrated in high-speed rail, energy, water conservancy, and other industries.[67] Apart from their business functions, SOEs also show their distinctive linkage with the Party-state and state-directed capitalism.[68] Although it is not possible to simplify or synergize the Belt and Road Initiative completely, it can be seen that China's foreign investment in large-scale infrastructure projects has absorbed China's surplus production capacity to a certain extent, which is conducive to the development of its own economy.[69] At the same time, it has also driven the rapid development of infrastructure and construction projects along the Belt and Road. Apparently, the Belt and Road Initiative presents great opportunities to enhance a win-win investment cooperation between China and its counterparts.[70] Therefore, the foreign investment under the Belt and

Road Initiative is basically driven by the Chinese government and the countries, with heavy reliance on the economic activities and participation of Chinese SOEs. This type of cross-border investment cooperation, although not inseparable from legal texts such as BITs, is more based on economic complementarity and political mutual trust.

China now has larger outbound FDI than inbound FDI, which thanks to China's regulatory framework for outbound FDI, notably government policies, laws, and regulations as well as incentive schemes. Consequently, China's outbound investment even surpassed that of several major developed economies in the past decade.[71] A holistic review of this outbound FDI-friendly framework unveils its two interconnected objectives: to help Chinese firms, in particular, SOEs, to be more competitive in the global market and to implement China's development strategy through some consorted regulatory and policy efforts. However, China's legal framework is not flawless. While it benefits SOEs the most, it also creates a discriminatory environment and damages other market players.[72]

2. Free Trade Zone and New Reformist Measures

2.1 Free Trade Zone and Negative List

In recent years, China has begun to actively explore the ways of reforming its economic governance regime, in particular through the Free Trade Zones (FTZs). This is the typical experimentalist approach towards reform and governance. Before conducting profound reforms of the trade and investment legal framework, China often started with the reforms on a small scale, in specified geographic zones as testing grounds. FTZs are used as pilot projects to achieve multiple objectives, including testing how to upgrade China's trade and investment laws, boosting China's economy in new normal, and preparing China for international law-making and high-standard BITs/FTAs negotiations.[73] In this sense, the experimental experiences accumulated in the FTZs provide a better approach or even solution to challenges faced by China in transforming and upgrading its economic governance model. This domestic–international law interaction or reconciliation is a unique perspective of transnational law process in China's context.

Since the establishment of Shanghai FTZ on 19 September 2013, China has established FTZs in 12 regions, including Guangdong, Tianjin, and Fujian, and has begun to focus on promoting the construction of Hainan Free Trade Port. The FTZ is viewed by the business community and analysts as the Chinese government's most important policy move for economic reform in more than a decade. Both internal and external factors are pushing for a deeper reform of China's legal and regulatory regime and a substantial change in China's economic growth model.[74] At home, soaring wages and an aging workforce are forcing China to move towards a "middle-income" trap. Abroad, rivals are rushing into regional free-trade deals such as the Trans-Pacific Partnership (now the CPTPP) and the TTIP without involving China. Both forces place pressure on China. Inefficient and cosseted service sectors must be further opened up in a globally competitive game. For example compared to Hong Kong, whose service sectors account for 90% of the whole economy, Shanghai's services were only 62% in 2013.[75] Shanghai can use its own economic strength and geographical and political advantages in China to achieve reform goals.

Thanks to the reform experience of Shenzhen Special Economic Zone,[76] the Chinese government has actively given local governments greater policy freedom in running the FTZs and authorized FTZs to break through the original economic management system. Therefore, in respect of foreign investment, the systemic reform of FTZs are mainly carried out through breaking the old system and establishing some new measures.

Prior to the official launch of the Shanghai FTZ on 30 August 2013, the National People's Congress Standing Committee authorized the State Council to operate the China (Shanghai) FTZ with some freedom. From 1 October 2013, the EJV Law, CJV Law, and WFOE Law were temporarily paused to be entirely applied to the set-up and operation of FIEs in the FTZ apart from some special measures for the implementation of the national regulations.[77] On 28 December 2014, the Standing Committee of the National People's Congress issued a decision to adjust relevant laws for the FTZs in Guangdong, Tianjin, Fujian, and the extended area of the Shanghai FTZ.[78]

According to the authorization of the Standing Committee of the National People's Congress, the State Council issued two decisions on 21 December 2013 and 4 September 2014 respectively, allowing some regulatory experiments over FIEs in the Shanghai FTZ. On 1 July 2016, the State Council decided to temporarily adjust 18 administrative regulations such as the Implementing Rules for the Foreign Investment Enterprise Law of the People's Republic of China and the Decision of the State Council on Investment System Reform in the Pilot FTZs, the Catalogue (2004), and other relevant provisions of the ministerial regulations approved by the State Council.[79] Relevant regulations were further amended by the State Council in December 2013, September 2014, and July 2016 to accommodate the special reformist needs in the FTZs. In 2016, the National People's Congress revised the relevant provisions of the FIE Laws –

> Where the establishment of a joint venture does not involve the implementation of special admission administration measures as per national regulations, record-filing management shall apply to the approval matters as specified. The special admission administration measures under the national regulations shall be issued by or upon approval of the State Council.[80]

Thus, the new practice of the Shanghai FTZ is extended to the whole country.

In terms of local legislation, taking the Shanghai FTZ as an example, at the beginning of the establishment of the Shanghai FTZ in September 2013, the Shanghai Municipal Government simultaneously formulated the *Special*

Management Measures (Negative List) for Access of Foreign Investment to China (Shanghai) Pilot Free Trade Zone (2013),[81] which clarified the scope and content of local regulation. In July 2014, the 14th Shanghai Municipal People's Congress reviewed and approved the *Regulation on the China (Shanghai) Pilot Free Trade Zone,*[82] which were implemented on 1 August of the same year. This is China's first local regulation concerning the FTZ. The Regulations outline the regulatory system over investment, trade, finance, and taxation as well as comprehensive supervision in the FTZ, further condensing the content of institutional innovation with the aim of providing strong institutional support for the reform in the FTZ.

After the local legislation clarifies the basic framework of the FTZ's economic management system, the central government mainly focused on the negative list reform in regulating foreign investment. China pledges to provide equal treatment of foreign investment putting foreign investors on equal footing with domestic ones in the Chinese market and giving them equal protections and market access. However, in certain sectors and industries, such treatment and market access can be limited for foreign investors, which has been administered by the Chinese government by its publication of the negative list from time to time. Under this system, foreign investment is either prohibited or limited in sectors only if they are covered under the negative list; and for any sectors that are not identified in the negative list, foreign investors are treated equally as domestic investors, and no additional restrictions on market access will apply.

As a matter of fact, the so-called list system (or blacklist) applied in foreign investment regulation can be traced back to the *Provisional Regulations on Direction Guide to Foreign Investment* in 1995 and the corresponding Catalogue, which were the rudimentary form of the negative list mechanism for the market access of foreign investment in China.[83] Since 1995, after nearly over two decades' development as shown in Table 3.1, the list mechanism related to foreign investment's market access has gradually been turned to its current form as shown in

TABLE 3.1 Evolution of Negative List in China

Title	Effective Date	Legal Status	Issuing Authority(ies)
Provisional Regulations on Direction Guide to Foreign Investment	20/06/1995	Expired	State Development Planning Commission and State Economic and Trade Commission
Catalogue of Industries for Guiding Foreign Investment	28/06/1995		
Catalogue of industries prohibited from foreign investment	31/12/1997		

(*Continued*)

TABLE 3.1 (Continued)

Title	Effective Date	Legal Status	Issuing Authority(ies)
Catalogue of Industries for Guiding Foreign Investment (1997 Revision)	01/01/1998		
Catalogue of Priority Industries for Foreign Investment in Central and Western China	06/16/2000		
Provisions on Guiding the Orientation of Foreign Investment	01/04/2002	Effective	State Council
Catalogue of Industries for Guiding Foreign Investment (2002 Revision)	01/04/2002	Expired	National Development and Reform Commission and State Economic and Trade Commission
Catalogue of Priority Industries for Foreign Investment in Central and Western China (2004 Revision)	01/09/2004		National Development and Reform Commission and Ministry of Commerce
Catalogue of Industries for Guiding Foreign Investment (2004 Revision)	01/01/2005		
Catalogue of Industries for Guiding Foreign Investment (2007 Revision)	01/12/2007		
Catalogue of Priority Industries for Foreign Investment in Central and Western China (2008 Revision)	01/01/2009		
Catalogue of Industries for Guiding Foreign Investment (2011 Revision)	30/01/2012		
Catalogue of Priority Industries for Foreign Investment in Central and Western China (2013 Revision)	10/06/2013		
Special Management Measures (Negative List) for Access of Foreign Investment to China (Shanghai) Pilot Free Trade Zone (2013)	29/09/2013		People's Government of Shanghai Municipality
Special Management Measures (Negative List) for Access of Foreign Investment to China (Shanghai) Pilot Free Trade Zone (2014)	30/06/2014		

Title	Effective Date	Legal Status	Issuing Authority(ies)
Catalogue of Industries for Guiding Foreign Investment (2015 Revision)	10/04/2015		National Development and Reform Commission and Ministry of Commerce
Opinions of the State Council on Implementing the Market Access Negative List Regime	01/12/2015	Partially Expired	State Council
Draft Negative List for Market Access (Trial Version)	02/03/2016		National Development and Reform Commission and Ministry of Commerce
Catalogue of Priority Industries for Foreign Investment in Central and Western China (2017 Revision)	20/03/2017	Effective	
Special Administrative Measures (Negative List) for the Access of Foreign Investment in Pilot Free Trade Zones (2017)	10/07/2017	Expired	State Council
Catalogue of Industries for Guiding Foreign Investment (2017 Revision)	28/07/2017	Partially Expired	National Development and Reform Commission and Ministry of Commerce
Special Administrative Measures (Negative List) for the Access of Foreign Investment (2018)	28/07/2018	Expired	
Special Administrative Measures (Negative List) for the Access of Foreign Investment in Pilot Free Trade Zones (2018)	30/07/2018		
Special Management Measures (Negative List) for Access of Foreign Investment to China (Shanghai) Pilot Free Trade Zone (2013)	01/11/2018		People's Government of Shanghai Municipality
Market Access Negative List (2018)	21/12/2018	Effective	National Development and Reform Commission and Ministry of Commerce
Catalogue of Industries Encouraging Foreign Investment (2019)	30/07/2019		
Special Administrative Measures (Negative List) for the Access of Foreign Investment (2021)	01/01/2022		
Special Administrative Measures (Negative List) for the Access of Foreign Investment in Pilot Free Trade Zones (2021)	01/01/2022		

Source: Compiled by the author.

TABLE 3.2 China's Current Negative List System

Title	Key Characteristics
Market Access Negative List (the Negative List)	A nationwide negative list for all market players.
Special Administrative Measures (Negative List) for the Access of Foreign Investment (the China Negative List)	A nationwide negative list for all foreign investors.
Special Administrative Measures (Negative List) for the Access of Foreign Investment in Pilot Free Trade Zones (the FTZ Negative List)	A FTZ negative list for all foreign investors.
Catalogue of Industries for Guiding Foreign Investment (the Catalogue)	A positive list for foreign investors in the nation and special regions.

Source: Compiled by the author.

Table 3.2. It reflects the trend of the Chinese government to streamline its regulatory system for foreign investment with less governmental intervention but greater transparency and predictability, indicating the Chinese government's attempt to "leave (its sovereignty)."

Since the first FTZ Negative List was issued in Shanghai FTZ in 2013, some experience has been gradually spread to other FTZs and even to the whole country. The negative list model of the Shanghai FTZ has been affirmed by the State Council and promotes the "big negative list" of unified market access. On 2 October 2015, the State Council issued the *Opinions of the State Council on Implementing the Market Access Negative List Regime,* which clarify that the negative list system for market access refers to the list of industries, fields, and businesses that the State Council prohibits and restricts foreign investment within the territory of the People's Republic of China. The governments at all levels adopt corresponding management measures according to law. Except for those industries, fields, and businesses which are not opened for market access of foreign investors, all other industries are opened up for foreign investors. The negative list includes prohibition of access (such as pornography and gambling) and restricted access, which is applicable to investment behaviours of various entities based on voluntary investment, expansion of investment, and mergers and acquisitions.[84] From 1 December 2015 to 31 December 2017, the market entry negative list system in some areas (i.e. the provinces where the FTZ is located) was put in place to accumulate experience. The negative list and the corresponding institutional mechanisms will formally implement a unified negative list system for foreign investors' market access in the entire country from 2018. On 25 December 2018, with the approval of the Central Committee of the Communist Party of China and the State Council, the National Development and Reform Commission and the Ministry of Commerce issued the China Negative List (2018). This indicates that China's FDI regulatory model has shifted from the comprehensive control over FIEs to a negative list system,[85] and it has a great impact on the liberalization of China's foreign investment supervision model.[86]

On the one hand, the negative list basically changed the government-centred approval regime which was framed by the EJV Law, CJV Law, and WFOE Law. The extent of state control is best evidenced by the approval regime in the admission of foreign investment. The government authorities are involved in all the stages of foreign investment projects, from the formation, operation, to termination. Challenges of securing administrative licences and business approvals and navigating China's licensing and regulatory procedures have been in existence since the inception of foreign investment.[87] The area of law and practice is deeply problematic. Unreasonable delays take place too often. The licensing and approval procedure may take much longer than it should take. Confusion arises very often when various authorities interpret and apply laws differently. Discretionary administrative powers and local standards often make it difficult for applicants to do preparation and paperwork and predict the results. Most foreign investors may have to devote much more management time and workforce to handling approvals and licensing issues.[88]

As far as the EJV Law, CJV Law, and WFOE Law are concerned, preliminary approval is required for the feasibility study even before the negotiation and conclusion of the actual foreign investment contract (either in the form of the Sino–foreign joint venture agreement or the foreign investment agreement). Chinese parties to the joint ventures may need to obtain approval for a project proposal, the purpose of which is to list the project in the local economic plan. Without the approval for a project proposal, the Chinese party may even not be able to commence formal negotiation with the foreign party for the project.[89] The articles of association and joint venture contract (or the foreign investment agreement for the WFOE Law) also are subject to the approval by the Ministry of Commerce or its local branch.[90] Until these documents are registered with the State Administration of Industry and Commerce, and the business licence is issued by the company registry, the EJV, CJV, or WFOE is not formally established. This whole process may take three to six months depending on the size and location of the project.

The actual business activities of the EJV Law, CJV Law, or WFOE Law are limited by the business scope specified in the articles of association and business licence. Unlike some common law jurisdictions, the objects clause in the articles, together with the principle of *ultra vires*, is no longer restricted and the company is basically able to conduct any commercial activities. However, this is not the case in China. The parties to the joint ventures or WFOE Law need to specify the business scope explicitly in the project proposal, feasibility study report, joint venture contract, and articles of association. The scope of business in the business licence will not only affect the scope of business activities the EJV Law, CJV Law, or WFOE Law is about to conduct, but also influence the treatment the project may receive from competent government authorities.[91] For instance the availability of import/ export licences, customs duties, investment incentives, preferential tax rates, market access, and other treatments largely depends on the scope of business set out in the business licence. The business scope also may affect the way the company operates the business in terms of environmental protection and labour management.[92] Like the operation of object clauses in a common law jurisdiction, the conduct of business activities outside the scope of business does not necessarily become void to a bona fide third party. However, the conduct of legally prohibited or restricted business may be void from the very early beginning.

Moreover, the negative list has effectively promoted the liberalization of China's regulatory model for foreign investment. The negative list system is "more demanding in terms of resources" and requires "a sophisticated domestic regulatory regime and sufficient institutional capacity for properly designing and negotiating the scheduling of liberalization commitments."[93] The number of special management items in the FTZ Negative List, from 2013 to 2020, was reduced from 190 to 30.[94] The sharp shrinking of the negative list shows the Chinese government's attempt to open wider to foreign investors and promote investment liberalization. This demonstrates a clear trend of China's "leaving" its sovereignty and police power.

In terms of the content, the negative list 2018 is a list of industries into which foreign investment is either prohibited or restricted, and contains restrictions or prohibitions on foreign investment in 34 sectors. The negative list had already been published and in use nationwide since mid-2018 and is no longer a new concept. The FTZ Negative List (2019) eliminates investment restrictions in agriculture, mining industry, manufacturing industry, and transportation.[95] This demonstrates the Chinese government's firm position of enhancing the freedom and convenience of investment and conforms to its "leaving" gesture in the field of investment. Further, the China Negative List (2019) shows the leading role of FTZ in liberalizing restrictions over foreign investment. For example in the FTZ Negative List (2018), performing brokers, oil and gas exploration and development, as well as other opening measures in the China Negative List (2019) were pushed to the whole country in 2019.[96] This gesture shows the Chinese government's willingness to stick less to its sovereignty (in the form of regulatory power) when it comes to regulate foreign investment.

The FIE negative list can better serve its function – to provide instructions specific to foreign investments. Foreign investors must consult both the FIE or FTZ negative list and the Market Access Negative List before entering into the market.[97] The negative list has become an exhaustive list of special management measures for foreign investments. Therefore, it is more investor-friendly and easier for both foreign investors and the authorities to interpret. Consequently, effective implementation can be better guaranteed. Clarity and transparency reduce transaction costs and legal barriers to market entry, and therefore they can probably encourage more foreign investment flows and contribute to the goal of opening up the Chinese investment market.[98] A gradually shortened negative list boosts China's integration into the global market as it opens China's market to foreign investments, especially high-end and intelligent manufacturing like aviation, shipping, and pharmaceutical that can contribute to the goal of building technological capacity, and green industries that can benefit the goal of environmental protection, like newly established electric passenger vehicles manufacturing. It also limits room for the discretion of the authorities in their supervision of foreign investments.[99] Meanwhile, mobile surveying[100] and research institutions of humanities and social sciences[101] are added onto the list. These industries closely relate to the national security that China intends to safeguard, like geographical information security and cultural security.[102] Consequently, the protection of national security is largely strengthened.[103]

Although the negative list will continue to be shortened (thus opening more industries), its current implementation is insufficient as the list still follows its previous category model with various industrial classification, which differs from international practices and might cause confusion for foreign investors.

2.2 Further Leaving of the State Under Outside Pressures

The key reason for China vigorously promoting the reform of its foreign investment regulatory supervision system with negative list as the core lies in the pressure exerted by developed countries such as the US and EU in relevant BITs negotiations. The Chinese authorities have published a keenly awaited negative list of sectors, similar in concept to the US' mooted Trans-Pacific Partnership Agreement, establishing which business lines will be closed to foreign companies in the zone, while all others will be open.[104] The move is expected to give foreign investors much more freedom. A short list merely banning a small number of sectors including guns, drugs, and pornography to foreign investors is theoretically investor-friendly.

On the other hand, while the Shanghai FTZ legislation incited China's foreign investment legislation, it also had a huge impact on China's negotiation and signing of investment treaties. On the issue of market access, for a long time under the investment approval mode led by administrative examination and approval authorities, Chinese BITs only provide for the post-establishment treatment. With this differentiated treatment to domestic and foreign investment, China has never "leaved" its sovereignty behind. However, as the investment liberalization promoted by developed countries has become the mainstream norm in international investment law, the gap between China and developed economies in investment policies has become quite prominent. Especially on the issue of market access, due to the Chinese domestic laws, it has also become a major issue in the negotiation of BITs between China and the US[105] and the EU.[106] With the establishment of the Shanghai FTZ, the National People's Congress authorized the suspension of FIE Laws and gradually promoted the pre-entry national treatment plus negative list model, which is a new development in Chinese law thereby affecting China's BIT regime as well. Since 2013, China has changed its consistent attitudes towards foreign investment in its BITs negotiations with the US and the EU and has clearly expressed its willingness to engage in substantive negotiations with the US on the basis of pre-entry national treatment and negative list.[107]

In the negotiations of the China–Europe BIT (in the form of the EU-China Comprehensive Agreement on Investment, which has not been ratified), the EU further requires the State party not to impose restrictions on technology transfer, investment ratio, and investment volume on the basis of pre-entry national treatment, in an effort to promote China's lifting of its foreign investment protection standards.[108] With the development of FTZ in recent years and the passing of the Foreign Investment Law (FIL), China is indeed showing a more open treaty negotiation posture, a shift to promote investment liberalization. It appears that the reform carried out in the free trade zones in China has been a stepping stone for China's further opening up to foreign investment as its commitment to bear a higher level of obligations towards foreign investors.[109] Likely, these reformist measures taken in China's FTZs can be the connecting points between China's domestic law and its BIT regime as indicated in Figure 3.3.

Just as China further transforms its investment legislation and policies, the developed economies represented by the US are questioning China's current trade, investment, and economic policy. In the 301 Report published by the Office of the US Trade Representative in 2018, there are many criticisms of China's investment policies. The main problems are the following. First, in view of foreign investment access, the United States believes that China has long imposed legislation and administrative means to require technology transfer by foreign investors in areas such as automobile manufacturing and aviation manufacturing, which has seriously damaged US investors and their rights. This reflects China's problems in the protection of intellectual property rights, national treatment, and MFN status.[110] Second, in response to China's foreign investment, the US believes that the Chinese government has highly controlled the foreign investment activities of Chinese enterprises through foreign investment approval and foreign exchange control measures and does not meet the requirements of the market economy in terms of policies. At the same time, most of China's foreign investment enterprises are SOEs, and the areas they invest in involve military industry, equipment manufacturing, and high-tech

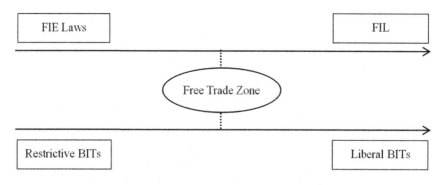

FIGURE 3.3 Moving Direction of FIL and BITs

Source: Compiled by the author.

industries. Therefore, in the eyes of the US, China's current foreign investment is an unfair economic act against the key US interests supported by the government, threatening the national security and industrial competitiveness of the US.[111]

Judging from the statistics of relevant international organizations, there is also a big gap between China and the US in the field of foreign investment supervision. According to the Foreign Investment Restriction Index released by the OECD, among the 68 countries in which it counts, the 2017 China Foreign Investment Restriction Index reached 0.316, ranking fourth, only superior to the Philippines, Saudi Arabia, and Indonesia. The US index is 0.089, which is at the midstream level.[112] From the perspective of specific industries, China currently has clear restrictions on the proportion of foreign equity in automobile manufacturing, telecommunications services, medical care, education, and finance, and the restrictions include prohibiting foreign investment in internet culture businesses and news information services, news broadcasting and other industries, and securities companies. The ratio of foreign shares of securities investment fund management companies shall not exceed 51%. In addition, China currently has many hidden barriers to market access, including industry regulation and business licences in areas such as banking and insurance services, securities fund business, telecommunications network-related services, and express delivery services. In contrast, the current US foreign investment regulation does not have special restrictions on the industries. The US restrictions are case-based review of related transactions based on national security exceptions under the CFIUS regime.

From the perspective of the investment policy since 2018, both China and the US have seen more obvious changes. In recent years, the US has continuously strengthened the supervision of foreign investment, showing the tendency of its "return of the state." In contrast, in 2018, President Xi Jinping announced to the world at the Boao Forum for Asia and China International Import Expo that China is determined to open up to the outside world. China will relax market access for industries such as finance and automobiles and will accelerate the opening up of telecommunications, medical care, education, and culture. Specifically, the China Negative List (2018) in June 2018 further narrowed the scope of restrictions and proposed that financial companies such as securities companies and insurance companies cancel the restrictions on foreign shares in 2021.[113] At the beginning of 2019, China had begun to liberalize the market for foreign investors in the field of finance and telecommunications services and gradually promoted the opening of relevant industries.[114]

China's National Reform and Development Commission and the Ministry of Commerce jointly issued the China Negative List for year 2019 that set out the sectors where foreign investment is either limited or prohibited, along with a consolidated encouraged list of sectors for foreign investment, both of which will come into effect on 30 July 2019 and further remove restrictions and facilitate foreign investment in China. The China Negative List (2019), like the previous ones, are composed of two separate lists that are applicable in the designated pilot free trade zones respectively. The China Negative List (2019) specifically ease restrictions on market access in agriculture, mining, infrastructure, and manufacturing industries as well as multiple service sectors. The China Negative List (2019) contained 40 items, down from 48 in the 2018 version. For FTZs, the FTZ Negative List contained 37 items, down from 45. In 2021, the nation-wide Negative List contained 31 items and the FTZ Negative List contained 27 items. Compared to their old versions, these two lists have already been substantially shortened.

The China's National Development and Reform Commission and the Ministry of Commerce also issued in their Joint Order No. 27 a new Catalogue of industries where foreign investment is encouraged. As a replacement of the encouraged industries section under the Catalogue (2017) and the *Catalogue of Priority Industries for Foreign Investment in Central and Western China (2017 Revision)*, the new Encouraged List, now containing 1,108 sectors in total with 415 sectors of encouraged industries nationwide and 693 region-specific sectors, not only combines the previously mentioned two catalogues but also expands the preferential policies for foreign investment to certain new sectors. Being updated annually, the negative list gradually eases the control on foreign access and streamline the administrative process with regard to foreign investment. The 2019 version of the China Negative List signals the extent to which China is seeking to loosen its control over foreign access to its markets.

In the automobile manufacturing industry, China will remove the restrictions on foreign-invested shares of special-purpose vehicles and new-energy vehicles. In 2020, the restrictions on foreign-invested shares in commercial vehicles will be lifted. In 2022, the restrictions on the foreign-invested shares of passenger vehicles were eliminated, and the same foreign company could establish no more than two joint ventures that produce similar vehicle products in China.[115] The reforms since 2018 also include drastically reducing tariffs on pharmaceuticals, automobiles, consumer goods, and industrial products, accelerating the pilot of free trade zones and free trade ports, and promoting a new pattern of high-level reform and opening up.[116] In addition, the rapid advancement of the Foreign Investment Law is also a declaration of policy stance and a response to the US concern. The widening of industrial sectors in the 2019 version of the China Negative List to foreign investors reflects China's positive gesture to cool the tension between China and US.

By empowering the FTZ with the autonomy to reform, the Chinese government has broken the existing approval-led system and established a new model with a negative list as the core in the field of foreign investment. The negative list system is not only a continuation of the "list system" established by China since the 1990s, but also a response to TPP and other models in the negotiation of relevant BITs with developed countries. The negative list model has changed China's foreign investment regulatory model and profoundly affected China's stance on BITs, thus promoting China's liberalization and transformation of domestic law as well as international investment law in the form of BITs.

3. China's New Foreign Investment Law

China's National People's Congress approved a new Foreign Investment Law in March 2019 which can be viewed as a great attempt to address key issues raised by the US government as part of the US–China trade war.[117] The FIL came into effect on 1 January 2020, and is to abolish the EJV Law, the CJV Law, and the WFOE Law. The purpose of the FIL is to replace and unify these three FIE Laws.

The existing regulatory regime was established with the promulgation of the EJV Law in 1979. In 1986 and 1988 respectively, the WFOE Law and the CJV Law were promulgated, thereby completing the trio of the so called Three FIE Laws, which constitute the three pillars of the foreign investment regulatory regime that governed foreign investment matters for the past three decades.[118]

Under the three FIE Laws, all foreign investments into China and their subsequent changes require prior, case-by-case approval from MOFCOM (the Ministry of Commerce) or its local branches.[119] In its deliberation of each case submitted for approval, MOFCOM would review not only the background of the foreign investor, the industry, and project that the foreign investor intends to engage in, but also the corporate governance terms of the FIEs to be established. Joint venture contracts and articles of associations of FIEs are to become effective only after MOFCOM approval is granted. As a result, FIEs have been subject to a parallel series of regulations in addition to the Company Law, which was promulgated in 1993 and was quite exclusively applied to domestically owned enterprises.

The approval regime, which played a pivotal role in the initial opening up of China to the external world and in bringing in foreign capital and technologies into the Chinese market, had long seemed excessive and inefficient.[120] It prolonged the approval process, increased regulatory costs for foreign investors, and to some extent, impeded free competition and liquidity flow.

The FIL basically transforms the approval system for the set-up of FIEs to a record filing system under which FIEs, like domestically owned enterprises, would come into existence only with registration with the company registrar.[121] This change of the approval system would reduce the level of government intervention into the establishment of FIEs and offers an equal procedural treatment to foreign investors. In terms of transaction costs, the record filing system certainly helps save transaction costs for foreign investors which no long need to spend cost and resources on the approval system which is less predictable due to the discretionary powers exercised by the government authorities. Compared with the current FIE Laws, the FIL has undergone a fundamental change in foreign investment. The FIL ceases to be a law governing various forms of foreign investment enterprises, leaving the task to the Company Law and the Partnership Enterprise Law.[122]

A final unclear aspect lies on two dimensions. One is the failure in specifying which actual special management measures are imposed on foreign investments in a number of restricted industries.[123] Therefore, the approval authorities enjoy wide discretion to decide the conditions for approval. Accordingly, the oversight of key investments largely relies on the competence of the authorities. Since proper implementation of the negative lists is essential to achieving the development goals, it is necessary to specify the measures imposed on restricted investments in different industrial sectors as well as which departments are responsible for formulating these restrictions. An example that can be followed is the negative list attached to the US–Uruguay Bilateral Investment Treaty[124] that specifies the measures imposed on different sectors, the applicable norms, and the competent level of governments. This method can significantly increase transparency and unify the administrative measures imposed on a particular sector, provide instructions for both foreign investors and competent authorities, and thus ensure effective management of the negative lists.[125]

Another unclear aspect on both negative lists is the administrative regime regarding national security, public order, and financial prudence. These measures are stipulated in the applicable regulations and imposed by authorities other than the commerce departments, which might be the reasons for their being omitted from the lists. Consequently, to ascertain the applicability of the specific measures imposed on their investments, foreign investors must search every related law. Most applicable rules are hidden in various normative legal documents and only have rough rules on the issues; this makes it burdensome for investors to assess the investment environment and will probably frustrate their motivation for entering China's market. To remedy this scenario, the FIL, as a unified foreign investment law, should either include all applicable rules for a certain class of investments, or provide a clear regulatory road map. This would considerably improve transparency and facilitate investment, thus fulfilling the requirements of the development goals.

The FIL is designed to focus on investment promotion and protection which is supplemented by foreign investment management, and to level domestic playing field for foreign investors by addressing various concerns raised by the global investment community such as forced technology transfer to Chinese partners, unfair treatment in terms of market access and government procurement, and the theft of commercial secrets from foreign businesses in China.[126] For instance foreign investors are treated the same as domestic investors not only at the set-up period when their business entities are established but also after the establishment of the entities. Foreign investors are ensured of equal opportunity to government procurement between both domestic and FIEs.[127] The big ticket item, in terms of foreign companies, is IP theft in the form of the handover of technological secrets as the price of entry to the massive Chinese market – which takes place when the multinational firm partners up with a local entity. According to the FIL, the officials are obliged to protect commercially confidential information they obtain from overseas businesses. The FIL makes it illegal for officials to misuse critical information or to provide it to local firms. The FIL imposes criminal penalties for sharing sensitive foreign company information, adopts a much tougher deterrent against counterfeiting and IP theft, and also offers new avenues for the enforcement of IP protection. There is a clear ban on illegal government interference in the activities of foreign business.[128] These changes came after the US' accusation of Chinese authorities' linking market access to technology transfer from US companies to Chinese partners[129] and can be viewed as an effort to appease the tension between the US and China over the issue of protection of foreign IP rights.

Unfair subsidies to Chinese companies are also addressed by the FIL. However, foreign investors may need to be wary of some requirements. For instance one of the provisions includes a requirement for the local subsidiaries of international firms to report various details of their operation to Chinese officials. This could include performance indicators relating to labour relations, overall staffing numbers, pollution records, and the like.[130]

One issue which may be a structural difference between the US BIT and China BIT[131] is the pre-establishment national treatment plus a negative list instead of relying on a case-by-case approval model. In Chinese BITs, the definition of "investment" usually does not cover the "pre-establishment" phase of investment.[132] This means that only "post-establishment" investment can be protected by the BIT, and foreign investors, to enjoy BIT benefits, must obtain the permission from the government to invest in an industry or sector on a case-by-case basis according to the industrial policies. Clearly, post-establishment rights dilute the value of investor protections under the BITs. Pre-establishment rights instead tend to reduce discretionary requirements and bureaucratic obstacles. Together with the pre-establishment rights is a negative list allowing foreign investors to invest into most industrial sectors as domestic investors on the basis of national treatment. There is a China Negative List of 40 sectors that will not be open to foreign investment or, in some cases, not open without conditions or special permission. For instance there is a complete ban on investing in fishing,[133] gene research,[134] news media and television broadcasting,[135] and religious education.[136] Non-renewable energy automobile production will require partnerships for a few years but then be phased out.[137] The general principle established by the FIL is that foreign companies will receive and enjoy the same treatment as their Chinese counterparts for the industries that are not listed in the negative list.[138]

Nevertheless, many in the business community in China see the FIL as a kind of sweeping set of intentions rather than a specific, enforceable set of rules. As the wording of the FIL is still vague and general – which is the characteristics of Chinese legislation, many details may have to be left to be addressed in the future regulations and rules. It is fair for the international business community to fear it could be open to different and changing forms of interpretation. Besides, enforcement will be the key metric for evaluating the success of the FIL. Enforcement, at the end of the day, relies upon structural changes and an independent judicial system.[139]

A very important change in the FIL is to strengthen investment promotion and protection by providing more solid legal protection for foreign investors and FIEs.[140] The FIL includes clauses concerning the expropriation, profit remittance, intellectual property protection, and non-forced technology transfer, local government compliance, and other issues. Foreign investors are also ensured of equal opportunity to government procurement between Chinese enterprises and foreign investment enterprises.

Following increasing frustration by foreign businesses about their inability to compete fairly with Chinese companies, the US and China became embroiled in trade tensions in 2018. Under the US President Donald Trump, the rhetoric about the spat initially focused on the American trade deficit with China. That resulted in the application of tariffs on $250 billion worth of imported goods from China, to which Beijing countered with duties on $110 billion worth of goods from the US. In the last several months, the negotiations between both sides have increasingly centred on issues of intellectual property protection and claims of forced technology transfer.[141] The FIL may not be enough to appease the demands of the US in ongoing trade negotiations. Passing the law is a clear attempt to translate some of the concerns expressed by the US and EU into legislation. It is a step in the right direction. But the trade tensions are wider than that.

The State Council may establish a security review system for foreign investment, under which a security review shall be conducted for any foreign investment affecting or having the possibility to affect state security.[142] The law gives China the right to retaliate against a particular country for restricting Chinese companies there. Such a clause essentially reinforces the unequal footing that foreign and Chinese companies have in accessing each other's countries. US companies have complained that they get less access in China than Chinese companies have in America.

The FIL can be seen as a strong signal sent by the Chinese government to the global community that it remains an attractive investment destination. The FIL emphasizes the protection of foreign investors' rights and interests, limits the government's right to intervene in reporting, and clarifies the full implementation of pre-entry national treatment and negative list.[143] In terms of foreign investment supervision, on the one hand, the FIL highly emphasizes the importance of administrative agencies in formulating negative list. However, from the current negative list, there are still many areas that prohibit or restrict foreign investment, and there is a big gap with developed countries. In the ongoing BITs negotiations between China and the US and the EU, the specific content of the negative list is always the focus of disputes between the parties, especially the clarity of the negative list, the distribution of power between the central government and local governments, and the negative list for specific industries. Some scholars also believe that clarifying the negative list is a difficult point in the negotiation of BITs between China and the US.[144]

On the other hand, although the foreign-funded review mechanism established by the FIL clearly defines the position of restricting the administrative power of the government, the provisions still have great ambiguity, and there is also great uncertainty in the specific interpretation and application, which reduces foreign country investors' expectations of investment risks and makes them still afraid of investing.[145] Generally speaking, the FIL is not only a summary and effective integration of China's foreign investment legislation in the 40 years of reform and opening up, but also a recitation of internationally accepted investment standards in the basic position of the CCP's Central Committee to continue to promote reform and opening up. In particular, the pre-entry national treatment, the super-vision of the negative list as the core, and the legislation of specific measures such as the protection of intellectual property rights demonstrate the basic position of China to continue to promote investment liberalization and facilitation. The new FIL is a big step forward in China's investment liberalization.

In short, from the perspective of China's foreign investment legislation for 40 years since the reform and opening up, it has experienced a system build-up from scratch, highlighting the basic position of constantly restricting the govern-ment's regulatory power and safeguarding the interests of foreign investors,[146] and showing the country's "leaving of the state" gesture. However, this "leaving of the state" is not sufficient in terms of speed, scope, and strength, especially in terms of national treatment, MFN status, and intellectual property protection,[147] and the standards expected by developed economies such as the US and the EU. From the policy direction of 2018, China has begun to pay attention to reforms in the previously mentioned areas, and it continues to highlight the trend of continuously pushing the country's "leaving" (the sovereignty) posture both at the legislative and administrative levels.

4. Mixed Image of China's Foreign Investment Law

At the time of global financial crisis, China appeared on the course of marketiza-tion, liberalization, and facilitation evidenced by its political will to adhere to the open-door policy and the increasing amount of outbound FDI.[148] However, the global financial crisis also made a perception among China's policy makers that the state-driven model is a solution to regulatory failure and market failure. As a result, China seemed to rely more on state intervention than market disciplines to manage macroeconomy.

As long as China continues to regulate foreign investment comprehensively and closely, policy may remain and dominate the laws in regulating foreign investment and businesses. Meanwhile, the economic reforms that have signifi-cantly transformed China have made necessary development of the legal frame-work for foreign trade and investment. The evolution of law, legal institutions, and legal infrastructure remains slow and uneven. While the laws and regula-tions are more available than before, the law enforcement remains the key hurdle to the rule of law in a Western sense. The administrative organs and officials, even if not granted, are used to exercising their discretionary power to interpret and enforce laws, which create more uncertainty, inconsistency, and complexity in enforcement. Recent years may have witnessed China's more authoritarian and paternalist image in terms of its regulation, policy, and governance.

China has been heavily criticized to implement and advocate a state-directed economic model which has distorted fair competition in the global market. This has been one of the heatedly contested issues between China and its Western coun-terparts. During the trade war negotiations, the US administration demanded reforms of SOEs, but China appears to reinforce its state-directed economic model by increasing the influence of SOEs as well as CCP intrusions into boardrooms of private enterprises.[149] Apparently, the US and China represent two opposing systems for running an economy. The US adopts a liberal economy model. But China was labelled as a revisionist state running state capitalism.[150] China's past four decades reveal the close linkage between the state and the market amid its economic miracle. The state played a triple role in the economy – it is a planner, a regulator, and a player. In Chinese terminology, the state has a triple role in the game: it is a soccer player, it is an arbitrary, and it is a coach. As a result, the domestic legal system underpins the distinctive market–state relationship. This may work in the Chinese context but contradicts the political economy orthodox and the essential norms of international economic law and global economic governance.

Locally, this state–market paradox hinders China's economic growth and transformation from a labour-intensive to an innovation-based one. Globally, it causes controversy between China and its Western counterparts. The Chinese government is highly involved in guiding its economy. In cross-border investment, China's intervention makes it hard to discern whether outbound FDI is driven by policy or the market.[151] International economic order is also challenged as its inherent market–state dichotomy has a clear boundary which makes it hard to justify China's economic governance model. Policy tools run contrary to the principles of free trade. Despite China's efforts to convince the rest of the world it is actually offering the world an alternative model, the world may either need a fresh perspective to comprehend the market–state relationship or take for granted that the market and the state have a mutually exclusive relationship.[152]

Notes

1 See Jonathan Bonnitcha, Lauge N. Skovgaard Poulsen & Michael Waibel, *The Political Economy of the Investment Treaty Regime* (Oxford University Press 2017) 57.
2 Helen V. Milner, "Introduction: The Global Economy, FDI, and the Regime for Investment" (2014) 66 *World Politics* 1, 7.
3 See Richard C. Chen, "Bilateral Investment Treaties and Domestic Institutional Reform" (2017) 55 *Columbia Journal of Transnational Law* 547, 554.
4 Huiping Chen, "China's Innovative ISDS Mechanisms and Their Implications" (2018) 112 *American Journal of International Law* 207, 211.
5 Y. Y. Kueh, "Foreign Investment and Economic Change in China" (1992) 131 *China Quarterly* 637–690.
6 Shirley Ayangbah & Liu Sun, "Comparative Study of Foreign Investment Law: The Case of China and Ghana" (2017) 3 *Cogent Social Sciences* 1–22.
7 Kate Hadley, "Do China's BITs Matter? Assessing the Effect of China's Investment Agreements on Foreign Direct Investment Flows, Investors' Rights and the Rule of Law" (2013) 45 *Georgetown Journal of International Law* 255.
8 See Deng Xiaoping, "Emancipating the Mind, Seeking Truth from Facts, Looking Forward Together", in *Selected Works of Deng Xiaoping* (Vol. 2) (Foreign Language Press 1994) 146–147.
9 Michael J. Enright, "China's Inward Investment: Approach and Impact", in Julien Chaisse (ed), *China's International Investment Strategy: Bilateral, Regional, and Global Law and Policy* (Oxford University Press 2019) 28.
10 Sherif H. Seid, *Global Regulation of Foreign Direct Investment* (Routledge Taylor & Francis Group 2017) 30.

11 Michael J. Enright, "China's Inward Investment: Approach and Impact", in Julien Chaisse (ed), *China's International Investment Strategy: Bilateral, Regional, and Global Law and Policy* (Oxford University Press 2019) 30.

12 Ibid., 35.

13 UNCTAD Data Center, *available at* https://unctadstat.unctad.org/wds/ReportFolders/ reportFolders.aspx??sCSChosenLang=en (last visited 30 October 2022).

14 EJV Law (1979), Article 1.

15 EJV Law (1979), Article 2.

16 EJV Law (1979), Articles 3, 6 and 9.

17 EJV Law (1979), Article 14.

18 Constitution of the PRC (1982), Article 18.

19 WFOE Law (1982), Article 1.

20 CJV Law (1988), Articles. 3, 5, 6, 7 & 9.

21 CJV Law (1988), Article 26.

22 Li Wanqiang, "Chinese Foreign Investment Laws: A Review from the Perspective of Policy-oriented Jurisprudence" (2011) 19 *Asia Pacific Law Review* 35, 41.

23 Joseph C. H. Chai & Kartik C. Roy, *Economic Reform in China and India: Development Experience in a Comparative Perspective* (Edward Elgar Publishing 2006) 51.

24 Constitution of the PRC (1993), Article 15.

25 EJV Law (1990), Article 3.

26 EJV Law (1990), Article 14.

27 EJV Law (1990), Article 7.

28 In 1993, China further revised the 1982 Constitution, clarifying that China will implement a socialist market economic system.

29 Final Version of the 14th CPC National Congress Report, FBIS Daily Report – China, 21 October 1992.

30 EJV Law (1990), Article 2.

31 Michael J. Enright, "China's Inward Investment: Approach and Impact", in Julien Chaisse (ed), *China's International Investment Strategy: Bilateral, Regional, and Global Law and Policy* (Oxford University Press 2019) 26–27.

32 See Meichen Liu, "The New Chinese Foreign Investment Law and Its Implication on Foreign Investors" (2018) 38 *Northwestern Journal of International Law and Business* 285, 288–289.

33 Songling Yang, "China's Administrative Mode for Foreign Investment: From Positive List to Negative List" (2015) 33 *Singapore Law Review* 93, 96–97.

34 Provisions of the State Council for the Encouragement of Foreign Investment (1986).

35 EJV Law, Articles 5 and 9; EJV Law Implementing Rules, Articles 4, 28, and 62. CJV Law, Article 8.

36 Wang Wei, "Super-national Treatment: A Misconception or a Creation with Chinese Characteristics?" (2010) 5 *Frontiers of Law in China* 376–396.

37 EJV Law, Article 7; Joint Venture Income Tax Law, Article 5.

38 Provisions of the State Council for the Encouragement of Foreign Investment.

39 Ibid.

40 WFOE Law, Article 3.

41 To be more detailed, these industries refer to machinery, automobiles, telecommunications, construction, iron and steel, and non-ferrous metals. "Control Over Key Industries 'Crucial'", *China Daily*, 19 December 2006, *available at* http://english. people.com.cn/200612/19/eng20061219_333839.html (last visit 18 January 2019).

42 For details, see Shen Wei, "Is SAFE Safe Now? – Foreign Exchange Regulatory Control over Chinese Outbound and Inbound Investments and a Political Economy Analysis of Policies" (2010) 11 *The Journal of World Investment and Trade* 227, 245–250.

43 Mure Dickie, "Chinese Takeover Fears Grow", *Financial Times*, 4 August 2006, 6; Geoff Dyer, Sundeep Tucker and Tom Mitchell, "Forbidden Country? How Foreign Deals in China Are Hitting Renewed Resistance", *Financial Times*, 8 August 2006, 11.

44 The most high-profile and lasting battle was Carlyle's bid to take stake in Xugong, China's leading machinery maker, which was finally defeated. Sundeep Tucker, "Carlyle

Concedes Defeat in Battle to Take Stake in China's Xugong", *Financial Times*, 23 July 2008.

45 The liberalizing trend was not extended to most publishing activities. Also, genetically modified organisms were also moved to the "prohibited" category.

46 *Decision of the State Council on Reforming the Investment System*, issued by the State Council on 16 July 2004, *available at* https://policy.asiapacificenergy.org/sites/default/files/Decision%20of%20the%20State%20Council%20on%20Reform%20of%20the%20Investment%20System.pdf (last visited 24 September 2022).

47 See Pravin Jadhav, "Determinants of Foreign Direct Investment in BRICS Economies: Analysis of Economic, Institutional and Political Factor" (2012) 37 *Procedia-Social and Behavioral Sciences* 5, 12.

48 China Briefing, "New Catalogue for the Guidance of Foreign Investment Industries Released," 7 November 2007, *available at* https://www.china-briefing.com/news/new-catalogue-for-the-guidance-of-foreign-investment-industries-released (last visted 15 November 2022).

49 United States Trade Representative, "Report to Congress on China's WTO Compliance 6" (2005), *available at* https://china.usc.edu/sites/default/files/article/attachments/2005%20China%20Report%20to%20Congress.pdf (last visited 24 September 2022).

50 NPC Standing Committee of PRC, *Decision of the Standing Committee of the National People's Congress on Amending Four Laws Including the Law of the People's Republic of China on Foreign-funded Enterprises*, 3 September 2016, *available at*http://www.lawinfochina.com/display.aspx?lib=law&id=4687 (last visited 24 September 2022).

51 EJV Law, Article 2; WFOE Law, Article 5.

52 See Shen Wei, "Expropriation in Transition: Evolving Chinese Investment Treaty Practices in Local and Global Contexts" (2015) 28 *Leiden Journal of International Law* 579, 600–601.

53 See Xinli Zheng, *China's 40 Years of Economic Reform and Development: How the Miracle Was Created* (The Commercial Press Ltd. and Springer Nature Singapore Pte Ltd. 2018) 151.

54 See Zhang Jianhong & He Xinming, "Economic Nationalism and Foreign Acquisition Completion: The Case of China" (2014) 23 *International Business Review* 212, 224–225.

55 Susan L. Shirk, *The Political Logic of Economic Reform in China* (University of California Press 1993) 21.

56 See generally Lucian Pye, *The Mandarin and the Cadre* (University of Michigan Press 1988).

57 See generally Kenneth Lieberthal and Michel Oksenberg, *Policy Making in China: Leaders, Structures, and Processes* (Princeton University Press 1988).

58 Yong Wang, "China's Domestic WTO Debate" (2000) 27 *China Business Review* 54, 56.

59 Law is the most overtly culture-bound of all the disciplines. Comparative legal study has not been successful in developing culturally neutral legal concepts. Therefore, the assumption of the universality of Western legal forms and legal ideals or a complete ignorance of cultural bias may not be a good technique to comparative legal study. See Gunter Frankenberg, "Critical Comparisons: Re-thinking Comparative Law" (1985) 26 *Harvard International Law Journal* 411, 434–440.

60 See Jiang Zemin, Open Strategy for the Implementation of "Introduction" and "Going Global", in *Selected Works of Jiang Zemin* (Vol. 2) (Foreign Language Press 2006) 91–94.

61 Jiang Zemin, *Highly Holding the Great Banner of Deng Xiaoping Theory and Pushing the Construction of Socialism with Chinese Characteristics into the 21st Century, in Selected Works of Jiang Zemin* (Vol. 2) (Foreign Language Press 2006) 27.

62 Since the 15th National Congress of the Communist Party of China in 1997, "going out" has always been the basic line that the Chinese party and government have adhered to in the field of opening up to the outside world. Until the party's 19th National Congress in 2017, General Secretary Xi Jinping still emphasized the need to 'One Belt and One Road'. "Building as the focus, adhere to the introduction and go out and pay equal attention, follow the principle of joint construction and sharing, strengthen the openness and cooperation of innovation capabilities, and form an open pattern of linkage between the

land and the sea, and between the east and the west." See Xi Jinping, "Decisive Victory to Build a Well-off Society in an All-round Way to Win a Great Victory in Socialism with Chinese Characteristics in the New Era – Report at the 19th National Congress of the Communist Party of China", *People's Daily*, 28 October 2017, 1st edn.

63 On 24 October 2014, the finance ministers and authorized representatives of the first batch of 21 intent-initiating member countries including China, India, and Singapore signed a contract in Beijing to jointly decide to establish an investment bank. On 25 December 2015, the Asian Infrastructure Investment Bank was formally established. From 16 to 18 January 2016, the opening ceremony of the AIIB and the inaugural meeting of the Board of Directors and the Board of Directors were held in Beijing.

64 See National Development and Reform Commission, Ministry of Foreign Affairs, Ministry of Commerce, "Vision and Action to Promote the Construction of the Silk Road Economic Belt and the 21st Century Maritime Silk Road", *People's Daily*, 29 March 2015, 4th edn.

65 Hui Yao Wang and Lu Miao, "China's Outward Investment: Trends and Challenges in the Globalization of Chinese Enterprises", in Julien Chaisse (ed), *China's International Investment Strategy: Bilateral, Regional, and Global Law and Policy* (Oxford University Press 2019) 47.

66 See *Ministry of Commerce of the People's Republic of China: China Foreign Investment Cooperation Development Report (2017)*, 124. For the relevant data of 2018, see the Department of Foreign Investment and Economic Cooperation of the Ministry of Commerce of the People's Republic of China, *Island Investment and Cooperation in the Countries Along the Belt and Road from January to December 2018*, 22 January 2019, *available at* http://hzs.mofcom.gov.cn/article/date/201901/20190102829086.shtml (lasted visited 5 February 2019).

67 According to relevant officials of the Chinese government, as of the first half of 2018, more than 80 SOEs in China have undertaken 3,116 investment projects and projects in the countries along the "Belt and Road", involving high-speed rail, water conservancy, and energy, which have effectively promoted the local Economic growth. See Wang Wei, "In the Second Half of the Year, SOEs 'Anti-Risk' Five-Way Progress", *Economic Information Daily*, 19 July 2018, 4th edn.

68 Nana de Graaff, "China Inc. Goes Global. Transnational and National Networks of China's Globalizing Business Elite" (2020) 27(2) *Review of International Political Economy* 208–233.

69 Tristan Kohl, "The Belt and Road Initiative's Effect on Supply-chain Trade: Evidence from Structural Gravity Equations" (2019) 12 *Cambridge Journal of Regions, Economy and Society* 77, 90.

70 Dragana Mitrovic, "The Belt and Road: China's Ambitious Initiative" (2016) 59 *China International Studies* 76, 81–82.

71 Wang and Miao (n 65), 43.

72 Karl P. Sauvant & Victor Zitian Chen, "China's Regulatory Framework for Outbound Foreign Direct Investment" (2014) 7(1) *China Economic Journal* 141–163.

73 Jie Huang, "Challenges and Solutions for the China-US BIT Negotiations: Insights from the Recent Development of FTZs in China" (2015) 18 *Journal of International Economic Law* 307–339.

74 Gladie Lui, "Shanghai Pilot Free Trade Zone: Shaping of China's Future Foreign Investment Environment" (2014) 40 *Journal of International Taxation* 31.

75 People's Government of Shanghai Municipality, *Statistical Bulletin on National Economic and Social Development of Shanghai in 2013*, 26 August 2014, *available at* https://tjj.sh.gov.cn/tjgb/20140225/0014-267416.html (last visited 29 October 2022).

76 See Deng Xiaoping, "Make a Success of Special Economic Zones and Open More Cities to the Outside World", in *Selected Works of Deng Xiaoping* (Vol. 3) (Foreign Language Press 1994) 61–62.

77 NPC Standing Committee of PRC, *Decision of the Standing Committee of the National People's Congress on Authorizing the State Council to Temporarily Adjust the Relevant*

Administrative Approval Items Prescribed in Laws in China (Shanghai) Pilot Free Trade Zone, 30 August 2013, *available at* http://en.pkulaw.cn/display.aspx?cgid=aff2ae6e2040c7a6b dfb&lib=law (lasted visited 5 June 2019).

78 NPC Standing Committee of PRC, *Decision of the Standing Committee of the National People's Congress on Authorizing the State Council to Temporarily Adjust the Relevant Administrative Approval Items Prescribed in Laws in China (Guangdong) Pilot Free Trade Zone, China (Tianjin) Pilot Free Trade Zone, China (Fujian) Pilot Free Trade Zone, and the Extensions of China (Shanghai) Pilot Free Trade Zone,* 18 December 2014, *available at* http://lawinfo china.com/display.aspx?id=e1293ff74c8e3a4dbdfb&lib=law (lasted visited 5 June 2019).

79 PRC State Council, *Decision of the State Council on Temporarily Adjusting the Provisions of Relevant Administrative Regulations, Documents of the State Council, and Departmental Rules Approved by the State Council in Pilot Free Trade Zones,* 1 July 2016, *available at* http:// en.pkulaw.cn/display.aspx?id=4456b97685822112bdfb&lib=law&SearchKeyword=& SearchCKeyword (lasted visited 5 June 2019).

80 NPC Standing Committee of PRC, *Decision of the Standing Committee of the National People's Congress on Amending Four Laws Including the Law of the People's Republic of China on Foreign-funded Enterprises,* 3 September 2016, *available at* www.fdi.gov. cn/1800000121_39_4849_0_7.html (last visited 26 January 2019).

81 Local People's Congresses (incl. Standing Committees) and Governments at Various Levels, Shanghai Municipality, People's Government of Shanghai Municipality, *Measures for the Administration of China (Shanghai) Pilot Free Trade Zone,* 29 September 2013, *available at* http://en.pkulaw.cn/display.aspx?id=eda25915d2ee977cbdfb&lib=law&Sea rchKeyword=&SearchCKeyword (last visited 26 January 2019).

82 Local People's Congresses (incl. Standing Committees) and Governments at Various Levels, Shanghai Municipality, Shanghai Municipality People's Congress (incl. Standing Committee), *Regulation on the China (Shanghai) Pilot Free Trade Zone,* 25 July 2014, *available at* http://en.pkulaw.cn/Display.aspx?lib=law&Cgid=17657380 (last visited 26 January 2019).

83 See the earlier relevant discussions in Section III(I)1(1).

84 Jiaxiang Hu, "FTZs, Can They Initiate a New Round of Reforms in China?" (2016) 59 *Boletim Ciencias Economicas* 9, 13–14.

85 Baihua Gong, "The Change of the Perspective of Rule of Law from China's Free Trade Pilot Zone to Free Trade Port" (2019) 190 *Journal of Political Science and Law* 109, 113.

86 Louise Watt and Kelvin Chan, *China Pilot Free Trade Zone Opens in Reform Push,* 29 September 2013, *available at* www.ksl.com/article/27048736/china-pilot-free-trade-zone-opens-in-reform-push (last visited 26 March 2019).

87 Yuwen Li & Cheng Bian, "A New Dimension of Foreign Investment Law in China – Evolution and Impacts of the National Security Review System" (2016) 24 *Asia Pacific Law Review* 149, 161.

88 United States-China Business Council, *Administrative Licensing and Business Approvals, United States CBC 2007 Member Priorities Survey Executive Summary: United States Companies' China Outlook: Continuing Optimism Tempered By Operating Challenges, Protectionist Threats,* November 2007, *available at* https://www.ids.trade/files/news/2007/ uscbc-member-survey-2007.pdf (last visited 24 September 2022).

89 EJV Law, Article 3; CJV Law, Article 5.

90 WFOE Law, Articles 6 and 7.

91 EJV Law, Article 6, CJV Law, Articles 7–15, WFOE Law, Articles 9–13.

92 PRC Environment Protection Law; Joint Venture Labor Regulations; Provisional Regulations on Environmental Control for Economic Zones Open to Foreigners.

93 UNCTAD, Investment Policy Framework for Sustainable Development 2012, 61; UNCTAD, Investment Policy Framework for Sustainable Development 2015, 113.

94 See National Development and Reform Commission and Ministry of Commerce, *Special Administrative Measures (Negative List) for the Access of Foreign Investment in Pilot Free Trade*

Zones (2019), available at http://wzs.mofcom.gov.cn/article/n/202006/20200602976957.shtml (lasted visited 3 September 2020).

95 Compared with the FTZ Negative List (2018), the FTZ Negative List (2019) has removed investment prohibitions of the fishing (Article 4), printing (Article 8), production of xuan paper and ink ingots (Article 12), domestic vessel agencies (Article 17), development of state protected wild fauna and flora resources native to China (Article 34) and construction and operation of cinemas (Article 42). Meanwhile, the FTZ Negative List (2019) has simplified investment prohibitions in mining industry (Articles 5–7) and telecommunications (Article 23).

96 Chinese Government News Web, "Updating the Negative List for Foreign Investment, What Restrictions Should be Cancelled? Which Industries Should be Encouraged?", 6 July 2019, *available at* www.gov.cn/fuwu/2019-07/06/content_5406718.htm (last visited 9 July 2019).

97 Yawen Zheng, "China's New Foreign Investment Law and Its Contribution Towards the Country's Development Goals" (2021) 22 *Journal of World Investment & Trade* 388, 410.

98 Ibid.

99 Ibid.

100 The FTZ negative list (2019) number 30; 2019 FTZ negative list (effective 30 July 2019) number 27.

101 2019 FIE Negative List number 29.

102 National cultural security consists of four main aspects: security of language, values, lifestyle, as well as customs and manners, which can be influenced or threatened by foreign culture, and thus damaging the soft power of a State. Lin Han, "Chinese Cultural Security in the Information Communication Era", *Focus Asia*, 6 February 2014, *available at* https://www.files.ethz.ch/isn/184242/2014-lin-han-chinese-cultural-security-information-communication-era.pdf (last visited 24 September 2022).

103 Yawen Zheng (n 97).

104 Heng Wang, "The Differences Between China's Recent FTA and the TPP: A Case Study of the China-Korea FTA", in Julien Chaisse, Henry Gao & Chang-fa Lo (eds), *Paradigm Shift in International Economic Law Rule-Making* (Springer 2017) 299.

105 Karl P. Sauvant & Huiping Chen, "A China-US Bilateral Investment Treaty: A Template for a Multilateral Framework for Investment?" (2013) 5 *Transnational Corporations Review* 1, 2.

106 See Wei Yin, "Challenges, Issues in China-EU Investment Agreement and the Implication on China's Domestic Reform" (2018) 26 *Asia Pacific Law Review* 170, 176–179.

107 See Jie Huang, "Challenges and Solutions for the China-US BIT Negotiations: Insights from the Recent Development of FTZs in China" (2015) 18 *Journal of International Economic Law* 307, 316.

108 Jun Xiao, "How Can a Prospective China-EU BIT Contribute to Sustainable Investment: In Light of the UNCTAD Investment Policy Framework for Sustainable Development" (2015) 8 *Journal of World Energy Law and Business* 521, 525–528.

109 See Lin Xiao, *National Test: System Design of China (Shanghai) Pilot Free Trade Zone* (Springer 2016) 421–422.

110 See Office of The United States Trade Representative Executive Office of The President, *Findings of The Investigation into China's Acts, Policies, And Practices Related to Technology Transfer, Intellectual Property, and Innovation Under Section 301 of The Trade Act of 1974*, Mar. 22, 2018, pp. 29–35, *available at* https://ustr.gov/sites/default/files/Section%20301%20FINAL.PDF (last visited Jan. 12, 2019).

111 See Office of The United States Trade Representative Executive Office of The President, *Findings of The Investigation into China's Acts, Policies, And Practices Related to Technology Transfer, Intellectual Property, And Innovation Under Section 301 of The Trade Act of*

1974, Mar. 22, 2018, pp. 62–153, *available at* https://ustr.gov/sites/default/files/Sec tion%20301%20FINAL.PDF (last visited Jan. 12, 2019).

112 See OECD, *OECD FDI Regulatory Restrictiveness Index*, *available at* https://stats.oecd.org/ Index.aspx?datasetcode=FDIINDEX&_ga=2.141403184.380646240.1547967192-364793636.1547707704# (last visited 8 January 2019).

113 The China Negative List (2018), Articles 21 and 22.

114 BT Group announced on January 24, 2019, that it has obtained two value-added tele-communications licenses from China's Ministry of Industry and Information Technol-ogy, marking the beginning of China's opening up to the telecommunications services industry. See BT Official Website, *BT First Global Telco to Receive Domestic Telecoms Licences in China*, 29 January 2019, *available at* www.chinadaily.com.cn/a/201901/29/WS5c4fbdfca3106c65c34e70b2.html (last visited 30 January 2019). The Business Man-agement Department of the People's Bank of China issued an announcement on 28 January 2019, announcing the completion of the S&P Credit Rating (China) Co., Ltd. completion of the credit rating agency filing, marking the beginning of the overseas financial rating agencies in China. See the Business Management Department of the People's Bank of China (Beijing), 28 January 2019, *available at* http://beijing.pbc.gov.cn/beijing/132024/3753866/index.html (last visited 30 January 2019).

115 The China Negative List (2018), Article 8.

116 See Xi Jinping, "Opening, Creating, Prospering, Innovating, Leading the Future – Keynote Speech at the Opening Ceremony of the 2018 Annual Meeting of the Boao Forum for Asia", *People's Daily*, Apr. 11, 2018, 3rd edition; Xi Jinping, "Building Inno-vation Inclusive Open World Economy-Keynote Speech at the Opening Ceremony of the First China International Import Expo", 15 November 2018, *available at* www.xinhuanet.com/2018-11/05/c_1123664692.htm (last visited 1 January 2019).

117 The Chinese government rushed the legislation through the National People's Con-gress to fend off complaints from the US and EU about unfair trade practices. The new law was first introduced as a draft in 2015, but its progress picked up markedly from the middle of last year. Apparently, this was an attempt to address issues identified by the US in the ongoing trade war. If there is pushback against a draft bill and amendments so made, this happens before the NPC sits at a series of standing committee meetings behind closed doors. The process can take years. This time, the passing of the bill only took three months.

118 See Martin Endicott, "China and International Investment Law: An Evolving Rela-tionship", in Wenhua Shan (ed), *China and International Investment Law: Twenty Years of ICSID Membership* (Brill – Nijhoff 2014) 220–221.

119 EJV Law, Articles 1, 3; CJV Laws, Article 5; WFOE Law, Article 6.

120 See Jacques Morisset & Olivier Lumenga Neso, "Administrative Barriers to Foreign Investment in Developing Countries", 17–18 May 2012, *available at* http://documents.worldbank.org/curated/en/556581468766823917/pdf/multi0page.pdf (last visited 14 July 2019).

121 FIL, Articles 29, 30 and 31.

122 Bao Zhi, et al., "China Issues a New Consolidated Law on Foreign Investment", 9 May 2019, *available at* https://globalcompliancenews.com/china-issues-new-consoli dated-law-foreign-investment-20190318/ (last visited 20 July 2019).

123 For example 2019 FIE Negative List (n 63) number 10 and 2019 FTZ negative list (effective 30 July 2019) number 7: Manufacturing of satellite telecasting ground receiv-ing facilities and key components.

124 United States–Uruguay BIT (signed 11 April 2005, entered into force 31 October 2006) annex III.

125 Yawen Zheng (n 97) 415.

126 BBC, *China Foreign Investment Law: Bill Aims to Ease Global Concerns*, 15 March 2019, *available at* www.bbc.com/news/business-47578883 (last visited 15 June 2019).

127 FIL, Articles 15 and 16.

128 FIL, Articles 22, 23.
129 US companies often license their IP rights to their Chinese subsidiaries formed together with the Chinese partners. In exchange, the Chinese partners and local governments may prefer to see some technology transfer with the aim of fostering economic and technological development by offering some incentives in land, infrastructure, tax, and loans on more favourable terms. Although it is true that the Chinese partners may be in a better position to negotiate more favourable terms, it is the US investors that eventually decide to make a deal on a cost-benefit analysis basis. Previously, the US investors may be willing to transfer technology as the Chinese counterparties' ability to adapt and master this transferred technology may be somehow limited. Nevertheless, when the Chinese entities' capability for indigenous innovation has progressed substantially in recent years, the US investors may feel pressured to continue this practice as they see Chinese counterparties as genuine and serious competitors. As a result, the US investors want to change this strategy and accuse this practice of unfair competition or forced technology transfer.
130 FIL, Articles 32, 33, 34.
131 C. Fred Bergsten, Gary Clyde Hufbauer, and Sean Miner, *Bridging the Pacific: Toward Free Trade and Investment Between China and the United States* (Peterson Institute for International Economics 2014).
132 Chapter 3.
133 The China Negative List (2019), Articles 2, 4.
134 The China Negative List (2019), Article 3.
135 The China Negative List (2019), Articles 6, 10, 34–37.
136 The China Negative List (2019), Article 32.
137 The China Negative List (2019), Article 9.
138 FIL, Article 28.
139 *China Issues a New Consolidated Law on Foreign Investment*, 9 May 2019, *available at* https://globalcompliancenews.com/china-issues-new-consolidated-law-foreign-investment-20190318/ (last visited 13 July 2019).
140 FIL, Articles 9–21.
141 Lee Branstetter, "China's 'Forced' Technology Transfer Problem – And What to Do About It", 2–3, 31 May 2018, *available at* www.uscc.gov/sites/default/files/Branstetter. Forced%20Technology.China%205-24%20US-China%20Commission.pdf (last visited 11 July 2019).
142 FIL, Article 35.
143 FIL, Articles 3 and 4.
144 See Jie Huang, "Challenges and Solutions for the China-US BIT Negotiations: Insights from the Recent Development of FTZs in China" (2015) 18 *Journal of International Economic Law* 307, 318–319.
145 FIL Article 35.
146 Chunlai Chen, "The Liberalisation of FDI Policies and the Impacts of FDI on China's Economic Development", in Ross Garnaut, Ligang Song & Cai Fang (eds), *China's 40 Years of Reform and Development* (ANU Press 2018) 612.
147 See Guiguo Wang, "China's Practice in International Investment Law: From Participation to Leadership in the World Economy" (2009) 34 *Yale Journal of International Law* 575, 577.
148 Wangqiang Li, "Chinese Foreign Investment Laws: A Review from the Perspective of Policy-Oriented Jurisprudence" (2011) 19(1) *Asia Pacific Law Review* 35–52.
149 Frank Tang, "China Ignoring US Demand for Trade War Reform by Reinforcing State-Directed Economic Model", *South China Morning Post*, 13 July 2019, *available at* www.scmp.com/economy/china-economy/article/3018120/china-ignoring-us-demand-trade-war-reform-reinforcing-state (last visited 5 September 2020).
150 Barry Naughton, *State Capitalism, Institutional Adaptation, and the Chinese Miracle* (Cambridge University Press 2015).

151 Joerg Wuttke, "Vetting China's State-Directed Investments", *Wall Street Journal*, 6 March 2017, *available at* www.wsj.com/articles/vetting-chinas-state-directed-invest ments-1488822328 (last visited 5 September 2020).
152 Luyao Che, *China's State-Directed Economy and the International Order* (Springer 2019) (exploring the legal underpinnings of the state–market economic model and its challenge to the international economic order).

4

INTELLECTUAL PROPERTY PROTECTION IN DOMESTIC AND BILATERAL CONTEXTS

1. Introduction

The United States and China, the two largest economies in the world, have been locked in a bitter trade battle since early 2018. The US has long accused China of unfair trade practices and intellectual property theft[1] while China views this as the US' efforts to curb its rise as a global economic power. Although the Economic and Trade Agreement between the United States of America and the People's Republic of China (Phase One) (hereinafter the "Phase One Agreement") that has been concluded in January 2020 offers a symbolic truce, it leaves many important questions unanswered. Compliance uncertainty is accompanied by deteriorating economic relationships between the two countries during the COVID-19 pandemic.

While it is tempting to focus on the texts of the Phase One Agreement alone, doing so could ignore the much more important role of the legal interactions between the US and China in a transnational legal setting. It would overlook the fact that, by importing and reconstructing American legal norms, China made various changes during and after the Trade War. It would also fail to consider China's series of promises to carry on structural reforms in its legal and regulatory regime, promises aimed at addressing numerous long-standing concerns raised by the Trump administration, US industrial sectors, and business communities. These concerns included raising its domestic intellectual property rights ("IPR") protection standards, increasing transparency of foreign investment regulations, opening up more industrial sectors such as banking,[2] credit rating,[3] and electronic payment services,[4] and taking more effective enforcement actions against counterfeit pharmaceuticals and related products.[5] Nevertheless, the Phase One Agreement is not a zero-sum game to China. Characterizing China's concessions as due solely to economic and diplomatic pressures from the US is oversimplification, undermining the dynamics and complexities of a transnational legal process.

DOI: 10.4324/9781003130499-4

This chapter seeks to conceptualize the current US–China trade tension by providing an alternative narrative with a focus on IPR standards. Most scholars see the Phase One Agreement as weak and as non-binding on either party. In fact, it was already in partial breach due to the escalation of US–China diplomatic tension and an ongoing pandemic.[6] Despite this, we believe that it has paved the way for further US–China trade and investment talks, possibly leading to a conclusion of a US–China BIT or a separate IPR chapter of a minilateral Free Trade Agreement ("FTA"). It does demonstrate the strength of bilateralism (in the form of bilateral negotiations and bilateral agreement) within a WTO-centric multilateral trade framework. Through the most-favoured-nation ("MFN") treatment provided under Article 4 of the Agreement on Trade-Related Aspects of Intellectual Property Rights ("TRIPS"), this framework will strengthen China's commitment to its other trading partners that are members of the WTO, such as EU member states and Australia. Although this driving force was surely not contemplated by WTO framers, it has provided a partial solution to the current deadlock caused by the US' shift to unilateralism and the deadlock of WTO reform. Against the backdrop of anti-globalization and rising populism,[7] bilateralism effectively induced China's behavioural changes without multilevel intervention, but it still operates within limits, since China will implement changes and make adjustments based on its own interests. Fortunately, with China's concession, it might be easier for advocates of multilateralism to pull trading partners back to renegotiate within the WTO framework.

The chapter will proceed as follows. Section 2 will provide a thorough review of unilateral trade warfare conducted by the US to exert pressures on China. It will briefly discuss the legality of US approaches within the international legal framework. Section 3 will provide a thorough analysis of IPR chapters (Chapters 1 and 2) in the Phase One Agreement, with references to China's aftermath changes to domestic law to achieve timely compliance. Section 4 will provide an overview of US continuous demands of a TRIPS-plus standard in its IPR-related trade policy making. It will show that bilateralism is central to US IPR treaty making almost as early as the conclusion of TRIPS. Then it will discuss in detail how China has started to implement terms of the Phase One Agreement by rapidly upgrading its domestic laws. Considering the effectiveness of the US' bilateral approach to China's IPR regime, Section 5 will further assess US–China IP bilateralism and its implications regarding transnational legal ordering and the multilateralist trade regime. The latter seeks ways to maintain a proper balance between preservation of policy space and regulation of protectionist measures, an approach better-aligned with the WTO framework.

2. IPR-Related Tactics During Trade War

As China's early economic development relied on the mass production of cheap goods based on foreign prototypes, creating and enforcing a strict IPR regime was not desirable for its manufacturing industry.[8] Along with China's economic development of greater reliance on IP-intensive industries, the Chinese government is openly seeking to become competitive in a range of advanced technologies and industries in accordance with some industrial policies, the latest and most well-known being Made in China 2025.[9]

At the heart of China's industrial policy lies a vaguely defined "forced technology transfer" policy. Such a policy can take different shapes. Generally, it is for the benefit of Chinese innovation industries as manufacturers gain access to advanced Western technologies. The type of government measures that enable such a policy may range from direct acts of economic espionage to domestic laws requiring foreign firms to disclose certain technologies in exchange for access to the Chinese market.[10] In particular, forced technology transfer is a practice harshly criticized by the US administration as unfairly infringing upon the rights of American IPR holders.[11]

At the early stage of economic reform starting from 1978, China took a strategy known as "market-for-technology" to absorb foreign technology in order to speed up China's technological development in pillar industries such as the automobile industry. The notion underscoring this strategy was China's huge market in exchange for much-needed technologies from foreign investors who wanted to obtain market access to some industrial sectors not yet opened to them.[12] Under this strategy, it was believed that foreign investors were allowed to form joint ventures in some strategically important but legally restricted sectors with Chinese state-owned enterprises on the condition of technology sharing.[13,14]

When the EJV Law was promulgated in 1979, it was mandated that the technology and equipment contributed by foreign investors must be really advanced technology and equipment that suit China's needs.[15] In 1983, the State Council adopted the Regulations for the Implementation of the EJV Law, according to which a joint venture must meet one or more of the following requirements: (i) it employs advanced technology and equipment; (ii) it provides benefits of technical innovation; (iii) it enables to expand exports of the produced products; and (iv) it provides for the training of technical and operation management personnel.[16,17]

In addition, according to Article 27 of the 2001 State Council's Regulations for the Administration of the Technology Import and Export (RATIE), during the term of technology import contract, the results of improvement to the imported technology belong to the party making the improvement.[18] This provision appears detrimental to foreign parties as Chinese parties own improvements they make to technology involved in research and development of foreign-owned technologies.[19,20]

Commercial theft or stealing of intellectual property is a quite common phenomenon in the arena of international business transactions. However, it has been deemed as a massive threat to the US economy. China is categorically labelled as the primary culprit.[21] According to US federal law enforcement officials, China "relies on an army of domestic computer hackers, traditional spies overseas and corrupt corporate insiders in U.S. and other companies."[22] It is also claimed that "Chinese thefts of U.S. commercial software and technology are relentless, growing and hitting on multiple fronts-with hackers penetrating corporate and government email and digital networks, and Chinese operatives recruiting U.S. executives and engineers to spill juicy secrets."[23]

The previously mentioned strategy and relevant provisions have been criticized as forced technology transfer or FTT – an infamous practice in which the domestic government forces foreign businesses to share their technology with the domestic counterparts in exchange for market access.[24] Despite China's strong denial of any such practice in the country,[25] the complaints from foreign companies were widely spreading. In 2018, the EU took a WTO action against China on the FTT. A report in 2019 revealed that one-fifth of EU companies operating in China said they were compelled to transfer technology to maintain access to the Chinese market.[26] The FTT issue was also on the top list of US–China trade negotiations in 2019.[27,28]

Since 1978, the incoming FDI has promoted remarkable economic growth and social development over the past four decades by creating new business opportunities; introducing advanced technologies and managerial skills; promoting legal, social, and other reforms; intensifying competition; and enhancing efficiency and competitiveness of domestic industries. Statistics have indicated the significant role of foreign investment in China's economic and social development.[29] For instance at least 40% of China's total import and export value and an average of about 18% of national tax revenue are contributed by foreign-invested enterprises each year.[30] To continue such rapid growth while improving the quality of its development, China has set various development goals closely related to the proper utilization of inward foreign investment. These goals are (i) building technological capacity, (ii) deepening integration into the global economy, (iii) promoting green development, (iv) protecting public security, and (v) participating in global economic governance and rulemaking.[31] These economic development goals somehow shaped China's FDI and IP polices.

In the past decade, US federal agencies, including the United States Trade Representative ("USTR") and the International Trade Commission, have conducted extensive investigations into such matters. Many of their policy briefs have pointed out the prevalence of unfair trade practices occurring in China, mostly in a state-sponsored manner.[32] On 18 August 2017, the USTR initiated an investigation under Section 301 of the Trade Act of 1974 against China's practices. Based on the results of this investigation, President Trump ordered that China be put on USTR's Special 301 "Priority Watch List." On 3 April 2018, the USTR released a list of Chinese products that would be subject to an additional *ad valorem* tariff. This action provoked the US–China Trade War based on retaliatory tariffs without explicit authorization from the WTO. On 5 September 2020, a WTO panel ruled that tariffs unilaterally imposed by the US violated the General Agreement on Tariffs and Trade (GATT).[33]

Also at the core of Special 301 sanctions is the Specially Designated Nationals and Blocked Persons List ("SDN") maintained by the Office of Foreign Asset

Control.[34] Using Chinese corporations as proxies of the Chinese state, some of these actions provide tactical support for the government's tariff measures, doubling or tripling Chinese corporations' costs of doing business in the US.[35] Huawei, China's 5G telecom industry worldwide giant, is a primary target of the wide-reaching Trade War. In 2012, the US had already banned domestic companies from using Huawei equipment.[36] The Department of Commerce issued a Final Rule in May 2019, adding Huawei Technologies Co. Ltd. (Huawei) and its 68 non-US affiliates to the Bureau of Industry and Security ("BIS") "Entity List." This cut off Huawei from the supply chain, making it unable to acquire US-originated hardware, software, and technology directly or indirectly. As an aftermath of the Trade War, the list has been further expanded to include more Huawei affiliates and subsidiaries across the world.

In addition to putting a ban on Huawei and its affiliates for engaging in any form of business relationship with US entities without securing a special export licence from the EAR, the US has requested the extradition of Huawei's Chief Financial Officer, Wanzhou Meng. Ms Meng is charged with bank fraud and violation of the US sanctions on Iran.[37] In July 2019, the US imposed a sanction measure on two Chinese executives of Zhuhai Zhenrong company, prohibiting them from conducting financial activities through any institution of the US, including foreign currency exchange. These actions are highly unusual, as these prosecutions are often issued against foreign corporations rather than on corporate executives, and have led to criticisms of the Trump administration both in the public media and in scholarly communities. These actions have also caused panic among Chinese business executives who fear the dire consequence of isolation from access to US capital markets.

The Trade War was largely motivated by technology competition, unilateral sanctions, extraterritorial corporate regulations, and cross-border legal enforcement. These issues became major weapons the American government utilized to exert additional economic burdens and compliance costs on the Chinese government and Chinese entities. The result was the creation of functional pressures and political incentives that have a profound impact on the domestic laws of China.

In the US–China trade war that began in early 2018, the US has accused China of forcibly requiring foreign investors to transfer advanced technology according to some FDI laws and other laws.[38] China adopted two paths countering the US' complaints. First, to avoid the misinterpretation, the related articles in some laws on foreign investment have been removed during the legislative process of the FIL.[39]

The FIL explicitly prohibits government authorities and their staff from "using administrative means to force the transfer of technology."[40] The reference to "forced technology transfer" is the first in Chinese legislation. It can be viewed as a gesture of compromise in the trade war, considering that Beijing has never admitted the existence of the problem.[41] According to Article 22 of the FIL, the State encourages technical cooperation based on the principle of voluntariness and commercial norms in the process of foreign investment.[42] To implement Article 22 of the FIL and Article 24 of the Implementation Regulations further prohibits any administrative agency, including an organization authorized by law or regulations to administer public matters, and their staff from compelling directly or in a disguised form a foreign investor or an FIE to transfer technology through administrative licensing, inspection, penalty, coercion, or other administrative means.[43]

The FIL promises to strengthen their protection, through intensifying the punishment of infringement, reinforcing the enforcement of pertinent laws, and establishing diversified mechanisms for the resolution of disputes over IPRs.[44] Moreover, government authorities are prohibited from divulging trade secrets to which they have had access while performing their duties.[45] These rules – at least on their surface – address the widespread concerns over forced technology transfer and the leak of sensitive commercial information[46] and thus encourage more investment flows – especially those from technology companies.[47] The ban imposed under Article 22 of the FIL on the FTT is limited to the administrative measures and applicable to administrative agencies and their staff.

However, concerns from foreign businesses remain. Some expressed concerns about the effectiveness of Article 22 because they believed that the FTT is not an issue of statute but a matter of practice.[48] Others viewed Article 22's focus on administrative methods as an implication that government officials may still be free to use other tactics to pressure companies to hand over know-how.[49] Article 22 also clarifies that administrative agencies and their staff members may not use administrative means to force the transfer of technology.[50] This is couched in very high-level and vague terms, and it takes time to see whether it will be effective to tackle this widespread issue.[51] The criticism is that Article 22 may deter lower-level members of the bureaucracy, but it may not change anything substantial on the ground.[52]

Article 22 (of FIL) stipulates that the State protects the intellectual property of foreign investors and FIEs, as well as legitimate rights and interests in intellectual property and other relevant obligations. Under that same article, any intellectual property infringement will be investigated for legal liability, and the State will encourage technical cooperation in the process of foreign investment on the basis of free will and business rules. It also provides that conditions for cooperation between Chinese and foreign investors concerning technology shall be negotiated by following the principle of fairness for all investment parties. Principles of voluntariness and commerce established by the FIL provide a flexible space for cross-border technology licensing and transfer arrangements. Foreign investors as licensors also will have more avenues to protect their technology, which should help ease the concerns of foreign investors.[53]

Capital contributions to an LLC can be made in-kind but the cash contribution must not be less than 30% of the total registered capital of a company. Accordingly, equity interest can be one kind of contributable asset. Previously, opposite to the current approach, there was no minimum cash contribution but a 20% cap on the value of industrial property rights and non-patented technology (35% in the case of capitalization of technology in an "advanced technology entity" with the aim of attracting more high-technology investment). This 70%

cap on "non-cash assets which can be monetarily valued and legally transferred" once offers more flexibility to shareholders who plan to contribute capital in kind. It remains to be seen how these rules will affect the approval process of FIEs.

The Company Law 2013 no longer requires that at least 30% of the registered capital of a limited liability company be contributed in cash. This means that (i) shareholders of a company can decide the ratio between cash and other assets in their initial capital contribution; and (ii) it will be legally permissible to establish a company without cash contribution after 1 March 2014. Nevertheless, investors are still required to evaluate the non-monetary assets and determine the contribution amount accordingly.

Capital in kind contributed to the company limited by shares or LLC can also be in form of land-use rights, machinery, equipment, and other moveable or immoveable properties.

According to the Company Law 2013, where a promoter contributes the capital by non-monetary properties, he or she shall go through the formalities for the transfer of his or her rights in those properties to the company according to law. The Company Law, however, offers little guidance concerning legal formalities.

Previously, under the Company Law 1995, only five kinds of assets may be contributed to the registered capital of a company limited by shares or LLC, that is cash, tangible assets, industrial property rights, non-patented technology, and land-use rights. For other kinds of property-related rights such as equity interest, receivables, or copyright, government practice varies from one place to the other. The Company Law 2005 provides a clear-cut rule on the available contribution methods by allowing contribution of any non-cash asset which can be monetarily valued and legally transferred and which covers tangible and non-tangible assets. The Company Law 2013 specifically uses the concept of "intellectual property" as a contributable asset, in lieu of the "industrial property rights and non-patented technology," which means that intellectual property such as copyrights will now be allowed to be contributed under the Company Law.

Labour, credit, goodwill, franchising rights, and secured assets are still prohibited from being contributed as capital under Chinese law.[54]

The Company Law 2005 is silent on the permissibility of human capital contributions. The Regulations on the Administration of Company Registration 2005 forbid the contribution of labour services.[55] Some local courts such as the Shanghai Higher People's Court forced the Shanghai legislature to issue the Pudong New District Provisional Measures on Human Capital Contributions, which set forth two legal mechanisms for the valuation of human capital contributions, one being evaluated by a third-party certified appraiser or agreed upon by the entire shareholders' meeting. Local courts have been cautious about very obvious defects in human capitalization.

The Company Law is still highly conceptual and declaratory and fails to provide standards and procedures for non-cash contribution. There remains a controversial issue under Chinese law as to how to determine whether a non-cash capital contribution obligation has been duly performed.

The Supreme People's Court on 16 February 2011 issued the Provisions Regarding Certain Issues Concerning the Application of the Company Law (III), which provides clarification of various widely disputed issues in practice, including equity contribution and verification of equity interests.

It is clarified in the Judicial Interpretations III that, as to certain kinds of non-cash property which are subject to registration requirement for transfer of ownership, the completion of ownership change registration and actual delivery of such property are both required for equity contribution.

If the properties have been delivered to the company for use but the formalities of title transfer have not been completed, the court may order the contributor to transfer titles to the company within a specified period of time. The contributor will be deemed by the court to have fulfilled its capital contribution obligation from the time when the properties are actually delivered to the company for use if the titles are transferred within the specified period.[56]

Where a capital contributor makes a non-cash capital contribution and has transferred titles but failed to actually deliver it to the company for use, if the company or any other shareholder claims the capital contributor should deliver the property to the company and should not enjoy the corresponding shareholders' rights prior to the actual delivery, the court should support such a claim.

On 2 March 2019, the State Council issued a decree to amend, among others, the Regulations for the Administration of the Technology Import and Export.[57] An important item in the amendment is to delete the controversial Article 27 which used to give the Chinese partner the statutory right to improve and own technology licensed from foreign partners as a condition to technology import. The deletion of this controversial requirement is to help optimize the environment for foreign technology transfer in the country.[58,59] However, the abolition did not expressly apply to certain interpretations of the PRC Contract Law by the Supreme People's Court, which may continue to have a similar practical effect on technology sharing agreements governed by PRC law.[60]

These provisions on intellectual property rights protection in the FIL and its Implementation Regulations are a direct response to the US–China trade war, where the US has been accusing China of theft on intellectual property rights. The ban on the FTT is indeed also an effort China made to address the fear of foreign companies doing business in China. The FIL and its underlying IP policy will play a positive role in encouraging a more innovative environment.[61]

The FIL-makers appear too eager to please foreign investors and stretch to address issues not properly included in an FDI law. The protection of intellectual property rights is a good example. FIL explicitly prohibits government officials to force intellectual property transfers or to reveal foreign investors' business secrets acquired in exercising their authority to any third party. However, this issue might be better addressed through amending the intellectual property law and related mechanisms. On this sense, FIL is used by the Chinese government to relieve the concerns expressed by the US government in the trade war. In the 2015 Draft FIL, there was no mention of forced technology transfer through administrative measures and a one-sentence reference to the "protection of intellectual property of foreign investors and foreign-invested enterprises in accordance with the law."[62] Both issues were specifically addressed in Article 22 of the FIL.[63] Even the much-publicized restriction on forced technology transfer was considered more form than substance. "The identification of 'forced' is very ambiguous, and there are many ways for Chinese government to do forced technology transfer even after the law is passed."[64]

Facing the mounting criticism on the commercial theft, China, on the one hand, denied all charges, and, on the other hand, has to take certain measures to cope with this matter. Reflected in the FIL are the provisions that tend to prevent commercial theft. Chapter III of the FIL strengthens the constraints on the formulation of normative documents concerning foreign investment.[65] The FIL states that administrative organs and their staff members shall keep confidential the business secrets of foreign investors and foreign-invested enterprises they receive in the course of performing their duties and shall not disclose or illegally provide them to others.[66] The government at all levels and their relevant departments shall comply with the provisions of laws and regulations in formulating normative documents concerning foreign investment. Unless authorized by laws and administrative regulations, they shall not derogate from the legitimate rights and interests of foreign-invested enterprises or increase their obligations; set forth conditions for market access and exit; and interfere with normal production and operation of foreign-invested enterprises.[67,68]

Specifically, there are three articles in the FIL that have the function of anti-commercial theft. The first one is Article 22. In addition to its ban on the FTT, Article 22 of the FIL is also considered a bar on Chinese JV partners from stealing IP and commercial secrets from their foreign counterparts.[69] Since Article 22 is a general provision of IP protections, it remains questionable whether Article 22 may effectively resolve the commercial theft problem with regard to Chinese JV partners.

The second article that prohibits government officials from disclosing business secrets is Article 23. Under Article 23, the administrative agencies and their staff shall keep confidential the business secrets of foreign investors and foreign-invested enterprises known to them during the performance of their duties and shall not disclose or illegally provide these business secrets to others.[70] Article 23 seems quite specific on the protection of commercial secrets, but once again like the ban on the FTT in Article 22, it has a focus on the administrative conducts and applies only to the government organs and their staff. There is a similar provision in the Implementation Regulations. According to Article 25 of the Implementation Regulations, where there is a need for an administrative agency to request a foreign investor or an FIE for materials or information involving trade secrets, the materials or information so provided shall be constrained within the scope necessary for the administrative agency to perform its duty, and the access to the materials or information should be strictly restricted and any relevant to performing such duty shall not have access to the said materials or information. In addition, Article 25 requires all administrative agencies to establish and improve an internal administration system and adopt effective measures to protect the foreign investors or FIEs' trade secrets obtained during performing of their duties.[71]

The third article is Article 39, which provides statutory assurance for the application of Articles 22 and 23 of the FIL. According to Article 39, if staff of an administrative agency abuses his or her power; neglects his or her duty or engages in malpractice in the promotion protection, or management of foreign investment; or leaks or illegally provides others with trade secrets known to him or her during the course of performance of his or her duties, the staff will be punished under the law.[72] Article 39 also makes the administrative staff criminally liable if a crime is found to be committed in this regard.[73]

The FIL includes other important provisions that will give better protection for foreign investors and their subsidiaries in China, including technology cooperation shall be conducted on the basis of fairness, equity, free will, and progressive business practices. The FIL confirms that China will establish a compliance mechanism to promptly address the issues raised by FIEs and their foreign investors. When FIEs and their foreign investors consider that their legal rights have been infringed by governmental authorities or their officials, FIEs and their foreign investors may apply for administrative review or initiate legal actions in courts, in addition to lodging complaints via the compliance mechanism.[74]

As a legislative response to the concerns of foreign investors, the FIL contains a special chapter consisting of eight articles for investment protection. Attempting to improve the country's environment for foreign investment, the FIL set forth several rules that not only provide protection of foreign investors' legitimate rights and interests but also impose restrictions on the government at both central and local levels. These rules constitute the statutory basis to safeguard foreign investors and their investment from being harmed.[75]

Regarding improving the protection of IP rights, China has emphasized – as much for its internal development as to placate overseas rights holders – on improving the rights of IP holders as well as the enforcement of such rights.[76] There are enhanced remedies for IP infringement. The high-level sentiments in the FIL have been implemented in an amendment to the PRC Trademark Law and the PRC Patent Law that both included arising punitive damages for malicious trademark infringement from three times to five times the actual losses and raising the cap on statutory damages from RMB 3 million to RMB 5 million. The actual force of these provisions will need to be tested in court and in commercial negotiations between foreign investors and Chinese parties in the coming years.[77]

Ultimately, along with its domestic legal reform, in January 2020, China entered into a symbolic truce with the US by immediately concluding the Phase One Agreement. The Phase One Agreement has internalized and consolidated most of the US demands in the arena of IPRs. It offers a valuable case study to understand the dynamic process of cross-border IPR rulemaking.

3. Reinforced Bilateralism: A Critical Assessment of the Phase One Agreement's IPR Chapters

As Alan Sykes noted, the Phase One Agreement resembles less a bilateral treaty than a one-way deal because it has unevenly imposed duties mostly on China.[78] This section provides a brief recap of major provisions concerning intellectual property and technology transfer in the Phase One Agreement, collectively called IPR chapters in this chapter. In general, these IPR chapters cover broad issues related to trade secrets, such as patents, IP enforcement, e-commerce, geographical indications, trademarks, copyright, and related rights, that are contentious between the US and China. Of particular interest are three interconnected aspects: (i) non-incorporating of existing international standards; (ii) enforcing uniquely US norms, and (iii) an inadequate dispute settlement system.

3.1 Departure From International Standards

A shift to unilateralism by the US, especially with respect to China, seems a sensible and final aspect of the Phase One Agreement with the aim of realizing some of its policy priorities to change China's behaviour. Compared with the recent US Free Trade Agreement with Mexico and Canada (the United States-Mexico-Canada Free Trade Agreement, or "USMCA"), as well as the earlier version of the Trans-Pacific Partnership Agreement (the "TPP"), it is quite surprising that the Phase One Agreement has not a single reference to international IPR treaties such as the Berne Convention, the Paris Convention, or the TRIPS. Moreover, none of these IPR provisions have borrowed the language of TRIPS or international IPR agreements in general, including their flexibilities, exceptions, or limitations, all of which carve out necessary regulatory space. The lack of references to multilateral commitments comes as an additional surprise, taking into account scholarly views that China could take a more assertive role at the WTO, whereas there is no mention of such in the Phase One Agreement at all. The lack of multilateral IP agreements seems to justify a bilateral effort made by the US and China to reach a deal quickly.

3.2 Enforcement of US Norms

Instead, IPR chapters of the Phase One Agreement are mainly driven by the US interest in making China compliant with the substantial and procedural norms of US IP law. Therefore, various US standards were further defined, elaborated on, and incorporated into those provisions.

Trade secrets are a particular concern of US investors investing in China and a key claim against China in pre-Trade War USTR Special 301 Reports. There is no prevailing multinational framework on trade secret protection, and China does not have a trade secret law per se. In the US, cybersecurity devices and physical protective measures are generally seen as part of the trade secret protection regime, keeping technology out of the hands of competitors.[79] The Obama administration launched strategies for mitigating the theft of US trade secrets, which saw Chinese cyber intrusion and cyber-attacks as threats.[80] Outside cyber areas, traditional trade secret remedies are enforced through Section 337 of the Tariff Act of 1930, which mainly relies on private enforcement and has gained extraterritorial power.[81]

Trade secrets occupy the Phase One Agreement's first section, signifying its primary importance in the Agreement. Under Section B, "trade secret" is broadly defined as including all "confidential business information," which can touch upon almost anything of commercial value.[82] Acts concerning trade secret misappropriation have been prohibited, regardless of whether they are electronic intrusion, breach, or inducement of breach of a duty of confidence, or unauthorized disclosure after acquiring a trade secret.[83] These are all made in accordance with US legal constructs.

The same trend can be found in copyright protections (Section E). Section E does not only aim to reduce piracy and counterfeiting by providing enforcement against e-commerce platforms but is simultaneously interested in "reducing barriers, if any, to making legitimate content available in a timely manner to consumers and eligible for copyright protection."[84] Unlike any existing WTO obligations, the measures that China should take to reduce online infringement include "notice and takedown" in a similar spirit as the U.S. Digital Millennium Copyright Act.[85] China commits to require "expeditious takedowns" and "eliminate liability for takedown notices submitted in good faith," among others.[86] Similar provisions can be found in the push for US-style civil and criminal enforcement measures, as seen in the Transfer from Administrative Enforcement to Criminal Enforcement of Judgment (Art. 1.26), Deterrent-level Penalties (Art. 1.27), Burden Shifting in Civil Proceedings (Art. 1.5), and Early Resolution of Patent Disputes in pharmaceutical-related intellectual property (Art. 1.11),[87] which all contain distinctive US law standards and are difficult to be transposed onto existing Chinese laws bluntly.

3.3 Ineffective Dispute Resolution Mechanism

Unfortunately, the Dispute Resolution chapter of the Phase One Agreement, primarily aiming to facilitate the implementation of such normative changes in China, has been criticized as weak, ineffective, and non-reciprocal.[88] These dispute resolution provisions are placed to allow the US to monitor the Chinese government's compliance with the Phase One Agreement, and, as a result, are favourable only to the US.

According to Chapter 7 (Bilateral Evaluation and Dispute Resolution), a Trade Framework Group will be created to monitor and discuss implementation of related issues, and a Bilateral Evaluation and Dispute Resolution Office for each Party will be established to facilitate a dispute resolution mechanism via consultation.[89] When consultation fails, the Parties will take the issues back into their own hands.[90] Scholars remain suspicious towards the true monitoring effect of such an ADR-style dispute resolution mechanism with neither an independent adjudication body nor an appeals mechanism, which suggests the difficulty of having an enforcement scheme in a bilateral context.[91] The mechanism itself involves coercion, in the sense that political pressures are constantly required to ensure China's compliance. Such enforcement mechanism is not only hard to implement but may be viewed as lacking international law legitimacy because it is one-sided in favour of US unilateralism. When US force intensifies, the mechanism easily transfers to trade sanctions under Section 301, which defeats the purposes of the Phase One Agreement; when US influence in international affairs dwindles, it opens up the possibility of a Chinese backlash.

4. Efficacy of a Bilateral Approach to Inefficiencies of China's IPR Framework

4.1 Regionalism and Bilateralism in US-led IPR-Treaty Making

Trade and economic matters are at the heart of US engagement with international law.[92] However, as the US gained its sole superpower status in the 1990s, its attitude towards international law became much more mixed.[93] Even though US efforts were central to reforming the GATT and establishing the WTO, it developed a skeptical attitude towards the TRIPS soon after its adoption.[94] Unlike many other areas in trade, there has not been an overly satisfactory cross-border IPR regulatory scheme within the TRIPS framework.[95] It only imposes an obligation on WTO members to maintain a minimum level of protection and enforcement of IPRs. The US skepticism of TRIPS was soon shown in its decision to not dismantle its domestic trade-related tools to seek higher standards of IPR through unilateral pressures. Congress enacted Special 301 as part of the 1988 amendments to the Trade Act of 1974, establishing a mechanism under which foreign countries might be placed on a special priority IP violators list for non-TRIPS compliant behaviours. Special 301 authorized the USTR to investigate countries with weak IP protection and subject them to accelerated sanctions.[96] Between the 1970s and 1990s, the US deployed Special 301 against more than a dozen countries.[97]

Furthermore, the US maintains that Section 337 of the Tariff Act 1930 intended to prevent the importation of goods that would infringe upon patents enforced in the US.[98] Until today, Section 337 continues to be actively used by holders of US patents in various industry sectors as a means to prevent entry of infringing goods into US commerce.[99] The trend has been intensified due to the 2011 decision of the U.S. Court of Appeals for the Federal Circuit in *TianRui Group Co. Ltd. v. International Trade*, which expanded the applicable scope of Section 337 to misappropriation of trade secrets committed overseas.[100]

The US has been very active in pushing TRIPS-plus standards in bilateral and regional FTAs.[101] In its bilateral trade template, the US seeks to fill a number of gaps left open in the TRIPS.[102] Still, Brazil, India, and other major emerging countries have been unwilling to enter into bilateral negotiations with the US because doing so would mean acceptance of TRIPS-plus IPR standards that harm their young innovation industries. The US has also pursued pluralist agreements in the form of Anti-Counterfeiting Trade Agreement ("ACTA") and the TPP. The TPP negotiations included many of the US' substantial efforts seeking TRIPS-plus standards, as well as its attempts to ring-fence China. After the Trump administration's abrupt withdrawal from the TPP, some limited successes lie in "gold standards" of IPR protection in the EU–US FTA negotiations, although there has been very limited concrete discussion about what such gold standards might entail. The USMCA represents improved IPR standards more in line with the current US expectations in its trade treaties. It includes, in part, extensive provisions of trade secret protections, extension of patent and copyright terms, IPR protections in digital environment, stronger regulatory enforcement, and international coordination.[103] Nonetheless, in accordance with Article 4 of the TRIPS, whatever IP "benefits" or "concessions" are conferred on the parties to the Agreement, these must be extended on an MFN (most favoured nation) basis to other US trading partners. In this sense, the US seems to have strategically opted for bilateralism, pluralism, and minilateralism as its IPR-related treaty-making strategy to support US industries in its relentless campaign to increase the IPR standards worldwide.

4.2 Failure of Restraining China's "Unfair Competition"

Apart from the US' continuous pursuit of implementing TRIPS-plus standards widely, there is a strong political current in the US supporting protection against what is portrayed as "unfair competition" from abroad, particularly from China. The Chinese government's interest in building up its national technological infrastructure is self-evident, and the government's capability of shifting supply of labour, finance, and other resources into certain prioritized industries is unparalleled. In early years, China's economic development relied more on the mass production of cheap goods based on foreign imported technology and management know-how, and creating a strict IPR enforcement regime was less desirable. Gradually, as China's economy started to host a higher-portion of technology-intensive industries, domestic demand for stronger IPR protection increased.[104] These bottom-up efforts were met with top-down efforts that focused on developing "indigenous IP," which created new incentives of IPR regime development. The Chinese model of governmental aggregation of capital seems to neutralize to a certain extent the historical investment-related technological advantages held by the US. Made in China 2025 is rather successful, and international patent databases confirm China's status of being a technological power.[105] Additionally, new legal institutions were built. Since 2014, specialized IP courts were established in Beijing, Shanghai, and Guangzhou, and they have witnessed an update in number of litigations.[106]

At the heart of the US–China contention is the issue of forced technology transfer, which has longer historical roots. There is no universal definition of forced technology transfer, but many investors claim that China's industrial policy allows mandatory technology transfer as a condition to market entry into China's restrictive but highly lucrative industries, such as the telecommunications and financial sectors, before and even after it joined the WTO.[107] Despite this, for a long period of time there was no national government policy in the US restraining US-based businesses from transferring their valuable technologies to China.[108]

Back in 2001, China's WTO accession prompted a major revamp in China's foreign investment and innovation laws and policies. As a result of US pressures, China committed itself to implementing the TRIPS obligations immediately upon succession, with no transition period. The TRIPS Agreement itself, though, is silent on the issue of mandatory technology transfer. Therefore, beyond the generally applicable GATT, GATS, and TRIPS obligations, China made a special WTO commitment not to condition the approval of foreign investment on "the transfer of technology" or "the conduct of research and development in China."[109]

Nonetheless, removing the "market-for-technology" type of requirements from the rulebook is not the same as the elimination of such requirements in practice.[110] Actually, the old policy can still be easily implemented, often through three routes. First of all, Chinese officials require the transfer of technology as a prerequisite to regulatory approval or access to the Chinese market. This is linked to the Foreign Investment Industrial Catalogue used in China for almost two decades to guide foreign direct investment in China according to the government's planning, under which foreign investment remains subject to equity restrictions and specific government approvals.[111] To gain approval to enter into the Chinese market, foreign investors often need to enter into some form of joint venture with local companies, during which process technology may be transferred. Second, Chinese officials often require submission of excessive confidential business information for regulatory approval purposes, and, in some cases, submissions of such information are unnecessary and not related to the approval process.[112] Third, cyber-intrusions, cyber-attacks, or other unauthorized activities result in technology theft. The US has claimed that some of these activities are state-sponsored. These practices were neither covered by China's TRIPS obligations nor specifically applied by the Protocol of Accession. In the following decades, forced technology transfer gained notoriety and has become the core contention between China and Western industrialized nations.[113]

4.3 Implementation of Phase One Obligations

During the Trade War, China kept denying claims made by the US and other developed states against it based on alleged unfair trade practices. In complying with its Phase One Agreement obligations, China has agreed to deploy a defensive strategy to satisfy the US' demands by selectively importing legal principles from American law, such as damages for wilful infringement, shifted burden proof, and abolition of forced technology transfer. Improving its IPR protection system is a strategic choice to frame IPR reforms as a domestic necessity so as to fit into its strong pro-economic development state rhetoric.

Within two years' time, China initiated significant changes in reforming its domestic legal systems by quickly passing the 2019 Foreign Investment Law ("FIL") and amending the existing Patent Law, Trademark Law, and trade secret provisions in the Anti-Unfair Competition Law. China also promised to further amend some of its pharmaceutical patent registration systems and early patent dispute resolution by entering into the Phase One Agreement.[114] This section offers an in-depth review of how China has implemented and internalized the Phase One Agreement obligations by speedily updating its domestic legislation in its general IPR regime, and by banning forced technology transfer and improving civil and criminal infringement enforcement.

4.3.1 General Duties

Pressured by the US, several quick legal changes of IP laws took place in China during and shortly after the Trade War. A few significant first changes were made in trade secret areas. Trade secrets made to Article I of the Phase One Agreement signify its core importance during the US–China economic standoff. China did not have a clear legal framework for protecting trade secrets as a form of IPR until very recently. Rather, it borrowed trade secret protection rules from other civil law countries, in which private remedies sought for stolen confidential business information could only be requested by direct business competitors in tort law.[115]

On 23 April 2019, the Standing Committee of the National People's Congress (the "Standing Committee") passed amendments to PRC Trademark Law and the PRC Anti-Unfair Competition Law ("AUCL"). The amendments to the Trademark Law mainly target curbing and increasing damages assessed against bad-faith application and registration in China, or alleged counterfeit products.[116] The AUCL has been most concerned with trade secret protection, which is relevant to the Trade War because of key findings in the Section 301 Report 2018 on the leakage of trade secrets and confidential business information. These changes have been reflected in the PRC Civil Code promulgated in 2020.[117] In addition to general trade secret provisions, Article 1 prohibits acts concerning trade secret misappropriation including "electronic intrusions," "breach or inducement to breach a duty of confidence," and "unauthorized disclosure after acquiring a trade secret" (Article 1.4). These are likely dealt with in China's series of revised statutes in digital security areas, which have already been included in the 2020 legislative plans of the Standing Committee.[118]

In other areas of IPR, on 25 June 2019, the amendments to the Patent Law were passed after its second read. The amended Patent Law will become effective in June 2021. A revised draft of the Copyright Law was released for public consultation in April 2020 on schedule, a few months after the Phase One Agreement was closed. Most changed provisions found in proposed amendments to the Patent Law and Copyright Law turned on revisions in civil and criminal enforcement and will be analyzed in detail in Section 4.3.3.

Requirements and demands of the US were fixed into the Phase One Agreement only to ensure that China deals with existing problems, such as Early Resolution for Pharmaceutical Patents[119] and counterfeit medicines.[120] Nonetheless, China remains reluctant to increase IPR protection standards for pharmaceuticals notwithstanding its relatively fast advancement in selected areas of biotechnology. This shows that the economic coercion of the US has its limits. At the same time, it points out China's challenge: how to incorporate selected foreign norms based on its need to justify its actions and policy choices on the global stage, meanwhile carefully balancing the party-state's political will, governmentality, and institutional capacity.

4.3.2 Forced Technology Transfer

Technology transfer occupied one chapter in the Phase One Agreement, but the issue itself was dealt with a bit earlier than the conclusion of the Phase One Agreement in the newly promulgated FIL. Earlier drafts of the FIL contained no provisions to ban forced technology transfer.[121] One new version of Draft FIL was released in March 2019 in the midst of the Trade War. Contrary to early approaches, it took a full step forward and fully addressed common complaints from the US businesses and government by explicitly banning forced technology transfer, promising better IPR protection, and ensuring equal treatment for foreign firms in government procurement. It is unambiguously stipulated that no government authority can, through administrative means, force technology transfer or disclosure of business secrets by foreign investors to China. This timely movement directly responds to the US allegations that Chinese officials play a secondary role in forced technology transfer and disclosure of trade secrets improperly gained in administrative proceedings.[122] Even so, many foreign investors still doubt whether forced technology transfer will be eliminated even after the enactment of the new FIL. Some of them suspect that China will continue the practice of forced technology transfer via secretive or hidden means other than through administrative procedures.[123] If that happens, it will be more challenging for foreign investors to attack these new schemes, and China may easily use the FIL as *prima facie* evidence proving its official stance against forced technology transfer.

4.3.3 Civil and Criminal Infringement Enforcement

During these sweeping amendments to all major IP laws in China, within one year (which is a very short even in Chinese legislative standards), several common themes emerged. The first is the introduction of punitive damage systems based on wilful infringement. The AUCL provides punitive damages for malicious

TABLE 4.1 Changed Provisions in Chinese IPR Laws

	Trademark Law (April 2019)		Trade Secret (April 2019)		Amendments to Patent Law (December 2019)		Amendments to Copyright Law (Draft) (April 2020)	
	Before	After	Before	After	Before	After	Before	After
Maximum Statutory Damages (yuan)	3 million	5 million	3 million	5 million	1 million	5 million	0.5 million	5 million
Punitive Damages	3 times	5 times	0	5 times	0	5 times	0	5 times

trade secret infringement and increases the cap on civil liability from three million yuan to five million yuan.[124] As to the amended Patent Law, which for the first time introduced punitive damage rules, the increased penalty amount was five times the actual damages. On the copyright end, the increased maximum statutory punitive damage of copyright infringement was set at five million yuan in the proposed amendment, a ten-fold increase from previous statutory maximum, and quintuple damages for wilful and malicious infringement was introduced (summarized in Table 4.1).[125]

The introduction of punitive damage rules was a highlight of the Opinion on Strengthening Intellectual Property Protection passed by the State Council in November 2019, and it is considered an important gesture to incorporate and reinforce the punitive damage system in the US law and especially in China's own patent law. Punitive damages in IP infringement are not commonly seen in civil law jurisdictions, where, under traditional principles, punitive damages are considered a form of punishment that is appropriate only in criminal proceedings and generally prohibited in private actions.[126] The US, on the other hand, has always complained of the insufficiency of China's IPR system when it comes to damages, alleging that China has failed to effectively penalize counterfeiters and other IPR infringers from "damages adequate to compensate for the injury from the infringement" nor to "deter future intellectual property theft or infringements."[127] Amending its laws to increase both statutory maximum and punitive damages is probably among the few options to avoid further coercive tactics from the US.

Another very much acclaimed provision, a shifted burden of proof, is a signature heritage of the US laws and has been described by legal commentators as the most promising change among trade secret legislative developments, since it

> involves shifting the burden of proof in cases where the circumstantial evidence seems strong – such as the development of a similar product in an unusually short time after access to the plaintiff's secrets – and requiring the defendant to prove independent development.[128]

However, to implement such a change in a country with inquisitive courts and civil law style rules is not an obviously optimal choice, and the lack of discussion is quite striking. As somewhat of a compromise, Article 32 of the amended AUCL states that a rights holder who has preliminarily proven that it has taken reasonable confidentiality measures on the claimed trade secrets and has preliminary evidence reasonably demonstrating that its trade secrets have been infringed upon can shift the burden of proof to the infringer to prove that the trade secrets claimed by the rights holder do not belong to those as prescribed in this law.[129] This type of shifted burden of proof with Chinese characteristics revamped existing civil procedural rules, which put the whole weight of proving the case on alleged trade secret holders, a drastically difficult approach based on Chinese judicial practices. It was already suggested by field practitioners that the introduction of such provisions is going to lead to widely diverse interpretations in different regions and levels of Chinese courts, opening for Supreme People's Court interpretative guidelines to fill in the gap.[130]

5. Assessing US–China IP Bilateralism and Implications on the International Economic Governance Order

From the US perspective, one achievement of the Phase One Agreement was the successful imposition of higher IPR standards on Chinese legal systems, promoting the rights of American investors. This bilateral approach may be combined with some multilateral efforts, for example the joining of the EU and Japan to push for further reforms of WTO rules leading to a spillover effect into other arenas.[131] With China yielding to US pressures by incorporating significantly higher IPR standards in its domestic laws, negotiating a newer multilateral TRIPS-plus agreement would be more feasible. Yet the use of a bilateral treaty to engage China has some significant weaknesses. This section provides a critical analysis of the shift towards IPR-bilateralism between the US and China and its short-term and long-term implications on the international trade governance order.

5.1 Costs of Negotiation and Spillover of TRIPS-Plus Standards

The classical rationale for entering into bilateral trade negotiation is bargaining cost.[132] International cooperation suffers, ranging from severe collective action to coordination problems.[133] Modern multilateralist trading schemes have complicated structures, multiple incentive schemes, deliberate rulemaking processes, and low efficiency. Any bargaining process is usually lengthy and involves substantial costs due to each party's attempts to try to obtain the best possible deal on its own favoured terms. Moreover, bargaining breakdowns and deadlocks arise due to either asymmetric information or "incomplete information," causing counterparties to be unable to determine what demands would leave the other party with inadequate returns and induce it to walk away.[134]

Consequently, the hegemony preference of bilateralism in treaty making is easily explicable. Bilateral negotiations are far more likely to be influenced or even manipulated by the stronger party than by multilateral ones. In addition, the bilateral form is more receptive to exceptional rules for powerful states. Because of more direct reciprocity, these treaties often do not have to create the same or equal rights and obligations for both parties, as in the Phase One Agreement, which almost created no additional obligations to the US. bilateral norm construction is consequently a much easier tool to reflect and translate the will of the dominant party in the negotiation.

One of President Trump's first actions was to withdraw the US from the TPP, setting the tone for a new approach to trade – less multilateral cooperation and more asymmetric bilateralism. In the newly concluded USMCA, for example with little bargaining power on the negotiation table, both Canada and Mexico have given in by accepting more US-dominated IPR standards, by removing provisions in the TPP template, including "Public Domain,"[135] "Cooperation in the Areas of Traditional Knowledge,"[136] and "Balance in Copyright and Related Rights Systems" provisions, and by elevating highly diffusible standards favouring US interests.[137] The steady expansion of IPR under the USMCA – which goes further than the TPP in providing IP protections, has been linked to victories of not only the US state but also US corporations to advance investor interests in trade negotiations, at the cost of Mexican auto industries.[138] USTR has made clear that the USMCA's IP provisions will be used as the new template to renegotiate with EU and Japan in new FTAs.[139]

In the U.S.–China context, the benefits of a bilateral approach were obvious. In actively pushing its IPR reforms in recent years, China has been very tactical in changing laws favouring its domestic industries. It is more willing to change its downstream IP laws to protect electronic and internet-related patents where its industries grow faster but has been slow in changing its trade secret regime and removing its various routes of forced technology transfer. Moreover, China has been very critical of any potential improvement of TRIPS, citing its WTO Accession Protocol and its "developing country" status.[140] By opting for a bilateral formulation, the US was able to tailor normative contents of IP rules to the problems it wanted solved, for example to mandate China's change in its foreign investment regulations on issues of forced technology transfer which would have been otherwise difficult. The bilateral formula avoided the transaction costs of including additional parties while maintaining the possibility of engaging countries like the EU and Japan based on the MFN treatment. On the other hand, by going bilateral, the United States sent a signal that it had specialized interests in China's behaviours and suggested it had less concern with similar actions by other actors. To better engage China, bilateralism might seem to be the only viable option in IPR.[141] The ensuing transnational legal process temporarily enhances the US' dominance over China in trade and IPR negotiations, helping the US to re-grasp sustainable leverage over China in the long run.[142] Since such a process never stops at the moment when foreign rules are being imported to Chinese written laws, the US–China bilateral legal construction in the IPR area will transcend the recipient state by enhancing its judicial practices and legal professionalism.[143]

Even though multilateralism is stagnant, China's giving in to US demands under the Phase One Agreement's bilateral IP construct has affected some of its trade negotiation strategy with others. The recently concluded China-EU Comprehensive Agreement on Investment contains specific provisions banning China's forced technology transfer practices.[144] On one hand, EU can be seen as a free rider of economic benefits reaped from an ongoing US–China tension; on the other hand, for countries with economic association to China while strategically allied with the US, straddling the trench between both will become easier. However, China's commitments to the US were less reflected by the contents of the Regional Comprehensive Economic Partnership (RCEP) Agreement, the newest mega-regional FTA in the Asia-Pacific, because RCEP was more led by ASEAN member economies that have little interest in robust IP protections for more advanced technology. For instance RCEP merely mentions the TRIPS Agreement but does not impose any TRIPS-plus obligations on member states. This further demonstrates that IP bilateralism, even driven by United States coercion, has its limits. Without interlocked accountabilities seen in multilateralist arrangement, it is easier for China to depart from its promises and engage in strategic treaty-negotiation choices solely favouring self-interest.

5.2 (Mis)Perception-Based Legitimization

In pursuing bilateral deals with China, the assumption is that China has the capacity to conform to cross-border IPR norms. In this section, we argue that perception-based legitimacy has played a large role in China's quick implementation of international legal duties, including some of its seemingly unfair obligations under the Phase One Agreement. During the process, domestic actors, including local communities, government officials, legal and economic experts, and other members of civic groups, have started to exert more influence on legal reforms, inspired by external incentives, in manners consistent with China's authoritarian legitimacy.

5.2.1 Prestige

One of the most frequently cited explanations for the implementation of international norms is the prestige and effectiveness of stronger foreign models.[145] Internalizing foreign legal norms is nothing new to postmodern China. The turn to economic liberalization starting in the late 1970s made foreign legal norms and practices acceptable and even attractive, giving China a more modernized and liberalized image to the rest of the world. The rise of neo-institutional economics was highly influential, leading the public to believe that reforming existing laws is conducive to better economic proficiency and, as a result, can be seen as beneficial and legitimate. Like many countries with less intricate legal structures, legal reforms in China often involve transplanting rules or practices that were successful in the Global North. Even inside China, it is generally believed among scholars and political elites that the construction of an Americanized legal system is conducive to economic growth and regime modernization.[146] More natural and gradual forms of norm import already occurred in IPR,[147] accelerated by market-oriented economic reforms built on recognizable rule of law principles.

The effectiveness of these constructs is heavily influenced by perceptions of the purpose and content of foreign norms and practices.[148] Obviously, the US technology strength, its prestige in IPR standards, and its unparalleled complicated legislative processes have all contributed to the selection as a model for China to imitate.[149]

Since the early 2000s, the Chinese government has been paying a fair amount of attention to the development of a consumption- and knowledge-based economy, which was necessary to sustain growth. Therefore, a stronger focus on IPR and technological developments fits this incremental approach. An effective IPR regime is essential for ensuring inventors' capability to reap the benefits, albeit possible limitations over any economic benefit derived from such innovation. A dilemma that China and developing nations may face is direct import of standards devised by any foreign system, particularly the US. This challenge draws forth lessons learned from the import nation's experiences. Since the borrowed provisions have contributed greatly to the US' technology advancement, they are easy accepted and reinforced in China.[150]

As discussed in Section 4.3, legal changes based on the Phase One Agreement terms offer examples of how such prestige-based legitimacy works. In 2019, Chinese legislative decisions to incorporate in both the amended AUCL and the Trademark Law quintupled punitive damages if bad faith infringement is found, based on the wilful infringement doctrine of the US law. These have been further demanded in the Phase One Agreement, wherein China promised that it shall "increase the range of minimum and maximum pre-established damages, sentences of imprisonment, and monetary fines to deter future intellectual property theft or infringements" and, at the same time, cooperate with the United States under a "bilateral Intellectual Property Criminal Enforcement Working Group."[151] These changes are questionable in terms of current stages of Chinese IP laws because it is not certain if these new provisions will have their desired effect of deterring infringement. First, statutory damages remain the principal remedy in most IP cases in China; second, cases in which actual damages are imposed and could be multiplied are very rare. Nevertheless, these provisions receive infrequent opposition and even discussion throughout the legislative process, because Chinese legislators were persuaded that wilful infringement demonstrates some valuable experiences of the US in promoting innovation while effectively converting the US judicial forum as the transnational battlefield for IP infringement cases. Specialized IP courts, established in Beijing, Shanghai, and Guangzhou shortly before the Trade War, already benefited from liberalized US judicial practices in raising their adjudication standards to better protect rights holders.[152]

Another very much praised provision in the Phase One Agreement, the shifted burden of proof in civil infringement cases, is also a signature heritage of the US IPR system. In actuality, to implement such a change in a country with inquisitive courts and civil law style rules is not a straightforward practice. These concerns did not stop these legislations from being quickly passed at the height of US–China trade tension and are perceived as strengthening China's IPR regime and eventually benefitting its innovation- or knowledge-based economy. Both of the highlighted changes in Chinese IP laws illustrated the importance of economic prestige in transplanted norms, especially if the norm settlement processes took place in a short time span.

5.2.2 Competition

As in many other places, Chinese citizens' judgements and choices are deeply affected by limitations on their ability to acquire, process, and digest information and are primarily determined by implicit attitudes and automatic reactions.[153] The state media has played a big role in shaping and manipulating public perception, framing public preferences, and structuring public discourse by engaging in a combination of legitimacy strategies promoting its adopted legal norms as fair, reasonable, and self-interest motivated whilst continuing to have a strong standing in its defense of national and sovereign interests in front of the Chinese public, giving rise to a form of competition-based social legitimacy.

In times of crisis, a common strategy is to use nationalist sentiment to influence public opinion so as to build up a psychological and ideological basis for political legitimacy.[154] Due to the Chinese government's capacity to shape domestic opinions, the rising anti-US sentiment will help some of these newly implemented norms to better diffuse.[155] China's public rhetoric grew increasingly anti-America sometime prior to the Trade War. Somewhat like in the United States, the Trade War is prominently framed in China as a fierce competition between the United States and China for the world's leadership, as well as an ideological contest between the Western and Eastern camps.[156] Framing the trade friction as a "war" and the US as a sole hegemon in addition to an "enemy" can recast popular public perceptions, amassing support for the government based on overwhelming patriotism. Numerous instances leading to top Chinese tech companies such as Huawei being sued in the United States and FBI arrests of Chinese American scientists and engineers are repeatedly reported and broadcasted by state media.[157] These incited animosities have helped major media in China to form a strong competition-based narrative that the US is a primary obstacle China needs to overcome in its further development and competition for the world's leadership. This likely explained the reason that during the Trade War the television debate between CCTV hostess Liu Xin and the Fox News's Trish Regan generated more than 130 million overall views in China.[158]

Knowing that China is under extreme pressures to overcome the US in the Trade War, reforms leading to stronger rule of law and market-oriented economy, even based on importing US standards, earned the Chinese government much respect and favouritism. China was able to comply with most requests demanded by the US without appearing weak or incapable, making any transnational lawmaking hassle-free.

The sustained anti-US rhetoric, despite generating deep skepticism among intellectuals and social elites, has made not only a lasting and profound impression on the general public, but also a positive feedback loop in which the government can reap further legitimacy benefits. This type of propaganda campaign gained the government further grounds of legitimacy and discretion in policy making. Following that logic, any type of norm transplant that is framed on "competing with the U.S. for world leadership" easily earned the government's support.[159] As the legality of enacted rules and the rights of these elevated to authority under such rules to issue commands, a competition-based rhetoric could also be used to generate legitimacy of the transplanted norms.[160]

To sum up, by quickly transplanting selected US norms into its own legal system, the Chinese government was able to avoid blame and accusations of failing to comply superficially with its international obligations, allowing them to escape a toothless image. Domestic perception based on American economic prestige, international reputation shaming, and competition-based anti-US rhetoric help add legitimacy to these newly enacted rules, helping norm distribution and promotion. These tools do not necessarily exclude each other or other factors such as China's domestic political agenda, the "pull power" of rule qualities and right processes,[161] or the growing convergence of foreign and domestic legal norms. It is more probable that they work together to create a conducive environment for US-led legal principles and standards to be imported into China in a time of crisis. Meanwhile, China's Party leadership keeps earning popularity and social legitimacy in any of their reform or non-reform efforts through legislation, propaganda, policy choice, and change of governance strategies. Potentially, these new laws are about to have a much longer perpetual effect on China, working to strengthen its post-Trade War legal scheme and competitiveness in the international economic order.

5.2.3 Resolving the US–China IPR Clash: Weaknesses of Current Scheme

Some significant weaknesses can be seen in bilateralism between the US and China over the IPR terms. There is a rather weak dispute resolution system that excludes a neutral third-party assessment process and is independent from the WTO DSM. Thus, the terms are hard to enforce and sustain. As discussed earlier, the current implementation of the Phase One Agreement in China is the combined interaction of US coercion and China's domestic legitimization. This has left the US with few check mechanisms when China has refused to comply with the terms, and, theoretically, vice versa. A good example occurred during the COVID-19 pandemic, when the ineffective anti-virus battle conducted by the US government further tainted its world leadership image in the international governance system. Concurrently, political changes in the US have made it difficult to constantly keep an eye on China's compliance.

As one of the existing monitoring strategies, Section 301 proceedings will still play an active part at the bilateral treaty implementation stage and become a checkpoint for outside observers to get a sense of China's compliance status. Immediately after the conclusion of the Phase One Agreement, the USTR Report was released in April 2020. It indicates some positive impact by recognizing expected changes in the Chinese legal system.[162] More importantly, it suggests how the US might wish to see the implementation of the Phase One Agreement and the need to further negotiate for a Phase Two Agreement.[163] The USTR Report addresses issues that the Phase One Agreement did not, such as "poor quality patents," "the presence of competition law concepts in the patent law," and challenges faced in trademark prosecution.[164] The Report notes, too, that there are "obstacles in establishing actual damages in civil proceedings,"[165] including a lack of "preliminary injunctive relief"[166] and issues spurred by amended laws based on US intellectual property law principles. It goes on to state that "Chinese judicial authorities continue to demonstrate a lack of transparency,"[167] including publishing only "selected decisions rather than all preliminary injunctions and final decisions."[168] By taking these steps, the US still undeniably wishes to exercise certain forms of continued monitoring power over China's law-making, pulling China towards standards and/or practices favoured by US industries. Hence, China's obligations in the Phase One Agreement serves as an interlocutor that links the domestic and unilateral approach monitoring mechanism to a transnational and bilateral accountability process. Although these measures may constrain China's policy choice and compliance behaviour for a certain period time, for it to work more effectively, the US must maintain a strong will and resources to keep up economic incentives long enough for norm internalization processes to cause an impact. China's possible backlash towards the US depends on its perception of the American economic prestige or geo-economic power, the fading of which may reduce any perceived legitimacy of imported norms, and China's retreat from the commitments is a second-priority optimal scenario.

Second, from a trade law perspective, US–China IPR bilateralism will probably lead to further fragmentation of the cross-border IPR regime under the TRIPS. Bilateral arrangements are inherently inconsistent with the objectives of the multilateral trading system. By attempting to impose regulatory elements in trade relations, obligations not multilaterally agreed upon may unfairly disfavour less competitive developing countries, obviating the purpose of trade liberalization. Even further fragmentation might help the US to successfully export its TRIPS-plus vision to the world. With strong pressures coming from developing countries such as India and Brazil, let alone China, the international IPR regime faces the danger of falling back to pre-TRIPS broken pockets. WTO members did not intend WTO rules to be a self-executed regime without regard to other obligations under international law.[169] Losing international coordination will make cross-border enforcement of IPR a lot more expensive.[170]

While China's industrial policies and state capitalism generate considerable concerns to its trading partners and the world economy more generally, the use of unilateral and confrontational approaches to address these concerns has proved to be counterproductive. An alternative is to return to the WTO framework, which seems difficult to accomplish though constantly advocated by many Chinese scholars. The US must be willing to again campaign a multilateralist approach and significantly reduce frequencies of trade-based sanctions. For this to happen, the US needs to forgo broader gains from bilateral norm making and incur tradeoffs and compromises that dilute its ability to focus on its most preferred outcomes, providing allies with sufficient incentives to collectively seek leverage over China. Unfortunately, as the United States has reduced its support to multilateral treaty-making, the current prospect for negotiations under the WTO is far from bright, and the fate of a regional solution like CPTPP is uncertain. The Trump administration's refusal to approve new appointees to the vacant Appellate Body seats has made itself excluded from the new Interim Appeal arbitration mechanism advocated by Canada, China, and the EU. The theoretical implication is a slim possibility of the US reinventing multilateralist coercive measures to ensure China's longer-term compliance.

6. Conclusion: Beyond Trade War Bilateralism

The traditional US-led multilateral trade order, such as the WTO, was incredibly successful in transforming and engaging countries like China. International law used to serve a much more critical and delicate function in constraining unilateral approaches solely benefitting national interests over foreign and global ones. More recently, there have been challenges to realigning national and global interests, leading to the failure to reach a common ground for legal norms in various areas. With the US' gradual departure from the WTO and dedicated return to unilateralism or minilateralism,[171] building a coordinated international trade order seems to end up as a big setback. This dissonance has an especially devastating impact on IPR protection, when an effective enforcement mechanism under the TRIPS has been lacking and US interests were never fully satisfied.

The US–China relationship will remain a key theme in the incoming decade's diplomacy. As the world's two biggest economies, both the US and China are compelled to maximize their political and economic interests through technology innovation. Undeniably, in the past, China has utilized its unique economic structure to its advantage, including to access and acquire foreign and particularly US IPR and other confidential information, which became an important underlying cause of the Trade War. By entering into the Phase One Agreement and having China make straightforward commitments on how it would improve its IPR protection scheme based on US demands, bilateralism seems to have smoothed out trade and IPR frictions between the two nations, bringing them back to the negotiation table. At the same time, with China continuing to narrow the US' economic and technological advantage in the next decade, no one should overestimate the benefit of a rigid bilateral agreement, despite a weak enforcement mechanism undermining its implementation certainties.

By offering one of the first thorough scholarly evaluations of the Phase One Agreement IPR chapters, this chapter made two additional contributions. First, the chapter demonstrated that the Trade War and its associated bilateral tactics generated new incentives in transnational legal ordering. Situations of target states sometimes warrant quick acceptance of foreign legal norms to balance its governance and foreign policy interests. Even though China's IPR reform was not entirely built on transplanted norms, nor did it entirely rely on external stimuli, the successes of the Trade War-induced behavioural changes did stimulate wider domestic acceptances of US IPR norm in China in a short time span. The second contribution is showing that, while IPR bilateralism was able to impose quite a number of US demands on China in a seemingly cost-effective fashion, in light of further trade fragmentation it will cause, bilateralism is unlikely to be the final cure of US–China IPR disputes. How normative outcomes inspired by US interests affect and shape Chinese behaviours still largely depend on China's strategic choices – and some aftermath were already observed in China's post Trade War treaty negotiation practices. To achieve a better result, returning to multilateralism is probably the most conducive way to promote long-term economic prosperity in the US–China relationship, despite all challenges.

This chapter argues that US-reinforced IPR rules have potentially paved the way for further US–China trade and investment talks. However, to better maintain long-term balance between preservation of policy-making autonomy and regulation of protectionist measures, an approach better-aligned with the WTO framework needs to be pursued. As far as China is concerned, the goal of further integrating China into the global economy requires further openness of the Chinese market, gradual dismantlement of bureaucratic barriers, and relaxation of restrictions on China's inward investment. The goal of innovation in technology can also be attained by admitting high-volume foreign investment. Successful innovations in the investment regime can be used as a model of investment rule-making, thereby enabling China to participate in global economic governance.

Notes

1 USTR Special 301 Report (April 2019) [*hereinafter* Section 301 Report 2019], at 5; 2018 Report to Congress on China's WTO Compliance, at 9, 11, 28 (February 2019); Office of the USTR Update Concerning China's Acts, Policies and Practice Related to Technology Transfer, Intellectual Property, and Innovation (20 November 2018) [*hereinafter* Section 301 Report 2018 Update]; Office of the USTR Findings of the Investigation into China's Acts, Policies, and Practices Related to Technology Transfer, Intellectual Property, and Innovation under Section 301 of the Trade Act of 1974 (22 March 2018) [*hereinafter* Section 301 Report 2018].

2 Economic and Trade Agreement Between the United States of America and the People's Republic of China, Article 4.2, 15 January 2020 [hereinafter *Phase One Agreement*].

3 Phase One Agreement, Article 4.3.

4 Ibid., Article 4.4.

5 Ibid., Articles 1.12, 1.13–14.

6 See U.S.-China Economic and Security Review Commission, Economics and Trade Bulletin (13 January 2021), p. 2, quoting Chad Brown, senior fellow at the Peterson Institute for International Economics, 'China's purchase at $82 million in covered goods through November 2020 – far below the year-to-date target of $141.7 billion.'

7 Judith Goldstein and Robert Gulotty, "The Globalization Crisis: Populism and the Rise of an Anti-Trade Coalition", 6(3) *European Review of International Studies* 57 (2019), at 59–60.

8 Yi Wen, *The Making of an Economic Superpower: Unlocking China's Secret of Rapid Industrialization* (Singapore: World Scientific Publishing, 2016) 26, 93; William Weightman, "Is the Emperor Still Far Away? Centralization, Professionalization, and Uniformity in China's Intellectual Property Reforms", 19 *UIC Review of Intellectual Property* 145 (2020), 148–151.

9 国务院关于印发<中国制造 2025>的通知》(2015) [Notice on the Printing and Release of "Made in China 2025" 2015], Order No. 28 of the State Council, issued on 8 May 2015, effective on the same date.

10 Julia Ya Qin, "Forced Technology Transfer and the U.S.-China Trade War: Implications for International Economic Law", *Wayne State University Law School Legal Studies Research Paper Series* (2020), 2–7, https://papers.ssrn.com/sol3/papers.cfm?abstract_id=3436974.

11 Section 301 Report 2019, *supra* n 1, at 12; Section 301 Report Update 2018, *supra* n 1, at 5, 22; Section 301 Report 2018 Summary of Submissions, *supra* n 1, at 9.

12 *See* Lv Fuyuan, *Talks to the "Angry Youth" on the "Market-for-Technology"* (13 February 2006), http://auto.sina.com.cn/news/2006-02-13/1114167094.shtml [https://perma.cc/N5U9-TCN2].

13 *See* Yu Zhou, "US. Trade Negotiators Want to End China's Forced Tech Transfers. That Could Backfire", *The Washington Post* (28 January 2019), www.washingtonpost.com/news/monkey-cage/wp/2019/01/28/u-s-trade-negotiators-want-to-end-chinas-forced-tech-transfers-that-could-backfire/?noredirect=on&utm term=.929dddda9da4.

14 Mo Zhang, "Change of Regulatory Scheme: China's New Foreign Investment Law and Reshaped Legal Landscape", 37 *UCLA Pacific Basin Law Journal* 179 (2020).

15 *See* the EJV Law, Article 5.

16 *See* Regulations for the Implementation of the Law of China on Sino-Foreign Joint Ventures (promulgated by the St. Council, 20 September 1983, effective 20 September 1983, as revised 2001), http://english.mofcom.gov.cn/article/lawsdata/Chineselaw/200301/20030100064563.shtml.

17 Mo Zhang, "Change of Regulatory Scheme: China's New Foreign Investment Law and Reshaped Legal Landscape", 37 *UCLA Pacific Basin Law Journal* 179 (2020).

18 *See* Regulations for the Administration of the Import and Export of Technology (promulgated by the State Council, 10 December 2001, effective 1 January 2002).

19 *See* Jane Cai and Keegan Elmer, "Is the US Right to Cry Foul About Forced Tech Transfer to Do Business in China – and What is Beijing's Position?", *South China Morning Post* (10 January 2019), www.scmp.com/news/china/diplomacy/article/2181528/us-right-cry-foul-about-forced-technology-transfer-do-business.

20 Mo Zhang, "Change of Regulatory Scheme: China's New Foreign Investment Law and Reshaped Legal Landscape", 37 *UCLA Pacific Basin Law Journal* 179 (2020).

21 *See* Conor Mercadante, "Secrets, Secrets: The Trump Administration and Chinese Intellectual Property Theft", *Columbia Business Law Review* (13 August 2019), https://journals.library.columbia.edu/index.php/CBLR/announcement/view/180, accessed 25 September 2022.

22 *See* Del Q. Wilber, "China 'Has Taken the Gloves Off' in the Thefts of US Technology Secrets", *L.A. Times* (16 November 2018), www.latimes.com/politics/la-na-pol-china-economic-espionage-20181116-story.html.

23 *See id.*
24 *See* Jake Frankenfield, "Forced Technology Transfer (FTT)", *Investopedia* (3 May 2021), www.investopedia.com/forced-technology-transfer-ftt-4687680.
25 *See* "China Paper Says US 'Fabricated' Forced Tech Transfer Claims", *Bloomberg* (18 May 2019, 10:31PM), www.bloomberg.com/news/articles/2019-05-18/china-paper-says-u-s-fabricated-forced-tech-transfer-claims.
26 *See* John Lappin, "China Compels Technology Transfer, Say EU Firms, Expert", *Investor Europe* (27 May 2019), https://expertinvestoreurope.com/china-compels-technology-transfers-say-eu-firms.
27 *See* Dean A. Pinkert and Hughes Hubbard, "Inside Views: US Complaints About Technology Transfer in China: Negotiating Endgame", *Intellectual Property Watch* (24 January 2019), https://www.ip-watch.org/2019/01/24/us-complaints-technology-transfer-china-negotiating-endgame/, accessed 25 September 2022.
    See also, James Politi and Tom Mitchell, "US.- China Trade Talks: What Does the US. Want?", *Financial Times* (24 January 2019), https://www.ft.com/content/a747e98e-1f5c-11e9-b126-46fc3ad87c65, accessed 25 September 2022.
28 Mo Zhang, "Change of Regulatory Scheme: China's New Foreign Investment Law and Reshaped Legal Landscape" 37 *UCLA Pacific Basin Law Journal* 179 (2020).
29 China's GDP growth has been on average 10% a year in the last three decades, while more than 500 million people have been lifted out of poverty. World Bank and Development Research Centre of the State Council of the People's Republic of China (PRC), *China 2030: Building a Modern, Harmonious, and Creative Society* (World Bank, 2013) 3–4.
30 MOFCOM 2019.
31 "Suggestions of the Central Committee of the CPC on Formulating the 14th Five-Year Plan for National Economic and Social Development and Long-Range Objectives Through the Year 2035" (adopted by the Fifth Plenary Meeting of the 19th Central Committee of the CPC, 29 October 2020) (*People's Daily Online*, 4 November 2020), http://politics.people.com.cn/n1/2020/1104/c1001-31917678.html, accessed 29 October 2020.
32 How China's Economic Aggression Threatens the Technologies and Intellectual Property of the United States and the World, White House Office of Trade and Manufacturing Policy (June 2018), at 5; Section 301 Report 2018, *supra* n 1, at 6.
33 Panel Report, *United States – Tariff Measures on Certain Goods from China*, WTO Doc. WT/DS 543/R.
34 Court E. Golumbic and Robert Ruff III, "Leveraging the Three Core Competencies: How OFAC Licensing Optimize Holistic Sanctions", 38 *North Carolina Journal of International Law & Competition Regulation* 729 (2013), at 732–33.
35 Jill I. Goldenziel, "Law as a Battlefield: The U.S., China, and the Global Escalation of Lawfare", 106 *Cornell Law Review* (2021), https://papers.ssrn.com/sol3/papers.cfm?abstract_id=3525442#.
36 Ibid.
37 *Indictment of United States of America v. Huawei Technologies* (E.D.N.Y., Brooklyn, N.Y.), 24 January 2019, at 11–14.
38 Min Zhao, "Analysis and Interpretation of the New Foreign Investment Law of the People's Republic of China" 2 *CWY* 351, 353 (2019).
39 Article 3 of the Law of People's Republic of China on Foreign Capital Enterprise stipulates that the state encourages the establishment of the enterprises with foreign capital that export their products or are technologically advanced. Article 4 of the Law of People's Republic of China on Sino–Foreign Contractual Joint Ventures stipulates the same rule. Article 5 of the Law of People's Republic of China on Sino–Foreign Equity Joint Ventures stipulates that the technology or equipment contributed by any foreign party as investment shall be truly advanced and appropriate to the needs of China. These articles are actually not about imperative technology transfer but have always been misinterpreted that way. So the Foreign Investment Law has removed such stipulations.

40 FIL, Article 22; Implementation Regulations, Articles 24 and 25.
41 See State Council Information Office, China's Position on the China–US Economic and Trade Consultations (June 2019) (stating the accusation of forced technology transfer is 'utterly unfounded').
42 FIL, Article 22.
43 Implementation Regulations, Article 24.
44 Ibid. Article 23.
45 FIL, Articles 22–23.
46 For example see the Office of the United States Trade Representative, "Section 301 Report into China's Acts, Policies, and Practices Related to Technology Transfer, Intellectual Property, and Innovation" (2018), https://ustr.gov/sites/default/files/Section%20301%20 FINAL.PDF, accessed 20 July 2019.
47 Yawen Zheng, "China's New Foreign Investment Law and Its Contribution Towards the Country's Development Goals" (2021) 22 *Journal of World Investment & Trade* 388.
48 *See* Keegan Elmer, "Will China New Forced Technology Transfer Law Satisfy US. Concerns?", *South China Morning Post* (26 December 2019), https://amp.scmp.com/news/china/diplomacy/article/2179556/will-chinas-new-forced-technology-transfer-law-satisfy-us. *See* Julie Wernau, "Forced Tech Transfers Are on the Rise in China, European Firms Say", *The Wall Street Journal* (20 May 2019), https://www.advfn.com/stock-market/stock-news/79951364/forced-tech-transfers-are-on-the-rise-in-china-eu, accessed 25 September 2022.
49 *See* "China Approves Law Against Forced Tech Transfer to Appeases US", *Market Watch* (14 March 2019), https://www.marketwatch.com/story/china-approves-law-against-forced-tech-transfers-to-appease-us-2019-03-14, accessed 19 March 2014.
50 McDermott Will and Emery, "China's New Foreign Investment Law: What's New and What's Next" *McDermott Will & Emery* (9 April 2019), https://www.mwe.com/insights/chinas-new-foreign-investment-law-whats-new-and-whats-next/, accessed 25 September 2022.
51 Morrison Foerster, "China's Foreign Investment Law: Are You Ready for It?", *Morrison Foerster* (3 January 2020), https://www.mofo.com/resources/insights/200102-chinas-investment-foreign-law, accessed 25 April 2022.
52 *See* Austin Lowe, "China's Foreign Investment Law Fails to Address U.S. Concerns", *Lawfare* (7 March 2019), www.lawfareblog.com/chinas-foreign-investment-law-fails-address-us-concerns.
53 McDermott Will and Emery, *supra* n 50.
54 Company Registration Regulations, Article 14.
55 Regulations on Administration of Company Registration, Article 14(2).
56 Judicial Interpretations III, Articles 8 and 10.
57 *See* the State Council, Announcement of the Issuance of Decree No. 709 (18 March 2019), www.gov.cn/guowuyuan/2019-03/18/content_5374742.htm [https://perma.cc/JKE6-TALD]. *See also* "Morgan Lewis' Lawflash Alert: China Introduces Amendments to Address Fear of Forced Technology Transfer", *JD Supra* (25 March 2019), www.jdsupra.com/legalnews/china-introduces-amendments-to-address-21378.
58 *See* the State Council Decree No. 709 (promulgated by the St. Council, 2 March 2019, effective 2 March 2019), Article 38, www.gov.cn/zhengce/content/2019-03/18/content_5374723.htm.
59 Julia Ya Qin, "Forced Technology Transfer and the US–China Trade War: Implications for International Economic Law", 22 *Journal of International Economic Law* 743 (2019).
60 Morrison Foerster, "China's Foreign Investment Law: Are You Ready for It?", *Morrison Foerster* (3 January 2020), https://www.mofo.com/resources/insights/200102-chinas-investment-foreign-law, accessed 25 April 2022.
61 Xuebing Dong, Hui Zhu, and Charlotte Q. Hu, "Protection of Intellectual Property Rights and Industrial Agglomeration: Evidence from the Creative Industries in China", 48 *Chinese Economy* 22–40 (2015).
62 FIL 2015 Draft, Article 116.

63 Xiaojun Li, "Durability of China's Lawmaking Process under Xi Jinping: A Tale of the Two Foreign Investment Laws" (2020) *Issues and Studies* 1.

64 Ibid.

65 Zhe Mou, "A Comparative Study of Foreign Investment Enterprise Law and Foreign Investment Law (draft for comments)", *Business* (2 September 2015), at 234.

66 FIL, Article 23.

67 Ibid. Article 24.

68 Min Zhao "Analysis and Interpretation of the New Foreign Investment Law of the People's Republic of China", 2 *China and WTO Review* 351 (2019).

69 *See* Alexander C. Koty, "China's New Foreign Investment Law", *China Briefing* (20 March 2019), www.china-briefing.com/news/chinas-new-foreign-investment-law.

70 FIL, Article 39.

71 *See* the Implementation Regulations, Article 25.

72 FIL, Article 39.

73 Id.

74 Barbara Li, "Great Expectations: China's New Foreign Investment Law Unpicked", 3 *International Financial Law Review* 48 (2019).

75 Mo Zhang, "Change of Regulatory Scheme: China's New Foreign Investment Law and Reshaped Legal Landscape", 37 *UCLA Pacific Basin Law Journal* 179 (2020).

76 Mark Schaub, Atticus Zhao, Dai Xueyun and Zheng Wei, "China Foreign Investment Law: How Will It Impact the Existing FIEs?", *King & Wood Mallesons* (3 June 2019), www.chinalawinsight.com/2019/06/articles/foreign-investment/china-foreign-investment-law

77 Z. Alex Zhang and Vivian Tsoi, "China Adopts New Foreign Investment Law", *White & Case* (29 March 2019), www.whitecase.com/publications/alert/china-adopts-new-foreign-investment-law, accessed 25 April 2022.

78 Stanford's Alan Sykes on the New U.S.-China Trade Agreement, 16 January 2020, https://law.stanford.edu/2020/01/16/al-sykes-on-the-new-phase-one-u-s-china-trade-agreement/; Pratyush Upreti and Maria Callo-Müller, "Phase One U.S.-China Trade Deal: What Does it Mean for Intellectual Property?", 69(4) *Journal of European and International IP Law* 389 (2020).

79 Frederick M. Abbott, "The United States Response to Emerging Technological Powers", in Fredrick M. Abbott (ed.) *Emerging Markets and the World Patent Order* (Cheltenham: Edward Elgar, 2014).

80 Cyber Espionage and the Theft of U.S. Intellectual Property and Technology: Hearing before the S. Comm. On Oversight and Investigations of the Comm. on Energy and Commerce, 113th Cong, 1 (2013), Opening Statement and Prepared Statement of Hon. Tim Murphy, a Representative in Congress from the Commonwealth of Pennsylvania.

81 Elizabeth A. Rowe and Daniel Mahfood, "Trade Secrets, Trade, and Extraterritoriality", 66 *Alabama Law Review* 63 (2014), at 64, 66.

82 Phase One Agreement, Sec. B.

83 Ibid., Article 1.4.

84 Ibid., Sec. E.

85 Ibid., Article 1.13.

86 Ibid.

87 China's Draft Patent Law Amendment Introduces Patent Linkage for Pharmaceutical Patents and Patent Terms Extension, www.lexology.com/library/detail.aspx?g=9cc1f828-0aa7-45c1-9a75-e460064c9bc1.

88 Weihuan Zhou and Henry Gao, "US-China Phase One Deal: A Brief Account" *Kluwer Regulating for the Globalization Blog* (22 January 2020), http://regulatingforglobalization.com/2020/01/22/us-china-phase-one-deal-a-brief-account/?doing_wp_cron=15890 90481.9717640876770019531250.

89 Phase One Agreement, Ch. 7.

90 Ibid.

91 See Zhou and Gao, *supra* n 88.
92 Nico Krisch, "International Law in Times of Hegemony: Unequal Power and the Shaping of the International Legal Order", 16(3) *The European Journal of International Law* 369 (2005), at 384.
93 Nico Krisch, "Weak as Constraint, Strong as Tool: The Place of International Law in U.S. Foreign Policy", in David M. Malone and Yuen Foong Khong (eds.) *Unilateralism and U.S. Foreign Policy* (Boulder, CO: Lynne Rienner Publishers, 2003), at 41, 45–53.
94 Nico Krisch, ibid.; Frederick M. Abbott, *supra* n 79; Carlos M. Correa, "Bilateralism in Intellectual Property: Defeating the WTO System for Access to Medicines", 36 *Case Western Reserve Journal of International Law* 79 (2004), at 79–82.
95 J. Michael Finger, "The WTO's Special Burden on Less Developed Countries", 19 *CATO Journal* 425 (2000), at 435.
96 Special 301 Section of the United States Trade and Tariff Act of 1984, 19 U.S.C. 2114c(2)(A)(1984).
97 Paul Katzenberger and Annette Kur, "TRIPs and Intellectual Property", in Friedrich Karl Beier and Gerhard Schricker (eds.) *From GATT to TRIPs: The Agreement on Trade-Related Aspects of Intellectual Property Rights* (New York: Weinheim, 1996).
98 Frederick M. Abbott, *supra* n 79, at 393.
99 Ibid.
100 Marisa Anne Pagnattaro and Stephen Kim Park, "The Long Arm of Section 337: International Trade Law as A Global Business Remedy", 52 *American Business Law Journal* 4 (2015); Rowe and Mahfood, *supra* n 81; William Dodge, "Jurisdiction, State Immunity, and Judgments in the Restatement (Fourth) of U.S. Foreign Relations Law", 19 (1) *Chinese Journal of International Law* 101 (2020), at 115.
101 Y.S. Lee, "Bilateralism under the World Trade Organization", 26(2) *Northwestern Journal of International Law & Business* 357 (2006), at 372.
102 Frederick M. Abbott, "Intellectual Property Provisions of Bilateral and Regional Trade Agreements in Light of U.S. Federal Law", *UNCTAD–ICTSD Project on IPRs and Sustainable Development*, Issue Paper No. 12, February 2006.
103 David Gantz, "USMCA Provisions on Intellectual Property, Services and Digital Trade", *Arizona Legal Studies Discussion Paper No. 20-03*, https://papers.ssrn.com/sol3/papers.cfm?abstract_id=3524943
104 Weightman, *supra* n 8, at 148–149; Gregory Shaffer and Henry Gao, "A New Chinese Economic Order", 23(3) *Journal of International Economic Law* 607 (2020), at 612–613.
105 Jyh-An Lee, "Shifting IP Battle Grounds in the U.S.-China Trade War", 43(2) *Columbia Journal of Law & Arts* 147 (2020), at 158.
106 See Nari Lee and Liguo Zhang, "Specialized IP Courts in China – Judicial Governance of Intellectual Property Rights", 48 *International Review of Intellectual Property & Competition Law Journal* 900 (2017), at 910; Beijing Specialized IP Court Witnessed an Annual Filing Increase of 30% in the Last Five Years ('近五年北京知识产权案件年均增幅超过30%') (24 September 2020), *Beijing News*, www.bjnews.com.cn/news/2020/09/24/772126.html.
107 Weihuan Zhou, Huiqin Jiang and Qingjiang Kong, "Technology Transfer Under China's Foreign Investment Regime: Does the WTO Provide a Solution?" 54(3) *Journal of World Trade* 455 (2020), at 457.
108 See Frederick M. Abbott, *supra* n 79.
109 Accession of the People's Republic of China (23 November 2001), at 5.
110 See Qin, *supra* n 10.
111 Section 301 report (2018), at 25.
112 USTR, Update Concerning China's Acts, Policies and Practices, at 25.
113 Qingjiang Kong, "China's WTO Accession: Commitments and Implications", 3(4) *Journal of International Economic Law* 655 (2000), at 675
114 China started to actively amend its pharmaceutical patent system since October 2020, which included Patent term extension for pharmaceutical patents and patent linkage system similar to the one under the United States Hatch-Waxman Act, and it is

currently under public consultation. See Melanie Rupert et al., "China's Proposals to Provide a Patent Linkage System and Patent Term Extensions – Considerations for Drug Companies", Paul Hastings LLP publications (27 July 2020), www.paulhastings. com/publications-items/details/?id=0011c06f-2334-6428-811c-ff00004cbded.

115 Peter K. Yu, "The Transplant and Transformation of Intellectual Property Laws in China", in Nari Lee (ed.) *Governance of Intellectual Property Rights in China and Europe* (Cheltenham: Edward Elgar Publishing, 2016), at 20–42.

116 Shang Biao Fa [Law on the Protection of Trademark] (promulgated by the Standing Committee National People's Congress, 23 August 1982, amended 23 April 2019, effective 23 April 2019), Article 4.4.

117 Min Fa Dian [Civil Code] (promulgated by National People's Congress, 28 May 2020, effective 1 January 2021), Article 123.

118 Luo Sha, The Standing Committee of the National People's Congress Adjusts the 2020 Legislative Work Plan (20 June 2020), *Xinhua News*, www.xinhuanet.com/2020-06/20/c_1126139779.htm.

119 Phase One Agreement, Article 1.11.

120 Ibid., Article 1.18.

121 Wai Guo Tou Zi Fa (Cao An Zheng Qiu Yi Jian Gao) [Foreign Investment Law (Draft for Public Consultation)] (promulgated by the Ministry of Commerce of the People's Public of China, 17 February 2015), http://tfs.mofcom.gov.cn/article/as/201501/2015 0100871010.shtml.

122 See Y.S. Lee, *supra* n 101, at 170.

123 Ibid.

124 Fan Bu Zheng Dang Jing Zheng Fa [Anti-Unfair Competition Law] [*hereinafter* amended AUCL] (promulgated by the Standing Committee of the National People's Congress, 2 September 1993, amended 23 April 2019), Article 17.

125 Zhu Zuo Quan Fa Xiu Zheng An Cao An [Amended Copyright Law (Draft)] (released on 26 April 2020 for public consultation), Article 52.

126 John Y. Gotanda, "Punitive Damages: A Comparative Analysis", 42 *Columbia Journal of Transnational Law* 391 (2004), at 396; Volker Behr, "Punitive Damages in American and German Law – Tendencies towards Approximation of Apparently Irreconcilable Concepts", 78 *Chicago Kent Law Review* 105 (2003), at 106–107.

127 Phase One Agreement, Article 1–14.

128 Mark Cohen, "The Changing Legislative Landscape of Trade Secret Protection", *China IPR Blog* (27 April 2019), https://chinaipr.com/2019/04/.

129 Amended AUCL, Article 32.

130 To promote consistent application of amended IP laws, the Supreme People's Court promulgated several judicial interpretations in late 2020, including Opinions of the Supreme People's Court on Legally Imposing Heavier Punishments for Infringements of Intellectual Property Rights ('最高人民法院关于依法加大知识产权侵权行为惩治力度的意见') (14 September 2020), and Provisions of the Supreme People's Court on Several Issues Concerning the Application of Law in the Trial of Civil Cases of Infringement of Trade Secrets ('最高人民法院关于审理侵犯商业秘密民事案件适用法律若干问题的规定') (12 September 2020).

131 TRIPS Council discusses IP and Innovation, *New eTRIPS Portal Under New Chair*, www.wto.org/english/news_e/news19_e/trip_06jun19_e.htm.

132 Abram Chayes and Antonia Chayes, "Compliance without Enforcement: State Behavior Under Regulatory Treaties", 7 *Negotiation Journal* 311 (1991), at 311.

133 Tom Ginsburg and Gregory Shaffer, "How Does International Law Work? What Empirical Research Shows", in Peter Cane and Herbert Kritzer (eds.), *Oxford Handbook of Empirical Legal Studies* (Oxford: Oxford University Press, 2010), at 3.

134 Robert H. Mnookin, "Strategic Barriers to Dispute Resolution: A Comparison of Bilateral and Multilateral Negotiations", 8 *Harvard Negotiation Law Review* 1 (2003), at 15.

135 TPP IP Chapter, Article 18.15.

136 Ibid., Article 18.16.

137 Ibid., Article 18.66.
138 Sergio Puig, "Can International Trade Law Recover? The United States-Mexico-Canada Agreement: A Glimpse into the Geoeconomic World Order", 113 *AJIL Unbound* 56, 56–57 (2019).
139 Trade Policy Agenda and 2019 Annual Report, USTR (2020), pp. 6–7.
140 See Zhou and Gao, *supra* n 88.
141 Margot E. Kaminski, "The Capture of Intellectual Property Law Through the U.S. Trade Regime", 87 (4) *Southern California Law Review* 979 (2014).
142 See Gregory Shaffer and Terence Halliday, "With, Within and Beyond the State: The Promise and Limits of Transnational Legal Ordering", in Peer Zumbansen (ed.) *Oxford Handbook of Transnational Law* (Oxford: Oxford University Press 2017).
143 Ibid.
144 EU and China Comprehensive Agreement on Investment Fact Sheet, "Clear Prohibition of Investment Requirements that Compel Transfer of Technology", *European Commission*, https://ec.europa.eu/commission/presscorner/detail/en/FS_20_2544.
145 Jonathan Miller, "A Typology of Legal Transplants: Using Sociology, Legal History and Argentine Examples to Explain the Transplant Process", 51 *American Journal of Comparative Law* 839 (2003), at 854.
146 Kevin E. Davis and Michael J. Trebilcock, "The Relationship between Law and Development: Optimists versus Skeptics", 56 *American Journal of Comparative Law* 895 (2008), at 899–901.
147 Simin Gao and Qianyu Wang, "The U.S. Reorganization Regime in the Chinese Mirror: Legal Transplantation and Obstructed Efficiency", 91 *American Bankruptcy Law Journal* 1 (2017).
148 See Miller, *supra* n 145, at 9.
149 Alan Waston, "Aspects of Reception of Law", 44 *The American Journal of Comparative Law* 335 (1996).
150 See Miller, *supra* n 145.
151 Phase One Agreement, Article 1, 27 2(b), 3.
152 Dmitry Karshtedt, "Enhancing Patent Damages", 51 *UC Davis Law Review* 1427 (2008); Mark Cohen, Statements of Mark Allen Cohen before the U.S.-China Economic and Security Review Commission, June 8, 2018 (ass observed by Cohen, the Beijing IP court has conducted reforms such as "citation to cases and use of case law; drafting of shorter and more to-the-point judicial opinions; the introduction of dissenting opinions and *en banc* decisions by judges; experimentation with amicus briefs; and diminished role of behind-the-scenes adjudication committees," many of which have long been sought after by US bar and businesses).
153 Pitman B. Potter, "Globalization and Economic Regulation in China: Selective Adaptation of Globalized Norms and Practices", 2 *Washington University Global Studies Law Review* 119 (2003), at 119–150; Wenwei Guan, "Beijing Consensus and Development Legitimacy: The Evolution of China's Foreign Direct Investment (FDI) Regime from a Law & Development Perspective", 12 *Asian Journal of Comparative Law* 115 (2017), 115, 138, 139.
154 Huisheng Shou, "Nationalism and State Legitimacy in Contemporary China", 1 *Journal of Washington Institute China Studies* 2 (2006), at 2.
155 Ibid.
156 Feiteng Zhong (钟飞腾), "Transcending Hegemony, The Political-Economy of U.S.-China Trade War" ('超越霸权之争：中美贸易战的政治经济学逻辑'), 6 Wai Jiao Ping Lun (《外交评论》) (2018).
157 Margaret Lewis, "Criminalizing China", 111 *Journal of Criminal Law and Criminology* 1 (2021).
158 Tony Munroe and Huizhong Wu, "Fox Host, Chinese State TV Anchor Face Off Over Trade War", *Reuters* (29 May 2019), www.reuters.com/article/uk-usa-trade-china-debate/fox-host-chinese-state-tv-anchor-face-off-over-trade-war-idUKKCN1T00B2.

159 See Wei Shi, "The Cat and Mouse Saga Continues: Understanding the US-China Trade War", 55 *Texas International Law Journal* 187 (2020), at 214 (suggesting that Chinese public vent grievances on American enterprises fueled by nationalist sentiment).
160 See Waston, *supra* n 149.
161 Thomas M. Franck, "Legitimacy in the International System", 82 *American Journal of International Law* 705, at 712 (1998).
162 2020 Special 301 Report (April 2020), USTR.
163 Ibid.
164 Ibid. 40–45.
165 Ibid. 42.
166 Ibid.
167 Ibid. 41.
168 Ibid. 42.
169 Ernst-Ulrich Petersmann, "De-Fragmentation of International Economic Law through Constitutional Interpretation and Adjudication with Due Respect for Reasonable Disagreement", 6 *Loyola University of Chicago International Law Review* 209 (2008), at 217.
170 Peter Yu, "TRIPS Enforcement and Developing Countries", 26 (3) *American University International Law Review* 727 (2011), at 781.
171 Chris Brummer, *Minilateralism: How Trade Alliances, Soft Law, and Financial Engineering Are Redefining Economic Statecraft* (Cambridge: Cambridge University Press, 2014) 165.

5

ANOTHER HOLE IN CHINA'S "GREAT WALL OF MONEY"? CONCEPTUALIZING THE INVOLVEMENT OF FOREIGN INVESTMENTS IN THE CHINESE NON-PERFORMING LOANS MARKET UNDER THE US–CHINA TRADE DEAL

1. Introduction

China's banking system has been struggling with a staggering amount of non-performing loans (NPLs). The risk of a rise in NPLs, coupled with corporate vulnerability and inefficient insolvency system, could lead to a surge of firm failure and cause world trade disruptions. Currently, disposal of NPLs is not only an attention-drawing domestic issue of China but also a battlefield for the trade tensions between China and the US. China's NPLs market is massive and remains attractive to foreign investors. The treatment of foreign firms in the Chinese NPLs market is generally considered beyond China's commitments under the General Agreement on Trade in Services (GATS) and should be subject to bilateral or multilateral agreements external to the World Trade Organization (WTO) regime. One of the recent developments in this area is the US–China Phase One Trade Deal (the US–China Trade Deal) which allows participation of US firms in NPLs primary market trading in China and a larger role of these firms in the secondary market.

Under Chinese law, foreign investors may access the Chinese NPLs market through various established channels such as the Qualified Foreign Institutional Investor (QFII), the RMB Qualified Foreign Institutional Investor (RQFII) schemes, and direct investment in China's inter-bank bond market (CIBM Direct) and Bond Connect. The US government considered these channels insufficient and sought to enlarge the participation of the US firms in China's NPLs market through Article 4.5 of the US–China Trade Deal which reads:

1   The Parties acknowledge the mutual beneficial opportunities in the distressed debt services sector and will work together to promote further opportunities in this sector.

DOI: 10.4324/9781003130499-5

2   China shall allow U.S. financial services suppliers to apply for asset management company licenses that would permit them to acquire non-performing loans directly from Chinese banks, beginning with provincial licenses. When additional national licenses are granted, China shall treat U.S. financial services suppliers on a non-discriminatory basis with Chinese suppliers, including with respect to the granting of such licenses.

3   The United States will continue to allow Chinese financial services suppliers to engage in acquisition and resolution of non-performing loans in the United States.

One way of understanding Article 4.5 is its intention to grant foreign investors the right to purchase NPLs in bulk directly from commercial banks in China, which seems to many observers an attempt to remove major regulatory hurdles for US buyers of NPLs. It will create pricing, quality of supply, and other advantages associated with foreign investors' participation in the primary market, and, therefore, loads a new page of China's NPLs industry. Likely, local asset management companies (AMCs) will face mounting competition posed by the increase in the number of foreign investors, which will potentially increase the viability and efficiency of the NPLs market and then challenge financial stability and state ownership in China to an extent.

Contrary to the previously mentioned view, the opposing observation is that, since the provision does not contain much detail about the criteria, requirements, procedure, and timeline for US financial services suppliers to obtain local AMC licences, Article 4.5 of the US–China Trade Deal is a policy watchword (used by China to soften the US stance in the trade war) rather than a solid plan. The argument on this side also underlines the fact that 'regulatory hurdles have never been the primary gating factors for foreigners hoping to invest in Chinese NPLs'. The disposal of local NPLs, especially when it involves leading players, triggers problems related to public policies, livelihood issues, and other societal complications. Local governments may hesitate to involve foreign investors in the NPLs disposal procedure. Foreign investors may also find it difficult to obtain information that is important for a fast-track solution for NPLs, especially when such information is associated with the public interest and financial security. They may lack networks for disposal of NPLs that take years to set up. The establishment of such networks often requires cooperation from local authorities. Arguably, the non-discrimination principle is of little help in mitigating this situation since this principle is only invoked when national licences are granted. Local authorities have considerable discretion in formulating rules biased towards Chinese AMCs.

A contextual analysis of Article 4.5 of the US–China Trade Deal may indicate that this provision alone is unlikely to promote earth-shattering changes that could rock the dominant position of the state-owned AMCs. In the context of the NPLs disposal scheme in China, the role of legal instrument is rather minor when compared to that of economic and political factors. Without proposing that China should be more analogous to its Western counterparts regarding policies for trading in financial services, we only aim to achieve some moderate goals, namely to demystify the misunderstandings of Article 4.5 of the US–China Trade Deal and of China's financial reform measures, and on this basis, to predict the possible policy moves that may be taken by the Chinese authorities, mostly local authorities, to diminish the effect of Article 4.5.

The chapter is organized as follows. Section 2 offers a review of China's NPLs market involving the definition of NPLs in international instruments and that in Chinese law and the severity of the NPLs problems in China. NPLs disposal channels are discussed in Section 3 to set the ground for analysis of China's NPLs disposal policies in Section 4. Section 5 sheds light on the regulatory tendencies of the Chinese authorities following the US–China Trade Deal and the underlying legal, economic, and political considerations. Section 6 concludes this chapter.

2. China's Non-performing Loans (NPLs) Market: An Overview

Worldwide, there is no universal definition of NPLs. In simple terms, NPLs are loans that are in default or close to being in default.[1] The Basel definition of NPLs is said to be the most widely used. Accordingly, NPLs should be identified based on delinquency status (90 days past due) or the unlikeness of repayment. Namely loans become NPLs when (i) payments of principal and interest are past due by three months (90 days) or more, or (ii) the debtor is unlikely to pay its credit obligations in full without realization of collateral, regardless of the existence of past-due amount or the number of days past due.[2] Before the Basel Guidelines where the previous definition is contained,[3] there was no universal way of categorizing problem loans.[4] Therefore, the Basel Guidelines contributed significantly to the promotion of consistency in supervising the reporting and disclosures of banks. The European Banking Authority adopted the Basel definition of NPLs. So did some other regional banking regulatory authorities.

China claimed that it would follow suit. It has updated the definition of NPLs since 2019 to bring its financial regulation in line with the international standard. Based on the Interim Measures for Classification of Asset Risks of Banks (商业银行金融资产风险分类暂行办法), a five-level classification of financial assets is implemented, requiring assets overdue for more than 90 days to be classified as substandard, doubtful, and loss regardless of the adequacy of security.[5] This definition is built upon elements of the Basel definitions of NPLs. Specifically, debts that are more than 90 days past due must be categorized as "substandard,"[6] those that are more than 270 days past due must be classified as "doubtful," and those that are more than 360 days past due must be categorized as "losses."[7] In practice, this definition is known as a loose one. Chinese banks could push the loose boundaries. The Basel definitions and regional financial regulations have promoted the harmonization of the NPL definition.[8] But they have not prevented countries or their banks from tightening or loosening their rules on regulating problem loans.[9] A lack of a uniform definition of NPL hinders cross-country comparison of NPLs disposal measures.

Although China's financial system and banking system per se survived the global financial crisis and challenges posed by the pandemic, excessive debt has been and is always a serious problem in China. The country's total borrowing rose to 335% of GDP by the end of June 2020,[10] from 162% in 2008.[11] China's US$34 trillion pie of public and private debt is an explosive threat to China's economy. Of China's nearly US$13 trillion in outstanding domestic debt (that is publicly traded), the financial sector holds the largest piece at US$4.9 trillion (39%), US$2.7 trillion non-financial debt (22%), US$2.7 trillion in local government debt (22%), and US$2.2 trillion in national government debt (17%).[12] A high non-performing loans (NPLs) ratio is considered by China as one of the most significant threats to its financial stability and prosperity and has previously triggered several rounds of policy changes. China is sitting on a record amount of bad loans as the COVID-19 pandemic unfolded since the end of 2019. The NPLs ratio of the banking sector was 1.92% by the end of 2020.[13] Views and expectations in relation to the impact of COVID-19 on the NPLs market vary. But commentators all agree on the urgency of addressing NPLs-related problems. Measures must be implemented to prevent widespread distrust that could impose a kind of "tax on all forms of economic activity."[14]

China's standards for NPLs classification contain ambiguities, leaving room for the provincial authorities to either tighten or loosen their NPLs regulations.[15] The Zhejiang division of the China Banking Regulatory Commission, for instance initiated the experiment of recognizing debts that are more than 60 days past due as NPLs.[16] In other areas of China, the bank is allowed to look beyond the 90-day period in determining whether it expects to suffer a loss, which might lead to a lower level of NPLs on the balance sheet.[17] NPLs problems may be hidden if the NPLs transactions conducted by the banks are defined otherwise.[18] Ultimately, these transactions involving a huge amount of NPLs are resolved outside the banking sector. China Banking and Insurance Regulatory Commission in early 2022 raised its tolerance level to NPLs in response to the COVID-19 pandemic as part of the supporting scheme for micro, small, and medium-sized enterprises.[19] This undoubtedly increases the opaqueness of NPLs disposals and resolutions in the Chinese context.

China's NPLs market is massive and is getting even bigger due to the slowing economy caused by structural issues, which is being further aggravated by the ongoing trade war with the US since 2018 as well as the global pandemic. As of June 2018, China's commercial banks reported nearly RMB 2 trillion (US$ 282 billion) of NPLs on their balance sheets.[20] Adding the approximately RMB 4.3 trillion (US$ 620 billion) of NPLs on the books of the AMCs, China's distressed asset market is the world's largest one.[21] In the three months ended 30 September, the NPLs ratio rose to 1.96%, the highest level in at least six years, according to the study of foreign analysts.[22] This indicates a need for a more vibrant NPLs disposal market while the market and the larger context have not displayed signs of significant changes. Despite partial privatization (or commercialization in the Chinese government's official terminology), the Chinese government still largely retains ownership and control over massive state-owned enterprises. As the government continues to intervene in the real economy and equity markets, it leaves an impression to the public and foreign investors that it would implicitly guarantee the safety and solvency of the critically important state sectors and national champion companies including the Big Four banks. Effectively the government, through its ownership, offers its sovereign creditability to the Big Four banks and other state-owned enterprises (SOEs), a "too-big-to-fail" case in China. This so-called hard repayment principle (in Chinese, *gangxing duifu*, literally meaning the debtors will pay off debts for sure) creates a moral hazard problem failing to discipline both banking and state-owned sectors, thereby worsening the NPL problem. On the one hand, China relies upon cheap credit from state banks and depositors to help indigenous state-owned companies survive and grow. On the other hand, executing this "too-big-to-fail" norm in China amasses excessive government debts and impedes the economy from becoming less dependent on state spending.

The US–China Trade Deal includes China's commitment to making changes to its economic and trade regimes in not only the area of financial services but also other areas such as intellectual property, technology transfer, agriculture, and currency and foreign exchange.[23] It is found by the National Trade Estimate Report released by the US Office of Trade Representative in April 2021 that the US–China Trade Deal has not led to significant changes to China's investment regulations for foreign investors, except in financial services sectors.[24] Nonetheless, the report has not specified the changes to the financial services sectors. This chapter seeks to fill the gap by investigating whether the impact of the US–China Trade Deal on the position of foreign asset managers in the Chinese NPLs disposal market is substantial.

3. NPL Resolutions by Chinese AMCs and Foreign Entities

At the outset of China's effort of dealing with NPL problems, it had to choose between disposal inside or outside the banking system. Eventually, due to both legal and economic reasons, it chose the latter and accordingly assets management companies (AMCs) were established on the national and local levels. Before 2012, Chinese law only relied on four national state-owned AMCs, Huarong, Orient, Great Wall, and Cinda, to manage and dispose of NPLs from state-owned commercial banks. These AMCs keep expanding their business scope over the years. Now this scope is wide enough to cover investment in NPLs of banks, non-bank financial institutions, and non-financial institutions. There is a tendency that these AMCs shift away from their core NPLs disposal business and have become true financial conglomerates, with direct lending arms and interests in banks, securities, trust, and financial leasing companies. While to a certain extent the diversification is natural and market-oriented, the AMCs have been overextending themselves and straying from their intended purposes.[25] Consequently, they may act like banks channelling funding and likely involve systemic risks with overburdened debts. As AMCs are not legally characterized to be banks, they effectively turn themselves into shadow banking institutions to circumvent banking regulations, thus making themselves more vulnerable to systemic risks and regulatory failures.

In 2012, AMCs at the provincial level were allowed to be established by the Ministry of Finance and the CBRC.[26] At the initial stage, each provincial government was allowed to establish one local AMC to participate in the bulk acquisition and disposal of NPLs from financial institutions within its own province, with the disposal method being limited to debt restructuring.[27] In December 2013, the CBRC released its requirement of additional qualifications for the set-up of provincial AMCs, including (i) RMB1 billion in paid-up registered capital; (ii) professional teams with requisite experience in the financial field; and (iii) good corporate governance. Since 2016, the central government has introduced a series of supportive policies, permitting each provincial government to establish one more local AMC, which is allowed to dispose of NPLs by, among other methods, transferring the NPLs to other investors without being subject to geographic limitation (including offshore investors).[28]

China's NPL market can be classified into the primary and secondary markets. In the primary market, banks and other financial institutions sell their NPLs to AMCs, and AMCs then disposed of the NPLs via multiple means, one of which is to sell the NPLs in the secondary market to other investors (including both onshore and offshore investors).[29] The sale process is subject to a diverse set of laws and regulations in China, and special approval requirements are applicable to the transaction involving offshore investors.[30] The bank determines the amount and type of NPLs to be sold and carries out due diligence on the NPLs to evaluate the NPLs and form the transfer or sale plan. After the transfer plan has been reviewed and filed, the bank invites interested AMCs to conduct due diligence on the target NPLs. The sale is required to be conducted via competitive means (such as bidding and auction) in order to maximize the sales proceeds. The winning bidder enters into an NPLs transfer agreement with the transferor. Both parties should, within the agreed period, issue a public announcement to inform the debtors and the guarantors of NPLs regarding the occurrence of the transfer. Without proper announcement, debtors and guarantors may challenge the validity of the sale.

To trade NPLs in the secondary market, an AMC is required to disclose the basic information of the target NPLs including the nature, size, and maturity of the NPLs on its public website as well as a designated newspaper. For any disposal of NPLs whose book value is more than RMB 10 million but less than RMB 50 million, an announcement must be made in a newspaper at the municipal level or above. For any disposal of NPLs whose book value is more than RMB 50 million, an announcement must be made in a newspaper at the provincial level or above.[31] The announcement period should generally last for at least ten to 20 working days.

The transfer process in the secondary market should also be carried out by competitive means, including but not limited to bidding, auction, invitation to offer, and public inquiry/solicitation. AMCs must transfer NPLs to non-state-owned transferees in the public competition process. The NPLs transfer agreement after the process is concluded between the AMC and the winning bidder. Public announcement regarding the transfer needs to be issued by the AMC to notify the debtors about the repayment of outstanding debts to the relevant transferee. A public announcement is a precondition for a valid sale that binds the buyers and debtors.

Aside from direct sales and securitizations, the main NPLs disposal methods adopted by the AMCs include debt collections, sales, or lease of real property, restructuring of debt terms, and bankruptcy settlement. One of the main obstacles that AMCs encounter in their debt collection efforts is created by their own and debtors' status as SOEs. The state ownership creates a moral hazard issue inhibiting effective recovery and collection. Another impediment is the AMC's inability to seek a remedy when companies, typically SOEs, reneged on the debt restructuring contracts they entered into.

Foreign investors may access the Chinese domestic NPLs market through the established channels, such as the QFII, the RQFII schemes, the CIBM Direct, and Bond Connect. They may also purchase NPLs portfolios from AMCs, or from commercial banks through the Pilot Program.[32] Foreign investors can set up joint ventures with Chinese AMCs for the purpose of managing NPLs. The latter could use NPLs as their contribution. They could also transfer their interests of the NPLs to foreign investors through joint ventures while remaining as the owner. Some of the foreign investors choose to establish wholly owned AMCs in China. Such entities are generally not allowed to participate in the primary market. Article 4.5 of the US–China Trade Deal is expected to enable a new legal structure that could improve the disposal of NPLs with the involvement of foreign investors, which help lower the concentration level of financial assets in China's economy to foster diversification and competition in the financial markets. The US investors may be granted the licence to establish licensed wholly owned foreign AMCs to compete with national AMCs in the primary market. Nevertheless, there has been no US firm being given such a licence.

4. Chinese Financial Policies for the NPLs Market Through a Comparative Lens

China has established its own model of development, which differs or even challenges the Western liberal market economy theories. The Chinese model is largely driven by political factors and accordingly its NPLs market is policy-oriented, despite the regulatory movement to open the market to foreign investors and to enhance the function of market elements. Part of this section is dedicated to the analysis of the key political norms that centre the discussion of the unique features of the Chinese NPLs market. To deepen the readers' understanding of the aforementioned features, some regulatory experiences beyond the Chinese borders are introduced. It is revealed that the concept of financial liberalism does not lead the reform of the law or policies for NPLs disposal in the discussed countries, although it has a role to play. There is generally a lack of headlines outside China about a country's concerns over selling NPLs to foreign investors. Given the unique features of the Chinese NPLs market, some upcoming regulatory changes may be anticipated. The discussion has largely concentrated on the potential impact of the US–China Trade Deal but has also paid attention to other international trade deals to which China has committed, such as the China-EU Comprehensive Agreement on Investment (CAI) and the Regional Comprehensive Economic Partnership (RCEP).

4.1 The Unique Features of Chinese Financial Policies

Before cheering for the various ways that foreign investors must enter the NPLs market, there is a more fundamental question: how Chinese financial policies are structured politically and how the Chinese NPLs market is shaped by key political concerns. Previous study suggests that the market-based theory only explains a fraction of the Chinese economy,[33] which implies the importance of investigating the non-market factors in Chinese context. The discussion of foreign investors' participation in the Chinese NPLs disposal market takes note of the fact that China has a strong preference for development-oriented finance, "a finance entity that aims to realize government objectives and promote the sound, rapid and sustainable development of the economy and society."[34] The key factor to the success of Article 4.5 of the US–China Trade Deal largely depends on the suitability of foreign investors' investment strategies in the context of China's development-oriented finance, that is to facilitate economic development while eliminating financial activities completely separate from the real economy for self-loop. Certainly, the Chinese government's sincerity to implement its open-up policy is also a determinative factor in shaping and realizing foreign investors' strategy in being involved in China's NPL market.

It is widely recognized that China has more control over its economy than other countries. China can get a tight hold over the banks to finance investment projects when growth is sluggish. Thus, the Big Four banks and other Chinese commercial banks have never really been freed from policy-loan responsibilities. For example Bank of China and others are involved in pet political projects, that is China's spectacular railroad expansion plan. Chinese banks' commercial lending activities are always influenced by the government's economic policy changes. When the government calls, Chinese commercial banks must lend money to those designated entities which shall not be eligible for the loans in accordance with normal review procedures of the banks. Thus, the banks are indeed creating mounting NPLs every year from a government-directed lending boom to maintain the growth of economy. This dilemma effectively reminds us the old problems and new challenges that underdeveloped and state-dominated Chinese banks may still have and face despite a decade of frenetic and large-scale reform in the banking sector. It might be still the case that Chinese banks are *de facto* instruments of the state's economic and monetary policy, and the commercialization has a long way to go. After the global financial crisis, the Chinese government has relied upon the persistent credit expansion policy to pursue economic growth. Although China's credit easing policy raises the production of infrastructure goods, it increases the probability of credit default.[35] The mounting NPLs resulting from irregularity and policy lending force Chinese banks to manage this issue. These banks are not afraid of bank failures given China's "too big to fail" principle, namely that the Chinese government rescues Big Four banks and major commercial banks from bank runs and financial instability under any circumstances. The resolution of the NPLs-related problems relies on joint efforts of the banks and the government.

Financial stability is an important political concern in China and ensuring financial stability will continue to be China's paramount policy consideration,[36] or public interest. Article 4.5's expectation of fewer state elements in the primary market for NPLs will surely trigger political concerns. State-ownership is another feature that is relevant to the topic of NPLs disposal. In China, state-owned enterprises are more prevalent in some strategic sectors, such as financial services, than in others. Although China allows the market to play a decisive role in resource allocation, state-ownership still occupies a particularly important role in China's economy. As such, one must view China's NPLs market from the perspectives of state-managed market economy. While foreign investment benefits the viability and efficiency of the NPLs market, it is not entirely in line with China's state interest. The Chinese government still believes that the strong and efficient financial system led by state-owned banks and financial institutions is a primary prerequisite for continuous financial growth and economic success.

The opening and deregulation of financial markets, a controversial topic in China and beyond, has encountered more resistance in China since the financial crisis of 2008, originating from US subprime mortgage derivatives. It is understood by Chinese authorities that the cause of the crisis was too many innovative products of subprime mortgage derivatives targeted at retail investors and there was no much needed financial regulation.[37] Therefore, it is understandable that China is cautious in adopting elements of a haphazard or free market approach when allowing new participants to enter the primary NPLs disposal market. Widely accepted, the involvement of the state in the financial sector has proved to be a necessity in safeguarding financial safety and stability, protecting the public from unexpected losses, limiting concentrations of wealth and monopoly power, and so on.[38] State shareholding of China's banking sector offers a guarantee of safety to the financial sector albeit its side effect on fair competition or competitive neutrality.

4.2 Regulatory Experiences Beyond Chinese Borders

Commentators often give their analyses of China's reforms in various domestic areas a political bias. For instance Victor Shih has said the following in an article regarding political constraints on NPLs in China: "Reform is crossing the river by feeling for stones *(moshi guohe)*. Yet the stones that Chinese leaders feel for are not sound economic policies but political survival."[39] Here, we also highlight political norms related to the financial sector, but do not agree with the oversimplified theory that changes to the Chinese financial regulations are merely a result of political calculation. Shih's finding has neglected the fact that state-ownership and state-controlled regulations have been pervasive not only for China but also across many other countries for much of the modern era in the process of enabling an ideal environment for NPLs disposal. Many regulatory measures taken in the times of global financial crisis indicate the need of governmental intervention in the field of financial regulation. It is hard to rationalize a complete laissez faire approach in modern economy.

Financial liberation or financial deregulation, especially the questions of how far and how fast, has been one of the most topical issues in both academic discussion and in the practice of reforming financial laws. We believe that a review of regulatory experiences from other parts of the world is helpful. As a matter of fact, the set-up of four AMCs is a transplant from the US experience tackling the savings and loans crisis during the 1990s which witnessed the set-up of the Resolution Trust Company established by the US government for the same purpose. Different from their US peers which were wound up once the cleanup of debts was done, Chinese AMCs extended their life and branched out to other financial areas not identified in their original mandates, and therefore have become financial conglomerates touching upon many financial sectors ranging from trust, insurance to mutual fund, securities blockages. Due to the difference in the ideological dimension and the financial performance of other countries, it is hard for the authors to propose that foreign experiences could be used as China's reference. But China's understanding of the US subprime market, the European countries' examples, and some lessons from Asia has been influential in its decision-making over the regulation of NPLs disposal.

NPLs-related problems in Europe have received ever increasing attention from both academic and practicing areas since the European banking and sovereign debt crisis. These problems call for reflection on reforms of law and regulation on both public and private levels. Different from China, many European countries face a situation in which foreign banks provide most of the credit and possess most of the NPLs, and therefore, cross-border non-performing exposures could be severe. In addition to that, commercial banks in Europe are market-oriented and are normally expected to manage NPLs through private solutions such as internal workouts, the recovery of collaterals, direct sales through various trading platforms, and so on. In this sense, lessons from the European regulatory experience may not be applicable in China. But due to market failure, the lack of sufficient market for NPLs transaction, and the potential moral hazard within the domestic banking sectors, Europe has seen proposals being made to introduce public solutions, such as state AMCs, so that consistent and efficient disposal of NPLs can be achieved.[40] Both Europe and China must deal with concerns arising from the implementation of public solutions. For instance will the state AMCs become too big to fail when state organ could not find sufficient market demand?[41] How and to what extent should state AMCs share risks with other interested market participants? Europe is currently struggling with the choice between a "state-centred" approach and a "corporate-centred" approach in monitoring and managing NPLs.[42] The relevant debate may enlighten China in its way forward to reform its regulations on NPLs disposal. This warrants a valid comparative study between China and the relevant European countries. By comparison, this chapter identifies country characteristics that enable the implementation of the relevant strategies.

Some European countries suffer more severe bad loans problems than others. For instance data from European Banking Authority for end-2016 has revealed a high NPL ratio of around 45% in Cyprus and Greece, and of around 15% in Italy.[43] This section first focuses on Greek and Italy where NPLs problems are system-wide. As argued, there is a strong call for coordinated response to NPLs-related problems with the understanding that the bank-by-bank approaches could be counterproductive in dealing with NPLs problems on the systemic levels. In these countries, governments feel the responsibility of bailing out banks and other non-banking institutions which are considered essential to the domestic financial stability.[44] A good example is the GACS bad loan scheme which offers state guarantee that can be purchased by banks from the Treasury for the benefit of the holders of the senior class of asset-backed securities.[45] This scheme was introduced in 2016 and was updated in 2019. It has received applause while its cost-benefit ratio of granting the state guarantee should be subject to further assessment.[46] Greece followed suit by introducing the Hercules Asset Protection Scheme (HAPS) in the late 2019. This scheme helps banks to pack non-performing loans into asset-backed securities.[47] In the previously mentioned countries, addressing NPL issues into broader market is considered the main solution within which government intervention is the key factor. Particularly, securitization converts NPLs to securities which could be attractive to foreign investors.[48] All European countries allow sales of NPLs from the banks to foreign investors.[49] Within the Italian and Greek legal systems, there are very few restrictions on foreign investors' participation in NPLs disposal activities.[50] In fact, foreign investors are major players in the whole European market,[51] which differs greatly from the situation in China. But dealing with overseas banks and institutions is still a great challenge in both Europe and China.

Europe also has countries with low NPL ratio, such as Germany and the Netherlands.[52] In these countries, NPLs could be disposed of through roughly two routes, namely a decentralized model and a centralized model. In Germany, the government, on the one hand, encourages banks to change their credit policy and their controlling mechanisms in order to avoid the accumulation of a large amount of NPLs. On the other hand, it creates optimal conditions for NPLs transactions between German banks and domestic and foreign investors.[53] Some foreign investors even acquire German banks to conduct their NPL disposal business more flexibly. According to the study by Schwarze and Storjohann, most German banks' NPLs portfolios were acquired by Anglo-Saxon or US investment banks and investment fund companies.[54] Through acquiring a single name NPLs portfolio or debt-equity swap, foreign investors are allowed to gain control of many companies. The Netherlands with a low NPL ratio does not always embrace measures facilitating NPL disposal. The Dutch banks have the option of assigning loan portfolio to the investors. But there are legal limits created either by the law or by the contractual arrangement between the parties that have to be applied to the aforementioned investors.[55] Priorities are given to consumer interests and/or other considerations. Generally speaking, a desire to ensure that the domestic financial system is not controlled by foreigners is much weaker in European countries than in China. Other Western developed economies' attitudes towards the involvement of foreign investors are quite similar. Beyond Chinese borders, there is generally a lack of headlines about a country's concerns over selling NPLs to foreign investors who care more about their financial interests than the national interests of the home country of the NPLs.

However, with the reality that financial crises come and go with increasing frequency, countries tend to implement stricter regulations and introduce state intervention into transactions involving foreign investors. Using Germany as an example again, as the strongest economy in the EU, Germany is considered the ideal investment destination by some Chinese investors. The rise of Chinese investment did not trigger much-needed market transparency but rather the striving for protectionism.[56] The German foreign investment framework changed from an afterthought, namely the proceedings were only initiated in relatively few cases and were no issue at all in the vast majority of international transactions, to aforethought that requires a notification duty for transactions in so-called critical business sectors, extensions of the time periods for an assessment of transactions as well as an extension of the information obligations for the parties to the transaction.[57] In both Germany and beyond, it is becoming clear that the government is more willing than previously to intervene in the market to protect key industries. In light of the Chinese perceptions of the functions of financial systems, it is likely that the pace of foreign investors' entry and expansion in the NPLs market will continue to be tightly monitored and contained.

The US has abundant experience in disposing of NPLs through government-led non-banking institutions and public programmes. For instance, in the S&L crisis in the 1990s, Resolution Trust Corporation (RTC) was established to resolve the problem loans possessed by failing and failed institutions. This practice received much applause but was also criticized as being too late.[58] The Federal Deposit Insurance Corporation (FDIC) is another important establishment for resolving problems presented by troubled banks and thrifts during the financial crisis of the 1980s and early 1990s. Various measures have been implemented by these establishments in the process of disposing of NPLs, such as loan sales, auctions, securitizations, and partnerships with private firms.[59] Among these measures, there was a clear shift of disposal method from holding non-performing assets to maturity to selling non-performing assets so as to write off them from balance sheets. Gradually, private firms became the major players in evaluating, packaging, and marketing NPL portfolios.[60] But the law required the public agent to limit the use of the private sector to the extent that the strategy needed to be "efficient and cost-effective."[61] The trend of expanding the universe of investors, including foreign investors, was apparent. The involvement of foreign investors has not been deemed a significant risk.

In the Asian market, Korea may be an ideal research target, since it has well-known experience of taking advantage of international auctions to deal with domestic NPLs problems.[62] The problems of bad loans became severe in Korea in 1997 as the consequence of the country's unprepared financial liberation policies.[63] Korea established the Korea Asset Management Corporation (KAMCO) and the Non-Performing Asset Management Fund (NPA Fund) as the key component of the rescue programme. Korea's efforts of disposing of NPLs in the late 1990s are considered successful, especially the effort to issue asset-backed securities. KAMCO created a special purpose vehicle to purchase special bonds and sold them to overseas investors.[64] In the meanwhile, the Korean authorities lifted restrictions on foreign investment to take advantage of the international investors. But the inclusion of outside investors could not become effective in solving problems related to NPLs without the implementation of policies to enhance the efficiency and soundness of the domestic financial market and the financial institutions.[65] As one of the implications of Korea's experience of regulating financial market shocks, emerging economies are encouraged to be vigilant about risks arising from global financial market.[66] Their ability to respond quickly and effectively to financial turmoil is required to be enhanced. In the process of Korea's financial reform, taking major steps still rely on state support in the form of state-backed AMC and public fund. Similar to China, the operation of the Korean state-backed AMC was challenged by the difficulty of pricing NPLs. The government has to deal with the risk that the profits from disposing of NPLs could not cover AMC's operating expenses.[67]

That said, although the Basel Committee and other cross-border authorities have made efforts to harmonize and coordinate regulatory activities, the character and scope of NPLs resolution measures remain domestic. It appears that the introduction of a fiscal backdrop in the form of a state-backed bad bank is a quite common and universal approach to some other countries confronting high levels of NPLs. Examples include Sweden, Spain, and Ireland, just to mention a few.[68] By contrast, an outright bail-in of creditors could raise concerns that could delay the triggering of resolutions.[69] The effect of the aforementioned measures often depends upon how much direct power of intervention the domestic authorities have over local banks and other interested participants. Other complex factors may obscure the resolution of NPLs problems. The loopholes, as rightly pointed out by others, are the lack of punitive, ex post bank management sanctions, as well as the absence of full managerial incentives leading to managerial forbearance.[70] These factors should be considered when contemplating the results of the comparative study. Overall, disposal of NPLs requires timely and mixed measures. Granting foreign investors the right to market access by itself could not be a stand-alone solution. As a matter of fact, it has already been confirmed that a combination of systemic (macroeconomic) and idiosyncratic factors contributes to the accumulation of NPLs and other non-performing bank exposures.[71]

5. China's Regulatory Tendencies After the US–China Trade Deal

Without doubt, Article 4.5 of the US–China Trade Deal will loosen China's control over its NPLs market and will subsequently trigger some regulatory changes. But this provision does not necessarily imply massive deregulation of foreign investment or the change of dominant actors in the Chinese NPLs disposal market. Foreign investors may anticipate potential upcoming regulatory mechanisms that are likely to moderate the liberalizing commitments made by Article 4.5. These mechanisms might, on the one hand, reflect the state's intent to exert stricter supervision over disposal of NPLs, and on the other hand, encourage the participation of foreign investors with advanced investment know-how.

One can see this approach in the recently adopted regulation issued by the CBIRC on licensing for non-banking financial institutions, that is *the Implementation Measures on Administrative Licensing for Non-bank Financial Institutions (Implementation Measures 2020)*, which modified the *Implementation Measures 2015*, with the aim to upgrade the thresholds for qualified investors in the nationwide market. Noticeably, China has adopted a dual path approach in regulating state-owned AMCs. Regional AMCs are not subject to the previously mentioned measures but to a set of rules issued by both CBIRC and the local governments.[72] The recent example is Notice No. 153 issued by CBIRC that aims to enhance the scrutiny of NPLs purchases by local AMCs. In brief, the *Implementation Measures 2020* prepares for the second stage opening-up promised by Article 4.5 of the US–China Trade Deal, namely to grant foreign investors national licences.

Local authorities are likely to pursue a lighter-touch regulatory approach in dealing with local AMCs. Since 2012, local AMCs have become another means of tackling China's debt problem. At the preliminary stage, they were established for the bulk acquisition and disposal of NPLs from financial institutions within its province, with the disposal method being limited to debt restructuring.[73] CBIRC made clear the qualification requirements of local AMCs in 2013: 1 billion RMB in paid-up registered capital, professional teams with the requisite experience, and good corporate governance. Regulations affecting the business model of local AMCs were relaxed in 2016 when the central regulators expected local AMCs to sell NPLs to entities outside their home provinces. Over time, while some local AMCs had their focus on the disposal of NPLs, other local AMCs operated diversified business lines, including trusts, venture capital funds, small loan companies, and so on. In 2019, China's banking regulator sought to enhance the scrutiny of local NPLs disposal activities. Among other goals, this move aimed to encourage the use of assessment and valuation procedures to achieve fair market pricing and implement real and complete transfers of assets and risk. The participation of foreign investors may serve this purpose. In reality, local AMCs were relying heavily on shadow banking activities due to the limit on disposal methods. A lighter-touch regulatory approach is expected to continue when local government has no intention of eliminating shadow banking or other regulatory arbitrage.

Foreign investors are likely to face restrictions in areas where public interest and livelihood issues prevail. Chinese law currently restricts foreign entities from directly owning Chinese real estate. This rule may be expanded by local authorities to limit the ability of foreign entities to dispose of NPLs. The potential impact is expected to be significant since, at this stage, real estate occupies an important part of NPLs portfolios.

In addition, foreign investors may expose themselves to various tax risks. The tax environment in China is unstable, mainly due to the reality that tax policies are in a constant change, and there is a variety of tax practices. Guo Shui Fa [2003] No. 3 represents the primary attempt to regulate tax rules on the disposal of NPLs. It sets out a preferential taxation framework for foreign investors in the Chinese NPLs disposal market, which allows the recovery to be recognized on "a cost recovery method under a total portfolio basis."[74] This regulation was invalidated by an announcement issued by the State Taxation Administration.[75] Due to the lack of any official guidelines at the central level, it falls under the discretion of local authorities allowing foreign investors to enjoy the preferential treatment offered by Guo Shui Fa [2003] No. 3.

The state has authorized preferential tax policies for the national AMCs. As an illustration, the Ministry of Finance and the State Administration of Taxation issued a notice regarding the tax policies applicable to the national AMCs.[76] Accordingly, national AMCs were exempted from the duty to pay VAT. In 2017, the Ministry of Finance and the State Administration of Taxation jointly issued Cai Shui [2017] No. 56, which relates to asset management products. Despite the fact that VAT replaced business tax and is applied to all sectors of business, Cai Shui [2017] No. 56 set out guidelines for certain asset management products to be subject to a simplified VAT calculation method, but at the same time, again postponed the effective date to 1 January 2018. As a result, VAT taxable activities happening during the operation of asset management products before that date would not be affected by VAT-related matters.[77] Since 2018, asset management products in various asset classes have been subject to 3% VAT on income derived from the invested assets.[78] Currently, preferential policies for regional AMCs have not been made clear. The tax policies biased towards Chinese asset managers may be used by local authorities as a reference when they have to grant provincial licences to foreign entities for participating in the primary NPLs market.

Last but not least, there may be inconsistent NPLs regulations across different provinces. An experimental pilot programme has been allowed in Shenzhen, through which foreign investors may directly purchase NPLs from Chinese banks. In May 2018, this programme was upgraded by a simplified process.[79] Some areas of China may be more prepared for foreign participants in the NPLs primary market than others. Foreign investors will have to deal with the scenario where understanding the disposal processes across China's different localities is key to their success.

In light of these regulatory tendencies, the US–China Trade Deal will force some changes to the business model of regional AMCs, who seem content for now with their ad hoc approach.[80] Foreign investors will have to address the potential tax risks posed by the previously mentioned legal ambiguities.

China has thus far not seen one single US firm being granted provincial licence for directly acquiring NPL portfolios from Chinese banks, which already implies that China may not plan to let the US–China Trade Deal lead to a great change to its NPL disposal market. This view is further grounded when CAI and RCEP are considered. Both are currently attracting broad attention and contain China's commitments to improve the market access conditions for foreign companies. RCEP does not have a direct impact on the NPL disposal. CAI, the landmark investment deal between China and EU, provides provisions that are much more moderate than those in the US–China Trade Deal regarding the regulation of the financial assets management companies. Under "Annex I Entry 33" of CAI, national treatment is applied with restrictions to foreign companies in terms of requirements for foreign investors to invest in existing financial assets management company. To be more specific, foreign investors concerned shall be "financial institutions" and the total assets of a foreign investor shall be "no less than USD 10 billion by the end of the year prior to its application." Beyond that,

> a foreign investor who cumulatively acquires no more than 5% of the shares of a financial assets management company solely through securities transactions in domestic and overseas secondary markets shall not be subject to the restrictions set forth in this Entry.

These legal instruments barely indicate significant steps in liberating China's financial market. Therefore, the NPL-related provision in the US–China Trade Deal is an expediency responding to the pressure facing China at the peak of the US–China trade war rather than an attempt to welcome greater participation of foreign investors in the Chinese NPL disposal market.

6. Conclusion

From the earlier analysis, Article 4.5 of the US–China Trade Deal, as an attention-drawing regulatory catalyst for changes to the position of foreign investors in the Chinese NPLs disposal market, is unlikely to promote earth-shattering changes that could rock the dominant position of the state-owned Chinese AMCs in the targeted market. But foreign investors' advanced business know-how may force local AMCs to improve their approaches to NPLs disposal. As a sideline point to add, increase in international trade relies largely on the stability of the world's trade law. The US–China Trade Deal is an unpleasant development since it only demonstrates the tendency of major trading parties to weaponize international trade for political reasons and will encourage further departure of the trade policies in China and in the US from a rule-based approach to allow a power-based bargaining model.

Moving forward, local authorities will play an important role in supervising and regulating foreign investors' activities in the NPLs disposal market, especially in the primary market, and for this reason, these authorities' autonomy and manoeuvrability could not be overlooked. It is apparent from Article 4.5 of the Trade Deal that the non-discrimination principle is only applied when national licences are granted. Local authorities are left with a wide regulatory space in which to delay or impose extra restrictions and burdens on foreign applicants, driven by a strong preference for domestic NPLs buyers. This is likely to be the case since it aligns with the gradualist and experimental approach favoured by the central government of China. Foreign investors might encounter, for instance lighter-touch regulatory approvals for local AMCs, restrictions on foreign investment in dealing with some classes of assets, and tax risks.

Among provinces, there will be different, and potentially contradictory, policies regarding the entry-level and market access conditions for the involvement of foreign investment in the NPLs primary market. We try to evaluate the previously mentioned regulatory tendencies by making a comparison between the US–China Trade Deal and China's recent treaty practice with EU and some Asian countries, especially CAI and RCEP which have received broad attention and have significant implications on China's internal reforms. On the appearance, the US–China Trade Deal allows licences to be granted to US firms for NPL trading in the primary market, while the other two treaties fend off foreign investors in the same market. A logical assumption is that the policy objective of levelling the playground for the NPLs primary market is dubious. China's view of the foreign investors in disposing of NPLs has also been compared to that of the chosen foreign countries. The research results demonstrate that the chosen countries do not concern the involvement of foreign investors as much as China does. It is found that the disposal of NPLs requires timely and mixed measures, and granting foreign investors the right to market access by itself could not be a stand-alone solution.

The heavy burden of NPLs has forced the Chinese government to seek revolutions by different means. While asset disposals, bankruptcies, and debt-for-equity swaps[81] have a patchy record, they have not resolved the structural problems embedded in China's financial system. The US–China Trade Deal opens a window for foreign investment to directly join the game of the Chinese NPLs business. However, the conservative and piecemeal approach of the government policy emphasizing financial stability will undoubtedly set up strict standards and obstacles for the foreign capitals. Seeking the approval from multiple regulators could generate unexpected transaction costs to foreign investors unfamiliar with China's legal, regulatory, and commercial processes. Backed up by the support from local governments, the state-owned AMCs are and will be the dominant players in the market. Any foreign investors who are interested in the NPLs business could surely have an optimistic expectation upon the future of the Chinese NPLs market. They should keep in mind that as for now, this market is not a fair game. Perhaps the foreign investors need to weigh the potential risks hidden inside before swarming into the mist. Looking ahead, China is advised to make comprehensive plans for reforming the regulations of NPLs disposal to make the NPLs market more vibrant and legitimate. Thus far, some positive moves have been identified. For instance Shenzhen has implemented its local personal insolvency law which improves the legal framework for dealing with individuals' bad debts. Some other provinces followed suit but by installing judicial implementing measures instead of statutory law.

We are not sanguine about the prospect of bilateralism, that is bilateral trade deal, becoming an effective approach to solving differences regarding transaction in China's NPLs market. In the traditional trade area, bilateralism as well as regionalism are often criticized for causing more trade diversion than trade increase and for enabling strong counties to take advantage of the weaker ones.[82] In recent years, the tendency that countries choose to use bilateral treaties as a temporary solution to their political disputes[83] have further decreased the credit of bilateralism in managing international trade. The US–China Trade Deal is only another demonstrative example of this tendency. A more positive move would be the two parties' attempt to have provided in this trade deal a framework within which one may assess when it should yield to multilateralism. The key provisions of the US–China Trade Deal, however, only reflect the primary notion of the post-2018 US trade policy, that is protectionism, and China's willingness to employ outflanking strategies.

China's attitude towards multilateralism varies among fields. In dealing with trade issues, its preference for multilateralism is rather observable. When the US blocked the nomination of the members of the Appellate Body of the WTO and eventually caused the paralysis of the WTO Dispute Resolution Body, China worked with many member states to install a temporary arbitration appeal procedure. To resolve the US–China trade disputes, before major retaliatory actions, China filed claims to a WTO panel and won the case. The US branded the decision of the panel as "deeply disappointing" and reiterated the necessity for a reform of the WTO law. When China continues to support multilateralism and the US shifts away from it, the former will grow a larger role in decision-making from the latter and its allies within multilateral institutions. A reasonable option for the US, therefore, is to incorporate China's strategic preference for multilateralism into the trade policy and to actively engage through multilateral regimes in the discussion of what China means to be a "reasonable global shareholder" and how it will build a more open and fairer "immunity for all mankind."[84]

Notes

1 *Non-performing Loan, available at* https://en.wikipedia.org/wiki/Non-performing_loan.
2 Guidelines - Prudential treatment of problem assets – definitions of non-performing exposures and forbearance. (2016); Basel Committee on Banking Supervision, *Prudential*

Treatment of Problem Assets – Definitions of Non-performing Exposures and Forbearance (2016), *available at* www.bis.org/bcbs/publ/d367.htm.

3 Basel Committee on Banking Supervision, Prudential treatment of problem assets – definitions of non-performing exposures and forbearance. 2016.

4 Basel Committee on Banking Supervision, Guidelines - Prudential treatment of problem assets – definitions of non-performing exposures and forbearance. 2016; Basel Committee on Banking Supervision, Prudential treatment of problem assets – definitions of non-performing exposures and forbearance. 2016.

5 Basel Committee on Banking Supervision, Guidelines - Prudential treatment of problem assets – definitions of non-performing exposures and forbearance. 2016; Interim Measures for Classification of Asset Risks of Banks (商业银行金融资产风险分类暂行办法).

6 A delinquent loan is not necessarily recognized as a NPL as long as the value of the collateral backing it is sufficient to pay off the loan, even if the loan is more than 90 days past due.

7 § Articles 11, 12, 13.

8 IMF Working Paper: The Dynamics of Non-Performing Loans During Banking Crises: A New Database (WP/19/272). (2019).

9 Dalvinder Singh, *European Cross-Border Banking and Banking Supervision* 103 (Oxford: Oxford University Press, 2020).

10 Evelyn Cheng, *China Is Open to Taking on More Debt If That's What It Takes to Support the Economy*, *available at* www.cnbc.com/2020/10/16/china-is-open-to-more-debt-to-support-its-economy.html.

11 Enda Curran, *China's Debt Bomb* (2018), *available at* www.bloomberg.com/quicktake/chinas-debt-bomb.

12 The largest share of debt in the US is Treasury securities, which account for US$14.8 trillion (36%). Corporate debt (financial and non-financial) account for under US$10 trillion (23%).

13 *2020: Chinese Banks Dispose $467b in Non-performing Assets* (2021), *available at* https://news.cgtn.com/news/2021-01-22/2020-Chinese-banks-dispose-467-bln-in-non-performing-assets-XggBVOE492/index.html. Taking into account implied NPL based on methods used by the IMF, the balance of implied NPLs held by Chinese financial institutions at the end of 2015 can be ten times more than the figure stated in the official statistics. Shinichi Seki, "The Growing Problem of Excessive Debt in China: Estimating the Implied Non-Performing Loan Ratio and the Amount of Bad Loans", XVI *Pacific Business and Industries* No. 61 (2016).

14 Francis Fukuyama, *Trust: The Social Virtues and the Creation of Prosperity* 28 (The Free Press, 1995).

15 中国经营报 (China Business Journal), 地方监管部门窗口指导 逾期60天贷款纳入不良 [Local Regulatory Authority Window Operation: Debts 60 Days Due Can be Deemed as Non-performing Loans], *available at* https://baijiahao.baidu.com/s?id=1630661952798802954&wfr=spider&for=pc.

16 逾期60天贷款进 "不良"？官方统一回复来了！, *available at* www.zichanjie.com/article/463329.html.

17 PwC, "China's Non-Performing Loans Are Rising Fast - Are There Now Opportunities for Investors?" (December 2015), *available at* https://doczz.net/doc/8586081/china-s-non-performing-loans-are-rising-fast, accessed 3 October 2022.

18 Ben Charoenwong, Meng Miao and Tianyue Ruan, *Hidden Non-Performing Loans in China* (April 2021), *available at* https://abfer.org/media/abfer-events-2021/annual-conference/papers-immb/AC21P1054_Hidden-Non-Performing-Loans-in-China.pdf, accessed 3 October 2022.

19 Notice by the China Banking and Insurance Regulatory Commission, the People's Bank of China, the National Development and Reform Commission, and other Departments of Implementing Temporarily Deferred Repayment of Principal and Interest for Loans to Micro, Small, and Medium-sized Enterprise (2020).

20 2019: A sunnier outlook for international China NPL investors (2018).

21 Id. at 2.

22 Rebecca Isjwara and Francis Garrido, *Chinese Banks Set to Clean Up Balance Sheet More Quickly in Q4* (2020), *available at* www.spglobal.com/marketintelligence/en/news-insights/latest-news-headlines/chinese-banks-set-to-clean-up-balance-sheet-more-quickly-in-q4-61427131.

23 2021 National Trade Estimate Report on Foreign Trade Barriers.

24 Id. at 103.

25 China Banking Regulatory Commission has issued the *Notice of the China Banking Regulatory Commission on Issuing the Measures for the Capital Management of Financial Asset Management Companies (for Trial Implementation)* to help AMCs refocus on NPLs disposition. See *The Banking Regulatory Commission issued the Notice of the China Banking Regulatory Commission on Issuing the Measures for the Capital Management of Financial Asset Management Companies (for Trial Implementation) (*银监会印发《金融资产管理公司资本管理办法（试行）》*) (2018), *available at* www.gov.cn/xinwen/2018-01/01/content_5252176.htm.

26 The Administrative Measures for the Bulk Transfer of Financial Enterprise Non-performing Assets（金融企业不良资产批量转让管理办法）(2012).

27 Investment in Non-performing Loans in China. (2017).

28 Circular on Properly Adjusting Relevant Policies of Local Asset Management Companies by CBRC (中国银行监督管理委员会办公厅关于适当调整地方资产管理公司有关政策的函) (2016).

29 Bing Wang and Richard Peiser, "Non-Performing Loan Resolution in the Context of China's Transitional Economy", in Y. Song and C. R. Ding (eds), *Urbanization in China* (Lincoln Institute of Land Policy, 2007), Chapter 13, pp. 206–239, *available at* SSRN: https://ssrn.com/abstract=2093441.

30 Id.

31 Id.

32 The programme was initiated in 2017 to allow commercial banks in Shenzhen to sell NPLs directly to foreign investors for a testing period of one year. During the one-year pilot period, NPLs of face value of renminbi 6.8 billion were sold to foreign investors. In May 2018, the pilot program was upgraded by removing the one-year restriction and changing the pre-approval to pre-filing process. This pilot programme is applicable to banks in Shenzhen only. It is expected to be extended to commercial banks nationwide if the pilot programme proves successful.

33 China's development model is unique. The understandings of the Chinese economic system among countries diverse greatly. For instance the US has labelled China as "state capitalism" while China disagrees. See Wei Li, "Towards Economic Decoupling? Mapping Chinese Discourse on the China–US Trade War", 12 *The Chinese Journal of International Politics* 519, 532–533 (2019).

34 Lixing Zou, *China's Rise: Development-Oriented Finance and Sustainable Development* xxxviii (World Scientific Publishing Pte. Ltd., 2014).

35 Huixin Bi, Yongguan Cao and Wei Dong, Non-Performing Loans, Fiscal Costs and Credit Expansion in China. IDEAS Working Paper Series from RePEc, IDEAS Working Paper Series from RePEc (2018), *available at* https://www.bankofcanada.ca/wp-content/uploads/2018/11/swp2018-53.pdf, accessed 3 October 2022.

36 Anne-Marie Neagle, Andrew Fei, Richard Mazzochi and Xiaoxue (Stella) Wang, *China's NPL Market: Implications of the China-U.S. Trade Deal*, 186 (2020) *available at* https://www.kwm.com/global/insights/latest-thinking/chinas-npl-market-implications-of-the-china-us-trade-deal.html; Wei Ping He, "Why China's Banking Sector Remains Closed to Meaningful Foreign Competition", 27 *Journal of International Banking Law and Regulation* 186 (2012). According to Wei Ping He, the essence of the socialist market economy lies in government control and, where necessary, government intervention to maintain economic growth and economic, social, and political stability. Maintaining

economic stability conventionally involves avoiding high inflation and preventing excessive volatility in the financial market.

37 Zou, 418.

38 Gerard Caprio, et al., *Financial Liberalization: How Far, How Fast?* 4 (Cambridge University Press, 2001).

39 Victor Shih, "Dealing with Non-Performing Loans: Political Constraints and Financial Policies in China", (2004) *The China Quarterly* 922.

40 Singh, 110–111.

41 Id. at 112.

42 Id. at 114.

43 FSI Insights on policy implementation No 3: Resolution of non- performing loans – policy options. (2017).

44 Peter Cincinelli and Domenico Piatti, "Non-Performing Loans, Moral Hazard & Supervisory Authority: The Italian Banking System" (Gennaio–Giugno 2017) *Journal of Financial Management, Markets and Institutions* 5–6.

45 Vittorio Pozzi, *Guarantee Scheme for Non-performing Loan Securitisations: Latest Developments* (7 May 2019), *available at* https://www.lexology.com/commentary/banking-financial-services/italy/legance-avvocati-associati/guarantee-scheme-for-non-performing-loan-securitisations-latest-developments#Main%20innovations, accessed 3 October 2022.

46 Id.

47 European Commission, *State Aid: Commission Approves Prolongation of Market Conform Asset Protection Scheme for Banks in Greece* (2021), *available at* https://ec.europa.eu/commission/presscorner/detail/en/ip_21_1661.

48 Recent developments in tackling the Greek non-performing loans problem - Keynote speech at IMN's 2nd Annual Investors' Conference on Greek & Cypriot NPLs. (2019).

49 Risk reduction through Europe's distressed debt market (2018).

50 Id. at 9–10; John Mourmouras, "Recent Developments in Tackling the Greek Non-Performing Loans Problem – Keynote Speech at IMN's 2nd Annual Investors' Conference on Greek & Cypriot NPLs 5" (2019) 8, *available at* https://www.bis.org/review/r190214b.pdf, accessed 3 October 2022.

51 Patrizia Baudino and Hyuncheol Yun, "Resolution of Non-Performing Loans - Policy Options", *Financial Stability Institute* (9 October 2017), *available at* https://www.bis.org/fsi/publ/insights3.pdf, accessed 3 October 2022.

52 Mourmouras, *supra* note 50, 5.

53 Torsten Schwarze and Jürgen Storjohann, "The Sale and Acquisition of Non-performing Loans Under German Law", 21 *Journal of International Banking Law and Regulation* 77 (2006).

54 Id. at 79.

55 Tim Elkerbout and Ivo van Dijk, *Dutch Loan Portfolio Transactions: Supreme Court Judgment* (2020), *available at* https://transactions.freshfields.com/post/102gbhh/dutch-loan-portfolio-transactions-supreme-court-judgment, accessed 3 October 2022.

56 Tilmann Becker, Hui Zhao, Christian Cornett and Sandra Link, "Recent Development to German Foreign Investment Control", *King & Wood Mallesons* (5 February 2019), *available at* https://www.kwm.com/global/en/insights/latest-thinking/germany-further-tightens-transaction-environment-for-foreign-investors.html, accessed 3 October 2022.

57 Id.

58 European Systemic Risk Board, *Resolving Non-performing Loans in Europe*, 46 (2017), *available at* https://www.esrb.europa.eu/pub/pdf/reports/20170711_resolving_npl_report.en.pdf, accessed 3 October 2022.

59 The Federal Deposit Insurance Corporation (FDIC), Managing the Crisis: the FDIC and RTC Experience 1980–1994. Vol.1. District of Columbia: Federal Deposit Insurance Corporation (1998), *available at* https://babel.hathitrust.org/cgi/pt?id=mdp.39015043145542&view=1up&seq=1, accessed 3 October 2022.

60 Id. at 299.

61 Id. at 300.

62 Korea's experience in dealing with non-performing loans has generated important implications for China. See Wang Bing, *Non-Performing Loan Resolution in the Context of China's Transitional Economy (2007). Urbanization in China, Y. Song, C. R. Ding, eds. (Cambridge, MA: Lincoln Institute of Land Policy, 2007), Chapter 13, pp. 206–239., Available at SSRN* https://ssrn.com/abstract=2093441, *in* Urbanization in China 271, (Y. Song & R. Ding eds., 2007).

63 Resolution of Non-performing Assets: Experiences of Korea. (2018).

64 Baudino and Yun, 17.

65 Twenty years after the financial crisis in the Republic of Korea (ADBI Working Paper, No. 790) (2017).

66 Id.

67 European Systemic Risk Board, 49 (2017).

68 Douglas W. Arner, Emilios Avgouleas and Evan Gibson, "Overstating Moral Hazard: Lessons from Two Decades of Banking Crises", University of Hong Kong Faculty of Law Research Paper No. 2017/003 (2017), *available at* https://hub.hku.hk/bitstream/10722/239333/1/Content.pdf, accessed 3 October 2022.

69 Id.

70 Steven L. Schwarcz, "Too Big to Fool: Moral Hazard, Bailouts, and Corporate Responsibility", *Minnesota Law Review* 761 (2017); Charles Nolan, Plutarchos Sakellaris and John D. Tsoukalas, 'Optimal Bailouts of Systemic Banks', *Adam Smith Business School University of Glasgow Working Paper* (2017).

71 Emilios Avgouleas and Charles A.E. Goodhart, "Bank Resolution 10 Years from the Global Financial Crisis: A Systematic Reappraisal", Edinburgh School of Law Research Paper (2019) *available at* https://papers.ssrn.com/sol3/papers.cfm?abstract_id=3396888.

72 Notice by the General Office of China Banking and Insurance Regulatory Commission on Enhancing Supervision on Local AMCs (中国银保监会办公厅关于加强地方资产管理公司监督管理工作的通知) 银保监办发[2019] 153号 (2019).

73 *Administrative Measures on the Batch Transfer of Distressed Assets of Financial Enterprises* issued by CBIRC and the MoF stipulated that NPL disposition activities of local AMCs have to comply with the following conditions: "1. A batch transfer of 10 or more accounts is allowed; 2. Provincial AMCs are not allowed to sell distressed assets to third parties; 3. Distressed assets can only be restructured, meaning that bankruptcy is off-limits." See: Local Asset Management Companies in China: The Next Frontier to Tackle China's Local Debt Problem. (2014).

74 Patrick Yu, "The Future of Asset Management in China 2020," *Fleishmanhillard* (2020), *available at* https://fleishmanhillard.com/wp-content/uploads/2021/03/The-Future-of-Asset-Management-in-China-2020.pdf, accessed 3 October 2022.

75 Announcement No. 2 [2011] of the State Administration of Taxation – List of Tax Regulatory Documents Repealed in Full or in Part.

76 Notice of the Ministry of Finance and the State Administration of Taxation on Issues concerning Tax Policies on the China Cinda Asset Management Co., Ltd. and Other Three Financial Asset Management Companies (财政部 国家税务总局关于中国信达资产管理股份有限公司等4家金融资产管理公司有关税收政策问题的通知) No. 56 [2013] of the Ministry of Finance (2013).

77 Surprise?! VAT Supplementary Circular in Asset Management Sector Released at the Last Minute. (2017).

78 PwC, Seizing Opportunities from China-US Trade Deal and Managing Tax Risks: A Game-changer for US Asset Managers to Improve Access to China Financial Market (2020).

79 Gulong Ren and Jiaqi Zhang, *How to Invest in China's NPLS – A Legal Review* (2019) *available at* https://www.lexology.com/library/detail.aspx?g=9c9b6c0b-ae16-42ca-9249-675f2f1c57cb.

80 The Chinese NPL market in 2020: Regulatory Catalyst May Lead to Higher Volumes. (2020) *available at* https://www.pwccn.com/en/deals/publications/the-chinese-npl-marekt-in-2020.pdf.

81 Debt-for-equity swaps were promoted by China's National Development and Reform Commission and China Banking Regulatory Commission (now China Banking and Insurance Regulatory Commission) in 2016 to lower SOEs' debt level and strengthen banks' balance sheets as banks can digest overdue loans with limited capital charge and manageable risks. However, execution has been slow. As of June 2018, the amount of signed contracts was renminbi 1.7 trillion but only 20% of the contracts had been implemented. DBS Group Research, China Banking Sector, 14 August 2018.

82 Arie Reich, "Bilateralism versus Multilateralism in International Economic Law: Applying the Principle of Subsidiarity", 60 *The University of Toronto Law Journal* 263–287, 265, 266 (2010).

83 Yong-Shik Lee, "Weaponizing International Trade in Political Disputes: Issues Under International Economic Law and Systemic Risks", *Journal of World Trade* 405–428, 405–407 (2022).

84 Hui Zhang, "A Community of Shared Future for Mankind - The Contemporary Development of the Social Foundations Theory of International Law", 40 *Social Science in China* 186, 187–188 (2019).

6

WHY DID THE DOOR NOT OPEN WIDER IN THE AFTERMATH OF ALIBABA? – PLACING (OR MISPLACING) FOREIGN INVESTMENT IN A CHINESE PUBLIC LAW FRAME

China became the second-largest economic power in the world in 2010.[1] As the world's fastest-growing and most populous telecommunications and internet market,[2] China's overall telecoms business volume revenues in 2021 were 1.4 trillion yuan (about US$232.43 billion).[3] Foreign investors have long been attracted to this market while Chinese entrepreneurs hope to capitalize on the foreign funding.[4] Nevertheless, foreign investment in China's telecommunications industry has always been in the global spotlight. Google search engine's pull out of China in 2010 (mainly due to its dispute with the Chinese government over censorship of search results)[5] and Alibaba, Yahoo, and Softbank's dispute over Alipay in 2011 were two major events that brought China's telecoms industry and, more importantly, foreign investment policies into the global spotlight. The centre of the Alipay dispute is the legality of the "variable interest entity" structure or the VIE structure, a transactional model or device most foreign investors adopted in investing into China's telecoms sector, which is now under much tighter scrutiny of Chinese authorities.

This chapter examines China's regulatory measures in tackling the "variable interest entity" structure which has been widely adopted by foreign industrial players and investors to access China's telecommunications market and tries to "rationalise" these regulatory movements by offering a political economy analysis.

This chapter is structured as follows. Section 1 focuses on China's telecommunication laws and policies relating to foreign investment in the 1990s. Section 2 discusses China Unicom's use of the CCF structure in attracting foreign investment in the 1990s and the Chinese government's crackdown. Key Chinese laws and policies in the first decade of the 21st century are outlined in Section 3. Section 4 details the recent dispute among Alibaba, Yahoo, and Softbank over Alipay's ownership. Section 5 discusses the creation and utility of the VIE structure

DOI: 10.4324/9781003130499-6

by foreign investors to sneak around restrictive Chinese laws governing foreign investment in the telecoms sector. The VIE structure will be analyzed in terms of its functions and foreign investors' incentives of doing so against China's regulatory background. Section 6 outlines recent regulatory measures tightening up the regulatory space of the VIE structure. Section 7 offers an insight into the underlying rationale of these regulatory movements and an outlook of possible future developments based on a political economy line of thinking. Section 8 discusses some legislative attempts made by the Chinese government in the draft Foreign Investment Law to "legalize" the VIE structure. However, these attempts eventually were not materialized. A short conclusion follows in Section 9.

1. Chinese Telecommunications Laws and Policies in the 1990s

China adopted the open-door policy in 1978[6] and speeded up its economic reform in 1992, three years after the Tiananmen Square accident. The entire 1990s witnessed differential liberalization dominance as well as a departure from the conventional state planning system of the old days to a more market-oriented macroeconomic regulation and control.[7]

The laws and regulations of China in the 1990s exercised very tight control over the telecommunications industry, especially concerning the involvement of foreign capital into the sector. The PRC Wholly Foreign Owned Enterprise Law Implementing Rules, promulgated in 1990, provides that establishing wholly foreign owned enterprises (WFOEs) in the following industrial sectors shall be prohibited: "(c) post and telecommunications. . . ." It is evident that WFOEs cannot be established in the telecommunications service sector.[8] The Ministry of Post and Telecommunications Reiterating the Prohibition to Enter into Joint Operation in Post and Telecommunications Business with Foreign Investor Circular, issued on 20 June 1992, refers to the fact that "in some localities foreign investors attempted to enter into joint operation in wireless paging service and mobile phone telecommunications." The Ministry of Posts and Telecommunications in 1993 issued the Further Strengthening the Administration of the Telecommunications Market Opinion[9] and clearly provided that foreign merchants shall not operate or participate in the operation of telecommunications businesses within the Chinese territory.[10] More specifically, foreign entities, foreign enterprises, foreign individuals, WFOEs, Sino–foreign joint ventures, or cooperative joint ventures already established within the Chinese territory were excluded from the scope of players who can lawfully participate in the operation of the cable and/or wireless telecommunications business offered by the public and specialized telecommunication networks within China. The State Council's earlier notice in 1993 provided explicitly

> in order to avoid creating disorder in the telecommunications industry and to avoid influencing or interrupting the normal operation of telecommunications businesses, various regions and departments shall not establish

companies or other economic entities that engage in basic telecommunications business without the approval of the State Council.

Furthermore, the

> Chinese Communist Party (CCP) Central Committee and the State Council have clearly provided that foreign investors are prohibited from operating or participating in the telecommunications business within Chinese borders. All regions and departments including China Unicom shall strictly implement this policy of the State in the operational activities of their telecommunications business.[11]

The Ministry of Post and Telecommunications promulgated the Issues Relating to the Operation of Basic Telecommunications Business Circular on 5 September 1994 which also prohibited foreign investors from investing in the telecommunications industry.

The foreign investment regime in China has evolved significantly since its inception immediately after the adoption of the "open door" policy in 1978. Policy plays a very critically important role in this regime. Unlike other jurisdictions, policy in China not only affects the content and application of laws but also the day-to-day life of individuals and corporates. The conceptual approach drove the Chinese government to rely upon industrial policies in regulating and directing foreign investment. The then State Planning Commission, State Economic and Trade Commission and Ministry of Foreign Trade and Economic Cooperation (the predecessor of Ministry of Commerce, MOFCOM) jointly issued the Foreign Investment Industrial Guidance Catalogue in June 1995. The Catalogue is a list of investment guidelines that classified foreign-invested projects into four categories: "encouraged," "permitted," "restricted," and "prohibited." The "restricted" category limited the equity share that foreign firms could have in certain industries. The Catalogue signalled the state policies in attracting foreign investment.

The State Council approved a revised Catalogue on 9 December 1997 and the new Catalogue came into force on 1 January 1998. The 1997 Catalogue favoured those enterprises that were willing and able to bring high technology to China or promote exports and offered tax exemptions and other benefits to foreign-invested enterprises (FIEs). The 1997 Catalogue removed barriers to foreign participation in some restricted sectors such as distribution, infrastructure, energy, and power generation. However, the 1997 Catalogue's list of prohibited industries still included the operation and administration of telecommunications business. These "industries prohibited from foreign investment" should be interpreted in accordance with the Directing of Foreign Investment Tentative Provisions, which clearly prohibit any foreign companies, enterprises, other economic organizations or individuals from participating in investment in the industries where foreign investment is prohibited.

2. CCF Structure: Foreign Investors' Earliest Attempt to Access to Chinese Telecommunications Market and Chinese Government's Crackdown

In the 1990s, foreign investors made great efforts to sneak around the law restricting the involvement of foreign investment in the telecoms industry by adopting a so-called Chinese-Chinese-foreign structure ("CCF structure"). China Unicom was the first Chinese entity that used the CCF structure. When China Unicom was initially set up, it desperately needed a large amount of capital to expand its business operation. However, neither the PRC Joint Venture Law nor the PRC WFOE Law allows China Unicom to alleviate its capital shortage difficulties through establishing either equity or cooperative joint ventures with foreign investors. Nor does the WFOE work for this purpose. As a result, China Unicom adopted the CCF structure which assisted China Unicom in circumventing relevant restrictive provisions of the PRC Equity Joint Venture Law, PRC Cooperative Joint Venture Law, and PRC WFOE Law.

In China Unicom's CCF structure, an onshore joint venture between a local company and a foreign investor is set up first and the joint venture then makes the investment into a local telecoms company, which can either be a subsidiary of China Unicom or a company chosen by China Unicom with the approval of a China Unicom shareholder or a government authority close to the physical location of the project. China Unicom would then enter into project contracts with the joint venture according to the principle of "cooperative investment, China Unicom construction, China Unicom operation, and the sharing of interests and risks."[12] A simple CCF structure is indicated in Figure 6.1.

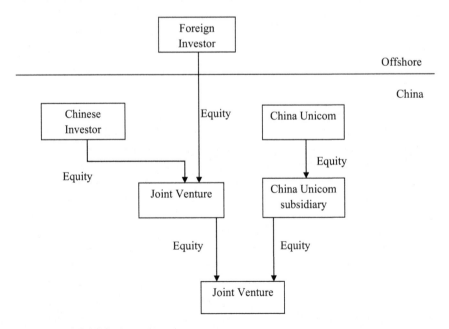

FIGURE 6.1 CCF Structure

The joint venture entered into by China Unicom in the CCF structure was technically viewed as a joint venture between two Chinese entities, which did not fit in the regulatory space of PRC foreign investment law. Hence, through the CCF structure, China Unicom was able to attract and utilize foreign capital into domestic telecoms projects. The rights and obligations of both foreign parties and China Unicom are clearly stipulated in the cooperation agreements. From 1995 and 1999, China Unicom executed around 46 cooperative projects in the form of CCF structure, including projects with French Telecom and Japan's NTT, and involved planned investments totaling US$1.5 billion and actual investments of US$1 billion.

The Chinese government disregarded this arrangement for a while but denounced this transactional model in 1999 claiming that the arrangement was illegal. The then Ministry of Information Industry issued an official document that eventually rejected China Unicom's CCF structure on 30 August 1999. In the spirit of the then validly effective Chinese laws and regulations which entirely ruled out foreign investment's participation in China's telecoms sector, the CCF structure was regarded as an unlawful tool to avoid Chinese regulatory barriers even though the CCF structure involved a joint venture between Chinese legal persons. Furthermore, the government required local companies to redress the CCF structure by buying out the foreign investors' stake. Although some affected foreign investors were big names in the marketplace such as Deutsche Telekom, the Chinese government firmly adhered to its clear-out crackdown policy. To terminate these CCF structure projects, China Unicom negotiated with various foreign investors including French Telecom, US Sprint, and Hong Kong First Pacific and eventually paid RMB 9.8 billion in capital, of which over RMB 4 billion was for compensation. The CCF incident indicated that any form of foreign investment in the telecommunications service industry in mainland China remains strictly prohibited in the 1990s.

3. Chinese Telecommunications Regulatory and Policy Regime in the Early 21st Century

China's accession to the World Trade Organization (WTO) on 11 December 2001 marked a new chapter of foreign investment in China. The significance of this event was that it unravelled a legally binding road map for China to further liberalize and modernize the economy and foreign investment regime per se. As a result, many remaining restrictions on foreign investment were removed, the principle of national treatment was more expansively implemented, and the regulation and supervision of foreign investment activities were subject more to legal rather than administrative means. The Chinese government has been focusing on adapting its industrial guidelines and regulations to its WTO commitments in the new century. However, these rules and regulations in relation to the information and telecommunications industry largely remain unchanged and the administrative measures remain as the main tool for the government to wield.

The key legislation governing the telecommunications industry is the PRC Regulations of Telecommunications (the "Telecoms Regulations"), issued by the State Council on 25 September 2000. Under the Telecoms Regulations, all telecommunications services businesses in China are categorized as either basic[13] or value-added telecommunications services businesses. A "value-added telecommunications business" is defined as a business that provides telecommunications and information services by using the basic facilities of public networks, which include internet information services (ICP services), content services, entertainment/gaming, commercial information, and positing services. The Telecoms Regulations further provide that the then Ministry of Information Industry (MII, the predecessor of the Ministry of Industry and Information Technology, MIIT) shall be responsible for the nationwide supervision and administration of telecommunications, including the issuance of the appropriate business licences for the conduct of telecommunications businesses. Under the Telecom Regulations, commercial operators of value-added telecommunications services must first obtain an operating licence from the MII (now MIIT) or its provincial level counterparts. Although the Telecoms Regulations do not in any way limit the scope of foreign investment in the telecoms service industry, it does provide that "specific procedures for investing and operating in the telecoms business in the PRC by foreign organizations or individuals as well as organizations or individuals of Hong Kong, Macao and Taiwan shall be separately formulated by the State Council."[14]

The Administrative Measures for Telecommunications Business Operating Licenses (the "Telecoms License Measures"), issued by the MII on 26 December 2001 and amended by the MIIT on 1 March 2009, is another piece of legislation which sets forth the types of licences required to operate the value-added telecoms business and the procedures for obtaining such licences. Under the Telecoms License Measures, an e-commerce service provider must obtain an inter-province operating licence, which is issued by the MII, in order to provide wireless value-added services nationally; or an intra-province operating licence to provide such services within a province.

It is clear that foreign investment was not welcome in China's telecoms service industry prior to China's entry into the WTO. Foreign investment in operating networks was not allowed. After its accession to the WTO, China is obligated to open to foreign investment some sectors of its economy that were previously closed. Telecommunications is one area that was closed to but has to be opened to foreign investment under China's WTO commitments. Under China's WTO Agreement, foreign investors shall be allowed ownership of a 25% equity in telecoms businesses. This ratio would be increased to 49% within three years after China's accession to the WTO. China also agreed that foreign businesses would be permitted to operate inter-city networks, meaning that foreigners would no longer be limited to furnishing operational activities in China's urban areas. In addition, China would open its lease services market for telecommunications cables.

China's State Council introduced regulations on the administration of foreign-invested telecommunications enterprises allowing joint ventures to invest and conduct activities in a broad range of areas which are to be phased in over a period of years. The most influential legislation relating to foreign investment in China's telecoms industry is the Regulations for the Administration of Foreign-Invested Telecommunications Enterprises (the "Foreign Invested Telecoms Regulations"), issued by the State Council on 11 December 2001 and further amended on 10 September 2008, according to which the ultimate foreign equity ownership in a value-added telecoms services business must not exceed 50%. The Foreign Invested Telecom Regulations set forth detailed requirements for the application for foreign investment, and such requirements include capitalization requirements, investor qualifications, and other application procedure. A foreign investor must demonstrate a good track record and experience in operating value-added telecoms services and the Chinese partner must submit an application to the MII (now MIIT) for procedural purposes. Foreign investors that meet these requirements must obtain approvals from the MIIT and the MOFCOM (the watchdog in charge of approving foreign investment projects), or their authorized local branches, and the relevant approval application process usually takes six to nine months.

Nevertheless, in practice, it has been extremely difficult for FIEs to obtain telecommunications operating licences even though the foreign equity is less than 50%. Based upon this author's no-names basis enquiries to MIIT, practically speaking, the MIIT has rarely approved an application for foreign investment into a PRC telecommunications business. It was reported that China had granted 22,000 telecoms operating licences but only seven of them were granted to FIEs.[15] This may attribute to the Chinese government's fear of foreign participation in the media and publishing industries, which may make the control and censorship of information more difficult,[16] and eventually make the CCP's ruling less manageable. The Chinese government occasionally tried to justify its prohibitive policy with the excuse of protecting the State's sovereignty as foreign dominance in the telecoms industry may bring negative impacts to China. To have a bite of the profitable telecoms business in China, foreign investors have worked out an artful transactional model to participate in Chinese telecommunications industry while avoiding regulatory barriers prohibiting foreign investment from being involved in the telecommunications sector.[17]

4. Episodes of Alibaba's Alipay

The episode of Alipay brought the VIE structure into the global spotlight. On 10 May 2011, Yahoo! Inc, which is a 43% shareholder of Alibaba.com Corporation ("Alibaba"), one of the largest Chinese internet companies, disclosed in its quarterly report that Alibaba's online e-commerce payment processing business, Alipay (similar to eBay Inc's PayPal), had been restructured: 100% of Alipay's ownership was transferred to a Chinese domestic company.[18] Next day, Yahoo!

Inc released a press statement indicating that Alibaba's spinning Alipay out of Alibaba occurred without the approval of Alibaba's board of directors or shareholders,[19] which was rejected by Jack Ma, the CEO of Alibaba.[20]

According to the notice of Alipay (China) Network Technology Company's application for the online payment business operating licence published by the Hangzhou Branch of the People's Bank of China (PBOC), China's central bank, on 22 December 2010, the current sole investor of Alipay was Zhejiang Alibaba E-Commerce Co., Ltd. ("Zhejiang Alibaba").[21] The basic information of Zhejiang Alibaba retrieved from the official website of Zhejiang Administration of Industry and Commerce, the local company registrar, shows that the legal representative of Zhejiang Alibaba is Jack Ma,[22] a 80% shareholder of the company.[23]

Prior to the Alipay dispute, Alipay was a subsidiary of Alibaba.[24] On 24 July 2009, the board of Alibaba decided by passing board minutes to transfer 70% of shares in Alipay (then incorporated in Cayman Islands) from Alibaba to Zhenjiang Alibaba. However, Alibaba maintained its control over Alipay through a VIE structure, which was used to circumvent the Chinese telecoms laws and rules under which a telecoms business operation licence can only be lawfully and validly held by a pure Chinese company rather than a foreign-invested enterprise (FIE). Through the VIE structure, Yahoo and Softbank can continue to control and enjoy economic benefits of Alipay via various contractual arrangements while Alipay would be safe to secure a valid operating licence from competent Chinese authorities. Zhejiang Alibaba, labelled as a consolidated affiliate of Alibaba in Alibaba's 2009 Annual Report,[25] was under control of Alibaba via the VIE structure until the first quarter of 2011.

Fearing that Alipay, being an FIE, might not be duly licensed in accordance with a new set of administrative measures[26] issued by the PBOC in 2011, Alibaba then transferred the remaining 30% of equity to Zhejiang Alibaba on 6 August 2010 so that Alipay was able to secure the licence it needed to continue operating. In this sense, having Alipay owned 100% by a domestic entity is a necessary move. In an interview with the *China Entrepreneur* magazine, Jack Ma disclosed that Alibaba's board had been in discussions of reorganizing Alipay for almost three years to comply with China's regulatory restrictions on foreign investment in e-payment operators. After the spinoff, Zhejiang Alibaba owns 100% of Alipay, which satisfies the regulatory requirement that Alipay is not owned by any foreign investor, via equity or contracts. At this point, Zhejiang Alibaba became Alibaba's VIE, whose beneficiary is Alibaba though its equity is owned by Jack Ma et al.

Things have changed dramatically since 26 January 2011 when the PBOC sent a fax to Alipay requesting it to declare whether or not it had a VIE arrangement with any foreign investor. This fax implicitly indicated that Alipay's application would not be accepted unless it is a pure Chinese-owned company without any VIE type of arrangement.[27] The PBOC's fax indeed left Alibaba with no options as the validity and effectiveness of Alipay's existing VIE structure triggers the endorsement of the State Council, which is almost an impossible mission in

China's bureaucratic system. Consequently, Jack Ma decided to terminate the VIE structure,[28] with the sole purpose of complying with Chinese law governing online payment businesses, and securing a valid licence to maintain the normal operation of Alipay.[29]

Thereafter, Alibaba, Yahoo, and Softbank (a 29.3% shareholder) have been under negotiation to monetize Alipay and eventually reached a compensation agreement, under which Alibaba would participate in the distribution of Alipay's future profits but would be subject to a cap on the amount of money it could receive in a sale or initial public offering (IPO) of Alipay. Alibaba will receive between $2 and $6 billion in proceeds from an IPO or any other type of liquidity event (i.e. the evaluation of Alipay is $1 billion, or the sale of entire Alipay's assets).[30] The amount to be paid to Alibaba in such events will be calculated by multiplying Alipay's equity value by 37.5%. Although there is no visibility into a timeline for Alipay's IPO, Yahoo, as a major shareholder, is entitled to force a liquidity event after ten years from now on. Under the deal, Alipay will pay to Alibaba, prior to a liquidity event like an IPO, a royalty and software technology services fee, which consists of an expense reimbursement and a 49.9 % share of the consolidated pre-tax income of Alipay and its subsidiaries.[31] In addition, Alipay will continue to offer payment services to Alibaba on preferential terms. This settlement agreement reduced both the ownership and the share of earnings as Alibaba is no longer a beneficiary under a VIE structure after the restructuring given the fact that Alipay is the largest online platform in the world in terms of its registered users (550 million compared to PayPal's 94.4 million), transactions, and total payment volume.[32] Although the VIE structure has been abolished, this compensation agreement continues to entitle Yahoo and Softbank to enjoy Alipay's economic benefits before and after its IPO or any other liquidity event. Hence, the compensation agreement may, at least economically, serve the function the VIE structure has played before Alipay's latest restructuring.

5. "Creative Compliance" – How and Why Is a VIE Structure Used?

The centre of the dispute among Alibaba, Yahoo, and Softbank is the VIE structure, which is essentially a set of contracts between a foreign entity and an internet company in China. In practice, foreign investors often utilize the VIE structure to circumvent the entrance barriers imposed by Chinese laws[33] in some heavily regulated, highly restricted but lucrative industrial sectors, which have not been entirely opened to foreign investors.[34]

A VIE structure (as illustrated in Figure 6.2) is set up so that foreign investors can invest in an offshore holding company, that is a special purpose vehicle (SPV) that channels equity capital into a wholly foreign-owned enterprise (WFOE) while Chinese shareholders of the local telecoms entity will own shares of the SPV. Meanwhile, as the WFOE, due to its foreign equity, is not qualified to apply for a telecoms operating licence from the Chinese government authority,

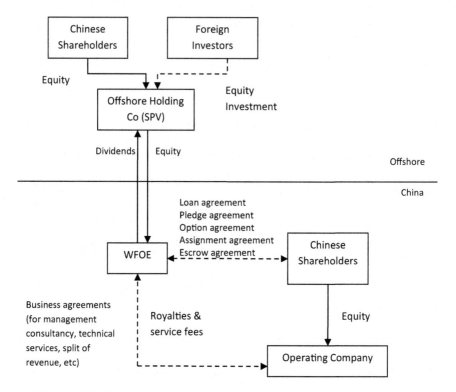

FIGURE 6.2 VIE Structure

it nominates the Chinese shareholders to own the operating entity that possesses a valid telecoms operating licence necessary for a business and operates telecoms assets in China.

A control mechanism, involving use of pledges, proxies, and powers of attorney, will be established between the WFOE and the nominee shareholders, thereby securing the WFOE's control through contracts and exercise all corporate controls over the operating company whilst a shareholding control is not able to be achieved under the current law. The nominee shareholders will also grant an option to purchase their interest in the operating company to the WFOE or the SPV, to be exercised at the optionee's discretion when relevant PRC laws relax the regulatory restrictions and allow foreign investors to directly and solely invest in the industry. A voting agreement may be necessary so as to enable the nominee shareholders to take instructions from the WFOE or SPV when they cast votes in the shareholders' meetings. These contracts make the nominee shareholders contractually act on behalf of the WFOE as the shareholders of the operating company.[35]

Meanwhile, a cash extraction mechanism is put in place between the operating company and the WFOE in the form of a bundle of contracts by and between the WFOE and the operating company. Pursuant to these contracts, the operating company engages the WFOE as its exclusive technology consultant and service supplier to provide the technological consulting, technical training, and other services to the operating company in return for an annual fee in the form of royalties or licensing fees. Other contracts such as accounting services agreement and know-how or trademark licensing contract can be entered into so that an increased revenue stream can be secured. These commercial contracts can help the WFOE not only capture the operating company's profits in the form of service fees and royalties, but also effectively control Chinese shareholders in exercising their shareholder power in the voting process in the operating company. The VIE structure may allow a foreign investor to be paid for its equity investment (through the WFOE) based on the performance of the Chinese telecoms company.

Through the VIE structure, the SPV invested by both Chinese and foreign investors can successfully get access to the operating assets in China, lawfully owned by the Chinese shareholders, which in turn helps secure the telecoms operating licence. More importantly, Chinese laws and regulations are technically complied with.

A less complicated transactional device, the "round-trip investment" model, has been used by Chinese investors in restructuring their businesses located in mainland China with the aim of achieving various tax, regulatory, and legal purposes. In a "round-trip investment" model (as illustrated in Figure 6.3), an SPV needs to be incorporated in a "satellite" common law jurisdiction, typically Hong Kong, Cayman Islands, British Virgin Islands, or Bermuda. The SPV, owned or controlled by Chinese investors, then controls an onshore operating entity either through direct acquisition or contractual arrangement. If direct

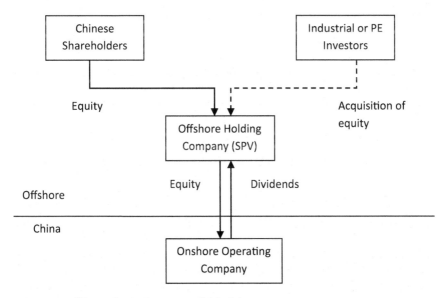

FIGURE 6.3 "Round-trip Investment" Model

acquisition, the SPV acquires and owns the equity capital in the onshore operating company, which retains ownership and operates existing business assets. Thus, the original Chinese investors own both the offshore SPV and the onshore operating company. After the restructuring is completed, foreign investors invest into the offshore SPV. In essence, the "round-trip investment" model is a less advanced variation to the VIE structure.

Both the VIE structure and the "round-trip investment" model reflect the local business community's preference to be "packaged" as foreign investment,[36] and thereby (i) achieving a preferential tax treatment;[37] (ii) circumventing rigid Chinese FIE laws and thus attracting foreign investment;[38] (iii) smoothening the overseas listing process;[39] and (iv) utilizing concepts of preferred shares and preferential rights and thus facilitating execution of merger and acquisition or private equity (PE) transactions.

The VIE structure has now become the prevailing market practice for foreign investors to invest into a China venture. Many China-based internet search engines or e-commerce sites such as Baidu.com, Sohu.com, Alibaba.com, 51job.com, eLong.com, and KongZhong.com adopted the VIE structure, and these e-portals have been successfully listed in either New York or Hong Kong. As of April 2011, 42% of Chinese companies listed in the United States have used the VIE structure to run an internet search engine or an e-commerce platform in China, and thousands of unlisted companies continue to operate through the use of the VIE structure.[40]

As a "forum shopping" strategy, foreign investors land investments into China through offshore vehicles because the offshore regime is more flexible and has higher standards, thus better supports multiple rounds of debt and equity financings. The VIE structure, like a "locked-in" market norm, is the result of efficient bargaining in a series of transactional events.[41] The advantages of this model are the possibility of avoiding the burdensome Chinese corporate law and regulatory regime and, in spite of the "switching costs," reducing transaction costs. This transactional device, as a type of an informal sanction, has helped more and more Chinese companies "piggyback" on more user-friendly offshore jurisdictions to facilitate private placement and future overseas listings in Hong Kong, New York, or elsewhere, thereby partially replacing formal legal institutions in China.

6. Legality of the VIE Structure and Recent Regulatory Countermeasures

Although VIEs have been widely used for years in China, the recent Alipay case reaffirmed that the VIE structure, having an *ad hoc* character, is a matter of dubious legality, enforceability, and sustainability. To date, the VIE structure has never been tested in a PRC court[42] and there is therefore no certainty that the legality of such structure will be recognized or that such a structure will not encounter regulatory scrutiny (or even a crackdown) at a later stage. Foreign industrial and PE investors seem to have taken the commercial view that the adoption of the VIE structure is a business risk worth bearing.

The broad use of the "round-trip investment" model *per se* has had a damaging impact on China's tax pool, state-owned assets, foreign exchange control, and regulatory efficiency. In addition, the "round-trip investment" model has been used in money-laundering activities speculating on renminbi-denominated assets.[43] Essentially, both devices are instruments used by Chinese and foreign businesses to exploit both regulatory law and practice to resist control and are typical examples of "creative compliance" whereby investors play the system through tax and regulatory arbitrage. Chinese authorities have incrementally been tightening up regulatory loopholes in the past several years. The new regulations promulgated by China's central bank can be viewed as one of the latest regulatory attempts.[44]

6.1 Foreign Exchange Control Rules in 2005

The State Administration of Foreign Exchange (SAFE, the Chinese watchdog in charge of foreign exchange control) issued two sets of rules in January and April 2005 respectively: the Circular on Relevant Issues in Perfecting Foreign Exchange Control in Mergers and Acquisitions by Foreign Investors ("Circular 11") and the Circular on Relevant Issues in the Registration of the Offshore Investments of Individual Domestic Residents and Foreign Exchange Registration in respect of Mergers and Acquisitions by Foreign Investors ("Circular 29"). These two Circulars required Chinese residents, for the purpose of making an investment in China through an offshore SPV, to carry out approval and registration formalities with the SAFE or its local branches. In particular, these two circulars required residents to obtain approval from the national-level SAFE but failed to provide any procedural guidance to applicants to follow with. These two circulars, therefore, made obtaining approval from SAFE an impossible mission, and *de facto* froze PRC investments involving offshore companies controlled by PRC residents, considerably slowing the flow of PRC-related private and foreign investments into China and red-chip listings.

The foreign investment community lobbied against both Circular 11 and Circular 29 due to the lack of procedural guidance and regulatory certainty. In October 2005, the SAFE issued the Circular on Relevant Issues in the Foreign Exchange Control with respect to the Financing and Round-trip Investment through Offshore Special Purpose Companies by Residents Inside China ("Circular 75") to repeal Circular 11 and Circular 29.[45] Under Circular 75, Chinese residents[46] need to register[47] their round-trip investments[48] with the local SAFE office: (i) before forming or taking control of a special purpose company[49] abroad;[50] (ii) when injecting a domestic enterprise's assets or equity into an SPV;[51] (iii) when conducting an equity financing exercise abroad after injecting assets or equity into an SPV;[52] or (iv) within 30 days of a material change in the capital structure – including external guarantees – of an SPV controlled by the residents.[53]

In addition, a domestic resident must go through the approval, or registration procedure, for the domestic enterprise's receipt of the round-trip investments or loans from an SPV's financing proceeds like any other domestic enterprise engaging in similar foreign exchange transactions.[54] The consequence of failing to register the round-trip investment with SAFE, or its local branch, or comply with other SAFE rules is two-fold. The offshore parent company's Chinese subsidiary will be prohibited from distributing "profits, dividends, liquidation proceeds, equity transfer proceeds, capital reduction proceeds" out of China[55] and will bear liability under Chinese law for violation of the relevant foreign exchange rules. Compared to Circulars 11 and 29, Circular 75 reopened the door to Chinese residents who are able to use an offshore SPV to conduct offshore financings.

SAFE issued the Operating Procedures Regarding Issues Concerning Foreign Exchange Control on Financing and Round-trip Investment Through Offshore Special Purpose Companies by Domestic Residents ("Circular 106") on 29 May 2007 to clarify Circular 75. Circular 106 works to implement Circular 75 by not only outlining a road map of the documentation and intricate registration requirements for the multiple stages of SPV financing, but also imposing new compliance burdens on Chinese residents' use of SPVs in offshore jurisdictions. Accordingly, a domestic target company in a round-trip investment is required to have a three-year operating history and the registration requirement is extended to Chinese residents "greenfield" investments. The scope of "Chinese residents" is further expanded to any foreigner who "has permanent residence in China, owns onshore assets or interest in the Chinese company, or beneficially owns offshore asset or interest converted from his assets in the Chinese company."[56]

6.2 MII's Value-added Telecoms Business Rules in 2006

The Ministry of Information Industry (MII, the predecessor of the Ministry of Industry and Information Technology, MIIT) on 13 July 2006 issued the Circular on Strengthening the Administration of Foreign Investment in and Operation of Value-added Telecommunications Business (the MII Circular), which introduces three elements in the way the law is to be interpreted and enforced: (i) the holder of a value-added telecoms service (VATS) licence[57] cannot (a) lease, transfer, or sell the VATS licence to a foreign investor or (b) provide resources, premises, facilities, and other conditions for the illegal operation of telecoms business by a foreign investor in the PRC;[58] (ii) the VATS licence holder must own the domain name and trademark that it uses, have the necessary premises and facilities to operate the VATS business, and have in place its own security system;[59] and (iii) a VATS licence holder must make a filing stating that it is in compliance with the requirements of the MII Circular.[60] A licence holder will be subject to a "self-investigation and self-rectification" programme, meaning that it must itself report any non-compliance with the requirements of the MII Circular by 1 November 2006. If a licence holder fails to comply with these requirements and cure such non-compliance within a specified time frame, the MII or its local counterparts have discretion to take measures against such licence holders, including revoking their VATS licences.

The mischief that the prohibition, that is "a holder of a VATS licence cannot lease, transfer or sell the VATS license," is aimed at those structures where the VATS licence holder is merely a shell, holding the licence with no real operations. In effect, the MII Circular is intended to attack the licence holder who has leased out or transferred the licence to the FIE.

6.3 Mergers and Acquisitions Rules in 2006

The most influential piece of legislation which had an immediate and widespread effect on the VIE structure is the Provisions on the Acquisitions of Domestic Enterprises by Foreign Investors ("M&A Rules") in 2006.[61] To restore a higher level of scrutiny and streamline the approval procedure, the M&A Rules require domestic companies to disclose the offshore shareholding structure to and obtain approval from the MOFCOM before setting up an offshore SPV;[62] meanwhile no trusteeship, holding through agency or other means, is allowed to be used to circumvent these procedural requirements.[63] After receiving preliminary approval from the MOFCOM, a domestic company is entitled to submit application documents for the overseas IPO by the SPV to China Securities Regulatory Commission (CSRC), China's securities regulator. Following the CSRC's approval, the domestic company is required to apply to the MOFCOM for an FIE approval certificate – bearing the legend "equity held by an overseas SPV" – valid for one year from the date of issuance of the business licence. The domestic company must submit both a report of its overseas IPO through an SPV and the IPO proceeds repatriation plan to MOFCOM within 30 days following the IPO.[64] In addition, an SPV must restore the domestic firm to its initial shareholding composition if the listing does not take place within one year. The M&A Rules make the entire registration/approval regime more clumsy, burdensome, uncertain, time-consuming, and costly. Under the M&A Rules, the VIE structure is overall unworkable and the flow of new PE-backed companies and the route of red-chip listings have been effectively closed off.[65] As a matter of fact, MOFCOM and CSRC have not approved any related transactions and overseas IPOs since the promulgation of the M&A Rules. Almost all the offshore restructurings of the VIE structure may have to stop.[66]

6.4 Tax Notice 82 in 2009

The new PRC Enterprise Income Tax Law, effective as of 1 January 2008, for the first time introduced the concept of Tax Resident Enterprise ("TRE"). In early 2009, looking to secure a sensible tax pool, the State Administration of Taxation issued a Notice 82[67] to clarify the concept of "establishment" in the "round-trip investment" structure.[68] Under the Enterprise Income Tax, an enterprise that is established outside the PRC but has its "place of effective management" in the PRC is regarded as a PRC tax resident enterprise. Notice 82 set out certain proposed interpretative guidance on what constitutes a place of effective management. Under the Notice 82, overseas enterprises that are "controlled" by PRC enterprises may be deemed to be PRC tax residents when certain conditions are satisfied.[69] With the passing of the Notice 82, the non-residency status of the offshore SPV in the "round-trip investment" structure may be difficult to maintain. An offshore SPV may be regarded as a PRC tax resident under the Notice 82. As an overriding consideration, the Notice 82 laid down the substance-over-form principle as the basis for determination of the place of effective management. Notice 82 is the PRC authority's major tax rules to tighten up control over "round-trip investments" and may push industrial and PE investors to reconsider the use of the "round-trip investment" model, or other protective strategies, in their China-related deals.[70]

With the aim of further standardizing the tax administration for the CCCFCs which obtained Chinese TRE status (known as overseas registered Chinese-capital controlled tax resident, or "deemed overseas TREs" in short), the State Administration of Taxation released the Administrative Measures for Overseas Registered Chinese-capital Controlled TREs (Trial) on 27 July 2011. The Measures, effective from 1 September 2011, cover the major tax matters concerning deemed overseas TREs including application procedures of the TRE status, documentation requirement, CIT treatments, administration and collection matters, and application of double tax treaty provisions.

6.5 Online Game Rules in 2009

The Notice of Implementing the Provisions of the State Council on "Three Determinations" and the Relevant Explanations of the Central Commission Office for Public Sector Reform and Further Strengthening the Administration of the Pre-approval of Online Games and Examination and Approval of Imported Online Games (the "Online Game Notice") came into effect on 28 September 2009.[71] The Online Game Notice merely has six loosely drafted articles, one of which deals specifically with the VIE structure and clearly prohibits foreign investors from investing in the online game service industry by "actually controlling or participating in the online game operations of domestic enterprises in such indirect ways as establishing another joint venture company, signing relevant agreements or providing technical support."[72] Any violation of these prohibitive rules will lead to the revocation of a business licence or a telecoms operating licence.[73] As such, contractual control, the substance of the VIE structure, is ruled out as an indirect method foreign investors may rely upon for market access.[74]

6.6 PBOC Measures on Online Payment Services in 2010

The immediate cause of the Alipay case can be traced back to 21 June 2010 when a nationally unified administrative permit, the Payment Services License,[75] was introduced by the Administrative Measures on Payment Services of Non-financial

Institution, issued by the PBOC.[76] It will be mandatory for all non-financial institutions which provide payment services (including online payment services, prepaid card issuance services, and bank card acceptance services) to apply for a payment services licence.[77] No one is allowed to operate online payment businesses without obtaining such a licence after 1 September 2011. The applicant for a payment service licence shall be a limited liability company or joint-stock company legally formed inside the PRC.[78] Where the applicant is an FIE, its business scope, the eligibilities of overseas investors, the investment ratio of the overseas investors and other such matters shall be determined by the PBOC in other initiatives and the applications made by FIEs will be subject to the approval of the State Council.[79] Even with this exception, the administrative measures effectively rule out the possibility for an FIE to obtain the appropriate licence.[80] In other words, the online payment services licence will only be granted to Chinese-owned entities. The PBOC's Measures directly led to the transfer of equity in Alipay and the removal of the VIE structure coined in Alibaba's corporate structure, which in turn sparked the dispute among Alibaba, Yahoo, and Softbank.

6.7 National Security Review Rules in 2011

The Alipay case is not the end of the story. For the purpose of guiding foreign investors' mergers and acquisitions of domestic enterprises and safeguarding national security, the General Office of the State Council issued the Notice on Establishment of the Security Review System for Mergers and Acquisitions of Domestic Enterprises by Foreign Investors ("State Council Circular 6") on 3 February 2011.[81] The national security regime focuses on foreign investors' mergers and acquisitions of all types of enterprises such as military industry enterprises and their ancillary enterprises, the enterprises around the key and sensitive military facilities and other units which have impact on national defense security, and which may result in foreign investors' acquisition of actual control over the enterprises.[82]

New security review rules from the MOFCOM,[83] effective on 1 September 2011, clarify national security reviews of foreign investments in Chinese companies and bar them from using arcane investment structures or techniques such as "multi-level reinvestment," "nominee shareholders," and "control by agreement" to evade China's security review process. The relevant provision reads:

> Whether a merger or acquisition of a domestic enterprise by a foreign investor falls within the scope of merger and acquisition security review shall be determined on the basis of the substance and actual impact of the transaction. No foreign investor shall substantially evade the merger and acquisition security review in any form, including but not limited to proxy, trust, multi-level reinvestment, lease, loan, variable interest entities (agreement-based control) and offshore transaction.[84]

Although the rules are vaguely worded for application, they implicitly target the VIE structure and explicitly leave regulators with more discretionary powers. The term "agreement-based control" is explicitly highlighted as a form used by foreign investors to evade the security review regime. It is clear that the VIE structure will be deemed as a domestic enterprise actually controlled by a foreign investor and thus will be subject to a security review. Both the State Council Circular and MOFCOM rules have adopted a clearly restrictive approach to applying the security review rules to foreign investment projects and signalled the authorities' intention to place the VIE structure under deeper and heavier regulatory scrutiny and supervision. Nevertheless, given the vagueness of rules, the exact scope of implementation remains unclear. The foreign industrial players and PE investors should no longer base their business operations and deal designing on the assumption of Chinese government's tacit approval of the VIE structure. More likely, the VIE structure may be subject to closer scrutiny in future transactions.[85]

The loss suffered by Yahoo! and Softbank may happen to every single foreign investor who invests into the PRC telecoms companies through the VIE structure. Any further tightening on foreign investment policy could seriously affect Chinese web companies which utilize the VIE structure, such as Baidu (China's largest online search engine by revenues), Sina (China's leading miroblog), YouKu (the biggest online video company by revenues), RenRen (the biggest Facebook clone by revenues), and Tencent (the owner of QQ, an instant messaging tool). The more heavily controlled regime also risks crippling any upcoming Chinese web's IPOs in an offshore stock exchange, which would become nearly impossible in the face of ministry-level approval for each VIE. Both foreign investors and Chinese companies may have to face a crisis due to a possible abolishment of their VIE arrangements. In this sense, the Alipay drama sent an alarming signal that the VIE structure may not be safe for foreign investors, and the risk surrounding the use of the VIE structure is real and pressing.

7. Understanding Chinese Law – Placing Foreign Investment in a Chinese Public Law Frame

One of the major regulatory headaches both in China and abroad nowadays is creative compliance. No longer remains as an issue the compliance in form, but non-compliance in substance, in that the regulated seeks to resist regulation by working out an "artful" structure that technically complies with the law, compared to that of an outright/flagrant breach. Investors find imaginative means to interpret rules or package deals such that their activities can be categorized to comply with regulations at the same time as avoiding any disadvantageous impact or consequence they would otherwise have had. The use of the "round-trip investment" model or the VIE structure is creative compliance as both of them involve advantageous interpretations of grey areas, seeking out loopholes in specific rules, complying with letter not spirit, with form not substance, or dreaming up devices which regulators had not even thought of, let alone regulated.

7.1 Microviewed Legitimacy in Private Law

On a literal reading of Circular 75, M&A Rules, Circular 106, and Tax Notice 82, it is getting more and more difficult, if not entirely impossible, for Chinese residents to take advantage of SPVs to inflow round-tripping investments or make public or private offerings in the overseas capital markets. These regulatory changes significantly tighten the regulatory environment for offshore restructurings in potential telecoms projects or PE transactions. The motives of MOFCOM, SAFE, Taxation Bureau, and other authorities appear to prevent China's high-quality assets from being listed overseas, to monitor the foreign currency flows and – probably more importantly – to secure domestic listings and tax revenues.

Circular 75 and M&A Rules, together with other regulatory measures, are a revival of previous regulatory attempts to address the disguised foreign direct investment (FDI) in the form of the "round-trip investment" model or the VIE structure, either of which causes a huge loss to the national welfare. For instance businessmen and top corrupt officials may use SPVs to transfer state-owned assets, launder corruption proceeds, and avoid tax liabilities, as SPVs are easily packaged as shell companies without any substantial assets. Where the nominee structure, SPVs, trust, and bearer shares are used, the ultimate shareholders of the business may be covered or disguised well through various layers of corporate veils and cannot be easily tracked down. If the "round-trip investment" truly constitutes 25% to 50% of the total FDI into China,[86] it exaggerates China's foreign exchange reserves.[87] This could increase the political pressure on China to re-evaluate the exchange rate between renminbi and US dollars.[88]

An array of rules and circulars from the MOFCOM, SAFE, and Taxation Bureau from 2005 to 2009 were some examples of the tension between China's regulatory concerns addressing high-quality domestic assets being drained overseas and the motivation of foreign investors to "vote with their feet" for an international standard regime in which the transaction can be structured in a highly automated and structured manner. It signals the regulatory body's intention to, with a "responsive" or "tit for tat" approach,[89] integrating offshore transactions into the Chinese regulatory framework. Nonetheless, various additional governmental approval requirements and procedural delays may cause a chilling effect on many legitimate transactions that actually sustain FDI flows that might otherwise slow because increasing transaction costs and inefficiency costs make China less attractive for FDI.[90] The regulatory intervention may ultimately deter PE or other investment activities essential to improving the efficiency of the corporate law regime, which is in line with findings that government programmes often hinder rather than help the growth of FDI activities and PE markets.[91]

7.2 Macroviewed "Rationale" in Public Law

Judging from a series of regulatory responses to the telecoms sector from 2009 onwards, it appears clear that regulatory restrictions curbing foreign investment remain in legislation and practice. It is not promising, at least in a short term, that foreign investment and financing will find its way into China's telecoms sector sooner or easier than expected. This makes economic sense. The whole foreign investment environment is changing: China is no longer desperate for cash. Rather, the European Union and other developed countries turned to China for possible funding of the Eurozone bail-out fund.[92] Foreign investment nowadays may contribute to inflation, trade imbalance,[93] and local corruption.[94] Correspondingly, the pro-foreign investment atmosphere has changed which is more obvious from the recent tension between the US and China over Google's business operation in China[95] as well as between Australia and China concerning Rio Tinto's four employees arrested on charges of taking bribes and stealing commercial secrets.[96] The less favourable foreign investment policy towards the VIE structure is in line with a rising chorus of complaints from the foreign business community concerning China's protectionist regulatory environment and increasing hostility to foreign multinationals.[97]

As discussed earlier, the regulatory actions to scrutinize the "round-trip investment" model and the VIE structure have some legitimate grounds. Why then have various regulators been keen to firm up the regulatory space covering the VIE structure more recently? The more hostile policy towards the VIE structure and foreign telecoms investors indeed makes more political sense. Chinese laws and regulations that limit foreign investors from engaging in industrial sectors are considered related to national security such as agriculture, real estate, media, and telecommunications. A more restrictive approach taken by the Chinese government towards the VIE structure *per se* is mainly related to, among others,[98] the Chinese government's national security concerns.[99] This may be attributed to the Chinese government's fear of foreign participation in the media and publishing industries, which may make the control and censorship of information more difficult,[100] and eventually make the Chinese Communist Party's (CCP) ruling less manageable. In line with this line of argument, the Chinese government occasionally tried to justify its prohibitive policy with the excuse of protecting the state's sovereignty, as foreign dominance in the telecoms industry may bring negative impacts to China. The tightening regulatory regime of the VIE structure is also attributable to Chinese authorities' way of looking at and understanding the internet and telecoms sector.

The contemporary era is one where information flow and access touch upon every single aspect of our life, be it public or personal. Therefore, the regulation of the exchange and dissemination of information has become an important part of overall governmental control and societal management in the face of continuous global economic downturn. This is particularly true in China. Maintaining social stability and national security and controlling the flow of information are the priority of the Chinese government. Hence, to curb foreign investment, participation in the operation of the telecoms industry is an inherent part of this policy strategy. The Chinese government's conservative and cautious approach to tackling the information industry has been consistent and long standing. For example as early as on 25 September 2000, the State Council issued the Administrative Measures on Internet Information Services,[101] which specify that the internet information services regarding, among others, news, publication, education, medical and health care, pharmacy, and medical appliances are required to be examined, approved, and regulated by the relevant authorities. ICP service providers are prohibited from providing services beyond those included in the scope of their ICP licence or the registration information. Furthermore, the measures specify a list of prohibited content. ICP service providers must monitor and control the information posted on their websites. If any prohibited content is found,[102] they must cease dissemination of the offending content immediately, keep a record, and report to the relevant authorities. To the extent that PRC regulatory authorities find any content displayed on or through the website objectionable, they may require ICP service providers to limit or eliminate the dissemination or availability of such content on the website or impose penalties, including the revocation of operating licences or the suspension or shutdown of online operations.

Chinese authorities no longer merely regard the internet sector as an industry or business generating lucrative profits. Rather, the internet and websites are powerful forms of media, which China always controls tightly and leaves no space for foreign investors to participate in or intervene with. For young netizens *per se*, microblog (Weibo platform, a Chinese substitute for Twitter) or QQ[103] is much more powerful and influential than conventional newspapers and state-run TV and radio programmes. In the eyes of the Chinese government, a sharper economic slowdown and double-digit inflation may lead to serious domestic social unrest, including labour strikes over layoffs, unemployment or cuts in overtime, and outbreaks of violence caused by land confiscations or police abuses,[104] which could pose risks for the CCP ruling and spark large-scale political protests.[105] Modern technologies such as mobile phones and QQ have been recently used to coordinate and organize labour strikes in southern China.[106] This political element triggers much heavier regulatory scrutiny and policing response than before. For instance China's broadcasting watchdog, the State Administration for Radio, Film and Television, has recently stepped up censorship and control of local television programmes by warning local TV stations to focus more on "quality, responsibility and values" rather than exclusively on "entertainment."[107] Some bloggers and internet activists campaigning for social justice through internet and online messaging have been sentenced to imprisonment for the charge of "provoking quarrels and creating disturbance." Activist Zhao Lianhai, who helped parents whose children (including Zhao's own son) fell ill after drinking formula milk tainted with the industrial chemical melamine and called on supporters to protest via internet, was sentenced to two and a half years jail.[108] The Chinese government is reclaiming at least part of its propaganda authority by introducing a government edition of microblog with 19,000 or so officials and government departments' tweeting and 5,000 police accounts.[109] In the near future, China may grow more heavy-handed in policing the internet, telecommunications, and media sectors given its social management and political governance system.

Currently, censorship is a state policy in China where foreign social networking sites such as Facebook, YouTube, and Twitter are blocked[110] since they are viewed by the Chinese authorities as potential vehicles for fomenting opposition to the CCP ruling.[111] To this end, the Chinese government has engaged both local and foreign researchers and technology companies to tailor hardware and software such as the Great Firewall programme used for internet blocking and surveillance.[112] China's strict internet censorship system has kept many Western internet competitors out of the Chinese market. The most dramatic and high-profile case is Google, which relocated its China search service from its mainland website to its Hong Kong website in 2010, arguing that it could no longer put up with growing censorship demands from Chinese authorities.[113] Broad restrictions and constraints on the internet and telecoms have the effect of preventing free trade both for internet companies and companies that rely on the internet for customer services, and favouring local players (in particular state-owned enterprises) under the guise of censorship.[114] As to the online third-party payment processing business, there is a stronger reason to see the Chinese government take more intervening measures as the business may be more related to sensible financial information and financial security. Against this background, it is not surprising to see the PBOC stepped in by passing the online payment business rules, which resulted in the Alipay's ownership change.

8. Draft Foreign Investment Law's Attempt to "Legalize" the VIE Structure

The Ministry of Commerce issued the Draft Foreign Investment Law in 2015 for public comment.[115] The draft law continued to limit foreign investment in restricted industries and tried to eliminate the VIE structure which helps foreign investors access restricted sectors, in particular the telecommunications sector.

The draft law limits foreign investors' ability to invest or operate business in sensitive industries. The draft law defines foreign investors to include non-citizen individual, any enterprise incorporated under foreign laws, any organ of a foreign government, international institution, and any domestic entity which is controlled by any of these.[116] An additional criterion for identifying foreign investors is added to regulate indirectly foreign controlled business. The draft law introduced a new concept of actual control to determine the foreign or local nature of an invested enterprise on the basis of the origin of the invested capital.

Article 18 of the draft law states as follows:[117]

1   A person holds, directly or indirectly, more than fifty percent of the shares, equity, property shares, voting rights or other similar rights on the company;

2   In a case where directly or indirectly owned share equity, property shares, voting rights or other rights on the company are less than fifty percent, a company is deemed to be controlled under any of the following circumstances:

   (a) The controlling entity has the right to appoint, directly or indirectly, more than half of the members of the board of directors or similar decision-making bodies;

   (b) The controlling entity may ensure that its nominee obtains more than half of the seats of the board of directors or similar decision-making bodies;

   (c) Its voting rights are sufficient to have a significant impact on the resolutions of the decision-making bodies, such as the shareholders' meeting, the shareholders' general meeting or the board of directors;

3   A person exercises a decisive influence on the business operations, financial strategy, personnel or technology of the enterprise through contracts, trusts.

Control under this law means, in regards to an enterprise, a situation that conforms to one of the following conditions:

(1) directly or indirectly holding 50 percent or more of the shares, equity interests, property shares, voting rights or other similar rights and interests in that enterprise;

(2) directly or indirectly holding less than 50 percent of the shares, equity interests, property shares, voting rights or other similar rights and interests in such enterprise but fulfilling one of the following criteria: (a) having the right to directly or indirectly appoint one half or more of the members of the board of directors or similar decision making organ of that enterprise; (b) having the ability to ensure that the personnel nominated by it will obtain one-half or more of the seats on the board of directors or similar decision making organ of such enterprise; or (c) possessing the voting rights to exert a substantial influence on the resolutions made by the shareholders' meeting, shareholders assembly, board of directors or similar decision making organ; or having the ability to exert a decisive influence over the operations, finance, human resources or technology, and others of that enterprise by contract, trust arrangement or other means;

(3) a person exercises a decisive influence on the business operations, financial strategy, personnel or technology of the enterprise through contracts, trusts or other means.

It appears that Article 18(3) explicitly refers to the VIE entities, insofar as they allow foreign companies to exercise a decisive influence on business operations, as described in the norm. This does not necessarily mean that all investments imputable to VIEs will be invalidated. Although VIEs absorb capital in foreign markets, they do not grant governance powers to foreign investors. As was seen in the Alibaba case, the company's articles of association often provide mechanisms that allow the founders of the company to maintain control, despite subsequent capital investments. In other words, these companies are under the actual control of Chinese investors.

This means that any domestic entity controlled by a foreign entity or individual – such as nominally independent domestic companies that are controlled contractually through VIE structure – will be characterized as controlled by a foreign investor and its investment will be subject to the foreign investment restrictions. This would present a material impediment for both foreign investors and Chinese businesses in the restricted category (or prohibited sectors on the negative list).

The draft law also for the first time specified the legal consequence of such companies that adopt the VIE structure in the future, including terminating business, mandatory disposal of shares or assets, confiscation of illegal gains, a fine of up to approximately US$140,000 or 10% of the investment amount, and imprisonment or criminal detention.[118]

In the draft Implementation Regulations, an attempt was made to recognize the VIE arrangement. Under Article 35 of the draft Implementation Regulations, a VIE structure is allowed if it meets two requirements: (i) a wholly owned enterprise, and (ii) approval by the State Council.[119] This provision, however, was deleted from the adopted Implementation Regulations due to the lack of consensus over how the VIE structure should be regulated and what restrictions should be imposed. One critic view, for example, is that the "wholly owned" requirement significantly narrows the scope of the VIE structure for legal recognition.[120] Thus, as a result of the deletion, the status of the VIE structure remains uncertain under the provisions of the FIL.

If the draft law were passed, Chinese companies with VIE structures would no long need to disguise foreign investments, since, unlike the laws that are currently in force, the Foreign Investment Law does not take capital investments into account, as long as these capital investments do not exceed the 50% quota set out by Article 18.1. It is worth mentioning that this limitation could be easily circumvented by only offering shares that are not granted voting rights to foreign investors.[121]

If the 2015 Draft FIL had been passed into law as drafted, this would have meant that these companies (including those China-based TMT players listed overseas which have adopted VIE Structures), and their foreign controllers, would have had to revisit the use of the VIE Structure.[122]

The passage of the draft law, however, may have a devastating effect on those companies that incorporated the VIE structure. Destructing the VIE structure would make foreign investors suffer economic losses as they would be forced to exit from the target company. Meanwhile, the regulated assets would have to be spun off from the VIE structure without the involvement of foreign investors. This would be a lose–lose scenario to both foreign investors and Chinese entity. Given the fact that eliminating the VIE may cause hues and cries from the foreign investment community and make the Chinese government suffer reputational losses, the final version of the Foreign Investment Law does not incorporate any relevant clauses on the VIE structure. Effectively, the government leaves this bomb untouched. The Chinese government should have tried to remove more restrictions on the shareholding caps imposed on some industrial sectors. By doing so, foreign investors can have full market access to these previously restricted sectors without trying to avoid legal restrictions through any VIE structure or alternative walk-around solutions.

Looking forward, when the government is determined to resolve the VIE structure, it may have two options. One is to declare the VIE structure valid and grandfather all the VIE structures so that the interests of foreign investors will not be affected. The other option is for foreign investors (through the WFOE) to legalize their shareholding control over the operational companies (holding regulated assets). The feasibility of this option depends on the Chinese government's further opening up the restricted sectors to foreign investment.

The Shanghai Free Trade Zone appeared to take the second approach by opening up some restricted sectors to foreign investment. The Ministry of Industry and Information in its 2015 document allowed foreign investors to hold up to a 100% equity ratio in online data processing and e-commerce businesses.[123] This allows foreign investors to legally own the equity in the operational entity.

The door is still left open under the FIL to regulate the VIE structure in the future. Article 2 of FIL defines foreign investment to include both "direct" investment and "indirect" investment by foreign investors. Indirect investment can be those investment in which foreign investors obtain shares, equities, property shares, or other similar rights and interests of enterprises in China[124] or other investment prescribed by laws, administrative regulations, or specified by the State Council,[125] which catches various forms of foreign investment that are not listed. However, there has been no official confirmation on these understandings.

This means that any domestic entity controlled by a foreign entity or individual – such as nominally independent domestic companies that are controlled contractually through VIE structure – will be classified as controlled by a foreign investor and its investment will then be subject to the foreign investment restrictions. This can be a material impediment for both foreign investors and Chinese businesses in the restricted category. Industries appearing on the negative list will be prohibited outright or subject to specified restrictions.[126]

What constitutes "indirect investment" is important with respect to the implementation of the negative list system. One of the objectives of foreign investment regulation is to prevent foreign investors from evading the negative list restrictions through various indirect investment methods or structures. Therefore, whether China will adopt the "penetration principle," to which level the "penetration principle" will be used, whether "control" will be used as a criterion, whether it is limited to the fields specified in the negative list, and the administration methods (licensing or filing) are all pending to the relevant authorities' further clarification.[127]

It remains open whether other government authorities would take action to explicitly regulate or challenge domestic enterprises which are controlled by foreign investors via the VIE structure or through other means.[128]

Different regulators are also likely to adopt a different approach to the treatment of foreign investment more generally. For example the authority regulating the telecommunications industry takes the view that whether a company should be viewed as an FIE and thus subject to the Negative List depends on the identity of the ultimate shareholder of such company, while some other authorities consider that only the identity of the direct shareholder of such company should be looked at when determining whether the relevant company is an FIE.[129]

9. Replacing Foreign Investment Law – Improving China's Regulatory Space

After more than four decades of rapid economic growth, China again stands at a crossroad on the development path. Regulatory countermeasures towards the "round-trip investment" model and the VIE structure are a vivid example indicating many fundamental problems China is faced with, that is improving rule of law, policy making, regulatory techniques, and ideology.

The legal environment or legal system of a country is generally considered a decisive factor in shaping the size and volume of a country's foreign investment.[130] The quality of a legal system has many facets including, but not limited to better and fairer laws, stronger property rights protection,[131] greater enforcement of commercial contracts,[132] more efficient and transparent administrative operation, fewer bureaucratic delays, and less bribery and corruption.[133] All of these aspects have a significant impact on the inbound movement and governance of investments and the national economy as a whole.[134] China is making progress in improving its legal institutions and governance quality; however, progress appears slower than anticipated, especially given China's accession to the WTO.[135] According to the World Bank's Worldwide Governance Indicators (WGI), China's governance rankings were lower in the indicators of voice and accountability, political stability, governance quality, and control of corruption in 2010 than in 1996, except the indicators of government effectiveness and rule of law.[136] China is often criticized for its lack of a functioning legal (judicial) system,[137] *inter alia*, weaker property rights protection[138] and less vigorous contract enforcement mechanisms.[139] In a recent survey conducted by the American Chamber of Commerce in China, 29% and 28% of respondents ranked "unclear laws and regulations" and "inconsistent regulatory interpretation" as one of top risks facing their business respectively.[140]

9.1 Current Approach – Deficiencies

Foreign investment law is inevitably complex. This is particularly true of PRC law, with its massive legislative sources and multiple regulators (often termed as "mothers-in-law" in Chinese legal culture). This deficiency, the problem of legislative overload, has grown worse in recent years and does not have a solution while many regulatory bodies are yearning for regulatory powers and discretions. Chinese law has opted for the micro-regulation of companies (including foreign investee companies), which differs from US-based systems preferring a more fluid and overarching matrix of general principles. However, such a micro-regulation approach fails to strike a balance between flexibility and certainty. A multiple-regulator approach confuses masses of detail and fails to promote transparency, clarity, and efficiency.

At a deeper down level, how far should state control intrude into the mainstream of regulation, bearing in mind that the fundamental aim of business regulation is to enable companies and investors to grow and prosper, whether that be a private acquisition, friendly merger, or offshore restructuring? A tightened regime for foreign industrial players and PE investors may ruin a fair playing field leading to a detriment to national economy in a long run. There are secondary questions that must be discussed. How are the regulations to be enforced? The proliferation of regulators has brought with it the necessity for Chinese regulators to achieve regulatory efficiency. How satisfactory the relationships among various regulators are and how they can be strengthened is a significant issue of concern. When combined, as it is, with truly astonishing legal developments such as those arising in the telecoms industry or caused by regulatory harmonization or competition, Chinese regulators are now faced with a speedily changing and increasingly complex regulatory world.

The view underpinning China's policy-making process and environment in the field of foreign investment is that it is a product of bargaining dynamics,[141] clientelism,[142] and bureaucratic processes.[143] This process is now more contested than before among various domestic and foreign interest groups and constituencies as well as champions of global capitalism, notwithstanding the CCP's reliance upon a continuous growth for legitimacy, new goal of realizing a harmonious society,[144] and urgent needs to protect socially and economically vulnerable groups. The debate in China, that is, economic nationalism vs. liberal treatment towards foreign investment, has been ongoing for decades[145] which may explain, if not rationalize, the policy change wavering. In contrast to the growing liberalization, a Chinese economic nationalism appeared in recent years. The legislation, that is the M&A Rules, which block foreign purchases of Chinese companies involving "key industries" described as those whose operations influence or might influence "state economic security,"[146] gradually shows concerns that foreign interests are acquiring domestic assets at undervalue,[147] seizing control of strategic industrial sectors,[148] and taking up market share in China without adequate oversight and control.[149] The debate of liberalism vs.

economic nationalism also mirrors the objective and direction of economic, legal, and/or political reform itself in a larger context.

9.2 New Approach – "Responsiveness"

In practice, how should the regulatory body more effectively respond to regulatory circumvention or non-compliance of the regulated? The use of foreign exchange control mechanism to steer and reshape the industry players' investment and operational behaviours does not solve the real obstacles to the growth of FDI, telecoms industry, or PE market in China. The practical culture prevailing in the business sector or the pressing forces of competition more often drive or shape corporate behaviour rather than regulatory pressure.[150] It would be more effective if the regulators would take a truly responsive approach, that is a target-analytic approach. This could entail investigating into and tailoring regulatory measures on the basis of the regulatees' own operating and cognitive settings, the broader institutional environment of the regulated industry, the differing logics of regulatory tools and strategies, and even the regime's own performance and functioning.[151] Instead of a "pure" responsive strategy,[152] a more effective means may lie in the reformulation, or reform, of an industry-friendly corporate law regime and institutions in China, which would likely be more responsive to the business sector's concerns and expectations as a whole.[153]

Technically, it is a promising move to see Chinese authorities make various efforts to eliminate grey areas by having more rules and legislation in place so that all the market players can correctly assess legal risks and financial returns in adopting a transactional model, and regulators will also have clear-cut jurisdictions. However, there have been legitimate concerns in the international investment community that foreign investment would be gradually squeezed out of Chinese web companies by more and more recently promulgated rules and legislation if the Chinese government tends to clamp down on VIEs.

An appropriate approach now is to "think business (or market economy) first" (or "think business (or market economy) more")[154] and improve the situation by laying out general standards and principles of behaviour, without leaving too much discretion to regulators. There is a need to bring in line what business community needs and the ideology underlying legal policies. It is important to bear in mind the potential diversity of users including foreign investors who are entitled to expect clarity. A careful investigation of how law and policy operate in practice is required before corrective measures can be envisaged as a viable solution to many problems in the marketplace.

Placing foreign investment law in a Chinese public law frame seems a path-dependent phenomenon in the Chinese legal context. Going forward, a more constructive approach, streamlining different strands of regulations with a more market-oriented focus and less public law manoeuvre, will much better serve the needs of the business community and environment, and more importantly, Chinese legal development, including the rule of law. Paradoxically, China appears to have taken a hard call on foreign investment at a time it opens itself more than ever to the world. However, oddly it may seem, it ought not to detract us from the general trend, that is movement towards more openness and a more market-oriented economy, albeit with some "Chinese socialist characteristics."[155]

Notes

1 China overtook Japan and became the second-largest economy in normal terms in the world in 2010. In purchasing power terms, China's economy surpassed Japan's nearly a decade ago. David Pilling, "China at Number Two . . . and Counting," *Financial Times*, 19 August 2010, p. 7.
2 China had the world's largest internet population at 420 million in 2010. Kathrin Hille, "Social Networks Steer China Web Evolution," *Financial Times*, 29 November 2010, p. 22.
3 Xinhua, "China's Telecom Sector Sees Robust 2021 Growth with Better IT Environment," 2 February 2022, available at http://english.www.gov.cn/archive/statistics/20 2202/02/content_WS61f9df49c6d09c94e48a49a9.html (accessed on 19 April 2022).
4 Bruce Einhorn, "China's Tangled Web: Will Beijing Ruin the Net by Trying to Control It?," *Business Week International*, 17 and 28 July 2000, p. 28.
5 In August 2018, The Intercept, the investigative journalism website, reported that Google was working on a secret prototype of a new, censored Chinese search engine, Project Dragonfly. US Vice President Mike Pence called on Google to kill Dragonfly on the grounds that it would "strengthen Communist Party censorship and compromise the privacy of Chinese customers." Google suspended this project in response to complaints from human rights activists and its own privacy team. Matt Sheehan, "How Google Took on China—and Lost," 19 December 2018, available at www.technologyreview.com/2018/12/19/138307/how-google-took-on-china-and-lost/ (accessed on 19 April 2022).
6 The Third Plenum of the 11th Central Committee of the Chinese Communist Party formally, though scantly, introduced the "open door" policy.
7 The 14th CPC National Congress Report, FBIS Daily Report – China, 21 October 1992.
8 The PRC Joint Ventures Law Implementing Rules, promulgated on 20 September 1983, provide that the main industrial sectors in which joint ventures are allowed to operate within the territory of China, include the electronics and computer industries, as well as the manufacturing of communication equipment. Strictly speaking, the information industry and the information service industry are not explicitly mentioned in this clause. Therefore, the joint ventures cannot be established to engage in the information service industry.
9 State Council Guo Fa [1993] No. 55.
10 Ibid., Article 5.
11 State Council Guo Han [1993] No. 178.
12 Request for Instructions on Standardizing, "Foreign-Chinese-Chinese," Funding Structures Used by China United Telecommunications Co., Ltd. (Ji Jiao Neng [1998] No.405), jointly promulgated by the State Planning Commission, State Economic and Trade Commission and Ministry of Finance on 18 March 1998.
13 "Basic telecommunications business" refers to any business that provides basic facilities for public networks, public data transmission, and basic speech communication.
14 Telecoms Regulations, Article 80.
15 See Qingjiang Kong, "EU's Monitoring of China's Compliance with WTO Obligations" (December 2008) *EAI Background Brief* No. 417.
16 China's long-established policies in the publishing industry are to limit the scope of players and eventually to control the free expression and exchange of ideas. Similarly,

there have been restrictions on advertising content. Political sensitiveness also affects the monitoring model of market research players, which were required to register with the State Statistical Bureau and submit all surveys for prior approval and share their research products with security forces. There is no surprise that China failed to implement its trading rights commitments insofar as they relate to the importation of books, newspapers, periodicals, electronic publications, and audio and video products and continued to reserve the right to import these products to state trading enterprises. United States Trade Representative, 2007 Report on China's WTO Compliance, 11 December 2007.

17 Notice on Strengthening the Administration of Foreign Investment in the Operation of Value Added Telecoms Services (issued by the PRC Ministry of Information Industry in 2006).

18 SEC filling Form 10-Q of Yahoo! Inc, 29 April 2011, www.sec.gov/Archives/edgar/data/1011006/000119312511134295/d10q.htm. Unless otherwise indicated, website materials were checked in November 2011.

19 Press Release of Yahoo! Inc, 12 May 2011, www.sec.gov/Archives/edgar/data/1011006/000119312511139078/dex991.htm.

20 "Xinhua Insight: Alipay Case Shows VIE Structure May Not be Safe Anymore," available at http://news.xinhuanet.com/english2010/china/2011-06/22/c_13944523.htm.

21 The Original source is no longer available on the website of Hangzhou Branch of the People's Bank of China. For a screen shot, see "Is Alipay Disturbance a False Alarm?," available at http://seekingalpha.com/instablog/911206-ichinastock/178174-is-alipay-disturbance-a-false-alarm.

22 Ibid.

23 "Alipay's Buy-back," *Southern China Weekend* (in Chinese), 4 August 2011, D17.

24 Jack Ma's interview with *China Entrepreneur Magazine*, available at www.slideshare.net/stevenmillward/jack-ma-interview-july-2011.

25 Alibaba.com Limited Annual Report 2009, 82, available at https://www1.hkexnews.hk/listedco/listconews/sehk/2010/0408/ltn20100408544.pdf (accessed on 3 October 2022).

26 For details, see section 3.6.

27 O'Melveny & Myers, "VIE Structures in China: What You Need to Know" 1 November 2011, available at https://www.omm.com/resources/alerts-and-publications/publications/omelveny-myers-publishes-paper-vie-structures-in-china-what-you-need-to-know?sc_lang=zh-CN.

28 Min Li and Changsheng Wang, Jack Ma's interview with *China Entrepreneur Magazine*, available at www.slideshare.net/stevenmillward/jack-ma-interview-july-2011; "Jack Ma Terminated Alipay's VIE Structure in Q1 2011," 11 July 2011, available at http://tech.sina.com.cn/i/2011-07-11/11315761634_4.shtml?wm=3049_0015.

29 John W. Spelich, "Alibaba Group Clarification with respect to Alipay Status and Related Statements by Yahoo!," 13 May 2011, available at https://www.semanticscholar.org/paper/Alibaba-Group-Clarification-with-Respect-to-Alipay-Spelich/abc667a1a21e-18fa5bcc3041ade9545ef41f391d (accessed on 3 October 2022).

30 Ibid.

31 Alibaba Group Holding Limited, Yahoo! Inc. and Softbank Corp, "Alibaba Group, Yahoo and Softbank Reach Agreement on Alipay," 29 July 2011, available at https://group.softbank/en/news/press/20110729 (accessed on 3 October 2022).

32 Eric Savitz, "Yahoo Discloses Jack Ma Takes Control Of Alipay From Alibaba," available at www.forbes.com/sites/ericsavitz/2011/05/11/yahoo-discloses-jack-ma-takes-control-of-alipay-from-alibaba/.

33 The most influential legislation relating to foreign investment in China's telecoms industry is the Regulations for the Administration of Foreign-Invested Telecommunications Enterprises, issued in 2001 and amended in 2008, according to which the ultimate foreign equity ownership in a value-added telecoms services business must not exceed 50%. PRC law remains, on paper, compliant with the PRC's WTO obligations. However,

this has effectively proved to be illusory since in practice it has been extremely difficult for FIEs to obtain telecoms operating licenses even though the foreign equity is less than 50%. Based upon this author's no-names basis enquiries to the Ministry of Industry and Information Technology (MIIT), practically speaking, the MIIT has rarely approved an application for foreign investment into a PRC telecoms business. It was reported that China had granted 22,000 telecoms operating licenses but only seven of them were granted to FIEs. Qingjiang Kong, "EU's Monitoring of China's Compliance with WTO Obligations" (December 2008) *EAI Background Brief* No. 417.

34 Apart from the telecoms industry, China still maintains ownership caps on foreign investors in such industries as banking and construction. Shen Wei, "Financial Services Regulation in China," in Andrew Halper and Carl Hinze (eds), *Financial Services Regulation in Asia Pacific* (Oxford: Oxford University Press, 2nd ed., 2008) 58, 91–92.

35 Nominees are customarily used to structure corporate transactions in order to circumvent some regulatory or corporate default rules. One of the earliest company law cases probably was *Pender v Lushington* (1877) 6 Ch D 70 (Court of Chancery), in which nominees were appointed by the shareholder to defeat a provision in the articles that fixed the maximum number of votes to which any one shareholder was entitled. The chairman of the company refused to accept the nominees' votes and declared lost a resolution proposed by the shareholder who appointed the nominees. The Master of the Rolls granted the shareholder an injunction restraining the directors from acting on the basis of that the nominees' votes had been bad. The ruling was treated as an exception to the *Foss v Harbottle* rule, under which the company is the proper plaintiff in an action relating to a wrong done to the company, and no action could be brought if the wrong would be ratified by shareholders in general meeting.

36 Terry Sicular, "Capital Flight and Foreign Investment: Two Tales from China and Russia" (1998) 21 *World Economy* 589–602.

37 Prior to the promulgation of the uniform Enterprise Income Tax Law, the income tax rate for an FIE was 15–25%, while a tax rate of 33% was applicable to a pure domestic entity. By adopting a VIE structure or "round-trip investment" model, Chinese companies and domestic shareholders may capture a tax break and enjoy more preferential tax treatment. Even after the enactment of the Enterprise Income Tax Law, under which both FIEs and Chinese enterprises are subject to the same enterprise income tax rate of 25%, these transactional structures still enable shareholders to enjoy more preferential tax treatment. The SPV is only subject to a withholding tax on the distribution of dividends from the WFOE. The withholding tax rate is 10% depending on the application of a tax treaty and can be as low as 5% if the SPV is incorporated in Hong Kong. Any payments of interest or dividends made by the SPV, and/or capital gains derived from the exiting investment through the sale of shares in the SPV, are free of PRC tax. By contrast, sales proceeds in a share transfer for a purely domestic company in China are deemed to be taxable income. Together with other taxable incomes received in the same fiscal year, the proceeds are subject to a 25% enterprise income tax after the deduction of the deductible costs in that fiscal year.

38 For example if a foreign investor directly invests into a Chinese company and becomes a shareholder afterwards, any amendments to the articles of association of the company, transfer of equity capital, increase and reduction of the equity capital, and liquidation and dissolution of the company are subject to unanimous consent of all the board members (appointed by the shareholders in proportion to their respective equity percentages) and approval of the original approval authority, which can be a painful and time-consuming exercise. Exiting through a sale of equity in a company will also trigger approval from the competent Chinese authority, that is the Ministry of Commerce, (MOFCOM) or its local branch depending on the total investment amount. Moreover, under the PRC Equity Joint Venture Law or PRC WFOE Law, other shareholders have a pre-emptive right to acquire the equity of the selling shareholder and have the absolute consent right to any general transfer. No transfer of an interest in an equity joint venture (EJV) or cooperative joint venture (CJV) – including transfers of interests

between the joint venture shareholders – can be made without an amendment to the articles of association, the other parties' consent, unanimous consent of the board, and approval of the original approval authority. In the VIE structure or "round-trip investment" model, however, the amendments to the articles of association of the SPV, transfer of equity capital, increase and reduction of equity capital, and liquidation and dissolution of the SPV do not require unanimous consent of all shareholders or the approval of any governmental authority. This partially motivates both Chinese and foreign investors to utilize these transactional structures.

39　Chinese companies seeking to list abroad generally prefer to use an offshore SPV as the listed company due to various tax, legal, and regulatory concerns. Taking Alibaba as an example, the listed company is Alibaba, which is incorporated in Cayman Islands. Then, this offshore holding company would be listed to finance from an offshore stock exchange. This can avoid the troublesome securities regulations in China and the problematic stock exchange in the domestic market.

40　Kathrin Hille, "China in New Push on Web Ownership," *Financial Times*, 2 September 2011, p. 14.

41　This assumption is largely based on the efficiency theory that lawyers, as a transaction-cost engineer, are well-compensated and sophisticated enough to structure the transaction in the most feasible and efficient way. As a result, transaction costs in negotiating a new transactional structure changing the existing equilibrium among the parties may be high in an economic sense. See Ronald J. Gilson, "Value Creation by Business Lawyers: Legal Skills and Asset Pricing" (1984) 94 *Yale Law Journal* 239, 243; Ian Ayres and Robert Gertner, "Filling Gaps in Incomplete Contracts: An Economic Theory of Default Rules" (1989) 99 *Yale Law Journal* 87, 91–93.

42　The dispute between GigaMedia Limited, an online gaming company using the VIE structure to do business in China, and Wang Ji, the shareholder of the VIE entity, was brought to both Chinese and American courts. GigaMedia Limited lost its control over the VIE as Wang Ji took away the company seal, finance chop and business license of the VIE entity. However, GigaMedia Limited only sued Wang Ji on the ground of the latter's breach of his fiduciary duty in the Chinese court. On its face, the lawsuit in the Chinese court has nothing to do with the legality and enforceability of the VIE structure. In the US court, Wang Ji made a claim that the VIE structure is not effective and valid under Chinese law. It appears that the effectiveness of the VIE structure in this case will only be adjudicated by the US court rather than the PRC court. For details, see SEC Filing FORM 6-K of GigaMedia Limited (30 August 2010), available at http://sec.gov/Archives/edgar/data/1105101/000134100410001910/giga_6k.htm; SEC Filing Form 20-K of GigaMedia Limited (2010), available at www.sec.gov/Archives/edgar/data/1105101/000095012311063164/c19286e20vf.htm; Leodis C. Matthews, "Its VIE structure Claimed a Sham: Allegations against China Variable Interest Entity (VIE) Operations," available at www.eworldwire.com/pressreleases/212206.

43　See CLPSTAFF, "Round-trip Investments Key to Reversing FDI Decline," available at https://www.chinalawandpractice.com/2009/05/08/round-trip-investments-key-to-reversing-fdi-decline/ (accessed on 3 October 2022).

44　It has been reported that some Chinese companies still rely on the VIE structure to secure the PBOC license. For instance Tenpay, an online payment service subsidiary of the overseas listed Chinese Internet company, Tencent, has been specifically mentioned. Tenpay, however, rejected this allegation by saying that it is a pure Chinese-owned company and has never used the VIE structure.

45　Circular 75 was issued by SAFE on 1 October 2005 and came into effect on 1 November 2005.

46　According to Section 1 of Circular 75, the term "residents" covers both "domestic resident natural persons" including individuals holding a China domestic identity document and other individuals who "habitually reside in China for reasons related to their economic interests" and "domestic resident legal persons" including the enterprises, other economic organizations and the newly recognized "domestic venture investment enterprises."

47 Although Circular 75 only requests the domestic residents to register the transactions with the SAFE, the information required to be submitted to the SAFE is so substantive that registration is same as approval or verification, where the SAFE will conduct a substantive review and exerts its discretion in the registration process. Circular 75, Section 3.

48 The definition of "round-trip investment" under the foreign exchange rules is in great breadth and detail to cover "purchasing or swapping for the equity of a Chinese shareholder/owner in a domestic enterprise; establishing a foreign-invested enterprise in China and through such an enterprise purchasing or reaching agreement to control domestic assets; purchasing through agreement domestic assets and using such assets to invest in and establish a foreign-invested enterprise or for increasing the capital of a domestic enterprise." Circular 75, Section 1(2).

49 The definition of a "special purpose company" in Circular 75 is narrow and only covers those entities "conducting . . . financing abroad [with] the assets of the domestic enterprise or equity." Circular 75, Section 1. This definition seems to suggest that Circular 75 does not apply to the SPV with cash investment from the domestic resident or without the purpose of raising financing abroad.

50 Circular 75, Section 2.

51 Circular 75, Section 3.

52 Circular 75, Section 3.

53 Circular 75, Section 7.

54 Circular 75, Section 5.

55 Circular 75, Section 6.

56 SAFE issued a Circular 19 on 1 July 2011. Circular 19 eliminates most of the overlap between SAFE and MOFCOM and simplifies foreign currency registration of round-trip investments and fundraising, while increasing the pressure and urgency on investors to rectify previous non-registration. SAFE's procedures are conditional upon the applicants having complied with MOFCOM's requirements.

57 All telecoms services businesses in China are categorized as either basic or value-added telecoms services businesses. A "value-added telecoms business" is defined in the PRC Regulations of Telecommunications, issued by the State Council on 25 September 2000, as a business that provides telecoms and information services by using the basic facilities of public networks and includes internet information services (ICP services), content services, entertainment/gaming, commercial information, and positing services.

58 The Circular on Strengthening the Administration of Foreign Investment in and Operation of Value-added Telecommunications Business, Article 1 para 2.

59 Ibid. Articles 2(1), 2(2), and 2(4).

60 Ibid. Article 4.

61 The M&A Rules were jointly issued by six ministries including SAFE, SAIC, and MOFCOM on 8 August 2006 and came into effect on 8 September 2006.

62 SPV is defined as any overseas company controlled, directly or indirectly, by a domestic company or Chinese natural person inside China for overseas listing of its/his/her share interests. M&A Rules, Chapter IV.

63 M&A Rules, Article 15.

64 M&A Rules, Articles 45 and 47.

65 Article 11 of the M&A Rules provides that, where a foreign company established or controlled by a domestic company, enterprise, or natural person intends to take over its domestic affiliated company, it shall be subject to the examination and approval of the MOFCOM. The parties concerned are not able to get around these requirements by making investments within China through a foreign-funded enterprise or other means. Certainly, this hinged on how liberal the MOFCOM would be in approving the VIE structure. Within the first year of enacting the Provisions, there were no approvals for restructurings of Chinese companies into offshore holding companies.

66 While SAFE increases its focus and coordination by passing Circular 19 (see *supra* note 56), MOFCOM's uncertainties under the M&A Rules remain.

67 The Notice concerning the Recognition of Chinese-controlled Overseas Incorporated Enterprises as Resident Enterprises according to the Actual Management Entity Standard, issued by the State Administration of Taxation on 22 April 2009.

68 For example the determination criteria of Chinese TRE for Chinese-capital controlled foreign companies ("CCCFC").

69 These conditions include, for example senior management are in charge of day-to-day activities and the place for senior management to execute their duties is mainly located in China; strategic management over finance and personnel decisions are made or approved by an establishment or individual in China; the enterprise's major asset, accounting records, corporate seals, and minutes of board of directors and shareholders' meetings are located or maintained in China; and at least 50% of the board members with voting rights or senior management habitually reside in China. Notice 82, Article 2.

70 The latest movement in the PE circle is to set up renminbi-based funds in China which may help foreign PE investors create more inroads into China. Sundeep Tucker and Jamil Anderlini, "Carlyle to Set up Renminbi-based Fund in Beijing," *Financial Times*, 13 January 2010, p. 17.

71 The Online Game Notice's full Chinese title is 关于贯彻落实国务院〈"三定"规定〉和中央编办有关解释，进一步加强网络游戏前置审批和进口网络游戏审批管理的通知, issued by the General Administration of Press and Publication, the State Copyright Bureau and the Office of the National Work Group for "Combating Pornography and Illegal Publications."

72 Ibid. Article IV.

73 Ibid. Article IV.

74 Ironically, NetEase.Com Inc, a NASDAQ listing company using the VIE structure, announced on 17 August 2010 that it had gone through all the PRC authorities and obtained all approvals for the purpose of operating a new online game product World of Warcraft, in spite of the clear prohibition. Tao Liang, "Worst Seems to Have Passed for Online Game Operators" (2010) *China's Foreign Trade* 61, available at https://www.chinaqikan.com/thesis/pdf/908644 (accessed on 3 October 2022).

75 Administrative Measures on Payment Services of Non-financial Institutions, Article 3.

76 In most cases, it is the MOFCOM, State Administration for Radio, Film and Television, and MIIT that regulate and supervise different respects of the telecoms industry. The PBOC's involvement may be attributed to its jurisdiction over online payment businesses.

77 The Administrative Measures on Payment Services of Non-financial Institutions, Article 3.

78 Ibid. Article 8.

79 Ibid. Article 9.

80 Ibid. Article 9.

81 The Notice of Establishing the Security Review System for Mergers and Acquisitions of Domestic Enterprises by Foreign Investors （国务院办公厅关于建立外国投资者并购境内企业安全审查制度的通知）, promulgated by the General Office of the State Council, effective as of 3 March 2011.

82 Ibid. Article 1.

83 Ministry of Commerce's Regulations on the Implementation of the Security Review System for Mergers and Acquisitions of Domestic Enterprises by Foreign Investors, Announcement [2011] No. 53, Article 9, available at www.gov.cn/gzdt/2011-08/26/content_1934046.htm.

84 Ibid., Article 9.

85 Confusingly, Google's license was renewed by the Chinese authority less than a week after the MOFCOM's new mergers and acquisitions rules. Theoretically, Google, due to its falling-out with the Chinese authority in 2010, may be more vulnerable to risk of regulations. See *infra* notes 77 and 95 as well as accompanying texts. Kathrin Hille, "Google Secures Renewal of China License," *Financial Times*, 8 September 2011, p. 16.

86 Empirically, it is very difficult to quantify the amount of "round-trip investments" in a dollar value. The World Bank estimated that the "round-trip investments" are at least 25% of China's total foreign direct investment (FDI) while other commentators may have claimed a higher percentage up to 50%. See respectively, World Bank, "Private Capital Flows to Emerging Markets," in *Global Development Finance* (New York: World Bank Publication, 2002) 41 (Box 2.3: Round-tripping of Capital Flows between China and Hong Kong), available at https://documents1.worldbank.org/curated/en/876431468140678171/pdf/multi0page.pdf; Geng Xiao, "People's Republic of China's Round Tipping FDI: Scale, Causes and Implications" (July 2004) Asian Development Bank Institute Discussion Paper (Tokyo) No. 7, available at https://www.hiebs.hku.hk/wp-content/uploads/2020/09/wp1137.pdf (claiming that the "round-trip" investment constitutes 30% to 50% of the total FDI); David Dollar and Aart Kraay, "Neither a Borrower Nor a Lender: Does China's Zero Net Foreign Asset Position Make Economic Sense?" (2006) 53(5) *Journal of Monetary Economics* 943–971 (estimating that round-tripping represents as much as one-third of China's FDI).

87 China's foreign exchange reserves reached US$853.7 billion in February 2006, surpassing those of Japan to become the largest in the world, available at the website of the PBOC: www.pbc.gov.cn and SAFE's website: www.safe.gov.cn/model_safe/index.html.

88 Renminbi or yuan, the Chinese currency, has been a highest profile and longest-running subject of controversy between China and its trade partners, especially the United States, the European Union, and Japan. China has been accused of intentionally manipulating renminbi's exchange rate to the US dollar to gain its competitive advantage and keep its export artificially cheaper. The undervalued renminbi, as often asserted, is the key reason of China's growth in its unparalleled foreign exchange reserves and trade surpluses as well as for global economic imbalances. As to how much renminbi is misaligned, substantial disagreement appears in various research, ranging from 1% to 56% undervaluation. See W.L. Chou and Y.C. Shih, "The Equilibrium Exchange Rate of the Chinese Renminbi" (1998) 26(1) *Journal of Comparative Economics* 165–174 (claiming that renminbi was about 10% undervalued at the beginning of the 1990s); Fred Bergsten, "We Can Fight Fire with Fire on the Renminbi," *Financial Times*, 4 October 2010, p. 13 (claiming that renminbi is still undervalued by at least 20% after its appreciation from 2005 to date); Morris Goldstein, "Adjusting China's Exchange Rate Policies" (2004) Institute for International Economics Working Paper 04–1 (arguing that renminbi is undervalued by at least 30–35%); Ernest H. Preeg, "Exchange Rate Manipulation to Gain an Unfair Competitive Advantage: The Case Against Japan and China," in C. Fred Bergsten and John Williamson (eds), *Dollar Overvaluation and the World Economy* (Washington DC: Institute for International Economics, 2003) 267–284 (estimating that renminbi exchange rate undervaluation is about 40%). There are also proponents against the idea that China should alter its exchange rate. See Ronald McKinnon and Gunther Schnabl, "China: A Stabilizing or Deflationary Influence in East Asia? The Problem of Conflicted Virtue" (2003), available at https://papers.ssrn.com/sol3/papers.cfm?abstract_id=753385. US lawmakers, led by Senators Charles Schumer and Leslie Graham, threatened to sanction China by imposing a 27.5% tariff on Chinese imports in order to pressure China to raise the value of Renminbi. See "US Lawmakers Turn up Yuan Beat" The Standard (Hong Kong), 13 June 2007. The US House of Representatives passed legislation that would punish China for undervaluing its currency and damaging the competitiveness of US manufacturers and exporters. The US administration however preferred to pursue a policy of engagement with China with the view of persuading China to allow the Renminbi to strengthen while enhancing its own negotiating position by mounting congressional pressure. See James Politi, "House to Hit Back on Renminbi," *Financial Times*, 30 September 2010, p. 2. Meanwhile, the US administration also sought to organize a coalition in the framework of G20. Alan Beattie, "A Heated Exchange," *Financial Times*, 5 December 2011, p. 7. The US Senate passed a

bill in October 2011 that would allow the US to levy retaliatory across-the-board tariffs on Chinese imports according to estimates of currency misalignment. However, the Republican leaders opposed to the move and resisted bringing a similar bill to a vote in the House of Representatives. Alan Beattie, "Renminbi's Threat to Dominant Dollar Grows," *Financial Times*, 17 November 2011, p. 6.

89 See generally, Ian Ayres and John Braithwaite, *Responsive Regulation* (Oxford: Oxford University Press, 1992).

90 See "Round-trip Investments Key to Reversing FDI Decline," available at https://www. chinalawandpractice.com/2009/05/08/round-trip-investments-key-to-reversing-fdi-decline/ (accessed on 3 October 2022).

91 John Armour and Douglas Cumming, "The Legislative Road to Silicon Valley" (2006) *Oxford Economic Papers* 58, 596–635.

92 Guy Dinmore, Mure Dickie, and Rachel Sanderson, "Italy Spoils Mood after EU Deal," *Financial Times Weekend*, 29/30 October 2011, p. 1.

93 The current account imbalances are the mirror image of international investment flows. In the wake of financial crisis, China faces pressure to curb "hot money" or "abnormal" amounts of speculative capital from flowing into China given the widespread expectation on the appreciation of renminbi. Frederic Neumann, "Flood Control," *South China Morning Post*, 6 May 2011, A19. The inflow of "hot money" also causes inflation and accumulation of foreign exchange reserves. Reuters, "Asia Braces for Next Flood of Hot Cash from West," *South China Morning Post*, 10 September 2011, B5. While SAFE continues to supervise cross-border fund flows by imposing stricter capital control rules, the Ministry of Housing and Urban-Rural Development has been trying to cool the hot property market by only allowing foreigners living in China to buy one home for their own use. For details, see "Hot Money: A Burning Issue in China," available at www.chinadaily.com.cn/bizchina/2010-12/14/content_11697596.htm (accessed on 20 June 2022).

94 Foreign investors have been reportedly involved in corrupt practices due to their lack of confidence in the fairness of Chinese legal system and business environment as well as their fear of retaliation. Michael A. Santoro, *China 2020: How Western Business Can – and Should – Influence Social and Political Change in the Coming Debate* (Ithaca: Cornell University Press, 2009) 113.

95 "Google v China," *Financial Times*, 23 March 2010, p. 14 (remarking Google's closure of Google.cn and debate on internet freedom with China); Kathrin Hille, et al. "China Gets Tough on Google," *Financial Times*, 24 March 2010, p. 1 (reporting Google's decision to end compliance with local censors and move search engines to Hong Kong).

96 Patti Waldmeir and Peter Smith, "Rio Tinto's Top Iron Ore Salesman in China Admits Bribe Allegations," *Financial Times*, 23 March 2010, p. 1 (arguing that Rio's practice in China was in line with industry practices but one of the biggest problems for foreigners operating in China is vague and ill-forced law); William MacNamara and Patti Waldmeir, "Rio Seeks to Rebuild Relations with Beijing," *Financial Times*, 23 March 2010, p. 17 (alleging that the "arrests were payback for Rio's touch stance in negotiation of iron ore sales with the Chinese steel industry").

97 Guy Dinmore and Geoff Dyer, "GE Chief Accuses China of 'Hostility'," *Financial Times*, 2 July 2010, p. 1; Jamil Anderlini, "Demand for Market Access," *Financial Times*, 20 July 2010, p. 3; Alan Beattie and Jamil Anderlini, "'Foreign Friends' Lost Reluctance to Criticize China," *Financial Times*, 20 July 2010, p. 3; Geoff Dyer, "Wen Is Able to Call the Bluff of the Moaning Multinationals," *Financial Times*, 21 July 2010, p. 2. Meanwhile, the Western countries such as the United States have been hostile to Chinese telecoms players who have been trying to make huge strides into these markets. For instance US diplomats tried to stop sensitive technology being acquired by Huawei, the key Chinese telecommunications equipment maker, by putting pressure on European suppliers such as Spirent Communications in the UK and Philips in the Netherlands. Martin Arnold and Stephanie Kirchgaessner, "US 'Tried to Press Huawei Suppliers'," *Financial Times*, 15 February 2011, p. 17.

98 Arguably, protecting China's own telecommunications industry is one of the major motivations behind the Chinese government imposing restrictions on foreign investment. Chinese information industry, though making great progress in the past decade, still lags behind advanced global standard. Chinese internet companies are often criticized by Western observers as mere clones of their Western peers. Lionel Barber and Kathrin Hille, "Baidu Plans Operating System for Mobiles," *Financial Times*, 23 March 2011, p. 13. Lax corporate governance and managerial system of Chinese enterprises also contribute to the competitive disadvantage.

99 This may be very different from the US' security concern over the sale and dispersal of telecommunications technology, equipment, and products for military applications, which also frustrates commercial transactions. Stephanie Kirchgaessner, "Huawei Confident of US Plans," 15 November 2010, *Financial Times*, p. 22. Chinese companies' plan to inroad into the American market also encountered similar barriers. The Committee on Foreign Investment, the US body that scrutinizes cross-border deals for potential national security implications, refused to endorse Huawei's $2 million acquisition of patents from 3Leaf. Kathrin Hille and Paul Taylor, "Relief for Huawei after It Settles Suit with Motorola," *Financial Times*, 14 April 2011, p. 16.

100 China's long-established policies in the publishing industry are to limit the scope of players and eventually to control the free expression and exchange of ideas. Similarly, there have been restrictions on advertising content. Political sensitiveness also affects the monitoring model of market research players, which were required to register with the State Statistical Bureau and submit all surveys for prior approval and share their research products with security forces. There is no surprise that China failed to implement its trading rights commitments insofar as they relate to the importation of books, newspapers, periodicals, electronic publications, and audio and video products, and it continued to reserve the right to import these products to state trading enterprises. United States Trade Representative, 2007 Report on China's WTO Compliance, 11 December 2007.

101 These measures in particular regulate ICP services. Commercial ICP service operators must obtain an ICP license from the relevant government authorities before engaging in any commercial ICP operations within the PRC.

102 ICP service providers are required to monitor their websites in accordance with relevant PRC laws and regulations, including but not limited to the Internet Measures. They may not produce duplicate, post, or disseminate any content that falls within the prohibited categories and must remove any such content from their websites, including any content that opposes the fundamental principles stated in the PRC constitution; compromises national security; divulges state secrets; subverts state power or damages national unity; harms the dignity or interests of the state; incites ethnic hatred or racial discrimination or damages inter-ethnic unity; undermines the PRC's religious policy or propagates heretical teachings or feudal superstitions; disseminates rumours, disturbs social order or disrupts social stability; disseminates obscenity or pornography, gambling, violence, murder, or terror or incites the commission of a crime; insults or slanders a third party or infringes upon the lawful rights and interests of a third party; or is otherwise prohibited by law or administrative regulations.

103 QQ is a very popular and convenient messaging tool. Tencent's QQ, for instance, has 638 million active accounts at the latest count. Kathrin Hille, "Social Networks Steer China Web Evolution," *Financial Times*, 30 November 2010, p. 22.

104 Rahul Jacob, "China's Migrants Face Struggle," *Financial Times*, 13 September 2011, p. 6.

105 David Pilling, "Could China's Rulers be Right to be Jittery?," *Financial Times*, 24 February 2011, p. 9.

106 Justine Lau and Patti Waldmeir, "Fears Grow Over China Labor Unrest," *Financial Times*, 11 June 2010, p. 16.

107 Kathrin Hille, "Beijing Steps up TV Censorship as Political Crackdown Broadens," *Financial Times*, 31 March 2011, p. 1.

108 Verna Yu, "Activist Jailed Over Blogger Protest," *South China Morning Post*, 10 September 2011, p. A7.

109 Kathrin Hille, "Chinese Police Tweet to Keep the Peace," *Financial Times*, 6 December 2011, p. 2.
110 Kathrin Hille, "Social Networks Steer China Web Evolution," *Financial Times*, 30 November 2010, p. 22.
111 Andrew Jacobs, "Eggs and Shoes Lobbed at Web Censor for China," *International Herald Tribune*, 21–22 May 2011, p. 4.
112 Joseph Menn, "Lawsuit Links Cisco with China Crackdown," *Financial Times*, 24 May 2011, p. 18 (reporting that Cisco has been engaged by the Chinese government to design, implement, and support a project of Golden Shield to facilitate internet censorship).
113 Kathrin Hille, "Beijing Appears Uncertain on Google," *Financial Times*, 25 March 2010, p. 4.
114 Baidu alone accounts for more than three quarters of the Chinese online search market after Google's relocation out of mainland China. Lionel Barber and Kathrin Hille, "Baidu Plans Operating System for Mobiles," *Financial Times*, 23 March 2011, p. 13. China Telecom and Unicom, two major state-owned players (fixed line carriers), combined account for more than two-thirds of the market for internet access business. However, the National Development and Reform Commission, China's antitrust authority and economic regulator, is investigating whether they conducted any monopolistic practices in the broadband access sector by abusing their dominant market position to keep other competitors out of the broadband business. Kathrin Hille, "Beijing Probes Telecoms Groups," *Financial Times*, 10 November 2011, p. 17.
115 Practical Law China, Draft Foreign Investment Law Open for Comment Until February 17, Prac. L. China (19 January 2015), available at https://uk.practicallaw.thomsonreuters.com/9-596-4525?transitionType=Default&contextData=(sc.Default)&firstPage=true (accessed on 3 October 2022).
116 Article 11 defines Foreign Investors as (i) individuals who do not have Chinese nationality; (ii) businesses incorporated under the laws of other countries or regions; (iii) governments of other countries or regions or their subordinate departments or authorities; (iv) international organizations; and (v) domestic businesses controlled by the aforesaid subjects, which shall be deemed as foreign investors.
117 Article 18.
118 Draft Foreign Investment Law 2015, Articles 144–145.
119 Article 35 of the Implementation Regulations provides that the wholly owned enterprises formed overseas by Chinese natural person, legal person, or other organizations which make investment within the territory of China may, subject to the review of relevant government authority and approval by the state council, be exempt from the restrictions under the special administrative measures for the market access contained in the negative list.
120 *See* Corporate Alert, "The Foreign Investment Law Gets Wings: Draft Implementation Regulations Released for Public Consultation," *Hogan Lovells Publication*, 5 November 2019, available at https://www.hoganlovells.com/en/publications/the-foreign-investment-law-gets-wings (accessed on 3 October 2022).
121 Giulio Santoni, "Foreign Capital in Chinese Telecommunication Companies: From the Variable Interest Entity Model to the Draft of the New Chinese Foreign Investment Law" (2018) 4 *Corporate and Financial Market Law* 589, 606–608.
122 Clifford Chance, "China's New Foreign Investment Law – What Does This Mean for Foreign Investors in China?" *Clifford Chance*, 22 March 2019, available at www.cliffordchance.com/briefings/2019/03/china_s_new_foreigninvestmentlawwhatdoe.html (accessed on 25 April 2022).
123 David Livdahl and Jenny Sheng, "China Opens Up to Wholly Foreign-Owned E-Commerce Cos.," *Law360*, 14 July 2016, available at www.law360.com/articles/817517/china-opens-up-to-wholly-foreign-owned-e-commerce-cos.
124 FIL, Article 2(2).
125 FIL, Article 2(4).

126 Meichen Liu, "The New Chinese Foreign Investment Law and Its Implication on Foreign Investors" (2018) 38 *Northwestern Journal of International Law & Business* 284, 293.

127 Jindu Research Institute Public Account, "Foreign Investment Law: Highlights and Challenges" available at https://mp.weixin.qq.com/s/3RcPjm4YKUA71wrcWpU-zw (accessed on 17 March 2019).

128 It is worth noting that some PRC government authorities have been scrutinizing the use of VIE structures in certain business sectors. For instance the PRC State Council issued the *Certain Opinion on In-depth Reform of the Pre-School Education* on 7 November 2018, explicitly prohibiting any listed company from acquiring or otherwise controlling (whether or not through nominee or contractual arrangements) non-profit kindergartens.

129 Rui Bai Law Firm, Xin Bai Law Firm and Tiang & Partners, "China Welcomes Investors with New Foreign Investment Law," *News Flash*, 13 February 2020, available at https://www.hoganlovells.com/en/publications/the-foreign-investment-law-gets-wings (accessed on 3 October 2022).

130 See generally, Rafael La Porta et al., "Legal Determinants of External Finance" (1997) 52 *Journal of Finance* 1131–1150; and "Law and Finance" (2002) 57 *Journal of Finance* 1147–1170.

131 Mihir Desai et al., "Institutions and Entrepreneurial Firm Dynamics: Evidence from Europe" (2006) Harvard NOM Research Paper 03-59; Simon Johnson et al., "Property Rights, Finance and Entrepreneurship" (1999) SSRN Working Paper 198409; and Jakob Svensson, "Investment, Property Rights and Political Instability: Theory and Evidence" (1998) 42 *European Economic Review* 1317–1341.

132 Simeon Djankov et al., "Courts" (2003) 118 *Quarterly Journal of Economics* 453–517; and "The Law and Economics of Self-dealing" (2005) NBER Working Paper 11883.

133 Simeon Djankov, "The Regulation of Entry" (2002) 117(1) *Quarterly Journal of Economics* 1–37.

134 Douglass C. North, *Institutions, Institutional Change and Economic Performance* (Cambridge: Cambridge University Press, 1990) 35.

135 World Bank's Worldwide Governance Indicators (WGI) measure six dimensions of governance between 1996 and 2008: voice and accountability, political stability and absence of violence/terrorism, government effectiveness, regulatory quality, rule of law, and control of corruption. See Daniel Kaufmann, Aart Kraay and Massimo Mastruzzi, "Governance Matters VIII: Aggregate and Individual Governance Indicators 1996–2008" (June 2009) World Bank Policy Research Working Paper WPS 4978. However, it should be pointed out that Kaufmann et al. conceded the difficulties of assessing trends in a particular country indicator given the large margins of error. The decrease indicated in the diagram may be attributable to the addition of new data sets and more margins of error. Besides, WGI aggregates results from some other data sources that rely on subjective judgements made by public organizations, private institutions, and NGOs, which may be out of line with objective circumstances and may not be necessarily expert assessments. Also, according to WGI, China outperforms or at least performs as well as the average country in the same income class on these core indicators.

136 China ranked 34th out of 131 countries in the 2008–2009 World Economic Forum's Global Competitiveness Index and 57th out of 127 countries in the Business Competitiveness Index. China ranked 99th out of 122 countries on transparency of government policy making. The World Economic Forum's index is based on 12 pillars: institutions; infrastructure; macroeconomic stability; health and primary education; higher education and training; goods market efficiency; labour market efficiency; financial market sophistication; technical readiness; market size; business sophistication; and innovation, available at https://www3.weforum.org/docs/WEF_GlobalCompetitivenessReport_2008-09.pdf.

137 See generally, Randall Peerenboom, *China's Long March Toward Rule of Law* (Cambridge: Cambridge University Press, 2002); and Margaret Y.K. Woo, "Law and Discretion in the Contemporary Chinese Courts" (1999) 8 *Pacific Rim Law & Policy Journal*

581, 584. A road map of upgrading and reconstructing the judicial system in China is also provided in Yang Xiao, "A New Chapter in Constructing China's Legal System," in Laurence Brahm (ed), *China's Century: The Awakening of the New Economic Powerhouse* (John Wiley & Sons (Asia) Pte Ltd, 2001) 219–233.

138 Donald C. Clarke, "Economic Development and the Rights Hypothesis: The China Problem" (2003) 51 *American Journal of Comparative Law* 89.

139 Donald C. Clarke, "Power and Politics in the Chinese Court System: The Enforcement of Civil Judgments" (1996) 10 *Columbia Journal of Asian Law* 43.

140 Kathy Chu, "Is China Turning Against Foreign Businesses?," *USA Today*, 25 October 2011, p. 8A.

141 Susan L. Shirk, *The Political Logic of Economic Reform in China* (Berkeley: University of California Press, 1993).

142 Lucian Pye, *The Mandarin and the Cadre* (Ann Arbor, MI: University of Michigan Press, 1988).

143 Kenneth Lieberthal and Michel Oksenberg, *Policy Making in China: Leaders, Structures, and Processes* (Princeton: Princeton University Press, 1988).

144 See generally, http://en.wikipedia.org/wiki/Harmonious_society, and Maureen Fan, "China's Party Leadership Declares New Priority: 'Harmonious Society'," *The Washington Post*, 12 October 2006. A harmonious society is of higher standards, not only trying to fill in the gap between the wealthy and poor but also providing an opportunity to the people for self-fulfilment, which is akin to the capabilities approach advocated by, that is Martha C. Nussbaum, *Frontiers of Justice: Disability, Nationality and Species Membership* (Cambridge, MA: Belknap Press Harvard University Press, 2007) Chs 3, 5 & 7; and Amartya Sen, *Developments as Freedom* (Oxford: Oxford University Press, 1999).

145 Yong Wang, "China's Domestic WTO Debate," (January/February 2000) 27(54) *China Business Review* 54.

146 To be more detailed, these industries refer to machinery, automobiles, telecommunications, construction, iron and steel, and non-ferrous metals. "Control Over Key Industries 'Crucial'," *China Daily*, 19 December 2006, available at http://english.people.com.cn/200612/19/eng20061219_333839.html.

147 Shen Wei, "Is SAFE Safe Now? – Foreign Exchange Regulatory Control over Chinese Outbound and Inbound Investments and a Political Economy Analysis of Policies" (2010) 11(2) *Journal of World Investment and Trade* 227, 245–250.

148 Mure Dickie, "Chinese Takeover Fears Grow," *Financial Times*, 4 August 2006, p. 6; Geoff Dyer, Sundeep Tucker and Tom Mitchell, "Forbidden Country? How Foreign Deals in China are Hitting Renewed Resistance," *Financial Times*, 8 August 2006, p. 11.

149 The most high-profile and lasting battle was Carlyle's bid to take stake in Xugong, China's leading machinery maker, which was finally defeated. Sundeep Tucker, "Carlyle Concedes Defeat in Battle to Take Stake in China's Xugong," *Financial Times*, 23 July 2008.

150 Robert Baldwin, "Why Rules Don't Work" (1990) 53 *Modern Law Review* 321.

151 See generally, Ian Ayres and John Braithwaite, *Responsive Regulation: Transcending the Deregulation Debate* (Oxford: Oxford University Press, 1992); Malcolm K. Sparrow, *The Regulatory Craft – Controlling Risks, Solving Problems, and Managing Compliance* (Washington, DC: Brookings Institution Press, 2000) Ch 19; Julia Black, "New Institutionalism and Naturalism in Socio-Legal Analysis: Institutionalist Approaches to Regulatory Decision Making" (1997) 19 *Law and Policy* 51.

152 For a general attack on the shortcomings of a "responsive" approach such as lack of formalism, fairness, proportionality, and consistency, see generally, Karen Yeung, *Securing Compliance: A Principled Approach* (Oxford: Hart Publishing, 2004); Keith Werhan, "De-legalizing Administrative Law" (1996) 58 *University of Illinois Law Review* 423.

153 See John Braithwaite, "Rewards and Regulation" (2002) *Journal of Law and Society* 29, 12, 21–22; "Responsive Regulation and Developing Economies" (2006) 34 *World Development* 885.

154 This is largely not the case in China. However, the Chinese government has adopted pro-private-investors policies and rules more recently due to the slowdown of the national and global economy. The State Council issued the Several Opinions of Encouraging and Guiding Private Investment's Healthy Development in May 2010. Thereafter, 17 ministries or commissions have promulgated administrative rules to open up more previously restricted industries such as banking, energy, health care, and infrastructure sectors to private investors. The State Council is also trying to reform the banking sector and curb shadow banking (i.e. avoiding a large amount of domestic deposits being steered from bank loans into opaque, off-balance-sheet and risk-laden vehicles) by allowing Wenzhou to test how to channel more funding to the private sectors. Reuters, "Shadow Bank Reform Needed to Fight Bubbles," *South China Morning Post*, 12 January 2012, p. B3. The latest move was that China Banking Regulatory Commission took a more favourable position towards private sectors while implementing Basel III to Chinese banks. According to the newly passed Commercial Banks' Capital Regulations (Trial), issued on 8 June 2012, Chinese banks would be motivated to obtain better quality credit and extend more lending to small and medium-sized enterprises (SME) as the Chinese version of Basel III lowers the risk weighting assigned to SME loans in calculating banks' capital ratios. Simon Rabinovitch, "Beijing Puts Back Date for Enforcing Basel III," *Financial Times*, 7 June 2012, available at www.ftchinese.com/story/001044938/en/?print=y (accessed on 22 June 2012). For more details on China's shadow banking, see generally Shen Wei, *Shadow Banking in China: Risk, Regulation and Policy* (Cheltenham, UK: Edward Elgar, 2016); "Three Paradoxes of Shadow Banking: A Political Economy Paradigm," in Shen Wei (ed.), *Conceptualizing the Regulatory Thicket: China's Financial Markets After the Global Financial Crisis* (Oxford and New York: Routledge, 2021) Ch 6.

155 PRC Constitution (Article 15) defines the model as a "socialist" market economy.

7

FOREIGN INVESTMENT LAW IN THE CONTEXT OF BILATERAL INVESTMENT TREATY

1. Introduction

Protection of foreign investment is a long-standing issue facing China. On the one hand, China wants to absorb more foreign investment in order to help modernize its economy. On the other hand, there are outstanding concerns from the foreign investors about the adequacy of investment protection. Apart from its domestic law, in particular, the FIE Laws and now the FIL, bilateral investment treaties are also important vehicles codifying China's foreign investment protection standards.

China did not conclude agreements on mutual protection of investment with foreign countries until 29 March 1982 when its first bilateral investment treaty ("BIT") was concluded with the Kingdom of Sweden. Up to 2022, China has already concluded 125 BITs (106 in force) and 25 TIPs (22 in force), which ranks first in the number of BITs and TIPs concluded.[1] Nevertheless, there has not been a single arbitration case brought by any foreign investor against China until 2009, when a Hong Kong-based investor brought a BIT claim against Peru at the International Centre for Settlement of Investment Disputes (ICSID).[2]

This chapter mainly outlines a framework about China's BIT law and practice by focusing on (i) substantive standards and (ii) procedural rules under Chinese BITs.

2. Bilateral Investment Treaty Protection of Foreign Investments

2.1 Definition of "Investment"

BITs only provide protection to covered investments. Chinese BITs define the term "investment" widely, which regularly encompasses:

DOI: 10.4324/9781003130499-7

every kind of asset invested by investors of one Contracting State in accordance with the laws and regulations of the other Contracting State in the territory of the latter and in particular, though not exclusively, includes (a) moveable and immovable property as well as any other property rights such as mortgages, liens and pledges; (b) shares, stock, debentures and any other form of participation in a company; (c) claims to money, or to any performance under contract having an economic value associated with an investment . . .; (d) intellectual property rights, including copyrights, patents, industrial designs, trademarks, trade names, technical processes, know-how and goodwill; (e) business concessions conferred by law or under contract permitted by law, including concessions to search for, cultivate, extract or exploit natural resources.[3]

With little difference, the vast majority of Chinese BITs, such as the Singapore–China BIT,[4] the Philippines–China BIT,[5] Laos–China BIT,[6] Indonesia–China BIT,[7] and Cambodia–China BIT,[8] include this all-embracing definition of "investment," which guarantees that all rights and interests involved in economic activities in China are covered by the substantive protection supplied by the relevant BIT.

The Agreement on Investment of the Framework Agreement on Comprehensive Economic Cooperation (the "Treaty") between China and ASEAN defines the term "investment" as "every kind of assets which are invested by the investors of a Party in accordance with the relevant laws, regulations and policies of another Party."[9] The "in accordance with its laws, regulations and polices" requirement is a common qualification attached to the definition of "investment" in Chinese BITs. This qualification sets a jurisdictional limit (or a restriction on admissibility),[10] which may be a *de facto* blocking element to the utility of substantive protections offered in the BITs and which has been arbitrated in some recent cases.[11] For instance *Inceysa Vallisoletana v. El Salvador* indicates that investments that were made fraudulently and therefore not in accordance with the law do not fall within the ICSID jurisdiction embodied in the BIT between El Salvador and Spain (2005).[12] This qualification, however, is rarely clarified in Chinese BITs except for one amendment to the Cuba–China BIT (1995), which provides that:

> the expression "pursuant to the laws and regulations" shall mean that for any kind of invested asset to be considered as an investment protected in this Agreement, it shall be in accordance with any of the foreign investment modalities defined by the legislation of the Contracting Party receiving the investment and registered as such in the correspondent registry.

This amendment is clear in that the investment made by a natural or legal person from a foreign state must take one of the accepted forms of foreign investment in China. The Treaty, conforming to the WTO's transparency requirement, makes a further clarification in this regard by providing that "policies shall refer to those affecting investment that are endorsed and announced by the Government of a Party, and made publicly available in a written form."[13]

The Treaty adopts a broad asset-based definition of "investment."[14] The definition is supplemented by an illustrative list of particular assets covered by the Treaty, ranging from movable and immovable property, interests in companies, intellectual property rights ("IPRs"), to business concessions and contractual rights.[15] This list is broader than the one in the Netherlands–China and Germany–China BITs, particularly in its references to contract rights. However, this list fails to reflect some positive changes adopted in recent Chinese BITs. For instance, the Treaty fails to differentiate debts as an investment and debts from normal trade transactions. The New Zealand–China Free Trade Agreement (FTA) (2008) is progressive in making a distinction between trade and investment debts in that "bonds, including government issued bonds, debentures, loans and other forms of debts, and rights derived therefrom" are parallel to the category of "investment" which normally covers the forms of shares and stocks.[16] Differentiating the two categories of debts may potentially avoid certain unintended claims being brought under a BIT. This differential approach has gained some popularity in BIT practice. For instance a bank guarantee, being a contingent liability, was not regarded by the tribunal in the *Joy Mining* case as an "investment" within the meaning of the investment treaty.[17] Among others, the US Model BIT has adopted this differential approach.[18]

The list of specific IPRs contained in the definition of "investment" is a lengthy one, which is in line with the recent practice that more IPRs will be protected under the BITs.[19] This also reflects China's confidence in being able to provide foreign investors with more IPR protections of international standard.

In terms of the category of business concessions, Chinese BITs vary in their wording but mainly target business concessions for the exploration of natural resources. The Treaty adopts the typical language "including concessions to search for, cultivate, extract or exploit natural resources," as seen in the Netherlands–China BIT (2001), Germany–China BIT (2003), and Finland–China BIT (2004). A new version of the "business concession" term has emerged in the Australia–China BIT which includes "rights to engage in agriculture, forestry, fisheries and animal husbandry" and "rights to manufacture, use and sell products" in addition to "rights to search for, extract or exploit natural resources."[20]

Reinvestment of returns is also covered in the definition of "investment" in the Treaty. Most Chinese BITs are silent on this point. However, several recent BITs make clear that reinvestment of returns are also covered. The Finland–China BIT provides that "reinvested returns shall enjoy the same treatment as the original investment."[21] The Treaty's wording is slightly different but broad enough to confirm that "returns that are invested should be treated as investments and any alteration of the form in which assets are invested or reinvested shall not affect their character as investments." The legal significance of adopting such an extensive approach needs to be further observed. The term "returns" is defined as "amounts yielded by or derived from an investment particularly, though not exclusively, profits, interests, capital gains, dividends, royalties or fees."[22] This definition is substantially same as the one that appears in other BITs such as the Cambodia–China BIT.[23]

The definition of "investment" in the Treaty is in line with the Chinese BIT practice. The Treaty does not include "licences and permits pursuant to law,"[24] "payable services"[25] or "goods that, under a leasing agreement, are placed at the disposal of a lessee in the territory of a Party in conformity with its laws and regulations"[26] in the illustrative list of the "investment."

More notably, the Treaty has not absorbed the concept of "indirect investment," which was first introduced into the Gabon–China BIT, under which the "investment" includes "every kind of investment invested directly or indirectly by the investors of one Party in the territory of the other Party in accordance with its laws and regulations." The Germany–China BIT (2003) defines the term "invested directly" as "invested by an investor of one Contracting Party through a company which is fully or partially owned by the investor and having its seat in the territory of the other Contracting Party."[27] Thus, investments made by an investor in the home country but effectuated via a subsidiary in the other contracting state are also covered by the BIT. The Argentina–China BIT (1992) included the concept of "indirect investment" but through a third-party construction approach as follows:

> If natural or juridical persons of a Contracting Party have an interest in a juridical person which was established within the territory of a third State, and this juridical person invests in the other Contracting Party it shall be recognised as a juridical person of the former Contracting Party.[28]

The New Zealand–China FTA provides that "investments" extend to investments of legal persons of a third party which are owned or controlled by investors of one Party, provided the third country has no, or disclaims its, right to claim compensation for expropriation. As a result, investments made by a New Zealand or Chinese investor may still be covered even if directly made through an offshore vehicle. To be clear, a denial of benefits clause is included in the FTA with respect to investments made by investors of one Party, where the investment is made through a legal entity owned or controlled by nationals of the other Party or a third party.[29]

Even in the absence of explicit provisions in BITs, tribunals may still recognize the protection of indirect investment either through a non-controlling shareholder[30] or indirect shareholder.[31] The right to claim for alleged infringements of indirect investment is available to the investor within the meaning of the BITs[32] and has been supported by the case of *Tza Yap Shum v. Peru*, in which a Hong Kong citizen's indirect investment in Peru through a BVI company was well recognized by the tribunal to fall in the scope of "investment" under the China–Peru BIT.[33]

The concept of "indirect investment" is important in the Chinese law context in two respects. First, those investors whose home jurisdictions have not signed any BIT with China may consider structuring their investments through a subsidiary which is incorporated in a country having a BIT with China.[34]

Second, the utility of the "indirect investment" concept may clarify the status of holding companies incorporated in Hong Kong or Macau. A Hong Kong- or Macau-based investor can secure investment protections under the BIT entered into between China and the investment forum if it invests in that country through a China-incorporated subsidiary. Unfortunately, the Treaty does not make a reference either to the "indirect investment" concept or the third-country construction.

2.2 National Treatment

National treatment is the core standard that underpins the principle of non-discrimination and requires the host state to accord equal treatment under BITs. The purpose of this standard is to promote equal treatment between foreign and domestic investors while avoiding arbitrary or discriminatory measures. A typical clause requires the host states to grant foreign investors treatment that is "no less favourable than" or "as favourable as" that accorded to the host state's own citizens.[35] The difficulty in applying this treatment in reliance upon the "no less favourable than" criterion is to properly determine when foreign and domestic investors are in a comparable situation so as to judge whether the foreign investor has been unjustifiably discriminated against. The other way of describing this standard is to use the phrase "same treatment," which does not prevent foreign investors from enjoying more favourable treatment.

2.2.1 Qualified National Treatment Provision

Some earlier Chinese BITs including the Singapore–China BIT (1985) and the Philippines–China BIT (1992) did not mention the national treatment doctrine at all. Less than half of Chinese BITs grant a national treatment standard by merely adopting the phrase "no less favourable than." China was historically hesitant to apply a full-scale national treatment doctrine, which explained the reason why Chinese BITs often add various qualifications to the national treatment standard. The first Chinese BIT which incorporated the national treatment standard was the United Kingdom–China BIT (1986), which, however, is subject to substantial qualifications: a soft "best effort" obligation and a local law caveat. The United Kingdom–China BIT (1986) states the following:

> either Contracting Party shall to the extent possible, accord treatment in accordance with the stipulations of its laws and regulations to the investment of nationals or companies of the other Contracting Party the same treatment as that accorded to its own nationals or companies.[36]

This provision fails to bind the host country to eliminate existing discriminatory measures or not to take new discriminatory actions, provided that these actions are in the form of local "laws and regulations." Moreover, the limitation "to the extent possible" reduces the effect and goodwill of the host state's undertakings to guarantee equal competition among foreign and domestic investors. As a result, national treatment granted by the BIT remains symbolic and is not able to provide sufficient guarantees to foreign investors.

2.2.2 Full-Scale National Treatment Provision

Very few Chinese BITs include a full-scale national treatment provision. The typical example is the provision in the Japan–China BIT as follows:

> the treatment accorded by either Contracting Party within its territory to nationals and companies of the other Contracting Party with respect to investments, returns and business activities in connection with the investment shall not be less favorable than that accorded to nationals and companies of the former Contracting Party.[37]

This provision applies not only to the "business activity," *inter alia*, "the maintenance of branches and other establishment necessary for the business activity, the control and management of companies, the employment and discharge of personnel and the making and performance of contracts"[38] but also to "the purchase of raw materials, power and fuel, marketing of products, obtaining loan, etc."[39] However, the significance of this provision cannot be over-exaggerated as its efficacy was substantially reduced by the BIT's Additional Protocol which provides that:

> it shall not be deemed treatment less favourable for either Contracting Party to accord discriminatory treatment, in accordance with its laws and regulations, to nationals and companies of the other Contracting Party, in case it is really necessary for the reason of public order, national security or sound development of national economy.[40]

This caveat included in the Protocol and other Chinese BITs, such as the Czech and Slovak Republic–China BIT, is in broad terms since such concepts as "public order" and "sound development of national economy" are not explicitly defined. Besides, the application of these terms is subject to the tribunal's interpretation and discretion. Even worse, these catch-all terms give China considerable leeway to implement existing discriminatory measures against foreign investors, or even adopt new ones.

Moving away from the United Kingdom–China BIT type of restrictions, China has been gradually more willing to accept general national treatment since late 2001. In the new Germany–China BIT, for example a more general national treatment provision is offered. Accordingly, China "shall accord to investments and activities associated with such investments by the investors of the other Contracting Party treatment not less favourable than that accorded to the investments and associated activities by its own investors."[41] Nevertheless, this "full" national treatment standard is still subject to a "grandfather" clause, under which the national treatment standard does not apply to:

(a) any existing non-conforming measures maintained within its territory;
(b) the continuation of any such non-conforming measure;
(c) any amendment to any such non-conforming measure to the extent that the amendment does not increase the non-conformity of these measures.

> The People's Republic of China will take all appropriate steps in order to progressively remove the non-conforming measures.[42]

This "grandfather" clause appeared in the Cyprus–China BIT[43] and various Chinese BITs with European states.[44]

The Treaty includes a wider national treatment clause as follows:

> Each Party shall, in its territory, accord to investors of another Party and their investments treatment no less favourable than it accords, in like circumstances, to its own investors and their investments with respect to management, conduct, operation, maintenance, use, sale, liquidation, or other forms of disposal of such investments.[45]

The inclusion of a "full" national treatment provision in the Treaty constitutes a major development. However, the Treaty's national treatment standard is subject to a similar "grandfather" clause, which allows the preservation of existing non-conforming measures, that is legislation inconsistent with the national treatment obligation:

1 National Treatment . . . shall not apply to:

> (a) any existing or new non-conforming measures maintained or adopted within its territory;
> (b) the continuation or amendment of any non-conforming measures referred to in sub-paragraph (a).

2 The Parties will endeavour to progressively remove the non-conforming measures.[46]

There are several significant differences between the Treaty and the Germany–China BIT in terms of the "grandfather" clause. First, the "grandfather" clause in the Germany–China BIT establishes a one-way right, and only China can enjoy the "grandfather" clause to maintain non-conforming measures. By contrast, the "grandfather" clause in the Treaty allows both sides to preserve a limited right to discriminate between domestic and foreign investors. This difference makes sense given the fact that China and the majority of ASEAN member states are developing states. Second, the scope of exceptions granted by the "grandfather" clause in the Germany–China BIT is narrower. The exception only allows the preservation of existing measures and amendments that do not increase the non-conformity level.

In other words, the "grandfather" clause is a "standstill" clause which prohibits new non-conforming measures or changes to the existing non-conforming measures that would increase the degree of discrimination. The Treaty's approach to the "grandfather" clause, however, is a wider one. In addition to "grandfathering" those non-conforming measures, the clause also waives the national treatment obligation to the new non-conforming measures. This has been so far the only Chinese BIT which adopts this unique wider approach. Third, China made a commitment in the Germany–China BIT to take all appropriate steps in order to progressively remove the non-conforming measures. The language and context indicate a "rollback" commitment of a soft law nature, which arguably lacks a binding effect but may be enforced by means of reputational costs. The Treaty's language is explicit in that the endeavour to remove the non-conforming measures is a non-binding posture rather than a legally binding obligation. Although the language in the Treaty avoids any potential debate on the legal effect and enforceability of "endeavour to remove the non-conforming measures," the legal significance of such commitment to remove the non-conforming measures may unfortunately deteriorate to zero.

2.2.3 "In Like Circumstances" Qualifier

Unlike the European BITs, the North American BITs normally contain an "in like circumstances" qualification.[47] In assessing whether a national treatment standard has been breached or not, the tribunals often apply a three-step approach: to identify the subject of comparison (a "comparator" or "like investor"); to compare the treatment received by the foreign and the "comparator" investors with a view to establishing any discrimination; and to ascertain whether there is any justification for such differential treatment.[48] First, the tribunal must identify a "like investor" and compare the treatment this "like investor" receives with that received by the foreign investor concerned. Under the NAFTA, tribunals will resort to the phase "in like circumstances" in determining the scope of the subject of comparison. For instance the tribunal in *SD Myers v. Canada* ruled that the term "like circumstances" invited an examination of whether a non-national investor complaining of less favourable treatment was in the same "sector" as the national investor.[49] The tribunal in *Methanex v. United States*, in applying a narrower approach, decided to choose only entities that were in the most closely "like circumstances" rather than comparators that were in less similar circumstances to the comparator.[50] Although the inclusion of the "in like circumstances" caveat can be used by the tribunal to determine the breach of national treatment standard, there is no uniform approach to the comparator in arbitration practice. The "in like circumstances" caveat may justify differences in treatment. Tribunals in several NAFTA cases left host states significant flexibility in applying different treatments to domestic and foreign investors as long as the policy considerations were rational. In *SD Myers v. Canada*, the tribunal confirmed that the assessment of "like circumstances" needed to take into account circumstances that would justify governmental regulations that treated investors differently to protect the public interest.[51]

Chinese BITs usually follow the European approach and tend not to include a "like circumstance" qualification (except in the case of a few BITs).[52] The Treaty adopts this caveat as follows:

> Each Party shall, in its territory, accord to investors of another Party and their investments treatment no less favourable than it accords, in like circumstances, to its own investors and their investments with respect to management, conduct, operation, maintenance, use, sale, liquidation, or other forms of disposal of such investments.[53]

The adoption of this caveat seems to be a trend in recent years. The New Zealand–China FTA contains similar language, requiring "treatment no less favourable than that accorded, in like circumstances, to the investments . . . by its own investors."[54] The utility of this better-crafted language may avoid potential confusion. In the absence of this phrase, the textual interpretation may suggest that the comparison may be made to a broader group of domestic investors.[55] With the "like circumstances" caveat, the tribunal may interpret the national treatment standard to imply the requirement of "comparability" between two investors. The national treatment standard granted in the Treaty is not necessarily a great leap forward as the standard is still subject to both the "grandfather" clause and the "in like circumstances" qualification. In this sense, the national treatment standard is of limited, symbolic value.

2.2.4 Scope of Application

In terms of the scope of application, some Chinese BITs adopt a wider formula by applying the national treatment obligation not only to "investments of investors" but also to "investments and activities associated with investments"[56] and to other issues such as legal remedies and compensation for losses due to war.[57] The Treaty appears closer to the rather narrower formula by defining, in a non-exhaustive manner, that the national treatment obligation applies to "the investors and their investments with respect to the management, conduct, operation, maintenance, use, sale, liquidation, or other forms of disposal of such investments." The function of the list appears to be two-fold. First, even though the Treaty does not explicitly use the wording "associated activities," the non-exhaustive list enables it to extend the national treatment obligation to "activities associated with investments." The loose language effectively broadens the limited scope of investment and provides a certain level of flexibility. Second, the list also indicates that the national treatment obligation may also apply at the pre-establishment phase as there is no mention of "establishment" or "acquisition" in the list. Yet it has to be pointed out that the stance taken by China so far is to limit the application of BITs to post-establishment measures, which is in contrast to the US approach of applying BITs to both pre-establishment and post-establishment measures.[58] Therefore, an investor is not able to bring a claim against China for any measures restricting the establishment of an investment in China. The investment can only be "admitted subject to its right to exercise power conferred by its laws"[59] or "in accordance with [the Contracting State's] laws and regulations."[60] Based on these provisions, the admission of foreign investment, or in Chinese terminology, the approval of foreign investment, is at the discretion of the Chinese government. This is also the arrangement under the WTO framework, where the Chinese government is permitted to exclude foreign investors from a limited number of specific sectors.

The Treaty's position on the national treatment standard reflects its recent departure from a conservative to a more liberal stance in offering foreign investment protections.[61] This move makes sense as China (as indicated in Figure 7.1) is now expanding its FDI activities overseas while remaining the largest capital-importing state. China's outbound investment amounted to US$183.97 billion by 2008 and was in the amount of US$43.3 billion in 2009.[62]

Along with more and more Chinese nationals and companies going abroad to invest in other natural resources rich countries, mainly in Africa, Latin America, and the Middle-East region, the Chinese government is also eager to enter into BITs with these countries and bargain for a full national treatment clause in BITs. China has in fact signed more BITs with developing than developed countries. Africa, along with Latin America, has replaced Europe as the most important partner region for China to sign new BITs.[63] This changing pattern, as shown in Figure 7.2,[64] is attributable to the growing importance of developing countries, in particular, Africa, as the key destinations absorbing Chinese outbound FDI. Other factors which have contributed to the appearance of a full-scale

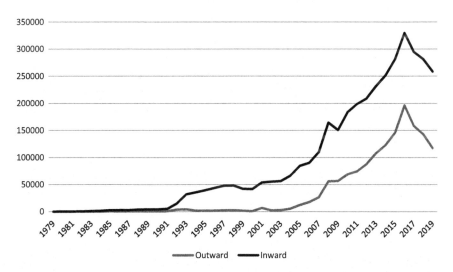

FIGURE 7.1   China's FDI Flows (1979–2019)[65]
(USD Millions)
Source: Compiled by the author.

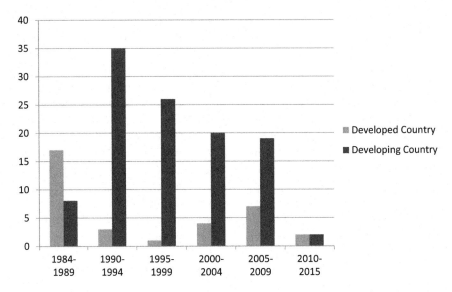

FIGURE 7.2 Growth in Number of Chinese BITs With Trading Partners[66] (1984–2015)

national treatment provision in recent Chinese BITs include (but are not limited to) China's accession to the WTO,[67] its rapid economic growth and the positive development of a "socialist market economy"[68] and the rule of law.[69]

FIL's Chapter II starts with Article 9, which introduces the principle of equality between domestic and foreign enterprises: the state's various policies shall equally apply to foreign-invested enterprises. This may somehow address the US' complaint over China's lack of reciprocity. Comments and suggestions from foreign investors should be considered "in a proper manner."[70] More cooperation is needed which might be multilateral or bilateral between China and other countries, regions, or international organizations.[71]

But a condition is attached to the special economic areas. To boost investments, the government can establish special economic areas to promote foreign investment[72] or guide foreign investors to invest in specific industries, fields, and areas, taking into account national economic and social development.[73]

The FIL lays an emphasis on the equal treatment of foreign and local investors and seeks to increase the level of investment promotion and protection. As the first comprehensive legal basis for China's inward foreign investment, these objectives can further encourage investment flows and thus contribute to the development goals.[74]

Unlike the three laws on FIEs that barely mentioned equal treatment, various clauses in the FIL place foreign investments on equal footing with domestic investments and cover four main aspects.

The FIL grants foreign investors pre-establishment national treatment. Foreign investors investing in sectors falling outside the negative list will be entitled to national treatment at the time of making the investment. With respect to the national treatment for sectors not covered by the negative list, the FIL further clarifies that the market access requirements applicable to foreign investors will be no less favourable than those applied to domestic investors.[75] In addition to the grant of pre-entry national treatment to foreign investments not being included in the negative lists, the FIL also explicitly requires the authorities to examine the licensing applications of foreign investors under the same conditions and procedures as those for domestic investors.[76]

Above all, the FIL substantially alters the existing monitoring system of foreign investment and instead sets forth a new mechanism of market access for foreign investment. The new mechanism has two components: pre-entry national treatment and negative list.[77] The adoption of the new market access mechanism in the FIL signifies the change of policies in handling foreign investment from approval to registration and from management of investors to regulation of investment activities.[78,79]

As to the management of foreign investments, the complaints that industrial standards have disadvantaged FIEs[80] can be solved, as the FIEs' right to equally participate in the formation of these standards is guaranteed. Meanwhile, the compulsory standards enacted by the government should be applied equally to both foreign and domestic investments.[81] Moreover, the FIL stipulates that the views of foreign investors must be collected when subsequent rules applying to their investments are formulated.[82] However, considering that China often allows a very short comment period for the public,[83] the lack of a requirement for a time frame may impede the functioning of this rule. Additionally, FIEs are equally covered by the policies supporting the development of enterprises as are domestic enterprises.[84]

Pre-entry national treatment is defined as treatment given to foreign investors at the stage of entry in which the investment standards are not lower than that of domestic investors and their investments.[85] Article 4 of the FIL makes it clear that the country will "implement the management scheme of pre-establishment national treatment plus negative list with respect to foreign investment."[86]

Pre-establishment national treatment grants to foreign investors a national treatment before their presence or establishment in the country. Under the FIE Laws, foreign investors are treated differently until after they have gained market access. The FIL extends national treatment to the pre-entry-stage prior to the actual establishment of the FIE.[87] As provided in Article 4 of the FIL, the pre-entry national treatment is a "treatment given to foreign investors and their investments at the stage of investment admission no less than that given to the domestic investors and their investments."[88,89]

National treatment is considered the single most important standard of treatment in international investment[90] and is also believed to be the most difficult standard to achieve given both economically and politically sensitive issues it may touch upon.[91] According to the United Nations Conference on Trade and Development (UNCTAD), national treatment refers to "a principle whereby a host country extends to foreign investors treatment that is at least as favorable as the treatment that it accords to national investors in like circumstances."[92] The very purpose of the national treatment standard is "to ensure a degree of competitive equality between national and foreign investors."[93]

The national treatment only extends to the post-entry treatment of foreign investors; there has been a new trend that the standard is expanded to apply to the pre-entry stage.[94] The FIL follows this trend. As a statutory requirement under the FIL, China undertakes a policy of high-level investment liberalization and facilitation.[95] The underlying notion is the principle of equality under which foreign and domestic investors are on an equal footing at both pre- and post-entry stages. The expansion of national treatment is deemed essential to achieving "a stable, transparent, predictable and fair market environment."[96]

A centrepiece of the pre-entry national treatment is the equal competition among all investors, foreign or domestic. For that purpose, the FIL contains several articles that are intended to maintain and promote the equality principle as a basic incentive to attract more foreign investments. For example under the FIL, it is required that the management of foreign investment in the areas not in the negative list be made in accordance with the principle of equality between domestic and foreign investments.[97] In addition, if permission is needed for business operation in a certain industry or sector, the government authorities are required to review and examine foreign investors' application for permission under the equal conditions and procedures as applied to domestic investment, except as otherwise provided by the laws and administrative regulations.[98]

Other provisions in the FIL that are aimed at implementing the equality principle include (i) the state policies concerning the support of enterprise development are equally applied to the FIEs;[99] (ii) the FIEs are equally entitled to participating in the standard-setting work, and the mandatory standards established by the state are equally applicable to the FIEs;[100] (iii) the FIEs have equal access to the government procurements through fair competition, and the FIEs' products and services within the territory of China are treated equally with the domestic enterprises' products and services in the government procurement;[101] and (iv) like domestic enterprises, FIEs may also raise funds through public offerings, and issuance of corporate bonds or other securities.[102]

The Implementation Regulations reinforce the equality principle as between domestic and foreign investments in at least three aspects. The first aspect concerns equal application of the state policies in supporting the enterprise development. According to Article 6 of the Implementation Regulations, the government and its relevant departments shall treat FIEs and domestic enterprises equally in funds arrangement, land supply, tax reduction or exemption, qualification licensing, standard setting, project application, or human resource policies. It is also required that all policies adopted by the government to support enterprise development, and the condition, procedure, as well as time limit pertaining to application for the support be publicized. The government is mandated to treat the FIEs and domestic enterprises equally when reviewing their applications.[103]

The second aspect is about equal participation in the process of standard setting. Under Article 13 of the Implementation Regulations, the standard setting in which the FIEs' equal participation is required includes the state, industry, local, and group standard. In addition, the FIEs may, based on needs, make industry standard on its own initiative or jointly with other enterprises. On the other hand, an FIE may propose for setting a standard and may make comments and suggestions during the periods of approval of the standard setting, drafting of the standard, technology examination, and the feedback and evaluation of the implementation of the standard. The FIEs may also engage in standard drafting, technology examination, and other relevant works as well as the translation of the standard into foreign languages.

Article 13 makes it a statutory requirement that transparency and the complete publicity of the information on standard setting and revision be observed. Furthermore, according to Article 14 of the Implementation Rules, any mandatory standard made by the state shall equally apply to the FIEs and domestic enterprises. Article 14 prohibits the government and its departments at all levels from imposing solely on the FIEs any technical requirements exceeding the mandatory standard.

The third aspect relates to equal access to government procurements. There are three articles in the Implementation Regulations concerning the FIEs' access to government procurements. Under Article 15 of the Implementation Regulations, FIEs shall not be obstructed or restricted from freely entering into the government procurement market in the local area or in a specific industry. The review and determination of the qualification of suppliers shall not be made on the basis of differentiation or discrimination against FIEs. No unreasonable conditions such as the suppliers' ownership type, organizational form, equity structure, the nationality of the investors, or the brand of product or service shall be imposed. For the purpose of government procurement, the product manufactured or service provided within China by an FIE should not be differentiated from those manufactured or provided by its domestic counterpart.

Article 16 of the Implementation Regulations provides that an FIE may, in accordance with the government procurement law and regulations of China, inquire or question the purchaser about a government procurement matter and file complaints with the authority supervising government procurement. After receiving the inquiry, question, or complaint, the purchaser or the authority supervising government procurement shall reply or make a decision within the legally required period of time. Article 17 demands strengthening the supervision of government procurement so that an action differentiating or discriminating against FIEs will be corrected and punished.

In addition, Article 35 of the Implementation Regulations requires an equal treatment for FIEs in obtaining licences for particular sectors. It is provided in Article 35 of the Implementation Regulations that where a foreign investor invests in an industry or sector which requires obtainment of a licence, unless otherwise provided by law or regulations, its application for such licence shall be viewed under the same conditions and procedures applicable to domestic enterprises, and no discriminatory requirements shall be allowed concerning the conditions for the licence, application materials, review steps, and time limits.

Article 35 also provides that where an FIE applies for a type of licence that meets the stated conditions and requirements, the application may be handled by simplified procedure known as "notification and promise" in accordance with the law. The notification and promise refers to an application and approval process in which government departments disclose specific standards or conditions, the applicant promises in writing to have met the standards or conditions, and based on the applicant's promise, the administrative authority directly grants an approval.

The core of the national treatment with regard to foreign investors is "no less than" or "no less favorable than" the treatment granted to domestic investors. The term "no less" does not necessarily mean the "same." In other words, the treatment given to foreign investors could be the same or better. Therefore, it is legally permissible to provide foreign investors with preferential treatment. In fact, the preferential treatment has been widely used in many countries as a useful policy tool to draw in foreign investment. In China, with the national treatment, foreign investors may still enjoy investment incentives that are not applicable to domestic investment. The supernational treatment enjoyed by foreign investors sometimes is the target complained of by domestic businesses.

According to the FIL, foreign investors and FIEs may enjoy preferential treatment when making investment in the industries, sectors, and regions specified by the state for the needs of national economic and social development. Under the FIL, local governments at or above the county level may within their statutory competence adopt policies and measures for promotion and facilitation of foreign investment. This provision actually empowers local governments to provide foreign investors with certain preferential treatment on the basis of local needs. Article 12 of the Implementation Regulations further provides that a foreign investor or an FIE may enjoy a preferential treatment in areas such as finance, tax, banking, and land use. Pursuant to Article 13 of the Implementation Regulations, foreign investors who expand their investment in China with their investment proceeds in China shall enjoy corresponding preferential treatment.

On the other hand, the national treatment is subject to certain limits. As a continuing effort to promote foreign investment, Article 13 of the FIL provides that the state may establish special economic zones where needed or adopt pilot policy or measures for foreign investment in selected regions. Both "special economic zones" and "pilot policy measures" may apply certain preferential treatments or incentives to foreign investments in these areas. Article 10 of the Implementation Regulations defines the "special economic zone" as a specific area established with the approval by the state for which more vigorous opening-up policy and measures for foreign investment will be implemented. Further, under Article 10 of the Implementation Regulations, the pilot policy or measures applied to foreign investment may be extended to other regions or nationwide under particular circumstances if proven to be feasible in practice. In addition, the application of national treatment is paired with a "negative list," which renders the national treatment inapplicable to the "excepted areas" of foreign investment. Put differently, the national treatment applies only to the investment activities in the positive areas or sectors. Certain exceptions to the national treatment exist concerning public health, safety and morals, and national security.

Equal participation and fair competition of FIEs in government procurement activities are also guaranteed.

As for the organization and operation of FIEs, the Company Law and the Partnership Enterprise Law, which previously applied only to domestic-invested enterprises, have extended to FIEs,[104] thus doing away with any restrictions resulting from the separate regime.[105] These provisions can effectively level the playing field and ensure fairer competition between domestic and foreign investments, thus improving China's foreign investment environment.[106]

Any expectation that the laws would remain unchanged after the establishment of an investment is not legitimate,[107] especially since China's foreign investment legal regime has changed frequently over the past decades. Moreover, the proposed reform has been tested and adjusted in the FTZs, and the removal of preferential treatments has been gradually implemented in various aspects like tax,[108] along with the abolishment of inferior national treatment, with the aim of achieving a fair competitive environment for both domestic and foreign investments. Therefore, foreign investors that have acted with due diligence should not rule out changes like those entailed by the recent reform.

The problem remains with specific commitments made to foreign investors by local authorities in contract or undertakings under the previous legal regime. For instance the Implementation Regulations of EJVL authorized provincial governments to grant foreign investors preference in land use.[109] Such commitments may form the basis of legitimate expectations, and thus their cancellation can violate the FET.[110]

Therefore, it is advisable to leave the commitments unaffected by the reform until their expiry dates. As for undertakings that are difficult to observe after the change, the *Vivendi v Argentina II* tribunal suggested that a government can seek to renegotiate their terms in a transparent and non-coercive manner after the implementation of new policies.[111] Moreover, the adoption of transitional measures can also reduce the impact of the regulatory change on existing investment projects and contribute to the consolidation of existing foreign investments.

Similarly, investors also fear changes in laws that increase the cost to business operations, especially those related to the election and turnover of prefecture-level city officials who have both authority and incentive to design and implement new policies,[112] as well as the obligation to accept unfavourable modifications of contractual terms. Accordingly, the FIL prohibits authorities from promulgating normative measures that derogate from investment.

Any change to treatments due to the changing policies or adjustment of government officials requires that contractual amendments imposed by the authorities can be made when necessary, in accordance with their statutory powers and applicable procedures, and against compensation for the investor's losses.[113]

Ultimately, the FIL appears to tackle certain major concerns of foreign investors in China. Together with the investment promotion mechanism, this reform is in regulatory alignment with, and can contribute to, the goal of creating an improved regulatory environment for foreign investors. The extent to which this goal can be attained depends in part on the implementation of the FIL.

2.3 Most-Favoured-Nation Treatment

MFN treatment is the most commonly adopted standard in international investment treaties.[114] The purpose of this standard is to create a level playing field among different foreign states regardless of foreign investors' nationalities, as the relevant parties undertake to treat each other in a manner that is at least "as favourable as" or "not less favourable than"[115] they treat a third-party national under this standard. A foreign investor is then able to invoke benefits, that is the admissibility of an investor-state claim, that the host state offers to a third party on the basis of an MFN clause. This has been largely confirmed by case law.[116] In this sense, the MFN clause has considerable weight in the Chinese context.

New-generation BITs with a full range of substantive protections give the protected investor a significant competitive advantage. Therefore, investors in China may prefer to seek protection under one of such new-generation BITs by channelling the investment through a country that is a signatory to a new-generation BIT. Such restructuring, however, must be made before the dispute arises.

As for investors from countries with an old-generation Chinese BIT, they might rely on the more advantageous provisions of the new-generation BITs, including the full scope investor-state arbitration clause, for example not only concerning the amount of compensation for expropriation, but also the violation of other substantive rights. Such an option, however, is not necessarily reliable since MFN treatment obligations with respect to foreign investment and investors are not customary international law obligations but only arise on the basis of an express treaty obligation,[117] largely depending on how the tribunals may likely interpret relevant MFN provisions. While arbitrators advocating the broad interpretation of the MFN clause might be supportive, it may be squarely rejected by other arbitrators advocating a more restrictive or conservative jurisprudence on binding non-signatories to an arbitration clause in a BIT.[118] As a result, investors may need to look for other alternatives because the outcome of an arbitration based on the relevant line of argument is not predictable or sustainable.[119]

All Chinese BITs adopt the MFN standard. In some Chinese BITs, the MFN treatment is offered alongside other standards such as national treatment and fair and equitable treatment standards. In these BITs, the MFN standard is linked with the fair and equitable treatment standard and used as a reference point of the latter.

The Slovenia-China BIT includes the following:

1   Investments and activities associated with investments of investors of either Contracting State shall be accorded fair and equitable treatment and shall enjoy protection in the territory of the other Contracting Party.
2   The treatment and protection referred to in Paragraph 1 of this Article shall not be less favourable than that accorded to investments and activities associated with such investments of investors of a third State.[120]

Other Chinese BITs such as Denmark-China contain more 'standard' MFN provisions as follows:

1   Neither Contracting Party shall subject investments made by nationals or companies of the other Contracting Party or returns of such investments to treatment less favourable than that which it accords to investments or returns of nationals or companies of any third State.
2   Neither Contracting Party shall in its territory subject nationals or companies of the other Contracting Party, as regards their management, maintenance, use, enjoyment or disposal of their investments or returns, to treatment less favourable than that which it accords to nationals or companies of any third State.[121]

Many BITs enumerate the substantive areas to which the MFN clause is limited to apply, such as the 'admission, expansion, management, conduct, operation, maintenance, use, enjoyment and disposal' of investments.[122] The MFN treatment in most Chinese BITs covers both "investment" and "investment-related activities" (or "any activity connected with these investments").[123] While some BITs tend to stipulate them in two separate sections,[124] other BITs merge the two sections and confirm that the host state shall not "subject investments and activities associated with such investments by the investors of the other Contracting Party to treatment less favourable than that accorded to the investments and associated activities by the investors of any third State."[125] Several Chinese BITs, however, restrict the application of the MFN treatment obligation to the "investments" only.[126]

The MFN treatment clause appears in the Treaty as follows:

Each Party shall accord to investors of another Party and their investments treatment no less favourable than that it accords, in like circumstances, to investors of any other Party or third country and/or their respective investments with respect to admission, establishment, acquisition, expansion, management, conduct, operation, maintenance, use, liquidation, sale, and other forms of disposal of investments.[127]

Although the Treaty does not explicitly use the term "activities associated with such investments," the list of "respective investments" supplements this omission and extends the MFN treatment obligation to a series of investment-related activities. The Treaty's MFN provision again uses an 'in like circumstances' comparison.

Like other developing states' BITs,[128] the MFN treatment clauses in most Chinese BITs are not applied to market access but only to the post-admission stage. The first Chinese BIT that extended this standard to investment admission was the Japan–China BIT (1988), which included the following provision:

> Nationals and companies of either Contracting Party shall within the Territory of the other Contracting Party be accorded treatment no less favourable than nationals and companies of any third country in respect of the admission of investment and matters in connection therewith.[129]

Some recent BITs also extend the MFN treatment standard to the investment admission stage but in a different form. The Finland–China BIT (2004) provides that investors from the other contracting party shall receive no less favourable treatment than that accorded to investments of investors from any third state relating to the "establishment, acquisition, operation, management, maintenance, use, enjoyment, expansion, sale or other disposal of investments." The distinction between the terms "establishment" and "expansion" may be expansively interpreted to include the pre-admission treatment within the ambit of MFN treatment.

It is obvious that the Treaty not only follows this pre-admission route but also makes some new changes. First, the Treaty clearly includes the "admission" in the list, which is in line with the Japan–China BIT approach. Second, the Treaty further extends the MFN treatment to "liquidation." Given the fact that "admission," "establishment," "acquisition," and "liquidation" are all included in the list of national treatment standard, it can reasonably be interpreted that these are deliberately included in the list by the Treaty to widen the scope of the MFN and national treatments. The Treaty's approach to applying the MFN treatment is the widest approach so far and has appeared in a small number of the latest Chinese BITs, such as the New Zealand–China FTA.[130]

A number of Chinese BITs expressly impose the MFN treatment obligation on specific matters such as expropriation and compensation,[131] repatriation of investments and returns,[132] treatment of gains resulting from subrogation,[133] measures taken to deal with losses resulting from war or civil disturbance,[134] and judicial and administrative remedies.[135]

China's new-generation BITs such as the Germany-China BIT (2003) covers "indirect" investment. This MFN clause has considerable weight in the Chinese context. The MFN clause in the old-generation Chinese BITs, given the uncertainty and narrower scope, is not a reliable means for foreign investors to enjoy the favourable benefits under other BITs. China's new-generation BITs with a full range of substantive protections give the protected investor a significant competitive advantage. Therefore, foreign investors in China may prefer to seek protection under one of such new-generation BITs by channelling the investment through a country that is a signatory to a new-generation BIT. Such restructuring, however, must be made before the investment dispute arises.

There has been significant controversy over to what extent MFN clauses should apply to substantive rights or procedural rights, or both. Some Chinese BITs expressly impose the MFN treatment obligation on specific matters such as expropriation and compensation,[136] repatriation of investments and returns,[137] treatment of gains resulting from subrogation,[138] measures taken to deal with losses resulting from war or civil disturbance,[139] and judicial and administrative remedies.[140] Unfortunately, the Treaty does not explicitly specify the matters which are subject to the MFN treatment obligation. In this respect, the Treaty is clearly restricted and vague in scope as compared with the BITs that provide an express list. It is reasonably anticipated that a future protocol may improve this matter by providing for a detailed list of activities covered by the MFN treatment obligation.[141]

All the Chinese BITs include express exceptions to the application of the MFN clause. These exceptions are generally fairly identical and mostly relate to benefits for the investor that might be found in other international economic treaties entered into by the host states. The typical exceptions are concerned with economic integration organizations such as customs unions and free trade zones, taxation treaties, and frontier trade arrangements.[142] Some treaties also brought "common market," "economic multilateral or international agreement,"[143] and "regional or sub-regional arrangement"[144] into the list of exceptions. However, not all Chinese BITs include all the three common exceptions. For instance the France–China BIT (1984) and Sweden–China BIT (1982) only included one exception of economic integration; the Korea–China BIT (1992) and Iceland–China BIT do not have the exception for frontier trade arrangements; and the Turkey–China BIT does not cover taxation exceptions. The Treaty refers to economic integration as the only exception as follows (Article 5(3)):

> [MFN] treatment . . . shall not include:
>
> (a) any preferential treatment accorded to investors and their investments under any existing bilateral, regional or international agreements, or any form of economic or regional cooperation with any non-Party; and
>
> (b) any existing or future preferential treatment accorded to investors and their investments in any agreement or arrangement between or among ASEAN Member States or between any Party and its separate customs territories.[145]

Regional economic integration units such as customs unions and free trade zones are one of the most commonly found exceptions to the MFN treatment obligation under the BITs. The WTO does not prohibit such regional economic integration agreements as long as they are compatible with the multilateral trading system.[146] The wording in the Treaty on the economic-integration exception is a relatively broad one covering "bilateral, regional or international agreements, or any form of economic or regional cooperation." Apparently, this expression can be widely interpreted to cover "economic and monetary union, regional economic cooperation or other similar agreements,"[147] "economic union, organisation of mutual economic assistance,"[148] or "any arrangement with a third State or States in the same geographical region designed to promote regional cooperation in the economic, social, labour, industrial or monetary fields within the framework of specific projects."[149]

The Treaty's economic integration exception has some distinguishing features. Unlike some Chinese BITs which extend this exception to both existing and future arrangements,[150] Article 5(3)(a) confines the economic integration exception to agreements entered into before the Treaty. This clears up any doubt about its potentially wider application. Further, the Treaty's language seems to go beyond "regional" arrangements. As a result, the benefits of MFN treatment are not extended to arrangements covered by "existing . . . international agreements."

Apart from the economic integration exception, the Treaty attaches to the MFN treatment the same "grandfather" exception applicable to national treatment. The "grandfather" clause relates to "any existing or new non-conforming measures or continuation or amendment of any non-conforming measures."[151] The Treaty's "grandfather" provisions are almost identical to those in the Czech Republic–China BIT (2005)[152] and the Belgium–Luxembourg–China BIT (2005). The "grandfather" clause in the Treaty merely confirms that the MFN treatment does not apply to existing or new non-conforming measures in both contracting parties. Similarly, there is no obligation imposed on both contracting parties to eliminate any such measures, even though both have promised to progressively remove these non-conforming measures, which would be beneficial to all investors.

Despite Article 5(3)(b) allowing for preferential treatment between a contracting party and its separate customs territories, it is still a conventional economic integration exception. A typical taxation treaty exception generally refers only to any "international agreement or arrangement relating to taxation."[153] Arguably, this exception may be interpreted as a tax treaty exception as the arrangement between a contracting party and its separate customs territory may address issues such as the customs concession or avoidance of double taxation. Judging from the language, this subsection is intended to exclude any arrangement between China and its separate customs territories such as Hong Kong and Macau from the coverage of the MFN treatment. This is important, as mainland China concluded the Closer Economic Partnership Arrangement (CEPA) with Hong Kong and Macau in 2003 respectively, which are designed to be permissible regional free trade agreements under the WTO rules.[154]

As the MFN treatment clauses in the BITs usually grant investors, as regarding "management, maintenance, use, enjoyment or disposal of their investment," no less favourable treatment, it is always controversial if the investor can invoke the MFN obligation to invoke the more favourable dispute resolution provisions in other BITs, which may include consent to ICSID arbitration as an option for all disputes. Arbitration practice indicates that the broader the language used, the more likely that the tribunal will extend the MFN standard to cover procedural rights. For instance the investor may use the MFN treatment to bypass purely procedural matters, that is the requirement to resolve the dispute in the local courts.[155] It has been also confirmed that the MFN treatment may be relied upon to broaden the tribunal's jurisdiction, from disputes relating to the amount or payment of compensation as under the basic treaty, to all disputes including the existence of expropriation under a third-party BIT.[156] The case law in this respect is divergent. In response to debate on MFN clauses and procedural rights, the Treaty tries to eliminate all potential controversies by making clear that the MFN treatment does not cover the procedural rights.[157] Accordingly, an investor in a contracting party cannot claim MFN treatment in resolving the dispute according to the dispute resolution procedures other than those set out in the Treaty. This reflects China's recent stance on this issue, and it continues to include this caveat in other more recent BITs including the New Zealand–China FTA, the relevant provision of which reads:

> For greater certainty, the obligation in this Article does not encompass a requirement to extend to investors of the other Party dispute resolution procedures other than those set out in this Chapter.[158]

2.4 Fair and Equitable Treatment of Investment

Fair and equitable treatment is a commonly used but the least specific substantive protection standard. This standard requires the host country to treat foreign investment in a manner that appears, from the perspective of the international community, fair and equitable under the circumstances of each case. Although the exact content and scope of this standard have not been authoritatively determined and is often decided on a case-by-case basis,[159] the standard is often interpreted as an "absolute standard" or "minimum standard," the violation of which may include any "arbitrary, grossly unfair, unjust or idiosyncratic, discriminatory" conduct or conduct that "exposes the claimant to sectional or racial prejudice, or involves a lack of due process leading to an outcome which offends judicial propriety."[160] Nevertheless, the level of fairness and equity is not supposed to be a baseline for foreign investment protections as the application of the standard also involves the claimant's reasonable reliance on the representations made by the host state.[161] Hence, the standard should be at a level generally acceptable to the international commercial community. In other words, a purely local concept of fairness and equity under domestic law may be likely to be rejected by the international commercial community.[162] Due to its less specific content and vague scope, this treatment has emerged as a "catch-all" ground of investment treaty claims and has often become associated with the concept of legitimate expectations.

The prevailing interpretation of the required standard of fair and equitable treatment is relatively stringent on the host country given its wide coverage. It has been interpreted to protect foreign investors against unjustified or unpredictable adverse changes in regulatory rules,[163] non-transparent or inconsistent decision-making in administrative procedures, the government's failure to negotiate in good faith, or gross deficiencies in the host country's judicial system.[164] These misconducts may violate the standard even if it is not motivated by a specific discriminatory or any other malevolent intent. From a conceptual perspective, the standard is overarching for all legislative, administrative, and judicial branches of the host state. Thus, the possibility of invoking protections under fair and equitable treatment will be more substantial, not only for the protection of foreign investors in their economic and commercial activities but also for shaping the host state's rule of law.

In the Chinese law context, to invoke the fair and equitable treatment standard in investor–state arbitration is likely to touch upon systematic deficiencies in law enforcement by the administrative agencies and courts which enjoy wide discretion and arbitrariness.[165] Although China is making progress in improving its legal institutions and governance quality, progress appears slower than often anticipated, especially given China's accession to the WTO. According to the World Bank's Worldwide Governance Indicators (WGI) (as indicated in Figure 7.3), China's governance rankings (including political stability and absence of violence) are all lower in 2020 than in 1996 except the indicator of voice and accountability.[166]

Most Chinese BITs include a fair and equitable treatment provision, accompanied by a "full protection and security" clause.[167] The standard often appears in the section of "treatment of investment" which creates a concrete legal obligation on the contracting parties. However, these Chinese BITs do not make an express reference to a particular body of law or other standards. As such, the treatment may be assessed against other provisions in the BIT, and then against general international law and domestic law of the host state. In a number of Chinese BITs, references are made to such criteria as domestic law,[168] the present BIT,[169] international treaties to which both parties are contracting parties,[170] generally recognized principles of international law accepted by both parties, and universally accepted principles of international law.[171] More recent Chinese BITs tend to abolish the qualifications of domestic law[172] and accept international law as a qualification. These qualifications generally are still vague in determining

Indicator	Country	Year	Percentile Rank (0 to 100)
Voice and Accountability	China	1996	
		2020	
Political Stability and Absence of Violence/Ter..	China	1996	
		2020	
Government Effectiveness	China	1996	
		2020	
Regulatory Quality	China	1996	
		2020	
Rule of Law	China	1996	
		2020	
Control of Corruption	China	1996	
		2020	

FIGURE 7.3 Comparison of China's Governance Quality Between 1996 and 2020[173]

and applying "fair and equitable treatment." The Treaty makes an attempt to define and substantiate the standard by providing the following in Article 7(1):

> For greater certainty:
>
> (a) fair and equitable treatment refers to the obligation of each Party not to deny justice in any legal or administrative proceedings;[174]

This is a seemingly new and distinct variation to the existing practice but is of great help in reducing the scope of "fair and equitable treatment," which has been conventionally regarded as a broad concept covering the requirement of stability, predictability, and consistency of the legal framework, the principle of legality, the protection of investor confidence, or legitimate expectations, apart from the rule of law components such as procedural due process and denial of justice, substantive due process or protection against discrimination and arbitrariness, the requirement of transparency, and the requirement of reasonableness and proportionality.[175] The thrust of this Article suggests that the "fair and equitable treatment" merely refers to access to justice in legal or administrative proceedings and arguably extends to procedural due process if it is interpreted in a wider sense. It is hard to explain why this provision is crafted to define "fair and equitable treatment" more narrowly. The only sensible reason may be that the contracting parties to the Treaty are not able to unanimously accept other qualifications, such as references to the principles of international law, but are able to reach consensus by following the general investment treaty jurisprudence. The New Zealand–China FTA takes a similar approach by defining "fair and equitable treatment" as including "the obligation to ensure that, having regard to general principles of law, investors are not denied justice or treated unfairly or inequitably in any legal or administrative proceeding affecting the investments of the investor."[176] The United States–Uruguay BIT defines treatment, based on customary international law, to include the obligation not to deny justice in criminal, civil, or administrative adjudicatory proceedings in accordance with the principle of due process.[177] Compared to the New Zealand–China FTA and the US–Uruguay BIT, the Treaty's definition of "fair and equitable treatment" is much narrower and exclusively refers to procedural justice. In any event, the Treaty's approach reduces the "catch-all" nature of fair and equitable treatment by providing that "a breach of another provision in the [Treaty], or of a separate international agreement" does not "establish that there has been a breach of [fair and equitable treatment and full protection and security provision]."[178]

The Treaty's method of bringing the prohibition against "denial of justice" within the ambit of "fair and equitable treatment" may be treated as a new attempt to clarify the scope of the term by setting a "floor." This approach approximates the fair and equitable standard to the international minimum standard, which has the merit of relative clarity as there is a substantial body of jurisprudence concerning the elements of the international minimum standard, including due process and access to justice in administrative or legal proceedings.[179] The advantages of this provision are two-fold. First, it prevents the possibility of an interpretation of "fair and equitable treatment" to allow a standard that is lower than the "access to justice in legal or administrative proceedings." Second, it closes the door to an expansive interpretation of the standard covering obligations beyond "access to justice in legal or administrative proceedings." In applying this test, the right to access to justice in any legal or administrative proceedings should be sufficient to meet the investor's "legitimate expectations," which is generally regarded as the central or "dominant" element in "fair and equitable treatment."[180] In some arbitration cases, the tribunals have attempted to limit the application of "fair and equitable treatment" to a "reasonable and legitimate" level.[181] The Treaty's language seems in line with this arbitration practice.

The "no denial of justice" doctrine does not refer to any established body of international law or legal principles. This omission, however, may constitute an advantage as it will clearly avoid any potential confusion. The application of principles of international law or domestic law, on the contrary, still relies upon the tribunal in judging what is "fair and equitable." The case law has indicated that an express reference to any body of law is of little help and may well require the tribunal to resort to other elements in the case law or sources of law. *Middle East Cement v. Egypt* is a good example, in which the tribunal ruled that the "fair and equitable treatment" provision "must be given particular relevance in view of the special protection granted by Article 4 against measures 'tantamount to expropriation', and in the requirement for 'due process of law' in Article 4.a."[182] In the absence of any reference to a body of law or principles in the BIT, the tribunal is able to apply international law in arbitration cases. As *Siemens v. Argentina* demonstrated, the tribunal was still "bound to find the meaning of these terms under international law" even if the governing BIT did not refer to "international law."[183]

Regarding other elements or sources, some Chinese BITs try to establish a linkage between the BIT and other international agreements. The United Arab Emirates–China BIT makes reference not only to the present treaty but also other treaties to which both contracting parties are members, providing in relevant part that:

> Once the investment is established, it shall at all times enjoy the full protection and security that is in conformity with relevant international agreements to which both Contracting Parties are members.

This provision will create the effect of extending the reference from the current BIT to all other relevant treaties, such as regional or multilateral investment agreements to which both parties are members. The Treaty takes a clear-cut approach against this by providing that "a breach of another provision of this Agreement, or of a separate international agreement does not establish that there has been a breach of this 'fair and equitable treatment.'"[184]

There are 149 (96%) IIAs with FET clauses, leaving 6 (4%) IIAs without FET clauses, which instead merely emphasize fair and reciprocal treatment to investors. The China–Australia FTA (2015) may be a special case as its investment chapter does not have FET clauses[185] but leaves minimum treatment (possibly including the FET)[186] for future negotiation and only mentions NT and MFN treatment clauses in its main body and does not include the FET clause. In terms of timeline, except for the China–Slovak BIT Additional Protocol (2005), which retained the relevant provisions in the BIT 1991, other BITs were signed in the late 1980s and early 1990s,[187] showing a trend of offering better protection to foreign investors.

The FET provisions often make the compliance with the host state's law or public order a condition to exceptional measures. These FET clauses are more conservative than others. For example the China–Belgian and Luxembourg BIT 1984 states that "Protection and equitable treatment shall be accorded as regards management, operation, use or liquidation of the above said investment unless necessary measures should be taken for the maintenance of public order and in defense of the State law."[188] This is a typical qualified FET standard, opposite to an unqualified one which usually makes a reference to the minimum standard of treatment of aliens under customary international law,[189] and which is said to be minimalist, autonomous and self-standing.[190]

Of the 149 IIAs with FET provisions, 34 (23%) of them provide for exceptions (qualified FET standard) while 115 (77%) IIAs make no exceptions to the FET provisions (unqualified FET standard), showing China's willingness not to place considerable constrain in the state's sovereignty while granting FET to foreign investors.

Implementing national treatment in an all-round manner as stated in the FIL removes the previous preferential treatments for foreign investments and thus raises the concern on the compatibility of the change with the fair and equitable treatment (FET) that is widely stipulated in China's investment treaties. Although the specific definition of the treatment is controversial due to its broad wording,[191] various tribunals have held that one of the key elements is the protection of legitimate expectations,[192] created by the conduct of the host state and relied upon by foreign investor to make investing decisions.[193] Accordingly, the change of legal framework may violate investors' legitimate expectation of a stable and predictable legal framework[194] – especially if their legal rights acquired under the previous laws are significantly affected – and thus breach the FET obligation.[195] Such a scenario can trigger investment claims, undermining the reform's attempt to entice foreign investments.

2.5 Full Protection and Security Standard

The full protection and security standard is often combined with the "fair and equitable treatment" standard in BITs[196] and appears in virtually all Chinese BITs.[197] As a result, the standard is sometimes treated as part of "fair and equitable treatment." The doctrine underscores "fair and equitable treatment" by obliging the host country to commit to protect the investment against civil unrest, public disturbance, threats, and attacks targeting it by reason of its foreign nature.[198] In essence, the standard is a "police protection" obligation on the part of the host state to make good faith efforts to protect the foreign-invested properties.[199] The case law in this respect is more expansive in requiring the host country not only to provide physical protection (saving the foreign-owned commercial property from being destroyed by the host state's armed forces),[200] but also to ensure "the stability afforded by a secure investment environment."[201]

The Treaty tries to substantiate the standard by providing the following:

> For greater certainty:
>
> (b) full protection and security requires each Party to take such measures as may be reasonably necessary to ensure the protection and security of the investment of investors of another Party.[202]

The thrust of this provision is to suggest that the police protection or taking reasonably necessary measures would satisfy the "full protection and security" standard under the Treaty. In this sense, the approach has the merit of relative clarity and has made some improvements to the old-generation Chinese BITs, some of which only required the host state to "at all times" provide "adequate protection and security" to foreign investors in its territory.[203] Arguably, this approach is in line with case law which clarifies that the "protection and full security" obligation is not only applicable to "physical interferences" but also to "any act or measure which deprives an investor's investment of protection and full security."[204] The uncertainty in this provision is that the Treaty does not clarify the level or magnitude of police protection required under customary international law.

2.6 Expropriation

The origin of expropriation can be traced back to the international law standards for the protection of aliens. In modern international investment protection law, expropriation is permitted only if it is carried out on a non-discriminatory basis, for a public purpose, in compliance with due process and the principle of payment of compensation. BITs regulate the exercise of the state's power to expropriate investments. As discussed later, the elaboration of these key elements may provide useful clarification and guidance to tribunals, but they add little to international expropriation law. In fact, the chance of an investor succeeding in a claim against a state for expropriation is somewhat slim, in particular in cases where the disputed expropriation is a regulatory one. Tribunals have always found it difficult to conclude either that the state's action amounts to an actual taking, or that there is evidence of the cumulative effect of the state's acts reaching the threshold of expropriation. In some cases, tribunals may look into a technical side of the dispute, for example whether there is "a sufficient causal link between an actual breach of the BIT and the loss sustained," to determine the grant of compensation.[205]

Expropriation is a critically important BIT issue considering China's history of nationalizing foreign investment soon after the founding of the PRC[206] and China's "new state order" and "creeping renationalisation" to "attack private enterprises" by grabbing state land from privately owned coal mines.[207] In line with general BIT practice,[208] most Chinese BITs contain a generic expropriation clause covering "nationalisation," "expropriation," and any other "similar measures," without providing any detailed definitions of these terms. The Treaty basically adopts the following structure in outlining the expropriation term:

> A Party shall not expropriate, nationalise or take other similar measures ("expropriation") against investments of investors of another Party.[209]

Like other Chinese BITs, the Treaty covers "investments of investors," which is broad enough to cover both tangible and intangible assets. It is likely that this provision can be to a great extent applied to the contract rights in concession agreements[210] and other non-discriminatory regulatory actions taken by the state government. While this provision is able to provide a full-scale protection for the investors, the disadvantage is also obvious in that the catch-all expropriation clause effectively prohibits all measures that have an effect equivalent to expropriation and do not include special exemptions for the right of states to regulate.

2.6.1 "Indirect Expropriation"

Under investment treaty jurisprudence, it is almost settled that (subject always to the precise words of the BIT) expropriation extends to both direct and indirect measures as well as to "creeping expropriation."[211] Some Chinese BITs such as the Germany–China BIT touch upon "indirect expropriation" by stipulating that:

> investments by investors of either Contracting Party shall not directly or indirectly be expropriated, nationalised or subjected to any other measure the effects of which would be tantamount to expropriation or nationalisation in the territory of the other Contracting Party.[212]

The Mexico–China BIT expressly refers to expropriation being made directly or "indirectly through measures tantamount to expropriation or nationalisation."[213] The Mauritius–China BIT provides that the parties shall not "take any measures depriving, directly or indirectly, nationals and/or companies . . . of their investments."[214] A large number of Chinese BITs have other variations to similar effect. Examples are the Czech Republic–China BIT, Denmark–China BIT, Indonesia–China BIT, and Iceland–China BIT, which include the phrase "having an effect equivalent to";[215] the Greece–China BIT, which includes the caveat "tantamount to";[216] and the France–China BIT, which uses the phrase "same effect." Based on the extensive jurisprudence, any of these formulations may be held by the tribunals to have the effect of bringing indirect expropriations into the ambit of a treaty,[217] when the state's actions or measures effectively "neutralise the benefit of the property of the foreign owner."[218] The most sophisticated definition of "indirect expropriation," drawing on recent BIT case law, appears in the New Zealand–China FTA, under which it is confined to measures which are (i) equivalent to direct expropriation, in that "[they] deprive . . . the investor in substance of the use of the investor's property"; (ii) either severe or indefinite; and (iii) disproportionate to the public purpose.[219]

In comparison with other Chinese BITs, the Treaty is silent on "indirect expropriation." This silence adds to the uncertainty that an investor may face when it considers whether to bring a claim in investor–state arbitration. The phrase "other similar measures" in the Treaty may be interpreted by the tribunal to cover "indirect expropriation" simply because the term "expropriation" alone can be interpreted to cover both direct and indirect expropriation, or where a tribunal wishes to apply a more expansive approach to interpreting the Treaty's wording. Due to the lack of guidance in the Treaty in applying the treaty standard to specific circumstances, the application of international law to relevant disputes seems to be an option. Investment arbitration jurisprudence has already indicated that tribunals usually "look to international law in determining the relevant criteria for evaluating the claim of expropriation,"[220] and expressed the general view that "no distinctions have been attempted between the general concept of dispossession and the specific forms thereof."[221]

2.6.2 Preconditions to Lawful Expropriation

Expropriation is not unlawful under international law as long as certain conditions are complied with by the state. This is a highly formalistic area of law. Under customary international law,[222] the well-recognized conditions include four elements, namely the expropriation must be in the public interest, under domestic legal procedure, non-discriminatory, and provide compensation. These four elements consistently appear in almost all Chinese BITs[223] (with the exception of a few BITs such as the United Kingdom–China BIT[224] and the Italy–China BIT).[225] The Treaty, in a fairly traditional fashion, reproduces the Chinese treaty practice by imitating these four elements. Accordingly, a signatory state is able to expropriate, nationalize, or take other similar measures against investments of investors of another Party, so long as the following conditions are met:

(a)   for a public purpose;
(b)   in accordance with applicable domestic laws, including legal procedures;
(c)   carried out in a non-discriminatory manner; and
(d)   on payment of compensation.[226]

A "public purpose" is relevant to expropriation as it can be authorized by the government for diverse reasons. However, the term "for a public purpose" has not been defined, nor has it been explained in the form of illustrative grounds. Thus, the application of this criterion in the expropriation analysis leaves the tribunal with some discretion. Variations on the term "for a public purpose" include "for the public interest," adopted by a large number of Chinese BITs such as the Cyprus–China BIT, Cambodia–China BIT, Myanmar–China BIT, and Benin–China BIT, and "for public benefits," which appears in the Germany–China BIT. These terminologies do not indicate substantial differences. The formula of "public purpose, security or national interests" adopted by the Belgium–Luxembourg–China BIT, "for a public purpose related to the internal needs of the expropriating Contracting Party" adopted in the Indonesia–China BIT, or "as necessitated by the public interest" adopted in the Laos–China BIT makes this criterion more effective by placing the host state in a more advantageous position, as such an operative criterion is easier to satisfy even though it may seem to be somehow harsher. Other variations, such as "the need of social and public interest" and "national security and public interest" (appearing in the Argentina–China BIT[227] and the Philippines–China BIT[228] respectively) are less effective due to their wide or vague coverage. But these varied terms indicate the scope and nature of the "for a public purpose" criterion and would entail consideration of detailed facts in the specific case.

Some Chinese BITs[229] contain an exemption for the reasonable exercise of a state's "police powers," which is intended to offer a safe harbour for regulation that is reasonably justified in the public interest. Given the lack of a "police powers" exemption in the Treaty, the "for a public purpose" condition may function as a safe harbour for expropriation regulations. A "public purpose" may serve a local protectionist purpose and may be difficult to discern from an international perspective. The tribunal must weigh such elements as bad faith, arbitrariness, or discrimination heavily in determining whether a "public" but more domestic "purpose" is acceptable or not.

Some BITs prescribe that the expropriation must be effected according to notions of due process. Different from the Western terminology, a large number of Chinese BITs use the term "under domestic legal procedure"[230] instead of "in accordance with due process." In a few Chinese BITs, the phrase "due process" is used but with some Chinese characteristics. For instance the expropriation may need to be carried out in accordance with the "due process of national laws"[231] or "due process of law."[232] However, the meaning of "due process of national laws" or "due process of law" has never been clarified in these BITs. The distinction between these two similar terms seems clear: "due process of law" is closer to "due process" whereas "due process of national laws" leans more towards "national laws." The investor will be better off if "due process of law" is adopted as the investor may rely upon customary international law for protection, whilst "due process of national laws" may give the investor less leeway. Therefore, it is easy to understand why some Chinese BITs used the term "in accordance with its laws"[233] or "relevant domestic laws"[234] instead. The reference to the "domestic law" or "national laws" provides the state with more flexibility and control over the legal process, as the expropriation process will be subject to the domestic laws of the expropriating state. In any event, this criterion should be relatively easy to satisfy by the expropriating state where domestic review of the expropriatory act, a fair hearing and impartial tribunals are available.[235]

Under some Chinese BITs, the norm "due process of national laws" or "in accordance with its laws" is more effective as the investor is granted the right to a judicial review of a completed expropriation and of the amount of compensation due. The United Kingdom–China BIT, for example provides that

> the national or company affected have a right, under the law of the Contracting Party making the expropriation, to prompt review, by a judicial or other independent authority of that Party, of his or its case and of the valuation of his or its investment in accordance with the principles set out in this paragraph.[236]

Similar rights are granted under other Chinese BITs, such as the Germany–China BIT, according to which the investor may request "the legality of any such expropriation and the amount of compensation shall be subject to review by national courts."[237] Unfortunately, the Treaty did not follow this route by providing the investors with a right to a review. As a result, the investor may have to rely upon investor–state arbitration for making a claim against expropriation.

The non-discriminatory requirement appears in many Chinese BITs and is only absent from a small number of BITs between China and Austria, Germany, Indonesia, Italy, Oman, and the United Kingdom. This requirement adds more value to the investor protection if the BIT does not offer national treatment protection to investors or the expropriatory act is not conducted in due process. In practice, discrimination complaints are more likely to be raised with regard to due process and payment of compensation. However, the discriminatory factor is "extremely difficult to prove in concrete cases."[238] Thus, the blanket exception for non-discriminatory measures may create a "gaping loophole in international protections against expropriation."[239]

Payment of compensation is an essential condition to validate expropriation. It is difficult to reach consensus on an acceptable standard of compensation for lawful expropriation. The North–South divide on this is clear: whilst the developed countries insist on the full compensation according to the so-called Hull Formula, that is, "prompt, adequate, and effective compensation,"[240] the developing countries prefer either "appropriate" compensation or no compensation at all.[241] Investment treaty jurisprudence in this area has shown an increasing level of convergence that the compensation needs to be equivalent to the "market value"[242] or the "fair market value."[243] On a few occasions, variations such as "real value"[244] and "genuine value"[245] are used instead. These formulae refer to the price voluntarily reached by the seller and buyer in an arm's-length transaction. As such, modern BIT jurisprudence appears to support full or "adequate" compensation.[246]

Under old-generation Chinese BITs, the standard of compensation is usually not clarified. The Chinese stance was clear: the Hull Formula was not acceptable as it was the standard demanded by developed countries. Rather, Chinese BITs preferred to endorse "reasonable," "fair," "appropriate,"[247] or "effective"[248] compensation. The new-generation Chinese BITs make an attempt to address the compensation issue in clearer terms. A number of Chinese BITs link compensation to the "value of the expropriated investment."[249] Some BITs clarify the "value" by reference to "genuine,"[250] "actual,"[251] "market,"[252] or "fair market"[253] value. The reliance upon the "value of the expropriated investment" demonstrates the host state's willingness to provide the investors with "just compensation." At the technical level, the tribunal is more capable of achieving a "just compensation" as the "value" formulation reflects the genuine value of the property affected.[254] Chinese BITs usually fix the valuation date as "immediately prior to the time when the expropriation became public,"[255] "immediately before the expropriation measures were taken,"[256] or "prior to the moment in which the decision to expropriate is announced or made public."[257] This helps guarantee that the "value of the expropriated investment" will not depreciate once expropriation is known to the public.

The Treaty is in line with the general "value" formula and stipulates that "such compensation shall amount to the fair market value of the expropriated investment at the time when expropriation was publicly announced or when expropriation occurred, whichever is earlier."[258] However, the Treaty's "value" formula is less operative in a practical sense. In this respect, some Chinese BITs took a lead by incorporating some practical valuation methods or introducing some valuation-related terms. For instance under the Zimbabwe–China BIT, the calculation is to be made taking "as may be appropriate, the net asset value as certified by an independent firm of auditors as well as the market value."[259] The valuation under the Guyana–China BIT is to be determined as "if the investments were to be sold as an ongoing concern on the open market."[260] To adopt more operative valuation methods and principles is the approach recommended by the World Bank, incorporated by the NAFTA, and endorsed by some tribunals to increase the transparency of the valuation method.[261] Another concern about the Treaty's compensation formula is that it is still not clear whether this wording actually refers to the full market value. In sum, the Treaty makes little substantial progress in clarifying the issue of how to evaluate the expropriated investment. Certainly, it may be arguable that the Treaty's approach gets closer to the Hull formula since the wording has absorbed some market-oriented factors.

The cut-off point for valuation purposes is clearer, as the caveat of "whichever is earlier" allows the choice of an earlier time between the occurrence of expropriation and the announcement of expropriation. The purpose of having such a caveat, as the Treaty provides, is that "the fair market value shall not reflect any change in market value occurring because the expropriation had become publicly known earlier."[262]

The appropriate date is also important in calculating interest, which is an integral part of the total compensation awarded by the tribunal for expropriation. The old-generation Chinese BITs usually do not provide for interest to be payable on compensation,[263] which is consistent with the earlier investment treaty practice not being specific on the payment of interest.[264] Starting from the late 1990s, a provision for interest appears in Chinese BITs with a reference to the "normal,"[265] "commercial,"[266] "appropriate,"[267] "fair and just,"[268] "usual bank,"[269] or "LIBOR"[270] rate of interest. The interest provision in the Treaty reads as follows:

> The compensation shall be settled and paid without unreasonable delay. In the event of delay, the compensation shall include interest at the prevailing commercial interest rate from the date of expropriation until the date of payment.[271]

The first sentence in the cited paragraph is not that meaningful as the term "delay" is not well defined even though "unreasonable delay" (or "undue delay") appeared in a number of Chinese BITs such as the Philippines–China BIT and Indonesia–China BIT. On its face, the sentence immediately following seems to suggest that it constitutes a delay when compensation is not made at the date of expropriation. This interpretation, however, does not seem sensible as the investor and state may be in dispute on the existence of expropriation. The Iceland–China BIT prescribes the exact meaning of a delay in payment by providing that "the delay begins with the submission of a relevant application and must not exceed six months."[272]

The term "prevailing commercial rate" also appears in other Chinese BITs, such as the Germany–China BIT and the Netherlands–China BIT. The reference to the "prevailing commercial" rate of interest is practically specific so as to avoid the situation that the interest rate may be determined by the tribunal in an over-subjective manner. The Treaty follows this general practice by specifying that the interest is payable between the "date of expropriation" and "date of payment." This may result in a fairer scenario whereby the arbitral tribunal awards interest from the date of the arbitral award, which may be earlier than the date of payment.

To make compensation more effective, compensation should be made in a form usable by the investor. Therefore, the currency of payment must be freely usable or convertible into a freely usable currency.[273] In this respect, the Treaty states that "the compensation, including any accrued interest, shall be payable either in the currency in which the investment was originally made or, if requested by the investor, in a freely usable currency." Although the "currency in which the investment was originally made" may not be satisfactory to the investor where that currency is not freely convertible, the Treaty leaves leeway to the investor who is entitled to choose a freely usable currency, which is defined by the Treaty as meaning "any currency designated as such by the IMF under its Articles of Agreement and any amendments thereto."[274] Technically, "freely usable currency" is limited to the US dollar, the euro, the pound sterling, and the Japanese yen, according to the IMF's definition.[275] As such, the Treaty makes compensation effective. Nevertheless, it has to be pointed out that this clause in the Treaty is not the most satisfactory arrangement to the investor. Some Chinese BITs confirm that "compensation will be convertible and realisable and freely transferable without delay,"[276] or "effectively reliable and freely transferable,"[277] which effectively gives the investors more protection from the risk of currency depreciation.

Unlike some other Chinese BITs, the Treaty fails to specify the way to determine the exchange rate between the local currency and the freely usable currency. Some Chinese BITs adopted several formulae, such as the "average of the daily exchange rates,"[278] the "official exchange rate" on the day of transfer,[279] and the "exchange rate applicable for the payment of the compensation . . . on the date used to determine the value of the investment,"[280] all of which are helpful in avoiding potential disputes in this regard.

The Treaty also contains the following provision:

> Where a Party expropriates the assets of a juridical person which is incorporated or constituted under its laws and regulations, and in which investors of another Party own shares, it shall apply the [expropriation] provisions . . . so as to ensure that compensation is paid to such investors to the extent of their interest in the assets expropriated.

This provision addresses the compensation issue in expropriation and makes compensation rules applicable to a foreign investor holding shares in a local company whose assets are expropriated. This reflects the more recent investment treaty practice whereby compensation is "paid to the investors in respect of the investments of the Contracting Party who are owners of those shares."[281] However, to grant compensation to the investor in expropriation triggers some criticisms as "it denies the defendant the option to defend itself against an indirect claim by referring to the different legal personality of the company and the claiming shareholder."[282] The underlying concern is that this may cast doubt on the "no double recovery" rule in international law as the investor, as the ultimate shareholder may be doubly compensated where expropriation of certain assets at the company level does not prejudice the value of shares owned by the investor.[283]

2.6.3 Compulsory Licence: The Case of Indirect Expropriation

IPRs have long been recognized as a form of "investment" entitled to protection under BITs. The Treaty, like most Chinese BITs, in the definition of "investment" provides a detailed list of the types of intellectual property that may be considered as a form of investment asset, for example "copyrights, patents and utility models, industrial designs, trademarks and service marks, geographical indications, layout designs of integrated circuits, trade names, trade secrets, technical processes, know-how and goodwill."[284] The inclusion of IPRs in the definition of 'investment' reflects the extent to which the issue of intellectual property has been the subject of recent attention in the investment protection field.

In authorizing a compulsory licence, the government authority, in response to a perceived need, may interfere directly with an IPR privately owned by the foreign investor by compelling the owner, on an *ex post* basis, to grant use of an IPR to the state or to other third parties in exchange for licencee payments.[285] Such a compulsory licence, a case of indirect expropriation, may cause a direct impact on FDI involving IPRs, by constituting a potential threat to the security of private property and to commercial innovation,[286] and trigger an alleged violation of the terms of the BIT.[287] Despite the standard inclusion of IPRs in the definition of "investment" and the increasing importance of IPRs in a more technologically oriented globalized economy, there have been surprisingly few publicly reported cases concerning IPR-centred investment disputes.[288]

Under international law, some form of compulsory licensing has been recognized. The Paris Convention, for example recognizes compulsory licensing as a means to address the abusive exercise of patent rights on "failure to work" grounds, thereby justifying issuance in limited cases.[289] Within the WTO framework, the Agreement on Trade-Related Aspects of Intellectual Property Rights ("TRIPS Agreement") also addresses compulsory licences, under the heading of "use without authorisation of the right holder," with an array of conditions. Article 31 of the TRIPS Agreement, together with Articles 7, 8, 40, and 42, permits the grant of a compulsory licence by WTO member states, so long as an overriding public interest is served,[290] certain procedures are followed and terms fulfilled.[291] The Doha Declaration on the TRIPS Agreement and Public Health, adopted by the WTO in 2001, confirms that member states have the right to grant compulsory licences to protect public health.[292] In any event, issuing a compulsory licence may involve contentious, fact-specific, and case-by-case decisions,[293] placing the IPR owner at odds with the host state authorizing the compulsory licence. The foreign investor may consider claiming its rights under the international standards either under the WTO system or through investment arbitration.

By definition, a compulsory licence does not deprive the IPR owner of ownership over the protected IPR. Thus, the government's authorization of a compulsory licence does not fall within the scope of direct expropriation. Despite the lack of a "mechanical formula" in determining whether a compulsory licence amounts to an indirect expropriation, the fact that the compulsory licence has a potential impact upon an investor's rights in its investment may allow it to be viewed as a form of government interference in the wider context of indirect or regulatory expropriation.

The case law jurisprudence in this respect is relatively restrictive. The "sole effect doctrine" adopted by the tribunal for the case of *Starrett Housing Corp.* set a high threshold under which a compulsory licence constitutes an indirect expropriation if "measures . . . can interfere with property rights to such an extent that these rights are rendered so useless that they must be deemed to have been expropriated."[294]

The Treaty contains a more important provision that directly addresses compulsory licences but complicates the matter in Article 8(6):

> The [expropriation clause] shall not apply to the issuance of compulsory licences granted to intellectual property rights in accordance with the TRIPS in Annex 1C to the WTO Agreement.[295]

The Treaty's provision brings the WTO disciplines directly into play in the investment dispute context. To the extent that a compulsory licence is TRIPS Agreement compliant, the expropriation provision will not apply at all. This "cross-reference" approach bears some significance. First, it manifests the linkage between compulsory licence and investment arbitration. Second, it ties the question of validity of a host state's issuance of the licence to compliance with the TRIPS Agreement. Third, the wording is clear enough that the tribunal should "apply" the TRIPS Agreement rather than simply rely on it for "interpreting" the regulatory treatment standard in this respect. In other words, the WTO Agreement here does not just provide an interpretive context or suggestive guidance to a certain point on the detailed aspects of a compulsory licence that can be considered. Rather, Article 8(6) requires an investor–state arbitration tribunal to give a decision on the basis of WTO substantive rules. Yet this does not end the argument. Article 8(6) only excludes TRIPS-compliant compulsory licences, which may imply that TRIPS-incompatible compulsory licences may still be subject to expropriation rules. Meanwhile, even compliance with the TRIPS Agreement does not necessarily yield immunity. In this respect, the Treaty is of little help in guiding the future tribunals in issuing a sensible award. In any event, the possible reference to the TRIPS Agreement shows the complex interplay between two different treaty-based regimes providing different levels of protection and different types of remedies.

Article 8(6) of the Treaty closely follows (if not has identical wording to) the similar clause in the United States–Uruguay BIT which reads:

> This Article does not apply to the issuance of compulsory licences granted in relation to intellectual property rights in accordance with the TRIPS Agreement, or to the revocation, limitation, or creation of intellectual property rights, to the extent that such issuance, revocation, limitation, or creation is consistent with the TRIPS Agreement.[296]

The United States–Uruguay BIT language not only provides some leeway for governments in their regulation with respect to the compulsory licence, but also makes an attempt to define the scope of "compulsory licence," Nevertheless, as discussed, it does not explain how to deal with the TRIPS-incompatible compulsory licences under the BIT framework. Again, the Treaty, like the United States–Uruguay BIT, has the effect of importing WTO rules, as applicable law, into the context of the investment dispute regarding a compulsory licence.

Expropriation is a government action that takes privately owned property against the wishes of the owners.[297] International law does not prohibit expropriation.[298] On the contrary, the government's right to take private property, as a matter of both international norm and domestic principle, is regarded to be conceded.[299] Exercise of such right is subject to certain limitations. From the international law perspective, expropriation is limited (i) for public purpose; (ii) on a non-discriminatory basis, (iii) under due process; and (d) with compensation.[300]

Due to its commitment to the protection of foreign investment, China has put in place a rule against expropriation. When the 1979 EJV Law was amended, a non-expropriation provision was added into Article 2 of the EJV Law. China promised not to nationalize or expropriate Sino-foreign equity joint ventures but reserved the right to do so under extraordinary circumstances for social public interests according to legal procedures with appropriate compensation.[301] The non-expropriation rule under the amendment, however, was viewed as a simple "lip service" due to the vagueness of social public interests and inadequate compensation.

To protect the legitimate rights and interests of foreign investors, Chapter III of the FIL provides comprehensive and principled provisions.[302] Chapter III strengthens the protection of property rights of foreign-invested enterprises. Article 20 stipulates that the state does not expropriate foreign investment. Under extraordinary circumstances, the state may expropriate and requisition the investment of foreign investors in accordance with the law and for the needs of public interest. Such expropriation and requisition shall be conducted in accordance with legal procedures; timely and reasonable compensation shall be given.[303] Further, foreign investors' capital contribution, profits, capital gains, assets disposal income, intellectual property licence fees, legally obtained damages or compensation, liquidation proceeds, may be freely remitted overseas in RMB or foreign exchange according to law.[304] The state protects the intellectual property rights of foreign investors and foreign-invested enterprises, protects the legitimate rights and interests of intellectual property rights holders and related rights holders, and holds intellectual property rights infringers legally accountable in accordance with the law.[305,306]

The FIL in providing relevant guarantees against expropriation of foreign investments enumerates protection of various other rights related to those investments like protection of intellectual property rights. In encouraging technological cooperation through foreign investment, the FIL emphasizes on voluntariness and specifically prohibits administrative organs and their employees from forcing technology transfer through administrative measures.[307] Moreover, the FIL mandates administrative organs and their employees to maintain confidentiality of the trade secrets related to foreign investments learnt in the course of performing their duties[308] The rules governing foreign investments formulated by administrative bodies are required to be in conformity with laws and regulations and should not derogate from the lawful rights and interests of foreign-invested enterprises without a legal basis[309,310]

The FIL includes specific provisions designed to address certain issues that foreign investors may previously have had regarding investment into China. In particular, the FIL provides specific protections such as no expropriation of foreign-owned assets other than in special circumstances free transfer of renminbi or foreign currency into and out of China, for returns of capital, profits, capital gains, royalty payments, and other lawfully obtained compensation requirements that the local governments honour contractual and other commitments lawfully made lawful protection of foreign investors' intellectual property rights in China.[311]

The FIL reaffirms the notion of non-expropriation and creates a general rule against expropriation of foreign investment. Article 20 of the FIL explicitly provides that the government does not expropriate foreign investors' investment.[312] In the meantime, under Article 20 of the FIL, under extraordinary circumstances, the state may expropriate or requisition the investment of foreign investors in accordance with the law and for the needs of the public interests.[313] Article 20 requires that the expropriation or requisition be conducted pursuant to legal procedures and a fair and reasonable compensation be made promptly.[314]

The Implementation Regulations seem to have modified Article 20 of the FIL. As provided in Article 21 of the Implementation Regulations, the state does not expropriate foreign investors' investment. Under extraordinary circumstances where the state expropriates the investment of foreign investors for public interests, the expropriation shall be made in accordance with the legal procedure and in a non-discriminatory manner, and compensation shall be made promptly on the basis of the market value of the investment expropriated.[315]

In contrast to Article 20 of the FIL, Article 21 of the Implementation Regulations (a) drops the word "requisition" and (b) uses the "market value" to implicate "fair and reasonable" in terms of compensation. In addition, under Article 21 of the Implementation Regulations, foreign investors who disagree with the expropriation decision may seek for administrative review or file an administrative lawsuit in accordance with the law.[316]

The rule against expropriation under the FIL and the Implementation Regulations has several important features. First, no expropriation shall be made in general. Second, as an exception, an expropriation may take place if (i) there exist extraordinary circumstances; (ii) the expropriation is authorized by the law; and (iii) the needs of the public interests arise. Third, the expropriation, once needed, must follow the legal procedure, must be made on a non-discriminative basis, and compensation must be made promptly according to the market value. Fourth, the legal procedure and compensation applied to the expropriation equally applies to requisition, if any.[317] It is important to note that the FIL and the Implementation Regulations change the compensation standard as provided in previous laws for expropriation. As noted in the EJV laws, the compensation was required only to be "appropriate." In the Property Law, with regard to an expropriation of private premises or other real property, the standard is simply "compensation."[318] The FIL and the Implementation Regulations for the first time demand a compensation for the expropriation to be "fair, reasonable," or "at market value," and "prompt."[319]

However, there are some issues that will arise in the application of Article 20 of the FIL. The first question is what circumstances could be characterized as "extraordinary" to justify an expropriation. During the review of the draft FIL, some legislators raised the same question with a concern that the undefined "extraordinary circumstances" would adversely affect protection of foreign investment as intended by the FIL.[320] But when the NPC passed the FIL, this question remained open, which gave the government leeway to deal with it on a case-by-case basis.

The second issue is how to determine the public interests in case of expropriation. Chinese scholars have long debated on this issue ever since the Property Law was drafted in the mid-2000s. Some suggested a specific approach to define the public interests in the law in order to avoid confusion and prevent abuse of it. Others, however, preferred a general approach to provide it broadly so that the different public needs in the constantly changing environment can be met.[321] Like the Property Law, the FIL follows the general approach and leaves the public interests undefined.[322]

The third issue concerns requisition. Although both expropriation and requisition involves "taking" of privately owned property by government, a requisition mainly refers to an exercise of sovereignty to secure or dispose of some property or services primarily from its subjects for the performance of government function.[323] In China, requisition is generally defined as the mandatory use of collectively and privately owned property by an exercise of government power.[324] The requisition is authorized in the FIL but not mentioned in the Implementation Regulations. It then becomes a question whether requisition is still an allowed device in terms of taking.

2.7 Capital Transfer and Repatriation

Capital transfer and repatriation provisions guarantee the free flow of funds, which is the most fundamental right which foreign investors want to secure under a BIT. In many instances, however, the capital absorbing states, like China and some ASEAN member states, enact foreign exchange control laws due to their need to retain foreign exchange to pay for essential goods and services.[325] Therefore, the capital transfer provisions in BITs often attempt to balance the conflicting interests between the investors and host states.[326] This is the main reason that old-generation Chinese BITs explicitly ensured China's right to implement its foreign exchange control measures.[327]

2.7.1 Free Transfer Provision

The host state's obligation to ensure the free transfer of funds into and out of the host state is a common feature in BITs, which usually set out a non-exhaustive list of the types of payment. The host state's obligation is materialized in a relatively standard manner: specified types of payment can be transferred without delay in the convertible currency of the original investment and at the rate of exchange fixed on the transfer date. The Treaty contains a detailed free transfer of payments provision with an illustrative list of the types of payments, which should be especially welcome, given China and some ASEAN member states' foreign exchange control. This list operates in the same way as the illustrative list used in the definition of "investment." The Treaty covers the flows of funds both "into and out of its territory,"[328] which signals a move away from the old-generation BITs which exclusively addressed outward transfers.[329] Free inward transfers are covered by the transfer provisions in more new-generation BITs, such as Chinese BITs with Finland, Mexico, and Turkey.[330]

The Treaty's free transfer provision includes a wide range of payments.[331] It is clear that the profits from the investment or proceeds generated on a sale of investments are payments relating to the "investment" and returns.[332] The Treaty also explicitly refers to "the initial capital" as well as "any additional capital" used to maintain or expand the investment.[333] This reference combines features in both the Mexico–China BIT, which clarifies that the free transfer of payments covers those payments relating to "establishing, maintaining or expanding the investment" and the Portugal–China BIT, under which both the initial capital and additional capital are freely transferable.[334] In addition, payments under loan agreements, royalties, and for technical assistance all relate to an investment as well.[335] Net earnings and other compensations of natural persons are also payments relating to the "investment."[336] While returns, loan payments, liquidation proceeds, or payments from licences and royalties are guaranteed free transfer, the transfer of salaries is a qualified right.[337] The usual qualification is that the natural person who is employed and permitted to work in connection with an investment in the territory is entitled to this right.[338] This qualification appears in other Chinese BITs, such as the Indonesia–China BIT[339] and Malaysia–China BIT.[340] Some Chinese BITs are intended to be wide enough to cover other income earned by the employees. For instance the Finland–China BIT covers "earnings and other remuneration," while the Cyprus–China BIT and the Norway–China BIT make a reference to "unspent earnings" or "legitimate incomes."[341] The Treaty is broader in scope, covering not only net earnings but also "other compensations," which is likely to be interpreted to cover bonus payments and other benefits earned by the employees. The list in the Treaty also makes reference to free transfers of compensation awarded under the expropriation provisions and compensation for damages and losses provisions.[342] The transfer provisions in Chinese BITs, including the Treaty, reflect the general treaty practice with little deviations.

To make the transfer obligations more meaningful to foreign investors, BITs impose other substantive criteria on the transfer. First, the transfer is carried out in a freely convertible currency. Most commonly, BITs use a "freely convertible currency"[343] or "freely usable currency," as the Treaty does.[344] Although these terms are rarely defined in BITs,[345] the general consensus is that any "hard" currency can be regarded as a "freely convertible currency."[346] Second, the exchange rate between the local currency and the "freely usable currency" must be made at an acceptable rate, namely an "official rate of exchange"[347] or "the prevailing market rate of exchange."[348] Chinese BITs use the "official"[349] or "market"[350] rate of exchange. References to "Special Drawing Rights"[351] and "an official exchange rate determined by the Central Bank of the Contracting State"[352] also appear in some Chinese BITs. In a few BITs, the "currency of the original investment" is also used.[353] Certainly, the "prevailing market rate of exchange [of the Contracting Party accepting the investment on the date of transfer]" is probably the most popular option.[354] The Treaty follows this formulation. Third, the transfer must be free[355] and carried out without delay. Some Chinese BITs set a cap on the time frame to clarify the term "without delay." For instance the time limits set out in the Protocols to the Portugal–China BIT, Brunei–China BIT and the Korea–China BIT are two, four, and six months respectively.[356] The France–China BIT does not impose a time limit. Rather, it interprets the term "without delay" to be "a period normally required for the completion of transfer formalities according to the international financial practice."[357] The Italy–China BIT not only defines the meaning of "without delay" but also sets a time limit. The Protocol defines "undue delay" as meaning "within such period as is normally required according to international financial practice and not later, than six months." The Treaty does not clarify its position on this particular matter.

2.7.2 Limitations on Free Transfer Obligations

It is not uncommon to see some limitations imposed on the freedom of transfer of funds, for example compliance with bankruptcy measures. These limitations often appear in the form of a list of exclusions to free transfer in BITs. Accordingly, the host state may take some currency control restrictions or other measures. Usual limitations include the fiscal,[358] financial,[359] "due,"[360] or tax obligation on an investor seeking to make a transfer. The Treaty includes specific exclusions in Article 10(3), which states:

> a Party may prevent or delay a transfer through the equitable, non-discriminatory and good faith application of its law and regulations relating to:
>
> (a) bankruptcy, loss of ability or capacity to make payments, or protection of the right of creditors;
> (b) non-fulfilment of the host Party's transfer requirements in respect of trading or dealing in securities, futures, options or derivatives;
> (c) non-fulfilment of tax obligations;
> (d) criminal or penal offences and the recovery of the proceeds of crime;
> (e) social security, public retirement or compulsory saving schemes;
> (f) compliance with judgements in judicial or administrative proceedings;
> (g) workers' retrenchment benefits in relation to labour compensation relating to, amongst others, foreign investment projects that are closed down; and
> (h) financial reporting or record keeping of transfers when necessary to assist law enforcement or financial regulatory authorities.

The Treaty's exclusion list is extensive, not only covering the investor's fiscal, tax, and financial obligations but also including other "social" obligations such as the recovery of the proceeds of crime, settlement of social security, and compliance with judgements. The advantage of having such an extensive list is to make the non-transfer provision more effective, increasing predictability for the investor in bringing a claim against the host state's non-transfer decision, action, or measure. China is still implementing an exchange control policy and the Chinese currency, renminbi, is not freely convertible. Some Chinese BITs confirm such practice. The Protocol to the Syria–China BIT, for example provides that particular types of payments, liquidation amounts, and royalties will be subject to the approval of the appropriate foreign exchange authority for China. In the process of slowly but systematically liberalizing its laws and regulations on capital transfers and foreign exchange control, China has also demonstrated its flexibility in BIT negotiations by lifting the "subject to its laws and regulations" limitation on transfers, which often appeared in old-generation Chinese BITs.[361]

The utility of the free transfer of payments provision is set off to some extent by the "domestic laws and regulations" exemption. Unlike the old-generation BITs under which the freedom of capital transfer is often subject to "domestic laws and regulations,"[362] the Treaty does not directly include this exemption. Instead, the Treaty attaches the "domestic laws and regulations" qualification to the host state's prevention or delay of capital transfer.[363] As a result, when the host state prevents or delays a transfer,

> the transfers . . . shall comply with relevant formalities stipulated by the host Party's domestic laws and regulations relating to exchange administration, insofar as such laws and regulations are not to be used as a means of avoiding a Party's obligations.[364]

The application of the host state's "laws and regulations" must satisfy the qualifications of "equitable, non-discriminatory and good faith."[365] This signals a substantial move towards transparency and the rule of law in restricting the transfer of funds by the investors.[366] These two provisions clarify how the local law requirement should be interpreted and operated in practice. The local law requirement must be satisfied by the investor in transferring funds but cannot be intentionally created and used to circumvent the host state's commitments under the Treaty. In other words, the local law requirement cannot be applied in such a way as to frustrate the guarantee of free transfers. Yet it is unclear to what extent this can be relied upon to assist investors in practice. The Treaty's "domestic law" approach is different from the "grandfather" approach adopted in the Germany–China BIT, which envisages an abandonment of existing foreign exchange restrictions.[367] Accordingly, the introduction of new foreign exchange control restrictions is not permissible. From the foreign investment protection perspective, the Treaty's provisions are less protective than those in the Germany–China BIT. In addition, the Germany–China BIT obliges China's foreign exchange authority to handle the request for capital transfers within two months,[368] which does not appear in the Treaty either.

It is worth noting that the Treaty explicitly confirms that the transfer provisions should be applied in accordance with the MFN requirements. This allows the investors to avail themselves of the best treatment with regard to transfers. Under some Chinese BITs, such as the Oman–China BIT, "without restricting the generality of the [MFN clause]" the parties agree to accord any transfer "treatment as favourable as that accorded to transfer originating from investments made by investors of any third state."[369] The Treaty's wording is largely the same, except in having an "in like circumstances" caveat which also appears in the MFN clause in the Treaty. Accordingly, "each Party undertakes to accord to the transfer . . . treatment as favourable as that accorded, in like circumstances, to the transfer originating from investments made by investors of any other Party or third country."[370]

Exceptions to the freedom of transfer are allowed in times of financial crisis. For example the host state is permitted to temporarily restrict transfers out of the state when there are "serious balance of payments difficulties and external financial difficulties or the threat thereof."[371] The Treaty, possibly taking into account the phenomenon of "Argentine Currency Crisis Claims" in BIT arbitrations,[372] includes this exception, allowing the host state to "impose restrictions on any capital transactions inconsistent with its specific commitments [under the Treaty]."[373] This leaves some discretion to the host state to determine when a financial crisis exists or when there is a threat of such financial difficulties. However, recourse to the financial crisis exception is subject to several restrictions set out in the Treaty. First, the financial crisis exception only applies "in exceptional circumstances."[374] This restriction suggests that the financial crisis exception may not be relied upon by the host state very often or too easily. In terms of what constitutes an "exceptional circumstance," the Treaty does not provide a definition or an exhaustive list of events. Nevertheless, the Treaty gives two examples: where "movements of capital cause, or threaten to cause, serious economic or financial disturbance in the Party concerned"[375] and in "the event of serious balance of payments and external financial difficulties or threat thereof."[376] These two examples may provide some guidance to future tribunals. Second, the financial difficulties must reach the threshold of severity. The Treaty uses the wording that "movements of capital cause, or threaten to cause, serious economic or financial disturbance in the Party concerned." This qualification can be satisfied only if the "movements of capital" are causing or will cause serious consequences. The function or practical use of this threshold, however, is not crystal clear given some recent cases such as *CMS Gas Transmission Co. v. Argentina*, *LG&E v. Argentina* and *Enron v. Argentina*, in which the defense of necessity has been heavily debated but confusingly interpreted. Third, restrictions

> do not affect the rights and obligations of the Parties as members of the WTO under Paragraph 1 of Article XI of GATS, and the measures are taken in accordance with paragraph 2 of Article 11 of this Agreement, *mutatis mutandis*.[377]

Under the Treaty, balance of payments exceptions are also allowed at the request of the IMF[378] or under the article on Measures to Safeguard the Balance of Payments.[379] Where the host state relies upon the article on Measures to Safeguard the Balance of Payments to restrict the free transfer of funds, prompt notification must be served on the other party,[380] and restrictions are limited to those which:

(a) are consistent with the Articles of Agreement of the IMF;

(b) do not discriminate among the Parties;

(c) avoid unnecessary damage to the commercial, economic and financial interests of any other Party;

(d) do not exceed those necessary to deal with the circumstances [of serious balance of payments and external financial difficulties or threat thereof];

(e) are temporary and will be phased out progressively as the situation [of serious balance of payments and external financial difficulties or threat thereof] improves; and

(f) are applied such that any other Party is treated no less favourably than any third country.[381]

It appears that, given the intrinsically temporary nature of financial crises, the temporary restrictions on transfer must be imposed on an "equitable, non-discriminatory, and in good faith basis." In addition, the restrictions should reach the necessity threshold to deal with severe financial times.[382] These criteria effectively require the host state to impose restrictions, if not to the least extent, proportionately to the aims sought to be achieved. The Treaty's balance of payments exceptions are onerous in a practical sense, effectively leaving little room to the contracting party to invoke this exception, with the aim of not sacrificing too easily protections afforded to foreign investors in transferring funds. As the Treaty stresses, the balance of payments exceptions should not "affect the rights and obligations of the Parties as members of the IMF under the Articles of Agreement of the IMF."[383]

FIL reaffirms foreign investors' rights to free remittance of foreign exchanges. Pursuant to Article 21 of the FIL, foreign investors' capital contributions, profits, capital gains, asset disposal proceeds, IP licence fees, liquidation proceeds, legally obtained damage award, and compensation within the territory of China can be freely remitted inward or outward.[384] Article 22 of the Implementation Regulations further provides that no entity or individual may illegally impose restrictions on the type of currency, amount, or frequency of remittances inbound or outbound.[385] These provisions are interpreted as allowing a free transfer of foreign exchange into and out of China.

However, China is a country where its currency is not freely convertible. The flow of foreign exchange is restricted under a system known as "closed" capital account, meaning that no money can be moved in or out of the country except in accordance with strict rules.[386] The foreign exchange control in the country is regulated under the Regulation on the Administration of Foreign Exchange (Foreign Exchange Regulation),[387] and managed primarily by the State Administration of Foreign Exchange (SAFE).

The FIL places an emphasis on the free transfer of monetary funds,[388] clarifying that foreign investors' capital contributions, profit, capital gains, income from asset disposals, royalties from IP rights, lawfully obtained compensation or indemnity amounts, and proceeds from liquidation may be freely remitted in or out of China in RMB or foreign currency.[389] Specifically, FIL stipulates that foreign investors may freely remit into or out of China their capital contributions, profits, capital gains, income from asset disposal, intellectual property royalties, lawfully acquired compensation, and indemnity or liquidation income in renminbi or any foreign currency within the territory of China. Under China's current legal system, this provision is subject to foreign exchange control regulations. However, against the backdrop of the national treatment of foreign investors and the principle of equal protection, various regulatory measures for foreign exchange control should not be an obstacle to the normal commercial arrangements of foreign investors in investment activities. In past cross-border transactions, foreign investors often found that certain internationally common deal arrangements (such as purchase price adjustments, earn-outs, and others) were difficult to implement in China. This is in a stark contrast to the flexible arrangements available for purely domestic transactions in China.[390]

The FIL is intended to provide more protection for foreign investment. With that effort, the focus of Article 21 of the FIL is apparently on the "free" remittance of foreign exchange in and out. The Implementation Regulations also disallow any restrictions on the currency, amount, and frequency of such remittances.[391] But the FIL is not intended to displace or replace the existing foreign exchange control measures. Given the complexity of the existing legal structure of foreign exchange controls and difficulties posed by the remittance requirements and procedures, it remains to be seen how Article 21 of the FIL is to be implemented to the effect of free remittance and how the practical obstacles facing foreign investors and FIEs with respect to foreign exchanges are to be removed.[392]

The transfer of funds offshore is still restricted, but it is important to note that the Chinese authorities have not blocked legitimate repatriation of dividend payments. In recent years, measures have been tightened at times, but this situation may be greatly improved after the effectiveness of the FIL. According to Article 21 of the FIL, foreign investors will be free to remit funds such as profits, capital gains, income from asset proposal, or intellectual property royalties outside China in accordance with PRC law. We do not expect that the foreign investors can be "totally free" to remit funds in or outside China. However, foreign investors will enjoy more convenience when they remit their profits outside China.[393]

It is worth noting that foreign investors still need to fulfil the obligations with tax authorities, banks, or administration of foreign exchange when remitting funds outside China. Though the procedural requirement of remittance is being simplified, it does not eliminate such responsibilities or tax uncertainty.[394]

3. Settlement of Investment Disputes and Investment Treaty Arbitration Under BITs

Investment treaties commit the Chinese government to protect foreign investors from discrimination and certain unfavourable regulatory measures and offer a great deal of comfort to foreign investors.[395] However, the old generation of BITs fails to offer comprehensive protection to foreign investors from discrimination in favour of domestic firms or other abusive government practices. A recent wave of treaty negotiations involving China provides cause for optimism by foreign investors who may take maximum advantage of them. For example the BIT between Germany and China (2003) improves considerably on the terms of China's earlier BITs. Under the new BIT, German investors are entitled to treatment on a par with Chinese firms and also have the right to private arbitration against the Chinese government in response to treaty violations.[396]

3.1 Dispute-Settlement Venues

The meaningful protection granted by a BIT to the investors is dependent on the autonomy and efficacy of investment arbitration, which is an effective enforcement mechanism in the BITs. Chinese BITs traditionally did not include an effective investor–state arbitration clause.[397] For instance the Singapore-China BIT 1985 only made a reference to *ad hoc* arbitration.[398] Under these old BITs, investment arbitration can be conducted only with a separate arbitration agreement made by the investor and Chinese government, which made the investor–state arbitration less infeasible.

This practice has been changed since 1998. Most new-generation BITs to which China is a party since then have moved away from a restricted right to arbitrate and provided for an unrestricted access to international arbitration.[399] This dramatic change in BIT policies and practices coincided with an increasing growth of outbound investment made by Chinese companies abroad, and most of such investment is made in oil or other energy-related projects in other developing countries. Not surprisingly, the first new-generation BIT adopting such new policy was made between China and Barbados in July 1998. Among the subsequent 21 new BITs (excluding the China–Qatar BIT 1999 and China–Bahrain BIT 1999, both of which still adopted the traditional restrictive approach), only three were signed between China and other developed countries, that is the Netherlands, Finland, and Germany, and the rest are all between China and other developing countries.[400] In these 21 new BITs, resort to the national court is no longer the only option and both Chinese and foreign investors have the right of direct recourse for an international wrong for which the host state is responsible. Although most new BITs have not come into force, the liberal move has triggered both applauses and criticisms among Chinese legal scholars. While some scholars welcomed this move as "the most significant measure in Chinese BIT practice in recent years,"[401] other more conservative commentators called for a serious reconsideration by the Chinese government arguing that as an emerging economy and an investment-absorption country, the liberal dispute settlement provisions in the new BITs will leave developing China worse off.[402]

More recent Chinese BITs offer dual options to investors, even though this approach is not that popular in practice. Unlike the generally accepted principle that states unilaterally offer to all investors to settle disputes by arbitration,[403]

China's starting position has always been that disputes would be resolved in the local courts. A number of China's BITs provide for ICSID arbitration as an alternative to litigating the dispute in the competent local court. The relevant provision of the Uganda–China BIT reads as follows:

> If the dispute cannot be settled through negotiations within six months from the date it has been raised by either party to the dispute, it shall be submitted by the choice of the investor:
>
> (a) to the competent court of the Contracting Party that is a party to the dispute;
> (b) to International Centre for the Settlement of Investment Disputes.[404]

Some Chinese BITs make slight variations to this dual-option approach. The Malaysia–China BIT provides the investor with an option by choosing either filing a claim with the "competent administrative authority or agency" of the host state or the competent national courts.[405] The unique one appears in the Poland–China BIT. Where an investor disagrees with the amount of compensation for the expropriated investment, the BIT permits the investor concerned to file a "complaint with the competent authority of the Contracting Party taking the expropriatory measures" and to request the competent authority or *ad hoc* international arbitration tribunal to review the amount of compensation if it is not resolved within one year after the complaint is first filed.[406] This provision makes it a mandatory requirement that the investor seek recourse in the domestic courts first even for a dispute on quantum thereafter.[407]

The dual-option approach is largely in line with the traditional investor–state arbitration jurisprudence that the investor has to exhaust local remedies before it resorts to international arbitration such as ICSID arbitration. Under the ICSID Convention, consent to ICSID arbitration alone *de facto* excludes all other remedies, whether in domestic courts or before other international tribunals.[408] Several Chinese BITs follow this approach.[409] This restriction is applicable to the other contracting state of China's BIT. For instance the Cambodia–China BIT confirms that any disputes can be referred to the "competent court of the Contracting Party accepting the investment."[410]

The Ethiopia–China BIT also adopts a dual-option approach but, more liberally, allows arbitration by an *ad hoc* arbitral tribunal or under the auspices of ICSID even though arbitration is limited to the dispute involving the amount of compensation for expropriation. This dual-option arbitration clause appears in a large number of BITs, including the Jordan–China BIT, Kenya–China BIT, Tobago–China BIT, Congo–China BIT, and Benin–China BIT. The third approach and the most modern one is the provision in Chapter 11 of the Free Trade Agreement between New Zealand and China ("New Zealand–China FTA"),[411] which allows the investors to choose between ICSID arbitration and UNCITRAL arbitration.[412]

The ICSID Additional Facility was an invention of the ICSID in its early days when very few cases were filed and was used as a mechanism to provide an extended scope of the ICSID Secretariat as it covered those disputes that fell outside the competence of the ICSID Convention. The Additional Facility Rules play a very important role under the NAFTA since both Mexico and Canada were not signatory states to the ICSID Convention. The Energy Charter Treaty also includes the Additional Facility as one of the arbitration options.[413] China entered into several BITs that provide for ICSID Additional Facility. Both the India–China BIT and Mexico–China BIT, for example provide consent for ICSID Additional Facility as neither India nor China was a party to the ICSID Convention at the time of signature. An India or Mexican investor is accordingly able to commence the arbitration proceeding against China under the Additional Facility. The Treaty allows the investor to make a choice between the ICSID Convention and the ICSID Additional Facility Rules.[414]

Ad hoc arbitration under the UNCITRAL Arbitration Rules is a popular option for the settlement of large international investment disputes. The UNCITRAL Arbitration Rules gained its wide reputation in the international arbitration circle and are highly regarded as "modern, universally established set of international arbitration rules."[415] The Rules are currently under review by the UNCITRAL Working Group II and are proposed to be amended to impose additional obligations on investor–state arbitrations conducted under UNCITRAL Rules. Arbitration under the UNCITRAL Arbitration Rules is flexible, confidential, and free of any institutional requirements as to nominations for arbitrators, and no additional institutional administrative costs are payable. The Turkey–China BIT provides for *ad hoc* arbitration "in accordance with the Arbitration Rules of UNCITRAL." The other way to use the UNCITRAL Arbitration Rules, as the Cuba–China BIT indicated, is to use them as guidance in determining the procedure in *ad hoc* arbitration.[416] China's BITs heavily involve UNCITRAL Arbitration Rules if *ad hoc* arbitration is an option. The Treaty, for example makes a general reference to the rules of UNCITRAL in the investor–state dispute provisions. Therefore, UNCITRAL arbitration is an option to the investors in any ASEAN member state.

A few Chinese BITs have uniquely referred to the president of the International Court of Justice (ICJ) or the Stockholm Chamber of Commerce as the appointing authority. Under the Cuba–China BIT, one party to the dispute may invite the president of the ICJ to make the appointments if there is a default by the other party.[417] The Ghana–China BIT refers to the Stockholm Chamber of Commerce as the appointing authority.[418] Accordingly, the arbitration procedure can be determined by the tribunal with reference to the Stockholm Chamber of Commerce or ICC Rules.[419] Nevertheless, ICC arbitration does not appear in many Chinese BITs.

The Treaty provides a wide range of dispute-settlement options to the disputing parties as follows:[420]

> where the dispute cannot be resolved as provided for under Paragraph 3
> within 6 months from the date of written request for consultation and

negotiations, unless the parties to the dispute agree otherwise, it may be submitted at the choice of the investor:

(a) to the courts or administrative tribunals of the disputing Party, pro-vided such courts or administrative tribunals have jurisdiction; or

(b) under the International Centre for Settlement of Investment Disputes (ICSID) Convention and the ICSID Rules of Procedure for Arbitra-tion Proceedings, provided that both the disputing Party and the non-disputing Party are parties to the ICSID Convention; or

(c) under the ICSID Additional Facility Rules, provided that either of the disputing Party or non-disputing Party is a party to the ICSID Convention; or

(d) to arbitration under the rules of the United Nations Commission on International Trade Law; or

(e) if the disputing parties agree, to any other arbitration institution or under any other arbitration rules.

The Treaty is probably the most liberal and comprehensive BIT offering a widest range of venues to the disputing parties for resolving their disputes: the courts or administrative tribunals of the disputing party, ICSID arbitration, arbitration under the ICSID Additional Facility Rules, arbitration under the UNCITRAL Rules, or any other *ad hoc* arbitration.

The question of priority among various methods of dispute settlement arose in some cases, that is *Southern Pacific Properties Inc. v. Egypt.*[421] It was argued that the order in which these methods are mentioned indicates a hierarchic relation-ship. The sequence, it is said, reflects the *maxim generalia specialibus non derogant* – a principle that has been endorsed by publicists since Grotius and appears in the jurisprudence of the Permanent Court of International Justice such as Mavrom-mattis Palestine Concessions (Jurisdiction) and various international arbitral tribu-nals including *Saudi Arabia v. Arabian American Oil Company.*[422] However, a plain reading of the language in the Treaty, the list of dispute resolution procedures pre-scribed in the Treaty does not seem to imply a mandatory hierarchic relationship. The wording "or" and the "investor to choose" notion simply suggest that this is a negotiated list of possible alternatives. A mandatory construction of the priority order of the list would in effect deny the investor the right to international tribunals conferred by the BIT. This "textual" reading is important since it would help avoid conflicting awards on the jurisdiction or treaty interpretation.

Despite the top priority of local courts or administrative tribunals in the list of venues, the disputing parties do not have to first avail of the domestic courts or administrative tribunals. In other words, the investor does not have to exhaust local means in resolving its dispute before resorting to international arbitration for settle-ment. Controversy does exist as to the question of how to apply the general prin-ciple of exhaustion of local remedies in practice or how a BIT that is silent on the issue of the exhaustion of local remedies is to be interpreted. This question attains particular legal significance as it is a fundamental right in local procedural law. The prevailing view may be that the contracting states have waived the right to require the exhaustion of local remedies to the extent that nothing to the contrary has been expressly agreed upon[423] even though it has been opined that such a fundamental rule of international law should not be excluded without an explicit indication.[424] In any event, under the Treaty, the investor may have to obtain a final judgement or ruling in the domestic court or administrative tribunal if the investor's first choice is a domestic court or administrative tribunal. This can be confirmed by reference to subsection (5) in the same clause, which reads that:

> In case a dispute has been submitted to a competent domestic court, it may be submitted to international dispute settlement, provided that the investor concerned has withdrawn its case from the domestic court before a final judgment has been reached in the case.[425]

Some Chinese BITs may impose other requirements on the choice of the dispute settlement venue. The submission of the dispute to the local courts or administrative tribunals may be a precondition to the arbitral tribunal's having jurisdiction over the dispute. For instance under the Uganda–China BIT, the choice between the local court and ICSID arbitration is conditional upon one caveat that "provided that the Contracting Party involved may require the investor concerned to go through the domestic administrative review procedures specified by the laws and regulations of that Contracting Party before the submission to the ICSID."[426] The investor's right to arbitration is not limited in this BIT but has to comply with the host state's jurisdictional requirement. The Treaty does not follow this route by not imposing a precondition onto initiating international arbitration.

A large number of Chinese BITs have a three-month period within which the investor must pursue the domestic review procedure. However, not all of the Chinese BITs specify a grace period before the formal dispute settlement procedure. For instance the Latvia–China BIT is silent on the length of time an investor must exhaust the domestic administrative review procedure.[427] Alongside with the priority to the local courts or administrative tribunals for dispute settlement, this silence may suggest that an investor is able to commence the international arbitration proceeding against the host state even if the domestic procedure may take longer than three months. If the local procedure is still on after a three-month period, the investor can rely on the most-favoured-nation (MFN) treatment to resort to international arbitration under more favourable conditions, which is supported by the tribunal in *Maffezini* case.[428] The Treaty's approach on this grace period departs from the majority position. The Treaty did not set out a time limit for the local review procedure, under which the investor is free to move forward even if the disputing parties are still in the local review procedure.

3.2 Consent to ICSID Arbitration

The first BIT entered into between China and Sweden in 1982 did not include investor–state dispute resolution provisions at all. Instead, the disputes between the contracting parties on the interpretation and application of the BIT shall be referred to a three-member *ad hoc* tribunal.[429] The tribunal is usually composed of three members, two of them are appointed by each side and the third one is appointed by the two-party appointed arbitrators. In the event of a default of one of the parties, "either party to the dispute may invite the Secretary-General of the ICSID to make the necessary appointment."[430] Other early Chinese BITs such as the Singapore–China BIT 1985 also adopted *ad hoc* arbitration to resolve the dispute.[431] The emergence of this arrangement, as claimed, was due to the fact that China had not acceded to the ICSID Convention.[432] As a matter of fact, however, even after the ratification of the ICSID Convention, China continued to conclude some BITs without reference to ICSID arbitration. For instance the Slovenia–China BIT 1993 first required the dispute to be submitted by either party to the competent court of the Contracting State accepting the investment if the dispute cannot be settled through negotiations within six months. It goes on to direct the dispute to be submitted at the request of either party to an *ad hoc* arbitral tribunal.[433] The Qatar–China BIT 1999,[434] Indonesia–China BIT 1994,[435] and Egypt–China BIT 1994[436] contained the similar arrangement. In the 1990s, China only accepted ICSID arbitration in a very small number of BITs such as the Lithuania–China BIT 1993[437] and the Bahrain–China BIT 1999,[438] both of which only included a "limited ICSID clause" under which ICSID is only able to arbitrate the dispute over compensation from expropriation or nationalization. The limited use of ICSID arbitration by China in its BITs can only be sensibly explained by its capital-absorbing status which likely involves China in more international arbitration cases if it easily agrees to incorporate an ICSID arbitration clause in the BITs without any restrictions or qualifications. This may well explain the striking phenomenon that China has never become a respondent in any ICSID arbitration case. In fact, the limited scope of consent to ICSID arbitration compromised its effectiveness as a mechanism for investment protection.

Ad hoc arbitration often goes hand in hand with ICSID arbitration. However, *ad hoc* arbitration only appeared in half of China's early BITs, and some of these BITs were entered into by China after its ratification of the ICSID Convention. The Sri Lanka–China BIT 1986 and Uruguay–China BIT 1993 are two examples which did allow *ad hoc* arbitration but merely permitted quantum disputes to be referred to *ad hoc* arbitration. The Pakistan–China BIT also refers the investor to *ad hoc* arbitration if an investor challenges the "amount of compensation for the expropriated investment" and if the dispute has not been resolved after a year in the competent national authority of the host state.[439] *Ad hoc* international tribunal in some BITs is granted the jurisdiction to arbitrate all investor–state disputes.[440] There are other dispute-resolution mechanisms in a small number of Chinese BITs, but *ad hoc* followed by ICSID arbitration are the most popular combination.

ICSID arbitration is a popular option in many BITs due to its specialist expertise and reliable facility in resolving investor–state disputes.[441] In terms of the jurisdictional requirements, written consent must be given by both disputing parties.[442] Once consent has been given, it cannot be unilaterally withdrawn.[443]

This suggests that ratification of the ICSID Convention itself does not constitute a state's consent to arbitrate a dispute through ICSID procedures, and an express consent is a must. As far as the form of consent in the ICSID arbitration is concerned, there are few requirements except that consent is in writing,[444] leaving the parties otherwise free to choose the manner in which to express their consent. The case law, on the other hand, confirms that consent of a state can be incorporated by reference,[445] or given in a concession contract, its foreign investment domestic law,[446] BIT,[447] or multilateral treaty such as the Energy Charter Treaty and NAFTA.[448] The question of whether the parties have effectively expressed their consent to ICSID jurisdiction is not to be answered by reference to national law. Rather, the governing law on this point should be international law as set out in Article 25(1) of the ICSID Convention.[449]

The ICSID Convention is replete with the notion that it is the parties' consent that creates the arbitral tribunal's jurisdiction and competence. In the practice of ICSID arbitration, consent is the cornerstone of the jurisdiction.[450] The ICSID Convention and the model clauses that have been used by ICSID since 1969 are arguably intended to make consent to arbitrate legally binding.[451] The surge of the BITs brought out a new wave of arbitral consent, which is gradually developed towards a mechanism of indirect, non-simultaneous, and "staggered" consent to arbitrate. Under this mechanism, instead of having a direct contractual relationship on the basis of a traditional arbitration agreement, the disputing parties have a standing offer coupled with the subsequent exercise of an option to choose arbitration.

China has given its consent to arbitrate under the auspices of ICSID in many BITs. Nevertheless, some earlier Chinese BITs took a restrictive approach to give such consent. Under these BITs, disputes to be referred to ICSID must be quantum disputes even though the disputes that arise out of the investor–state relationship can be very broad ranging from the disputes concerning an alleged breach of an obligation of the state under the BIT which causes loss or damage to the investor or its investment, to the disputes concerning any obligation under some agreements concluded between the investor and the host state. For instance the Japan–China BIT refers quantum disputes to "a conciliation board or an arbitration board, to be established with reference to the ICSID Convention." As China has not ratified the ICSID Convention at that time, the effect of this provision is to merely make a reference to the ICSID Convention in the appointment process. Even in some Chinese BITs concluded after China's accession to the ICSID Convention including the Indonesia–China BIT 1994[452] and Cambodia–China BIT 1996,[453] a unilateral recourse to international arbitration is only confined to quantum disputes. This restriction was completely removed in a number of very recent BITs such as the Myanmar–China BIT 2001.[454] A number of older Chinese BITs attach other qualifiers to consent. For instance the Argentina–China BIT contains an arbitration provision creating a unilateral recourse to arbitration but protected investment is defined as those made "in accordance with the laws" of the host state. This makes the utility of consent more burdensome as arbitration can be triggered off to protect foreign investment only if all the extensive regulatory laws of China are complied with. In this sense, consent given here is a restricted one.

The Cambodia–China BIT not only took a restrictive approach but also confined ICSID arbitration to ancillary matters. It was provided that disputes on quantum are to be referred to *ad hoc* arbitration before a three-member tribunal. In the event of default in the appointment process, "either party to the dispute may invite the Secretary General [of ICSID] to make the necessary appointment."[455] While the clause allows the tribunal to determine the arbitral procedure, the tribunal may take the ICSID Arbitration Rules as guidance. The use of ICSID in dealing with "ancillary matters" is also the approach taken by other Chinese BITs such as Algeria–China BIT,[456] Azerbaijan–China BIT,[457] Croatia–China BIT,[458] Georgia–China BIT,[459] Indonesia–China BIT,[460] Mongolia–China BIT,[461] and Vietnam–China BIT.[462] Under the New Zealand–China BIT and Singapore–China BIT, the arbitral procedural rules can be determined by the tribunal with reference to the ICSID Convention.[463] The Peru–China BIT is a unique one in that it refers to ICSID arbitration only for quantum disputes but allows "any disputes concerning other matters" to be referred to ICSID "if the parties to the dispute so agree."[464]

Relevant clauses in some Chinese BITs (which were reached right after China's ratification of the ICSID Convention in 1993) allow the parties "by mutual agreement" to refer "any dispute concerning other matters to *ad hoc* arbitration."[465] On the contrary, some other Chinese BITs that predated China's ratification of the ICSID Convention included explanatory Protocols or exchange of letters required further negotiations to be arranged in order to decide the types of disputes that could be referred to ICSID. The Turkmenistan–China BIT 1992 is a clear example with such an arrangement, according to which when the parties become "Contracting States of ICSID, supplementary agreement may be reached to resolve relevant disputes accordingly." Thereafter, the two states would agree which disputes can be arbitrated at ICSID as both China and Turkmenistan have now ratified ICSID Convention. The similar arrangement also appeared in the Hungary–China BIT's Protocol which provides that the two states "will enter into a supplementary agreement concerning the scope of disputes" that could not submitted to ICSID after China becomes a party to the ICSID Convention.[466] Additional consent required for an international arbitration, in essence, reduces the effectiveness of the investor–state dispute settlement clause and makes this provision a mere symbolic other than an enforceable promise.

Consent can be conditional as well in that the parties to the dispute only include a reference to ICSID arbitration despite the non-satisfaction of the threshold requirements for jurisdiction. For instance the Australia–China BIT 1988 provides that "a dispute may be submitted to the ICSID for resolution in accordance with the terms on which the Contracting Party which has admitted the investment" in the event that both China and Australia become party to the ICSID Convention.[467] This clause came into effect only after Australia and China's ratification of the ICSID Convention in 1991 and 1993 respectively. A number of BITs such as the Turkmenistan–China BIT and Romania–China BIT included this condition plus a supplementary agreement by the host state.

More recent Chinese BITs included an express consent. The Belgo–Luxembourg–China BIT explicitly states that "each Contracting Party consents to the submission of the dispute at the investor's choice" if the dispute cannot be settled after six months.[468] The Israel–China BIT contained the same express consent provision but limited its application to "any legal disputes . . . concerning the amount of compensation in the case of expropriation."[469] The similar express consent appears in the Dutch–China BIT but in the term of "unconditional consent" to submit to arbitration. Those BITs China entered into in the 21st century often contain unconditional consent. The best example is the Netherlands–China BIT 2001 which clearly states that

> each Contracting Party gives its unconditional consent to submit the dispute at the request of the investor concerned to (a) the ICSID, for settlement by arbitration or conciliation under the ICSID Convention . . ., or (b) an *ad hoc* arbitral tribunal, unless otherwise agreed upon by the parties to the dispute, to be established under the Arbitration Rules of the UNCITRAL.[470]

A number of Chinese BITs with EU members in the 21st century often adopted this unconditional consent.[471]

Consent to arbitration usually has two components: the standing offer given by the state party to BIT in advance and the acceptance of the standing offer by the investor.[472] The Treaty included both components. First, by signing the Treaty, the contracting states give the standing offer subjecting future disputes with a foreign investor from the other state party to the jurisdiction of an arbitral tribunal "provided that . . . both the disputing Party and the non-disputing Parties are the parties to the ICSID Convention."[473] Second, the Treaty adopts the "investor to choose" model of accepting the standing offer in the jurisdictional clauses. Under the Treaty, it is the investor, not the host state, that has the right to choose one of several fora provided for in the Treaty by submission of its claim at its choice.[474] The advantage of having this arrangement is to gaining the trust and confidence of the investor to invest in a contracting state. The disadvantage is obvious too. The state may not have the certainty to foresee the extent and type of future dispute resolution proceedings it may have to participate in when it gives its consent in the form of a "standing offer." In this respect, the Treaty is clearly intended to provide the investor with adequate protection but puts the host state in a more passive position. By submitting a claim, the investor formally accepts the standing offer so as to perfect the consent. It is well established in both case law[475] and academic commentaries that the investor, through the institution of arbitration proceedings, has unequivocally expressed its will or consent to subject itself to arbitration. At the time when the submission is made by the investor, privity is created between the investor and the host state in a contractual sense.[476]

3.3 Amicable Settlement

Amicable settlement through either consultation or conciliation is almost the first option for settlement of investment disputes in nearly all the Chinese BITs. This is not only consistent with general treaty practice but also reflects China's willingness to resolve the dispute through friendly consultation or negotiation. Like almost all Chinese BITs, the Treaty includes a provision stating that:

> the parties to the dispute shall, as far as possible, resolve the dispute through consultations.[477]

The purpose of having this clause is obvious. The disputing parties may benefit from resolving the dispute through amicable settlement, which can often be conducted in a speedier, more cost-effective, and confidential manner. Like other Chinese BITs including the Singapore–China BIT 1985,[478] the Philippines–China BIT 1992,[479] and Indonesia–China BIT 1994,[480] the Treaty effectively imposes a mandatory obligation on both disputing parties to first resolve their dispute through negotiation or consultation, which is a significant move to incorporate mediation or ADR into the investment treaty regime. Furthermore, this ADR-type procedure is subject to a specified cooling-off period, normally six months, as the dispute-settlement provision indicates as follows:

> Where the dispute cannot be resolved within six months from the date of written request for consultations and negotiations, unless the parties to the dispute agree otherwise.[481]

The six-month period, as the waiting period, is supposed to have a binding effect on the investor if it wishes to bring the dispute to a formal dispute settlement venue. The waiting period varies from three months to one year. The Australia–China BIT, Finland–China BIT, and Sweden–China BIT's Protocol set a three-month period. The waiting period in the Bahrain–China BIT is five months. The Turkey–China BIT, Pakistan–China BIT, and Syria–China BIT have a longer waiting period of one year. Six-month is the usual practice adopted by other Chinese BITs such as the Singapore–China BIT[482] and Barbados–China BIT.

Despite the mandatory nature of amicable settlement and its waiting period, the case law jurisprudence on the application of these provisions has not been entirely consistent or clear cut.[483] The majority of case law on this matter confirms that the cooling-off period is merely a procedural requirement[484] and non-compliance is not fatal to the investor's claim.[485] Quite often, some investors, as claimants, have been able to "jump the gun" and initiate arbitration before the expiration of the waiting period.[486] In these cases, the cooling period did not deprive the tribunal of jurisdiction. However, some other cases have indicated that the tribunals may regard the obligation to conduct amicable settlement as a jurisdiction requirement rather than a pure procedural one.[487] The tribunal's

underlying rationale is obvious that amicable settlement may deserve more attention to make consultation or negotiation, as the pre-arbitration process, more
effective and meaningful. Therefore, the tribunal needs to attach more significance to amicable settlement and expect complete compliance with the waiting
period. Although the approach that the waiting period "is not of a jurisdictional
nature is preferable,"[488] the tribunals more often take a case-by-case approach to
take into account various circumstances in their rulings.

Some Chinese BITs would have some procedural formality requirements in
relation to amicable settlement. For instance under the Pakistan–China BIT, an
investor seeking to challenge the amount of compensation for an expropriated
investment may "file complaint with the competent authority of the Contracting
Party" within one year."[489] By contrast, more mandatory formality requirements
appear in the more recent New Zealand–China FTA, under which a "request for
consultations and negotiations shall be made in writing and shall state the nature
of the dispute."[490] A similar provision also appears in the Mexico–China BIT.
The procedural formality requirement in these provisions is more substantial in
nature and can be taken as a jurisdictional requirement in some sense. A prudent
investor needs to satisfy these procedural conditions within a specified time limit
rather than risk the chance of being rejected simply because of its failure to comply with such procedural requirements. No matter how the tribunal may view
this procedural requirement, the investor, at a minimum level, needs to ensure
that a written request with details of the dispute has been duly sent to the other
party prior to the commencement of the dispute-settlement proceeding. On
the contrary, even more substantial requirements may be imposed by the BITs.
The typical provisions appear in the Belgium–Luxembourg Economic Union–
China BIT, which stated that "the parties to the dispute shall endeavor to settle
the dispute through consultations, if necessary by seeking expert advice from a
third-party, or by conciliation between the Contracting Parties through diplomatic channels." This provision is prescriptive in nature but explicitly specifies
the involvement of third-party experts and diplomatic channels. The tribunals
may apply a more substantial approach to interpreting such provisions. In the
case of *Goetz and others v. Burundi*, the tribunal interpreted a similar provision
more extensively so that more substantial diplomatic intervention is required.[491]

The amicable settlement provision in the Treaty is less substantial. There are
only two procedural requirements. First, the parties shall resolve their dispute
through consultations "as far as possible." Unlikely, the tribunal will interpret
this "as far as possible" caveat more substantially or expansively as it is hard
to measure or quantify this requirement in practice. The "as far as possible"
caveat can hardly be interpreted as a requirement imposed on the investor to
exhaust local remedies, otherwise the Treaty, like the Pakistan–China BIT,[492]
may request the disputing parties to make more efforts to resolve the dispute
during the cooling-off period. Second, the parties may need to submit a "written request for consultations and negotiations." At the maximum level, the tribunal may require the initiating party to satisfy this requirement by serving a

written request, which does not impose any substantial obligation on the party. It is advisable that the investor prudently comply with this requirement before it decides to move forward.

3.4 Definition and Scope of "Dispute"

States, based on the investor–state arbitration clause, consent to arbitrate disputes that fall under the jurisdiction of the BIT. The jurisdiction of the arbitration clause varies depending on the states involved. Any dispute determined by a tribunal that falls outside its jurisdiction leaves an award open to challenge. Therefore, the tribunal must ensure that it has jurisdiction. In this regard, like the terms "investor" and "investment," the exact definition of "dispute" is critical in the practice of ICSID tribunals even though whether the dispute at issue was legal or not does not seem to have created problems and has never been seriously raised as a defence.[493]

In defining the term "dispute" under Chinese BITs, there are several formulae. Most old-generation Chinese BITs such as the UK–China BIT, Norway–China BIT, and Denmark–China BIT contained a restrictive clause which only refers to disputes "involving the amount of compensation for expropriation."[494] This restrictive definition of "dispute" appeared in more Chinese BITs prior to 1998. The France–China BIT combined a narrow term of "dispute" together with the requirement of exhausting local remedies in the fork-in-the-road provision.[495] The investor–state arbitration clause was not contained in the Sweden–China BIT, but Sweden expressed its intention to renegotiate this issue once China acceded to the ICSID Convention. Unfortunately, there did not seem to be any follow-up on this point thereafter.[496]

The Indonesia–China BIT's approach is even more restrictive and permits arbitration of disputes "involving the amount of compensation resulting from expropriation" to be referred to *ad hoc* arbitration.[497] This provision may leave no jurisdiction to the tribunal for determining the actual occurrence of any expropriation and potentially rules out the possible circumstance in such cases as *European Media Venture SA v Czech Republic*.[498] Similarly, the Qatar–China BIT provides that the dispute can be submitted to *ad hoc* arbitration if "the legal dispute is tied up with the amount of compensation for expropriation."[499] Other Chinese BITs such as the Lebanon–China BIT contain such a provision to absorb a narrow concept of compensation.[500]

Several Chinese BITs provide the parties with the option to agree with arbitration for "other disputes." The Greece–China BIT, for example materializes this option by stipulating that:

> Any other dispute between an investor and a Contracting Party may be submitted to an international arbitration tribunal, only by mutual consent. Each Contracting Party herewith declares its acceptance of such arbitration procedure.[501]

Instead of making a firm undertaking to allow all other disputes to be arbitrated, the intention of this provision is to show the contracting parties' willingness to consider any other disputes to be submitted to arbitration. However, the contracting parties' declaration of acceptance of the arbitration process is an absolute obligation with regard to the amount of compensation. As to "other disputes," the acceptance of arbitration is conditional upon "mutual consent." This requirement may technically make arbitration of "other disputes" difficult as the host state may refuse to give further consent to arbitrate.

Other BITs may allow "other disputes" to be arbitrated but in slightly different terms. The Lithuania–China BIT permits disputes relating to the amount of compensation and "other disputes agreed upon by both parties may be submitted" to ICSID.[502] This is an agreement to agree and imposes no obligation on the parties to submit other disputes to ICSID arbitration. The Philippines–China BIT is more specific: "any other dispute on the matter of this Agreement agreed by the two parties to the dispute for submission to international arbitration."[503] The provision is clearly so expansive that it subjects all disputes rather than only questions on quantum to arbitration. The enforceability of this provision, however, depends on whether the parties, in particular, the host state, agree to submit "any other dispute" to international arbitration, which indeed requires further consent from the host state.

Prior to 1998, the dispute between an investor and China which can be submitted to ICSID arbitration is limited to the "disputes over compensation resulting from expropriation and nationalization."[504] This was the case because the Chinese government filed a notification in accordance with Article 25(4) of the ICSID Convention at the time of ratification indicating that "the Chinese Government would only consider submitting to the jurisdiction of the ICSID over compensation resulting from expropriation or nationalization."[505] There have been some debates as to the legal effect of such Article 25(4) declaration on consent to arbitrate given in more recent BITs, which has been arbitrated in some ICSID cases such as *Kaiser Bauxite Co. v Jamaica*.[506] The declaration as such seems closer to a treaty reservation under the Vienna Convention on the Law of Treaties whereby a state purports to exclude or to modify the legal effect of certain provisions of a treaty in their application to that state. In *Kaiser Bauxite* case, Jamaica ratified the ICSID Convention in 1968 without reservation but filed a notification purporting to remove from ICSID's jurisdiction all disputes arising directly out of investments relating to minerals or other natural resources. When Kaiser initiated ICSID arbitration proceedings seeking a declaration that Jamaica's Bauxite (Production Levy) Act did not apply to it and seeking a return of taxes paid pursuant to this Act, Jamaica disputed the jurisdiction on the basis of its notification and refused to appoint an arbitrator and did not appear at the first meeting of the hearing.

It has been argued that the purpose of Article 25(4) is simply to give the state a non-binding opportunity to declare (or clarify) which disputes they may or may not submit to ICSID for arbitration.[507] In other words, as the basic ICSID norm, acceding to the ICSID Convention with an Article 25(4) declaration does not prejudice the effect of consent to the jurisdiction of arbitral tribunals,[508] as only ratification of the ICSID Convention and an express consent, rather than the declaration under Article 25(4) of the ICSID Convention, satisfy the treaty requirements for the tribunal to have the complete jurisdiction. In the case of *Kaiser Bauxite*, the tribunal ruled that it had jurisdiction over the case and, more importantly, Jamaica's notification did not affect the prior agreement to arbitration.[509] Article 25(4), at least in theory, does not represent a chance to the ICSID signatory to make a reservation in international treaty law.[510] By the same logic, the Article 25(4) declaration does not bind on jurisdictional decisions of arbitral tribunals constituted under the ICSID Convention, and consent given by China to the ICSID Convention, if given, is an unconditional consent.[511] This line of argument can be supported by the fact that more recent Chinese BITs rarely made a reference to its Article 25(4) declaration, which is different from the practice in some other "old" BITs where Article 25(4) declaration was mentioned.[512] Accordingly, an investor can rely on a new BIT to sue the Chinese government for any dispute before an ICSID arbitral tribunal in addition to the "disputes over compensation resulting from expropriation and nationalization."

In any event, China began to be more liberal in accepting a broader dispute resolution provision by giving general consent to arbitration of BIT disputes in 1998 when it entered into a BIT with Barbados.[513] According to international treaty laws,[514] recent BITs with non-restrictive consent to arbitrate *de facto* supersede China's earlier declaration under Article 25(4) of the ICSID Convention limiting its consent to the jurisdiction of ICSID to "disputes over compensation resulting from expropriation or nationalization" in the *inter se* relations between China and the counterparty, provided that the BIT does not exceed the scope of the ICSID Convention. A non-restrictive consent in a BIT entered into after China's Article 25(4) declaration may also be considered a unilateral withdrawal of earlier reservations or a new contractual consensus overriding the previous declaration.

In terms of the more recent treaty practice, a number of China BITs alternatively refer to "any legal dispute related to an investment."[515] The term of "legal dispute" appears in Article 25 of the ICSID Convention without definition, which was largely due to the negotiating history of the ICSID Convention.[516] The term may be explained as excluding moral, political, or commercial claims or as expressing the requirement that a legal right or obligation had to be involved and has been heavily considered by the ICSID tribunals. The case law confirmed that the "legal dispute" must "concern the existence or scope of a legal right or obligation, or the nature or extent of the reparation to be made for breach of a legal obligation."[517]

More recent BITs are more liberal by allowing "any investment dispute" to be referred to ICSID or *ad hoc* arbitration.[518] For instance the Botswana–China BIT 2000 explicitly allowed for transactional arbitration for "any dispute between an investor of one Contracting Party and the other Contracting Party" either under the ICSID Convention or before an *ad hoc* tribunal.[519] The Australia–China BIT confines the dispute to be "relating to an investment or an activity associated with an investment."[520] Although the wording seems to be broader than usual, the language in the same BIT still limits consent to arbitration to the amount of compensation awarded on expropriation.[521] The most recent New Zealand–China FTA limits the scope of the dispute provisions to disputes arising out of the specific investment under Chapter 11. The definition of "investment" therein is broad enough to cover "every kind of asset invested, directly or indirectly," including but not limited to property, shares, claims to money, intellectual property rights, concessions, bonds, and rights conferred by law or contract, such as licences.[522] More specifically, consent to arbitration in the Guyana–China BIT covers "investment disputes," which is defined as "a dispute between a Contracting Party and an investor of the other Contracting Party, concerning an obligation of the former under this Agreement to an investment of the latter."[523] Regardless of legal interpretation or application of these provisions, the wordings in these BITs no longer restricted the validity of the investor–state dispute settlement to the amount of compensation as the old-generation BITs had done. The wide-ranging language as such effectively allows the investors to invoke all substantive rights granted in the applicable BITs.

The widest formula so far probably is "all disputes" or "any disputes" followed by some caveat-outs. The Czech Republic–China BIT provides that:

> if any dispute between an investor of one Contracting Party and the other Contracting Party cannot be thus settled within six months of the date when the request for the settlement has been submitted, the investor shall be entitled to submit the case, at his choice, for settlement to

the competent court of the Contracting Party, or the ICSID or an ad hoc arbitration under the Arbitration Rules of the UNCITRAL.[524] This clause is broad in nature. As the wording does not specify the nature or type of dispute, it literally can be interpreted to cover "any dispute" between an investor and host state. The significance of "any (or all) disputes" should not be overestimated largely because most disputes between the investor and the host state are legal ones. In addition, the broad and vague term "any dispute" has been the source of controversies and arbitrated in various cases such as *Salini v Morocco*,[525] *SGS v Pakistan*,[526] and *SGS v the Philippines*.[527] The arbitral tribunals may take different approaches to apply this term. While some tribunals may extend the jurisdiction not only to a treaty violation but also contract claims by interpreting this term in a broad sense,[528] others may treat the broad formulation of "disputes with respect to investments" as a purely descriptive one without any indication of consent to arbitrate contractual disputes. Given the case law, it is reasonable to anticipate that investors may likely submit a contractual dispute to ICSID arbitration simply based on the broad dispute-resolution terms in China's BITs. Therefore, it is important to clarify this term in the BITs to the possible extent.

The Treaty takes a more expansive but specific approach by stating that

> the investment dispute concerning an alleged breach of an obligation of national treatment, most-favoured-nation treatment, treatment of investment, expropriation, compensation of losses, transfers and repatriation of profits,

which causes loss or damage to the investor in relation to its investment with respect to the management, conduct, operation, or sale or other disposition of an investment can be referred to international arbitration if the dispute.[529]

The term "investment dispute" reflects the wording adopted by the ICSID Convention.[530] Technically, this provision can be interpreted in either wide or narrow sense. The tribunal may apply the caveat of "loss or damage" in such a narrow way that it only focuses on the quantum, that is the amount of compensation as the "loss or damage" may strongly signal that the tribunal may not widen its jurisdiction to cover such matters as the occurrence of expropriation at the national level. Alternatively, the tribunal may place more emphasis on the cross-references to other treaty obligations and provisions such as expropriation, compensation of losses, and transfer and repatriation of profits to widen its jurisdiction resolving more substantial issues including whether expropriation occurs, whether such occurrence of expropriation constitutes a breach of treaty obligation, and whether the compensation should be made due to expropriation, and how much compensation is due. The wide sense of approach to expand jurisdiction is often adopted by the tribunals which are more willing to view it as giving itself substantive jurisdiction wide enough to determine whether an expropriation had in fact taken place, and whether the compensation should be awarded, rather than restricting its jurisdiction to the actual amount of compensation for an expropriation.[531] The way the Treaty deals with the scope of disputes is more straightforward and rules out any potential confusion. Based on the relevant provision of the Treaty, the dispute to be arbitrated must be specific and satisfies the definition of "investment dispute" in the Treaty. In terms of the consent, the contracting parties give clear consent to arbitration as long as the dispute to be arbitrated is a dispute defined by the Treaty.

The attempt has been made in recent years in concluding new-generation BITs by providing for more specific definitions of "dispute." The purpose of this attempt is to balance the need to broaden the scope of consent to arbitrate and the side effect of general consent. There has been a tendency that more and more new Chinese BITs will move towards a typical Western type investor–state arbitration mechanism whereby the institutional or *ad hoc* arbitration is available to foreign investors under the BIT without excessive restrictions. This is a significant progress with respect to China and ASEAN member states in the context of the Treaty.

3.5 Who Makes a Choice?

Relatively older Chinese BITs give "either party" the right to commence arbitration proceedings. However, the new-generation Chinese BITs such as the New Zealand–China FTA[532] have changed the approach and have been more accommodative to the investors by allowing the investor to initiate the proceeding and select the arbitration venue. The significance of this pro-investor approach is two-fold. First, it avoids any potential objection to jurisdiction based on the alleged lack of consent from the investor to submit the dispute to ICSID arbitration. In the case of *American Mfg. & Trading, Inc. v. Zaire*, for example the tribunal holds that "the requirement of the consent of the parties does not disappear with the existence of the treaty," and "the two States cannot compel any of their nationals to appear before the ICSID."[533] There must be an exchange of consents between "a State and a national of another State" according to Article 25 of the ICSID Convention.[534] When the investor exercises its right of option, the investor thus gives its consent to arbitration and "would be deemed to have accepted" the competence of ICSID.[535] Other ICSID cases confirmed this basic norm of ICSID arbitration that "consent by both parties is an indispensable condition for the exercise of the ICSID jurisdiction."[536] Second, the approach is consistent with the trendy BIT practice laid down by the US Model BIT and the Energy Charter Treaty. However, this may not necessarily truly reflect the trendy practice that investors, like multinational corporations, are under more social obligations. Therefore, the host states may be more litigious in the future to make the investors more socially responsible for their cross-border investment activities, for example environmental protection and sustainable development. The Norway Model BIT has already imposed environmental and other social obligations on the investors. The typical provisions are Articles 24 and 27 dealing with environmental exceptions and cultural exceptions respectively. The Treaty does not merely adopt a pro-investor approach. Whereas the Treaty allows the investor to initiate the proceeding and to make a selection among various dispute-settlement options after the dispute arises, it also allows both the investor and host state to reach an agreement on the arbitration venue.[537]

3.6 Limitation Period

Many states include a provision in their BITs imposing a limitation on consent to arbitration. The time limitation provision usually excludes arbitration if a certain period has elapsed from the date on which the claimant became aware of a breach of an obligation. For example, the North America Free Trade Agreement (NAFTA) has a three-year limitation period for claims to be made from the date "the investor first acquired, or should have first acquired, knowledge of the alleged breach."[538] The time limitation provision was invoked in the case of *Grand River Enterprise v USA* to strike out the investor's claim due to the elapse of the three-year period after the investor's awareness of the measures and loss or damage caused by such measures.[539] The time limitation of a claim depends on what the BIT provides. Some BITs including those concluded by the US with other states in recent years specify a three-year time limit.

A limitation period is neither standard practice nor the practice of China's BITs. However, some recent Chinese BITs have tried to import this practice. The New Zealand–China FTA provides that:

> no claim may be submitted to arbitration under this Chapter if more than 3 years have elapsed between the time at which the disputing investor

became aware, or should reasonably have become aware, of a breach of obligation under this Chapter causing loss or damage.[540]

The Treaty also included a three-year limitation period. The submission of a dispute to conciliation or arbitration is therefore conditional upon

the submission of the dispute to such conciliation or arbitration taking place within three years of the time at which the disputing investor became aware, or should reasonably have become aware, of a breach of an obligation under this Agreement causing loss or damage to the investor or its investment.[541]

The provision protects the host state from being sued for any event that takes place a long time ago. Thus, by having this time limitation provision, the Treaty eventually limits the state liability and curtails the admissibility of claims. Due to this restrictive effect to the claim brought by the investors, it is likely that China may more often incorporate this time limitation provision in more BITs.

3.7 Fork-in-the-Road Provision

The major purpose of a fork-in-the-road provision associated with the waiver provisions in a BIT is to preclude an investor from commencing other dispute-resolution proceedings if it has already made a choice among various dispute settlement options. Therefore, once a party has chosen a particular dispute-resolution forum, such a choice should be final and no other options can be used later on. By having this provision in the BIT, the finality and certainty can be strengthened for state parties. The host state can avoid ending up in a multiple-proceeding scenario by defending the same claim in different dispute settlement processes. In a same vein, attempts are also made to ensure the exclusivity of proceedings with the waiver clauses, whereby a choice in favour of a particular forum may be connected with a written waiver of the jurisdiction of any other forum. In essence, the fork-in-the-road and waiver provisions constitute the other side of the coin of the exhaustion of local remedies principle.

As the fork-in-the-road provision is "abound in BITs,"[542] a number of arbitration tribunals confirmed the intended function of such provision and disallowed the circumvention of such a provision by the disputing party's invoking the MFN clause.[543] For a fork-in-the-road provision to apply, the subsequent proceedings must concern the same legal and factual issues[544] and take place between the same parties.[545] Due to this "triple identity" requirement, very few cases have taken heed of the fork-in-the-road provisions with respect of barring claims. For instance in both *LG&E* and *Enron* cases, the fork-in-the-road provision of the US–Argentina BIT was held not to prevent minority shareholders from bringing arbitral claims in spite of the fact that the company they invested in had already brought ongoing proceedings in their own capacity before the Argentine courts.[546]

Not all Chinese BITs have a fork-in-the-road provision. The Norway–China BIT 1984 did not have this provision as the investor can only have the dispute over the amount of compensation reviewed by the national court or an international tribunal. As dual or multiple choices of forum are not offered to the investor, there is certainly no need to have a fork-in-the-road provision. The investor under the Philippines–China BIT is entitled to choose to have a quantum dispute arbitrated along with "other matters related thereto" and any other disputes under the BIT that the parties agree to submit to arbitration. The agreement between the disputing parties is required if the dispute to be arbitrated is not a quantum dispute or other related matters. As the agreement between the disputing parties is a precondition to arbitration, the aim of the fork-in-the-road provision of avoiding a multiplicity of claims is thus achieved.

The Jordan–China BIT retains a full fork-in-the-road provision under which the provision relating to international arbitration does not apply if the investor has already submitted the dispute to the competent court.[547] The Argentina–China BIT contains a provision making the choice of either the competent court or *ad hoc* arbitration "final."[548]

Despite the fork-in-the-road provision, the modern BIT may not prevent the investor from submitting the dispute to ICSID or *ad hoc* arbitration even if the investor has resorted to the local administrative review process. The Russia–China BIT has this qualified fork-in-the-road provision.[549] Most recent BITs are closer to adopting a qualified fork-in-the-road provision so that the investor is allowed to commence arbitration after the three-month domestic review.[550] The latest example is the New Zealand–China FTA which allows a dispute to be referred to arbitration even if it has already been referred to the competent domestic court "on the condition that the investor concerned has withdrawn its case from the domestic courts before a final judgment has been reached in the case."[551] This caveat-out is similar to a waiver obligation under the NAFTA that an investor must sign a written waiver of any right to commence or continue local court proceedings before resorting to arbitration. The Mexico–China BIT is odd in the sense that it does not have a fork-in-the-road provision but has a waiver requirement, according to which an investor can submit to arbitration only if a specific waiver on behalf of the investment enterprise has been given.[552] This waiver requirement must be interpreted as a mandatory obligation imposed on the investor to go through the local administrative review procedure of the host state prior to its pursuit of international arbitration.

The Treaty divides ASEAN member states and China into two groups and arranges two separate rules to be applied to them. First, the Treaty applies a more conventional approach, in line with general practice, by stipulating the following:

> In the case of Indonesia, Philippines, Thailand, and Viet Nam, once the investor has submitted the dispute to their respective competent courts or administrative tribunals or to one of the arbitration procedures [regarding

any of ICSID, ICSID Additional Facility Rules, UNCITRAL or *ad hoc* arbitration], the choice of the procedure is final.[553]

This fork-in-the-road provision obviously only has legal effect on Indonesia, the Philippines, Thailand, and Viet Nam but not China. A "qualified" fork-in-the-road provision is applicable to China and the rest of ASEAN member states. The investor is still able to submit the dispute to international arbitration even if the dispute has been submitted to a competent domestic court, provided that the investor concerned has withdrawn its case from the domestic court before a final judgement has been reached in the case.[554]

In China's 60 BITs (with the fork-in-the-road provisions), the fork-in-the-road clauses can be divided into two groups: no-U-turn and U-turn. The former refers to a scenario where the investor cannot switch to arbitration if it first chooses to rely on local remedy as long as there is no final decision in the proceeding made already, and vice versa. The latter gives the investor more flexibility by allowing the investor to switch to arbitration even if it first chooses to local remedy. Clearly, a varying level of flexibility is offered to investors by these two types of fork-in-the-road clauses.[555]

There is one multilateral investment agreement entered into between China and ASEAN which applies a no-U-turn fork-in-the-road clause to Indonesia, the Philippines, Thailand, and Vietnam while a U-turn fork-in-the-road clause applies to China and other ASEAN member states.[556] In the rest of the 59 BITs, 51 BITs (86%) include a no-U-turn fork-in-the-road clause, while eight BITs (14%) has U-turn ones. Eight BITs with a U-turn fork-in-the-road clauses were signed after 2000 but switched back to no-U-turn after 2010.

The composition of the-fork-in-the-road clauses and the switch between U-turn and no-U-turn fork-in-the-road clauses indicates a contracting state's open attitudes towards the ISDS, especially the reliance upon either local remedy or international arbitration.[557] China's changing stance on the fork-in-the-road matches its gradual "leaving (the sovereignty)" status in BIT patterns along with a fundamental shift in the nature and scope of international investment law, which in turn imposes limitations on the conduct of a nation-state's domestic policies.

3.8 Exhaustion of Local Remedies

The exhaustion of local remedies principle, as one of the safeguards to foreign investors' possible appeal to arbitration,[558] requires a claimant wishing to pursue an international arbitration to exhaust all domestic remedies first before resorting to diplomatic protection or bringing the claim to an international forum.[559] Such an obligation imposed on the claimant is to recognize the judicial sovereignty of the state over issues that fall within its jurisdiction.[560] In practice, the exhaustion of local remedies appears in BITs with Latin American states due to the popularity of the *Calvo* doctrine in Latin America. By contrast, neither NAFTA nor the overwhelming majority of modern BITs still require the exhaustion of local remedies for the disputing parties to initiate arbitration.

The principle of exhaustion of local remedies has been recognized to be a principle of customary international law.[561] It is also recognized by the ICSID Convention, which provides that consent to ICSID arbitration excludes all other remedies.[562] Under the ICSID Convention, "a Contracting State may require the exhaustion of local administrative or judicial remedies as a condition of its consent to arbitration."[563] This clause grants the contracting state to the ICSID Convention "the right to choose" if the exhaustion of local remedies is a pre-condition to arbitration. Technically speaking, the contracting state has to, up to the point of commencing arbitration, exercise this right to choose either by making an express requirement in an instrument, that is the BIT in which consent in the form of standing offer to ICSID Convention is given[564] or instituting local proceedings. A number of Chinese BITs including the Singapore–China BIT 1985,[565] Indonesia–China BIT 1994,[566] and Peru–China BIT 1996[567] entitle both the investor and the host state to submit the dispute to the competent court in the host state. According to this provision, the host state may exercise its option by initiating the proceeding in its domestic courts. Nevertheless, the ICSID Convention on the exhaustion of local remedies is not definite. In the absence of appropriately worded formulae in the BIT to the contrary,[568] there is no implicit agreement that local remedies must be exhausted before arbitration can be commenced. This is the other side of the "right to choose" rule. The other way of excluding the local remedies rule is that the host state and the foreign investor reach an arbitration agreement.[569]

There are two local remedies, judicial and administrative. The Barbados–China BIT only set out one local remedy: the right for international arbitration is not granted once the investor has chosen to access the host state's domestic judiciary.[570] Compared to the judicial remedy, the administrative remedy has more limited capacity which only involves an administrative review of decisions or actions made or taken by the administrative agency. The administrative remedy more often appears in more recent BITs, for example, the Germany–China BIT 2003, the Protocol of which indicates that

> [a German investor] may submit a dispute for arbitration under the following conditions only: (a) the investor has referred the issue to an administrative review procedure according to Chinese law, (b) the dispute still exists three months after he has brought the issue to the review procedure and (c) in case the issue has been brought to a Chinese court, it can be withdrawn by the investor according to Chinese law.[571]

This provision obviously combines the exhaustion of local remedies with the fork-in-the-road rule.

Resort to local courts is an entitlement rather than an obligation under both old and new Chinese BITs. For instance the Cambodia–China BIT 1996 explicitly states that "either party to the dispute shall be entitled to submit the dispute to the competent court of the Contracting Party accepting the investment."[572] The Myanmar–China BIT 2001 provides that "the investor of one Contracting Party may submit the dispute to the competent court of the other Contracting Party."[573] Chinese BITs often require an investor seeking to arbitrate to have explored, but not necessarily exhausted, the appropriate domestic administrative review process in the national courts. This is still the case even in recent BITs. The Czech Republic–China BIT 2005 makes it clear that:

> With respect to the possibilities of submission of a dispute to the international arbitrations set forth under this Article, the People's Republic of China will require the investor concerned to go through the domestic administrative review procedures specified by the laws and regulations of that Contracting Party before the submission of the dispute to the international arbitration. Such a procedure shall not exceed a period of three months.[574]

In some BITs, the exhaustion of local remedies is discretionary rather than compulsory. The Russia–China BIT 2006 has an exhaustion of local remedies provision in the Protocol, under which "the Contracting Party involved in the dispute may require the investor concerned to go through domestic administrative review procedures specified by the laws and regulations of that Contracting Party" before the submission of the dispute to arbitration.[575] Based on this provision, the state involved in the dispute may waive the exhaustion of local remedies requirement. The Protocol goes on to request that such review procedures take no more than 90 days. The time limit set out in the Treaty is much longer than the usual three-month period.[576]

Some Chinese BITs are even more liberal or flexible than the discretionary approach in dealing with the exhaustion of local remedies requirement by containing an "exit" or "opt-out" provision, allowing arbitration if a national court has not rendered its judgement within a specified period of time. For instance the Portugal–China BIT 2005 requires the investor to go through the local review process but also allows the investor to commence arbitration after the three-month period elapses even if the domestic review process has not been completed at the end of the three-month period. The "exit" mechanism is likely to render the option to go to national courts redundant as a vast majority of investors may opt for arbitration. The Iran–China BIT 2000 is unique in the sense that it does not include any reference to domestic review procedures as a precondition to arbitration.

The Treaty's approach dealing with the exhaustion of local remedies is a discretionary one in that "the disputing Party may require the disputing investor to go through any applicable domestic administrative review procedure specified by its domestic laws and regulations before the submission of the dispute" to arbitration under the ICSID Convention, the ICSID Additional Facility Rules, the UNCITRAL Rules, or *ad hoc* arbitration.[577] The "right to choose" is thus granted to the disputing state, which can waive this right by going ahead with arbitration directly. Procedurally, under the Treaty, the disputing state can exercise this "right to choose" "upon receipt of the notice" from the disputing investor.[578] Whereas the Russia–China BIT sets out the latest time frame for the disputing state to exercise the "right to choose," the Treaty indeed fixes the earliest time frame the disputing state can exercise the right. While the Treaty follows the trendy practice to incorporate an "exit" or "opt-out" mechanism in implementing the exhaustion of local remedies principle, the mechanism itself is quite different form the one in the Portugal–China BIT. Here, the Treaty adopts a semi-automatic "exit" route, which is not completely dependent on the elapse of a specified period of time but is more reliant upon a notice served by the investor making a choice between the local remedy and arbitration.

The notice must be submitted at least 90 days before the claim is submitted. This effectively suggests that the time limit for the exhaustion of local remedies is three months; and the failure to serve a valid notice may make the disputing investor lose its right to choose. The function of this requirement is to delay the proceeding until the elapse of the 90-day-notice period. Only after 90 days following the host state's receipt of the notice may the investor submit the dispute for resolution. During the 90-day notice period, the host state can be prepared for the incoming dispute resolution proceeding as the host state is in the passive position of defending to assess and judge the dispute.

As to the content of the notice, the Treaty imposes substantial requirements. Accordingly, in the notice, the disputing investor (i) needs to nominate either arbitration under the ICSID Convention, the ICSID Additional Facility Rules, the UNCITRAL rules, or *ad hoc* arbitration as the forum for dispute settlement and, in the case of the ICSID Convention arbitration, nominate whether conciliation or arbitration is being sought; (ii) waive the right to initiate or continue any proceedings, excluding proceedings for interim measures of protection before any of the other dispute settlement fora [that is arbitration under the ICSID Convention, the ICSID Additional Facility Rules, the UNCITRAL rules, or *ad hoc* arbitration] in relation to the matter under dispute; and (iii) briefly summarize the alleged breach of the disputing Party, including the Articles alleged to have been breached, and the loss or damage allegedly caused to the investor or its investment.[579] The notice, plus the 90-day notice period, enables the host state to gain knowledge in advance of the means of settlement being adopted, the arbitration rules to be followed, and the relief to be sought.

Of particular importance is the second requirement in the notice provision which requires the disputing investor to waive the right to initiate or continue any proceedings, excluding proceedings for interim measures of protection before the institution of the arbitration proceeding. Under the Treaty, the "interim measures of protection" can be taken by the disputing investor "for the preservation of its rights and interests" "prior to the institution of proceedings before any of the dispute settlement fora"[580] The term "interim measures of protection" is not defined by the Treaty in detail and, as clarified, does not involve "the payment of damages or resolution of the substance of the matter in dispute before the courts or administrative tribunals of the disputing Party."[581] The importance of the disputing investor's waiving interim measures of protection is that arbitration is the sole dispute settlement forum for the dispute concerned between the disputing investor and the host state so as to avoid the odd scenario that the host state may be subject to multiple proceedings for the same dispute.

Parallel to the precondition to arbitration that investor has to waive the right for proceedings, investors may have to withdraw from the ongoing proceeding under some BITs. For instance under the Finland–China BIT 2004, an investor that submitted the dispute to the national court may resort to international arbitration "if the investor has withdrawn his case before judgment has been delivered on the subject matter." The Latvia–China BIT 2004 has a similar provision to the effect that the investor may lose its right to bring the claim to arbitration in the event that he fails to withdraw the case before the delivery of a judgement.

The Treaty is closer to this route by stating that:

> In case a dispute has been submitted to a competent domestic court, it may be submitted to international dispute settlement, provided that the investor concerned has withdrawn its case from the domestic court before a final judgment has been reached in the case.[582]

This caveat suggests that access to an international arbitral tribunal will be allowed only if a unilateral withdrawal of the action before the national court will be still possible according to the domestic law of the host state.

In connection with the exhaustion of local remedies, the investor's waiver of diplomatic protection is also required by the Treaty to proceed with conciliation or arbitration.[583] In effect, the investor, if it has chosen to conciliate or arbitrate the dispute, must give up pressuring its home state to assist it in resolving the dispute with the host state. This largely reflects the tendency of modern international law and BIT practice to minimize the direct involvement of the home state by creating a right of action, usually under arbitration, for the disgruntled investor. Exclusion of diplomatic protection from the dispute settlement processes is a right direction and strategy in the field of international investment. For the avoidance of any doubt, the Treaty also clarified the term of "diplomatic protection" which "should not include informal diplomatic exchanges for the sole purpose of facilitating a settlement of a dispute."[584] To limit the use of local remedies and diplomatic protection not only allows investors' direct recourse to arbitration but also increases legal certainty and creditability of the BIT. As a result, the investors no longer have to rely on their home states to espouse claims, which potentially avoids political conflicts between the contracting states.

In summary, there is a two-stage procedure available to an investor from China or an ASEAN member state wishing to enforce its rights arising out of the Treaty against an ASEAN member state or China. First, at the choice of the host state, the dispute may need to undergo administrative review under its domestic law. Thereafter, international arbitration proceeding may commence at the earliest three months after the investor's submission of the claim. Nonetheless, where the investor has brought the claim to a domestic court in the host state, the arbitration proceeding may commence only if the action can still be withdrawn unilaterally by the investor under the domestic law.

In terms of the "exhaustion of local remedies" clause, prior to the China–Barbados BIT 1998 only the dispute over the amount of compensation from expropriation is allowed to be submitted to arbitration. This suggests that China possessed a restrictive stance towards international investment arbitration and maintained its sovereignty by not giving up its judicial sovereignty over investment disputes.[585] Here the focus is 60 BITs China signed after 2000.

Throughout these 60 IIAs, the contracting states allow foreign investors to choose to rely on local remedies (either administrative and/or court proceedings) or international investment arbitration. This has been a huge shift from China's previous position on the "exhaustion of local remedies" clauses where foreign investors cannot opt for arbitration without exhausting local remedies.[586] These 60 BITs can be further divided into three groups depending on the use of administrative review: no administrative review, optional administrative review, and administrative review, the difference of which indicates a varying degree of "leaving," surrendering sovereignty to arbitration or the ISDS mechanism.

In general, 60 IIAs are classified into two categories: reciprocal and non-reciprocal application of administrative review between the contracting parties of the BIT. The administrative review in 44 IIAs is reciprocally applied to investors from the contracting states of the BITs, while 16 IIAs include non-reciprocal clauses.

In 44 IIAs with reciprocity clauses, 4 IIAs (9%) stipulate that the parties may directly arbitrate without administrative review, and 37 IIAs (84%) stipulate that the Contracting State may require the investors to conduct administrative review in the host state before opt-in arbitration. Three IIAs (7%) subject foreign investors to administrative review. From the chronological point of view, the portions of these three types of IIAs are four (no administrative review), 28 (opt for administrative review), and three (compulsory administrative review). In the 2010s, the proportions changed to 0:9:0, meaning China's stance on administrative review softened and its growing recognition of the influence, universality, and de-territorial effect of the ISDS regime in the field of international investment.

Among the 16 IIAs that are not applicable reciprocally to investors from contracting states to the BITs, except for the 2009 China–ASEAN FTA, which allows investors, who are the ICSID member, to directly submit the dispute to international arbitration without administrative review[587] and this treaty is leaning towards a liberal stance,[588] China in the remaining 15 IIAs requires foreign investors to rely on administrative review first before arbitration. From the standpoint of the contracting states, in addition to the 2001 China–Cyprus BIT where Cyprus can require Chinese investors to conduct administrative review in the host country before arbitration[589] and the 2009 China–Malta BIT which requires Chinese investors to exhaust local remedies (court, arbitration, or administrative proceedings),[590] Chinese investors are not subject to administrative review in the other 13 IIAs.

It appears that China's leaving of its sovereignty in the 21st century is still not strong which is in line with China's conventional position on sovereignty as well as the nation-state as a meaningful unit of sovereign institution.[591]

Notes

1 UNCTAD, "IIAs by Economy", *Investment Policy Hub*, available at https://investment policy.unctad.org/international-investment-agreements/by-economy, accessed 30 September 2022. The second largest one is Germany which signed 121 BITs (115 in force) and 74 TIPs (58 in force).

2 Fernando Cabrera Diaz, "Chinese investor launches BIT claim against Peru at ICSID", *Investment Treaty News*, 2 March 2007; "First Chinese Claimant Registered at ICSID", in *Global Arbitration Law Review* (News), available at www.globalarbitrationreview.com/news/news_item.cfm?item_id=3739; Claire Wilson, "Protecting Chinese Investment Under the Investor-State Dispute Settlement Regime: A Review in Light of Ping An v Belgium" in Julien Chaisse (ed), *China's International Investment Strategy: Bilateral, Regional, and Global Law and Policy* (Oxford: Oxford University Press 2019) Ch 25.

    Tza Yap Shum v. *Republic of Peru*, ICSID Case No. ARB/07/6, available at www.worldbank.org/icsid/cases/pending.htm. The ICSID decision on jurisdiction has been heavily criticized by An Chen, 'Queries to the Recent ICSID Decision on Jurisdiction upon the Case of *Tza Yap Shum* v. *Republic of Peru*: Should China–Peru BIT 1994 be Applied to Hong Kong SAR under the "One Country Two Systems" Policy' (2009) 10(6) *Journal of World Investment and Trade* 829.

3 Trinidad and Tobago–China BIT 2002, Article 1(1).

4 Singapore–China BIT 1985, Article 1(1).

5 The Philippines–China BIT 1992, Article 1(a).

6 Laos–China BIT 1993, Article 1(1).

7 Indonesia–China BIT 1994, Article I(1).

8 Cambodia–China BIT 1996, Article 1(1).

9 The Treaty, Article 1(1)(d).

10 Gerold Zeiler, "Jurisdiction, Competence, and Admissibility of Claims in ICSID Arbitration Proceeding" in Christina Binder et al. (eds), *International Investment Law for the 21st Century* (Cambridge: Cambridge University Press 2009) 76–91 (thoroughly discussing the practical differences but unmarked distinctions between the concepts of jurisdiction and admissibility in international investment arbitration).

11 Ursula Kriebaum, "Illegal Investment" in Christian Klausegger et al. (eds), *Austrian Yearbook on International Arbitration 2010* (Bern: Wien 2010) 307–334.

12 *Inceysa Vallisoletana SL* v. *Republic of El Salvador*, ICSID Case No. ARB/03/26, Award of 2 August 2006. Cf: *Fraport AG Frankfurt Airport Services Worldwide* v. *Philippines*, ICSID Case No. ARB/03/25, Award of 16 August 2007 (in which the tribunal declined its jurisdiction based on the Germany–Philippines BIT 1997 due to the fact that the claimant had not made an investment "in accordance with the laws of the Philippines").

13 The Treaty, n. 1.

14 There are other ways such as enterprise-based, instrument-based, competence-based, and transaction-based approaches to define the "investment."

15 Civil engineering or construction contracts have sometimes been accepted by the tribunals as "investments." *Jan de Nul and Dredging International NV* v. *Egypt*, ICSID Case No. ARB/04/13, Decision on Jurisdiction of 16 June 2006, paras. 90–106; *Consortium RFCC* v. *Morocco*, ICSID Case No. ARB/00/6, Decision on Jurisdiction of 21 July 2001, paras. 37–58.

16 New Zealand–China FTA, Article 135. Footnote 8 thereof further clarifies that "loans and other forms of debt, which have been registered to the competent authority of a Party, do not mean trade debts where the debts would be non-interest earning if paid on time without penalty."

17 *Joy Mining Machinery Ltd* v. *Egypt*, ICSID Case No. ARB/03/11, Award on Jurisdiction of 6 August 2004, paras. 29–30, 41–63.

18 US Model BIT 2004, Article 1 and n. 1.

19 Earlier Chinese BITs cover only a few IPRs, such as copyrights, industrial rights, technical processes, and know-how. See Poland–China BIT (1988), Article 1(1).

20 Australia–China BIT, Article 1(1)(v).

21 Finland–China BIT (2004), Article 1(1).

22 The Treaty, Article 1(1)(g)(j).

23 Cambodia–China BIT 1996, Article 1(3); Laos–China BIT 1993, Article 1(3).

24 Kuwait–China BIT, Article 1(1); and New Zealand–China FTA, Article 135.

25 Turkmenistan–China BIT, Article 1(1).

26 Portugal–China BIT (2005), Article 1; Greece–China BIT, Article 19(1)(f).

27 Protocol to the Germany–China BIT (2003), Article 1(b); and the Germany–China BIT, Article 1(1).

28 Argentina–China BIT (1992), Article 1(1).

29 New Zealand–China FTA, Article 149. *Cf. Rompetrol Group BV* v. *Romania*, ICSID Case No. ARB/06/3, Decision on Jurisdiction of 18 April 2008.

30 *CMS Gas Transmission Co.* v. *Republic of Argentina*, ICSID Case No. ARB/01/8, Decision on Objections to Jurisdiction of 17 June 2003, para. 48.

31 *Siemens AG* v. *Republic of Argentina*, ICSID Case No. ARB/02/8, Decision on Jurisdiction of 3 August 2004, para. 137.

32 Germany–China BIT, Article 1(2); and ICSID Convention, Article 25(2)(b).

33 *Tza Yap Shum v Republic of Peru*, ICSID Case No. ARB/07/6, Decision on Jurisdiction and Competence, dated 19 June 2009.

34 As Christoph Schreuer rightly observed, "if you want to invest in China, I suppose it would be wise to do this through a company incorporated in Holland or in Germany for reasons that have to do with recent BITs." T.J. Grierson Weiler (ed), *Investment Treaty Arbitration and International Law*, Vol. 1 (New York: JurisNet, LLC 2008) 129.

35 Rudolf Dolzer and Margrete Stevens, *Bilateral Investment Treaties* (The Hague: Martinus Nijhoff 1995), 63–65, 82–83.

36 United Kingdom–China BIT, Article 3(3).

37 Japan–China BIT (1988), Article 3(2).

38 Ibid., Article 3(3).

39 Agreed Minutes to the Japan–China BIT (1988).

40 Japan–China BIT, Additional Protocol, Article 3.

41 Germany–China BIT, Article 3(2).

42 Germany–China BIT, Additional Protocol, Article 3(2).

43 Cyprus–China BIT, Article 3(3) and Protocol, Article 3.

44 Belgium–Luxembourg–China BIT (2005); Czech Republic–China BIT (2005); Finland–China BIT (2005); Netherlands–China BIT (2005).

45 The Treaty, Article 4.

46 Ibid., Article 6.

47 NAFTA, Article 1102.

48 UNCTAD, *Investor-State Dispute Settlement and Impact on Investment Rulemaking* (United Nations 2008) 48.

49 *SD Myers, Inc.* v. *Canada*, UNCITRAL, First Partial Award of 13 November 2000.

50 *Methanex* v. *United States*, UNCITRAL, Final Award of 3 August 2005, Part IV, Chapter B, para. 19.

51 *SD Myers v. Canada*, First Partial Award of 13 November 2000, para. 250.

52 Mexico–China BIT, Article 3; and New Zealand–China FTA, Article 138.

53 The Treaty, Article 4.

54 New Zealand–China FTA, Article 138.

55 *Cf.* Netherlands–China BIT, Article 3(3); Germany–China BIT, Article 3(2).

56 Belgium–Luxembourg–China BIT (2005); Cyprus–China BIT (2001); Latvia–China BIT (2004).

57 Korea–China BIT (2005), Articles 3(4) and 5(1); Japan–China BIT (1988), Article 4.

58 Kenneth J. Vandevelde, "US Bilateral Investment Treaties: The Second Wave" (1993) 14 *Michigan Journal of International Law* 621; Kenneth J. Vandevelde, "A Brief History of International Investment Agreements" (2005) 12 *UC Davis Journal of International Law and Policy* 157.

59 UK–China BIT (1986), Article 2(1).

60 Uruguay–China BIT, Article 2.

61 Locally, the playing field was indeed tilted in favour of foreign investors. Prior to the promulgation of the PRC Enterprise Income Tax Law, enacted on 16 March 2007 and effective as of 1 January 2008, the income tax rate for a foreign-invested enterprise (FIE) was 15–25% while a much higher tax rate of 33% was applicable to a pure domestic entity. In addition, China also offered a "two-year exemption and three-year half reduction" package to FIEs. Accordingly, an FIE was exempt from corporate income tax in the first two years of making profits and only needed to pay 50% of corporate income tax in the following three years. Unless grandfathered, FIEs are no longer entitled to such preferential tax treatment under the new PRC Enterprise Income Tax Law. FIEs located in national high-tech industrial zones were entitled to a 15% preferential tax rate.

62 *See* www.chinadaily.com.cn/china/2009-09/08/content_8668835.htm and http://hzs.mofcom.gov.cn/aarticle/date/201001/20100106752425.html. *See also,* Daniel H. Rosen and Thilo Hanemann, *China's Changing Outbound Foreign Direct Investment Profile: Drivers and Policy Implication,* Peterson Institute of International Economics Policy Brief No. PB09-14 (2009), available at www.ciaonet.org/pbei/iie/0017250/f_0017250_14753.pdf. According to UNCTAD, the share of outbound FDI from developing countries has increased to an average rate of 14 per cent, and China accounts for 10 per cent of such share. *See* UNCTAD's FDI Online Database.

63 China signed BITs with major Western European countries in the 1980s, and it is in the process of updating BITs with these countries.

64 BITs here include both old and new BITs concluded with developed countries, the Pakistan–China Free Trade Agreement of 24 November 2006 (Chapter 9), the New Zealand–China FTA of 7 April 2008 (Chapter 11), and the Treaty discussed herein.

65 UNCTAD Data Center, available at https://unctadstat.unctad.org/wds/TableViewer/tableView.aspx, accessed 17 September 2020.

66 Based on information available at UNCTAD's Online Database of International Investment Instruments, available at www.unctad.org/templates/page.asp.

67 Qingjiang Kong, "Towards WTO Compliance: China's Foreign Investment Regime in Transition" (2002) 3 *Journal of World Investment* 859–878.

68 PRC Constitution, Article 15.

69 *See generally,* Randall Peerenboom, *China's Long March Toward Rule of Law* (Cambridge: Cambridge University Press 2002).

70 FIL, Article 10.

71 FIL, Article 12.

72 FIL, Article 13.

73 FIL, Article 14.

74 Yawen Zheng, "China's New Foreign Investment Law and Its Contribution Towards the Country's Development Goals" (2021) 22 *Journal of World Investment & Trade* 401.

75 Terence Foo, "China's New Foreign Investment Law – What Does This Mean for Foreign Investors in China?", *Clifford Chance,* 22 March, 2019, available at www.cliffordchance.com/briefings/2019/03/china_s_new_foreigninvestmentlawwhatdoe.html, accessed 25 April 2020.

76 FIL, Article 30; Yawen Zheng, "China's New Foreign Investment Law and Its Contribution Towards the Country's Development Goals" (2021) 22 *Journal of World Investment & Trade* 401–402.

77 FIL, Article 4.

78 Mo Zhang, "Change of Regulatory Scheme: China's New Foreign Investment Law and Reshaped Legal Landscape" (2020) 37 *UCLA Pacific Basin Law Journal* 179.

79 Min Zhao, "Analysis and Interpretation of the New Foreign Investment Law of the People's Republic of China" (2019) 2 *China and WTO Review* 351.

80 Ashurst Corporate Briefing, "The New PRC Foreign Investment Law", 20 March 2019, available at www.ashurst.com/en/news-and-insights/legal-updates/the-new-prc-foreign-investment-law/, accessed 16 July 2019.

81 FIL, Article 15.

82 Ibid., Article 10.

83 US Department of State, "2020 Investment Climate Statements: China", available at www.state.gov/reports/2020-investment-climate-statements/china/, accessed 20 October 2020.

84 FIL, Article 9.

85 Łukasz Czarnecki, "The 2020 Foreign Investment Law of China: Confucianism and New Challenges for Social Development" (2019) 1 *Contemporary Central & East European Law* 94.

86 Xiaojun Li, "Durability of China's Law-making Process under Xi Jinping: A Tale of the Two Foreign Investment Laws" (2020) *Issues and Studies* 1.

87 Ibid.

88 FIL, Article 4.

89 Mo Zhang, "Change of Regulatory Scheme: China's New Foreign Investment Law and Reshaped Legal Landscape" (2020) 37 *UCLA Pacific Basin Law Journal* 179.

90 *See generally* U.N. Conference on Trade and Development, *National Treatment,* UNCTAD/ITE/IIT/11 (Vol. IV) (1999), available at https://authorzilla.com/KW9xV/unctad-ite-iit-11-vol-iv.html

91 Ibid.

92 Ibid.

93 Ibid.

94 FIL, Article 3.

95 Ibid.

96 Ibid.

97 FIL, Article 3.

98 Ibid., Article 90.

99 Ibid., Article 9.

100 Ibid., Article 15.

101 Ibid., Article 16.

102 Ibid., Article 17

103 Ibid.

104 Ibid., Article 31.

105 Ibid., Article 16.

106 Yawen Zheng (n 76), 402.

107 *Parkerings-Compagniet v Lithuania*, ICSID Case No ARB/05/8, Award (11 September 2007) 335.

108 See 2008 Notice of the State Administration of Taxation Regarding the Dealing with Relevant Matters After the Cancellation of Several Former Tax Preferential Policies on Foreign-Invested Enterprises and Foreign Enterprises (effective 5 March 2008).

109 2019 Implementation Regulation of EJVL (effective 2 March 2019) Articles 46–47.

110 Tribunals have held that regulatory changes did not violate the FET in the absence of specific commitments. Therefore, it can be inferred that FET is more likely to be violated with specific commitments made by the authorities. For example *Metalpar and Buen Aire v Argentina*, ICSID Case No ARB/03/5, Award on the Merits (6 June 2008) para 186.

111 *Compañiá de Aguas del Aconquija SA and Vivendi Universal SA v Argentina*, ICSID Case No ARB/97/3 (formerly *Compañía de Aguas del Aconquija, SA and Compagnie Générale des Eaux v Argentina*) Award (20 August 2007) para 7.4.31.
112 Danglun Luo, K.C. Chen and Lifan Wu, "Political Uncertainty and Firm Risk in China" (2017) 7(2) *Review of Development Finance* 85.
113 FIL, Articles 24–25; FIL Implementation Regulation, Article 28.
114 Rudolf Dolzer and Christoph Schreuer, *Principles of International Investment Law* (Oxford: Oxford University Press 2008) 186 (noting that the MFN standard is in "virtually all investment treaties").
115 Laos–China BIT 1993, Article 3(2); Indonesia–China BIT 1994, Article IV(2).
116 *MTD Equity Sdn Bhd and MTD Chile SA* v. *Republic of Chile*, ICSID Case No. ARB/01/7, Award of 25 May 2004, paras. 100 *et seq.*, 197 *et seq.*; *Pope & Talbot Inc.* v. *Canada*, UNCITRAL (NAFTA) Award on the Merits of Phase 2 of 10 April 2001, para. 105 *et seq.*
117 Andrew Newcombe and Lluís Paradell, *Law and Practice of Investment Treaties* (The Netherlands, Kluwer Law International 2009), 193–194.
118 *Cf. Emilio Augustin Maffezini* v. *Spain*, ICSID Case No.ARB/97/17, Decision on Objections to Jurisdiction of 25 January 2000; *Plama Consortium Ltd* v. *Bulgaria*, ICSID Case No. ARB/03/24, Decision on Jurisdiction of 8 February 2005, paras. 183, 200 and 205 (claiming that "the reference must be such that the parties' intention to import the arbitration provision of the other agreement is clear and unambiguous").
119 *Telenor Mobile Communications AS* v. *Republic of Hungary*, ICSID Case No. ARB/04/15, Award of 13 September 2006, para. 81 *et seq.*
120 Slovenia–China BIT (1993), Article 3.
121 Denmark–China BIT (1985), Article 3.
122 New Zealand–China FTA, Article 139.
123 Indonesia–China BIT 1994, Article IV(2).
124 The typical example is Austria–China BIT (1988), Article 3, which has two subsections: one relates to treatment no less favourable for "investments' and the other covers 'investment-related activities".
125 Belgium–Luxembourg–China BIT (2005); Australia–China BIT (1988), Article 3(c).
126 Sweden–China BIT (1982), Article 2(2).
127 The Treaty, Article 5(1).
128 India–Singapore Comprehensive Economic Cooperation Agreement (2005), Article 6.22.1 excludes market access disputes from the ambit of investor-state dispute settlement.
129 Japan–China BIT (1988), Article 2(2).
130 New Zealand–China FTA (2008), Article 139 para. 1.
131 Germany–China BIT (2003), Article 4(3).
132 Norway–China BIT, Article 6(2); Spain–China BIT (1992), Article 6(6).
133 Singapore–China BIT, Article 7; Kuwait–China BIT, Article 7(2).
134 France–China BIT, Article 4; Germany–China BIT (2003), Article 5.
135 Korea–China BIT, Article 4.
136 Germany–China BIT (2003), Article 4(3).
137 Norway–China BIT, Article 6(2); Spain–China BIT (1992), Article 6(6).
138 Singapore–China BIT, Article 7; Kuwait–China BIT, Article 7(2).
139 France–China BIT, Article 4; Germany–China BIT (2003), Article 5.
140 Korea–China BIT, Article 4.
141 Australia–China BIT (1988) is the best example.
142 Ibid., Article 3(3) included all three exceptions.
143 Indonesia–China BIT 1994, Article IV(3).
144 The Philippines–China BIT 1992, Article 3(3).
145 The Treaty, Article 5(3).
146 GATT 1994, Article 24; GATS, Article 5; and WTO Understanding on Article 24 of the GATT 1994.
147 Finland–China BIT (2004).
148 Poland–China BIT (1988).

149 Singapore–China BIT, Article 3(3); Philippines–China BIT, Article 3(3); and Mauritius–China BIT, Article 5.

150 Sweden–China BIT; Kyrgyzstan–China BIT; Ukraine–China BIT; Turkmenistan–China BIT; and Tajikistan–China BIT.

151 The Treaty, Article 6(1) and (2).

152 Czech Republic–China BIT (2005), Article 3(3).

153 Korea–China BIT (1992), Article 3(4); Greece–China BIT, Article 3(3).

154 The main text of CEPA covers three broad areas: trade in goods, trade in services, and trade and investment facilitation. CEPA is a "win-win-win" agreement, bringing new business opportunities to mainland China, Hong Kong, Macau, and all foreign investors. For Hong Kong, CEPA provides a window of opportunity for Hong Kong and Macau qualified businesses to gain greater access to the mainland market. CEPA also benefits mainland China, as Hong Kong or Macau serves as a "springboard" for mainland enterprises to reach out to the global market and accelerates mainland China's full integration with the world economy. CEPA is relevant to multinational investors with significant subsidiaries already established in Hong Kong or Macau. Foreign investors can leverage on the CEPA benefits through a Hong Kong or Macau holding company to explore the vast opportunities of the mainland China market. Similar to the CEPA, mainland China and Taiwan also signed an Economic Cooperation Framework Agreement on 29 June 2010, available at http://en.wikipedia.org/wiki/Economic_Cooperation_Framework_Agreement

155 *Emilio Agustin Maffezini* v. *Kingdom of Spain*, ICSID Case No. ARB/97/7, Decision on Objections to Jurisdiction of 25 January 2000.

156 *RosInvestCo. UK Ltd* v. *Russian Federation*, SCC Case No. Arb. V079/2005.

157 The Treaty, Article 5(4).

158 New Zealand–China FTA, Article 139(2).

159 *See* for example Rudolf Dolzer, "Fair and Equitable Treatment: A Key Standard in Investment Treaties" (2005) 39 *International Law* 87; Barnali Choudhury, "Evolution or Devolution? Defining Fair and Equitable Treatment in International Investment Law" (2005) 6 *Journal of World Investment and Trade* 297; Christoph Schreuer, "Fair and Equitable Treatment in Arbitral Practice" (2005) 6 *Journal of World Investment and Trade* 357.

160 *Waste Management, Inc.* v. *United Mexican States*, ICSID Case No. ARB(AF)/00/3, Award of 30 April 2004, para. 98.

161 Ibid.

162 *Saluka* v. *Czech Republic*, Partial Award of 17 March 2006, para. 291 *et seq.*

163 *CMS* v. *Argentina*, *supra* notes 283 at para. 283; *LG&E* v. *Argentina*, ICSID Case No. ARB/01/8, Award of October 3, 2006, at para 100.

164 *Compania de Aguas del Aconquija, SA and Compagnie Generale des Eaux (Vivendi)* v. *Argentina*, ICSID Case No. ARB/97/3, Award of 21 November 2000, para. 80; *Loewen Group, Inc. and Raymond L. Loewen* v. *United States*, ICSID Case No. ARB(AF)/98/3, Final Award of 26 June 2003, para. 132.

165 Randall Peerenboom, *China's Long March Toward Rule of Law* (Cambridge: Cambridge University Press 2002), 394.

166 World Bank's Worldwide Governance Indicators (WGI) measure six dimensions of governance between 1996 and 2008: voice and accountability, political stability and absence of violence/terrorism, government effectiveness, regulatory quality, rule of law, and control of corruption. *See* Daniel Kaufmann, Aart Kraay and Massimo Mastruzzi, *Governance Matters VIII: Aggregate and Individual Governance Indicators 1996–2008*, World Bank Policy Research Working Paper WPS 4978 (June 2009). However, it should be pointed out that Kaufmann et al. concede the difficulties of assessing trends in a particular country indicator given the large margins of error. The decrease indicated in Figure 7.3 may be attributable to the addition of new data sets and more margins of error. Besides, WGI aggregates results from some other data sources that rely on subjective judgements made by public organizations, private institutions, and NGOs, which may be out of line with objective circumstances and may not necessarily be expert assessments. Also, according to WGI,

China outperforms, or at least performs as well as, the average country in the same income class on these core indicators.

167 Laos–China BIT 1993, Article 3(1); Indonesia–China 1994, Article II(2); Brunei–China BIT 2000, Article 3.
168 Finland–China BIT, Article 3.
169 Sri Lanka–China BIT (1985), Article 3(2); Mauritius–China BIT, Article 3(2).
170 Singapore–China BIT (1985), Article 3(2).
171 Costa Rica–China BIT (2007), Article 3; Seychelles–China BIT (2007), Article 4(1).
172 For instance Finland–China BIT (2004), Article 3(1) removed the domestic law qualification.
173 Daniel Kaufmann, Aart Kraay and Massimo Mastruzzi, *The Worldwide Governance Indicators: Methodology and Analytical Issues*, World Bank Policy Research Working Paper No. 5430 (September 2010), available at https://papers.ssrn.com/sol3/papers.cfm?abstract_id=1682130; http://info.worldbank.org/governance/wgi/Home/Reports.
174 The Treaty, Article 7(1).
175 Stephan W. Schill, *Fair and Equitable Treatment under Investment Treaties as an Embodiment of the Rule of Law*, IILJ Working Paper 06 (2006).
176 New Zealand–China FTA, Article 143(1).
177 United States–Uruguay BIT, Article 5(1)–(3).
178 The Treaty, Article 7(3).
179 UNCTAD, Key Issue I, at p. 213; *Compania de Aguas del Aconquija, SA and Compagnie Generale des Eaux (Vivendi)* v. *Argentina*, ICSID Case No. ARB/97/3, Award of 21 November 2000, para. 80; *Loewen Group, Inc. and Raymond L. Loewen* v. *United States*, ICSID Case No. ARB(AF)98/3, Final Award of 26 June 2003, para. 132.
180 *Saluka Investments BV (The Netherlands)* v. *Czech Republic*, UNCITRAL Arbitration, Partial Award of 17 March 2006, para. 302.
181 *National Grid* v. *Argentina*, 1(17) IAI Reports, 17 December 2008, available at http://ita.law.uvic.ca/documents/NGvArgentina.pdf.
182 *Middle East Cement Shipping and Handling Co. SA* v. *Egypt*, ICSID Case No. ARB/99/6, Award of 12 April 2002, para. 143.
183 *Siemens AG* v. *Argentinean Republic,* ICSID Case No. ARB/02/08, Award of 6 February 2007.
184 The Treaty, Article 7(3).
185 Jean Ho, *State Responsibility for Breaches of Investment Contracts* (Cambridge: Cambridge University Press 2018), 227.
186 FET and the minimum standard of treatment are sometimes interchangeable, but their relationship is disputed for two reasons. First, the FET standard is a stand-alone term mentioned in many BITs, thereby constituting an autonomous rule. Second, there has been no consensus on the content of the minimum standard of treatment either in BIT law or in BIT jurisprudence. Amaud de Nanteull, *International Investment Law* (Edward Elgar 2020) 285.
187 There are China–Japan BIT (1988), China–Czechoslovakia BIT (1991), China–Korea BIT (1992), China–Belarus BIT (1993), and China–Romania BIT (1994).
188 Article 3.2.
189 China–Argentine Republic BIT 1994, Article 3(1); China–India BIT 2007, Article 3(2) (both having the concisely formulated language stating that "each Contracting Party shall at all times ensure fair and equitable treatment to investments"); China–Trinidad and Tobago BIT 2004, Article 3(2) and China–Egypt BIT 1996, Article 3(1) (both providing that foreign investments "shall be accorded fair and equitable treatment").
190 UNCTAD, "Fair and Equitable Treatment: UNCTAD Series on International Investment Agreements II", *New York*, 2012, available at https://unctad.org/system/files/official-document/unctaddiaeia2011d5_en.pdf, accessed 12 June 2020; OECD, "Fair and Equitable Treatment in International Investment Law" [2004] Working Papers on International Investment 2003/2004, available at https://www.oecd-ilibrary.org/

finance-and-investment/fair-and-equitable-treatment-standard-in-international-investment-law_675702255435, accessed 15 June 2020.

191 United Nations Conference on Trade and Development, *Fair and Equitable Treatment: A Sequel* (UN 2012) 1.

192 For example *Técnicas Medioambientales Tecmed v Mexico*, ICSID Case No ARB(AF)/00/2, Award (29 May 2003) 154.

193 Andrew Newcombe and Lluís Paradell, *Law and Practice of Investment Treaties: Standards of Treatment* (London: Kluwer Law International 2009) 280.

194 For example *Enron Corporation and Ponderosa Assets v Argentina*, ICSID Case No ARB/01/3, Award (22 May 2007) 264–66.

195 Newcombe and Paradell (n 193) 286.

196 This is also endorsed by case law, that is *Occidental Exploration and Production Company v. Ecuador*, London Court of International Arbitration, Case No. UN 346, Award of 1 July 2004 (holding that a breach of the fair and equitable treatment obligation amounted to a breach of the protection and security standard also).

197 For example Myanmar–China BIT 2001, Article 2(2).

198 Helge Elisabeth Zeitler, "The Guarantee of 'Full Protection and Security' in Investment Treaties regarding Harm Caused by Private Actors" in (2005) 1 *Stockholm International Arbitration Review* 3.

199 UNCTAD, *Investor-State Dispute Settlement and Impact on Investment Rulemaking* (United Nations 2008), 55.

200 *American Manufacturing and Trading, Inc. (AMT) v. Republic of Zaire*, ICSID Case No. ARB/93/1, Award of 21 February 1997, para. 6.04; *Asian Agricultural Products Ltd (AAPL) v. Republic of Sri Lanka*, ICSID Case No. ARB/87/3, Final Award of 27 June 1990, para. 45.

201 *Azurix v. Argentina*, ICSID Case No. ARB/01/12, Final Award of 14 July 2006.

202 The Treaty, Article 7(2).

203 Indonesia–China BIT 1994, Article II(2).

204 *Compania de Aguas del Aconquija SA and Vivendi Universal v. Argentine Republic*, ICSID Case No. ARB/97/3, Award of 20 August 2007.

205 *Biwater Gauff (Tanzania) Ltd v. Tanzania*, ICSID Case No. ARB/05/22, para. 779.

206 Laurie A. Pinard, "United States Policy regarding Nationalization of American Investments: The People's Republic of China's Nationalization Decree of 1950" (1984) 14 *California Western International Law Journal* 148.

207 Jamil Anderlini and Geoff Dyer, "Beijing Accused of Attacking Private Enterprise" and Geoff Dyer, "Crackdown on Coal Mines Ignites Fears of State Land Grab", *Financial Times*, 26 November 2009, p. 3.

208 Andrew Newcombe, "The Boundaries of Regulatory Expropriation in International Law" (2005) 20(1) *ICSID Review – Foreign Investment Law Journal* 8, 1–58.

209 The Treaty, Article 8(1).

210 *Compania de Aguas del Aconquija SA and Vivendi Universal v. Argentina*, ICSID Case No. ARB/97/3, para 7.5.4; *Waste Management, Inc. v. Mexico*, ICSID Case No. ARB(AF)/00/3, Final Award of 30 April 2004, paras. 163–167; *Parkerings-Compagniet AS v. Lithuania*, ICSID Case No. ARB/05/8.

211 For a general account discussing the concept of indirect expropriation, *see* Newcombe, *supra* note 208 p. 20; Rudolf Dolzer, "Indirect Expropriation of Alien Property" (1986) 1 *ICSID Review – Foreign Investment Law Journal* 41; George C. Christie, "What Constitutes a Taking of Property under International Law?" (1962) 28 *British Yearbook of International Law* 207.

212 Germany–China BIT, Article 4(2); Jordan–China BIT, Article 5(1); Uganda–China BIT, Article 4(1).

213 Mexico–China BIT, Article 7(1).

214 Mauritius–China BIT, Article 6.

215 Indonesia–China BIT, Article 6(1).

216 Germany–China BIT, Article 4(2).
217 *ADC Affiliate Ltd and ADMC Management Ltd* v. *Hungary*, ICSID Case No. ARB/03/16, para. 426; *Waste Management, Inc.* v. *Mexico (No. 2)*, ICSID Case No. ARB(AF)/00/3, Final Award of 20 April 2004, para. 143 (making a distinction between indirect expropriation and measures tantamount to expropriation).
218 *CME Czech Republic BV* v. *Czech Republic*, UNCITRAL Partial Award of 13 September 2001, paras. 6–4.
219 Annex 13 to the New Zealand–China FTA (providing clear interpretative guidelines on what actions constitute expropriation).
220 *LG&E* v. *Argentina*, ICSID Case No. ARB/02/1, para. 185; *Metalpar SA and Buen Aire SA* v. *Argentina*, ICSID Case No. ARB/03/5, para. 173; *Continental Casualty Co.* v. *Argentina*, ICSID Case No. ARB/03/9, para. 284.
221 *Lauder* v. *Czech Republic*, UNCITRAL Award, para. 200.
222 Dolzer and Schreuer, *supra* note 114 at p. 91.
223 For example Singapore–China BIT 1985, Article 6(1); the Philippines–China BIT 1992, Article 4(1); Laos–China BIT 1993, Article 4(1); Indonesia–China 1994, Article VI(1); Cambodia–China BIT 1996, Article 4(1); Brunei–China BIT 2000, Article 4(1); Myanmar–China BIT 2001, Article 4(1).
224 United Kingdom–China BIT, Article 5(1) (only specifying two conditions, that is public interest and reasonable compensation).
225 Italy–China BIT, Article 4(2) (making no reference to non-discriminatory basis and in accordance with the domestic legal system).
226 The Treaty, Article 8(1).
227 Argentina–China BIT, Article 4(1).
228 Philippines–China BIT, Article 4(1).
229 New Zealand–China FTA, Annex 13.
230 The Philippines–China BIT 1992, Article 4(1)(a); Laos–China BIT 1993, Article 4(1)(b); Cambodia–China BIT 1996, Article 4(1)(b); Myanmar–China BIT 2001, Article 4(1)(b).
231 Czech Republic–China BIT.
232 Austria–China BIT; Mexico–China BIT; Sweden–China BIT.
233 New Zealand–China BIT, Article 6(1), Singapore–China BIT, Article 6(1).
234 United Arab Emirates–China BIT, Article 6(1)(b); Guyana–China BIT, Article 4(1)(b); Kuwait–China BIT, Article 5(2).
235 Dolzer and Schreuer, *supra* note 114 at p. 91.
236 United Kingdom–China BIT, Article 5(1).
237 Germany–China BIT.
238 Malcolm N. Shaw, *International Law* (5th edn, Cambridge: Cambridge University Press 2003), 751.
239 *Pope & Talbot Inc.* v. *Canada*, Interim Award of 26 June 2000, para. 99.
240 *See for example* United States–Uruguay BIT, Article 6(1)(c).
241 UN Economic Charter 1974; Francesco Francioni, "Compensation for Nationalization of Foreign Property: The Borderland Between Law and Equity" (1975) 24 *ICLQ* 255.
242 ASEAN Treaty, Article VI(1).
243 NAFTA, Article 1110(2); Energy Charter Treaty, Article 13(1).
244 United Kingdom–USSR BIT; France Model BIT 2006, Article 6(2).
245 Czech Republic–Netherlands BIT, Article 5.
246 World Bank, *Report to the Development Committee and Guidelines on the Treatment of Foreign Direct Investment*, Article IV.3, reproduced in (1992) 31 ILM 1366 (confirming that compensation will be adequate "if it is based on the fair market value of the taken assets").
247 The Philippines–China BIT 1992, Article 1(c); Brunei–China BIT 2000, Article 4(1).
248 Laos–China BIT 1993, Article 4(1)(d).
249 Austria–China BIT, Article 4(1).
250 Mauritius–China BIT, Article 6(1)(c); Zimbabwe–China BIT, Article 4(2); Brunei–China BIT, Article 4(2).
251 Belgium–Luxembourg–China BIT.

252 Australia–China BIT; Barbados–China BIT; Spain–China BIT.

253 Netherlands–China BIT, Article 5(1)(c); Finland–China BIT, Article 4(2); Mexico–China BIT, Article 7(2)(a).

254 *CME Czech Republic BV* v. *Czech Republic*, UNCITRAL Final Award of 14 March 2003, para. 493.

255 Austria–China BIT, Article 4(1).

256 Netherlands–China BIT, Article 5(1)(c); New Zealand–China FTA, Article 145(2); Mexico–China BIT, Article 7(2)(a).

257 Indonesia–China BIT 1994, Article VI(1).

258 The Treaty, Article 8(2).

259 Zimbabwe–China BIT, Article 4(2).

260 Guyana–China BIT.

261 World Bank Guidelines on the Treatment of Foreign Direct Investment, Article IV.5 (1992) 31 ILM 1366; NAFTA, Article 1110(2) (listing a set of criteria that must be taken into account by the tribunal, for example "going concern value, asset value including declared tax value of tangible property, and other criteria, as appropriate to determine fair market value"); *CME Czech Republic BV* v. *Czech Republic*, UNCITRAL Final Award of 14 March 2003, para. 103 (recognizing that a discounted cash flow valuation is the most widely employed approach to the valuation of a going concern).

262 The Treaty, Article 8(2).

263 *See for example* Bulgaria–China BIT; Algeria–China BIT; Syria–China BIT.

264 Rudolf Dolzer and Margrete Stevens, *Bilateral Investment Treaties* (The Hague: Martinus Nijhoff 1995) pp. 112–114.

265 Chile–China BIT; Iceland–China BIT; United Kingdom–China BIT.

266 Jordan–China BIT; New Zealand–China FTA.

267 Denmark–China BIT; Greece–China BIT.

268 India–China BIT.

269 Lebanon–China BIT.

270 Oman–China BIT; Russia–China BIT.

271 The Treaty, Article 8(3).

272 Iceland–China BIT, Article 4.

273 World Bank Guidelines, *supra* notes 261, at Article IV.7.

274 The Treaty, Article 1(1)(b).

275 Article of Agreement of the International Monetary Fund, Article XXX(f).

276 Israel–China BIT, Article 4(1); Laos–China BIT, Article 4(2); Mongolia–China BIT, Article 4(2); Spain–China BIT.

277 Indonesia-China BIT 1994, Article VI(1).

278 Australia–China BIT.

279 Korea–China BIT.

280 Greece–China BIT, Article 4(2).

281 Czech Republic–China BIT, Article 4(3).

282 Markus Perkams, "Piercing the Corporate Veil in International Investment Agreements" in August Reinisch and Christina Knahr (eds), *International Investment Law in Context* (The Hague: Eleven International Publishing 2008), 93, 110.

283 *Gami Investments, Inc.* v. *Mexico*, UNCITRAL Final Award of 15 November 2004, paras. 123–129.

284 The Treaty, Article 1(1)(d)(iii).

285 Robert Bird and Daniel R. Cohay, "The Impact of Compulsory Licensing on Foreign Direct Investment: A Collective Bargaining Approach," (2008) 45 *American Business Law Journal* 283 n. 1; Carlos M. Correa, "Investment Protection in Bilateral and Free Trade Agreements: Implications for the Granting of Compulsory Licenses," (2004) 26 *Michigan Journal of International Law* 346.

286 Ronald A. Cass, *Compulsory Licensing of Intellectual Property: The Exception that Ate the Rule?*, Washington Legal Foundation Working Paper Series No. 150 (2007).

287 *Shell Brands International AG and Shell Nicaragua SA* v. *Republic of Nicaragua*, ICSID Case No. ARB/06/14.

288 Tsai-Yu Lin, "Compulsory Licenses for Access to Medicines, Expropriation and Investor-State Arbitration under Bilateral Investment Agreements: Are There Issues Beyond the TRIPS Agreement?" (2009) 40 *International Review of Intellectual Property Law* 152 (noting that no claim regarding compulsory licences has been brought before investor–state arbitration and led to an arbitral award).

289 Paris Convention on the Protection of Industrial Property, Articles 5A(2), (3), and (4).

290 In terms of "a public purpose," there is recognition in Article 31(b) of the TRIPS Agreement that a national emergency or circumstances of extreme urgency, that is dictated by national security or public health concerns, could justify a compulsory licence. TRIPS Agreement, Article 31(l), (k) on a broader anti-competitive rationale, respectively recognizes a more indirect public purpose, where a compulsory licence may be needed to permit the exploitation of an important "second" ("dependency") patent or to remedy anti-competitive practices.

291 The most important terms include (i) each compulsory licence must be considered on its individual merits; (ii) efforts must have been made to obtain authorization from the rights-holder on reasonable commercial terms and conditions but have failed; (iii) the licence is granted on a non-exclusive and non-assignable basis, with a scope and duration limited to the purpose for which the licence is issued, and it must cease if and when the conditions change to eliminate that purpose; (iv) the licence must be used predominantly for the supply of the domestic market of the authorizing state; and (v) the rights-holder must be paid adequate remuneration in the circumstances of each case, taking into account the economic value of the authorization. *See* TRIPS Agreement, Article 31(a)–(h).

292 WTO, Doha Declaration on the TRIPS Agreement and Public Health, adopted on 14 November 2001, WT/MIN(01)/DEC/2 (20 November 2001).

293 Carlos M. Correa, "Investment Protection in Bilateral and Free Trade Agreements: Implications for the Granting of Compulsory Licenses" (2004) 26 *Michigan Journal of International Law* 348.

294 *Starrett Housing Corp.* v. *Islamic Republic of Iran* (1983) 4 Iran–US CTR 122 at p. 154.

295 The Treaty, Article 8(6).

296 United States–Uruguay BIT, Article 6(5).

297 *See* U.N. Conference on Trade and Development, Expropriation: UNCTAD Series on Issues in International Investment Agreement 11 (2012), available at https://unctad.org/en/Docs/unctaddiaeia2011d7_en.pdf.

298 *See id.*, at 6–7.

299 *See* Ralph Folsom, Michael Gordon, John Spanogle, Peter Fitzgerald and Michael Van Alstine, *International Business Transactions: A Problem-Oriented Coursebook* 1077 (7th ed. Saint Paul, Minnesota: West Academic Publishing 2012).

300 *See* UNCTAD, Expropriation, Introduction, 9 October 2017, https://investment-policy.unctad.org/uploaded-files/document/Conference%20flow%20pp%208%20Oct%20(AU)_final.pdf.

301 *See* the EJV Law (as amended), Article 2.

302 FIL, Articles 20–27.

303 Ibid., Article 20.

304 Ibid., Article 21.

305 Ibid., Article 22.

306 Min Zhao, "Analysis and Interpretation of the New Foreign Investment Law of the People's Republic of China" (2019) 2 *China and WTO Review* 351.

307 FIL, Article 22.

308 Article 23.

309 Such rules should also not increase obligations, set market access or exit conditions, and interfere with normal business activities affecting foreign investments. See FIL, Article 24.

310 Muruga P. Ramaswamy, "The Impact of the New Chinese Foreign Investment Law 2019 on the Administrative Legal System Governing Foreign Investments and

Implications for the Investment Relations with Lusophone Markets" (2019) 9(2) *Juridical Tribune* 330.

311 Z. Alex Zhang and Vivian Tsoi, "China Adopts New Foreign Investment Law" *White & Case*, 29 March 2019, available at www.whitecase.com/publications/alert/china-adopts-new-foreign-investment-law, accessed 25 April 2022.

312 FIL, Article 20.

313 *See id.*

314 *See id.*

315 *See* the Implementation Regulations, Article 20.

316 *See id.*

317 Requisition commonly refers to a taking or seizure of property by government. *Requisition*, Black's Law Dictionary (6th ed. 1994). In the MOFCOM Draft, requisition was defined as taking foreign an investor or FIE's movable or non-movable property located with the territory of China under the provisions of the law for such emergent needs as rescues or disaster reliefs. *See* MOFCOM Draft, Article 112.

318 See Property Law of China (promulgated by the Fifth Session of the Tenth Nat'l People's Cong., 16 March 2007 effective 1 October 2007), Article 42. An English version of the Property Law is available at https://english.www.gov.cn/services/investment/2014/08/23/content_281474982978047.htm.

319 Mo Zhang, *supra* note 89, 213.

320 See "Legislators: The FIE Legislation Shall Clarify the 'Extraordinary Circumstances' for Expropriation of Foreign Investments," *Beijing News Report* (26 December 2018), available at www.bjnews.com.cn/news/2018/12/27/534228.html.

321 *See* Mo Zhang, "From Public to Private: the Newly Enacted Chinese Property Law and Protection of Property Rights in China" (2008) 5 *Berkeley Business Law Journal* 317, 361.

322 *See id.* at 361. There is a factor-based methodology proposed by some scholars in China to help identify public interests for purposes of expropriation. The factors to consider include (i) scope of beneficiaries, (ii) burden on the general public, (iii) priority of the interests involved, and (iv) availability of alternatives.

323 *See* Maurice Wise, "The Judicial Nature of Requisition" (1945) 6 *University of Toronto Law Journal* 58.

324 *See* Yao Hong (ed), *Detailed Explanations of the Property Law of the People's Republic of China*, 74 (Beijing: People's Publisher 2007).

325 Rudolf Dolzer and Margrete Stevens, *Bilateral Investment Treaties* (The Hague: Martinus Nijhoff 1995), p. 85.

326 Kenneth J. Vandevelde, *United States Investment Treaties: Policy and Practice* (Deventer: Kluwer 1992), 143.

327 United Kingdom–China BIT, Article 6(4).

328 The Treaty, Article 10(1).

329 *See for example* Korea–China BIT.

330 Finland–China BIT, Article 6(1); Turkey–China BIT, Article IV.

331 The Treaty, Article 10(1).

332 Ibid., Article 10(1)(b), (c).

333 Ibid., Article 10(1)(a).

334 Mexico–China BIT, Article 8(1)(a); Portugal–China BIT.

335 The Treaty, Articles 10(1)(f), (d), and (b) respectively.

336 Ibid., Article 10(1)(e).

337 Dolzer and Schreuer, *supra* note 114 at p. 193.

338 The Treaty, Article 10(1)(e).

339 Indonesia–China BIT, Article VII(1)(h).

340 Malaysia–China BIT, Article 6(1)(e).

341 Cyprus–China BIT, Article 6(1)(h); Norway–China BIT, Article 6(1)(d).

342 The Treaty, Article 10(a)(g).

343 Indonesia–China BIT 1994, Article VII(2).

344 The Treaty, Article 10(1).
345 The Energy Charter Treaty defines "freely convertible currency" as a currency which is "widely traded in international foreign exchange markets and widely used in international transactions". However, the Energy Charter Treaty does not specify any "freely convertible currency". Article 1.1(e) of the Egypt–Malaysia BIT defines "freely usable currency" as the "US dollars, pound sterling, Deutschemark, French Franc, Japanese yen and any other currency that is widely used to make payments for international transactions".
346 Article of Agreement of the International Monetary Fund, Article XXX(f).
347 UNCTAD, *supra* notes 300 p. 60.
348 Portugal–China BIT, Article 6(2).
349 The Philippines–China BIT 1992, Article 6 ("at the official rate of exchange prevailing at the time of transfer"); Malaysia–China BIT; Denmark–China BIT (without any reference to host state).
350 Czech Republic–China BIT.
351 Brunei-China BIT 2000, Article 6(2); Benin–China BIT, Article 6(4); Finland–China BIT, Article 6(4); New Zealand–China FTA, Article 142(2).
352 Ghana–China BIT, Article 6(1).
353 Indonesia-China BIT 1994, Article VII(2). Accordingly, the transfer "shall be made at the prevailing rate of exchange on the date of transfer with respect to current transaction in the currency to be transferred".
354 Laos–China BIT 1993, Article 5(2); Cambodia–China BIT 1996, Article 6(2); Brunei–China BIT 2000, Article 6(2); Myanmar–China BIT 2001, Article 6(3).
355 Singapore–China BIT 1985, Article 8(1).
356 Brunei–China BIT, Protocol, Article 6; Korea–China BIT, Protocol, Article 6.
357 France–China BIT, Protocol, para. 3.
358 Bulgaria–China BIT; Oman–China BIT; Ukraine–China BIT; and Yemen–China BIT.
359 Slovenia–China BIT, Article 5.
360 Yugoslavia–China BIT.
361 For example Finland–China BIT, Article 6.
362 Singapore-China BIT 1985, Article 8(1); Djibouti–China BIT, Article 6.
363 The Treaty, Article 10(3) and (4).
364 Ibid., Article 10(4).
365 Ibid., Article 10(3).
366 China has removed all restrictions on current account transactions according to Article VIII of the IMF Agreement. For the accounts of Chinese foreign exchange control on outbound and inbound investments, *see* Shen Wei, "Is SAFE Safe Now? – Foreign Exchange Regulatory Control Over Chinese Outbound and Inbound Investments and a Political Economy Analysis of Policies" (2010) 11(2) *Journal of World Investment and Trade* 227–258.
367 Germany–China BIT, Protocol, Article 6(a).
368 Germany–China BIT, Article 6(3); Ad Article 6(b).
369 Oman–China BIT, Article 6(2); Norway–China BIT.
370 The Treaty, Article 10(2).
371 Uganda–China BIT.
372 Michael D. Goldhaber, "Big Arbitrations" in *Focus Europe*, Summer 2003, at 22, available at https://www.transnational-dispute-management.com/article.asp?key=236.
373 The Treaty, Article 10(5).
374 Ibid., Article 10(5)(c).
375 Ibid., Article 10(5)(c).
376 Ibid., Article 11(1).
377 Ibid., Article 10(5)(c).
378 Ibid., Article 10(5)(b).
379 Ibid., Article 10(5)(a).
380 Ibid., Article 11(3).
381 Ibid., Article 11(2).

382 Ibid., Article 11(1).

383 Ibid., Article 10(5).

384 Ibid., Article 21.

385 See the FIL Implementation Regulation (n 85) Article 22. Under Article 22, the free remittance also applies to salaries and other lawful incomes earned by foreign employees, or employees from Hong Kong, Macau, or Taiwan working in an FIE.

386 See Dezan Shira, "Pre Investment Capital Planning for China's Foreign Exchange Control", *China Briefing*, 13 February 2018, available at www.china-briefing.com/news/pre-investment-capital-planning-for-chinas-foreign-exchange-control.

387 The Foreign Exchange Regulation was adopted by the State Council on 29 January 1996, and amended on 1 August 2008, available at https://www.registrationchina.com/articles/law/china-foreign-exchange-control-regulations/.

388 McDermott Will & Emery, "China's New Foreign Investment Law: What's New and What's Next" *McDermott Will & Emery*, 9 April 2019, available at https://www.mwe.com/insights/chinas-new-foreign-investment-law-whats-new-and-whats-next/, accessed 25 April 2022.

389 FIL, Article 21; Jones Day, "China Further Opens its Market with New 'Foreign Investment Law,'" *Jones Day*, February 2020, available at www.jonesday.com/en/insights/2020/02/chinas-new-foreign-investment-law, accessed 25 April 2022.

390 McDermott Will & Emery, "China's New Foreign Investment Law: What's New and What's Next," *McDermott Will & Emery*, 9 April 2019, available at https://www.mwe.com/insights/chinas-new-foreign-investment-law-whats-new-and-whats-next/, accessed 25 April 2022.

391 FIL, Article 22.

392 Mo Zhang, "Change of Regulatory Scheme: China's New Foreign Investment Law and Reshaped Legal Landscape" (2020) 37 *Pacific Basin Law Journal* 179, 235.

393 Mark Schaub, Atticus Zhao, Dai Xueyun and Zheng Wei, "China Foreign Investment Law: How Will It Impact the Existing FIEs?" *King & Wood Mallesons*, 3 June 2019, available at www.chinalawinsight.com/2019/06/articles/foreign-investment/china-foreign-investment-law

394 PriceWaterhouseCoopers, "China Welcomes Investors with New Foreign Investment Law", *News Flash*, 13 February 2020, available at https://thesuite.pwc.com/media/10831/china-foreign-investment-law-feb2020-en.pdf, accessed 25 April 2022.

395 For instance a relatively outdated Bilateral Investment Treaty between China and Japan of 1998 entitles Japanese-owned investments in China to treatment on a par with other foreign investments.

396 Even the new BIT between Germany and China may not be at the same level of protection provided by the BIT entered into by the US. The US investment treaties generally cover state-owned companies as well as national and local authorities, impose transparency obligations on regulatory agencies, and prohibit technology transfer and other performance requirements on investors. These terms are not acceptable to the Chinese government.

397 For example Thailand–China BIT, Article 10.

398 Singapore–China BIT, Article 13(3).

399 China entered into new-generation BITs with Belgium, Cyprus, Czech Republic, Finland, Germany, Latvia, Portugal, Slovakia, Spain, and Sweden. See United Nations Conference on Trade and Development at www.unctad.org.

400 Congyan Cai, "Outward Foreign Direct Investment Protection and the Effectiveness of Chinese BIT Practice" (2006) 7(5) *Journal of World Investment & Trade* 621, 646.

401 Ibid.

402 An Chen, *supra* note 2, 771–795.

403 Julian D.M. Lew, Loukas Mistelis and Stefan Kroll, *Comparative International Commercial Arbitration* (Alphen aan den Rijn, the Netherlands: Kluwer Law International 2003) paras 28–32.

404 Uganda–China BIT, Article 8(2).

405 Malaysia–China BIT, Article 7(3); and United Arab Emirates–China BIT, Article 9(2) (a) and (b).

406 Poland–China BIT 1998, Article 10(1).

407 The one-year waiting period may be eliminated if the investor relies on the most-favoured-nation treatment obligation. *Emilio Agustin Maffezini v Kingdom of Spain*, ICSID Case No. ARB/97/7, Award on Merits, 13 November 2000.

408 ICSID Convention, Article 26 (the first sentence of which states that "consent of the parties to arbitration under this Convention shall, unless otherwise stated, be deemed consent to such arbitration to the exclusion of any other remedies.")

409 Tunisia–China BIT, Article 9(2); Bosnia Herzegovina–China BIT, Article 8(2).

410 Cambodia–China BIT, Article 9(2).

411 The New Zealand–China FTA was signed on 7 April 2008 and came into force on 1 October 2008. The FTA not only extends to both goods (Chapter 3) and services (Chapter 9) but also contains an investment chapter (Chapter 11).

412 Ibid., Article 153(1).

413 The Energy Charter Treaty, Article 26(4).

414 The Treaty, Article 14(4)(b) and (c).

415 Rudolf Dolzer and Christoph Schreuer, *Principles of International Investment Law* (New York: Oxford University Press 2008), 228.

416 Cuba–China BIT, Article 9(4).

417 The Philippine–China BIT, Article 10(3).

418 Kuwait–China BIT, Article 8(3); the Protocol to the Norway–China BIT, Article 2(d); and Protocol to the Austria–China BIT, Article 4.

419 Ghana–China BIT, Article 10(2) and (3).

420 The Treaty, Article 14(4).

421 *Southern Pacific Properties Inc. v. Egypt*, ICSID Case No. ARB/84/3, Decision on Jurisdiction of 27 November 1985, 3 ICSID Reports 112, 137–145, 149–162 (1995).

422 Ibid. para. 83.

423 United Nations Conference on Trade and Development, *Investor-State Dispute Settlement* (2003) 33, 34; Zachary Douglas, "The Hybrid Foundations of Investment Treaty Arbitration" (2003) 74 *British Yearbook of International Law* 151, 179.

424 *Elettronica Sicula S.p.A.* (United States v. Italy), Judgment of 20 July 1989.

425 The Treaty, Article 14(5).

426 Uganda–China BIT, Article 8(2)(b).

427 The Protocol to the Latvia–China BIT, Article 9.

428 *Emilio Agustin Maffezini v the Kingdom of Spain*, ICSID Case No. ARB/97/7.

429 Sweden–China BIT 1982, Article 6.

430 Cambodia–China BIT 1996, Chile-China BIT 1994.

431 Singapore–China BIT 1985, Article 13(3).

432 Note of the Swedish Ambassador to China addressed to the Chinese Vice-Minister of Economics concerning the Sweden–China Agreement on the Mutual Protection of Investment dated 29 March 1982, available at https://edit.wti.org/document/show/pdf/a6d6d6eb-5198-4dab-a881-fbd8c8c4c69b.

433 The Slovenia–China BIT 1993, Article 8(2)(3).

434 Article 9.

435 Article IX.

436 Article 9.

437 Article 8, s 2.

438 Article 9, s 3.

439 Pakistan–China BIT, Article 10.

440 UK–China BIT 1986, Article 7; the Switzerland–China BIT 1987, Article 12.

441 See generally, Lucy Reed, Jan Paulsson and Nigel Blackaby, *Guide to ICSID Arbitration* (The Netherlands: Kluwer Law International 2004).

442 Christoph H. Schreuer, *The ICSID Convention: A Commentary* (Cambridge: Cambridge University Press 2001) paras 241–427; Report of the Executive Directors of the World Bank on the Convention (1993) 1 ICSID Rep 28.

443 ICSID Convention, Article 25, first sentence.
444 ICSID Convention, Article 25.
445 *Ceskoslovenska Obchodni Banka, AS v the Slovak Republic*, ICSID Case No. ARB/97/4, paras 49–59.
446 *Southern Pacific Properties Limited v. Egypt*, ICSID Case No. ARB/84/3, Decision on Jurisdiction of 27 November 1985, paras. 56–57, 116. 3 ICSID Reports 112, 137–145, 149–162 (1995).
447 *Asian Agricultural Products Ltd. v. Republic of Sri Lanka*, ICSID Case No. ARB/87/3 (1991) International Arbitration Report 6(5) 1. This is the first case in which ICSID tribunal found jurisdiction on the basis of an article on dispute settlement in a BIT submitting future disputes between a state party and a national of the other state party to ICSID for settlement.
448 Christoph H. Schreuer, *supra* note442, Article 25, paras 241–319.
449 *Ceskoslovenska Obchodni Banka, AS v. Slovakia*, ICSID Case No. ARB/94/7, Decision on Jurisdiction of 24 May 1999, para. 35.
450 *Autopista Concesionada de Venezuela, CA v Venezuela*, ICSID Case No. ARB/00/5, para 95; Executive Directors' Report, Report of the Executive Directors of the International Bank for Reconstruction and Development on the Convention on the Settlement of Investment Disputes between States and Nationals of Other States, 1 ICSID Reports 28 (1993); (1966) 60 *American Journal of International Law* 892; (1965) ILM 4, 524, available at www.worldbank.org/icsid/basicdoc/partB.htm
451 Model clauses are available at www.worldbank.org/icsid/model-clauses-en/main-eng.htm
452 Indonesia–China BIT, Article 9(3).
453 Cambodia–China BIT, Article 9(3).
454 Myanmar–China BIT, Article 9(3).
455 Cambodia–China BIT, Article 9(4); Qatar–China BIT, Article 9(4) and Iran–China BIT, Article 12(4).
456 Article 9(4) and (5).
457 Article 9(4) and (5).
458 Article 9(4) and (5).
459 Article IX(3) a and b.
460 Article 8(4) and (5).
461 Article 9(5) and (6).
462 Article 8(4) and (5).
463 Singapore–China BIT, Article 13(6).
464 Peru–China BIT 1994, Article 8(3).
465 Chile–China BIT 1994, Article 9(3), and Iceland–China BIT 1994, Article 8(3).
466 Protocol to the Hungary–China BIT.
467 Australia–China BIT, Article XII(4).
468 Belgo–Luxembourg–China BIT, Article 8(2); Mexico–China BIT, Article 14.
469 Israel–China BIT, Article 8(1)(a).
470 The Netherlands–China BIT 2003, Article 10(3).
471 Germany–China BIT 2003, Article 9(3); the Finland–China BIT 2003, Article 9.
472 Report of the Executive Directors on the Convention on the Settlement of Investment Disputes between the States and Nationals of Other States, ICSID Doc 2, 18 March 1965, para 24.
473 The Treaty, Article 14(4)(b).
474 The Treaty, Article 14(4).
475 *Ethyl Corporation v Canada*, Decision on Jurisdiction dated 24 June 1998 (1998) ILM 38, 708; Christoph H. Schreuer, *supra* note 442, Article 25, para 303.
476 Jan Paulsson, "Arbitration Without Privity" (1995) 10(2) *ICSID Review – Foreign Investment Law Journal*, 247.
477 The Treaty, Article 14(3).
478 Singapore–China BIT, Article 13(1).
479 The Philippines–China BIT, Article 10(1).

480 Indonesia–China BIT, Article 9(1).

481 The Treaty, Article 14(4).

482 Singapore–China BIT 1985, Article 13(3).

483 Christoph H. Schreuer, "Travelling the BIT Route: Of Waiting Periods, Umbrella Clauses and Forks in the Road" (2004) 5 *Journal of World Investment and Trade* 231, 232.

484 *Ronald S. Lauder v Czech Republic*, Final Award, UNCITRAL, para 187; *SGS Societe Generale de Surveillance SA v Pakistan*, ICSID Case No. ARB/01/13, para 184.

485 *Bayindir Insaat Turizm Ticaret Ve Sanayi AS v Pakistan*, ICSID Case No. ARB/03/29.

486 *Lauder v. Czech Republic*, Final Award, paras 187–191 (2001) (in which the claimant waited only 17 days before filing the request for arbitration), available at https://www.italaw.com/ cases/documents/611; *Ethyl Corp. v. Canada*, paras 74–88, 38 I.L.M. 708 (1999) (in which the claimant only waited for 9 days before filing its request for arbitration and its claim was not barred for failure to abide by the procedural rules set out in the BIT).

487 *Goetz v Burundi*, ICSID Case No. ARB/95/3 and *Enron Corporation and Ponderosa Assets, LP v Argentina*, ICSID Case No. ARB/01/3.

488 Rudolf Dolzer and Christoph Schreuer, *supra* note 114, 248.

489 Pakistan–China BIT, Article 10. Similar provisions also appear in the Malaysia–China BIT, Article 7(1) and Poland–China BIT, Article 10(1).

490 The NZ–China FTA, Article 152.

491 *Goetz and others v. Burundi*, ICSID Case No. ARB/95/3, Award (Embodying the Parties' Settlement Agreement) 10 February 1999; Christoph H. Schreuer, *supra* note 442, 237.

492 Pakistan–China BIT, Article 10 (under which an investor seeking to challenge the amount of compensation for an expropriated investment may file a complaint with the competent authority of the Contracting Party. If the matter is not resolved within a year, the investor can request either the competent national court or an international tribunal to review the amount of compensation).

493 Christoph H. Schreuer, *supra* note 442, para. 46.

494 Mongolia–China BIT, Article 8; Vietnam–China BIT, Article 8(3); Uruguay–China BIT, Article 9(3); Turkey–China BIT, Article VII(b); Peru–China BIT, Article 8(3); Lebanon–China BIT, Article 8(3).

495 See section 8.

496 Note of the Swedish Ambassador to China addressed to the Chinese Vice-Minister of Economics in relation to the Sweden-China Agreement on the Mutual Protection of Investments of 29 March 1982, available at https://edit.wti.org/document/show/pdf/ a6d6d6eb-5198-4dab-a881-fbd8c8c4c69b, at 6.

497 Indonesia–China BIT, Article IX(3).

498 *European Media Venture SA v Czech Republic,* UNCITRAL Award on Jurisdiction, 15 May 2007; *The Czech Republic v European Media Ventures SA* [2007] EWHC 2851.

499 Qatar–China BIT, Article 9(3).

500 Lebanon–China BIT, Article 9(3).

501 Greece–China BIT, Article 10(2); Kuwait–China BIT, Article 8(3); the Philippines–China BIT, Article 10(2)(b); Turkey–China BIT, Article 9(3).

502 Lithuania–China BIT 1993, Article 8(2)(b).

503 The Philippines–China BIT, Article 10(2)(b).

504 ICSID Convention, Article 25(4).

505 The text of the declaration is available at www.worldbank.org/icsid/pubs/icsid-8/ icsid-8.d.htm

506 *Kaiser Bauxite Co. v. Jamaica*, ICSID Case No. 74/3, Decision on Jurisdiction of 6 July 1975, 1 ICSID Reports. 296, 303 (1999).

507 Christoph H. Schreuer, *supra* note 442, Article 25, para 626.

508 ICSID, Report of the Executive Directors on the Convention of the Settlement of Investment Disputes between States and Nationals of Other States, para. 31, available at https://icsid.worldbank.org/sites/default/files/Report_Executive_Directors.pdf.

509 *Kaiser Bauxite Co. v. Jamaica*, ICSID Case No. 74/3, Decision on Jurisdiction of 6 July 1975.

510 Christoph H. Schreuer, *supra* note 442, Article 25, para 625.

511 Under OECD's Multilateral Agreement on Investment, the member state is not able to make any reservation or exception to the consent. However, the OECD's Multilateral Agreement on Investment allows the state to withhold its consent in cases in which the investor has previously submitted to local remedies.

512 South Korea–China BIT 1992, Article 9(10).

513 Congyan Cai, *supra* note 400.

514 The Vienna Convention on the Law of Treaties, Articles 30(3) and (4)(a) (confirming that the earlier treaty applies only to the extent that its provisions are compatible with those of the later treaty).

515 Jordan–China BIT, the Belgium–China BIT, and the Luxembourg–China BIT.

516 Christoph H. Schreuer, *supra* note 442, paras. 39–42.

517 *Azurix Corp v. Argentine Republic, Decision on Jurisdiction*, ICSID Case No. ARB/01/12, para 58; *El Paso Energy International Company v Argentina*, Decision on Jurisdiction, ICSID Case No. ARB/03/15, paras 61–2; and *Saipem SpA v People's Republic of Bangladesh*, ICSID Case No. ARB/05/7, para 95.

518 Barbados–China BIT 1998.

519 Botswana–China BIT, Article 9.

520 Australia–China BIT, Article XII(1).

521 Ibid., Article XII(1), paragraph 2(b).

522 The NZ–China FTA, Article 135.

523 Guyana–China BIT, Article 10(1).

524 Czech Republic–China BIT 2005, Article 9(2).

525 *Salini Construtorri SpA and Italstrate SpA v Morocco*, ICSID Case No. ARB/00/4, para 8.

526 *SGS Societe Generale de Surveillance SA v. Islamic Republic of Pakistan*, ICSID Case No. ARB/01/13, para 161.

527 *SGS Societe Generale de Surveillance SA v. Republic of the Philippines*, ICSID Case No. ARB/02/6, para 135.

528 *Salini Construtorri SpA and Italstrate SpA v Morocco*, ICSID Case No. ARB/00/4, para 61; *SGS Societe Generale de Surveillance SA v. Republic of the Philippines*, ICSID Case No. ARB/02/6, para 135.

529 The Treaty, Article 14(1).

530 ICSID Convention, Article 25(1).

531 *European Media Ventures v Czech Republic* [2007] EWHC 2851 (Comm).

532 The NZ–China FTA, Article 153(2).

533 *American Mfg. & Trading, Inc. v. Zaire*, ICSID Case No. ARB/93/1, Award of 21 February 1997, 36 ILM 1531, 1544–46, 1548 (1997).

534 Ibid.

535 *Ceskoslovenska Obchodni Banka, AS v. Slovakia*, ICSID Case ARB/94/7, Decision on Jurisdiction of 24 May 1999, para. 37.

536 Ibid. para 33.

537 The Treaty, Article 14(4).

538 NAFTA, Articles 1116(2) and 1117(2).

539 *Grand River Enterprises, Six Nations Ltd & Others v USA*, UNCITRAL Arbitration, Decision on Jurisdiction, 20 July 2006, para 103.

540 The New Zealand–China FTA, Article 154(1).

541 The Treaty, Article 14(6)(a).

542 Campbell McLachlan, Laurence Shore and Matthew Weiniger, *International Investment Arbitration: Substantive Principles* (New York: Oxford University Press 2007) para 4.75.

543 *Maffezini v Spain*, ICSID Case No. ARB/97/7 Jurisdiction Award.

544 *Azurix Corp v The Argentine Republic*, ICSID Case No. ARB/01/12, Decision on Jurisdiction of 8 December 2003, para 90.

545 *Gami Investments v The Government of the United Mexican States*, UNCITRAL Final Award of 15 November 2004, para 37.

546 *LG&E Energy Corp., LG&E Capital Corp. and LG&E International, Inc. v Argentine Republic*, ICSID Case No. ARB/01/1, Decision on Jurisdiction of 30 April 2004, para 76; *Enron*

Corporation and Ponderosa Assets, L.P. v The Argentine Republic, ICSID Case No. ARB/01/3, Decision on Jurisdiction of 14 January 2004, para 95.

547 Jordan–China BIT, Article 10(2), Botswana–China BIT, Article 9(3); Guyana–China BIT, Article 10(4).

548 Argentina–China BIT 1992, Article 8(3).

549 Russia–China BIT (2006) Protocol Ad Article 9.

550 Czech Republic–China BIT 2005, Article 9(4).

551 New Zealand–China FTA, Article 153(3).

552 Mexico–China BIT, Article 13(4).

553 The Treaty, Article 14(5).

554 The Treaty, Article 14(5), the first sentence.

555 Markus A. Petsche, "The Fork in the Road Revisited: An Attempt to Overcome the Clash between Formalistic and Pragmatic Approaches" (2019) 18 *Washington University Global Studies Law Review* 391.

556 China–ASEAN FTA (2009), Article 14.5.

557 Shu Zhang, "Developing China's Investor-State Arbitration Clause: Discussions in the Context of the 'Belt and Road' Initiative", in Wenhua Shan, Kimmo Nuotio and Kangle Zhang (eds), *Normative Readings of the Belt and Road Initiative-Road to New Paradigms* (New York: Springer International Publishing AG 2018) 160–161.

558 An Chen, *supra* note 2, 899–933.

559 Malcolm N. Shaw, *International Law* (Cambridge: Cambridge University Press, 5th edn 2003) 730; Ian Brownlie, *Principles of Public International Law* (Cambridge: Cambridge University Press, 7th edn 2008) 472.

560 M. Sornarajah, *International Law on Foreign Investment* (Cambridge: Cambridge University Press, 2nd edn 2004) 254.

561 *Norwegian Loans* Case [1957] ICJ Reports 9; *Interhandel* Case [1959] ICJ Reports 6.

562 ICSID Convention, Article 26, first sentence.

563 ICSID Convention, Article 26, second sentence.

564 Christoph H. Schreuer, *supra* note 442, Article 26, para 42.

565 Singapore–China BIT, Article 13(2).

566 Indonesia–China BIT, Article 9(2).

567 Peru–China BIT, Article 8(2).

568 For example Canada–the Philippines BIT 1995.

569 Chittharanjan Felix Amerasinghe, *Local Remedies in International Law* (Cambridge: Cambridge University Press 1990) 252.

570 Barbados–China BIT, Article 2(a)(b).

571 The Protocol of the Germany–China BIT 2003, Article 6(a); Germany–China BIT 2003, Article 9.

572 Cambodia–China BIT, Article 9(2).

573 Myanmar–China BIT, Article 9(2).

574 Czech Republic–China BIT, Article 9(3).

575 Russia–China BIT, Protocol, Ad Article 9(2).

576 Finland–China BIT 2004, Protocol Ad Article 9. Other Chinese BITs incorporating a three-month period are Belgium–China BIT 2005, Luxembourg–China BIT 2005, Latvia–China BIT 2004, Netherlands–China BIT 2001, and Spain–China BIT 2005.

577 The Treaty, Article 14(6)(b).

578 The Treaty, Article 14(6)(b).

579 The Treaty, Article 14(6)(b).

580 The Treaty, Article 14(7).

581 The Treaty, Article 14(7).

582 The Treaty, Article 14(5), the first sentence.

583 The Treaty, Article 14(8).

584 The Treaty, Article 14(8).

585 See Matthew C. Porterfield, "Exhaustion of Local Remedies in Investor-State Dispute Settlement" (2015) 41 *Yale Journal of International Law Online* 1, 5.

586 See Manjiao Chi & Xi Wang, "The Evolution of ISA Clauses in Chinese IIAs and Its Practical Implications" (2015) 16 *Journal of World Investment and Trade* 869, 890–891.

587 China–ASEAN FTA (2009), Article 14.4.

588 See Shen Wei, "Is This a Great Leap Forward? A Comparative Review of the Investor-State Arbitration Clause in the ASEAN-China Investment Treaty: From BIT Jurisprudential and Practical Perspectives" (2010) 27 *Journal of International Arbitration* 379, 417–418.

589 China–Cyprus BIT (2001), Article 9 and the Protocols.

590 China–Malta BIT (2009), Article 9.

591 The opposite view is that the nation-state is no longer a meaningful unit of social organization. See generally, Kenichi Ohmae, *The End of the Nation State: The Rise of Regional Economies* (New York: Simon and Schuster Inc Publisher 1995).

8

NATIONAL SECURITY REVIEW IN FOREIGN INVESTMENTS

A Comparative Context

1. Introduction

M&A transactions are one of the most important means through which foreign investors gain presence in a host country. In the United States, while mergers and acquisitions of US companies represent a small percentage of total foreign investment influx,[1] they had sizeable deal values of over $1 trillion during each peak year.[2]

Compared to greenfield investments, where foreign investors start on a clean slate, cross-border M&A activities have a greater impact on the host country in that foreign investors obtain an ideal conduit through which critical technology, know-how, sensitive information pertaining to existing client base, and market share are transferred. The other side of the coin, however, is that cross-border M&A transactions may become the Trojan Horse of foreign political goals, raising concerns on the national security of the host country. Thus, one of the regulatory challenges posed is national security concern accompanying the inflow of foreign capital in critical sectors. In response, regulators tend to initiate national security review as a regulatory instrument to scrutinize proposed cross-border M&A transactions.

National security review is a significant yet understudied regime in the regulatory framework governing foreign investment.[3] For law practitioners, national security review has become an increasingly important apparatus in any investment policy. For policy makers, the institutional design for national security requires a delicate balance between openness to foreign investment and protection of national security. In the trend towards globalization and free trade, most jurisdictions with national security review systems strive to avoid either extreme of the spectrum: unequivocal support of foreign investment or absolute protectionism. But where to draw the line between has always been a policy question.

DOI: 10.4324/9781003130499-8

The US national security review rubric, including most notably the Committee on Foreign Investment in the United States (CFIUS), has gained prominence over the years.[4] This is in part because of the heightened role that CFIUS has played,[5] represented in its expanding mandate and surge in enforcement activities. In comparison, China's national security review regime, modelled on that of the United States,[6] is relatively new on the horizon.

This chapter adopts a comparative perspective to evaluate the national security review regimes in the United States and China, the top two host countries for foreign investment in terms of monetary value. It considers the structural layouts of national security review regimes in these two countries, the economic backdrops, the political economies underlying institutional design, and their interplay with other regimes. It finds that while the US and Chinese national security review regimes bear a degree of formalistic resemblance due to China's transplantation of some mechanisms from the United States, they have contrasting effects in implementation. The divergence derives from nuanced differences in the two regulatory frameworks and the distinctive political economies behind institutional designs.

The assessment focuses on three vital aspects: (i) the criticism on the secrecy, unpredictability, and politicization in the decision-making process in national security review; (ii) relatedly, the scope and the standards of review that lead to under-inclusiveness and over-inclusiveness in enforcement, which add to the uncertainty and blur the line between national security and economic interests; and (iii) a few structural layouts that cause unreasonable delay, present undesirable deterrence effects, dampen efficiency, undermine comparative expertise of regulators, and create misplaced incentives for foreign investors.

This chapter proceeds as follows. Section 2 discusses the general regulatory frameworks concerning national security review regimes in the United States and China. It places the regimes in context by examining their interplay with other regulatory schemes relevant to foreign investment. Section 3 presents a critical examination on the scope and standards of national security review as enforced by CFIUS. It questions the validity of the arguments in favour of the CFIUS's current case-by-case adjudication approach by analyzing the regulatory environment under which the CFIUS enacted the approach. Section 4 states that while the Chinese regulatory framework may resemble its US counterpart, China's scope and standards face novel issues due to other schemes currently in place. China's policy makers fail to place adequate resources on more critical sectors, such as the financial sector, in the design of its national security review scheme. Also, China's relatively clear (but arbitrary) rules on the definition of "control" invite under-inclusiveness as well as over-inclusiveness in implementation. Section 5 contrasts several structural aspects of national security review regimes in the United States and China. It analyzes the structural layouts in national security review regimes that cause unreasonable delay, generate undesirable deterrence effects on foreign investors, dampen efficiency and institutional competence of regulators, and create misplaced incentives for foreign investors. Section 6 draws conclusions. Latest legislative developments in both countries in the past several years scatter throughout the chapter.

2. The Regulatory Frameworks Compared

2.1 Inward Investment in the United States: What CFIUS Is and How It Came Into Play in Acquisitions

CFIUS is an inter-agency committee that conducts national security review on inbound foreign investments in the United States, when investments take the form of mergers, acquisitions, or takeovers (M&A).[7] It does not review greenfield investments; only transactions involving a foreign investor[8,9] acquiring an existing "U.S. business," and gaining control[10] triggers the CFIUS process. As an inter-agency committee, CFIUS consists of representatives from seven cabinet-level executive branch departments, including the Departments of Treasury (which chairs the CFIUS), Defense (DoD), Homeland Security (DHS), State, Justice, Commerce, and Energy, as well as two White House offices: the Offices of the US Trade Representative, and Science and Technology Policy. In addition, the Director of National Intelligence (DNI) and the Secretary of Labor are non-voting, *ex-officio* members. The Department of Treasury and a Treasury-designated agency act as co-lead agencies on a case-by-case basis.

To retrace the history of CFIUS, President Gerald Ford established CFIUS in 1975, following the energy crisis from 1972 through 1975. In the 1970s, it was of concern that the Organization of the Petroleum Exporting Countries (OPEC) would use the surpluses gained in the oil embargo on the United States to buy up critical US assets. Originally, CFIUS merely functioned as a means of monitoring – requesting foreign investors to file preliminary reports regarding their foreign investment activities;[11] it did not possess the authority to block or divest a transaction during the period from 1975 to 1988.[12] In its first five years after its establishment, the CFIUS Committee had met only ten times,[13] making it unrealistic to respond to national security concerns of foreign direct investment in the United States.

In the 1980s, an increasing number of Japanese companies acquiring large US brands drew heightened attention from Congress. One of the salient cases at the time was Fujitsu's attempted acquisition of Fairchild Semiconductor in 1986.[14] The concerns over acquisition of US firms by Japanese companies prompted Congress to transform the review system from one of mere monitoring to one focused on systematic review. These concerns were exemplified through the Exon-Florio Amendment of 1988 to the Defense Production Act of 1950.[15] The Exon-Florio Amendment authorized the President to investigate the effect of foreign acquisitions on national security and to block a transaction that threatened to impair national security.[16] The President in turn delegated to CFIUS the authority to review transactions under the Exon-Florio Amendment.[17] In reality, the President has rarely been involved in the review of inbound M&A

transactions. Even when the President steps in, he acts on the recommendations made by CFIUS.[18] Thus, CFIUS plays a decisive role in deciding the fate of acquisitions by foreign entities that could result in control of a US business.[19] The cases at the time when the Exon–Florio Amendment was enacted already raised the question as to what, exactly, CFIUS deemed "national security." For example, it is hard to justify why and how Japan, a long-standing political ally of the United States, would pose threats to the national security of the United States in a wave of investments, as in the failed Fairchild acquisition attempt.

Subsequently, in 2007, Congress adopted the Foreign Investment and National Security Act (FINSA)[20] as part of the backlash from the 2006 United Arab Emirates-based Dubai Ports World's acquisition of Peninsular and Oriental Steam Navigation Company (P&O, a British firm). The proposed acquisition involved the sale of port management businesses in six major US seaports and its subsequent divesture of US port facilities.[21] FINSA and its follow-on regulations made significant changes to the Exon–Florio Amendment, including broadening the definition of national security[22,23] and creating a presumption of CFIUS investigation beyond the preliminary review stage in cases involving critical infrastructure as targets or government-owned investors as acquirers.

The evolvement of the CFIUS mandate against the changing political and economic landscape helps explain why CFIUS did not come into the spotlight until the 1990s; it was only after CFIUS had some real teeth – obtaining the power to block or unwind a transaction – that it gained prominence.

After the global financial crisis, there have been some great challenges facing the CFIUS. For instance the CFIUS's case volumes increased quite substantially, and new types of foreign investment came with more sovereign direction and complex fund structures appeared in the market. The average volume of CFIUS cases increased from fewer than 100 in the late 2010s to over 240 in 2017. However, the task force assessed by the Treasury and other member agencies to the CFIUS remained the same during the same period.[24] The level of complexity also increased which can be evidenced by the increasing number of cases in which CFIUS determined the mitigation[25] or prohibition[26] necessary to address national security concerns. These cases usually require substantial human resources and efforts.[27] New investment trends also affect the complexity of transactions. More sovereign objectives or rationales made the traditional CFIUS analysis of threats and vulnerabilities more painstaking. Investments through multilayered private equity, venture capital, sovereign wealth funds, and other kinds of investment funds made CFIUS harder to discern the ultimate control of the US target company it is supposed to investigate and monitor. As more military capabilities now build upon top of commercial innovations, the dual use of products with both commercial and military applications[28] also complicates commercial transactions. GPS, jet aircraft, artificial intelligence, driverless vehicles, and advanced semiconductors can be all used for both military and commercial purposes. The combination of both has led to a new evolution in the relationship between national security and commercial activity.

These new developments not only challenge the CFIUS's structural inadequacy but also its scope of jurisdiction. The US government felt a needed impetus for legislative changes to modernize CFIUS. The Trump administration joined the policy-making arena for reforming foreign direct investment review. The White House issued a Memorandum asking the Treasury Secretary to "propose executive branch action" for new regulations governing both foreign investments and exports in order to respond to investments "directed or facilitated by China" in US "industries or technologies deemed important to the US."[29] The White House also issued a statement in May 2018 stating the Administration would develop and implement "specific investment restrictions and enhanced export controls for Chinese persons and entities related to the acquisition of industrially significant technology" from US businesses.[30] Congress on 18 October 2017 introduced the Foreign Investment Risk Review Modernization Act of 2018 (FIRRMA) in the Senate to address the multitude of various concerns[31] and maintain its national security orientation. Unlike other bills which may encounter some fierce bipartisan resistance, the introduction of this bill received uniform welcome and praise in both Congress and the Executive Branch. Both the Treasury and the defense community are vocal in the support. The final version of the legislation was included in the annual National Defense Reauthorization Act,[32] with overwhelming bipartisan support in the House and the Senate. It was then signed into law on 13 August 2018.[33] President Trump praised the FIRRMA by emphasizing that "this new authority will enhance our ability to protect cutting-edge American technology and intellectual property vital to our national security."[34]

There are two policy goals FIRRMA tries to achieve a balance: the attraction of foreign investment, on the one hand, and the protection of national security, on the other hand. FIRRMA endorsed the idea that dangers to free trade and investment would jeopardize American well-being. This principle confines CFIUS review to national security, which rules out the possibility of turning CFIUS to a lever for pursuing other policy goals such as industrial or trade policy. To strike and maintain this balance, FIRRMA also stresses the methodological integrity of the CFIUS assessment of national security risks. For instance FIRRMA requires that any decision made by CFIUS to suspend a covered transaction, to refer a transaction to the President to be blocked, or to require mitigation "shall" be grounded on a "risk-based analysis . . . which shall include an assessment of the threat, vulnerability, and consequences to national security."

The following outlines key changes made by FIRRMA to the CFIUS system:

2.1.1 New Covered Transactions

Previously, CFIUS had the authority to review only those mergers, acquisitions, and takeovers that resulted in foreign "control" of a US business.[35] However, more transactions now do not involve the change of control. Non-controlling investments or joint ventures are more popular making this control requirement less meaningful than before. Other transactions use SPVs or offshore entities so that they can escape the jurisdictional hook of "US business."[36] As a result, more transactions fall outside of the jurisdictional ambit of CFIUS. These arouse more national security concerns especially when these deal-making strategies are viewed as a deliberate effort to evade CFIUS review.[37] Other loopholes have existed for a while. For instance the purchase of a US business in close proximity to a sensitive military installation was subject to CFIUS review, but the purchase of land at the same location was not. Such a gap is vulnerable to exploitation and national security threats.

The FIRRMA enlarged jurisdictional grant, equipping CFIUS with the authority to review new kinds of investments that could be used to weaken US national security.

FIRRMA not only retains the original authority for CFIUS to review "any merger, acquisition, or takeover" by or with any foreign person that could result in foreign control of any US business,[38] but it also expands CFIUS's authority beyond mere control by adding four new types of "covered" transactions in Table 8.1 as follows:

TABLE 8.1 FIRRMA's Four New Types of "Covered Transactions"

1	Non-controlling yet non-passive investments that afford a foreign person:

- "access to any material nonpublic technical information" held by the US business;[39]
- membership or observer rights on – or the right to nominate an individual to a position on – the board of directors of the US business;[40] or
- any other fundamental decision-making rights, other than shareholder voting rights, regarding:[41]
  - "the use, development, acquisition, safeguarding, or release of sensitive personal data of [U.S.] citizens."[42]
  - "the use, development, acquisition, or release of critical technologies;[43] or"
  - "the management, operation, manufacture, or supply of critical infrastructure."[44]

2	Any change in a foreign investor's rights resulting in control or a non-controlling yet non-passive investment;[45]
3	The purchase, lease, or concession of real estate located in proximity to sensitive US government facilities;[46] and
4	Any other action designed to be a circumvention of the jurisdiction of CFIUS.[47]

A new category of "other investments" relevant to critical technologies, critical infrastructure, and sensitive personal data of US citizens[48] is added in FIRMMA even though these investments may not reach the level of "control." Apparently, the FIRRMA eliminated the control requirement for certain kinds of investments. As a result, non-passive, non-controlling transactions (that provide access to certain nonpublic technical data in the possession of the US business; membership or observer rights on the board of directors or the right to nominate an individual to such a position; or any involvement, other than through voting of shares, in substantive decision-making of the business in connection with critical infrastructure, critical technology, or sensitive personal data) become covered transactions. FIRRMA includes within the definition of a covered transaction any investment that changes "the rights that a foreign person has with respect to a United States business in which the foreign person has an investment" if that change could result in "foreign control" of that business or would constitute an investment in critical infrastructure, critical technology, or a business involving sensitive personal data of US citizens. The definition of "covered transaction" quite substantially expands the jurisdictional ambit of CFIUS.

According to FIRRMA, "US businesses relevant to critical infrastructure" include expansively those that own, operate, manufacture, supply, or service critical infrastructure. Similarly, any investment in a US business that produces, designs, tests, manufactures, fabricates, or develops critical technologies is potentially subject to CFIUS review. An investment in a US company that maintains sensitive personal data, even if that company did not collect such data in the first place, could be subject to CFIUS review. The term "critical infrastructure" refers to "systems and assets, whether physical or virtual, so vital to the United States that the incapacity or destruction of [them] would have a debilitating impact on national security." "Critical technology" is defined to include a number of specific technologies relating to munitions, nuclear equipment, certain toxins, and certain emerging and foundational technologies, which may need a further clarification. "Critical technology" includes any technology on the Commerce Control List and controlled "pursuant to multilateral regimes, including for reasons relating to national security, chemical and biological weapons proliferation, nuclear nonproliferation, or missile technology" or "for reasons relating to regional stability or surreptitious listening." These wide definitions make CFIUS reach to a variety of businesses. A carve-out for indirect investment is made in FIRMMA to the effect that a foreign person's investment into an "investment fund" does not constitute an indirect investment. This means CFIUS jurisdiction does not extend to an investment fund managed exclusively by a non-foreign general partner; any advisory board membership associated with the investment without an ability to control the fund's investments or the activities of any portfolio company; and indirect investor's no access to "material nonpublic technical information" such as "knowledge, know-how, or understanding" concerning critical infrastructure or critical technology. Fund investment is excluded from "any other investment" subject to CFIUS jurisdiction.

Under the FIRRMA, Congress allows for CFIUS review of transactions triggering proximity issues. For instance where a piece of property is near enough to a sensitive site (i.e. specific airports, maritime ports, and military installations)[49] to raise national security concerns, CFIUS review is required. Accordingly, if a purchase or lease of real estate in or near an airport or maritime port, or in close proximity to a US military installation or other facility sensitive for national security reasons could provide a foreign person with the ability to collect intelligence or subject such a property to foreign surveillance, the transaction will be in the CFIUS jurisdiction. Certainly "close proximity" is a term that needs to be further defined. CFIUS has excluded many kinds of transactions within an "urbanized area" or "urban cluster."[50] CFIUS review does not extend to single-family residential properties and those in densely populated areas to prevent the CFIUS docket from increasing exponentially.[51]

CFIUS tends to prevent parties from exploiting legal loopholes and evading CFIUS review by extending the CFIUS reach to any transaction, transfer, agreement, or arrangement "the structure of which is designed or intended to evade or circumvent" CFIUS review. This means that any change in a foreign investor's rights would trigger a new round of CFIUS review so as to avoid a scenario that the foreign investor obtains CFIUS notice for a later transaction which substantially changes the original transactional arrangement.[52] CFIUS may reconsider transactions under changed circumstances. An anti-evasion jurisdictional prong to capture structures designed to circumvent CFIUS review is placed in the FIRMMA. This is different from legitimate structures adopted to ensure the passivity of the investment or otherwise reduce risks to US national security.[53]

The expanded CFIUS review powers have an impact on the formation of funds. Indirect investment made by foreign persons through investment funds is not viewed "covered investments" regardless of the investor's membership on an advisory board or fund committee.[54] This covers the case where (i) the fund is managed by a US general partner or a US managing member (or equivalent), (ii) the relevant advisory board or committee does not approve, disapprove, or control the fund's investment decisions, (iii) the foreign person does not otherwise have the authority to control the fund, and (iv) the foreign person does not have access to material nonpublic technical information as a result of its advisory board or committee membership.[55]

2.1.2 Abbreviated Declarations Process

FIRRMA created a new process involving "declarations" alongside the lengthy "notice" filings.[56] Prior to FIRRMA, all filings with CFIUS were voluntary.[57] CFIUS did not have the resources to proactively and systematically identify non-notified covered transactions.[58] Declarations is a streamlined filing that parties could voluntarily make in lieu of lengthier notices for covered transactions.[59] These declarations will be shorter than written notices (i.e. no more than five pages), and CFIUS is required to make responses to declarations within 30 days. FIRRMA requires mandatory declarations for transactions where a foreign government has a "substantial interest"[60] and transactions involving a US business that "produces, designs, tests, manufactures, fabricates, or develops one or more critical technologies."[61] CFIUS may notify the parties that they should file a complete notice, initiate a full review on its own, or clear the transaction.

Declarations do not automatically trigger a full CFIUS review. Rather, CFIUS may take one of four actions within 30 days: (i) request the filing of a regular notice; (ii) initiate a unilateral review of the transaction; (iii) inform the parties that CFIUS is unable to conclude action on the basis of only a declaration; or (iv) clear the transaction and notify the parties in writing. The advantage of declarations is to make the process smoother if the applications are filed by frequent filers and these transactions do not involve national security concerns. Then the parties may lower transaction costs as the CFIUS review may also have certainty. Effectively, the selective declaration is a de facto fast-track CFIUS review so that the parties may seek a confirmatory determination that CFIUS will clear the transaction.

Covered transactions that involve an investment of a "substantial interest" by a foreign person subject to significant "influence" by a foreign government must provide CFIUS with a declaration apprising the CFIUS of that transaction. "Less than a 10% voting interest" will not be considered a "substantial interest" in a US business to trigger a required declaration. The new declaration process provides procedure for transactions between private parties involving the potential background influence of a foreign government, and CFIUS will respond to some mandatory declarations with a request for a full notice.

FIRRMA provides an exception for investment-fund investments by parties that may be influenced by foreign governments. This exception parallels that which exempts fund investments from the category of "any other transactions."

FIRRMA lengthened the review period for a notice from 30 to 45 days.[62] This may give CFIUS staff more time for clearance. The lengthened period has already allowed more transactions cleared by CFIUS in the review phase.[63] CFIUS is required to provide comments on a notice it receives within ten days from the time a notice or draft notice is submitted.

2.1.3 Information Sharing

FIRRMA requires the Treasury Secretary (as CFIUS Chairman) to establish a formal process for the exchange of information in relation to "specific technologies and entities acquiring such technologies" with domestic government counterparts as well as with foreign allies[64] to the extent necessary "for national security purposes and subject to appropriate confidentiality and classification requirements." This indicates a trend towards international consultation and collaboration regarding perceived threats to address security concerns.

2.1.4 Reporting Requirements

FIRRMA requires additional detail on the volume and outcome of CFIUS notices, review, and investigations, which need to be reported by CFIUS to Congress. Other reported information includes the parties to transactions evaluated by CFIUS, the nature of their businesses, and continued analyses. There is also a China-specific requirement.[65] The Commerce Secretary needs to produce a biennial report through 2026 that includes statistics regarding all Chinese FDI into the US and an analysis of Chinese investment size, business categories, sectors, government investments, patterns in investments, and alignment with the objectives set forth in the Made in China 2025.[66] A comparison between the size of Chinese investment in the US and that of other countries must be included in the report.[67]

2.1.5 Process Enhancements

FIRRMA changes CFIUS review procedures, authorizes filing fees (which does not exceed the lesser of 1% of the value of the transaction or US$300,000 for notices, opposed to declarations which are free of charges), and provides for greater resources for CFIUS that may allow for both increased flexibility regarding mitigation and for more active monitoring of transactions not filed.

The time period for CFIUS investigations continues to be 45 days. FIRRMA authorizes CFIUS to extend any investigation for one 15-day period in "extraordinary" circumstances.[68] Therefore, the timeline for CFIUS review once a notice is accepted by CFIUS will be 90 days (from 75 days) or 105 days in extraordinary circumstances.

FIRRAM set up a new position within the Treasury Department, the Assistant Secretary for Investment Activity, to oversee the day-to-day CFIUS process on a full-time basis.[69] The CFIUS process, as the FIRRMA clarifies, can be used to identify technologies to be considered for enhanced controls under ECRA.[70] This also suggests a linkage between the export control regime and CFIUS review. Both share the same purpose of ensuring no US' most advanced and sensitive technologies are used by competitors without strict scrutiny.

2.2 National Security Review in China

The national security review regime in China is modelled on the CFIUS process. Compared to the relatively sophisticated practices in the United States, China's regime is still in its infancy, yet to mature into an effective regulatory framework, and a quick historical development of the regime can be seen in Table 8.2. In January 2015, China's Ministry of Commerce (MOFCOM) published a draft Foreign Investment Law to solicit public comments (hereinafter the "Draft Foreign Investment Law").[71] In the most optimistic scenario, the public anticipates at least 18 months before the formal Foreign Investment Law can be promulgated.[72] The Draft Foreign Investment Law aims to incorporate existing regulations on national security review into the new legal regime. It is expected that once finalized in the Foreign Investment Law, national security review will play a heightened role in China's foreign investment regulatory regime.

Similar to the institutional setting of CFIUS, the Draft Foreign Investment Law charges an inter-ministerial committee to conduct national security review.[73] The National Development and Reform Commission (NDRC, China's economic planning agency) and MOFCOM are designated as standing lead agencies ("conveners") in the review process, with a number of other agencies acting as member agencies

TABLE 8.2 Legislative History of China's NSRS[90]

No.	Laws and Regulations	Date Issued	Issuing Authority	Relevant Articles	Remarks
1	Anti-Monopoly Law of the People's Republic of China	2007.08.30	Standing Committee of the National People's Congress	Article 31 (now Article 38 in the amendments made on 24 June 2022): Where a foreign investor participates in any concentration of the business operators by merging with/acquiring a domestic enterprise or by any other means, and the national security is involved, the national security review shall also be conducted according to the relevant rules of the state.	The concept of the national security review is introduced into the law for the first time.
2	Provisions on M&A of Domestic Enterprises by Foreign Investors (2009 Revised)	2009.06.22	The MOFCOM	Item 1 of Article 12: If a foreign investor merges with/acquires a domestic enterprise and obtains the actual control over the enterprise, and if such merger with/acquisition involves any critical industry, affects, or may affect the security of national economy, the parties to the merger with/acquisition shall apply to the MOFCOM.	These provisions are the prototype of the Security Review System for M&A of domestic enterprises by foreign investors.
3	Notice on the Establishment of the Security Review System for M&A of Domestic Enterprises by Foreign Investors (the "Notice on M&A Security Review")	2011.02.03	General Office of the State Council	The Notice starts with the sentence: To guide the orderly development of M&A of domestic enterprises by foreign investors and safeguard national security, with the approval of the State Council, here are the relevant rules concerning the establishment of the security review system for M&A of domestic enterprises by foreign investors.	This notice and the other relevant laws and regulations are to build up the Security Review System for M&A of domestic enterprises by foreign investors.

4	Interim Provisions of the Ministry of Commerce on Issues Related to the Implementation of the Security Review System for M&A of Domestic Enterprises by Foreign Investors	2011.03.04	The MOFCOM	Item 1 of Article 1: A foreign investor who merges with/acquires a domestic enterprise that falls within the scope of the M&A security review specified in the Notice of the General Office of the State Council on the Establishment of the Security Review System for M&A of Domestic Enterprises by Foreign Investors shall apply to the MOFCOM for the M&A security review.	Same as aforementioned.
5	Provisions of the Ministry of Commerce on Implementing the Security Review System for M&A of Domestic Enterprises by Foreign Investors	2011.08.25	The MOFCOM	Item 1 of Article 1: Where a foreign investor's merger with/acquisition of a domestic enterprise falls within the scope of the M&A security review specified in the Notice of the General Office of the State Council on the Establishment of the Security Review System for M&A of Domestic Enterprises by Foreign Investors, the foreign investor shall apply to the MOFCOM for M&A security review.	These provisions aim to improve the provisions listed in Item 4.
6	Measures for the Pilot Program of National Security Review on Foreign Investments in Pilot Free Trade Zones (the "Security Review Measures in PFTZ")	2015.04.08	General Office of the State Council	The Measures start with this sentence: To effectively implement opening-up in the pilot free trade zones, implement the measures for the pilot programmes of the national security review on foreign investments adaptable to the negative list management mode, guide the orderly development of M&A of domestic enterprises by foreign investors and safeguard national security, these measures are hereby formulated.	These measures start the implementation of the Security Review System for foreign investments in some free trade zones.

(Continued)

TABLE 8.2 (Continued)

No.	Laws and Regulations	Date Issued	Issuing Authority	Relevant Articles	Remarks
7	Foreign Investment Law of the People's Republic of China	2019.03.15	National People's Congress	Item 1 of Article 35: The state establishes a foreign investment security review system to conduct a security review on foreign investments that impact or may impact national security.	The Security Review System is now required for all foreign investors into any place in China.
8	Measures for the Security Review on Foreign Investments	2020.12.19	The National Development and Reform Commission (NDRC) and the MOFCOM	Item 1 of Article 2: Foreign investments that affect or may affect national security shall be subject to the security review under these measures.	These measures make the Security Review System enforceable at the national level.

in the committee.[74] The Draft Foreign Investment Law does not specify the identities of member agencies apart from the NDRC and MOFCOM, but another set of rules implemented in China's pilot free trade zones provides us with a flavor of what the likely member agencies are.[75] As many as 30 agencies, including the Department of Justice, the Department of Finance, the Ministry of Industry and Information Technology (but ironically without China's Ministry of National Defense), may participate in the review process as member agencies.[76]

2.2.1 Before 2011

Prior to China's admission to the World Trade Organization (WTO) in 2001, policy makers in China did not pay specific attention to national security or economic security in the context of FDI. This was mainly due to the fact that China was at an initial stage of attracting FDI in large quantities, expecting to acquire advanced industrial technology and managerial expertise from Western economies at the cost of domestic market share. Further, due to the then case-by-case approval system for inbound FDI projects, the necessity for a national security review was not recognized.

Three significant developments in the post-WTO period have precipitated the incremental introduction of a national security review regime vetting inbound foreign investment projects in China: the swift increase of FDI in China in the post-WTO period; the expansion of Mergers and Acquisitions (M&As) of Chinese enterprises by foreign investors; and the failed attempts of China's outbound investment thwarted by national security implications in the recipient countries.[77]

Before 2011, China did not have a systematic national security review scheme in place, despite certain scattered provisions in foreign investment-related law and regulations. For example, China's Merger and Acquisition Rules 2006, namely that is a combination of *Provisions on Merger and Acquisition of Domestic Enterprises by Foreign Investors* and *Interim Provisions on Foreign Investors' Acquisition of Domestic Enterprises*, as amended in 2009,[78] state that parties should make a filing to the Ministry of Commerce (MOFCOM) when a foreign investor acquires a domestic Chinese company, obtains de facto controlling power, and the acquisition (i) concerns critical sectors or (ii) impacts, or has the possibility of impacting, China's national economic security.[79]

The national security review regime in China is modelled on the CFIUS process. Compared to the relatively sophisticated practices in the United States, China's regime is still in its infancy, yet to mature into an effective regulatory framework. China's national security review regime did not formally debut until 2011, over three decades after China opened up to foreign investments.

Another example of pre-existing foreign investment regulation is China's Anti-Monopoly Law of 2007,[80] which includes a clause skimming national security review. It provides that in the case of foreign investors acquiring domestic Chinese companies or in the event of other forms of undertaking business concentration, a national security review should be conducted.[81] A national security review provision in the Anti-Monopoly Law is misplaced; national security review should be separated out from antitrust review as the two regimes imply different policy considerations. It suggests that Chinese legislature had confusion about the distinctions between an antitrust merger control review and a national security review in an M&A transaction. The intertwining of national security review regime and the antitrust clearance regime led to the phenomenon that in China, antitrust lawyers concurrently handle national security analysis for their customers. Besides emphasizing the necessity of a national security review, the Anti-Monopoly Law does nothing to turn national security review into a feasible scheme; the policy statement in the Anti-Monopoly Law does not carry much beyond emphasizing the broad goal of establishing a national security review regime.

2.2.2 2011 Circular

To elaborate on the history of national security review in China, China's national security review regime did not formally debut until 2011 – more than three decades after China opened up to foreign investments.

The General Office of the PRC State Council on 3 February 2011 issued the *Circular Regarding the Establishment of National Security Review Mechanism for Mergers and Acquisitions of Domestic Enterprises by Foreign Investors* (the "Circular"), which would take effect 30 days after its promulgation. The Circular represents another major step that the Chinese government has taken in recent years in the area of regulating mergers and acquisitions (M&A) of domestic companies by foreign investors in China.

The Circular sets up a ministry-level intra-agency joint meeting as the national security review committee. It also lays out the scope and content of national security review as well as the mechanism and the procedures for the review. However, the declaration was made as a notice (an executive order in effect), not as a formal regulation. In spite of pointing out a policy direction, the State Council National Security Review Circular has a weaker force and effect than a regulation because violators do not face legal liabilities.

To implement the State Council's Circular, the Ministry of Commerce issued the Interim Rules on Issues Related to the Implementation of the Security Review System for Mergers and Acquisitions of Domestic Enterprises by Foreign Investors on 4 March 2011 and the Regulations on the Implementation of the Security Review System for Mergers and Acquisitions of Domestic Enterprises by Foreign Investors, effective as of 1 September 2011 (Announcement [2011] No.53). China's national security review regime was finally launched.

National security review covers the following areas as listed in Table 8.3:

- national defense security, including foreign investors' acquisition of military enterprises and military supporting enterprises, enterprises adjacent to important and sensitive military facilities, and other entities relating to national defense security; and

- other national security areas, including foreign investors' acquisition of enterprises involving important agricultural products, energy and resources, infrastructure, transport systems, key technology sectors, and important equipment manufacturers which may have an impact on national security and foreign investors may acquire *de facto control* of such enterprises.

TABLE 8.3 Targets Under the National Security Review

Category A	Category B
Where the target is a military industry enterprise	Where target involves agricultural products
A supporting enterprise for military industry enterprise	Where target is related to energy sources and resources
An enterprise located close to sensitive military facilities	Where target is related to infrastructure
	Where target is related to transportation services
	Where target is related to technologies
	Where target is related to equipment manufacturing

Under the Circular, the term "*de facto control*" refers to the following circumstances:

- a foreign investor and its parent company and subsidiaries hold in the aggregate more than 50% of total shares of a domestic company after acquisition;
- several foreign investors hold more than 50% of total shares of a domestic company after acquisition;
- a foreign investor holds less than 50% of total shares of a domestic company after acquisition, but the voting right of the foreign investor could have significant effect on the resolutions of the shareholder meeting or the resolutions of the board of directors; and
- other circumstances which may lead to a foreign investor's *de facto control* of a domestic company, including its operational decisions, financing, personnel, and technology.

Foreign investors' M&A activities in relation to domestic enterprises include the following circumstances:

- share purchase, including a foreign investor (i) purchasing the shares of a non-foreign-invested enterprise in China or subscribing to its the capital increase to convert it into a foreign-invested enterprise; and (ii) purchasing the shares from Chinese shareholders of a foreign-invested enterprise or subscribing to its capital increase.
- asset purchase, including a foreign investor (i) establishing a foreign-invested enterprise to purchase assets of a domestic company and operate such assets, or purchasing shares of a domestic company through such foreign-invested enterprise; and (ii) purchasing the assets of a domestic company directly to establish a foreign-invested enterprise with such assets.

The Circular describes the scope of review in a broad stroke and some of the products or sectors are not sufficiently described or defined and this may give the review committee a lot of discretion. For example, the term "important agricultural products" are not defined and thus it is difficult to ascertain what kinds of products are covered, whether agricultural products include agricultural products processing, etc.

The foreign investment security review committee will be guided by the State Council and led by the National Development and Reform Commission (NDRC) and MOFCOM, which will conduct reviews together with other agencies on a needed basis.

The national security review committee will review, approve, or block a transaction based on the following aspects if there is:

- any influence on national defense security, including influence on domestic manufacturing capabilities, services, and related facilities and equipment required by national defense;
- any influence on national economic stability;
- any influence on basic social order; and
- any influence on China's ability to research and develop key technologies for national security.

With respect to content of review, the Circular does not specify the criteria for evaluating influence on national economic stability and influence on basic social order. As the national security review gets tested in real-life cases, there will likely be questions raised on the review process and procedures. It is possible that further explanations or regulations will be issued by the State Council or relevant agencies to make the national security review more workable in the future.

It was unclear whether all foreign investors in all M&A transactions must file an application with the MOFCOM or whether it is only those transactions that fall within the scope of the Circular.

The review procedure and timeline are set out in Table 8.4.

TABLE 8.4 Procedure and Timeline for National Security Review

Steps	Timing
Notification to the MOFCOM	Not specified
The MOFCOM notifies the Ministerial Panel if the transaction falls within the scope of the security review	5 working days
A Ministerial Panel general review involves:	5 working days
	20 working days
	5 working days
• request of opinions from other departments;	
• opinions from other departments; and	
• decision (either dismissing or proceeding to a special review)	
Ministerial Panel special review	60 working days

a. Notification

Foreign investors shall make an application to MOFCOM when acquiring domestic companies. If the transaction falls into the scope of national security review, MOFCOM will submit the application to the committee for review within five working days. The Notice also permits the agencies of the State Council, national trade associations, competitors, suppliers, and upstream and downstream enterprises to apply to MOFCOM for review of a transaction.

b. Review Process

The review process starts with a "general review," and if a transaction fails to pass the general review, a "special review" will be required. If a transaction is deemed not have an impact on national security, the committee will send its review opinion to MOFCOM. Where a transaction is deemed to affect national security, a "special review" will be initiated by the committee and a security evaluation will be conducted and in the event of major disagreements, the committee will submit the transaction to the State Council for its final decision. After a final decision is made, MOFCOM will notify the applicant about the review result.

During national security review, the applicant may apply to MOFCOM to amend the transaction plan or cancel the transaction. Where the acquisition of domestic companies by foreign investors has had or may have a material impact on national security, the committee shall require MOFCOM, together with the relevant agencies, to terminate the transaction or transfer relevant equities/assets or take other effective measures to eliminate the transaction's impact on national security.

While China's national security review may add additional burden and costs on foreign investors as well as uncertainty for M&A transactions in China, the Circular also provides a timeline for the review process and some level of transparency on the review procedures. The requirement for national security review is already stipulated in the AML. However, there were no concrete rules in place until the newly issued Circular. In addition to the requirement for national review in respect of M&A activities, foreign investment in China must comply with the Catalogue for the Guidance of Foreign Investment Industries and, if required, complete anti-trust review in accordance with the AML. However, compared to developed countries, China's new requirement for national security review is not unique. For example, Australia has set up the Foreign Investment Review Board to review foreign investment projects, and the United States also has an intra-agency Committee on Foreign Investment in the United States, which reviews foreign investment in a US company that may result in foreign control or have an impact on national security.

Despite the grand declaration that national security review should be conducted, no further details were crafted out in the M&A Rules for how to carry out such a review. For example, terms such as "de facto control" and "national economic security" are not fleshed out by way of definition or guidelines. The result was that the M&A Rules did not enable national security review in China.[82] No penalties have ever been invoked in any M&A transactions.

Prior to the debut of national security review regime in China, the one and only notable case in which national security review concerns were raised was Carlyle Group, a US private-equity fund's attempted $375 million acquisition of 85% stake in Xugong Machinery, China's largest construction equipment manufacturer.[83] It is hard to know the extent to which national security concerns actually weighed on the failed acquisition;[84] more controversies over monopoly control and the sale of state-owned assets to foreign acquirers at an unreasonably low price hovered over the failed attempt.[85]

Since the implementation of national security review regime in 2011, there has not been any public information about its enforcement activities.[86] In particular, no one single case is made public, indicating that MOFCOM (alongside other agencies involved in the enforcement of the regime) has ever exercised the power to impose mitigation measures or block any inbound M&A transaction based on national security grounds. In accordance with the author's informal survey with practitioners in China, four years into the enabling of national security review in China, the invoking of the regime is still sporadic: only on occasional cases do foreign investors make national security filings with MOFCOM. Most of the time, foreign investors will not take actions to file until local offices of MOFCOM mandate doing so.

The legislative history of China's NSRS can be summarized in a chronological order as indicated in Table 8.2.

2.2.3 FIL

Unlike the FIL 2015 Draft, which attempted to establish a national security review system in the field of foreign investment through 27 articles in a whole chapter, the FIL only stipulates the "foreign investment security review system" in principle. The specific scope and process of the review is later regulated by the Notice of the General Office of State Council on Establishment of Security Review System for Foreign Investors' Mergers and Acquisitions of Domestic Enterprises[87] and the Notice of Trial Implementation Measures of Foreign Investment National Security Review in Free Trade Pilot Area.[88] Based on Article 2 of the Foreign Investment Law, it can be reasonably inferred that the national security review system in the field of foreign investment in the future will apply to all kinds of foreign investment instead of just foreign investment in mergers and acquisitions.

The FIL 2015 Draft presents the idea of "no administrative reconsideration and administrative litigation for the national security review decision made in accordance with this chapter."[89] Although the national security review is a special administrative function of the government and may involve more confidential information related to the national strategy, it may become a black hole in the field of foreign investment if it is completely exempted from administrative reconsideration and administrative litigation in accordance with the Draft FIL for Comment 2015. How to link the national security review with administrative reconsideration and administrative litigation conditionally will be an important issue in the future construction of the national security review system in the field of foreign investment.[91]

The FIL intends to facilitate foreign investments by creating a stable, transparent, and predictable investment environment. The FIL promises to treat foreign enterprises operating in China on an equal footing with domestic enterprises but reserves the right to "conduct security review of foreign investment affecting or possibly affecting national security." The national security review process will subject foreign investors to a more restrictive regulatory system. The lack of a clear legal definition and the regulatory overlay in the national security review process may undermine the legislative purpose of restraining access for foreign business interested in investing industries not open to foreign investment.[92]

Chapter III promotes local governments to abide by their promises. Article 25 provides that local governments at all levels and their relevant departments shall honor their commitments on policies and contracts concluded in accordance with the law. If policy commitments or contracts need to be changed for state interests and public interests, they shall be conducted in accordance with the statutory authority and procedures, and foreign investors and foreign-invested enterprises shall be compensated for the losses they suffered accordingly.[93]

Aside from steering clear of industries on the negative list, foreign investors will also need to ensure that their investments do not trigger concerns under the national security review which has already been in effect for a decade.[94] According to Article 6 of FIL, national security and public interest should be preserved and foreign investors and foreign-invested enterprises conducting investing activities within China shall abide by the laws and regulations, and neither compromise China's national security nor cause damage to public interest.[95]

The FIL also stipulates that foreign investors who merge Chinese enterprises or participate in the concentration of undertakings shall be subject to examining the concentration of undertakings in accordance with the provisions of the Anti-Monopoly Law.[96] Such provisions show that in the field of foreign investment, the concentration of operators should also be examined, but the scope and process of examination should be stipulated by a more advanced Anti-Monopoly Law.[97]

2.2.4 FISR Measures 2020

The success of the modified national security review in the Foreign Investment Law will largely hinge on whether it reverses its current image as a dormant regime. In other words, it is vital to ensure the regime will be actually enforced. In this regard, it is necessary to study why it has only been sporadically enforced so far. A convenient yet superficial excuse may be that it takes time for a regulatory mechanism to exert its full-fledged influence. CFIUS has been in existence for over four decades, during which transformations and evolvements phased in. China's scheme may likewise need time to develop after being fully exposed to political developments. But a more careful analysis shows the reasons go deeper than that. As further explored *infra*, China's national security review regime suffers several structural defects, creating an additional layer of approval requirements without properly securing national security.

On 19 December 2020, the NDRC and the MOFCOM jointly issued the Measures for the Security Review of Foreign Investment (FISR Measures 2020). FISR Measures 2020 follow China's Foreign Investment Law and demonstrate China's continuity of its "two-handed approach" promoting foreign investment while addressing security issues to take the country's opening to the next level.[98]

The purposes of FISR Measures 2020 are set out as follows:

(i) To broaden market access for foreign investors[99] and actively promote foreign investment;[100] and

(ii) To provide a clearer legal regime for national security review comparable to similar procedures in other developed economies[101] and scrutinize certain foreign investment transactions into China[102] to effectively prevent and defuse national security risks.[103]

The bolstered national security oversight of foreign investments is a response to the increased scrutiny Chinese companies now face abroad.[104]

a. Definition of "Foreign Investments"[105]

According to the FISR Measures 2020, "foreign investment" means the investing activities conducted by a foreign investor directly or indirectly in the territory of China, including the following circumstances:

(i) A foreign investor, alone or together with another investor, invests in a new project or invests by the formation of an enterprise in China;

(ii) A foreign investor acquires any equity or asset of an enterprise in China by means of merger or acquisition; or

(iii) A foreign investor invests in China by any other means.

Whether the variable interest entities (VIE) or control agreements shall be considered "foreign investment" remains uncertain. The Provisions on the Implementation of the Security Review System for M&A of Domestic Enterprises by Foreign Investors, which were issued by the MOFCOM in 2011, stipulated that

for mergers and acquisitions of domestic enterprises by foreign investors, the merger and acquisition transactions shall be analysed based on their substantial contents and actual impact to determine whether they fall within the scope of security review on mergers and acquisitions; foreign investors shall not substantially avoid security review on mergers and acquisitions in any way, including but not limited to holding shares on behalf of others, trust, re-investment at multiple levels, lease, loan, control agreement, overseas transactions, etc.

This means that the authority would look through the investment structures to determine whether the transaction shall be subject to security review under the de facto control principle. Subsequent regulations such as the Foreign Investment Law (FIL) and its implementation regulations failed to further clarify this. It remains unclarified in FISR Measures 2020 as to whether FISR Measures 2020's supervision on foreign investment will apply to the VIE structures or control agreements. However, from the perspective of judicial practice, the State Administration of Market Regulation recently conducted an investigation into three transactions involving control agreements,[106] and ultimately punished the party concerned after such party was found to have failed to file a merger control review in accordance with the Anti-Unfair Competition Law and other relevant regulations. Therefore, investments made by foreign investors through the VIE structures or other indirect methods are likely to be subject to the national security review.

What is also worth noting is that any purchase by foreign investors of domestic company stock at stock exchanges or elsewhere may also be subject to the national security review under FISR Measures 2020 if such purchase affects or may affect national security. The China Securities Regulatory Commission will formulate specific measures separately in accordance with FISR Measures 2020.[107]

According to FISR Measures 2020, rules for the implementation of FISR Measures 2020 for foreign investments in publicly traded companies will be formulated in the future. This is the first time that public M&A transactions are explicitly mentioned in the context of national security review. If the definition of "domestic company" under FISR Measures 2020 includes companies listed in China or companies listed overseas but with main or significant business operations in China, the implication of FISR Measures 2020 may extend beyond the usual concept of foreign investments security reviews.[108]

b. Reviewing Authorities[109]

Under FISR Measures 2020, the reviewing authority will be a Working Mechanism Office to be jointly led by NDRC and MOFCOM. The Working Mechanism Office will be responsible for the organization, coordination, and direction of security review of foreign investment in China and have the authority to review foreign investment transactions when an application for review is submitted or prompted by recommendations from other government agencies, enterprises, social groups, or the general public.[110]

Although the FISR Measures 2020 stipulate the location and the lead agencies of the Working Mechanism Office, the functions of different departments are not clear.

First, which departments can participate in the Working Mechanism Office is not defined by any laws or regulations. There are no clear regulations that state whether these departments are permanent members of the Working Mechanism Office or that they only join the Working Mechanism Office when they are involved in relevant cases. The regulations are also unclear as to the scope of cooperation required between the various departments within the State Council and the Working Mechanism Office.

Second, the relationship between other departments of the State Council and the two lead agencies is undefined. When these departments take responsibility for security review, the relationship between these departments is a parallel or a vertical one. In other words, other departments are cooperating with two leader departments or being managed by them to do review work in their respective fields.

Third, the internal relationship between the two lead agencies is undefined. The fact that the Working Mechanism Office is located in the NDRC does not mean that the other lead agency, the MOFCOM, will be guided by the NDRC. The respective responsibilities of leader agencies are undefined.

In brief, the vague regulations on the subjects of the security review could create confusion between power and responsibilities, such as buck passing, low efficiency, and others.[111]

c. Covered Sectors[112]

Before making investments, foreign investors or the relevant parties in China are bound to proactively report any foreign investment within the following scope to the Working Mechanism Office:

i   Investment in the arms industry, an ancillary to the arms industry, or any other field related to national defense security and investment in an area surrounding a military installation or an arms industry facility; and

ii Investment in important agricultural products, important energy and resources, critical equipment manufacturing, important infrastructure, important transportation services, important cultural products and services, important information technology and internet products and services, important financial services, key technology, or any other important field related to national security, resulting in the foreign investor's acquisition of actual control of the enterprise invested in.

The aforementioned "acquisition of actual control of the enterprise invested in" shall include the following circumstances:

(i) The foreign investor holds not less than 50% of the equities of the enterprise;
(ii) The foreign investor holds less than 50% of the equities of the enterprise but has voting rights that have a material effect on the resolutions of the board of directors or the members' or shareholders' meeting;
(iii) The foreign investor is otherwise caused to be able to have a material effect on the business decision-making, personnel, finance, and technology, among others, of the enterprise.

National security, as a state-of-art term, remains undefined, and there is no clear guidance on what elements the Working Mechanism Office will consider in determining whether there is national security concern.[113] What is considered "important" is not set out in any regulation, leaving the Working Mechanism Office with discretion to make a determination that may shift with changes in China's foreign investment policies or national security outlook from time to time. Certain businesses requiring a value-added telecommunications service operating licence could be subject to national security review. Further, with the recently revised technology export catalogue, foreign investment in Chinese big data or artificial intelligence companies may also be subject to national security review.[114]

In respect of "actual control," the concept of "material influence" remains to be clarified. Is "material influence" one and the same with "decisive influence" under the Anti-Monopoly Law for the purposes of assessing whether control has been acquired in the merger control context? Under China's previous national security review system, "actual control" includes the scenario where a number of unrelated foreign investors in the aggregate collectively hold 50% or more of the equity interests in the target. Is this still the case under the FISR Measures 2020? The answers to these questions are unclear at this moment.[115]

Under scenario 1 in Article 4, the FISR Measures 2020 do not provide guidance on the minimum threshold for the foreign investment, which means that even an extremely small percentage of shares or equity interests may trigger a security review for foreign investment in arms, national defense, military facilities, and other such sectors. FISR Measures 2020 fail to provide any express guidance on how "an ancillary to the arms industry," arms industry facility, and "surrounding areas" should be construed. A clear definition may be provided in the detailed rules subsequently promulgated or properly handled by the competent regulatory authority in practice on a case-by-case basis.

The investment sectors mentioned under scenario 2 in Article 4 have been broadened from those under the Pilot Free Trade Zone Security Review Measures issued by the State Council in 2015, by adding in the new terms "important internet products and services" and "important financial services," and also a catch-all wording of "other important fields," which grants authorities greater discretion in their interpretation. As to the definition of "obtaining the controlling stake," the FISR Measures 2020 notes that the actual controlling stake refers not only to the shareholding proportion (more than 50% of the equity interests), but also to the material impact on the decision-making of the enterprise in terms of operational decisions, human resources, finance and technology, among others.[116]

The lack of definition and the predictability this article provides for investors will likely give rise to some practical problems and confusions. It will result in a decrease in the inflow of foreign investment for the state. At the same time, the unclear regulations will result in the excessive discretion of the Working Mechanism Office, which brings uncertainty and unpredictability to foreign investors. In addition, the scope of the current Foreign Investment Security Review (FISR) is still too limited to include some important areas such as environmental area, which will lead to failure to fully protect national security.[117]

d. Review System[118]

(i)   The security review process has three steps:

Preliminary Review. The preliminary review can take up to 15 business days after the Working Mechanism Office receives a "complete" filing. A complete filing includes a filing form, an investment plan, a statement explaining how the investment will affect China's national security, and any other materials required by the Working Mechanism Office. At the end of the preliminary review, the Working Mechanism Office will notify the parties whether the investment requires a full security review. If a full security review is not required, the parties may complete the proposed investment subject to any other applicable regulatory approval.

General Review. If an investment requires a full security review, the Working Mechanism Office will open a "general review" which may take up to 30 additional business days. If following that review the Working Mechanism Office determines the investment will affect or may affect China's national security, the Working Mechanism Office will initiate a further review called a "special review"; otherwise, the parties may complete the proposed investment subject to any other applicable regulatory approval.

Special Review. The "special review" can last up to 60 additional business days and can be further extended under "special circumstances." The FISR Measures 2020 do not specify the "special circumstances" that trigger this extended form of review. As with the other reviews, if the Working Mechanism Office concludes that the investment will not affect China's national security, then it will clear the investment. If the "special review" concludes that the investment will affect China's national security, the Working Mechanism Office will prohibit the investment or impose conditions on the investment. The FISR Measures 2020 do not specify what types of conditions the Working Mechanism Office may impose.

During the review, the Working Mechanism Office may interview the parties or issue requests for information. Parties may consult the Office on relevant issues before submitting a filing. They are not allowed to complete the investment unless the Working Mechanism Office clears the investment or informs the parties that a security review is not needed.[119]

(ii) During the Working Mechanism Office's review, foreign investors are prohibited from making the proposed investment. In other words, the security review of a foreign investment transaction must be completed prior to the closing of a foreign investment transaction that is subject to such review.[120]

(iii) According to the FIL, the decision of security review shall be final, which means that a decision made by the Working Mechanism Office may not be administratively reconsidered or contested in court.[121]

(iv) Under FISR Measures 2020, the security review procedure may be triggered under the following circumstances:

(a) Voluntary reporting by the foreign investors or the relevant domestic parties prior to the commencement of investment for any investment subject to security review;

(b) The Working Mechanism Office issuing a demand for reporting within a set time period, applicable for those undeclared foreign investments that need to be declared; and

(c) Suggestions for security review by relevant government agencies, enterprises, social groups, or the general public to the Working Mechanism Office.[122]

There are some ambiguities surrounding these procedural rules.

Article 5 of the FISR Measures 2020 stipulates the consultation procedure that parties or applicants can choose to communicate and negotiate with relevant departments (the MOFCOM or the Working Mechanism Office) before formally reporting for Foreign Investment Security Review (FISR). But it uses the expression of "related problem" without clarifying the specific problem types, which confuses the foreign investors. Today, the FISR in China has been extended from the level of M&A to all forms of foreign investment. Therefore, the number of FISR cases is likely to surge in the coming period. For foreign investors, the costs of a FISR will rise as well. For the review subjects, the workload and the difficulty of the work will also increase. In conclusion, the pre-consultation process in China should be given a greater role in the security review process and also further refined.

Currently, the supervision procedure is in a blank state. From the perspective of legislation, the supervision measures in the process of FISR are not mentioned in FISR Measures 2020. It is only stipulated that reports should be submitted to the State Council only when opinions on the result are deeply divided or when decisions cannot be made within the prescribed working days. Although the 2015 FIL Draft suggested the establishment of a work reporting system, this proposal has not been adopted in the official law. Conclusively, in the procedure of FISR, who should supervise it and how to supervise it need to be further explored.

In recent years, the FISR in some developed countries is gradually politicized, which is closely related to the flexibility and ambiguity of the concept and scope of national security, and political discretion is exerted in the review process. According to the legislation of various countries around the world, the legal remedy for foreign investors has not been established under the FISR, and only some procedural provisions are provided. At present, Article 35 of the Foreign Investment Law stipulates that "A decision legally made upon a security review shall be final." Meanwhile, China has not provided for any actual remedy for foreign investors in any administrative legislation or normative documents. Thus, like most developed countries such as the United States, China has not offered legal remedy to foreign investors. However, as one of the most important recipients of FDI, if China hopes to establish a more comprehensive FISR while addressing concerns and maintaining the enthusiasm of foreign investors, it is necessary to increase the design of rights remedy in the system.

Apparently, more improvements should be made to the FISR system in order to make it more functional and enforceable not only to the government authorities but also to foreign investors.

Each department of the State Council related to the FISR should be included in the Working Mechanism Office. Moreover, how and when every department performs its duties should be stipulated in detail. Further, the relationships between the NDRC and the MOFCOM and the relationships between these two lead departments and other departments need to be specified. It seems that the NDRC, MOFCOM, and other departments should cooperate with each other to complete the review work since they are of the same rank. Other departments should not be led or directed by these two lead departments. Besides, this equal relationship between these review authorities contributes to mutual restraint and supervision, which is conducive to the efficiency and efficacy of the FISR system. To some extent, the checks and balances in the decision-making process is a guarantee to FISR's professionalism and efficiency. Last but not the least, the mechanism of supervision and accountability of the Working Mechanism Office should be established, which can form a complete system with procedural remedy. Therefore, the rights of foreign investors can be ensured.

The conception of "control" should be explained flexibly in the sensitive sectors such as in the areas of telecommunications, chips, and other key technologies. The threshold should be stricter in the fields of sensitive sectors for the purposes of discovering threats in time. Besides, it is necessary to making adjustments to the standard of holding 50% shares. The 50% shares of total control cannot be a standard. The practice of other countries can be used as references, which is holding 10%–20% shares.

e. Review Procedures

(i) Consultation Procedure There is a huge difference between the informal consultation procedure in the United States and the pre-consultation procedure in China. In the informal consultation procedure in the United States, the parties can communicate with CFIUS about substantive details and issues related to the investment. On this basis, CFIUS can directly give specific opinions on contracts

or arrangements so as to avoid the parties' entering into the complex formal review process.

China may fully use the US practice by adding substantive questions about the investment into the pre-consultation process and affirming the bonding force and validity of the consultation situation. In addition, matters of consultation, including substantive issues, should be clearly stated in the relevant documents. It should be noted that during the consultation process, the Working Mechanism Office should adhere to the principle of safeguarding national security and respond to concerns of foreign investors under the requirement of strictly guarding state secrets. These methods will not only effectively improve the efficiency of the review and save resources, but also help to save costs for foreign investors and protect the enthusiasm of investors.

(ii) Supervisory Procedure The lack of practical supervision system possibly leads to the rights abuse of the review subjects and inadequate supervision. As a result, the enthusiasm of investors may dampen. In the absence of a detailed system design, the most feasible approach to strengthen the supervision is the publication of the review work report. The publication of the work report can promote public supervision and prompt the review department to carry out the review work carefully and prudently. In addition, a work report system should be established so that Joint Conference and the Working Mechanism Office should be subject to the supervision of their superior administrative organs or the Standing Committee. The Joint Conference and the Working Mechanism Office will make regular work reports every year to summarize and reflect on the FISR in this year. Then the higher administrative organs and the Standing Committee of the National People's Congress will review the content of the report and form opinions for feedback.

(iii) Appeal Procedure According to Article 35 of the Foreign Investment Law, the review results are not open to appeal, and the relevant administrative legislation and normative documents do not provide any access. However, some scholars point out that the "A decision legally made" in Article 35 actually provides the possibility for foreign investors to seek legal remedy. According to the interpretation of this article, only decisions made in strict accordance with the law are final. Thus, decisions made in violation of legal provisions or procedural requirements can be changed. Since the review in administrative law is a kind of administrative act, China can establish a procedural re-review system on the basis of Article 35. Conclusively, foreign investors, as the counterpart of the administrative act, can bring an administrative suit to the court to safeguard their rights and interests.[123]

f. Liability

Any violation of the relevant requirements under the FISR Measures 2020 may bring severe legal consequences to a foreign investor and to the projects invested in.

Under the FISR Measures 2020, with respect to violations such as failure to report upon demand, provision of false information, or failure to satisfy the conditions imposed, the Working Mechanism Office is entitled to take measures:

(i) To demand disposal of relevant equity or assets within a specified time period and to restore the equity or assets to their original status prior to the implementation of the investment, and eliminate the impact on national security; and
(ii) To include a negative credit record in the relevant credit information system of the state and subject the relevant party to joint punishment in accordance with the relevant provisions of the state.[124]

Conditional clearance is available. Similar to the merger control review, a transaction may be conditionally cleared if remedial measures can be implemented to address the security concerns identified during the review. However, if there is no viable measure to eliminate the identified national security concern, the investment shall be prohibited.[125]

g. US v China: A Quick Comparison

A quick comparison between the CFIUS review and China's FISR can be seen in Table 8.5.

In a response to CFIUS review, before entering into definitive agreements, the parties need to consider the possibility of CFIUS filing and allocate the responsibility between them. Next comes the parties' informal contact with CFIUS staff, which usually takes place after the signing of definitive transaction documents. Following the informal contact is a pre-filing process. This process, in which CFIUS will provide comments and feedback regarding the pre-filing, typically occurs five business days prior to the formal filing. Next is a 30-day initial review, and if necessary, a 45-day investigation. During this initial review stage, lawyers at the Treasury Department undertake jurisdictional analysis to determine if the transaction is a covered transaction. This is usually completed within approximately 15 days. If it is a covered transaction, the Treasury determines whether it is a foreign-government controlled transaction. Approximately 20 days into the initial review period, CFIUS receives a "threat assessment" report from the national security agencies (including the Central Intelligence Agency, National Security Agency, Federal Bureau of Investigation) on the transaction, the parties, and the individuals. If there are unresolved national security concerns at the end of the initial review period, CFIUS will open an "investigation."

China's FISR resembles that of the United States. The review is carried out by an inter-ministerial joint committee chaired by both the NDRC and the MOFCOM, and it allegedly includes other ministries in charge of the industries and sectors related to the proposed foreign acquisition. There is a general review phase (analogous to the initial review phase in the CFIUS process), which is completed within 30 working days. If there is no national security concern found or confirmed, the transaction is cleared. Otherwise, the review enters a special investigation phase (analogous to the special investigation phase in the CFIUS

TABLE 8.5 Comparison Between FISR Measures 2020 and FIRRMA

Item	FISR Measures 2020	FIRRMA
Regulatory Body	Newly established Foreign Investment Security Review Working Mechanism, led by the NDRC and the MOFCOM.	Federal inter-agency committee (Department of the Treasury, Department of Justice, Department of Homeland Security, Department of Commerce, Department of Defense, Department of State, Department of Energy, Office of the US Trade Representative, Office of Science & Technology Policy) led by the US Department of Treasury, as part of the executive branch.
Investment Scope	FDI (including establishing subsidiaries in the PRC), equity or asset acquisition, investment through other means.	Direct or indirect investment in a US business (any person engaged in interstate commerce in the US), which includes investments in parent entities that have US subsidiaries. "Greenfield" safe harbor (i.e. a PRC entity that has not received investment establishing a US subsidiary).
Filing Obligation	"Active" (i.e. mandatory) filing for the following: • Military • "Important" (an undefined term) agricultural products, energy and resources, equipment manufacturing, infrastructure, transportation services, cultural products and services, information technology and online products and services, financial services, "critical" technologies (an undefined term) and other "important" fields where actual control over the invested enterprise is obtained (over 50% shareholding, less than 50% shareholding but where voting rights significantly influence the board and shareholders resolutions, other means whereby the foreign investor exercises significant influence over business decisions, personnel, finance, technology of the enterprise).	Voluntary filing control and national security (except Mandatory Declarations as set forth next): • Control: not necessarily determined by board control or over 50% equity ownership. Exists where a party has the right to determine, direct, or decide important matters affecting an entity, including without limitation the entry into significant contracts, major expenditures, the appointment and dismissal of officers, and relocating R&D facilities. • National security: never been defined (even under the old CFIUS law), at the discretion of CFIUS. Minority investment in a "TID" business (except mandatory declarations as set forth next): • "TID" business: critical technology (list provided, includes military dual use items and "emerging and foundational technology," which has not been defined yet), critical infrastructure (specific list provided), sensitive data (over 1 million US users).

(Continued)

TABLE 8.5 (Continued)

Item	FISR Measures 2020	FIRRMA
		• Minority investment: access to material nonpublic information, board or observer seat or involvement in "substantive decision making" (e.g. operational veto rights). Mandatory filing • Whether a control transaction or a minority investment, in a TID business, substantial interest (direct or indirect voting interest of 25% or more) by a government entity (other than the Canada, UK, Australia). • Whether a control transaction or a minority investment (including 25% ultimate beneficial owners along with the investor itself), in a TID business that involves "critical technology," which would require an export control licence if exported to the investor's jurisdiction.
Request by Governmental Authority	Permitted at the discretion of the Working Mechanism Office.	Permitted at the discretion of CFIUS.
Advance Consultation	Available prior to filing.	Available prior to filing.
Review Period	Step 1: Initial period of 15 business days from the date the submission is accepted to determine whether a review is necessary. If not, approval is granted. Step 2: If a review is deemed necessary in Step 1, 30 business days to determine whether there are national security concerns. If not, approval is granted. Step 3: If the review in Step 2. reveals national security concerns, 60 business days, which may be extended in "special circumstances." Decision may be approval, conditional approval, or denial. Conditional approval may involve follow-up compliance requirements.	Short-Form notice: 30 days from date of acceptance of submission. OR Long-Form notice: 45 days from date of acceptance of submission, with an additional 45-day investigative period if needed, and a 15-day presidential review if needed. Conditions may be attached to an approval with subsequent follow-up compliance requirements. Only the president can block a transaction where the parties do not voluntary withdraw the transaction.

Third-Party Feedback	General public may submit feedback on the security review of relevant transactions.	Not expressly permitted by law, but occurs in practice.
Retroactive Action	May order filing by parties who failed to file, may unwind unfiled transactions.	Permitted at the discretion of CFIUS.
Foreign Investment in Public Companies	Specific rules may be adopted by securities regulators.	Not within the remit of CFIUS, but restrictions may be instituted by the executive branch (e.g. executive orders, regulations from agencies such as the Securities and Exchange Commission) or the legislative branch (i.e. legislation passed by Congress).

process), to be completed within 60 working days. Before the conclusion of the special investigation, to avoid posing a national security risk, a foreign investor may propose mitigation measures, or the joint committee may recommend the State Council to make the final decision, including blocking the transaction (analogous to the presidential review phase in the CFIUS process).

2.3 Interplay of National Security Review With Other Foreign Investment Regulatory Regimes

To assess the practical implications of the Chinese and US national security regimes, it is helpful to view them through the lens of overall regulatory structure for inward foreign investments. This section assesses the purview of the regulatory framework governing foreign investments in the United States and China, putting national security review in context and examining its interplay with other regulatory apparatuses. One major difference in regulatory approach should be noted upfront: China is a regulatory state – its authoritarian government essentially regulates every aspect of economic activities until a deregulation initiative is launched, whereas in the United States, free entry into the market is the default rule unless a regulated industry is at issue. Certainly, some rules in the FIRMMA are politicized, targeting Chinese investors per se on the basis of national security concerns. As a result, investment from China to the US has plummeted since 2016 and dropped sharply after 2018, partly due to the FIRMMA as indicated in Figure 8.1, even though there were still some China-sourced M&A deals in 2017–2018 as indicated in Figure 8.2.

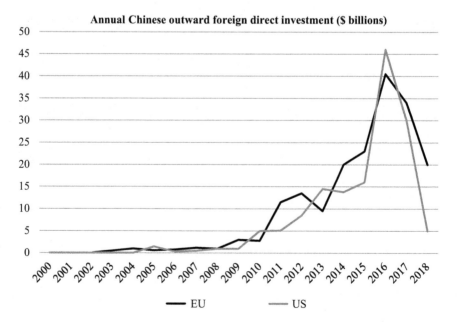

FIGURE 8.1 Chinese investment into the US and EU Has Plummeted since 2016

Target	Would-be acquirer	Country	When killed	Deal size
Qualcomm	Broadcom	Singapore	Mar 2018	$117 billion
Xcerra	Hubei Xinyan Equity Investment	China	Feb 2018	$580 million
MoneyGram	Ant Financial Services Group	China	Jan 2018	$1.2 billion
Cowen	China Energy Company Limited	China	Nov 2017	$100 million
Aleris	Zhongwang USA	China	Nov 2017	$1.1 billion
HERE	NavInfo	China	Sep 2017	$330 million
Lattice Semiconductor	Canyon Bridge	China	Sep 2017	$1.3 billion
Global Eagle Entertainment	HNA Group	China	Jul 2017	$416 million
Nocatel Wireless	T.C.L. Industries	China	Jun 2017	$50 million
Cree	Infineon Technologies	Germany	feb 2017	$850 million

FIGURE 8.2 China-Sourced M&A Deals (2017–2018)

Source: Data compiled by Bloomberg.

2.3.1 China's Transition From a Catalogue System to a Negative List System, Merger Control, and National Security Review

China's regulatory apparatus governing inbound foreign investment is composed of a nexus of complicated rules and regulations. A foreign investor aspiring to acquire a Chinese target company needs to abide by (i) the Catalogue system (to be superseded by the Negative List system),[126] (ii) the pre-approval requirements, and (iii) the merger control review, together with (iv) the new national security review regime. In a nutshell, Chinese authorities control the influx and outflow of foreign capital and closely monitor the establishment, ongoing operation, and termination of foreign investment projects. Central to its regulatory philosophy is the pre-screening of foreign investments – foreign investments that are above specified value threshold[127] or fall into certain restrictive categories[128,129] require pre-approval. Commentators expect the new Foreign Investment Law to bring about an overhaul in the pre-screening process by removing the pre-approval requirements in certain less critical sectors. But even with that, it will not be a full-blown free market access; access will be conditioned on monetary threshold and industrial sector.

So far, the substantial check on a foreign investor's entry into a domestic sector hinges on what is called the Catalogue system. The Catalogue system refers to the "Catalogue for the Guidance of Foreign Investment Industries," which is a catalogue promulgated by the NDRC and amended every few years (the 2015 version is hereinafter abbreviated as "2015 Catalogue"). The Catalogue lists the sectors in which foreign investment is "encouraged," "permitted," "restricted," or "forbidden." If the Catalogue specifies a sector as within the "encouraged" category, it is subject to relatively lenient approval requirements. And if one falls within the "restricted" category, the Catalogue imposes more stringent approval requirements or conditions (e.g. shareholding cap).

The pre-approval requirement kicks in after a transaction is characterized as falling into one of the "encouraged," "permitted," "restricted," or "forbidden" categories. Depending on the specific industrial sector and the deal size concerning the transaction, foreign acquirers will have to make filings with multiple agencies at different levels for their sequential pre-approvals. Without obtaining the pre-approvals, no foreign investor is able to complete the transaction or gain market access[130]

In recent years, largely out of external pressure from counterparties to the negotiation of bilateral investment agreements (notably the United States and the European Union), China has committed to a Negative List approach for replacing the Catalogue system.[131] A "Negative List" is expected to list all sectors in two categories: (i) the "prohibited" category in which foreign investment is completely prohibited and (ii) the "restricted" category in which foreign investment will be subject to various restrictions. Market access approval would be required for any foreign investment in a restricted sector. Commentators also expect the Negative List to set out a monetary threshold over which investments would require market access approval, regardless of sector. Once the Negative List is put in place,[132] it will lift regulatory hurdles for a number of foreign investment projects for which foreign investment approval would no longer be necessary[133]

Another relevant regulatory regime is merger control. Merger control review in an M&A transaction focuses on concentration and the anti-competitive effects of such transaction. It therefore has its stand-alone economic justification for playing a role in the regulation of foreign investments.

Besides the Catalogue system (or the Negative List), the pre-approval scheme, and the merger control review, the last layer of regulation governing inward foreign investment is the national security review, a regime in its infancy in China. As time has changed – free market entry by foreign investors has become the trend – policy makers seem to have an updated view towards national security review: to invoke it as a gatekeeper of foreign investments. This approach has its rationale – in any event, it is impossible for one host country to have full-fledged openness to foreign investments; at the minimum, it should strive to protect its national security. In this regard, while merger control has its stand-alone importance in the foreign investment regulatory framework, policy makers should deem national security review an indispensable supplement, particularly in the wake of removing entry barriers for foreign investment.

Further, a broader policy question regarding foreign capital is worth considering here. Since over four decades of openness to foreign capital, China has accumulated approximately $3.7 trillion of foreign-exchange reserves. Its thirst for foreign capital – an important drive behind its commencement of open-door policy in the late 1970s – is now an obsolete argument in favour of more foreign capital. Instead, China is stumbling in making profitable use of its excess foreign reserves. Its foreign reserves have yielded far from satisfactory investment returns due to its unsophisticated management strategies. On the other hand, it has witnessed a deep entrenchment of foreign capital into almost every aspect of its economy, giving rise to the criticism that excessive foreign capital has put its national security in jeopardy and endangered its vulnerable domestic enterprises. Chinese policy makers may therefore wish to address the question of whether China should slow down its pace in introducing foreign capital before hastily overhauling its regulatory framework solely in response to external political pressures.[134]

2.3.2 United States' General Openness, Merger Control, and National Security Review

Similar to China, national security review is an integral part of the overall regulatory framework governing inward foreign investments to the United States. The United States is generally open to foreign investments, imposing few restrictions on potential foreign investors unless the investments concern regulated industries such as banking, insurance, and aviation.[135] Unlike China, the United States does not require ex ante investment screening by regulatory agencies, unless certain regulatory issues are concerned, such as antitrust,[136] export control-related licences,[137] environmental issues, or compliance matters (e.g. securities law compliance).[138] Taken as a whole, regulators have limited tools to employ against foreign takeovers of US firms other than a declaration of national emergency by the President and the invocation of the aforementioned regulatory measures. This provides the US Congress with motivation to package policy concerns – for instance economic interests – beyond pure national security concerns in the CFIUS regime.

Merger control and national security review are two vital tools the regulators employ to scrutinize an inward M&A transaction in the United States.[139] Merger control focuses on the anti-competitive effects of concentration, that is monopoly, as a result of mergers and acquisitions. National security review, on the other hand, largely considers the impact of the transaction on US homeland security, acting as the last guard against detrimental inbound foreign investments. For example when a specific country desires to curb foreign investment due to suspected espionage, the hope would therefore be pinned on the invoking of national security regime. However, another source of concern over a foreign investment project may be the US economy. In this case, while it is hard to justify the employment of other regulatory tools, it is relatively easy to channel the economic concern into an ambiguous national security review regime. The layout of foreign investment regulatory framework hence helps explain why agencies within the CFIUS would want to package certain considerations that are apparently unrelated to genuine national security concerns into the grand basket of "national security review."

3. Scope and Standards of Review in the United States

3.1 Predictability in the CFIUS Process: Rulemaking or Adjudication

CFIUS is known for its broad power, secrecy, and unpredictability. These features are interlinked. Understanding these characteristics, their interplay, and their justifications is key to finding the right balance between clarity and flexibility.

CFIUS enjoys broad power because the "national security" that it is charged to protect is not defined: none of FINSA, the Exon-Florio Amendment, or the CFIUS regulations[140] define "national security." For example the Exon-Florio Amendment construes "national security" tautologically: "those issues relating to "homeland security,"[141] In lieu of defining "national security," the Exon-Florio Amendment sets forth an illustrative list of the factors for CFIUS and the President to consider when assessing a transaction's national security risks.[142] The listed factors raise interpretation issues, including overly broad and vague elements related to traditional military defense, to the technology the acquired business may possess, and to the effects of the acquisition on critical infrastructure, etc.[143] Further, by making these listed factors serve as non-exhaustive guidelines,[144,145] it leaves plenty of room for the President and CFIUS to consider other factors as deemed appropriate. The President and CFIUS therefore have considerable latitude in determining when to block or unwind an M&A transaction. To be sure, the Treasury Department published a "Guidance Concerning the National Security Review Conducted by CFIUS," but in terms of the national security considerations of CFIUS, it uses either vague terms such as "facts" and "circumstances" or merely illustrative examples.[146] For instance the Treasury expressly articulates that regulators should consider the nature of the US business being acquired by a foreign investor, and it enumerates several examples about the "nature of business" (such as whether the business has government contracts or whether it houses advanced technologies). However, an investor cannot rely on these examples to evaluate whether other occasions would similarly trigger the "nature of business" concern.

Secrecy marks the second feature of CFIUS. Information submitted to CFIUS is confidential.[147] Each CFIUS review – even the fact that a review is being conducted – is strictly confidential unless the transacting parties choose to disclose the information. This helps explain why CFIUS obstacles often are not widely known beyond the individual enterprises involved, let alone statistically computed.

The lack of clear definition, together with a secretive process in a black box exempt from judicial review, brings in vagueness and unpredictability, the third characteristic of CFIUS process. The CFIUS process shields the inner workings of its members from public knowledge; it therefore becomes purely case-by-case adjudication[148] and generates unpredictable review outcomes. The suboptimal level of clarity and predictability suggests the bolstering of CFIUS authority has outpaced the stifled definition. This may not be a huge issue in the old days when CFIUS merely assumed a monitoring function, but it is no longer apt now that it has major impact on virtually every cross-border M&A transaction involving a US target.[149]

3.1.1 Negative Effects

The combination of CFIUS's broad power, secrecy, and unpredictability gives rise to a series of negative effects. An unpredictable process means a "lottery" for potential foreign investors. Foreign investors now deem the CFIUS process the ultimate and major hurdle to their investments in the United States.[150] The costs imposed on foreign investors are tremendous: Foreign investors are unable to ex ante discern the national security implications of their potential transactions. This risks deflecting foreign investors from the United States to other jurisdictions.

To be sure, the case-by-case approach should not be confused with the common law adjudication process by judges. First, the judicial decisions are to a large extent open to the public, as are the reasons on which the rulings are based. Information about the rules or standards can therefore be summarized as doctrines and passed on to the public in the form of precedents. *Stare decisis* ensures that the court follows these doctrines, therefore promoting consistency between past and future cases.

Conversely, the black-box feature of the CFIUS works against the revelation and dissemination of information. On the one hand, since CFIUS keeps its decision-making process strictly confidential, no reason will be offered when blocking or divesting a transaction. On the other hand, companies going through CFIUS have every incentive to keep to themselves even the fact that they make the filing. After completing its review, CFIUS passes little information revealing the review standards to future investors.

When secrecy is at play, foreign investors will pause in the face of the potential CFIUS challenge when considering whether to invest in the United States. Admittedly, the CFIUS process generates tremendous deterrence effects; however, foreign investors are lost as to *what* they are deterred from. Therefore, the deterrence effect is unlikely to be associated with improved national security review compliance: future investors do not have much more of a clue even after one transaction has been penalized for threatening to impair the US national security. An increase in the number of cases going through the CFIUS process over the years does not necessarily lead to an increase in the supply of information about the standards enforced. In this sense, the CFIUS process has the negative effect of deterring foreign investments that should generally be welcomed because it places the burden of uncertainty and unpredictability on a wide array of foreign investors.

Second, judicial decisions are delivered by politically impartial judges, whereas CFIUS rulings are made by a group of political administrators and are thereby vulnerable to political influence. After all, CFIUS is an inter-agency committee composed of administrative agencies. CFIUS is not authorized to consider either political opposition or public opinion regarding a transaction.[151] But the institutional setting of CFIUS reflects that immunity from politics may merely be a hollow declaration; CFIUS's secrecy adds to the difficulty of monitoring the performance of CFIUS to make sure that it is competent and honest. The black-box process makes it possible for CFIUS to conceal political factors behind the mask of its broad mandate without having to expose its inner workings to the public.

Therefore, arguments in favour of case-by-case adjudication in the judicial process, as well as some conventional arguments in connection with rules versus standards, should not be applied in the context of CFIUS process by analogy. While as a general theory, a case-by-case adjudication process embraces more flexibility, the seemingly appealing rationale is a deceptive argument when applied to the CFIUS process.

3.1.2 Some Justifications for Flexibility and Secrecy

Admittedly, some justifications may exist for the flexible definition of national security and for preserving secrecy. For one, Congress may not want to expressly define the criteria for the CFIUS decisions in order to enable flexibility with an evolving concept of national security.[152] But it remains hard to justify such an extremely broad and vague mandate, especially if the general welcome of foreign investment is one of the stated policy goals.[153] The lack of any specific definition of what constitutes national security, as well as any standard of review, means that CFIUS can (and does) review many aspects of a transaction which may seem quite far strayed from accepted notions of national security.

As for secrecy, a few rationales may be offered. The CFIUS process involved classified and proprietary information. On the part of CFIUS, the agencies utilizing classified information in decision-making would not want to fully disclose their internal process. Specifically, the "risk-based analysis" – the report prepared by the agency with an equity interest in the transaction which forms the basis for mitigation conditions imposed on the parties – has its legitimacy in not being shared with the transacting parties. On the part of transacting parties, as CFIUS notices contain a great deal of private and proprietary information from both buy and sell sides of the transaction, the parties do not wish to make their submissions publicly accessible. Moreover, at times the parties may even prefer to keep the fact that the transaction is going through the CFIUS process, realizing any publicity could invite political intervention in the CFIUS process.

3.1.3 A More Plausible Approach

That said, in light of the broad (and seemingly infinite) reach of the CFIUS process and the high costs incurred to evaluate the CFIUS impacts on a specific transaction, promotion of clarity and predictability should be a goal. To achieve the proper balance between easing the undue burden on potential foreign investors and safeguarding national security, US policy makers should not pin hope on case-by-case adjudication of CFIUS. Instead, they should favour a direct regulation approach, meaning more clear-cut ex ante rulemaking.

For a completely secretive process like the CFIUS process, a case-by-case adjudication process is particularly unable to shed light on the review scope and standards. The case-by-case adjudication does not help potential foreign investors to better assess the national security consequence of their investments ex ante, so as to adjust their behaviour to ensure compliance.

To increase clarity and predictability, the CFIUS regime should lay out more black-letter rules or guidelines – it is time for CFIUS to adjust its regulatory approach. To facilitate predictability is to ensure continuity in the scope and standards of review enforced by CFIUS, and direct regulation in this sense should be a better candidate for the regulatory machinery.[154,155] CFIUS possesses proprietary knowledge and expertise in defining the elements that threaten to impair national security – it has accumulated sufficient information about inbound M&A activities and has the competence to tender a universal application now that it has been in operation for four decades.

3.2 Due Process: The Ralls Case and the Role of the Judiciary in National Security Issues

The frustrations from lack of clarity and unreviewability have led some foreign investors to challenge CFIUS on due process grounds, alleging that the secretive CFIUS process is in violation of the Fifth Amendment. For example in *Ralls Corp. v. CFIUS*, Ralls Corporation, a US company owned by two Chinese nationals (who are affiliated with a Chinese construction equipment company that manufactures wind turbines) acquired ownership interests in four Oregon wind farms as wind turbine demonstration projects.[156] The four wind farms were near a military training instalment.[157] Ralls did not make a voluntary notification of the transaction to CFIUS prior to closing.[158]

After the transaction closed, CFIUS requested that Ralls file a notice regarding the transaction.[159] With little or no advance notice or opportunity for discussion or negotiation of mitigating conditions, CFIUS ordered Ralls to cease all construction, sell the properties to a buyer that CFIUS would approve, remove all equipment on the properties, and destroy any construction that had been completed.[160] In 2012, based on the recommendation of CFIUS, President Obama issued an order unwinding the transaction.[161] Ralls filed suit against CFIUS. On appeal, the D.C. Circuit validated the Fifth Amendment due process claim of Ralls,[162] but left the *ultra vires* claim and other claims intact.[163] In October 2015, Ralls and the US government reached a settlement, putting an end to the continued litigation.[164,165]

According to the description of CFIUS's annual report to Congress, the important reason for the prohibition was that "[t]he wind farm sites are all within or in the vicinity of restricted air space at Naval Weapons Systems Training Facility Boardman in Oregon." An often overlooked fact, however, is that in the same restricted military area, there had already been a number of wind farms installed, some of which were owned by foreign entities, which nobody challenged on the basis of national security impacts.[166]

One should not read too much into the *Ralls* decision, or hope *Ralls* would help alleviate the secrecy clouding over the CFIUS process. The *Ralls* decision, in its essence, ruled that a foreign investor should be given the procedural protection to be notified of (i) the official action, (ii) the unclassified evidence on which the decision relies, and (iii) an opportunity to rebut the evidence.[167] What *Ralls* does not alter, however, is more important: a CFIUS or Presidential determination of national security risk, which deprives foreign investors of significant property interests, remains judicially unreviewable.[168]

The ruling of unreviewability is in line with the general *Chevron* deference to agencies based on their relative competence and the recognition of the institutional limitations of the courts.[169] Eric Posner and Cass Sunstein have noted that the *Chevron* deference is particularly apt in the domain of foreign affairs.[170] Courts have legitimate grounds for refraining from intervening in CFIUS substantive rulings and the Presidential orders: the relative competence of courts and executive officials to deal with national security issues.[171] Courts have limitations in their intellectual capacities to take sides in highly contested political issues such as national security. Judges should intervene in such areas as national security only if utterly convinced of the completely unreasonable character of the act or practice that they are asked to prohibit – a realism principle based precisely on the institutional limitations of the courts. As put by Judge Richard Posner,

> those of us who argue that courts should be extremely cautious about checking presidential initiatives in the current emergency do so in part at least on the basis of our assessment of the relative competence of courts and executive officials to deal with national security issues.[172]

Exactly because of the judicial passivity and self-restraint towards national security issues, the behaviour of CFIUS should be better guided by having more blackletter legislation and regulations. As the judicial branch refrains from intervening in national security review, when lack of certainty and predictability has taken a toll on potential foreign investors, more direct regulation becomes the most feasible option.

3.3 The Market's Ability to Help

While the *Ralls* decision on unreviewability is justifiable on *Chevron* grounds, the unpredictability of the CFIUS process remains unresolved. Whether CFIUS cloaks protectionism in the guise of national security in its adjudication becomes an open question. However, an important potential counter-argument is that market participants (intermediaries such as law firms, consulting firms, lobbying firms) can help bridge the information gap and bring a certain degree of predictability by collecting and analyzing precedents. This way, it may not be necessary for CFIUS to formulate, ex ante, the definition of national security or the scope and standards of review.

Law firms, lobbying firms, and consulting firms do come up with some generalizations as to the scope, the standards, and priorities of CFIUS review. In practice, firms have distilled some important elements as a rule of thumb: (i) nationality of acquirer,[173] (ii) extent of foreign government's involvement in acquirer,[174] (iii) industry sector,[175] (iv) particular products or services involved,[176] (v) types of assets involved,[177] (vi) contracts with the US government,[178] (vii) potential vulnerability of business,[179] (viii) defense-related issues,[180] and (ix) implicit political factors,[181] alongside some miscellaneous factors.[182]

Reliance on the interpretation furnished by the market has several inherent flaws, however. Above all, they are mostly rules of thumb, largely drawn from the law firms' past deal experiences. Individual firms may have some sample CFIUS cases as their know-how, but they are no more than sneak peeks at the scope or standards of review.[183] Such information in the possession of individual intermediaries is bound to be incomplete. Generally, it is very difficult to draw statistical inference from these cases scattered in separate law firms.

Still further, law firms, lobbying firms, and consulting firms have the incentive to keep confidential their proprietary analyses of the scope and standards of review enforced by CFIUS. They gained such know-how through their clientele relationship with foreign investors, their experience before CFIUS, or their employees who were previous CFIUS staff. They want to charge a high premium on the know-how next time when they advise new clients. The cost of information dissemination is therefore high.

More importantly, if one intends to apply knowledge gained from the past to predict the future, the premise is that all events (be it in the past or in the future) follow the same pattern, that is the scope and the standards of review are actually the same the whole time. But we are unable to ascertain whether the scope or the standards of review have remained the same throughout the history of CFIUS. Indeed, given its broad and vague mandate, CFIUS is under no obligation to ensure continuity or consistency in its decisions. In other words, CFIUS is *not statutorily required* to follow a consistent standard. If CFIUS is expected to play a dynamic role in national security review, it is implied that it will employ drifting and discriminative enforcement criteria over time. And we do see an expanding scope of "national security" purview: emphasis of hard assets in CFIUS review has given way to a close scrutiny on technology; proximity to strategic US operations had not become a salient issue until the *Ralls* decision. Last but not least, the information collected and revealed by market participants through private channels is at best helpful in shedding light on what kind of *information* is sought by CFIUS, not what kind of *standards* CFIUS is likely to implement.

3.4 The Value of Available Data

On a related subject, one may wonder whether empirical studies by scholarship or think tanks might lend a helping hand. Academics endeavor to decipher the standard of review through empirical studies by collecting data on CFIUS filing cases and conducting regression analyses.[184]

Valuable as they are, this strand of research similarly faces difficulty in overcoming the limitation on the source of data. First, the secrecy of the CFIUS process makes data collection a particularly challenging task. Second, researchers are prone to systemically underestimate the array of M&A transactions that are affected by CFIUS. Those companies that do not end up filing CFIUS notices but nevertheless incur high costs (attorney fees, lobbying efforts, etc.) in assessing the implication of CFIUS process on their specific transactions comprise a much larger population compared to what the datasets may represent. Essentially every cross-border M&A transaction involving a US target is covered by the CFIUS regime.[185] In contrast, the datasets compiled in research tend to be composed of observations collected from publicly available information.[186] The selection bias is two-fold. One is public M&As are overrepresented – information about public companies with SEC filing obligations is relatively easy to track down – whereas private M&A information is much harder to obtain. Another bias exists in that even for those private M&As reflected in the datasets, they tend to be high-profile cases that drew media attention. They are merely the tip of the iceberg and may not be representative of those medium or small-sized M&As that particularly suffer from the CFIUS process.[187]

Third, available data likely overestimate the success rate of CFIUS process. A large proportion of companies, deterred by the contingency of the CFIUS process, refrained from entering into a transaction with their desirable US target companies after assessing the CFIUS consequences.[188] Some other companies chose to withdraw after preliminary contacts with CFIUS or throughout the review phases and never made it to the finishing line.[189]

Last, the regression analysis may be useful in explaining past developments as covered in the time span of their datasets, but it may not be as helpful when making predictions. Again, when CFIUS is not bound by its past decisions or required to maintain consistency in its adjudicating process, a summary on the past behaviour of CFIUS does not do much help to shed light on CFIUS's behaviour in the future, providing foreign investors with limited guidance.

3.5 Vulnerability to Politicization and Protectionism

With no helping hands from the judiciary, the broadly mandated and highly secretive CFIUS process is vulnerable to political influence. National security has always been a profoundly contested political issue.[190] It is no surprise that high-profile M&A transactions feature politicization and media sensationalism, and the national security review regime adds to the politicization concern.[191,192]

National protectionism or even now popularism, a barrier to free trade, often fosters politicization. Openly advocating protectionism is sure to provoke protectionist backlashes in other countries, creating incentives to cloak their protectionist actions in the guise of other more glamorous claims. National security review regime is the perfect mechanism for that.

US economic interests have clouded the legislative history of the national security review regime. The possible economic protection function of CFIUS was raised as early as in 1979. In a congressional hearing, one legislator commented:

> the Committee has been reduced over the last 4 years to a body that only responds to the political aspects or the political questions that foreign investment in the United States poses and not with what we really want to know about foreign investments in the United States, that is: Is it good for the economy?

As of today, legislators have not formally addressed this concern in the national security regime, but the ambiguity in rules gives rise to the notion that the commercial nature of investment transactions is among CFIUS considerations in deciding on the fate of these cases.

Protectionism, be it in the open or hidden form, would greatly hamper the attractiveness of the host country. The CFIUS process is particularly vulnerable to abuse as a protectionist instrument.[193] Scholarship has long argued that overall protectionism is inefficient.[194] By raising the costs of entry in a domestic market for a subset of foreign firms and thereby putting them at a comparative disadvantage, protectionist measures leave the relatively high-cost players in the market. Deadweight loss is therefore present.[195] Empirical evidence has generally established that protectionism causes a series of adverse consequences that weaken the spillover effects – the positive outcomes – the host countries may have from foreign investment.[196] For fear of protectionism, foreign investors steer away their investment and look for possible substitute host countries.[197]

National security review can easily become a facially neutral, yet practically protective, regulatory instrument. Its secrecy may shield the selective protection of a certain group of investors from public scrutiny. If economic interests beyond national defense were involved in national security review, turning down certain group of investors may provide other groups of investors a competitive edge in winning over a desirable transaction.[198] The problem is the winner is not necessarily the most efficient acquirer.

If policy makers genuinely desire to eliminate protectionism or the criticism it facilitates protectionism from CFIUS review, they should aim to promote transparency in the decision-making process. Such an improvement would help confer more legitimacy on the national security review regime and reduce retaliation from other countries when its own enterprises seek to invest in other countries.[199] Indeed, countries may implement their own national security review programmes as retaliation instrument against the protectionism they experienced in the CFIUS process in the United States.[200] Retaliation will not only tarnish a country's reputation for openness to foreign investment but also distract the attention of policy makers from building the infrastructure for a genuine national security review.

4. How to Approach a Reviewable Transaction in China: Differences and Defects in the Review Standards of Two Systems

In contrast with an undefined rubric of national security in the CFIUS context, Chinese policy makers adopt a categorical list (albeit a very broad one) to narrow down the factors to be considered in a national security review.[201] In accordance with the list, regulators may review inward foreign investment transactions (not restricted to M&As) relevant to (i) national defense, (ii) critical technology, (iii) critical infrastructure, (iv) energy and other resources, and (v) economic safety.[202] However, such a broad and ambiguous list is, in effect, equivalent to the US approach of not furnishing a definition of national security. By the same token, the unpredictability of the Chinese system is equal to that of its US counterpart. What is worse, while each categorical element is broad and ambiguous, the list is far from a comprehensive one; for instance as discussed *infra,* the financial sector is completely missing. It unreasonably narrows the coverage of national security review and mistakenly renders large subsets of transactions immune from national security scrutiny.

Given the simultaneous narrowing and ambiguity in the list of reviewable transactions, it would be useful to understand policy makers' reasoning behind the list. The various regulations and rules possess striking inconsistencies in their wordings of reviewable transactions.[203] This indicates Chinese policy makers are undetermined as to what should be included in the list and what should be left out. One may therefore wonder where the list came from and whether there is a solid ground for it. Unfortunately, when retracing the steps, one would not be able to find any publicly available resources concerning the basis for such a list. Rather, the Chinese policy makers seemed to draw from a handful of salient US and Chinese cases while overlooking the danger that a salient-case approach is doomed to be under-inclusive and cannot evolve over time. For example "in the proximity of critical or sensitive military installations"[204] is likely a reciprocal provision in light of the *Ralls* decision in the United States. Recall that proximity to military installations was not a salient element in the CFIUS process until the Ralls acquisition. And "engaging in critical construction machinery industry" looks like a lesson drawn from the contested Xugong Machinery case (discussed *supra).*

Such a piecemeal list may suffer the deficiency of heuristic reasoning. China has long been criticized for, and has admitted, the poor quality of its legislation.[205,206] Empirical evidence supports the suspicion that a sizeable number of legislations were promulgated without prudent deliberation.[207] The rulemaking concerning foreign direct investment regulation was similarly based on the limited experience that China's top leadership had, and the legislative process was *ad hoc.*[208] Policy makers drafted the legislation largely by way of "water testing," wherein a legislative initiative is first rolled out despite lacking substantiated evidence in support of the legislation and is subsequently adjusted based on the lessons learned from the small-scale experiments.[209] When policy makers determine legislation by the views of individual leaders without prudent deliberation or rigorous empiricism, heuristic reasoning becomes a real danger. The issues spotted in national security legislation seem to suggest that Chinese policy makers have very limited experience regarding national security review. When first crafting the legal framework, Chinese policy makers chose the convenient way of directly borrowing from a sophisticated jurisdiction like the United States – convenient in a sense that it does not require cost-benefit analysis, data collections, or empiricism, a tradition lacking in China's policy-making process.[210]

The result is that Chinese policy makers have indeed transplanted many rules and structural arrangements from that of CFIUS. When it comes to the catalog of sectors that are reviewable, which should tailor to the Chinese conditions and is hard to copy (recall the United States does not promulgate a categorical list), the policy makers fell on the salient cases that came readily to mind and the availability heuristic then kicked in.[211] When the availability heuristic is at play, more concrete and vivid events tend to be perceived as more likely to occur.[212] Events that are not visible or salient to the policy makers are then systemically underestimated for their probability to occur. Systemic biases in the evaluation of possible cases that threaten to impair national security emerge.

To overcome the erroneous and dangerous reliance on heuristics, Chinese policy makers should get a helping hand from rigorous empiricism – an area under-appreciated in China[213] – so as to expand the canvas for the list by correctly assessing the probabilities of possible scenarios wherein foreign investment may hamper national security. It would be a huge project; however, it is a path the policy makers have to go down if the categorical list is the suitable approach in the context of China. Only in this way can they engage in a knowledgeable and informed rulemaking process.

The arbitrary rulemaking process invites two critical problems: (i) some critical sectors are missing from China's national security review, and (ii) the regulations are a mixture of under-inclusive and over-inclusive rules.

4.1 The Missing Critical Sectors: Financial Sector as an Example

One of the systemic errors in the list is the omission of certain critical sectors. Hard assets are the foci of the categorical list; services sectors, especially the financial services sector, are left out of the picture.[214] The Draft Foreign Investment Law briefly mentions national security in financial services sector but fails to recognize it as an imperative issue that warrants being included in the Foreign Investment Law.[215] Another deficiency in the salient case approach is a lack of vision that foresees the trend of the Chinese economy.

The utter absence of the financial services sector from the categorical list is at odds with the sector's strategic importance and sensitiveness in Chinese economy. China's financial services sector experienced substantial growth in the recent years.[216,217] Along with that came foreign investors' strong interests in the sector.

Of the $79 billion in foreign investment China received in 2005, around $12 billion "was for foreign banks' purchases of stakes in large state-owned commercial banks." Since 2009, foreign investment in the financial services sector has experienced a steady annual growth rate of 50%.[218] Figure 8.3 illustrates the exponential growth of foreign investment in the financial services sector in China. As of 2014, China's financial services sector has emerged to be one of the most active areas for M&A transactions.[219] A series of factors play a role in foreign investors, enthusiasm in the Chinese financial services sector, including the high profitability of the sector and the increasingly wider openness of the sector to foreign investment in recent years.[220]

Inter-agency political bargaining and compromise may account for the absence of the financial services sector from the list.[221] But the bureaucracy should by no means become any excuse for the insufficient attention to national security in the financial services sector. Policy makers should be alert to the possible catastrophic consequence: China may quickly lose the momentum, and the optimal timing, in systematically evaluating the national security risks of foreign investments in its financial services sector and consequently fail to safeguard its national security. It will be too late to reflect on the national security review policy once foreign investments have entrenched the financial sector. This is a high price to pay.

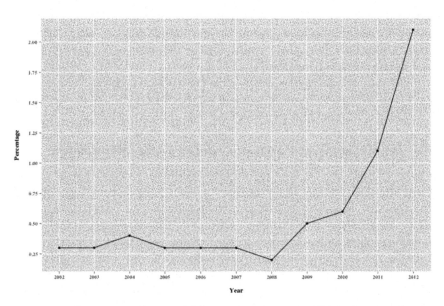

FIGURE 8.3 Percentage of Financial Sector Investment in FDI in Services Sector, 2002–2012

Source: MOFCOM

Put more generally, a heavy emphasis on the status quo – that manufacturing is by far the mainstream of foreign investments into China – leads to a focus on hard assets in China's categorical list for national security review.[222] With service sectors such as financial service sector becoming pillars in attracting foreign investment in China going forward, it would be a dangerous inertia if policy makers fail to develop a forward-looking vision. Chinese policy makers should not overlook that a transition from an industrial society to a service economy is the trend of China's economic development[223] and should factor this unavoidable trend in the formulation of the categorical list. The fragmentation of regulatory power should in no event constitute an excuse for an incomplete categorical list. A thoroughly deliberated list would create a truly uniform platform on which each ministerial-level regulatory agency could, as mandated, diligently perform its duty to assess the national security impacts, based on its unique expertise. This is key to the success of national security review regime.

In the case of the United States, in spite of criticism over an undefined "covered transaction," at least critical sectors are not inadvertently filtered out. FINSA merely requires assessment of the effect of covered transaction on US critical infrastructure,[224] energy assets, and critical technologies.[225] The effect is that the transactions filed with CFIUS involve a wide range of industrial sectors, as shown in Figure 8.4.

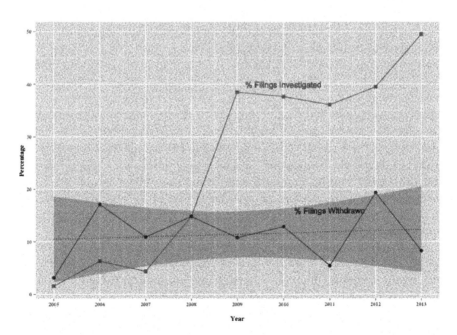

FIGURE 8.4 Percentage of CFIUS Filings Investigated Versus Withdrawn (2005–2013)

Source: CFIUS

During the 2008–2012 period, although more than one-third of CFIUS notices were in the manufacturing sector (223, or 41%), comprising the largest sector, another one-third of the notices were in the finance, information, and services sector (175, or 33%).[226] It covers a much wider spectrum of sectors compared to what is required under the Chinese categorical list.[227] Therefore, an incomplete coverage of sectors eligible for national security review is not a legitimate criticism on the CFIUS process.

4.2 Under-Inclusive Versus Over-Inclusive: The Definition of "Control"

In addition to the exclusion of the services sector from the list, another issue is the under-inclusiveness of China's definition of "control." To put the importance of defining control in context, a reviewable "covered transaction" should be one that may result in control of a US business by a foreign person, and so "control" becomes central to the definition of covered transaction.[228] The contour of "control" defines the threshold for national security review notices.[229] When using the term "control," on the one hand, no dollar threshold is set out for a covered transaction eligible for CFIUS review.[230] No matter how small the deal size, as long as "control" is found, an investor must file notice with CFIUS. On the other hand, CFIUS interprets "control" far more broadly than traditional corporate governance concepts.[231] By such standard, even foreign ownership of less than 10% in a US business may constitute foreign control unless it is "solely for the purpose of passive investment" with no elements of control (the safe harbor offered in the CFIUS regulation).[232]

The sweeping definition of "control" with no monetary threshold or shareholding percentage threshold for a transaction results in overly broad coverage of CFIUS review. A drawback of the expansive coverage is that it does not work to effectively filter out the chunk of transactions that are unlikely to pose national security risks; it is an over-inclusive list. Over-inclusiveness would not be a huge deficiency in the early era when CFIUS did not have its real teeth. In its nascent stage, its monitoring role did not add substantial burden on foreign investors. But times have changed. Now, because of the review's influential power to block or unwind M&A transactions, the delay as a result of the common heightened scrutiny,[233] and the global prominence of its increasing high-profile decisions, an over-inclusive list may not be justifiable anymore.

By contrast, the definition of "control" in the context of China is under-inclusive. China adopts a cutoff line of 50% equity interests as its national security review threshold: "control" is found where one or more foreign investors[234] hold more than 50% interests in a target company.[235]

The 50%-ownership threshold is documented in the rules promulgated by China's State Council, and as discussed *infra*, collides flagrantly with the Catalogue system which is primarily formulated by the NDRC. The failure to reconcile the national security review threshold with the Catalogue system may be a result of lack of prudent consideration of all possible consequences of a nexus of regulations.

The 50%-ownership threshold is arbitrary notwithstanding additional catchall provision where "control" may be found, including (i) where a foreign investor's equity interest is less than 50%, but equity interest voting rights exert substantial influences shareholders' meetings or the board of directors,[236] and (ii) a de facto control transfer from the target company (i.e. management decisions, finance, personnel, or technology) to foreign investors.[237]

At the outset, with the catchall provision in place, it seems not to make a substantial difference whether the threshold for national security review is a 10% or 50% equity interest. But the provision should not be understood in isolation. The catchall provision does not touch on the ownership threshold for "control," leaving it highly likely that the committee in its enforcement activities nevertheless relies on the 50%-ownership threshold as its benchmark for national security review.

The consequence of the legal rule is apparent when checking against the rules governing inward M&A activities. It is worrisome that the 50% threshold indeed functions to automatically filter out a subset of critical sectors – those sectors in which foreign ownership is restricted to minority interest such as financial service and telecommunication – granting them immunity from national security review.

Revisiting China's Catalogue system, we see a series of "sensitive" sectors of the Chinese economy have restrictions on foreign shareholding. In the telecommunications industry, basic telecommunications business (i.e. infrastructures or facilities of networks, data transmission), there is a cap on foreign shareholding of not exceeding 49%.[238] Likewise, in value-added communications business, foreign shareholding is capped at 50%.[239] In the financial services sector, foreign shareholding in banks is not allowed to exceed 25%;[240] in life insurance companies not to exceed 50%;[241] in securities companies not to exceed 49%;[242] in futures companies, foreign shareholders have to be minority shareholders.[243] In a nutshell, the Catalogue system enforces a different 50%-ownership threshold: in some of the most sensitive sectors, foreign shareholding should *not* exceed 50%.[244]

If we consider both the Catalogue system and the national security review regime as a whole, the over-50%-equity threshold renders the most critical sectors – those that are so vital that the Catalogue system imposes a cap on foreign shareholding – off the radar of scrutiny for national security threats. This is largely because a foreign investor has to *concurrently* abide by several layers of regulations. If it falls into a reviewable category according to the Catalogue system, it will have to comply with the shareholding limitation; meanwhile, if it intends to invest in a restricted sector, it will also have to file a national security notice. The collision between these two regimes leads to the doomed ineffectiveness of a national security review in certain sectors. Logic then implies that in these critical sectors, as long as a foreign investor complies with the shareholding

restrictions, the regulators do not have to assess the national security consequences of their investment. The seemingly neutral over-50%-equity threshold
deflects the correct focus of a national security review regime: the more critical
one sector is, the more heightened scrutiny a foreign investment in it the regulators should give.

Hence there is a misplacement of regulatory resources. The over-50%-equity
approach shifts the regulators' attention to less critical sectors – those that are
fully open to foreign investors with no shareholding limits, while systematically steering the regulators away from the most crucial ones in their screening
process – those that are so vital as to worth placing a restriction on shareholding.
A collision in legal rules risks nullifying the very purpose of national security
review regime.

5. Substantive Differences in Seemingly Similar Review Processes

United States. Overall, the CFIUS process resembles the two-stage Hart-Scott-
Rodino merger review process,[245] though it is less transparent. In the preliminary
Hart-Scott-Rodino review phase, parties to certain M&A transactions meeting
the filing thresholds file premerger notifications with both the FTC and the
DOJ and wait for a 30-day waiting period to expire.[246] During the preliminary
clearance period, the agencies decide whether to allocate the case to the FTC or
the DOJ for a 30-day second-phase review.[247] In the second-phase review, the
assigned antitrust agency will make additional "Second Requests" to the parties
and determine whether to clear the transaction.[248]

By contrast, the CFIUS process begins well before foreign investors file formal notices with CFIUS. Before entering into definitive agreements, the parties already need to consider the possibility of a CFIUS filing and allocate the
responsibility between them.[249] Next comes the parties' informal contact with
CFIUS staff, which usually takes place after the signing of definitive transaction
documents.[250] Following the informal contact is a pre-filing process. This process, in which CFIUS will provide comments and feedback regarding the pre-
filing,[251] typically occurs five business days prior to the formal filing.

Next is a 30-day initial review, and if necessary, a 45-day investigation.[252] During this initial review stage, lawyers at the Treasury Department undertake jurisdictional analysis to determine if the transaction is a covered transaction. This is
usually completed within approximately 15 days. If it is a covered transaction, the
Treasury determines whether it is a foreign-government controlled transaction.
Approximately 20 days into the initial review period, CFIUS receives a "threat
assessment" report from the national security agencies (including the Central
Intelligence Agency, National Security Agency, and Federal Bureau of Investigation) on the transaction, the parties, and the individuals.[253] CFIUS then proceeds
to conduct its formal due diligence.[254]

If there are unresolved national security concerns at the end of the initial
review period, CFIUS will open an "investigation."[255] The investigation phase

has no substantive or procedural difference from the review phase; the former is just an extension of the latter, allowing additional time for CFIUS to deal with national security issues if necessary.[256]

On rare occasions where national security issues are not resolved during the 45-day investigation phase, or the situation is sensitive enough that CFIUS agencies believe that the President should make the requisite national security determination, the Exon-Florio Amendment provides the President with an additional 15 days to issue a final determination.[257] When CFIUS cannot determine that the transaction lacks unresolved national security concerns, it refers the matter to the President for a decision, and at times includes a recommendation that he suspend or prohibit the transaction. The President's decision is likely to rely on CFIUS's opinion, as the President acts only after reviewing the record compiled by CFIUS and CFIUS's recommendation.[258] The CFIUS process triggering a presidential review is rare, and such cases usually draw heightened attention on an international scale. In the history of CFIUS, so far there have only been two incidents of presidential review, one of which being the *Ralls* case (discussed *supra*). The other incident traces back to 1990, when President George H. W. Bush unwound the sale of MAMCO Manufacturing to a Chinese agency, ordering China National Aero-Technology Import & Export Corporation to divest its interest in Seattle-based MAMCO on the grounds of national security threat.[259]

CFIUS has authority to take action to mitigate a threat posed by the covered transaction, but only the President has the authority to prohibit or unwind a transaction. If after going through the CFIUS process, CFIUS or the President determines that there is national security concern, either could ask the transacting parties to agree to conditions on a transaction to mitigate the national security concern. Mitigation agreement is a commonly used tool for CFIUS to address national security concern that it finds.[260] If an agency proposes mitigation, CFIUS will, by statute, prepare a confidential "risk-based analysis" describing the threat, vulnerability, and consequences and identify the risks that arise from the transaction.[261] The mitigation conditions imposed on the parties are negotiable. If approved by all of CFIUS, Treasury and lead agency will negotiate with the parties. Although more likely than a Presidential block, mitigation can undermine the business rationale for the transaction, as the parties may be required to restructure the transaction in question.[262]

China. National security review process in China resembles that of the United States. The review is carried out by an inter-ministerial joint committee chaired by both the NDRC and MOFCOM and allegedly includes other ministries in charge of the industries and sectors related to the proposed foreign acquisition.[263]

There is a general review phase (analogous to the initial review phase in the CFIUS process), which is completed within 30 working days.[264] If there is no national security concern found, the transaction is cleared.[265] Otherwise, the review enters a special investigation phase (analogous to the special investigation phase in the CFIUS process), to be completed within 60 working days.[266] Before the conclusion of the special investigation, to avoid posing a national security risk, a foreign investor may propose mitigation measures,[267] or the joint committee may recommend the State Council to make the final decision, including blocking the transaction (analogous to the presidential review phase in the CFIUS process).[268] Similar to the black-box process of CFIUS, there is essentially no public information about the inner workings of the inter-ministerial committee. Overall, the processing of filing is convoluted, making it susceptible to abuse and manipulation.[269]

5.1 Similar Delays in Both the CFIUS and China's Process

Practitioners have been complaining about the unreasonable delay caused by the pre-filing communications with CFIUS. The rationale behind such pre-filing process is that the parties now have the opportunity to submit their notice in draft form before the statutory time periods begin. In this way, CFIUS may determine early on whether they need more basic information for its review. Additionally, informal contacts with CFIUS staff before the official notice show an informal gesture of goodwill and avoid surprising the CFIUS staff with the submission of an unexpected notice.[270] Because of this, parties sensitive to their transaction's Exon-Florio implications routinely incorporate a pre-filing engagement strategy into their timetable and basic agreement.[271,272] On the part of CFIUS, it reduces its workload in reviewing the notices in the formal review stage (there is no evidence, however, that CFIUS is now overloaded; CFIUS typically reviews less than 150 filings per year, as depicted in Figure 8.5).

But pre-filing contacts also cause unreasonable delays. For instance, energy sector is hit hard by the delay in the prolonged review process. This is in part because FINSA broadened the scope of national security to explicitly include "critical infrastructure, including major energy assets." Energy assets are the only subcategory expressly mentioned in "critical infrastructure," and are therefore especially vulnerable to national security red flags if the parties choose not to file a CFIUS notice. In a sense, such spotlighting of energy assets forced more energy-related transactions to go through the CFIUS process – and more energy-related transactions became exposed to the delay problem. Moreover, the pre-notice process prolongs the CFIUS process because although it is "encouraged" by CFIUS, it has in practice turned into a "functionally mandatory" process.[273] Once an additional phase is introduced, along come new and unpredictable delays. Now, in addition to reviewing formal notices, CFIUS reviews draft notices – another round of review is added. To transacting parties, whether it is called a draft or a formal notice, it does not make a difference – both require the same level of care given they are under scrutiny by regulators.

Internally within CFIUS, new formality requirements and the bureaucratic process add to the time lag. Practitioners reported on CFIUS's slow pace of review.[274] This is understandable – policy-level approvals are bound to come slow when there are multiple agencies at work within CFIUS. In addition, while the Executive Order adopted by the Bush Administration to implement FINSA[275] established a more rigorous internal process that CFIUS must follow before adopting a mitigation measure, it creates an additional layer to the regulatory approval process.[276]

5.2 Deterrence Effects on Foreign Investors

Although the majority of CFIUS inquiries are completed in the 30-day initial review period, an increasing portion of filings have to go through the second investigation phase. As illustrated in Figure 8.4 (the grey curve depicts the percentage of notices to CFIUS that underwent the second investigation phase), prior to the enactment of FINSA in 2007, only a negligible portion of notices was required to proceed to the investigation phase. By 2008, among a total of 155 notices filed with CFIUS, approximately 15% of them underwent the additional 45-day investigation process. Since then, there has been a surge in the percentage of filings being investigated. Between 2009 and 2013, approximately 35–40% of all notices had to enter the investigation stage.[277] This percentage peaked at almost 50% in 2013. It has become routine for CFIUS to exceed the statutory time periods for its inquiry and to request that the parties accept such further delays before receiving a resolution and clearance. While this reflects the escalated importance of CFIUS process in recent years since the enactment of

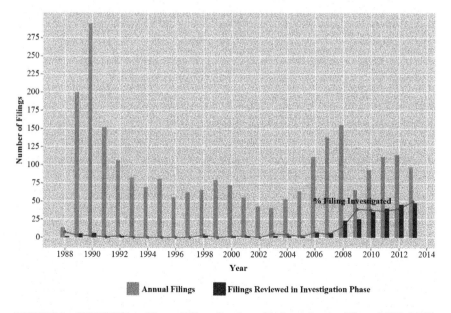

FIGURE 8.5 CFIUS Filings Versus Filings Reviewed in Investigation Phase (1988–2013)

Source: CFIUS

FINSA, it is an indication of delay in CFIUS review in addition to the delay in pre-notice consulting process.

Moreover, a sizeable number of withdrawn cases signify the amplified impact of CFIUS process on inbound M&A transactions in the United States. It is more than fear for delay in the withdrawn cases. Foreign investors may be deterred and choose to withdraw due to fear for reputation damages, the potential difficulties associated with completing the CFIUS process, and the cost of the process. As shown in Figure 8.6, in one of the peak years such as 2012 alone, 19% of the filings made were subsequently withdrawn. Although Figure 8.6 depicts that the withdrawal rate varies from year to year, in a typical year one would expect a median of 10% of the filings end up being withdrawn.

Withdrawals include two types of cases: those that withdraw to refile while having more time preparing for the answers, and those that withdraw because of high risk of rejection. The two types of cases both reflect the concerns of the parties regarding potential difficulties in passing the CFIUS clearance process. In cases in which the parties are unable to address all of CFIUS's outstanding national security concerns within the prescribed time frame, the parties might request to withdraw and refile their notice to provide themselves more leeway for addressing the remaining national security concerns.[278,279] In other cases, "the parties might request to withdraw their notice because they are abandoning

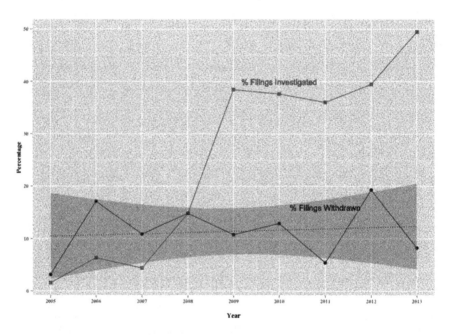

FIGURE 8.6 Percentage of CFIUS Filings Investigated Versus Withdrawn (2005–2013)
Source: CFIUS

the transaction for commercial reasons, or in light of a CFIUS determination to recommend that the President suspend or prohibit the transaction." From the business perspective, withdrawing a case after becoming aware of the high rejection risk does less reputational damage to a business than rejection in the later stage. Although a substantial part of the withdrawn cases would later be refiled with CFIUS after modification of transaction terms and conditions, the fact that an increasing number of parties choose to withdraw their cases suggests that CFIUS is having greater influence on the cross-border transactions and the parties are experiencing greater difficulties and need to put more efforts regarding national security reviews.

As with all transactions reviewed by CFIUS, all but a very few of these cases completed the process successfully. Generally, 80 to 90% of cases were approved without a mitigation agreement.[280] But one should read the clearance rate in conjunction with the withdrawal rate. Researchers tend to ignore the fact that there is a high clearance rate because a sizeable number of acquirers withdraw their filings, with or without subsequent re-filings. Merely looking at clearance rate of the cases that complete the whole CFIUS process can be misleading.

Although the increased percentage of investigated cases may be explained in part by the new presumption of CFIUS investigation extended beyond a preliminary review phase under FINSA for foreign government transactions and transactions involving critical infrastructure, the statistics suggest the CFIUS process has generated much greater impacts than before. To foreign investors, cross-border M&As in the United States become more difficult and more costly. It captures a broader array of foreign investors: absent clear definition, when in doubt, investors have to file. And the statistics do not reflect those investors deterred from investing; they spend considerable time and resources to weigh CFIUS implications and ultimately decide to invest elsewhere in light of the uncertainty posed. For those who nevertheless decide to make investments, it takes toll on the investors' investment costs – uncertain of CFIUS's reach, investors will have to file. Along the way of the CFIUS process, a sizeable group of investors withdraw their cases, which explains the high clearance rate for those who complete the long journey of review amid the delay and the deterrence effects.

As China's national security review mimics that of CFIUS, it is foreseeable that the delay derived from multiple bureaucratic layers would take a similar form in China. China already has a bloated bureaucratic structure in its administration, and an addition of three-tiered national security review will only deteriorate the problem. In this sense, the downsides of the three-tiered review such as more delay are likely to outweigh the potential benefits such as the arguably meaningful checks on national security threats. It is more worthwhile for Chinese policy makers to ponder on *what* exactly will national security review add to China's foreign investment regulatory regime, before rushing to build up more layers of approvals.

5.3 The "Two Lead Agencies" Schemes in Divergence

A few deviations of the Chinese national security review process from the CFIUS model are very puzzling, giving rise to suspicions about the existence of political compromises in the policy-making process. China's State Council designates both the NDRC and MOFCOM as standing lead agencies in the joint committee.[281] But why do we need two lead agencies in an inter-agency committee, if the purpose of having a lead agency is to coordinate among multiple agencies? When two standing lead agencies are in place, which has the say on coordination if they are at odds with each other? If the lead agency were a decision-maker having a say on which joint committee agency should handle a specific case, two parallel decision-makers would inevitably result in conflicts. Unnecessary complications and inefficiency therefore arise in the Chinese "two lead agencies" scheme.

The redundant "two lead agencies" scheme may be a result of political bargaining and compromise. The NDRC and MOFCOM are known to be in fierce jurisdictional competition. Long before the emergence of national security review as a regulatory regime up for grab by the agencies, the NDRC and MOFCOM had engaged in a long-lasting regulatory competition to fight for jurisdiction over foreign investment.[282] The outcome is the inefficient stacking of agencies; instead of being alternatives to each other, the NDRC and MOFCOM became additives to one another, each with veto power in signing off a foreign investment project.[283] For the regulated firms, it means onerous sequential approvals rather than an option to choose a preferred regulatory agency.

Such competition of power is common in China's legislative history. The difference this time seems to be that the State Council indulges the self-interested behaviours of the NDRC and MOFCOM by authorizing both of them to be lead agencies in the joint committee. This approach of reconciling the disputes between the two agencies is erroneous and likely furthers the agency turf warfare.

The harm goes beyond the tolerance of agency turf warfare at the price of efficiency in the regulatory structure. The rationale for an inter-agency committee in the national security review regime in the first place is the need for pooling relative institutional competence of multiple agencies. By reinforcing the dominant position of the NDRC and MOFCOM in the joint committee, other agencies are deprived of the opportunity to be designated to be a lead agency. Their opinions become less determinative and prone to be neglected.

When the decisive power belongs only to the two leading agencies and no other agencies is specifically referred in a list, it is hard to get the true opinions from other more informed and qualified agencies according to the specific circumstance. The reason is two-fold. First, when a subset of agencies in the joint committee is identified to be "lead agencies," essentially it forms a core group of decision-makers. A hierarchical structure is hence formed, and voices from other agencies will be peripheral; the NDRC and MOFCOM as lead agencies have the option of excluding agencies at their discretion when deciding on which agencies the joint committee would consult. Further, other than the NDRC and MOFCOM, no specific agencies are listed to be members to the joint committee – a signal that other agencies are likely to play a peripheral role in offering opinions when consulted. The pooling of comparative expertise from multiple agencies may be an institutional design on paper, but it is not so in action.

Second, in contrast with the process by which the CFIUS determines lead agencies in the CFIUS process (as described *infra*), the predetermined lead agencies take up the spot that should have been taken by other agencies on a case-by-case basis. The role that other agencies can play in the national security review process is doomed to be limited if the NDRC and MOFCOM are always the lead agencies despite the circumstances of individual transactions.

Having the NDRC and MOFCOM as predetermined lead agencies results in the over-representation of these two agencies and under-representation of other agencies (e.g. the Ministry of Science and Technology, the Ministry of National Defense). It creates a hierarchy among the agencies in the national security review process, which risks circumventing or sidelining of inputs of agencies other than the NDRC and the MOFCOM. If agencies other than the NDRC and MOFCOM are deprived of the opportunity to be designated lead agency and to play any decisive role in evaluating the national security impact of individual cases, the national security review regime essentially converges on other existing gate-keeping regulatory schemes and becomes a repetitive and useless layer of regulation. Ultimately, the dominance of one or two agencies in the decision-making process questions the credibility of the representative intent of the inter-agency involvement. The goal of having an inter-agency committee is severely undercut.

The determination process of lead agencies in the CFIUS process in the United States follows a more reasonable regulatory design. CFIUS is chaired by the Treasury Department. There is criticism that the Treasury Department acting as the chair renders economic concerns prevailing over national security concerns, but the scheme of co-lead agencies helps ease the potential defect.

While the Treasury Department acts as the standing chair, a co-lead agency is designated for each individual transaction filed with CFIUS.[284] Once a CFIUS notice is filed, the Treasury Department makes the decision as to which agency will join it as co-lead agency.[285] Such an agency generally has equity in the transaction. In practice, lead agencies are most common DoD and DHS when filings involve military-related equities or critical defense technology is at stake.[286] The lead agencies generally assume the obligation of monitoring the mitigation measures imposed on the transaction later on.[287] While there are a limited number of voting members of CFIUS, generally it operates on consensus, such that if one participant strongly objects to a transaction or seeks conditions, those demands are usually respected.[288] This is understandable, as CFIUS will wish to speak with the same voice.

By comparison, we can see that although the CFIUS process embraces the concept of two lead agencies, only the Treasury Department acts as the standing lead agency, playing the role of a coordinator in the inter-agency committee. The other spot for the lead agency is not predetermined; instead, it is assigned on a case-by-case basis. This way it adequately harnesses the expertise of agencies other than the Treasury Department. Moreover, unlike in the case of China where in theory an infinite array of agencies may be consulted in the national security review process – which ironically may imply that no agencies other than the NDRC and MOFCOM are consulted, the seven-member agencies in the CFIUS committee are announced, adding clarity to the CFIUS process.

Therefore, the similarity of "two lead agencies" in the context of the CFIUS process and China's national security review regime is deceptive. In terms of the effects, the scheme of two predetermined lead agencies in China bears no resemblance to the two-lead-agency scheme in the CFIUS review. The former nullifies the very purpose of creating a national security review regime and in turn renders the regime a useless repetition of existing regulatory structure. The latter, in contrast, has merits from an institutional design perspective.

5.4 Who Can Institute a Review Process? The Substantive Impacts of a Procedural Setting

Even nuances in procedural settings, such as how the national security review process can be initiated, may generate contrasting effects in the United States and China. The incentive structures in these two jurisdictions are indeed distinct from each other.

United States. In the United States, a national security review process is invoked mainly by voluntarily filing initiated by the transacting parties, in practice usually the acquirer.[289] Unlike Hart-Scott-Rodino antitrust clearance, CFIUS clearance is not a legal precondition to closing, nor is it mandatory. Neither the Exon-Florio Amendment[290] nor the CFIUS regulations[291] require that the parties to a covered transaction notify CFIUS of that transaction prior to closing.

But the voluntary filing mechanism functions well in encouraging CFIUS filings, and CFIUS employs a few tools to ensure this happens. First, under the Exon-Florio Amendment, CFIUS can initiate its own review and investigation of a covered transaction.[292,293] CFIUS personnel "routinely review the press and trade journals for transactions that have not be [sic] filed." Second, if CFIUS, in its review and investigation, determines that there is national security concern in a transaction, it can impose conditions on a transaction even after it is closed by demanding mitigation agreements or even ordering divestment to unwind the entire transaction.

In the face of the possibility that CFIUS undertakes reviews and investigations on its own initiative, parties that choose not to notify CFIUS are thus taking the risk that, either before or after closing, CFIUS will contact them and request that they submit information. Given CFIUS's authority to stop a transaction or even require divestment of US operations, the parties are not in a position to refuse such a request. The real danger of costly penalties is that it has deterrence effects and prompts the transacting parties to make the notification. Though CFIUS ultimately approves most investments that it reviews, at times investors have to accept significant conditions to obtain CFIUS approval.

Moreover, parties to a cross-border M&A transaction are usually prominent businesses. They risk their reputation if they choose not to voluntarily file and are subsequently chased by CFIUS. Also, by failing to voluntarily inform CFIUS, the parties have almost certainly forfeited the goodwill and cooperative climate that may result from a decision to fully engage with CFIUS in the first place (recall the *Ralls* scenario discussed *supra*). It will not be clear whether CFIUS will allow the transaction even if the parties file voluntarily, but it is certain that whatever the resolution CFIUS makes, it will probably be far less chaotic for the parties than an after-the-fact divestment. The aggregate effect is that transacting parties tend to file with CFIUS when there is a glimmer of doubt about whether to file.

China. Unlike the structural arrangement of CFIUS that induces transacting parties to file when in doubt, the incentive structure in China is the opposite: "when in doubt, do not file." The nuance lies in the identity of parties who can initiate a national security review process. If local MOFCOM branches decide the transaction in question involves national security concerns, the branches shall require transacting parties to make the filing with central MOFCOM when making approval decisions with respect to a proposed M&A transaction.[294] As background information, inbound M&A transactions need to be pre-approved by *local* offices of MOFCOM in the locality of the target company,[295] while a national security review filing is made with the *headquarters* of MOFCOM at the central ministerial level. The new Draft Foreign Investment Law removes pre-approval requirements for investments below a certain value threshold but nevertheless keeps pre-approval requirements for those above a value threshold irrespective of sector.[296]

Since local MOFCOMs can make judgements as to whether transactions are "covered transactions" or not during their pre-approval screenings, the dominant strategy of foreign investors would be to piggyback on the decision of local MOFCOMs. That is, they are reluctant to voluntarily make national security review filings until local MOFCOMs require so.

If in the pre-approval process with local MOFCOM, a foreign investor is not required to make a separate national security review filing with the central MOFCOM, it can claim that it has received endorsement from the authorities. The argument is this: local MOFCOM, as the approval authority, does not think my transaction triggers any national security concern, so why should I bother to make a national security review notification with central MOFCOM? Local MOFCOMs are then making decisions *for* transacting parties as to whether a national security filing needs to be made, and they affix their red stamps on such decisions. As a result, adding local MOFCOMs as possible requestors disincentivizes the parties from making voluntarily filings.

There is more danger to this. The approval authority for a transaction and the power to conduct a national security review lie in different branches of MOFCOM: the former with local MOFCOM and the latter central MOFCOM. The consideration behind such division of authority lies in the importance of national security review, and a realistic recognition of divergent incentives of local and central MOFCOMs. Local MOFCOMs align more with local governments with respect to the attraction of foreign investment in the locality. They are inclined to excessively focus on trivial details in a transaction so as to assert their authority and seek rents from the foreign investors. They are unlikely to turn down an incoming foreign investment project on the grounds of national security concern, as that implies steering foreign investment away from their locality. By bestowing local MOFCOMs the authority to provide a de facto safe harbor to foreign investors as to the question of whether there is a potential national security concern in a specific transaction, central MOFCOM is in fact delegating the power of judgement call to local MOFCOMs.

Even assuming local MOFCOMs are able to take a neutral stand on whether one individual transaction threatens to impair national security, they do not have the capacity or information advantage to do so. This is an example of over-regulation – the under-staffed MOFCOM branches are screening massive transactions in the market and make decisions for market participants that are better off making judgement calls on their own. What is more, the ability of local MOFCOMs to hand pick winners (i.e. the foreign investors who need not go through the additional expensive national security review process) and losers (i.e. those investors who will have to), creates ample room for rent seeking. Also, the capabilities of MOFCOM branches vary to a great extent in China, and therefore one would expect great disparity in the decision-making process.

Nor do local MOFCOM branches have the information advantage in making the decision for the transacting parties. Note that the local MOFCOM branches would make the judgement call as to whether the parties should make a filing *prior to* the revelation by the investors of comprehensive information about its national security implications. That is to say, foreign investors do not have to disclose their proprietary information about the possible national security impacts of their transaction, while they pass the obligation to decide whether to make a filing on to local MOFCOMs. The regulators, who have the least information and high costs in obtaining the information, are bestowed with the power to make the decision on behalf of market participants.

In China, wide arrays of administrative agencies are able to request the institution of a national security review,[297] an arrangement distinctive from the CFIUS process in the United States. Above all, the determination of whether a transaction is a "covered transaction" has already taken place when such "other agencies" make requests, well before the 30-business-day clock begins to tick. The introduction of agencies outside the joint committee adds another layer of review, which means more delay. Also, if one agency requests that a national security review process be instituted, it is signalling to other agencies that may later be involved in the review that *it* believes the transaction poses national security risks. The signal may affect the behaviour of other agencies. What is worse, subsequently if the NDRC and MOFCOM actually consult the same agency that instituted the review process in the first place, such agency's opinion may be biased. It is predictable that the preoccupation of such agency may lead it to leaning towards imposing mitigation conditions on the transaction, or even proposing to block the transaction. Otherwise it would have concerns over justifying the administrative costs and regulatory resources involved in the national security process, both internally in its institution and externally in other agencies involved in the review process.

Several other third-party requestors, such as competitors, upstream companies, or downstream companies, could initiate a national security review process.[298] The problem with these third-party requestors is that they have conflicting business interests that induce them to abuse the right. Policy makers may have good intentions in laying out such a structural arrangement: they hope to expand the pool of entities that keep an eye on any national security risks posed. This whistle-blowing setting borrows from its counterpart in Chinese antitrust enforcement, where regulators almost exclusively rely on whistle-blowing of disgruntled competitors, purchasers, and employees to decide on the antitrust cases to bring.[299]

As much as whistle-blowing helps mitigate the information asymmetry problem faced by national security reviewers and eases enforcement burdens on regulators, rival businesses in the marketplace are not the optimal parties to have the power of initiating national security reviews. The motivation of a competitor in instituting a national security review is likely to deter the potential entry by its rivals in the market, and it tends to abuse the right by strategically filing frivolous cases. It means substantial costs on the part of potential foreign investors and a deflection of regulatory resources on the part of the agencies.

Analogy can be drawn to sham litigation, that is anti-competitive litigation brought about by competitors with the purpose of imposing additional costs on the incoming entrant. Sham litigation, in particular in the areas of intellectual property and antitrust, is notably costly for defendants. In the antitrust realm, plaintiffs are prone to use antitrust litigation to exclude competitors or to extract a wrongful settlement payment.[300] The ability for a competitor to institute a national security review process, which is usually lengthy, is equivalent to imposing an injunction on the incoming foreign investors. It will be a good way to delay or deter entry, a result the competitor would like to see. What is worse, unlike litigation, which incurs costs (e.g. attorney fees) on the part of plaintiff competitors while taking a toll on the defendants, the institution of a national security review process essentially requires zero cost of competitors. That is to say, the competitors can easily trap their rivals in the lengthy national security review process by nothing more than simply making a request to institute the national security review. Thus, the stake is high for foreign investors, while the bar is low and pay-off high for their competitors as requestors; the system is inclined to induce competitors, opportunistic petitions.

Also, there is little benefit associated with bestowing competitors with the right to initiate the national security review process against their rivals. They lack superior information. Transacting parties usually keep private M&A transactions highly confidential before closing. And in China, a national security review process needs to be completed before a transaction is closed.[301] Furthermore, cross-border public M&As are rare in China.[302] Even in the case of public M&As, as the relevant information would become available to the public, it does not justify why the competitors need to be singled out as good candidates to kick-start the national security review process; the whole market then has the information.

To sum up, in the national security review process in China, bringing in more parties as possible requestors for the institution of a national security review process creates misplaced incentives. It would work as a better mechanism to encourage voluntary filings by transacting parties, who have the best information about the transaction's national security implications, while deterring filing by other third parties with their own divergent goals to pursue and who are prone to engage in self-interested, potentially egregious behaviour.

6. Conclusion

Walking a fine line between openness to foreign investment and the protection of national security is at the core of designing a foreign investment regulatory framework. While scholarship unanimously recognizes the delicate balance between free trade and the protection of national security, without a satisfactory certainty on what "national security" is and what the scope and the standards of national security review are, such a declaration merely pays lip service to the glorious notion.

When we look at the real-life national security programmes in action, while it appears that the Chinese counterpart of CFIUS resembles that of CFIUS, they are indeed two very different regimes with contrasting consequences. In the United States, while the CFIUS process sets the benchmark for national security review internationally and the degree of openness in foreign investment regulation, some reflections are necessary. CFIUS has experienced an expansion in its mandate (from "monitoring" to "blocking" or "unwinding" M&A transactions), an expansion in its scope of "national security" purview (all industries, all sectors, no dollar amount threshold), and has no obligation in ensuring the continuity of its standard of review (drifting standards of review over time, unreviewability of decisions) – all of which make the CFIUS especially challenging and unpredictable to potential foreign investors. The swift expansion of CFIUS power and its greatly heightened impact on companies has made it no longer apt to maintain a national security review system without a concrete definition of "national security," scope of review, or specific standards of review. As it stands, the CFIUS process does not facilitate compliance by foreign investors and generates negative consequences, including increased costs and undesirable deterrence effects on investors (yet the foreign investors are not entirely certain what they are deterred from). In light of the judicial self-restraint and deference to CFIUS as an inter-agency committee, as well as the inefficiency of case-by-case adjudication in shedding light on the criteria for review, policy makers should consider more direct regulation as a feasible regulatory approach to refine the CFIUS process. Otherwise, CFIUS will remain vulnerable to criticism that it may be abused for protectionist or political purposes.

In the case of China, while it strives to establish a national security review regime by modelling it on that of the United States, several structural and institutional loopholes lead to a failure in properly safeguarding national security. Above all, the poor draftsmanship implies difficulty in implementation. It does not factor in the institutional considerations that make the regime work in the United States; the twists and selective application due to unsophisticated draftsmanship, political compromises, and agency self-interested behaviours undermine the regime. Instead, China's regime becomes another layer of regulation that burdens the incoming foreign investors with no plausible positive effects. A more worrisome phenomenon is that it does not devote the appropriate proportion of regulatory resources to the critical sectors that are in the most need of national security review. This leads to a more profound question regarding the timing of its implementation of national security review programme. Its national security regime came into place too little too late: the sweeping wade of foreign investments in hard assets (including many of the valuable resources) has shown the trend of quieting down after foreign capital's wide penetration in a wide spectrum of economy.

The promulgation of the FISR Measures 2020 signals China's consolidated efforts to implement a more unified and comprehensive system to keep a close eye on investment and transactions that might have national security implications.[303]

Better certainty, predictability, and transparency for law compliance and enforcement can be seen in FISR Measures 2020. It can also be seen that the Chinese government strikes a balance between the promotion of foreign investment and the protection of national security as its core principle, rejecting foreign investment projects that potentially threaten national security in rare and exceptional circumstances.[304] The authorities involved in the national security review process should be responsible to guarantee the transparency of the procedure so as to make the system understandable and accountable for potential foreign investors.[305]

However, at the same time, the newly released measures have rattled the nerves of some foreign investors and Western media outlets, with some raising concerns that whether the Chinese government is trying to curb foreign investment and partially reducing China's opening up by practicing trade protectionism. These are baseless worries, because these new measures will reveal the Chinese leadership's determination to open the country's economy wider to the outside world. For example, military industries, as well as other national defense and security-related fields, are significant to a country's sovereignty. China has never before given the green light to foreign investment in these fields, or in locations surrounding military installations or arms industry facilities. Upcoming years will see these fields open up to and receive foreign investment.[306] So, the notion that FISR Measures 2020 are protectionist is quite biased. On the contrary, the measures align China with international practices.[307]

An increased degree of openness requires more stringent security measures. This is also the case in Western countries, which have laws such as the Foreign Investment Risk Review Modernization Act in the US and the EU's Foreign Direct Investment Screening Framework. The newly released rules have been put in place to strengthen China's security network during the process of opening up, as well as to prevent and remove national security risks while promoting and better protecting foreign investment.[308] Foreign investors and multinational corporations considering direct or indirect investments in China, including parties to offshore mergers and acquisitions involving business operations in China, will need to carefully assess whether their transactions trigger a national security review in China and factor the potential implications into their deals.

Besides China's opening up will be unsustainable without a strong security network. A stronger fence against various security risks is expected to ensure more extensive and deeper opening up to the rest of the world. Of course, on the precondition that security of foreign investment is ensured, the Chinese government will provide timely responses to foreign investors' misgivings so as to ensure the review process will not be too lengthy once the new measures are put into practice.[309]

As a broader lesson from legal transplantation in general, legal proposals to the Chinese national security review regime should embrace a presumption of skepticism over the institutional competence of regulatory agencies. The presumption should be different from that of general deference to administrative agencies deriving from the *Chevron* doctrine. Meanwhile legal framers should caution against the obsession with copying rules or procedures from developed jurisdictions, while disregarding the system-level effects and the institutional setting in which these rules and procedures operate.

Notes

1 See Comm. on Foreign Inv. in the U.S., Annual Report to Congress 30 (December 2013), www.treasury.gov/resource-center/international/foreigninvestment/Documents/2013%20CFIUS%2OAnnual%2OReport%20PUBLIC.pdf [hereinafter CHUS ANNUAL REPORT 2013].

2 See Wilmerhale, *2014 M&A Report 2* (2014), https://www.wilmerhale.com/-/media/files/shared_content/editorial/publications/documents/2014-wilmerhale-ma-report.pdf.

3 There is literature on national security review, a number of which are student notes and comments. For example George Stephanov Georgiev, 'Comment, The Reformed CFIUS Regulatory Framework: Mediating Between Continued Openness to Foreign Investment and National Security', 25 *Yale Journal on Regulation* 125 (2008); Cathleen Hamel Hartge, 'Note, China's National Security Review: Motivations and the Implications for Investors', 49 *Stanford Journal of International Law* 239 (2013); Souvik Saha, 'Comment, CFIUS Now Made in China: Dueling National Security Review Frameworks as a Countermeasure to Economic Espionage in the Age of Globalization', 33 *Northwestern Journal of International Law & Business* 199 (2012); Christopher M. Tipler, 'Note, Defining 'National Security': Resolving Ambiguity in the CFIUS Regulations', 35 *University of Pennsylvania Journal of International Law* 1223 (2014); Colin Stapleton, 'Note, The Global Colony: A Comparative Analysis of National Security-Based Foreign Investment Regimes in the Western Hemisphere', 92 *Washington University Law Review* 1647 (2015); *see also* David T. Zaring, 'CFIUS as a Congressional Notification Service', 83 *Southern California Law Review* 81 (2009); Karl P. Sauvant (ed) *Investing in the United States: Is the US Ready for FDI from China?* (London: Edward Elgar 2010); Matthew Aglialoro, 'Defend and Protect: National Security Restrictions on Foreign Investment in the United States', 83 *University of Cincinnati Law Review* 1261 (2015). As noted by David Zaring, national security is "the subject of little international scholarship." *See* David T. Zaring, 'CFIUS as a Congressional Notification Service', 83 *Southern California Law Review* 81, 129 (2009). Relatedly, there is literature on sovereign wealth funds and the prospect of a US–China bilateral investment treaty. *See, for example* Scott J. Shackelford, Eric L. Richards, Anjanette H. Raymond and Amanda N. Craig, 'Using BITs to Protect Bytes: Promoting Cyber Peace by Safeguarding Trade Secrets Through Bilateral Investment Treaties', 52 *American Business Law Journal* 1 (2015); David A. Gantz, 'Challenges for the United States in Negotiating a BIT with China: Reconciling Reciprocal Investment Protection with Policy Concerns', 31 *Arizona Journal of International & Comparative Law* 203 (2014); Daniel C.K. Chow, 'Why China Wants a Bilateral Investment Treaty with the United States', 33 *Boston University International Law Journal* 421 (2015); Paul Rose, 'Sovereigns as Shareholders', 87 *North Carolina Law Review* 83 (2008); Richard A. Epstein and Amanda M. Rose, 'The Regulation of Sovereign Wealth Funds: The Virtues of Going Slow', 76 *University of Chicago Law Review* 111 (2009).

4 The Dubai Ports World controversy was one of the most salient cases that symbolize the raised profile of CHUS, which led to the passage of FINSA. *See* Stephen K. Pudner, 'Moving Forward from Dubai Ports World – The Foreign Investment and National Security Act of 2007', 59, *Alabama Law Review* 1277 (2007).

5 *See* discussion *infra* Section IV.B.

6 *See* Andrew Batson and Matthew Karnitschnig, China Plans System to Vet Foreign Deals for Security, *Wall St. J.* (Aug. 26, 2008, 12:01 AM), www.wsj.com/articles/SB121968793079569903 (quoting lawyer Michael Han, who said that "[i]t looks like a national-security-review mechanism similar to CFIUS in the U.S., where several ministries are involved"); *see also* Saha, *supra* note 3, at 217–220.

7 50 U.S.C. app. § 2170(a)(3) (2015) ("The term 'covered transaction' means any merger, acquisition, or takeover that is proposed or pending . . . by or with any foreign person which could result in foreign control of any person engaged in interstate commerce in the United States."); *see also* 31 C.F.R. § 800.207 (2015) ("[A]ny transaction . . . by or with any foreign person, which could result in control of a U.S. business by a foreign person."); *id.* § 800.214 ("[A]ny covered transaction."); *id.* § 800.301 (clarifying the term "covered transaction").

8 31 C.F.R. § 800.216 (defining "foreign person").

9 *Id.* § 800.226 (defining "U.S. business").

10 *Id.* § 800.204 (defining "control").

11 Upon its establishment, CFIUS was charged with reviewing all inbound M&A investments that "might have major implications for United States national interests." Exec.

Order No. 11,858, 3 C.F.R. § 990 (1971–1975), amended by Exec. Order No. 12, 188, 3 C.F.R. § 131 (1981); Exec. Order No. 12,661, 3 C.F.R. § 618 (1989); Exec. Order 12,860, 3 C.F.R. § 629 (1994); Exec. Order 13,286, 3 C.F.R. § 166 (2004); Exec. Order 13,603, 77 Fed. Reg. 16651 (Mar. 22, 2012). It was to "monitor[] the impact of foreign investment in the United States.", Id. § 1(b).

12 See Joanna Rubin Travalini, 'Comment, Foreign Direct Investment in the United States: Achieving a Balance Between National Economy Benefits and National Security Interests', 29 *Northwestern Journal of International Law & Business* 779, 783–84 (2009).

13 H. COMM. on Gov't Operations, The Adequacy of the Federal Response to Foreign Investment in the United States, H. Rep. No. 96–1216, at 166–84 (1980); see also Matthew C. Sullivan, 'CFIUS and Congress Reconsidered: Fire Alarms, Police Patrols, and a New Oversight Regime', 17 *Willamette Journal of International Law and Dispute Resolution* 199, 211 (2009).

14 In 1987, Fujitsu Ltd. – a Japanese computer manufacturer – made an offer to buy Fairchild Semiconductor Corp. – a company that had supply contracts with US defense contractors. Many feared losing the technological edge to the Japanese and feared that the United States would have no other comparable microchip manufacturers if a Japanese company purchased Fairchild Semiconductor. In response, CFIUS instituted a review, and Fujitsu Ltd. withdrew its offer. See James K. Jackson, Cong. Research Serv., RL33388, The Committee on Foreign Investment in the United States (CFIUS) 4 (2014), www.fas.org/sgp/crs/natsec/RL33388.pdf; see also Pudner, *supra* note 4, at 1279.

15 50 U.S.C. app. § 2170 (2014).

16 §2170(d)(1).

17 §2170(b)(1)(A).

18 Id. § 2170(b)(3)(B), (d)(1). For an example of presidential action, see discussion of Ralls Corp. v. CFIUS, 758 F.3d 296 (D.C. Cir. 2014), infra Section II.B.

19 A US business refers to any business that operates in the interstate commerce of the United States. This means any business entity that has an office, some employees, and almost any type of operations in the United States. A US business can also be a collection of assets that could be considered to constitute an operating business.

20 Foreign Investment and National Security Act of 2007, Pub. L. No. 110–49, 121 Stat. 246 (codified at 50 U.S.C. app § 2170 (2014).

21 For further details about the Dubai Ports World transaction, see Thomas E. Crocker, 'What Banks Need to Know About the Coming Debate over CFIUS, Foreign Direct Investment, and Sovereign Wealth Funds', 125 *Banking Law Journal* 457, 459–60 (2008) (the author represented Dubai Ports World before CFIUS).

22 50 U.S.C. app. § 2170(a)(5), (f).

23 Id. §2170(b)(2)(B)(III).

24 U.S. Government Accountability Office, GAO-18-249, Committee on Foreign Investment in the United States: Treasury Should Coordinate Resources Needed to Address Increased Workload 19 (2018).

25 Mitigation requires the parties to negotiate measures approved by CFIUS for the transaction to be cleared. As a follow-up, CFIUS also devotes resources to monitoring compliance with mitigation agreements. U.S. Government Accountability Office, GaO-18-249, Committee on Foreign Investment in the United States: Treasury Should Coordinate Resources Needed to Address Increased Workload 19 (2020).

26 Transactions can be prohibited. The target US business may be required to divest a sensitive product line or a subsidiary before consummation of an investment by a foreign acquirer. U.S. Government Accountability Office, GAO-18-249, Committee on Foreign Investment in the United States: Treasury Should Coordinate Resources Needed to Address Increased Workload 19 (2018).

27 U.S. Government Accountability Office, GAO-18-249, Committee on Foreign Investment in the United States: Treasury Should Coordinate Resources Needed to Address Increased Workload 19 (2018) 20.

28 American Academy of Arts and Sciences, 'Introduction' in Elisa D. Harris (ed), *Governance of Dual-Use Technologies: Theories and Practices* 4 (Cambridge, Massachusetts: American Academy of Arts and Sciences 2010).

29 The White House, Presidential Memorandum on the Actions by the United States Related to the Section 301 Investigation (22 March 2018).

30 The White House, *Statement on Steps to Protect Domestic Technology and Intellectual Property from China's Discriminatory and Burdensome Trade Practices* (29 May 2018), https://trumpwhitehouse.archives.gov/briefings-statements/statement-steps-protect-domestic-technology-intellectual-property-chinas-discriminatory-burdensome-trade-practices/, accessed 2 October 2022.

31 Foreign Investment Risk Review Modernization Act of 2017, S. 2098, 115th Cong. (2017). Foreign Investment Risk Review Modernization Act of 2017, H.R. 4311, 115th Cong. (2017).

32 John S. McCain National Defense Authorization Act for Fiscal Year 2019, Pub. L. No. 115–232, 132 Stat. 1636, 2174 (2018).

33 John S. McCain National Defense Authorization Act for Fiscal Year 2019, Pub. L. No. 115–232, 132 Stat. 1636, 2423 (2018).

34 Remarks by President Trump at a Roundtable on the Foreign Investment Risk Review Modernization Act (FIRMMA), 2018 Daily. Comp. Pres. Doc. 1 (23 August 2018).

35 50 U.S.C. §4565 (2012).

36 Robert D. Williams, 'CFIUS Reform and U.S. Government Concerns over Chinese Investments: A Primer', *Lawfare*, 17 November 2017.

37 Evaluating CFIUS: Administration Perspectives: Hearing Before the Subcomm. on Monetary Policy & Trade, 115th Cong. 3 (2018).

38 §1703(a)(4)(B)(i), 132, Stat. at 2177 (2018).

39 §1703(a)(4)(D)(i)(I).

40 §1703(a)(4)(D)(i)(II).

41 §1703(a)(4)(D)(i)(III).

42 §1703(a)(4)(D)(i)(III)(aa).

43 §1703(a)(4)(D)(i)(III)(bb).

44 §1703(a)(4)(D)(i)(III)(cc).

45 §1703(a)(4)(A)(iv), 132 Stat. at 2180.

46 §1703(a)(4)(C)(ii).

47 §1703(a)(4)(B)(v), 132 Stat. at 2178.

48 §1703(a)(4)(B)(iii), 132 Stat. at 2178.

49 31 C.F.R. §802.

50 31 C.F.R. §802, app. A.

51 §1703(a)(4)(C)(i).

52 §1703(a)(4)(iv), 132, Stat. at 2178.

53 §1703(a)(4)(B)(v), 132 Stat. at 2178.

54 §1703(a)(4)(D)(i)(II), 132 Stat. at 2179.

55 §1703(a)(4)(D)(iv).

56 §1706.

57 50 USC §4565 (2012).

58 U.S. Government Accountability Office, GAO-18-249, Committee on Foreign Investment in the United States: Treasury Should Coordinate Resources Needed to Address Increased Workload 19 (2018).

59 §1706, 132 Stat. at 2184.

60 §1706(b)(1)(c)(v)(IV)(bb).

61 §1706(b)(1)(c)(v)(IV)(cc).

62 §1709, 132 Stat. at 2187–2188.

63 Committee on Foreign Investment in the United States, Annual Report to Congress 2–5 (2020).

64 §1713(3)(B)(ii) Stat. at 2191; §1713(3)(B)(ii).

65 §1713(3)(B)(ii) and §1719.

66 §1713(3)(B)(ii) and §1719(b).

67 §1719(b).

68 §1709, 132 Stat. at 2188–2189.

69 §1717.

70 §1703(a)(4), 132 Stat. 1636, 2177 (2018); 50 USC § 4565(a)(4).

71 *See* Waiguo Touzi Fa (Cao'an Zhengqu Yijian Gao)(外国投资法(草案征求意见稿)) [Foreign Investment Law of the People' s Republic of China (Draft for Comments)] (promulgated by the Ministry of Commerce, 19 January 2015) [hereinafter Draft Foreign Investment Law], http://tfs.mofcom.gov.cn/article/as/201501/20150100871010. shtml (China).

72 *See* Jie Guo, Zhongguo Fabu Waiguo Touzifa Cao'an (中国发布外国投资法草案) [China Publishes Draft Law on Foreign Investment Law], *Hong Kong Law* (April 2015), http://losangeles.mofcom.gov.cn/article/ddfg/tzzhch/201507/20150701035860. shtml (China).

73 See Draft Foreign Investment Law, *supra* note 71, at Article 49.

74 *Id.*

75 *See* Guowu Yuan guanyu Tongyi Jianli Guowu Yuan Ziyou Maoyi Shiyan Qu Gong-zuo Buji Lianxi Huiyi Zhidu de Pifu (国务院关于同意建立国务院自由贸易试验区工作部际联席会议制度的批复) [Approval Reply of the State Council Pertaining to the Establishment of the Working-Level Inter-Ministerial Joint-Committee System in Free Trade Zones That Were Set Up by the State Council] (promulgated by the State Council, 7 February 2015, Effective 7 February 2015), www.gov.cn/zhengce/content/2015-02/16/content_9486.htm (China).

76 *See id.* at Article 2.

77 Yuwen Li and Cheng Bian, 'A New Dimension of Foreign Investment Law in China – Evolution and Impacts of the National Security Review System', 24 *Asia Pacific Law Review* 149, 151–152 (2016), https://doi.org/10.1080/10192557.2016.1243212, accessed 19 April 2022.

78 Xingxing Li, 'National Security Review in Foreign Investments: A Comparative and Critical Assessment on China and U.S. Laws and Practices', 13 *Berkeley Business Law Journal* 255, 264 (2016).

79 Xingxing Li, 'National Security Review in Foreign Investments: A Comparative and Critical Assessment on China and U.S. Laws and Practices', 13 *Berkeley Business Law Journal* 255, 264 (2016).

80 Fan Longduan Fa (反垄断法)[Anti-Monopoly Law] (promulgated by the Standing Comm. of the Tenth National People's Congress, 30 August 2007, effective 1 August 2008), www.gov.cn/flfg/2007-08/30/content_732591.htm (China).

81 *Id.* at Article 31.

82 The M&A Rules set forth possible adverse consequences for any failure to make the national security filing, but the penalties are worded strongly and are vague on details. *See id.*

83 Denis McMahon, *Carlyle Agrees to Acquire Smaller Stake in Xugong*, Wall St. J. (26 March 2007, 12:01 AM), www.wsj.com/articles/SB117486672665348486; Sky Canaves, *Carlyle Moves On from Xugong Shadow*, Wall St. J. (12 January 2010, 3:56 AM), http://blogs.wsj.com/chinarealtime/2010/01/12/carlyle-moves-on-from-xugong-shadow.

84 By the time of the Carlyle-Xugong transaction, construction machinery had not been regarded as a sensitive sector in China. *See Chinese Companies: Over the Great Wall*, Economist (3 November 2005), www.economist.com/node/5121635.

85 *See Zhongguo Shi"Jingzheng"*(中国式"竞争")[A Chinese-styled "Competition"], NEW CENTURY WKLY. (新世纪周刊) (4 November 2013), https://topics.caixin.com/chinastyle/ (China); *see also Chinese M&A: Playing at Home*, Economist (3 August 2006), www.economist.com/node/7258903. *Cf.* Hairong Yu, *Waizi Binggou Anquan Shencha Chulu* (外资并购安全审查出炉)[Fresh Out of the Oven: National Security Review in M&As by Foreign Acquirers], Caixin Online (财新网)(28 February 2011), https://www.163.com/money/article/6TVQI68600253B0H.html (China).

86 No public information is available about the number of cases filed by parties in an inbound M&A transaction to the committee. MOFCOM does not make available the number of notices it receives to the public either.

87 State Department Office, No. 6 (2011), www.gov.cn/zwgk/2011-02/12/content_1802467.htm.

88 State Department Office, No. 24 (2015), www.gov.cn/zhengce/content/2015-04/20/content_9629.htm.

89 Foreign Investment Law (Draft for Comment 2015) www.mofcom.gov.cn/article/ae/ag/201501/20150100871007.shtml.

90 Rong Cai and Sean Lao, 'National Security Review on Foreign Investments into China', www.zhonglun.com/Content/2021/01-04/1708382620.html, accessed 19 April 2022.

91 Shuwen Chen, *Analysis and Suggestions on the Foreign Investment Law*, 1 Legal System & Soc'y 22 (2016).

92 Meichen Liu, 'The New Chinese Foreign Investment Law and Its Implication on Foreign Investors', 38 *Northwestern Journal of International Law & Business* 285 (2018).

93 FIL, Article 25.

94 Z. Alex Zhang and Vivian Tsoi, 'China Adopts New Foreign Investment Law' *White & Case*, 29 March 2019, www.whitecase.com/publications/alert/china-adopts-new-foreign-investment-law, accessed 25 April 2022.

95 Łukasz Czarnecki, 'The 2020 Foreign Investment Law of China: Confucianism and New Challenges for Social Development', 1 *Contemporary Central & East European Law* 94 (2019).

96 Anti-Monopoly Law, Article 33.

97 Article 31 of the Anti-Monopoly Law stipulates that "for participation in concentration of business operators by way of foreign-funded merger and acquisition of domestic enterprises or any other method which involves national security, the examination of concentration of business operators shall be carried out pursuant to the provisions of this Law and examination of national security shall be carried out pursuant to the relevant laws and regulations."

98 Thomas Heck and Katja Banik, 'Foreign Investment: China's Security Review Measures Take Effect', www.pwc.de/en/international-markets/german-business-groups/china-business-group/foreign-investment-china-s-security-review-measures-take-effect.html, accessed 19 April 2022.

99 Jenny (Jia) Sheng and Chunbin Xu, 'China Publishes New Rules on National Security Review of Foreign Investment', www.pillsburylaw.com/en/news-and-insights/china-rules-security-review-foreign-investment.html, accessed 19 April 2022.

100 Rui Bai Law Firm, Xin Bai Law Firm and Tiang & Partners, 'China Releases Foreign Investments Security Review Measures to Strengthen Regulatory Control over Foreign Investment', www.pwccn.com/en/china-tax-news/2021q1/chinatax-news-jan2021-2.pdf, accessed 19 April 2022.

101 Baker McKenzie, 'China Enacts New Foreign Investment Security Review Measures', www.bakermckenzie.com/en/insight/publications/2021/01/china-enacts-new-foreign-investment-security, accessed 19 April 2022.

102 Z. Alex Zhang, Vivian Tsoi, Charlie Zhu, and Chunlei Pang, 'The New FISR Measures – A Step Further in China's National Security Review of Foreign Investments', www.whitecase.com/publications/alert/new-fisr-measures-step-further-chinas-national-security-review-foreign?s=The%20New%20FISR%20Measures%20%E2%80%93%20A%20Step%20Further%20in%20China%E2%80%99s%20National%20Security%20Review%20of%20Foreign%20Investments, accessed 19 April 2022.

103 Rui Bai Law Firm, Xin Bai Law Firm, and Tiang & Partners, *supra* note 100.

104 O'Melveny & Myers LLP, 'China Expands National Security Review of Foreign Investments', www.omm.com/resources/alerts-and-publications/alerts/china-expands-national-security-review-of-foreign-investments/#, accessed 19 April 2022.

105 Measures for the Security Review of Foreign Investment (外商投资安全审查办法) 2020, Article 2.

106 State Administration for Market Regulation (2020) State Municipal Supervision Office No. 26 Administrative Penalty Decision; State Administration for Market Regulation (2020) State Municipal Supervision Office No. 27 Administrative Penalty Decision; State Administration for Market Regulation (2020) State Municipal Supervision Office Administrative Penalty Decision No. 28 (国家市场监督管理总局（2020）国市监处26号行政处罚决定书；国家市场监督管理总局（2020）国市监处27号行政处罚决定书；国家市场监督管理总局（2020）国市监处28号行政处罚决定书).

107 Rui Bai Law Firm, Xin Bai Law Firm, and Tiang & Partners, *supra* note 100.

108 Z. Alex Zhang, Vivian Tsoi, Charlie Zhu, and Chunlei Pang, '*supra* note 102.

109 Measures for the Security Review of Foreign Investment (外商投资安全审查办法) 2020, Article 3.

110 Z. Alex Zhang, Vivian Tsoi, Charlie Zhu, and Chunlei Pang, *supra* note 102.

111 Yizhu Chen, Zihan Ma, and Xiaoyu Wei, 'Investigation and Reflection on Foreign Investment Security Review: Focus on Current Legal Documents in China' (The 4th International Conference on Humanities Education and Social Sciences, Xishuangbanna, China, October 2021).

112 Measures for the Security Review of Foreign Investment (外商投资安全审查办法) 2020, Article 4.

113 Baker McKenzie, *supra* note 101.

114 Baker McKenzie, *supra* note 101.

115 O'Melveny & Myers LLP, *supra* note 104.

116 Rui Bai Law Firm, Xin Bai Law Firm, and Tiang & Partners, *supra* note 100.

117 Yizhu Chen, Zihan Ma, and Xiaoyu Wei, 'Investigation and Reflection on Foreign Investment Security Review: Focus on Current Legal Documents in China' (The 4th International Conference on Humanities Education and Social Sciences, Xishuangbanna, China, October 2021).

118 Measures for the Security Review of Foreign Investment (外商投资安全审查办法) 2020, Article 5, Article 7, Article 8, Article 9, Article 12, Article 13, Article 16, Article 17, Article 18.

119 O'Melveny & Myers LLP, *supra* note 104.

120 Z. Alex Zhang, Vivian Tsoi, Charlie Zhu, and Chunlei Pang, *supra* note 102.

121 Z. Alex Zhang, Vivian Tsoi, Charlie Zhu and Chunlei Pang, *supra* note 102.

122 Rui Bai Law Firm, Xin Bai Law Firm, and Tiang & Partners, *supra* note 100.

123 Yizhu Chen, Zihan Ma, and Xiaoyu Wei, 'Investigation and Reflection on Foreign Investment Security Review: Focus on Current Legal Documents in China' (The 4th International Conference on Humanities Education and Social Sciences, Xishuangbanna, China, October 2021).

124 Rui Bai Law Firm, Xin Bai Law, Firm and Tiang & Partners, *supra* note 100.

125 Jiang Huikuang, Scott Yu, and John Jiang, 'China Upgrades Security Review on Foreign Investment', www.lexology.com/library/detail.aspx?g=9c43eb56-c26d-441e-bcce-52cfcdfe9885, accessed 19 April 2022.

126 *See* Guowuyuan Guanyu Shixing Shichang Zhunru Fumian Qingdan Zhidu de Yijian (国务院关于实行市场准入负面清单制度的意见)[Opinion of the State Council on the Establishment of a Negative List System Pertaining to Market Entry] (promulgated by the State Council, 19 October 2015, effective 19 October 2015, www.gov.cn/zhengce/content/2015-10/19/content_10247.htm (China).

127 The Draft Foreign Investment Law is expected to alter the previous practice in foreign investment regulation that every aspect of foreign investment is regulated and subject to approval. Now a higher threshold is proposed for approval requirements, but it does not fundamentally change the screening and pre-approval nature of foreign investment regulation. *See* Draft Foreign Investment Law, *supra* note 71, at Articles 26, 27.

128 *Id*. at Article 26(2).

129 Waishang Touzi Chanye Zhidao Mulu (2015 Nian Xiuding)(外商投资产业指导目录(2015年修订))[Catalogue for the Guidance of Foreign Investment Industries (Amended in 2015)] (promulgated by Nat'l Dev. & Reform Common and Ministry of Commerce, 10 March 2015, effective 10 April 2015) [hereinafter 2015 Catalogue], http://www.gov.cn/gongbao/content/2015/content_2864060.htm (China).

130 For a more detailed narrative of the pre-approval requirements, see Xingxing Li, 'An Economic Analysis of Regulatory Overlap and Regulatory Competition: The Experience of Interagency Regulatory Competition in China's Regulation of Inbound Foreign Investment', 67 *Administrative Law Review* 685, 700–708 (2015).

131 *See* Ministry of Commerce, 2015 Nian Shangwu Gongzuo Nianzhong Zongshu, No. 1 (2015年商务工作年终综述之一)[2015 Year End Summary On Commerce-Related Work] (25 December 2015), www.mofcom.gov.cn/article/ae/ai/201512/20151201220159.shtml (China).

132 A nationwide Negative List has not been promulgated. One Negative List specifically applicable to China's pilot Free Trade Zones has taken effect. *See* Ziyou Maoyi Shiyan Qu Waishang Touzi Zhunru Tebie Guanli Cuoshi (Fumian Qingdan)(自由贸易试验区外商投资准入特别管理措施(负面清单)) [Special Administrative Measures Applicable to Free Trade Pilot Zones in Respect of the Entry of Foreign Capital (Negative List)] (promulgated by Gen. Office of State Council, 8 April 2015, effective 8 May 2015), http://www.gov.cn/gongbao/content/2015/content_2856650.htm (China).

133 For such investments, the investor may directly proceed to register the business with the competent Administration for Industry and Commerce (AIC), the Administration of Foreign Exchange (SAFE), and the Tax Bureau.

134 The pressure for more openness to foreign capital is in part transmitted from negotiations of BITs between China and developed jurisdictions such as the United States and the EU. *See, for example* Karl P. Sauvant and Huiping Chen, *A China – US Bilateral Investment Treaty: A Template for a Multilateral Framework for Investment?*, Colum. Fdi Persp., 17 December 2012, http://works.bepress.com/karl_sauvant/369/.

135 For a summary on the regulatory restrictions on foreign investment in the United States, see Michael V. Seitzinger, Cong. Research Serv., RL33103, Foreign Investment in the United States: Major Federal Statutory Restrictions (2013), www.fas.org/sgp/crs/misc/RL33103.pdf.

136 *See Merger Review*, FTC, www.ftc.gov/enforcement/merger-review, accessed 8 April 2016.

137 *See* 50 U.S.C. app. §2170(f)(9)(C) (2015). A target company in an M&A transaction is required to comply with export-control laws and sanctions laws. After the transaction, the Bureau of Industry and Security within the Department of Commerce, the Directorate of Defense Trade Controls within the Department of State, and the Office of Foreign Assets Control within the Treasury Department may hold a foreign acquirer liable for the target company's prior export controls and sanctions violations. For acquirer's successor liability, see Sigma-Aldrich Bus. Holdings, Inc., No. 01-BXA-06 (29 August 2002) (Fitzpatrick, A.L.J.) (Bureau of Industry and Security's approach); U.S. Dep't of State, Bureau of Political Military Affairs, General Motors Corporation Consent Agreement (22 October 2004), www.pmddtc.state.gov/compliance/consent_agreements/pdf/GeneralMotorsCorp_ConsentAgreem ent.pdf (Directorate of Defense Trade Controls, approach); Dep't of the Treasury, Office of Foreign Assets Control, Enforcement Information for 7 September 2007 (2007), www.treasury.gov/resource-center/sanctions/OFAC-Enforcement/Documents/09072007.pdf (Office of Foreign Assets Control's approach).

138 For example publicly traded companies must file Form 8-K with the SEC to disclose major events that may affect their businesses, which includes M&As. *See Fast Answers – Form 8-K*, SEC (10 August 2012), www.sec.gov/answers/form8k.htm; SEC, Form 8-K: Current Report Pursuant To Section 13 or 15(d) of The Securities Exchange Act of 1934 7, www.sec.gov/about/forms/form8-k.pdf, accessed 8 April 2016.

139 The United States has been persistent in including national security clauses when it enters into bilateral investment agreements with other countries. In its model bilateral treaty, the United States expressly reserves the right to scrutinize and invalidate a transaction through CHUS by "applying measures that it considers necessary for . . . the protection of its own essential security interests." Office of the U.S. Trade Representative, 2012 U.S. Model Bilateral Investment Treaty Article 18 (2012), www.ustr.gov/sites/default/files/BIT%20text%20for%20ACIEP%20Meeting.pdf.

140 Exec. Order No. 11,858, 3 C.F.R. § 990 (1971–1975), *as amended by* Exec. Order No. 13,456, 3 C.F.R. § 4677 (2008). The Regulations include 31 C.F.R. pt. 800 (2015), *as amended by* Regulations Pertaining to Mergers, Acquisitions, and Takeovers by Foreign Persons, 73 *Fed. Reg.* 70, 702 (21 November 2008).

141 50 U.S.C. app. § 2170(a)(5).

142 50 U.S.C. app. § 2170(f) (listing a total of 11 factors and also noting these factors are merely guidelines and not intended to be conclusive).

143 *Id.*

144 *Id.*

145 Office of Investment Security, Guidance Concerning the National Security Review Conducted by the Committee on Foreign Investment in the United States, 73 Fed. Reg. 74, 567 (8 December 2008).

146 *See* U.S. Dep't of the Treasury, CFIUS Reform: Guidance on National Security Considerations (1 December 2008), https://home.treasury.gov/system/files/206/GuidanceSummary-12012008.pdf (summarizing the Guidance).

147 50 U.S.C. app.§ 2170(c).

148 Regulations Pertaining to Mergers, Acquisitions, and Takeovers by Foreign Persons, 73 Fed. Reg. 70,702, 70,705 (21 November 2008) (discussing the case-by-case review approach as adopted in 31 C.F.R. § 800.101 (2015)).

149 After enabling CFIUS's function to block transactions, Congress complained that the CHUS review process is not sufficiently transparent and that the White House has taken a hands-off approach, resulting in reviews that are not sufficiently detailed. *See* Alan P. Larson & David M. Marchick, Foreign Investment and National Security: Getting the Balance Right 13–24 (2006), available at https://ciaotest.cc.columbia.edu/wps/cfr/0002843/f_0002843_2005.pdf last accessed 22 October 2022.

150 *See, for example* Harry L. Clark and Jonathan W. Ware, 'Limits on International Business in the Petroleum Sector: CFIUS Investment Screening, Economic Sanctions, Anti-Bribery Rules, and Other Measures', 6 *Texas Journal of Oil, Gas, and Energy Law* 75, 84–91 (2010) (discussing various regulatory regimes' impacts on inbound foreign investment in the United States and noting the particular challenges brought about by CFIUS's process); *see also* Christopher F. Corr, 'A Survey of United States Controls on Foreign Investment and Operations: How Much is Enough?', 9 *American University Journal of International Law and Policy* 417, 456 (1993) (noting that "mandatory submission of reports" such as CFIUS filings "are to some extent burdens on foreign investment, and in certain cases may deter potential investors concerned about negative political reaction or press coverage given the sensitivity of foreign investment").

151 A CFIUS decision "shall be based on a risk-based analysis, conducted by the Committee, of the threat to national security of the covered transaction." FINSA sec. 5, § 721(1) (1)(B), 121 Stat. at 254. Commentators interpret that "[n]ational security should be the prime consideration, presumably rather than political or diplomatic considerations, although the statute is not entirely clear on this score." Zaring, *supra* note 3, at 70, n.72.

152 *See* 134 Cong. Rec. S4833 (1988) (statement of Sen. Exon) (noting that "national security" was "to be read in a broad and flexible manner").

153 There is criticism that the broad and vague mandate of CFIUS, in combination with its secrecy, is an impediment to trade liberalization and a threat to economic productivity, and potentially in an arbitrary and capricious manner. *See, for example* Joseph Mamounas, 'Controlling Foreign Ownership of U.S. Strategic Assets: The Challenge of Maintaining National Security in a Globalized and Oil Dependent World', 13 *Law and Business Review of the Americas* 381, 393 (2007).

154 *See* Richard A. Posner, *Economic Analysis of Law* 493 (9th ed. 2014) (pointing out that direct regulation is continuous).

155 758 F.3d 296 (D.C. Cir. 2014).

156 *Id.* at 304.

157 *Id.*

158 *Id.* at 305.

159 A different version is that Ralls "submitted a CFIUS notice only after being told that the Department of Defense was preparing to file its own notice of the transaction and trigger review if Ralls did not." Ivan A. Schlager et al., *Court Finds CFIUS Violated Ralls Corporation's Due Process Rights*, Skadden (17 July 2014), https://www.skadden.com/-/media/files/publications/2014/07/courtfindscfiusviolatedrallscorporationsdueprocess.pdf.

160 CFIUS further prohibited Ralls from undertaking the equipment removal and demolition itself but instead ordered that only outside firms approved by CFIUS could do so.

161 The order directed Ralls Corporation to divest its interest in the wind farm project companies that it acquired in 2012 and to take other actions related to the divestment.

162 *Ralls Corp.*, 758 F.3d at 319–321.

163 *Id.* at 307 n.9 (noting that "Ralls [did] not appeal the dismissal of its *ultra vires* and equal protection challenges to the Presidential Order.").

164 Stephen Dockery, Chinese Wind Company Settles with U.S. in CFIUS Battle, *Wall St. J.* (9 October 2015, 6:45 PM), https://www.wsj.com/articles/BL-252B-8393.

165 *See* CFIUS Annual Report 2013, *supra* note 1, at 2.

166 Corrected Brief for Appellant Ralls Corporation at 6, *Ralls Corp.*, 758 F.3d 296 (No. 13-5315).

167 *Ralls Corp.*, 758 F.3d at 319.

168 *Id.* at 320 ("Our conclusion that the procedure followed in issuing the Presidential Order violates due process does not mean the President must, in the future, disclose his thinking on sensitive questions related to national security in reviewing a covered transaction. We hold only that Ralls must receive the procedural protections we have spelled out before the Presidential Order prohibits the transaction."). The *Ralls* decision made clear that although the statutory bar of judicial review does not preclude judicial review of due process challenge under the Fifth Amendment, the "final 'action[s]' the President takes 'to *suspend or prohibit* any covered transaction that threatens to impair the national security of the United States'" are barred from judicial review. *Id.* at 311 (quoting 50 U.S.C. app. § 2170(d)(1) (2015)).

169 *See* The Honorable Antonin Scalia, 'Judicial Deference to Administrative Interpretations of Law', 1989 *Duke Law Journal* 511, 511–12, 514 (1989) (noting one justification for *Chevron* deference is the expertise and competency of agencies); *see also*, Cass R. Sunstein, 'Law and Administration After Chevron', 90 *Columbia Law Review* 2071, 2083–84 (1990) (discussing the *Chevron* principle and deference to agency's relative competence in fact finding); Robert M. Chesney, 'National Security Fact Deference', 95 *Virginia Law Review* 1361, 1404–1419, 1434 (2009) (exploring "the judiciary's reluctance to overstep its bounds" in fact findings in such contested areas as national security, because of the executive branch's "comparative institutional accuracy").

170 *See* Eric A. Posner and Cass R. Sunstein, 'Chevronizing Foreign Relations Law', 16 *Yale Law Journal* 1170, 1170 (2007) (arguing for *Chevron* deference to the executive interpretation "in the domain of foreign affairs").

171 See Richard A. Posner, *Law, Pragmatism, and Democracy* 292–321 (Cambridge, Massachusetts and London, England: Harvard University Press 2003).

172 *See* Richard A. Posner, 'Reply: The Institutional Dimension of Statutory and Constitutional Interpretation', 101 *Michigan Law Review* 952, 957 (2003).

173 The identity and the home country of an acquirer loom large in a CHUS review process. Countries posing political or security challenges to the United States receive enhanced scrutiny. The home country's record on non-proliferation, counter-terrorism, and export controls is examined as well. A related issue is that during the CFIUS

review process, one common request addressed by CFIUS to foreign buyers is for a record of sales or other relationships involving countries on which the United States imposes trade restrictions. A combination of a suspect home country and physical proximity to sensitive US installations will magnify the chance of a transaction being closely scrutinized.

174 A related concern of CFIUS has been foreign governments' involvement in the buyer. This factor also marks the importance of the buyer's home country. Whether the entity is privately or publicly controlled is sensitive, and government-controlled entities receive heightened scrutiny.

175 Transactions involving the defense, energy, information and communications technology, financial markets and credit operations, and transportation sectors are more likely to raise CFIUS concerns.

176 More specifically, if CFIUS decides there is any critical technology involved, or transactions involving export-controlled products or nuclear related products, the transactions will be evaluated closely.

177 If the business being acquired controls technologies that are considered important to US strategic interests, CFIUS will usually closely scrutinize the transaction.

178 When the business being acquired does substantial business with the US government – especially when some of that business is classified – CFIUS will usually take a close look and may even seek to put conditions on the transaction.

179 CFIUS assesses potential vulnerabilities and whether the nature of the business creates susceptibility to the impairment of national security. This often involves asking whether the United States would face a critical shortage or emergency situation in a particular sector should the foreign parent decide to shut down or transfer its US operations abroad.

180 Other intelligence or defense-related issues include whether there is proximity to strategic US operations – "persistent co-location," for example military base. In recent years, the question of cybersecurity has also loomed large in CFIUS reviews.

181 Besides legitimate national security concerns, political considerations are embedded in CFIUS decisions. *See* discussion *infra* note 104 and accompanying text.

182 *See for example* Jeffrey R. Keitelman et al., *What Real Estate Cos. Need to Know About CFIUS Reviews*, LAW360 (5 January 2016, 3:44 PM), https://www.stroock.com/news-and-insights/what-real-estate-cos-need-to-know-about-cfius-reviews (enlisting such elements as the targeted asset's proximity to government facilities and accommodation of sensitive government tenants as some of the many factors that will draw CFIUS' s attention). There are numerous publications and newsletters alike released by third-party intermediaries, summarizing their views on the elements that CFIUS is likely to consider based on their respective experiences.

183 Almost all firms with international trade divisions have national security/CFIUS practices, and more than a handful of firms claim they have leading practices in the area. The market for CFIUS practice is fragmented, and proprietary information about CFIUS is disseminated within numerous firms. For a glimpse of leading players, see, for example *Foreign Investment in the US (CFIUS)*, Wilmerhale, www.wilmerhale.com/trade/cfius, accessed 8 April 2016; *Nationale Sicherheit/CFIUS*, Kaye Scholer, https://www.arnoldporter.com/en/services/capabilities/practices/national-security/cfius-and-exonflorio, accessed 2 October 2022; CFIUS, Covington & Burling, https://www.cov.com/en/practices-and-industries/practices/regulatory-and-public-policy/cfius, accessed 8 April 2016; *CFIUS and National Security*, Wiley Rein LLP, https://www.wiley.law/practices-national-security, accessed 8 April 2016; *Economic Sanctions and Foreign Investment*, Cleary Gottlieb, https://www.clearygottlieb.com/practice-landing/economic-sanctions-and-foreign-investments, accessed 8 April 2016.

184 *See, for example* Dustin H. Tingley et al., 'The Political Economy of Inward FDI Flows: Opposition to Chinese Mergers and Acquisitions', 8 *Chinese Journal of International Politics* 27 (2015); Paul Connell and Tian Huang, 'Note, An Empirical Analysis of CFIUS:

Examining Foreign Investment Regulation in the United States', 39 *Yale Journal of International Law* 131 (2014).

185 There are no specific data in direct support of this allegation, but given the broad and vague coverage of CHUS notification requirements, it is expected that a wide array of parties to M&A transactions would have to conduct CFIUS impact analyses even though they do not end up making the actual filings.

186 *See, for example* Connell and Huang, *supra* note 184, at 135 (using dataset composed of 76 transactions that underwent CHUS review); Tingley et al., *supra* note 184, at 27 (using "dataset of 569 transactions that occurred between 1999 and 2014 involving Chinese" investors attempted acquisitions of US targets).

187 For example one of the datasets was compiled from Bloomberg M&A database and newsletters of law firms (largely high-profiled cases) and the SEC EDGAR database (public companies). *See* Connell and Huang, *supra* note 184, at 152–153.

188 *See, for example* Joshua W. Casselman, 'Note, China's 'Latest Threat' to the United States: The Failed CNOOC-UNOCAL Merger and Its Implications for Exon-Florio and CFIUS', 17 *Indiana International & Comparative Law Review* 155, 161–64 (2007) (noting that in CNOOC's failed attempt to acquire Unocal, CNOOC withdrew its bid due to "mounting" political pressure before completion of the CFIUS process).

189 *See* CFIUS Annual Report 2013, *supra* note 1, at 20 (noting the parties' withdrawal from the CFIUS process for various reasons); *see also* Dick K. Nanto et al., Cong. Research Serv., RL33093, China and the CNOOC Bid for Unocal: Issues for Congress 14 (2006), www.hsdl.org/?view&did=460852.

190 *See* Posner, *supra* note 172, at 957.

191 CFIUS has been criticized as being unduly politicized. *See, for example* Maira Goes de Moraes Gavioli, *National Security or Xenophobia: The Impact of the Foreign Investment and National Security Act ("FINSA") in Foreign Investment in the U.S.*, 2 WM. Mitch-ellL. Raza J. 1, 33–36 (2011). Among the political considerations are the preservation of jobs, espionage of the home country of the acquirer, economic distress of the United States, and retaliation. Also, in recent years, inbound investment from China has become a particular target susceptible to political concerns. Hostility against acquirers from China is on the rise. Investment from China is treated as largely to transfer technology and know-how to Chinese firms but do little to help the US economy. *See* Wayne M. Morrison, Cong. Research Serv., RL33536, China-U.S. Trade Issues 17, 24 (2015).

192 *The Operations of Federal Agencies in Monitoring, Reporting on, and Analyzing Foreign Investments in the United States (Part 3 – Examination of the Committee on Foreign Investment in the United States, Federal Policy Toward Foreign Investment, and Federal Data Collection Efforts) Before the Subcomm, on Commerce, Consumer, & Monetary Affairs of the H. Comm. on Gov 7 Operations*, 96th Cong. 5 (1979) (statement of Mary P. Azevedo, M.A., M.A.L.D., Ph. D., & J.D. Candidate, the Fletcher Sch. of Law & Diplomacy, Tufts Univ.).

193 *See* W. Robert Shearer, 'Comment, The Exon-Florio Amendment: Protectionist Legislation Susceptible to Abuse', 30 *Houston Law Review* 1729, 1732–35 (1993) (discussing the danger that Exon-Florio Amendment may be abused for protectionist purposes).

194 *See generally* Alan O. Sykes, 'Regulatory Protectionism and the Law of International Trade', 66 *University of Chicago Law Review* 1 (1999).

195 *Id*. at 5.

196 *See* Magnus Blomström et al., 'The Determinants of Host Country Spillovers from Foreign Direct Investment: Review and Synthesis of the Literature' in Nigel Pain (ed) *Inward Investment, Technological Change and Growth: The Impact of Multinational Corporation on the UK Economy* 34 (London: Palgrave Macmillan 2001).

197 The fear for protectionism is genuine. *See, for example* Nagesh Kumar, *Multinational Enterprises, Regional Economic Integration, and Export-Platform Production in the Host Countries: An Empirical Analysis for the US and Japanese Corporations*, 134 Weltwirtschaftuches Archiv 450, 478–79 (1998) (discussing the scenario of multinational corporations'

utilization of host countries as platforms for export-oriented production – production made in the host countries will be shipped back to the multinational corporations' domestic markets).

198 *See, for example* CFIUS Annual Report 2013, *supra* note 1, at 147–50 (empirically showing that CFIUS decisions have significant positive effects on the stock prices of domestic companies in such sectors that may benefit from the denial of entry by foreign investors).

199 *See* Georgiev, *supra* note 3, at 126 ("If the United States is seen as using national security review to engage in protectionism, this could provoke a protectionist backlash in other parts of the world and hurt U.S. companies."). For some examples of retaliation by the United States against its international trade partners, see generally Thomas O. Bayard and Kimberly Ann Elliott, *Reciprocity and Retaliation in U.S. Trade Policy* (1994).

200 *See, for example* David M. Marchick & Matthew J. Slaughter, Global FDI Policy: Correcting a Protectionist Drift 12 (2008), https://www.cfr.org/sites/default/files/pdf/2008/06/FDI_CSR34.pdf ("[India] has considered creating new national security-related screening in the telecoms field – in part in reaction to a CFIUS review of an Indian company undertaking a U.S. acquisition).

201 Draft Foreign Investment Law, *supra* note 71, Article 57.

202 *Id.*

203 *Compare id.*, *with* State Council National Security Review Circular, at Article 1(1), *and* Ziyou Maoyi Shiyan Qu Waishang Touzi Guojia Anquan Shencha Shixing Banfa (自由贸易试验区外商投资国家安全审查试行办法)[Interim Measures on National Security Review Pertaining to Foreign Investments in Free Trade Pilot Zones] (promulgated by General Office of State Council, 8 April 2015, effective 7 May 2015), Article 1(1) [hereinafter Free Trade Zone National Security Review Rules], www.gov.cn/zhengce/content/2015-04/20/content_9629.htm (China).

204 State Council National Security Review Circular, Article 1(1); *see also*, Free Trade Zone National Security Rules, Article 1(1). In Draft Foreign Investment Law, the language has been modified to be "the impact on the safety of critical or sensitive military installations." See Draft Foreign Investment Law, Article 57(1).

205 State Council National Security Review Circular, Article 1(1); *see also* Free Trade Zone National Security Rules, Article 1(1).

206 *See* Yahong Li, 'The Law-Making Law: A Solution to the Problems in the Chinese Legislative System', 30 *Hong Kong Law Journal* 120, 122 (2000).

207 *See* Peng He, *Chinese Lawmaking: From Non-Communicative to Communicative* 21 (New York, Dordrecht, London: Springer 2014).

208 For an authoritative historical narrative of the legislative process of China's foreign investment regulatory apparatus, see Ping Jiang (江平)，Wei "Waiguo Touzi Fa" Shuo Jiju (为《外国投资法》说几句)(A Few Words on the Foreign Investment Law), Keynote Speech at the 2015 China International Investment Law Forum (17 September 2015), http://www.aisixiang.com/data/92660.html (China).

209 *Id.*

210 China's rulemaking process is more a top-down implementation of the intention of the leadership, rather than derived from empiricism or cost-benefit analysis. For an authoritative summary, see Dehuai Ma, *Woguo Lifa de Xianzhuang, Wenti yu Yuanyin Fenxi* (我国立法的现状、问题与原因分析)[The Current State of China Legislation, the Problems, and the Reasons Analyzed], People's Daily – Channel Theory (8 July 2008), http://theory.rmlt.com.cn/2015/0310/376277.shtml (noting the lack of cost-benefit analysis in rulemakings, the absence of procedural due process, and the top-down rulemaking process in which the drafters merely carry out the superior's will without scientific reasoning) (China). For a vivid illustration of China's legislative process, see Ta-kuang Chang, 'The Making of the Chinese Bankruptcy Law: A Study in the Chinese Legislative Process', 28 *Harvard International Law Journal* 333, 336–54 (1987), which discusses a Chinese bankruptcy law case. The legislative process for other legislations is analogous

throughout the years. For a summary of the interest parties that exert influence over the legislative process, see Stanley Lubman, 'Introduction: The Future of Chinese Law', 141 *China Quarterly*, 1, 3–4 (1995).

211 Availability heuristic refers to judgements on the accessibility or ease with which specific instances are brought to mind. For the classic paper on availability heuristic, see Amos Tversky and Daniel Kahneman, 'Availability: A Heuristic for Judging Frequency and Probability', 5 *Cognitive Psychology* 207(1973).

212 *See, for example* Ben R. Newell, Chris J. Mitchell, and Brett K. Hayes, 'Getting Scarred and Winning Lotteries: Effects of Exemplar Cuing and Statistical Format on Imagining Low-Probability Events', 21 *Journal of Behavioral Decision Making* 317, 320 (2008); Steven J. Sherman et al., 'Imagining Can Heighten or Lower the Perceived Likelihood of Contracting a Disease: The Mediating Effect of Ease of Imagery', 11 *Personality and Social Psychology Bulletin* 118 (1985); Paul Slovic, John Monahan, and Donald G. Mac-Gregor, 'Violence Risk Assessment and Risk Communication: The Effects of Using Actual Cases, Providing Instruction, and Employing Probability Versus Frequency Formats', 24 *Law and Human Behavior* 271 (2000).

213 *See* Ma, *supra* note 210.

214 *See* Draft Foreign Investment Law, Article 57; Free Trade Zone National Security Review Rules, Article 1(1).

215 The Draft Foreign Investment Law sets out that the national security review regime in financial services sector is to be formulated later, which usually means in an indefinite period. *See* Draft Foreign Investment Law, Article 74.

216 Pricewaterhouse Coopers HongKong, Chinese Bankers' Survey 2015 Executive Summary (2016), https://www.pwc.com/jp/ja/japan-knowledge/archive/assets/pdf/en-chinese-bankers_survey2015-1605.pdf. KPMG, Mainland China Securities Survey 2015, 26–33 (2015), www.kpmg.com/CN/en/IssuesAndInsights/ArticlesPublications/Documents/China-Securities-Survey-201510.pdf (discussing the securities sector's rapid development); *see also* Gabriel Wildau, *China Services Sector Key to Growth*, Fin. Times (6 December 2015), https://www.ft.com/content/0f6f0018-9817-11e5-bdda-9f13f99fa654 (discussing the rally of the services sector in China's GDP, with major contributions from the financial services sector, and foreign investor's zeal in investment in China's financial services sector).

217 *China's Economy: China Wants Higher-Quality Foreign Investment*, Economist (13 November 2006), www.economist.com/node/8162102.

218 *See* Ministry of Commerce, 2013 Zhongguo Waishang Touzi Baogao [2013中国外商投资报告] (China Foreign Investment Report 2013) 151 (13 December 2013) [hereinafter Chinese Foreign Investment Report], http://images.mofcom.gov.cn/wzs/201312/20131211162942372.pdf.

219 *See* PricewaterhouseCoopers, Going for Growth in Asia: Navigate the Way – Financial Services M&A – China 1–2 (2008), https://www.pwc.com/la/en/publications/assets/bulletin2008.pdf; PricewaterhouseCoopers, M&A 2014 Mid Year Review and Outlook Press Briefing 31 (26 August 2014), https://imaa-institute.org/docs/statistics/pwc_china_m-and-a_2014-mid-year-review.pdf.

220 *See* Deloitte, 'China Factors: A Guide for Investing in China', October 2018, https://www2.deloitte.com/content/dam/Deloitte/us/Documents/mergers-acqisitions/us-a-guide-for-investing-in-china.pdf, accessed 3 October 2022.

221 One explanation may be that due to the jurisdictional divisions between the NDRC, MOFCOM, and the financial regulators – for example the Ministry of Finance, CBRC, CSRC, CIRC, or China's central bank, the People's Bank of China – the NDRC and MOFCOM do not wish to intervene on the turfs of the financial regulators when it comes to national security review. But that argument has no merit. National security review, by its nature, is cross-sectorial. That is why there is need for an inter-agency committee to pool and harness the collective wisdom of various agencies in the enforcement. There is no excuse why, at the rulemaking process, one critical sector, as well as its regulators, is left out.

222 For the sectorial distribution of foreign investment in China in the early days during the 1980s and 1990s, see Harry G. Broadman and Xiaolun Sun, *The Distribution of Foreign Direct Investment in China*, 20 World Econ. 339, 355–59 (1997) ("At the same time, the Chinese manufacturing sector [was] fast becoming the most important field to foreign investors.")

223 China Foreign Investment Report 2013, ch. 4.

224 *See* 50 U.S.C. app § 2170(a)(6) (2014).

225 *Id.* § 2170(f)(6) and (7).

226 CFIUS Annual Report 2013, *supra* note 1, at 4 ("The remainder of notices were in the mining, utilities, and construction sector (96, or 18 percent) or the wholesale, retail, and transportation sector (44, or eight percent).")

227 *Compare* Draft Foreign Investment Law, Article 57, *with* Free Trade Zone National Security Review Rules, Article 1(1).

228 A covered transaction" is defined as a transaction, "by or with any foreign person, which could result in control of a U.S. business by a foreign person." 31 C.F.R. § 800.207 (2015).

229 50 U.S.C. app. § 2170(a)(3).

230 *Id.* § 2170(a)(2).

231 For instance "control" can be identified if a foreign investor (i) has the ability to determine or block important business matters, or (ii) has representation on the board of directors.

232 31 C.F.R. § 800.302(b).

233 *See* Tipler, *supra* note 3, at 1283–1284.

234 By itself, or through its parent holding company or its controlled subsidiary, individually or jointly with other foreign investor(s).

235 State Council National Security Review Circular, Article 1(3)(l)-(3). The Draft Foreign Investment Law is completely silent on the definition of control, which means one may need to fall back on the old rule – that is the State Council National Security Review Circular – when looking for a definition of "control."

236 State Council National Security Review Circular, Article 1(3)(3).

237 *Id.* at Article 1(3)(4).

238 2015 Catalogue, Article 6(20).

239 *Id.*

240 *Id.* at Article 8(24). Shareholding of one individual foreign investor (including its affiliates) is limited to 20% in a Chinese bank. The aggregate shareholding of multiple foreign investors investing in one Chinese bank is limited to 25%.

241 *Id.* at Article 8(25).

242 *Id.* at Article 8(26)

243 *Id.* at Article 8(27).

244 While the Catalogue system is expected to phase out of the foreign investment regulatory framework and superseded by a Negative List, the fact that the 2015 Catalogue was promulgated most recently indicates that the Catalogue system will not disappear at least in the short term.

245 *See* Hart-Scott-Rodino Antitrust Improvements Act, 15 U.S.C. § 18a (2015). Under the Hart-Scott-Rodino Act, parties to certain large mergers and acquisitions must file premerger notifications and go through the merger review process. For more explanations on the merger review programme, see *Premerger Notification and the Merger Review Process*, FTC, www.ftc.gov/tips-advice/competition-guidance/guide-antitrust-laws/mergers/premerger-notification-and-merger, accessed 8 April 2016.

246 *Premerger Notification and the Merger Review Process, supra* note 245.

247 Id.

248 Id.

249 The parties would consider CFIUS notification as one of the key factors for whether to proceed with the transaction. In negotiations, they allocate between themselves the responsibility to make CFIUS notice. Usually, the acquirer assumes the responsibility.

250 Specifically, the regulations rewritten following the enactment of FINSA explicitly encourage transacting parties to consult with CFIUS in advance of filing a notice. *See* 31 C.F.R. §800.401(f) (2015). Before and after the final agreement, the parties are able to give preliminary informal "heads up" to CFIUS, usually by phone. Besides informal contacts with CFIUS, the parties can, and are usually advised by their legal advisors, to address specific national security considerations with government agencies that may have specific jurisdiction over the particular industry sector, products, or services involved.

251 *Id.* §800.401(f).

252 *Id.* §800.503.

253 50 U.S.C. app. §2170(b)(4)(A) and (B) (2014).

254 CFIUS may address questions or requests for additional information to the parties regarding the transaction or any aspect of their operation or corporate structures. Questions posed by CFIUS would usually need to be answered within three business days.

255 *Id.* § 2170(b)(2)(A). Although the decision to open the investigation is largely at the discretion of CFIUS, the Exon-Florio Amendment requires that transactions involving foreign governments or vital infrastructures be subject to a mandatory 45-day investigation period. This relates to the presumption of investigation for foreign government transactions and transactions involving critical infrastructure, unless senior CFIUS officials sign off that no investigation is necessary. See Id. § 2170(b)(2)(C).

256 If the cabinet or sub-cabinet level representatives of the Treasury Department and the head of any lead agency or agencies agree that a foreign government-controlled purchase will not threaten national security, or that a vital infrastructure is not at risk, they may waive the mandatory investigation. *See* 31 C.F.R. §800.503(c).

257 50 U.S.C. app. § 2170(d)(2).

258 31 C.F.R. § 800.506(b)-(c).

259 *See* George Bush, *Message to the Congress on the China National Aero-Technology Import and Export Corporation Divestiture of MAMCO Manufacturing*, Incorporated (1 February 1990), http://fas.org/nuke/guide/china/contractor/90020112.html.

260 For a content analysis of mitigation agreements in the telecommunications sector between 1997 and 2007, see Zaring, *supra* note 3, at 110–116.

261 For example DoD may furnish CHUS with the "risk-based analysis" which assesses "threat, vulnerability, and overall risk including proposals to mitigate risks." *See* Inspector General, DoD, Assessment of DoD Processes in Support of Committee on Foreign Investment in the United States (CFIUS) Determinations and Foreign Ownership, Control, or Influence (FOCI) Mitigation (10 June 2014), at 2, www.fas.org/sgp/othergov/dod/cfius.pdf.

262 For a summary of mitigation measures adopted between 1997 and 2007, see Theodore H. Moran, Three Threats: An Analytical Framework for the CFIUS Process 42–43 (2009). *See also* Baker Botts LLP, A Guide to Demystify the CFIUS Process 7, http://www.bakerbotts.com/~/media/files/brochure-attachments/cfiusbookletenglishversion_000.pdf; CFIUS ANNUAL REPORT 2013, *supra* note 1, at 20 (noting some parties withdraw their notices with CFIUS altogether because they "[did] not want to abide by CFIUS's proposed mitigation").

263 Draft Foreign Investment Law, Article 49.

264 *Id.* at Article 61.

265 *Id.* at Article 62.

266 *Id.*

267 *Id.* at Article 65.

268 *Id.* at Article 64.

269 When a foreign investor intends to merge with or acquire a domestic enterprise, the investor is required to file an application with MOFCOM. *Id.* at Article 50. The modification under the Draft Foreign Investment Law is that screening and pre-approval are required only if the sectors that foreign investors invest in fall into the Negative List. *Id.*

at Article 27. If it deems the proposed transaction falls within the scope of a national security review, MOFCOM requests national security review to be initiated within five days. State Council National Security Review Circular, at Article 4(1).

270 In such an informal contact, usually the parties introduce themselves and their companies, describe the nature of their business, indicate whether the US business being acquired has government contracts and if so whether any classified information is involved, describe the transaction (stock or asset deal, merger, etc.), and note the estimated timetable for filing the draft CFIUS notice and for closing (subject to government approval).

271 On the side of foreign investors, it has been advised that foreign investors should aim to build relationships with key regulators and ensure adequate and practical disclosures are made to regulators to increase the prospects of a positive reception.

272 50 U.S.C. app. § 2170(a)(5), (1)(6) (2014).

273 For a description and criticism of the technically voluntary yet "functionally mandatory pre-notice process, see Joshua C. Zive, 'Unreasonable Delays: CFIUS Reviews of Energy Transactions', 3 *Harvard Business Law Review* 169, 173–174 (2013).

274 *See* Mark E. Plotkin and David N. Fagan, *Foreign Direct Investment and U.S. National Security: CFIUS Under the Obama Administration*, Colum. FDI Persp., 2, 7 June 2010, https://www.econstor.eu/bitstream/10419/253858/1/fdi-perspectives-no024.pdf.

275 Exec. Order No. 13,456, 3 C.F.R. § 4677 (2008).

276 For the "heightened formality of the internal mitigation process," see Plotkin & Fagan, *supra* note 274, at 2 (noting the "trade-off between fewer mitigations agreement but longer CHUS reviews").

277 U.S. Dep't of the Treasury, Covered Transactions, Withdrawals, and Presidential Decisions 2008–2012, https://home.treasury.gov/system/files/206/CFIUS-Summary-Data-2008-2020.pdf, accessed 8 April 2016.

278 The parties may also request to withdraw and refile their notice because a material change in the terms of the transaction warrants the filing of a notice. CFIUS Annual Report 2013, *supra* note 1, at 19.

279 *Id.*

280 *See* Comm. on Forhgn Inv. in the U.S., Annual Report to Congress 23 (February 2016), https://home.treasury.gov/system/files/206/CFIUS-Annual-Report-to-Congress-for-CY2014.pdf (noting from 2012 through 2014, on average only 8% of cases were subject to a mitigation agreement).

281 State Council National Security Review Circular, Article 3(2). An interesting contrast is that, in the subsequent MOFCOM National Security Review Rules, no reference is made to the NDRC as lead agency. *See* MOFCOM National Security Review Rules. The inconsistency in language was not reconciled until the Draft Foreign Investment Law was made public, in which it is reiterated that the NDRC and MOFCOM jointly act as lead agencies. *See* Draft Foreign Investment Law, Article 49.

282 *See* Xingxing Li, 'An Economic Analysis of Regulatory Overlap and Regulatory Competition: The Experience of Interagency Regulatory Competition in China's Regulation of Inbound Foreign Investment', 67(4) *Administrative Law Review* 700–708 (2015).

283 *Id.* at 730–34.

284 31 C.F.R. § 800, *as amended by* Regulations Pertaining to Mergers, Acquisitions, and Takeovers by Foreign Persons, 73 *Fed. Reg.* 70,702 (21 November 2008).

285 *Id.*

286 *For example see* Inspector General, *supra* note 261, Appendix B (setting out the internal CFIUS timeline and the internal working procedure when DoD acts as co-lead agency). For the active role of DoD in CFIUS, see Office of Under Secretary of Defense for Acquisition, Technology and Logistics, Annual Industrial Capabilities Report to Congress 12 (2006) (statistics of 2005); OFFICE of Under Secretary of Defense for Acquisition, Technology and Logistics, Annual Industrial Capabilities Report to Congress 45–47 (2013) (statistics of 1996 through 2012).

287 50 U.S.C. app. § 2170(k)(5) (2014) (addressing actions the co-lead agency should take).

288 For a glimpse over the inner workings of CHUS, see Plotkin & Fagan, *supra* note 274, at 2 (noting the trend to streamline inner-agency process within CFIUS); 153 Cong. Rec. 4800-01 (2007) (statement of Rep. Bachus); Stewart A. Baker and Stephen R. Heifetz, Addressing National Security Concerns 21–22 (September 2010), https://www.steptoe.com/a/web/2499/4149.pdf (the authors, as former officials of DHS, describing the weekly inter-agency discussions within CFIUS). *Cf. A Review of the CFIUS Process for Implementing the Exon-Florio Amendment: Hearing Before the S. Comm. on Banking, Housing, and Urban Affairs,* 109th Cong. 2–5 (2005) (statement of Katherine Schinasi, Managing Director, Acquisition and Sourcing Management; noting the existence of significant disagreements between CFIUS agencies in certain scenarios).

289 *See* 31 C.F.R. §§ 800.401(a), 402 (2015). Because the characteristics of the foreign acquirer, for example its nationality, are usually key determinants in whether a transaction poses threat to national security, in practice it is more often the acquirer that makes the voluntary filings. *See, e.g.,* Chelsea Naso, 5 *Tips for Ensuring a Smooth CFIUS Review,* LAW360 (10 November 2015, 3:54 PM), https://www.mayerbrown.com/-/media/files/news/2015/11/5-tips-for-ensuring-a-smooth-cfius-review/files/5tipsfore nsuringasmoothcfiusreview/fileattachment/5tipsforensuringasmoothcfiusreview.pdf.

290 50 U.S.C. app. §2170.

291 31 C.F.R. §800, as amended by Regulations Pertaining to Mergers, Acquisitions, and Takeovers by Foreign Persons, 73 Fed. Reg. 70, 702 (21 November 2008).

292 *Id.* § 800.401(b)-(c).

293 Stewart Abercrombie Baker, Navigating Joint CFIUS And DSS Jurisdiction (2015), https://www.steptoe.com/en/news-publications/navigating-joint-cfius-and-dss-juris-diction-1.html.

294 MOFCOM National Security Review Rules, Article 2; *see also* Draft Foreign Investment Law, Article 34.

295 The specific local office of MOFCOM – county-level, city-level, or provincial-level – is mainly determined based on the deal size and the subcategory – "permitted," "encouraged," or "forbidden" – within which the transaction is characterized to fall. *See* Shangwu Bu guanyu Xiafang Waishang Touzi Shenpi Quanxian youguan Wenti de Tongzhi (商务部关于下放外商投资审批权限有关问题的通知) [Circular of MOFCOM Concerning the Delegation of Pre-approval Authority in Respect of Foreign Investments] (promulgated by Ministry of Commerce, 10 June 2010, effective 10 June 2010), http://tfs.mofcom.gov.cn/article/ba/bl/gfxwj/201304/20130400106431.shtml (China).

296 *See* Draft Foreign Investment Law, Article 26(1).

297 *Id.* at Article 55.

298 *Id.*

299 *See* James K. Jackson, 'The Exon-Florio National Security Test for Foreign Investment' *Congressional Research Service,* 29 March 2013, p. 15, https://sgp.fas.org/crs/natsec/RL33312.pdf, accessed 3 October 2022.

300 *See* William J. Baumol and Janusz A. Ordover, *Use of Antitrust to Subvert Competition,* 28 J.L. & Econ. 247, 250–251 (1985). *Cf.* Frank H. Easterbrook, *Detrebling Antitrust Damages,* 28 J.L. & Econ. 445,461 n.31 (1985).

301 *See* MOFCOM National Security Review Rules, Article 6. The Draft Foreign Investment Law contains strong wording on the penalty the foreign investors may face if they complete the investment projects without prior national security clearance and are subsequently found to impair national security. *See* Draft Foreign Investment Law, Article 72.

302 Foreign investors were not permitted to purchase "A" shares, the most common types of shares listed on the two Chinese stock exchanges – that is Shanghai Stock Exchange and Shenzhen Stock Exchange – until the publication of Waiguo Touzi Zhe dui Shangshi Gongsi Zhanlve Touzi Guanli Banfa (外国投资者对上市公司战略投资管理办法)[Measures for the Administration of Strategic Investments in Listed Companies by Foreign Investors] (promulgated by the Ministry of Commerce et al., 31

December 2005, effective 30 January 2006), www.mofcom.gov.cn/article/swfg/swf-gbl/201101/20110107349072.shtml (China). Prior to that, the door for public M&As of Chinese A-listed companies by foreign investors was essentially shut, with a minor exception of QFII. Even after the promulgation of rules enabling public M&A by foreign investors in China, the qualification requirement is stringent. Foreign investors are subject to a three-year lock-up period, a minimum 10% shareholding in the listed company, and stringent approval requirements, making public M&A an unattractive option for foreign investors.

303 Jenny (Jia) Sheng and Chunbin Xu, 'China Publishes New Rules on National Security Review of Foreign Investment' www.pillsburylaw.com/en/news-and-insights/china-rules-security-review-foreign-investment.html, accessed 19 April 2022.

304 Yuwen Li and Cheng Bian, 'A New Dimension of Foreign Investment Law in China – Evolution and Impacts of the National Security Review System', 24 *Asia Pacific Law Review* 149, 175 (2016), https://doi.org/10.1080/10192557.2016.1243212, accessed 19 April 2022.

305 Ibid.

306 Xinzhen Lan, 'Foreign Investment Security Review Not Hurdle to Opening Up', 1 *Beijing Law Review* 29, 29 (2021).

307 O'Melveny and Myers LLP, 'China Expands National Security Review of Foreign Investments', www.omm.com/resources/alerts-and-publications/alerts/china-expands-national-security-review-of-foreign-investments/#, accessed 19 April 2022.

308 Xinzhen Lan, *supra* note 306.

309 Ibid.

9

IS UNRELIABLE ENTITY LIST RELIABLE?

1. Background

1.1 The Ongoing US–China Trade War

As the US–China trade war continues and unilateralism and protectionism are on the rise, the multilateral trading system is facing severe challenges.[1] Meanwhile, the world is witnessing China's increased influence in global economic governance.[2] For instance China pushes ambitiously its own version of internet governance towards becoming an international consensus.[3] In accordance with a plausible theory of Thucydides Trap, the US and China, two great powers, have been engaging in an inevitable war for global technological superiority along with the trade war.[4]

China first announced its plan to have its own version of Entity List, that is the Unreliable Entities List, in May 2019, shortly after the US added Huawei and many of its global affiliates to the US Commerce Department's Entity List,[5] which effectively bars Huawei and its affiliates from receiving US-originated goods, software, and technology as well as certain foreign-produced items that are the direct products of certain US-originated software and technology without a licence.[6]

Both the US Entity List and China's Unreliable Entity List create a legal conundrum for such firms that seek to operate with some targeted companies in the counterparty state. At the heart of the problem is the incongruity between the US and China perspectives on national security in their pursuit of global technological superiority.[7]

1.2 US Entity List System

The Entity List is a formidable administrative tool that prohibits listed foreign persons from receiving some or all items subject to the EAR unless the exporter,

DOI: 10.4324/9781003130499-9

re-exporter, or transferor receives a licence. The Entity List is used to block activities contrary to US national security and foreign policy.

The US Entity List system has been stipulated by the Export Administration Regulations (EAR), which takes its authority from the Export Control Reform Act of 2018. Publication of the Entity List helps US industry and foreign companies to identify restricted persons so as to reduce inadvertent violations of the EAR and increase compliance with the export controls.

The Bureau of Industry and Security (BIS) in the Department of Commerce established the Entity List in 1997 to inform the public of foreign entities that have engaged in activities that could result in an increased risk of the diversion of exported, re-exported, and transferred (in-country) items to weapons of mass destruction programmes, such as nuclear, missile, chemical, and biological weapons. BIS adopted foreign policy-based end use and end user controls that focus on foreign entities (e.g. business, research institutions, government and private organizations, individuals, other types of legal persons, and locations) that pose or could pose a threat to US national security or foreign policy interests. BIS implements the decisions of the End User Review Committee (ERC) by revising the Entity List to add, remove, and modify Entity List entries. The ERC is composed of representatives of the Departments of Commerce (Chair), State, Defense, Energy, and Treasury (where appropriate). The ERC adds entities by majority vote and removes or modifies entries by unanimous vote. The ERC conducts reviews and revise and updates the List as necessary. Persons on the Entity List may request the removal or modification of their entry.

The purpose of the Entity List is to protect and advance the US national security and foreign policy interests. To that end, the US is to resolve to restrict trade with persons that fail to comply with US export control and regulations or fail to adhere to acceptable norms of international behaviour, or whose conduct threatens US interests. The Entity List informs the public of entities that have engaged in activities that could result in an increased risk of diversion of items for use in weapons of mass destruction programmes or in other activities contrary to US national security and foreign policy interests.

A licensing requirement is applied to persons added to the Entity List to achieve the intended (and unilateral) foreign policy and national security objectives. The licensing requirement is intended to prevent the acquisition of certain items by persons who might engage in activities contrary to US interests. The Entity List enables BIS to target specific persons with export licence requirements, thereby avoiding the imposition of broad licence requirements on various items destined for many destinations.

These controls are in compliance with the US policy of prohibiting exports, re-exports, and transfers (in-country) when specific and articulable facts provide reasonable cause to believe that the persons to whom the items will be provided are involved in activities contrary to the national security or foreign policy interests of the United States, or pose a significant risk of becoming involved in such activities. BIS conducted some enforcement actions that are not in compliance with controls imposed by the Entity List. For instance BIS may impose penalties for violations of the licensing requirements on the Entity List.

The Trump administration used the BIS Entity List to restrict dual-use trade with China by placing certain Chinse state-tied firms of concern on the Entity List.

On 15 May 2019, the Trump administration issued the Executive Order 13873 on Securing the Information and Communications Technology and Services Supply Chain (EO 2019). The rationale is to prevent espionage activity and to protect US critical national infrastructure. Although the EO 2019 does not identify any particular entity, it is widely interpreted to target Huawei, an elephant of the room.[8]

Entities that handle US-originated goods are prohibited from supplying such goods and any other items that are subject to the EAR to Huawei. In principle, an entity may continue to deal with Huawei, so long as it does that without exceeding de minimis levels of the US components or using technology controlled on the grounds of national security purposes. The US Entity List requests a blacklisted Chinese company to apply for special permission to buy American components and technologies.[9] Likewise, US exporters need the same licence to sell designated components and technologies to those listed entities. However, blurring of distinctions between export controls and sanctions law, the Entity List has had enormous implications on suppliers' ability to engage in the development of new products and technology for Huawei.[10]

The Entity List has amplified the extraterritorial reach of America's law and geo-economic strategy.[11] It is aimed to prevent US technology from being used by foreign-owned entities in ways that potentially undermine US national security or foreign policy interests.[12]

While the EAR provides an illustrative, but non-exhaustive, list of activities that could be considered contrary to the public interests, any ruling will be assessed on a case-by-case basis. Once listed, the measures are detrimental to the operations of Chinese firms, some of which have already been labelled as national security threats by foreign governments around the world though such allegations have never been solidified. For instance that Huawei was placed on the Entity List is largely owing to an allegation that the firm has direct ties to the Chinese Communist Party for espionage.[13]

On 31 May 2019, MOFCOM announced to introduce an "Unreliable Entity List" regime, under which foreign entities or individuals that boycott or cut off supplies to Chinese companies for non-commercial purposes and causing serious damages to Chinese companies would be listed.[14]

In a number of interviews in mid-June and early July, MOFCOM officials and spokespersons stated that the Unreliable Entity List regime is undergoing required internal review with detailed rules/measures soon to be promulgated.[15]

Since then, the United States has taken a number of actions to push back on Chinese behaviour it considers unacceptable including revoking Hong Kong's "special status" in light of Beijing's crackdown on the city's pro-autonomy demonstrations, designating high-ranking officials for human rights abuses in Xinjiang, and Executive Orders targeting the popular Chinese mobile applications such as TikTok and WeChat.[16]

Since China first announced to introduce the list mechanism in May 2019, some US companies including Qualcomm, Cisco, Apple, and FedEx have been widely reported as potential targets for the list. In May 2019, a source close to the Chinese government told the *Global Times* that China was ready to put US firms on its Unreliable Entity List, imposing restrictions or probing US firms like Qualcomm, Cisco, and Apple and suspending airplane purchases from Boeing, in response to US threats to cut off foreign chip supplies to Huawei.[17]

On 19 September 2020, China's Ministry of Commerce (MOFCOM) published the Provisions on the Unreliable Entity List (UEL Provisions), which took effect on the same date.

In a question-and-answer session with media on 20 September 2020, an official with the MOFCOM's Department of Treaty and Law stressed that UEL was aimed at deterring certain foreign entities, organizations, and individuals from hurting Chinese interests, while reassuring those that abide by the law that their operations in China will not be affected. This may suggest that MOFCOM would be restrained from applying the UEL in practice as the scope of the provisions would not be expanded "at will." The official assures that there is no need whatsoever for credible and law-abiding foreign entities to worry about. The official also claims that there was no timetable or specific companies earmarked for the list.[18] Meanwhile, China would continue to welcome foreign companies that abide by laws and rules.

The UEL Provisions come on the heels of the US Department of Commerce posting on the Federal Registry on 18 September 2020 (US EDT) the regulations implementing the Executive Order that prohibits US companies from providing downloads or updates services for WeChat and TikTok apps.[19] Asked whether the release of the rules for the Unreliable Entity List is aimed at the US crackdown on Huawei, WeChat, and TikTok, the official said that the provisions have been in the works for more than a year and are not aimed at any particular country or entity.

Coincidentally, one day after MOFCOM published the UEL Provisions, WeChat and TikTok delayed the previously scheduled 20 September implementation of the new rules published by US Department for implementing the executive orders that ban WeChat and TikTok.[20] The prohibitions related to TikTok were subsequently delayed by the Trump administration and those related to WeChat were enjoined by a US federal court pending litigation challenging the prohibitions.[21] BIS can review and approve some licences for exports to Huawei.[22]

The "Unreliable Entity List" regime is established pursuant to China's Foreign Trade Law, Anti-Monopoly Law, and National Security Law. Such statutory authority includes the following:

Article 7 of the Foreign Trade Law provides in general terms that if a foreign country or region adopts prohibitive, restrictive, or similar measures on a discriminatory basis against China in trade, China may take corresponding counteractions against such country or region.

The Anti-Monopoly Law focuses on penalizing monopolistic conduct eliminating or reducing competition, including monopoly agreements, abuse of market dominance, and monopoly through concentration of business undertakings. Article 17 in particular prohibits abuse of market dominance by such means as refusal to trade or imposition of discriminatory conditions or prices.

Article 59 of the National Security Law provides that the state, to prevent and mitigate national security risks, shall establish a national security review and supervision system and conduct national security reviews on foreign investment, specific articles, key technologies, products, and services relating to network information technologies, infrastructure construction products, and other important transactions and activities that affect or may affect national security.

In addition to the three laws specifically referenced as the legal basis for the new regime, Article 40 of the Foreign Investment Law which enters into effect on 1 January 2020, also provides that China may take corresponding countermeasures against a foreign country or region if such foreign country or regime takes discriminatory measures against China, prohibiting or restricting investments.

Both Article 7 of the Foreign Trade Law and Article 40 of the Foreign Investment Law are directed against foreign governments, not specific companies. Therefore, a foreign company which complies with its own government's rules to restrict trade or investment with China may be treated as an "unreliable entity."[23]

On 28 June 2020, a new draft of the Export Control Law was submitted to the Standing Committee of the National People's Congress for a second review and is adopted on 17 October 2020, and effective as of 1 December 2020. China published a draft Export Control Law in June 2017 that introduced a blacklist system similar to the UEL. The second draft of the Export Control Law was published for public comment in December 2019.

The Export Control Law imposes restrictions on transactions with UEL-designated entities, including prohibiting exports of Chinese-origin controlled items to UEL-designated entities, revoking export licences related to transactions with such entities and imposing fines. China also updated its Catalogue of Technologies Prohibited and Restricted from Export on 28 August 2020, to enhance the protection of China's self-innovated high technologies.[24]

2. Key Particulars of China's Unreliable Entity List Provisions

2.1 Targeted Activities Triggering UEL Provisions

Article 2 The State shall establish the Unreliable Entity List System, and adopt measures in response to the following actions taken by a foreign entity in international economic, trade and other relevant activities:

(1) endangering national sovereignty, security or development interests of China;
(2) suspending normal transactions with an enterprise, other organization, or individual of China or applying discriminatory measures against an enterprise,

other organization, or individual of China, which violates normal market transaction principles and causes serious damage to the legitimate rights and interests of the enterprise, other organization, or individual of China.

The UEL Provisions do not specify whether a foreign entity or individual that suspend or stop conducting normal business with Chinese companies to comply with any applicable foreign laws, regulations, or government orders is considered covered by the previously described targeted activities.[25]

Some key terms, such as the "normal market transaction principles," are not defined in the UEL Provisions, nor have they been conceptualized in other Chinese laws.[26] To UEL Provisions, implementing rules and a blacklist are expected to be issued.

2.2 Factors to Be Considered for UEL Provisions

Article 7 The working mechanism shall, according to the results of the investigation and by taking into overall consideration the following factors, make a decision on whether to include the relevant foreign entity in the Unreliable Entity List, and make an announcement of the decision:

(1) the degree of danger to national sovereignty, security or development interests of China;
(2) the degree of damage to the legitimate rights and interests of enterprises, other organizations, or individuals of China;
(3) whether being in compliance with internationally accepted economic and trade rules;
(4) other factors that shall be considered.

The scope of sanctionable conduct appears potentially broad. While many other jurisdictions allow economic sanctions in response to threats to national security or national sovereignty, conduct endangering China's "development interests" might encompass a wide range of competitive practices clashing with industrial policy or trade policy goals.[27]

2.3 Working Mechanism

The UEL Provisions provide that the State will establish a "Working Mechanism" ("UEL Office") composed of relevant central departments to take charge of the organization and implementation of the UEL system. The UEL Office is organized by the MOFCOM. It is expected that MOFCOM will work together with other ministries such as the Ministry of Foreign Affairs and the Ministry of Public Security to implement the UEL system.

MOFCOM established a new "Bureau of Industry, Security, Import and Export Control" (BISIEC) in 2015 that has been relatively quiescent until now.

BISIEC's roles and responsibilities are to some extent similar to those of the Bureau of Industry and Security (BIS) in the US Department of Commerce, which, among others, administers the BIS "Entity List." BISIEC's key responsibilities include, among others, research and establishment of an import/export security review system involving national security and trade restrictions, tightening of the administration of import and export control systems, encouragement of relaxation of control on technologies exported to China, and establishment of bilateral export control and high-technology communication mechanisms.

2.4 Restrictions or Prohibitions on the Foreign Entities Designated in the UEL

Article 10 The working mechanism may, based on actual circumstances, decide to take one or several of the following measures (hereinafter referred to as "the measures") with respect to the foreign entity which is included in the Unreliable Entity List, and make an announcement of the decision:

(1) Restrict or prohibit it from engaging in China-related import or export activities.
(2) Restrict or prohibit it from investing in China.
(3) Restrict or prohibit its relevant personnel or vehicles from entering into China.
(4) Restrict or revoke its relevant personnel's work permit, status of stay, or residence in China.
(5) Impose a fine of the corresponding amount according to the severity of the circumstances.
(6) Other measures.

The UEL Provisions enable the Chinese government to use the threat or imposition of economic sanctions to deter and penalize conduct inimical to Chinese government interests and policies by foreign businesses, organizations, and entities.[28]

The PRC Administrative Litigation Law provides for the setting of different types of administrative penalty.[29] As a unilateral act within the statutory power, it is aimed to derogate from the entity's right or to create additional obligations for the entity.[30]

Restrictions on designated foreign entities' investment activities might apply to new investments, or might extend to orders requiring divestment or restructuring of existing investments.[31] The authorization of "fines" as a possible sanction, moreover, raises the possibility that actions contrary to Chinese government interests might result in administrative penalties.[32] However, the UEL Provisions do not explain how fines are calculated or when punitive measures are appropriate, noting only that this depends on the "actual circumstances."[33]

The Working Mechanism may allow a foreign entity to present a defence. However, where the facts are "clear," the Working Mechanism may proceed with a UEL designation. Where the facts are clear in one case, the Working Mechanism may, without conducting any investigation, decide to add a foreign entity to the UEL. The UEL Provisions, however, do not clarify what would be considered "clear facts," and it appears that the entities concerned will not have the opportunity to defend themselves before being listed. This is also similar to processes by which the US government makes decisions to list parties in certain cases with no advance notice.

US companies and other foreign entities that conduct business in or with China are caught between the crosshairs of both the Chinese and US governments,[34] considering the sanctions and export controls ramped up by the United States over various Chinese entities,

The UEL Provisions do not explicitly provide that foreign-invested enterprises in China may be sanctioned for the offshore conduct of foreign parent companies or affiliates. Theoretically, the sanctions may apply to both the underlying foreign entity and its affiliates and subsidiaries, including its subsidiaries in China. As stated by MOFCOM, foreign individuals may also be listed as "Unreliable Entities" which may include officers of foreign entities.[35]

The UEL Provisions allow sanctions to be imposed in response to conduct occurring outside China, making the UEL Provisions one of the few Chinese laws applying extraterritorially.[36]

The imposition of restrictions raises an issue of whether adherence to the US Executive Order (EO 2019) could constitute a valid reason and be considered as justifiable by the Working Mechanism. The Anti-Monopoly Law (2008) distinguishes between two kinds of breaches, one of which is undertaken "without a valid reason" highlighted under Article 17.[37] Although the Anti-Monopoly Law does not regard fault as a key determinant of a defence, a distinction, at least on face, can be drawn between whether the action is based on the entity's own initiative or its passive obedience.[38] If a foreign entity passively implements discriminatory measures within the limits required by the domestic law, such as the EO 2019, it may be a valid reason. In contrast, if the conduct carried out by a foreign entity exceeds the level required by the domestic law, it could not be a valid reason.[39]

The UEL Provisions do not include legal consequences for violation by any Chinese parties that continue to undertake prohibited or restricted transactions with the designated Foreign Entity in the UEL.[40]

Due to the catch-all clause, the Working Mechanism has broad discretion to investigate potential grounds for sanctioning foreign entities by collecting evidence through various channels.

The Working Mechanism may initiate an investigation against a foreign entity on its own, or based on suggestions or reports filed by other stakeholders.

Before a foreign entity is listed as an "Unreliable Entity," relevant procedures under the Administrative Licensing Law will need to be followed. A foreign entity will have the right to participate in hearings to rebut the allegations and have its views heard before a decision is made.[41] Once the Working Mechanism decides to proceed with the investigation, it should make such decision public while the UEL Provisions are silent about when and where such announcement will be made.

During the investigation, the Working Mechanism may ask the relevant parties and review relevant documents, as well as take other necessary means. The entity will also have the opportunities to make statement and defend its case during the investigation.

Given the lack of specifics, it is not clear whether the Working Mechanism would have ultimate authority to determine on including (or excluding) an entity to the UEL.[42] In theory, a decision to include an entity onto UEL is actionable as a specific administrative act. An entity may also initiate an administrative lawsuit, if it considers that the Working Mechanism abuses its administrative power.[43] Given the Working Mechanism's wide discretion, seeking relief through administrative reconsideration or litigation may not be an effective strategy.[44]

The Administrative Reconsideration Law 2018 provides that an entity may apply to a government department for administrative reconsideration if it does not intend to accept a specific administrative act.[45] When refusing to accept a decision made after administrative reconsideration, the applicant may bring an administrative lawsuit before a Court, or apply to the State Council for arbitration, which shall give a final ruling on the issue and no further litigation proceedings are allowed.[46] Accordingly, a foreign firm has a right to apply for administrative reconsideration, which examines specific administrative acts.[47] Further, the Administrative Procedure Law 2017 provides a negative enumeration of the scope of administrative litigation.[48] The Working Mechanism may decide to suspend or terminate the investigation based on the actual circumstances. It may also resume the investigation in case the facts have changed substantially.

2.5 Compliance Deadlines

In the announcement in which the relevant foreign entity is designated to the UEL, the Working Mechanism may include an alert about the risks of conducting transactions with the designated Foreign Entity.

The designation announcement may also set forth a curing period for the foreign entity to rectify its actions. During such curing period, the previously mentioned restrictions will not be implemented against the foreign entity but if the foreign entity fails to rectify its actions during the curing period, those restrictions or prohibitions will be imposed on the foreign entity.

2.6 Delisting From UEL

A foreign entity may apply for its removal from the UEL and the Working Mechanism shall decide whether to remove it based on actual circumstances.

Where the relevant foreign entity rectifies its actions within the curing period set forth in the designation announcement and takes measures to eliminate the consequences of its actions, the Working Mechanism will make a decision to remove it from the UEL.

The decision of removing a foreign entity off the UEL should also be made public and the imposed punitive measures should also cease to apply immediately upon such announcement.

That said, it is still at the discretion of the Working Mechanism whether such rectification and remedial measures are to its satisfaction.

2.7 Waiver System

The UEL Provisions provide that Chinese entities may apply for a waiver (or permit) to conduct otherwise-prohibited import or export transactions with foreign entities listed on the UEL. This is similar to the licensing procedures under the US economic sanctions and export control schemes.

3. Remaining Issues

3.1 Importance of UEL

The UEL is China's first list-based sanctions framework, which has been widely used in many other jurisdictions, including the US, the EU, and Australia.[49] The setup of the UEL system sends a stern warning to foreign entities that are seeking to hurt Chinese interests, as it gives officials more legal tools to punish them.[50] Previously, China sanctioned US defense firm Lockheed Martin following that company's arms sales to Taiwan. The Chinese government, however, did not articulate what the sanctions consisted of or how they would be applied. It could now do so more formally with the UEL.[51]

List-based sanctions enable the Chinese government to focus punitive measures on particular companies, organizations, and individuals engaged in conduct deemed objectionable.[52] However, it is unclear how a defence of "foreign sovereign compulsion" by a US or a third-country firm would be valid under the MOFCOM Regulation.[53] Ascertaining whether compliance with laws of the blacklisted firm's home state would be a valid defence, namely a "non-commercial consideration" in the UEL Provisions, is an essential issue to be clarified by the MOFCOM.[54]

The UEL constitutes a legal basis to be used in addition to the less formal instruments of "coercive diplomacy."[55] These provisions are a tit-for-tat step towards retaliating against the USA for denying vital American technology to Chinese companies.[56] The provisions constitute the basis for more comprehensive tit-for-tat retaliation by the Chinese government in response to a series of US executive orders and statutory sanctions. China's reaction is widely seen as a countermeasure in the context of the broader trade dispute, which increases the risk considerably of decoupling in the high-tech sectors. UEL Provisions also represent a latest response to the USA's long-arm jurisdiction, which refers to its use of extraterritorial sanctions against Chinese companies.[57]

The UEL Provisions increase tensions between the two countries that are already engaged in a trade war. It would force US entities to start navigating an increasingly complex minefield to avoid the growing animus between the two powers.[58]

Amidst escalating trade tensions and pressures to "de-couple" China from other markets, multinational companies active in Asia may face clashing directives from the sanctions regimes of China, the US, and other jurisdictions.[59]

For multinational companies that have already made great efforts addressing conflicting sanctions and export controls regimes, the UEL Provisions will be an important regime on the watch list. These multinational companies would be trapped in a dilemma. On the one hand, failure to comply with US restrictions on transacting with certain Chinese firms exposes foreign entities to potential criminal or civil penalties, including fines, the most draconian of which is the loss of US export privileges, and the ability to procure US goods. On the other hand, failure to comply with China's requirements of continued supply may result in fines and a ban from the Chinese market.[60] These companies should closely monitor the development of the UEL and navigate ways to ensure compliance with both Chinese laws and laws in other jurisdictions.[61]

3.2 China's Other New Sanction Tools

China's ongoing legislative activities demonstrate the Chinese government's efforts to enhance its export control regime and use export control as a policy tool to tackle the Trump administration's restrictions on US technology exports to China and a broader Western backlash against China's developments of new high technologies in various industries.[62]

The Catalogue of Technologies Prohibited or Restricted from Export was amended in August 2020 to include a wide range of technologies, and the new Export Control Law has completed its second reading before the National People's Congress.[63]

The issuance of the UEL Provisions is an important milestone towards the actual implementation of the UEL system in China. However, it remains unclear how the UEL Provisions will be implemented in practice. The broad language of several of the provisions means the Chinese government will maintain substantial flexibility in implementation and enforcement. Essentially, the UEL Provisions is blocking statutes. To what extent the UEL Provisions could have a "blocking" effect with respect to the sanctions and export control imposed by foreign countries against Chinese companies and individuals remain to be seen.[64] Until China starts to formally launch investigations and list foreign entities, it will be difficult to determine what conduct Beijing considers egregious enough to warrant the UEL's restrictive measures.[65] Since the Chinese government has been making great effort in promoting foreign investment, most of the existing foreign-invested companies should not be adversely affected by the UEL Provisions.

It must be pointed out that the UEL may be counterproductive and even hurt China's own interests more if the UEL Provisions are strictly implemented.[66] Although China's UEL system mirrors the US Entity List system, it may have nowhere close to the same effect, and it may not give the US tech behemoths the same survival risks as those upon on Huawei.[67] The more the UEL system is used, the more likely that foreign companies' confidence on operating in China will be undermined. We may see an unintended consequence for China that the UEL regime would likely hasten strategies by the US technology firms to diversify their supply chains away from China.[68] After the trade war was launched and escalates, a poll from the American Chamber of Commerce revealed that 40% of surveyed firms were considering moving manufacturing out of China to avoid future fallout.[69] This can become worse given the current foreign investors' deteriorating confidence on China's market and the US–China relationship.[70] Forcing foreign MNCs out of China's electronics supply chain could have a major impact on Chinese high-tech champion companies.[71]

Any measures under the UEL Provisions to shut down US tech firms' operations in China could hurt Chinese long-term tech upgrade.[72] Possible actions against those foreign listed MNCs' subsidiaries based in China under the UEL Provisions could lead to serious problems for China's economic growth. Given the US export control regime, some recent reactions with the US sanctions have been fairly toothless.[73] For instance sanctioning Lockheed Martin for US military sales does little damage to the firm.[74] As some commentators noted: "It would be unwise for China to lash out too severely, given it could see more doors close, particularly as it remains on the road to post-pandemic economic recovery."[75] In a short run, using countermeasures via the UEL regime may work as short-term bargaining chips.[76] Strategically, it will not be sustainable and viable in the longer run.[77]

Notes

1 Gao Feng, "China's Introduction of 'Unreliable Entities List' Regime", *MOFCOM Spokesman*, Beijing, 31 May 2019; "MOFCOM Spokesman Meets the Press on China's Introduction of 'Unreliable Entities List' Regime", 1 June 2019, available at http://english.mofcom.gov.cn/article/newsrelease/press/201906/20190602873151.shtml, accessed 24 April 2022.
2 J. Lawrence Broz, Zhiwen Zhang and Gaoyang Wang, "Explaining Foreign Support for China's Global Economic Leadership" (2020) 74(3) *International Organization* 417, 418–419.
3 Jasmine Hahm, "China: Overhauling the Internet", *Berkeley Political Review*, 2019, available at https://bpr.berkeley.edu/2019/02/14/china-overhauling-the-internet/, accessed 14 April 2022.
    Ariel (Eli) Levite, Lyu Jinghua, "Chinese-American Relations in Cyberspace: Toward Collaboration or Confrontation?", *China Military Science*, 25 January 2019, available at https://carnegieendowment.org/2019/01/24/chinese-american-relations-in-cyberspace-toward-collaboration-or-confrontation-pub-78213, accessed 24 April 2022.
4 Nouriel Roubini, "The Global Consequences of a Sino–American Cold War", *Project Syndicate*, 20 May 2019, available at www.project-syndicate.org/commentary/united-states-china-cold-war-deglobalization-by-nouriel-roubini-2019-05, accessed 20 April 2022.

5 Qingxiu Bu, "China's Bocking Mechanism: The Unreliable Entity List" (2020) 19(3) *Journal of International Trade Law and Policy* 159.

6 O'Melveny, "China Publishes 'Unreliable Entities' Rules Targeting Foreign Enterprises", 22 September 2020, available at www.omm.com/resources/alerts-and-publications/ alerts/china-launches-unreliable-entities-list-targeting-foreign-enterprises/, accessed 21 April 2022.

7 Qingxiu Bu, "Between a Rock and A Hard Place: Unreliable Entity List vis-à-vis the US Entity List" (2021) 1 *International Business Law Journal* 65–84.

8 Anthea Roberts, Henrique Choer Moraes and Victor Ferguson, "Toward A Geoeconomic Order in International Trade and Investment" (2019) 22(4) *Journal of International Economic Law* 655–676; Qingxiu Bu, "China's Blocking Mechanism: The Unreliable Entity List" (2020) 19(3) *Journal of International Trade Law and Policy* 161.

9 Alexandra Stevenson and Paul Mozur, "China Steps Up Trade War and Plans Blacklist of U.S. Firms", *New York Times*, 31 May 2019, available at www.sfgate.com/business/article/ China-steps-up-trade-war-and-plans-blacklist-of-13914598.php, accessed 21 April 2022.

10 Marianne Schneider-Petsinger, Jue Wang, Yu Jie, and James Crabtree, "US–China Strategic Competition: The Quest for Global Technological Leadership", *The Royal Institute of International Affairs, Chatham House*, November 2019, available at www.chathamhouse. org/sites/default/files/publications/research/CHHJ7480-US-China-Competition-RP-WEB.pdf, accessed 21 April 2022.

11 Robin Niblett, "The Struggle of Managing Trump", *The Royal Institute of International Affairs, Chatham House*, London, 3 June 2019, available at www.chathamhouse.org/ expert/comment/struggle-managing-trump, accessed 3 June 2020.

12 Gao Feng, "China's Introduction of 'Unreliable Entities List' Regime", *MOFCOM Spokesman*, Beijing, 31 May 2019.

13 Lindsay Maizland and Andrew Chatzky, "Huawei: China's Controversial Tech Giant", 12 June 2019, available at https://brewminate.com/huawei-chinas-controversial-tech-giant/, accessed 24 April 2020.

14 Jenny (Jia) Sheng and Chunbin Xu, "China's Ministry of Commerce Publishes 'Unreliable Entity List' Provisions", *Pillsbury*, 20 September 2020, available at www.pillsburylaw.com/ en/news-and-insights/china-publishes-unreliable-entity-list.html, accessed 21 April 2022.

15 Lester Ross and Kenneth Zhou, "China's Unreliable Entity List", *Wilmerhale*, 29 July 2019, available at www.wilmerhale.com/en/insights/client-alerts/20190729-chinas-unreliable-entity-list, accessed 21 April 2022.

16 Jenny (Jia) Sheng and Chunbin Xu, "China's Ministry of Commerce Publishes 'Unreliable Entity List' Provisions", *Pillsbury*, 20 September 2020, available at www.pillsburylaw.com/ en/news-and-insights/china-publishes-unreliable-entity-list.html, accessed 21 April 2022.

17 *Global Times*, "'No Timetable' for China's Unreliable Entities List: Official", *Global Times*, 20 September 2020, available at www.globaltimes.cn/page/202009/1201425.shtml, accessed 21 April 2022.

18 Ibid.

19 Jenny (Jia) Sheng and Chunbin Xu, "China's Ministry of Commerce Publishes 'Unreliable Entity List' Provisions", *Pillsbury*, 20 September 2020, available at www.pillsburylaw.com/en/news-and-insights/china-publishes-unreliable-entity-list.html, accessed 21 April 2022.

20 Ibid.

21 O'Melveny, "China Publishes 'Unreliable Entities' Rules Targeting Foreign Enterprises", 22 September 2020, available at www.omm.com/resources/alerts-and-publications/alerts/ china-launches-unreliable-entities-list-targeting-foreign-enterprises/, accessed 21 April 2022.

22 "U.S. Export Control Reforms and China: Issues for Congress", *Congressional Research Service*, 15 January 2021.

23 Lester Ross and Kenneth Zhou, "China's Unreliable Entity List", *Wilmerhale*, 29 July 2019, available at www.wilmerhale.com/en/insights/client-alerts/20190729-chinas-unreliable-entity-list, accessed 21 April 2022.

24 Jenny (Jia) Sheng and Chunbin Xu, "China's Ministry of Commerce Publishes 'Unreliable Entity List' Provisions", *Pillsbury*, 20 September 2020, available at www.pillsburylaw.com/en/news-and-insights/china-publishes-unreliable-entity-list.html, accessed 21 April 2022.

25 Ibid.

26 Qingxiu Bu, "China's Bocking Mechanism: The Unreliable Entity List" (2020) 19(3) *Journal of International Trade Law and Policy* 161.

27 Nathan Bush, Sammy Fang, John Zhang, and Ray Xu, "China Unreliable Entity List Provisions Fighting Fire with Fire", *DLA Piper*, 22 September 2020, available at www.dlapiper.com/en/australia/insights/publications/2020/09/china-unreliable-entity-list-provisions-fighting-fire-with-fire, accessed 21 April 2022.

28 Ibid.

29 He Haibo, "How Much Progress Can Legislation Bring? The 2014 Amendment of the Administrative Litigation Law of PRC" (2018) 13(1) *University of Pennsylvania Asian Law Review* 137–190.

30 Wei Cui, Jie Cheng, and Dominika Wiesner, "Judicial Review of Government Actions in China" (2019) 1 *China Perspectives* 29–38.

31 Nathan Bush, Sammy Fang, John Zhang and Ray Xu, "China Unreliable Entity List Provisions Fighting Fire with Fire", *DLA Piper*, 22 September 2020, available at www.dlapiper.com/en/australia/insights/publications/2020/09/china-unreliable-entity-list-provisions-fighting-fire-with-fire, accessed 21 April 2022.

32 Ibid.

33 O'Melveny, "China Publishes 'Unreliable Entities' Rules Targeting Foreign Enterprises", 22 September 2020, available at www.omm.com/resources/alerts-and-publications/alerts/china-launches-unreliable-entities-list-targeting-foreign-enterprises/, accessed 21 April 2022.

34 Hogan Lovells, "China Reveals the Provisions on Unreliability Entity List", *Lexology*, 16 October 2020, available at www.lexology.com/library/detail.aspx?g=a3fe7e11-61e4-4082-a9b6-e36bdb4912bf#:~:text=On%2019%20September%202020%2C%20China%27s%20Ministry%20of%20Commerce,List%20%28UEL%29%20at%20the%20end%20of%20May%202019, accessed 21 April 2022.

35 Lester Ross and Kenneth Zhou, "China's Unreliable Entity List", *Wilmerhale*, 29 July 2019, available at www.wilmerhale.com/en/insights/client-alerts/20190729-chinas-unreliable-entity-list, accessed 21 April 2022.

36 Nathan Bush, Sammy Fang, John Zhang and Ray Xu, "China Unreliable Entity List Provisions Fighting Fire with Fire", *DLA Piper*, 22 September 2020, available at www.dlapiper.com/en/australia/insights/publications/2020/09/china-unreliable-entity-list-provisions-fighting-fire-with-fire, accessed 21 April 2022.

37 Anti-Monopoly Law of the People's Republic of China (2008), Article 17 (3) and (4).

38 Christopher S. Yoo, Thomas Fetzer, Shan Jiang, and Yong Huang, "Due Process in Antitrust Enforcement: Normative and Comparative Perspectives" (2021) 94 *Southern California Law Review* 843.

39 Zhou Yong (Z.), Qin Yu (Bill), and Luo Shijing, "Legal Analysis of China's 'Unreliable Entities List'", *Junhe Law Review*, 18 June 2019, available at www.junhe.com/legal-updates/962?locale=en, accessed 18 June 2019; Qingxiu Bu, "China's Bocking Mechanism: The Unreliable Entity List" (2020) 19(3) *Journal of International Trade Law and Policy* 167.

40 Jenny (Jia) Sheng and Chunbin Xu, "China's Ministry of Commerce Publishes 'Unreliable Entity List' Provisions", *Pillsbury*, 20 September 2020, available at www.pillsburylaw.com/en/news-and-insights/china-publishes-unreliable-entity-list.html, accessed 21 April 2022.

41 Lester Ross and Kenneth Zhou, "China's Unreliable Entity List", *Wilmerhale*, 29 July 2019, available at www.wilmerhale.com/en/insights/client-alerts/20190729-chinas-unreliable-entity-list, accessed 21 April 2022.

42 Administrative Reconsideration Law of the People's Republic of China (2018), Article 13(4).

43 Ibid., Article 8, 12.

44 Zhou Yong (Z.), Qin Yu (Bill), and Luo Shijing, "Legal Analysis of China's 'Unreliable Entities List'", *Junhe Law Review*, 18 June 2019, available at www.junhe.com/legal-updates/962?locale=en, accessed 18 June 2019.

45 Yang Weidong, "Can the Introduction of Administrative Reconsideration Committees Help Reform China's System of Administrative Reconsideration?" (2018) 13(1) *University of Pennsylvania Asian Law Review* 107–136.

46 Administrative Reconsideration Law of the People's Republic of China, Article 14 (2018).

47 Ibid., Article 27.

48 Ibid., Article 13.

49 Nathan Bush, Sammy Fang, John Zhang and Ray Xu, "China Unreliable Entity List Provisions Fighting Fire with Fire", *DLA Piper*, 22 September 2020, available at www.dlapiper.com/en/australia/insights/publications/2020/09/china-unreliable-entity-list-provisions-fighting-fire-with-fire, accessed 21 April 2022.

50 *Global Times*, "'No Timetable' for China's Unreliable Entities List: Official", *Global Times*, 20 September 2020, available at www.globaltimes.cn/page/202009/1201425.shtml, accessed 21 April 2022.

51 K2integrity, "Policy Alert: China Announces 'Provisions on the Unreliable Entity List'", *K2integrity*, 24 September 2020, available at www.k2integrity.com/knowledge/policy%20alerts/china%20announces%20provisions%20on%20the%20unreliable%20entity%20list, accessed 21 April 2022.

52 Nathan Bush, Sammy Fang, John Zhang, and Ray Xu, "China Unreliable Entity List Provisions Fighting Fire with Fire", *DLA Piper*, 22 September 2020, available at www.dlapiper.com/en/australia/insights/publications/2020/09/china-unreliable-entity-list-provisions-fighting-fire-with-fire, accessed 21 April 2022.

53 Qingxiu Bu, "China's Bocking Mechanism: The Unreliable Entity List" (2020) 19(3) *Journal of International Trade Law and Policy* 162.

54 Qingxiu Bu, "Between a Rock and A Hard Place: Unreliable Entity List vis-à-vis the US Entity List" (2021) 1 *International Business Law Journal* 65–84.

55 Fergus Hanson, Emilia Currey and Tracy Beattie, "The Chinese Communist Party's Coercive Diplomacy", *Australian Strategic Policy Institute*, 1 September 2020, available at www.aspi.org.au/report/chinese-communist-partys-coercive-diplomacy, accessed 1 September 2020.

56 Alexandra Stevenson and Paul Mozur, "China Steps Up Trade War and Plans Blacklist of U.S. Firms", *Sfgate*, 31 May 2019, available at www.sfgate.com/business/article/China-steps-up-trade-war-and-plans-blacklist-of-13914598.php, accessed 21 April 2022.

57 Jeffrey A. Meyer, "Second Thoughts on Secondary Sanctions" (2019) 30(3) *University of Pennsylvania Journal of International Law* 905–967. Qingxiu Bu, "China's Bocking Mechanism: The Unreliable Entity List" (2020) 19(3) *Journal of International Trade Law and Policy* 164.

58 Kevin Rudd, "To Deal, or Not to Deal: The U.S.-China Trade War Enters the End-Game", *Asian Society Policy Institute*, 9 September 2019, available at https://asiasociety.org/policy-institute/to-deal-or-not-to-deal, accessed 9 September 2019.
   Qingxiu Bu, "China's Bocking Mechanism: The Unreliable Entity List" (2020) 19(3) *Journal of International Trade Law and Policy* 159.

59 Nathan Bush, Sammy Fang, John Zhang and Ray Xu, "China Unreliable Entity List Provisions Fighting Fire with Fire", *DLA Piper*, 22 September 2020, available at www.

dlapiper.com/en/australia/insights/publications/2020/09/china-unreliable-entity-list-provisions-fighting-fire-with-fire, accessed 21 April 2022.

60 O'Melveny, "China Publishes 'Unreliable Entities' Rules Targeting Foreign Enterprises", 22 September 2020, available at www.omm.com/resources/alerts-and-publications/alerts/china-launches-unreliable-entities-list-targeting-foreign-enterprises/, accessed 21 April 2022.

61 Tracy Wut, Zhi Bao, Jon Cowley, and Vivian Wu, "China Issues the Regulations on Unreliable Entity List", *Global Compliance News*, 27 October 2020, available at www.globalcompliancenews.com/2020/10/27/china-issues-the-regulations-on-unreliable-entity-list-22092020/, accessed 21 April 2022.

62 Jenny (Jia) Sheng and Chunbin Xu, "China's Ministry of Commerce Publishes 'Unreliable Entity List' Provisions", *Pillsbury*, 20 September 2020, available at www.pillsburylaw.com/en/news-and-insights/china-publishes-unreliable-entity-list.html, accessed 21 April 2022.

63 Nathan Bush, Sammy Fang, John Zhang, and Ray Xu, "China Unreliable Entity List Provisions Fighting Fire with Fire", *DLA Piper*, 22 September 2020, available at www.dlapiper.com/en/australia/insights/publications/2020/09/china-unreliable-entity-list-provisions-fighting-fire-with-fire, accessed 21 April 2022.

64 Tracy Wut, Zhi Bao, Jon Cowley, and Vivian Wu, "China Issues the Regulations on Unreliable Entity List", *Global Compliance News*, 27 October 2020, available at www.globalcompliancenews.com/2020/10/27/china-issues-the-regulations-on-unreliable-entity-list-22092020/, accessed 21 April 2022.

65 K2integrity, "Policy Alert: China Announces 'Provisions on the Unreliable Entity List'", *K2integrity*, 24 September 2020, available at www.k2integrity.com/knowledge/policy%20alerts/china%20announces%20provisions%20on%20the%20unreliable%20entity%20list, accessed 21 April 2022.

66 Eamon Barrett, "China Is Creating Its Own 'Entity List' to Avenge Huawei and Punish Foreign Firms", *Fortune*, 18 June 2019, available at http://businessfacts.epizy.com/china-is-creating-its-own-entity-list-to-avenge-huawei-and-punish-foreign-firms/, accessed 18 June 2019.

67 Zak Doffman, "China Threatens to Blacklist U.S. Firms Refusing to Supply Huawei", *Forbes*, 3 June 2019, available at www.oodaloop.com/briefs/2019/06/03/china-threatens-to-blacklist-u-s-firms-refusing-to-supply-huawei/, accessed 31 May 2019.

68 Alexandra Stevenson and Paul Mozur, "China Steps Up Trade War and Plans Blacklist of U.S. Firms", *Sfgate*, 31 May 2019, available at www.sfgate.com/business/article/China-steps-up-trade-war-and-plans-blacklist-of-13914598.php, accessed 21 April 2022.

69 Eamon Barrett, "China Is Creating Its Own 'Entity List' to Avenge Huawei and Punish Foreign Firms", *Fortune*, 18 June 2019, available at http://businessfacts.epizy.com/china-is-creating-its-own-entity-list-to-avenge-huawei-and-punish-foreign-firms/, accessed 18 June 2019.

70 Keith Bradsher, "China's Economic Growth Slows as Challenges Mount", *The New York Times*, 21 October 2019, available at https://www.nytimes.com/2019/10/17/business/china-economic-growth.html, accessed 17 October 2019.

71 Sarah Zheng and Wendy Wu, "Beijing to Blacklist 'Unreliable' Foreign Entities That 'Hurt Interests of Chinese Firms'", *South China Morning Post*, 1 June 2019, available at https://www.scmp.com/news/china/diplomacy/article/3012675/beijing-blacklist-unreliable-foreign-entities-hurt-interests, accessed 31 May 2019.

72 Alexandra Stevenson and Paul Mozur, "China Steps Up Trade War and Plans Blacklist of U.S. Firms", *Sfgate*, 31 May 2019, available at www.sfgate.com/business/article/China-steps-up-trade-war-and-plans-blacklist-of-13914598.php, accessed 21 April 2022.

73 Richard Nephew, "China and Economic Sanctions: Where Does Washington, DC Have Leverage?", *Washington International Trade Association*, 1 September 2019, available at www.wita.org/atp-research/china-sanctions-leverage/, accessed 21 April 2022.

74 Chun Han Wong, "China Threatens to Sanction Lockheed Martin over Taiwan Arms Deal", *The Wall Street Journal*, 14 July 2020, available at https://www.wsj.com/articles/

china-to-sanction-lockheed-martin-over-taiwan-arms-deal-11594727908, accessed 3 October 2022.

75 Veerle Nouwens and Raffaello Pantucci, "Huawei is No Way for British Strategy on China", *RUSI Commentary*, 17 July 2020, available at https://rusi.org/commentary/huawei-no-way-british-strategy-china, accessed 17 July 2020.

76 Z. Doffman, "China Threatens to Blacklist U.S. Firms Refusing to Supply Huawei", *Forbes*, 3 June 2019, available at www.oodaloop.com/briefs/2019/06/03/china-threatens-to-blacklist-u-s-firms-refusing-to-supply-huawei/, accessed 31 May 2019.

77 Qingxiu Bu, "China's Bocking Mechanism: The Unreliable Entity List" (2020) 19(3) *Journal of International Trade Law and Policy* 159.

10

CAN BLOCKING STATUTES BLOCK UNFAIR EXTRATERRITORIALITY?

1. Introduction

The newly installed *MOFCOM Order No. 1 of 2021 on Rules on Counteracting Unjustified Extra-territorial Application of Foreign Legislation and Other Measures* (the Blocking Statute or the Chinese Blocking Statute) represents the use of legal mechanisms to counter the effects of foreign extraterritorial legislation and measures. In the Chinese context, many scholars view this as a positive development as the Blocking Statute exemplifies a shift from the diplomatic approach to a more juristic one in dealing with foreign extraterritoriality.[1] China used to primarily rely on diplomatic agility to address all sorts of problems arising from or associated with the trade war. However, with the need for Beijing to ensure greater stability in its foreign policies and laws on trade due to the ever-increasing growth of Chinese businesses, the Blocking Statute has become an option.

The making of the Blocking Statute is said to satisfy the need of safeguarding national security, as Article 1 therein stated: "These Rules [the MOFCOM Order] are formulated in accordance with the National Security Law of the People's Republic of China and other relevant laws."[2] This seems to correspond to the American stand that the operation of some Chinese companies in the US and its allies, especially those already targeted by US extraterritorial jurisdiction, gives rise to national security concerns. The wider context is that the US has never faced a greater challenger than China since the 1880s when it began its rise as a superpower. To contain China's rise, the Trump administration waged a trade war, which involved ratcheting up tariffs and restricting Chinese high-tech companies on national security grounds. Many of these policies relied on the extraterritorial application of US laws and measures to be implemented. Now that the Biden administration has taken office, it remains to be seen whether the those policies will be overturned.[3] Noticeably, however, the past few decades

DOI: 10.4324/9781003130499-10

have witnessed the US increasingly seeking to weaponize economic sanctions to push through its public policy agenda,[4] without any signs that this will change in the near future.[5] Therefore, the discussion of the current Chinese Blocking Statute bears practical value, even though the new American administration will likely adjust its approach to China-related matters.

Some Chinese scholars suspect that the Blocking Statute is mainly targeting US secondary sanctions, which seek to "regulate" the relations between the target states and third countries and persons under their jurisdiction.[6] The Blocking Statute, however, does not contain a definition of secondary sanctions. According to the aforementioned scholars, both primary and secondary sanctions are essential components of the US economic sanction framework;[7] the former regulate the relations between the sanctioning states and the target states, while the latter focus on the relations between third states and the target states.[8] Secondary sanctions are particularly controversial because of their extraterritorial effect. Chinese scholarship tends to oppose the legitimacy of such sanctions because they have, in the past, imposed "unfair restrictions" on China's sovereign power. This view is shared by other countries. For instance the EU has imposed the blocking regulation with the effect of prohibiting EU companies from complying with US sanctions on third countries.[9] This regulation was recently updated in response to EU–US foreign policy clashes on Iran. The definition and legality of secondary sanctions are addressed in greater detail in Section 2 for the purpose of explaining the content of the Chinese Blocking Statute.

The provisions of the Blocking Statute contain many ambiguities. Assumably, this ambiguity is purposeful since "national security" is not well-defined in US law and therefore the scope of US rules on export and economic sanctions – which must be minded by Chinese companies – can be unreasonably broad. High-tech companies must be cautious if they rely on US-origin items or technologies, even if the contemplated transaction has otherwise no link to the US.[10] Moreover, threats to Chinese high-level administrative personnel for alleged contravention of US sanctions against a third country are also alarming. It is believed by Chinese officials that the new Blocking Statute lays a legal basis for China to take countermeasures to deal with the aforementioned effects and threats.[11] But it still remains to be seen if this is a pragmatic and justified vision. This chapter goes further to examine the potential impact of the Blocking Statute on the development of international law.

The rest of the chapter is structured as follows. Section 2 analyzes the core components of the Chinese Blocking Statute. Using comparative methods, it highlights the fact that this statute follows a practice that is familiar to the international community, although the blocking rules contained therein display some distinctive Chinese features that deserve attention. In the domestic context, these rules are compared to the blocking regulations implemented in 2018 and 2020 on international judicial assistance and the Unreliable Entity List (UEL) mechanism respectively.[12] This comparison enables the reader to gain a more comprehensive understanding of US–China lawfare and the "weapons" that have been employed. The comparative results lend justification to the author's critical views of the Blocking Statute presented in Section 3. The author is inclined to believe that this statute is neither effective in defining or countering "unfair US extraterritorial sanctions," nor capable of leading international law down the right path. Section 4 proposes the way forward. The final section concludes this chapter.

2. Key Components of the Chinese Blocking Rules

This section reviews the key components of the Chinese Blocking Statute. The analysis aims to reveal that the purpose of the Blocking Statute is not sufficiently clear because many key terms are not well defined. The working mechanism, which was established to take charge of counteracting the unjustified extraterritorial application of foreign legislation and other measures, is a main focus of this section.[13] This mechanism is viewed from a comparative perspective. Since the Chinese Blocking Statute borrowed heavily from EU law, in particular the EU blocking regulation and its most recent updates,[14] these have been accorded great weight. Both the EU and Chinese blocking laws have been referred to as "blocking mechanisms against "sanctions" in the literature.[15]

Blocking rules have existed in the EU's legal framework for decades. Such rules were first adopted by the EU in 1996 to counter the effects of the Iran Sanctions Act of 1996, and subsequently, to counter the effects of the Iran Freedom and Counter-Proliferation Act of 2012, the National Defense Authorizatiton Act for Fiscal Year 2012, the Iran Threat Reduction and Syria Human Rights Act of 2012, and the Iranian Transactions and Sanctions Regulations. It has been argued that those efforts were related to the Siberian pipeline case, where the US attempted to delay the construction of the West Siberian gas pipeline as a response to perceived Soviet responsibility for the declaration of martial law in Poland.[16] The sanctions were expanded in this case to companies operating abroad that were owned or controlled by US citizens or companies and to overseas licences of US technology,[17] which evoked strong objections from Europe. The US finally made compromises on the pipeline sanctions after European countries persistently resisted the US sanctions by implementing blocking statutes or resorting to the authority of international tribunals. It should be noted that the blocking legislation was not the only response to US laws with extraterritorial effects.[18] Other actions taken include lobbying US policy advisors, imposing pressure on the Regan administration through European governments, filing suits at federal courts, and forming cartels which American authorities attempted to break up.[19]

The US extraterritorial sanctions continued into the 1990s where these sanctions had more to do with the ideological hegemony of the US than Cold War survivalist thinking. The comprehensive legal framework for the US' position on Cuba, which includes embargoes and trade controls, for instance was framed to mitigate the perceived "increasing communist threat" posted by Cuba and to force a regime change in the country.[20] The US sanctions against Chinese businesses and individuals are the most recent demonstration of the American extraterritoriality and are believed to be the direct cause for China to issue the Blocking Statute.[21] These sanctions have happened in a novel era when conventional economic wisdom about China's current status and future is often wrong and mainstream scholarship has started casting doubt on the US metanarratives of political science. The US has to rely more on the preponderance of American businesses and technology rather than the anti-communism cliché in implementing extraterritorial legislations and measures.

The Chinese Blocking Statute is said to be a response to the risk of being sanctioned facing "Chinese persons and organizations,"[22] but "sanction" is not mentioned in the Statute. The legality of the specific sanction is subject to the judgement of the competent departments of the Chinese government.[23] Regarding the purpose of the Statute, Article 1 explains that it is formulated in accordance with the National Security Law of the People's Republic of China and aim to safeguard key international law norms. The Chinese authorities believe that the extraterritorial application of US laws results from the US' obsession with unilateralism and hegemony.[24] They articulate that some country-specific sanctions resulting from US judicial extraterritoriality could be challenged based on international law and principles of international relations.[25] It is confirmed in Article 2 of the statute that this piece of legislation is geared to counter extraterritorial application of foreign legislation and other measures in violation of international law and the basic principles of international relations and with the effect of unjustifiably prohibiting or restricting the citizens, legal persons, or other organizations of China from engaging in normal economic, trade, and related activities with a third state (or region) or its citizens, legal persons, or other organizations.[26] The previously mentioned provisions inevitably give rise to problems due to the lack of clarification on some key terms. The terms, such as "international law," "basic principles of international relations," "unjustifiable prohibition and restriction," "legal persons of China," etc., do not have commonly agreed definitions.

The Blocking Statute seems not to have sufficiently considered the reality that the term of "extraterritorial application of domestic laws" actually carries positive connotation. China has its own way in pursuing extraterritorial effect of Chinese law. The Chinese Anti-Monopoly law, for instance could block business mergers involving foreign companies.[27] But the effect of this law is rather unclear in a real extraterritorial context even though Article 2 thereof provides that the law is applicable to "monopolistic conducts outside the territory of the People's Republic of China for the purpose of eliminating or restricting competition on the domestic market of China."[28] Overall, the Chinese approach to asserting its judicial authority extraterritorially appears to be less aggressive, as compared to the US approach. Many have explained the reason by considering China's experience in the 19th century when foreign countries had the so-called consular jurisdiction and accordingly foreign citizens could live under their own laws in Chinese cities.[29] Others tend to find the reason from the existing Chinese foreign policies. As explained in Article 3 of the Blocking Statute, China pursues foreign policies with respect for "sovereignty, non-interference in each other's internal affairs, and equality and mutual benefit and for international treaty obligations."[30]

If reviewing the issue of extraterritorial application of domestic laws in the broader international law context, one may find that this issue largely falls within the discretionary power of the sanctioning state and, therefore, is less likely to run counter to international law. Arguably, it is not an easy task to reply on international law to prove the unlawfulness of the practice of applying domestic laws in the extraterritorial manner, no matter whether sanction is evoked.[31] There are even reasons to say that some extraterritorial sanctions might be necessary in the sense of avoiding military actions or other unwanted consequences.[32] Overall, conceptual analysis of "unlawful extraterritorial sanctions" is lacking in both the Chinese Blocking Statute and the current literature. This has created difficulties in assessing "the working mechanism" that has been established by the Statute to "take charge of counteracting unjustified extra-territorial application of foreign legislation and other measures."[33]

Although the Chinese rules seem to be more ambitious than their counterparts in other jurisdictions in the statement of purpose, the working mechanism is neither as strong nor as specific. This mechanism is led by "the competent department of commerce of the State Council" and the specific matters thereof are handled by the "competent department of commerce and the department of development and reform in conjunction with other relevant departments of the State Council."[34] There is nothing new in allowing governmental or administrative bodies to lead such a mechanism. The EU's blocking statute (Council Regulation (EC) No 2271/96), for instance allows submission of any effects on the economic and/or financial interests of the covered person caused by a measure blocked in the Annex to the European Commission and application to the Commission for an authorization to comply with the designated laws.[35] But without clarification on the extraterritorial legislations with which Chinese persons and organizations are prohibited from complying, it becomes a question whether those departments are capable of making sound decision on whether there exists unjustified extraterritorial application of foreign legislation and other measures.[36] Chief among the author's concerns is that those departments' decisions have a distinctly judicial character but it is not the case that they have organs within them that are charged with judicial impartiality.

The lack of provisions designating the prohibited laws represents a striking difference between the Chinese and EU blocking legislations. The 1996 EU blocking regulation specifies in the Annex that the following laws and regulations are targets of the regulation: Cuban Democracy Act 1992, Cuban Liberty and Democratic Solidarity Act of 1996, Iran and Libya Sanctions Act of 1996, and Cuban Assets Control Regulations.[37] The Annex was updated in 2018 to expand the listed extraterritorial legislations to which the protective measures contained in the regulation apply.[38] The updates were made for the Iran Sanctions Act of 1996, the Iran Freedom and Counter-Proliferation Act of 2012, the National Defense Authorization Act for Fiscal Year 2012, the Iran Threat Reduction and Syria Human Rights Act of 2012, and the Iran Transactions and Sanctions Regulations.[39] The extraterritorial reach of domestic laws is one of the most controversial topics in the international legal community. Therefore, in determining the laws being blocked, countries tend to leave the impression that the legislations are able to accommodate domestic regulatory interests and, in the meantime, to avoid impinging on the legitimate interests of foreign states. The lack of designation of the blocked laws in the Chinese Blocking Statute does not help move China in this direction.

The assessing procedure is expected to be initiated by the affected persons or organizations. Article 5 of the Blocking Statute has obliged these persons and organizations to truthfully report to the competent department of the State Council when they feel that the situation falls within the scope of the Blocking Statute.[40] The authorized departments have to consider and give weight to the following factors when deciding whether the affected parties have been "prohibited or restricted by foreign legislations and other measures from engaging in normal economic, trade and related activities:"[41] international law and basic principles of international relations; potential impact on China's national sovereignty, security, and development interests; potential impact on the legitimate rights and interests of the citizens, legal persons, or other organizations of China; as well as other relevant factors.[42]

It must be noted that the effect of the previously mentioned provisions may be hammered by the fact that the Blocking Statute fails to define "Chinese persons and organizations" upon whom this statute has imposed obligations and for whom it is designed to protect. Normally, subsidiaries and affiliates invested and established by foreign companies are also considered Chinese persons. Therefore, foreign multinational businesses should not overlook the risk that they will be left in a quandary. In some situations, they must make good use of the exemption mechanism provided in Article 8 of the rules when necessary. The EU regulation has taken a different path. Article 11 of the 1996 regulation states that the regulation shall apply to the following persons under EU jurisdiction:

(i) Any natural person being a resident in the Community and a national of a Member State;

(ii) any legal person incorporated within the Community;

(iii) Any natural or legal person referred to in Article 1(2) of Regulation (EEC) No 4055/86;

(iv) Any other natural person being a resident in the Community, unless that person is in the country of which they are a national;

(v) Any other natural person within the Community, including its territorial waters and air space and in any aircraft or on any vessel under the jurisdiction or control of a Member State, acting in a professional capacity.[43]

In the 2018 updates, the scope of the covered persons remained unchanged. As previously mentioned, the EU regulation was only updated to include the re-imposed American sanctions after the US' unilateral withdrawal from the Joint Comprehensive Plan of Action (JCPOA) in May 2018. The 2018 regulation continues serving the purpose of protecting EU operators that are engaged in international trade in a manner wholly compliant with EU law but in breach of sanctions imposed by other countries.[44]

Under Article 5 of the Chinese Blocking Statute, a "citizen, legal person, or other organization of China," who is prohibited or restricted by foreign legislation or other measures from engaging in normal economic activities, trade, or related activities with a third state or its citizens, legal persons, or other organizations, shall fulfil its reporting obligation within 30 days.[45] This provision, however, does not specify when the 30-day period starts. It is unclear whether the obliged persons should report when they notice the unfair circumstances, when the actual operation is restricted, or when they actually suffer damages and require protection from the Blocking Statute. The reporting parties may request the reported information to be kept confidential.[46] But therein contains no information regarding whether the competent authorities could request any other information or conduct their own investigation on the concerned situation on their own discretion. The EU blocking regulation contains similar informatory obligation. Article 2 of the 1996 regulation states that

> where the economic and/or financial interests of any person referred to in Article 11 are affected, directly or indirectly, by the laws specified in the Annex or by actions based thereon or resulting therefrom, that person shall inform the Commission accordingly within 30 days from the date on which it obtained such information.[47]

This provision further clarifies that this obligation applies to directors, managers, and other persons with management responsibilities. The same provision empowers the EU Commission to request any information in this regard according to its own discretion.[48]

Once the competent departments decide that the Blocking Statute should be applied to correct "unfair" extraterritoriality, there are two means of remedy. Under Article 7 of the Statute, the competent department may issue a "prohibition order" to the effect that "the relevant foreign legislation and other measures are not accepted, executed, or observed."[49] Alternatively, Article 9 offers the possibility for the affected persons or organizations to sue another person when the latter complies with the foreign legislation and other measures and therefore infringes the rights and interests of the former. The EU blocking regulation also has the effect of prohibiting the covered persons from complying with the extra-territorial effects of the US laws identified in the annex.[50] As to the impact of this regulation on the judicial system of the EU, the blocking legislation may nullify the effect in the EU of any foreign court judgements based on the re-instated

US laws and measures.[51] In the meantime, any affected person shall be entitled to recover losses due to damages to that person by the application of the laws specified in the regulation or by actions based thereon or resulting therefrom.[52] It is identified as a problem that the EU regulation does not clarify whether a covered person can seek damages directly from the US government. Thus far, it still remains an open question from whom the compensation can be sought.[53]

By allowing Chinese parties to sue "a person" who complies with "foreign legislation and other measures within the scope of a prohibition order" and who is thus infringing upon the rights and interests of the Chinese parties, the Chinese Blocking Statute likely changes the usual routine of dispute settlement. Cross-border transactions are often governed by contracts made according to international treaties or other application laws. In the international commercial law context, the favourable tendency is usually to allow transnational adjudication to transcend domestic litigation, not the reverse. It can be anticipated that it will be very difficult for judicial or administrative authorities in China to prove that the reason a certain company discontinued or reduced its business in a third country was linked to the compliance of US sanctions and not based on economic factors. The situation will be much complex when they consider the relevant choice-of-law mandate, the international law rules, and comity. In this setting, there is room to argue that a judicialized approach that relies on international dispute settlement mechanisms is more likely to result in convincing decisions. This position will be further explained in Section 4 regarding the way forward.

It is also worth considering one mechanism, that is an additional administrative support for persons who, by adhering to the prohibition order, have suffered significant losses, that appears in the Chinese Blocking Statute but not in its EU counterpart. Article 10 of the Blocking Statute provides that

> where, in adherence to the prohibition order, a citizen, legal person or other organization of China suffers significant losses resulting from non-compliance with the relevant foreign legislation and other measures, relevant governmental departments may provide necessary support based on specific circumstances.[54]

The ambiguous character of this provision makes it difficult to anticipate its real effect. It would be worthwhile for future research to explore whether such ambiguity is purposeful, as more empirical evidence arises.

Non-compliance of the prohibition may give rise to fine or warning in accordance with Article 13 of the Blocking Statute. Therein it states that, when an obliged person fails to comply with the prohibition order, the competent department may issue a warning, order he, she, or it to rectify within a period of time, and may concurrently impose a fine according to severity of the circumstances. The Chinese legislators may have been informed that, over the past few decades, the EU blocking regulation and the subsequent updates have been seldom used due to both political difficulties and technical defects.[55] Decades after the implementation of such a regulation, the EU is still facing the problem of the lack of guidance and advice to affected enterprises on how to comply with the regulation.[56] It is likely the case that the Chinese Blocking Statute will only function as the political and diplomatic tool that regulators in China can use to articulate their stands or force counter-parties to the negotiation table. Otherwise, the ambiguities anticipate the broad authority that will be granted to Chinese governmental authorities to regulate transnational transactions and businesses.

It is also interesting to compare the Chinese Blocking Statute and other blocking laws implemented domestically, such as the blocking regulations promulgated in 2018 that aim at preventing Chinese persons from engaging in unilateral cooperation with foreign criminal investigations in foreign countries and the UEL mechanism established in 2020 with the effect of enabling the government to include foreign entities on the list based on the results of an investigation.[57] These are all "legal weapons" that constitute part of the US–China lawfare[58] and are expected to supplement each other in their functions. They share certain features; for instance they are essentially countermeasures made on a unilateral basis against extraterritorial jurisdiction of foreign laws, and they only work well when they are widely supported by the international community and are backed by state powers.

In 2018, China enacted a new criminal judicial assistance statute, the International Criminal Judicial Assistance Law (the ICJA Law), which regulates judicial assistance requests from other countries in criminal proceedings. Under this law, documents, assets, and testimonies relating to criminal matters have to undergo a mandatory pre-approval process before they can be exported out of the Mainland of the People's Republic of China. As a direct response to the increasing tensions in the US–China relationship, the MOFCOM issued another blocking regulation in 2020, the "Provisions on the Unreliable Entity List" (the UEL), which provides procedures for designating non-Chinese operators including any "enterprise, other organization, or individual of a foreign country" that broadly acts contrary to China's national interests. The arrival of the those blocking laws represents the reinvigoration of unilateral countermeasures by China against extraterritorial jurisdiction. In the following section, this chapter reviews whether this is a positive development.

3. Critiques of the Chinese Blocking Statute

This section focuses on the major flaws inherent to the Chinese blocking rules which include both the new Chinese Blocking Statute and other blocking laws and regulations that are similar in terms of potential effects and legality. The discussion focuses on two questions: First, were the blocking rules efficient in achieving its goals? And second, does the application of the blocking rules favour the development of international law? The second question must be taken seriously by Chinese government and legislators if China desires to boost its image as a responsible player in global governance. The analysis intends to render two strands of arguments. One is that the blocking rules create more problems than they solve for both Chinese and foreign businesses due to the lack of clarification on key concepts and the underestimation of the political and legal barriers for implementation. The other is that the rules, which are essentially a unilateral countermeasure, may not lead international law down the right path.

3.1 The Inefficiency of the Chinese Blocking Rules

Despite China's hurried introduction of the Blocking Statute and other countermeasures that seek to minimize the impact of "unlawful" US extraterritorial jurisdiction in certain cases, this move may not be able to significantly shift the US' stand or to dissuade the covered persons from overcompliance with US secondary sanctions. The Blocking Statute does not negate the challenges faced by multinational companies, which are eager to avoid angering Chinese as well as American regulators. It, in fact, has left businesses between a rock and a hard place. It can at least be anticipated that some provisions of the Statute will lead to a considerable level of litigation risk and compliance risk for multinational companies which are already on the frontlines of US–China tensions, thereby facing considerable costs due to risk management. In this aspect, the EU experience with US extraterritorial sanctions is particularly relevant.

Previous EU studies have shown that countermeasures, including but not limited to the blocking regulation, have proved to be ineffective in reducing the regulatory risk facing European businesses.[59] The European Parliament in its 2020 report studied the status of the affected companies after the re-imposition of US sanctions on Iran and the implementation of the updated EU blocking regulation. The new regulation intends to help European firms improve their position in Iran. But the reality is that it has created severe problems for firms already invested in Iran and threatened companies which are trying to walk the line between US and EU laws.[60] It is, therefore, reasonable to foresee that the Chinese Blocking Statute will also place businesses in a compliance dilemma in which they will have to incur massive costs related to investigating and avoiding punishments from the application of US sanctions while simultaneously being seen to not be complying with these sanctions.

The year 2020 saw a few cases in which Article 5 of the EU blocking regulation, which contains a ban on compliance with US extraterritorial legislations and administrative measures, was applied. Therein, the courts' views were divided on whether there is a causal relationship between the alleged breach of contracts and the existence of extraterritorial sanctions.[61] These cases gave rise to issues that have been referred to the European Court of Justice (ECJ); in one such case, *Bank Melli Iran v Telekom Deutschland GmBH*,[62] the ECJ was asked for the first time to interpret Article 5 of the blocking regulation. This case arises from the situation in which the defendant terminated the service contract with the plaintiff following the reimposition of US sanctions on Iran, leading to the disruption of the plaintiffs' business activities at its German branch. The Hamburg

Regional Court ordered the defendant to perform the contract until the end of the ordinary notice period and held that the change of contractual relationship between the two parties did not entail Article 5 of the blocking regulation. The plaintiff was not satisfied with the result and appealed the case to a higher court. The appellate court made a request to the ECJ for a preliminary ruling. The review is currently pending. The ECJ ruling is expected to clarify some uncertainties surrounding the application of the EU blocking regulation, but it cannot significantly enhance the efficiency of the regulation or shift the US' stand on extraterritorial jurisdiction due to the reality of EU's vulnerabilities vis-à-vis US secondary sanctions, which is a result of its asymmetric interdependence with the US economy. China is facing a similar situation as the EU. Regardless of the severe impact of the US sanctions, such a backlash taking the form of blocking legislation has to consider the risk posed to the global supply chain and to the Chinese economy in general. From a pragmatic perspective, the possible conclusion may be that the blocking legislation is not preferred to remain or to be further escalated to some "sharper weapons."

3.2 The Legality and Rationality of the Chinese Blocking Rules as Unilateral Countermeasures Under International Law

With the new blocking rules, it seems that China finally has a legal instrument to counter technical blockage and suppression of China and its companies as the result of US extraterritorial sanctions. It can be argued that the Chinese blocking rules carry a positive connotation, as when one speaks of the legal countermeasure or legal instrument against extraterritoriality in the sense of conferring on a title or a normative proposition the legitimacy of law. Although the rules serve political agenda, it is not a mere assertion of Chinese sovereignty that pushes back against the long-arm jurisdiction of US economic laws and measures. Next to the positive connotation, there is a negative one, namely that unilateral action often turns out to be a political tool to force the opposing party to adjust their political preferences. It is doubtful that the Chinese blocking rules will help China to change US policy in its favour. Arguably, the efficiency of the blocking rules in large part depends upon China's relations with the rest of the world associated with a set of changing factors. More importantly, unilateral countermeasures are not the ideal solution if we sincerely aspire to move towards a sound and fair international legal system. As aforementioned, extraterritoriality has not been settled in international law. Through legislative activities, China is expected to build a different conceptual structure of the previously mentioned issue as the contribution to the establishment of an international legal order capable of accommodating and balancing conflicting legal requirements. However, it is doubtful that the new Chinese Blocking Statute and other blocking rules with similar effect will aid China in this project.

In debates on international law, there are ample comments on the legality of US sanctions, but scant comments on the legality of countermeasures.

Traditionally, views on sanctions and countermeasures made unilaterally are divided between developed and developing countries.[63] China, due to its unique cultural and historical features, used to believe that unilateral measures with extraterritorial effect, which were associated with imperialism, colonialism, and hegemonism, are illegal under international law.[64] But now it constantly resorts to unilateral measures in dealing with political opponents, which will potentially result in changes to the aforementioned stand. Countermeasures, including the newly imposed blocking rules by China, are essentially unilateral moves that are not instrumental in making international law more tenable. Such measures seem to contradict with the Chinese belief that coercion is not always or should not be the most commonly used mode of interaction between modern states. China has been trying to establish an image of itself as a defender of multilateralism.[65] Then it is required to carefully consider the compatibility (or lack thereof) of the countermeasures with multilateralism. Normally, countermeasures are used when diplomacy fails and when a military option is too radical. They are often issued on a retaliatory basis as a means of exerting pressure on a wrongdoing state to comply with certain international law norms or, in the current context, as a means of forcing the sanctioning state to comply with its international obligations. To achieve these purposes, the country, which adopts the countermeasures, has to violate certain obligations towards the sanctioning state. This raises the question of whether international law has left the choice of enacting countermeasures to the discretion of the state adopting it and whether international law imposes limits on such discretion.

Within existing international law, there is no prohibition on unilateral measures and extraterritorial jurisdiction, even though they are often a barrier for international law to evolve towards the universalization of certain values recognized by all humankind. The author notes that it would be wrong to assume that all secondary sanctions are technically violating international law.[66] Some scholars have argued that they may be legitimate when they only apply to operators who hold contracts with the enacting country or with nationals or residents within the enacting nation or have some other links to the enacting nation. Secondary sanctions are not necessarily the result of improperly exercising extraterritorial jurisdiction.[67] In some areas, secondary sanction is considered a useful tool to safeguard common values. Many human rights treaties, for instance have extraterritorial reach and can, in fact, reach beyond national borders,[68] even though there are disputes over how the respective treaties define the term "jurisdiction." The *Banković* case is a case in point, which concerns the violation of the right to life of victims from the 1999 NATO aerial bombardments in Kosovo. The court assumed a strict territorial or spatial model, leading to its decision that the European Convention on Human Rights (ECHR) was inapplicable. However, from the wording of Article 1, which states "the High Contracting Parties shall secure to everyone within their *jurisdiction* the rights and freedoms defined in Section 1 of this convention," reference to "jurisdiction" instead of "territory" seems to imply the drafters' intention to deviate from the territorial notion of jurisdiction. Subsequently, the European Court of Human Rights in the *Al-skeini* case, without completely abandoning the territorial meaning of jurisdiction, shifted somewhat towards the personal model of jurisdiction and held that Mr Al-Jedda's detention was attributable to and within the jurisdiction of the UK.[69] But increasingly, the negative consequences of applying human rights laws extraterritorially are subject to criticism. The sanctions regime is likely to cause damages to human rights conditions in the target state. As a disappointing fact, this may be the intention of the sanctioning state.[70] Such a state is less likely to guarantee due process and to offer judicial review for sanctions in the domestic laws. International law is required to place restrictions on the use of sanctions. Some scholars have even argued in favour of the "broad-based recognition of the unlawfulness of secondary extraterritorial sanctions."[71]

If there are still reasons for the existence of some unilateral sanctions, the centralization of the authority of issuing such sanctions is appreciated. The rules of the World Trade Organization (WTO) are particularly relevant in this context. According to the WTO rules, which are considered one of the most important components of international trade law, the key principle in the international trade domain is that states do not take retaliatory measures until they are authorized by a dispute settlement body to do so.[72]

An overall view of international law allows us to come to a preliminary conclusion that customary international law does not automatically relieve a state targeted by sanctions from performing its international obligations, nor does it immediately authorize the affected state to retaliate. The relevant theories are rather inconsistent and underdeveloped. One has to consult the applicable rules and the circumstances of the case for a fair and more conclusive decision. In the case of US sanctions against China, the related disputes at least have to be reviewed by competent authorities in accordance with relevant situations in order to distinguish between "restrictions of access to US market" and "penalties imposed on third countries engaging in the sanctionable activities."[73] It is doubtful that the Chinese government is capable of making a wise distinction considering that it has not paid sufficient attention to the tensions between unilateral sanctions and international law, and that the rules recently adopted do not contemplate at all the possibility of the full renunciation and prohibition of unilateral regulations and measures as a coercive tool. These findings culminate in the view that the Chinese Blocking Statute does not represent a step forward in the development of the rule of law and may have the unintended consequence of deterring the development of international law towards a more fair and comprehensive system favouring comity between states. What China urgently requires is a more judicialized and ethical approach, rather than a reckless tit-for-tat response. The author is inclined to believe that it is China's responsibility as a major player in the world economy to promote and facilitate the establishment of a multilateral regime that builds international consensus on the abolition of unilateral sanctions and related countermeasures.

4. The Way Forward Towards a More Judicialized Solution

The proposed way forward is to help correct China's strategic myopia in dealing with "unfair" extraterritorial application of US laws through blocking legislation. As a preliminary issue, as long as countermeasures do not involve the threat or use of military force, international law has as of yet not challenged their legality to a large extent. Countries continue moving back and forth between easing sanctions and countermeasures and between stagnation and reviewed intensification. Legislators pay little attention to the multifaceted relations between unilateral measures and the integrity of international law. This chapter does not contribute to the cost–benefit calculation concerning the making, duration, and termination of the countermeasures but, instead, argues that the policy of unilateral containment by activating the new Chinese blocking rules should not be encouraged for two reasons. First, the process of applying unilateral sanctions or countermeasures is highly volatile especially when international law has not developed legal principles in this regard, which has the effect of destabilizing the world order. As mentioned previously, many such measures have remained mostly dormant since their creation. Even when they are applied, the application gives rise to complicated issues that require decent judicial and political considerations. Second, unilateral containment contradicts China's policy of multipolarity and is not leading international law down the right path. For the Chinese Blocking Statute in particular, it has only yielded the vaguest of guidelines for administrative and court actions and had achieved little success in forging valuable international law norms into useful legal principles and methods for solving jurisdictional conflicts arising from economic laws. Moving forward, the author proposes a process-oriented, rational, and multilateral approach to sanction termination or to elimination of the negative effect of sanctions, which implies efforts to reform and improve existing multilateral judicial mechanisms.

The proposed approach represents a tendency to resort to domestic courts or, more ideally, international tribunals regarding disputes arising from unfair unilateral extraterritoriality. This approach is expected to advance the development of international law and in particular to provide a basis for China to partner with other nations to address US extraterritorial sanctions. It is expected to better account for the levels of intricacy of unilateral sanctions and the respective countermeasures. It should be more efficient in levying international resentment against unfair extraterritorial jurisdiction. It is a multilateral approach that is instrumental in creating a fair international legal order. Such an order can only exist when most states willingly practice certain legitimate principles in international affairs. Eventually, the application of the approach would lead to the ending of unjustified unilateral sanctions and help to ensure that countries' extraterritorial actions remain exceptional and follow widely recognized norms and multilateral rules, rather than unilateral policies.

China has thus far played an important role in reforming the WTO dispute settlement regime since the existential crisis broke out by the end of 2019. It has showed interest in using the WTO dispute resolution to solve problems arising from the US–China trade war, which, as implied by the proposed approach, is a step in the right direction. When the General Agreement on Tariffs and Trade (GATT) was signed by 23 nations in 1947, the goal was to establish a rules-based world trading system and to facilitate the settlement of disputes arising from trade activities.[74] This function has continued into the current era. In the course of the trade war, China lodged a complaint against the US at the WTO over US import duties.[75] Following that, a panel report was issued on 15 September 2020 with the view that the tariffs imposed by the US on China were inconsistent with WTO rules.[76] The US was dissatisfied with the results and appealed in accordance with Article 16 of the Understanding on Rules and Procedures Governing the Settlement of Disputes.[77] The effect of the rulings, especially when the two sides are still in negotiation on how to resolve trade issues, remains unclear. Because the WTO dispute settlement regime no longer has a functioning Appellate Body – due mainly to the US veto on AB member appointments, the US' subsequent appeal is likely to sabotage the whole dispute settlement procedure. As a result, at least in the short term, the panel's findings will not give rise to substantive changes in the tensions between the US and China. In any event, the case itself has conveyed some positive messages that the multilateral regime can be resorted to for the resolution of disputes over unilateral sanctions.

Even though considerable attention was paid to the US–Japan trade war before China sent its trade disputes to the WTO dispute resolution body in 2018 and also during the drafting of the Blocking Statute at the peak of the US–China trade war, Beijing has not taken lessons from the event and has not done better than Japan in justifying the introduction of blocking legislation. Undoubtably, the domestic and international environments that China faces today differs greatly from what Japan faced in the 1980s and 1990s. Therefore, to avoid a general comparison, the author limits the discussion mainly to Japan's experience related to the impact of the US Anti-Dumping Act of 1916 (the 1916 Act) and a few other relevant legislations which later either triggered Japan's retaliatory action of introducing blocking legislation or rendered unfair settlements.

The 1916 Act was designed to address the problem of transnational price predation and therefore contained an element of extraterritoriality. In 1999, Japan requested the WTO to review whether the 1916 Act substantially violated the WTO rules.[78] A panel report was issued in favour of Japan's position.[79] The relevant parties appealed and the Appellate Body eventually confirmed the violation of the 1916 Act.[80] Despite this ruling, the US failed to repeal the 1916 Act before the designated deadline,[81] which left Japan with no option within the WTO legal regime but to request the authorization to retaliate.[82] Japan chose to retaliate in the form of blocking legislation. The US requested for arbitration, pending which both parties agreed to suspend the arbitral proceedings while the US Congress reviewed the bill to repeal the concerned Act.[83]

It was reasonable and appropriate for Japan to resort to the WTO dispute settlement regime regarding the anti-dumping disputes related to extraterritoriality.

This effort rendered decisions from international tribunals, thereby enhancing the development of international trade law. Nevertheless, Japan's enactment of the blocking legislation looms over its attitudes towards multilateralism. The first blocking legislation in Japan, which is referred to as the Damage Recovery Act, allowed Japanese persons who had suffered from anti-dumping lawsuits in the US to recover the losses in the Japanese courts.[84] This Act denies the extraterritorial effect of the US 1916 Act by noting that "no final judgment of a foreign court entered in actions against any person in Japan under the United States Anti-Dumping Act of 1916 has any effect in Japan."[85] In the explanatory note, Japan clarified that this blocking legislation is not a WTO-related measure,[86] which inevitably casts doubt on the ability of the WTO to deal with the aforementioned trade differences.

Various and sometimes conflicting views have been expressed on the effect of the Damage Recovery Act. It has been considered a success in terms of articulating Japan's political views on the US trade restrictions but has not been justified in either domestic or international law. First, it represents a significant departure from the traditional Japanese conflicts of law rules. Second, beyond Japan's borders, its recognition was limited by the scope of bilateral or multilateral treaties, and, therefore, could contribute little to the elimination of US extraterritoriality. Scholars have also criticized the legislation for its lack of clarification on several key legal elements. For instance there was uncertainty whether the legal liability of the defendants was based on a tort or an enrichment.[87] Based on Japan's experience in dealing with the extraterritorial effect of US laws, it can be anticipated that, when the multilateral dispute resolution regime is absent and international law norms do not centre trade talks, unfair consequences will most likely arise. Small countries or countries that are politically isolated are usually forced into treaties with prolonged negative effect on their economy.

In addition to the blocking legislation, Japan took a series of acts with the US that threatened the multilateral trading system and the relevant principles of international law. For instance when disputes arose from trading in the automotive market, the two parties decided to sign an agreement without the adjudication of the WTO. The relevant law is the Trade Act of 1974 which was used by the US to "retaliate against foreign countries accused of unfair trade practices by imposing punitive penalties against the offending governments."[88] Prior to this agreement, Japan had already signed another deal with the US which was later referred to as the "Plaza Accord," an agreement that resulted in the yen's appreciation and subsequently triggered the bursting of Japan's economic bubble. This supports the following presumption: by taking the aforementioned disputes to international tribunals, the US and Japan may have forced the tribunals to deal with the problems, which would have likely created greater hostility towards US unilateral trade sanctions. In this sense, it is disappointing to see China's move to introduce the Blocking Statute.

China is not taking coherent actions in countering the US extraterritoriality. On the one hand, it is making unilateral legislation that contains many ambiguities. The consistency of this approach with the multilateral trade rules and international law is questionable. On the other hand, China is supporting the multilateral approach to trade and investment. By forging regional and global treaties, China has made great contribution to the development of international trade and investment laws as well as to global economic growth and efficiency.

Apart from resorting their disputes to international tribunals, domestic courts could be the supplementary means for private companies to seek remedies. Engaging private parties is an essential step in enforcing key legal norms on international trade. The recent case filed by Xiaomi Corp illustrated the possibility of such engagement. Xiaomi is the world's third-largest smartphone vendor. It sued the Defense and Treasury Departments of the US for their "arbitrary" decision on Xiaomi's alleged affiliation with Chinese military forces.[89] The Trump administration was empowered by the Defense Authorization Act of 1999 to include companies with a military background to the list. The result is that American investors are prohibited from buying the company's shares and related securities issued by the company. It is reported that Xiaomi's shares fell 10.6% on the day after the aforementioned decision was made.[90] Civil litigation can perform an important expressive function in shaping normative expectations for conduct, even if it is ultimately unsuccessful in obtaining compensation for the plaintiffs.[91] Professor Keitner has made this argument in the context of pandemic-related disputes, though it is still perfectly applicable to this context.[92]

The aim of this section is not to provide a comprehensive guide on how China can move forward to counter unjustified US sanctions. Instead, it was simply argued that resorting to judicialized mechanisms is a practical approach that is deserving of more attention. This section does not assert the primacy of the judicial approach over other efforts, such as quiet diplomatic negotiation or public international discussions to address concerns about extraterritorial sanctions and related countermeasure and to develop coordinated responses, nor does it expect that the proposed approach will replace research focusing on actors' cost–benefit calculations. The author has left the interplay of legal and non-legal approaches to future research. It is recommended that researchers characterize the nature of economic relations between China and many other states and also assess the magnitude of China's political will to act at the current stage. Comparative perspectives should be valued. It was reported that EU legislators have expressed interest in developing "a legislators' network that could encourage the respective executives to explain, defend and refrain from their respective views with regard to the – likely – effects of economic sanctions."[93] A promising starting point for future research could be to explore the means through which China could engage in such a network.

In the author's view, the proposed judicialized approach requires China to refrain from issuing all types of unilateral countermeasures. Many countries are concerned that, when China becomes the next prominent world power, the country's understanding of international law norms will result in overwhelming pressure upon other countries. The making of the recent unilateral countermeasures is not helping to ease this concern. Previous studies have shown that China used to have a preference for "informal coercive economic measures or sanctions" which was in contrast to US sanctions with highly formalized nature.[94] It was rare for China to publicly admit that it intended to impose unilateral economic measures in the context of a foreign policy dispute. The introduction of the blocking legislations, however, seems to be a turn in a direction that the author does not support. China's decision to take the unilateral route potentially ushers in a new era of disobedience and ignorance of multilateralism as well as international principles that are key to global stability, which indicates the need for a change of approach.

5. Concluding Remarks

The US' assertions of extraterritorial jurisdiction over the activities of Chinese businesses and individuals have long been a source of tension in US–China relations. The most recent arrests of high-level administrative personnel and trade sanctions against Chinese companies have provoked prolonged disputes and are assumed to be the direct cause for the making of the Chinese Blocking Statute. This chapter has studied the key provisions of the rules and has suggested that the lack of clarification on some key aspects of the rules will potentially underscore their benefits. On this basis, the chapter explores whether the rules are the ideal solution to the unfair application of foreign extraterritorial legislations and measures. It was argued that the rules are dubious in terms of effectiveness and legality. The application of the Blocking Statute as a form of countermeasure should not be a singular event based purely on cost–benefit calculation. A new approach is required to replace the blocking legislation issued on the unilateral basis. The new approach accounts for the need for a fair international order and is designed to fit China's policy of multipolarity. This approach does not represent a comprehensive plan on how to move forward but simply proposes a shift of focus to making greater use of existing multilateral judicialized mechanisms, such as the WTO, in both identifying and countering illegal extraterritorial laws and measures.

With the new blocking rules, it seems that China finally has a legal instrument to counter technical blockage and suppression of China and its companies by the US. The author agrees that the Chinese Blocking Statute carries a positive connotation, as when one speaks of the legal countermeasure or legal instrument against extraterritoriality in the sense of conferring on a title or a normative proposition the legitimacy of law. But this does not deny the fact that the making of such a law represents unilateral action. The particular vulnerability of this law to US extraterritorial sanctions is that that they are not conjoined with other key regulators of the international community, and the relevant decision resulting from the working mechanism is unlikely to be convincing beyond China's borders. Therefore, the author contends that the Chinese Blocking Statute does not have a considerable real effect other than intensifying the voicing of concern over the lack of legality of US extraterritorial sanctions and assuaging China's domestic audiences.

Extraterritoriality itself is essentially a phenomenon that is both resented and increasingly practised. Its existence in certain areas, such as human rights, environmental protection, antitrust, and global crime and terrorism, seems to have been accepted and somehow justified; however, one area has generated more controversy than the others. Therefore, a more judicialized approach is required to account for the complexities in identifying unlawful extraterritorial activities, allocating responsibilities, and rendering appropriate remedies. The WTO, as a multilateral trade regime, has contributed to minimizing the effects of unilateral decisions. Its function should be continued and enhanced in countering US sanctions. It is suggested that China assumes a more central role in reforming and updating the WTO rules in this aspect. It should be using its international influence to reinforce the idea that the answer to the question of how to end the unilateral and unfair extraterritorial application of foreign laws and measures can be found in the improvement of multilateralism, not retaliatory measures.

Notes

1 商舒, "中国域外规制体系的建构挑战与架构重点 – – 兼论《阻断外国法律与措施不当域外适用办法》(Carrie Shu Shang, Challenges and Keys to China's Extraterritorial Regulatory System: Also a Commentary on Rules on Counteracting Unjustified Extraterritorial Application of Foreign Legislation and Other Measures," 国际法研究 (*Chinese Journal of International Law*) 2021, no. 2: 63.
2 *MOFCOM Order No. 1 of 2021 on Rules on Counteracting Unjustified Extra-territorial Application of Foreign Legislation and Other Measures*, Article 1.
3 There is hope that the Biden administration will take a different approach from the Trump administration in dealing with Chinese high-tech companies. During the campaign, Biden promised that "the new administration will fight for tech supremacy by rebuilding its core strengths rather than slapping the restrictions on China." Yifan Yu, "Biden to counter China tech by urging investment in US: adviser," https://asia.nikkei.com/Business/CES-2021/Biden-to-counter-China-tech-by-urging-investment-in-US-adviser.
4 Ellie Geranmayeh and Manuel Lafont Rapnouil, "Policy Brief: Meeting the Challenge of Secondary Sanctions," 25 June 2019, https://ecfr.eu/publication/meeting_the_challenge_of_secondary_sanctions/.
5 Tom Ruys and Cedric Ryngaert, "Secondary Sanctions: A Weapon out of Control? The International Legality of, and European Responses to, US Secondary Sanctions," *The British Yearbook of International Law* (2020): 1–116; Jordan Tama, "Forcing the President's Hand: How the US Congress Shapes Foreign Policy through Sanctions Legislation," *Foreign Policy Analysis* 16 (2020): 397.
6 "低调公布的商务部一号令，背后设计有何考量? (What underlies the low-key MOFCOM Order No.1?)," https://news.sina.com.cn/c/2021-01-12/doc-iiznezxt2110178.shtml.
7 凌冰尧, "美国次级制裁的合法性分析 (Ling Bingyao, Analysis of the Legality of US Secondary Sanctions)," 武大国际法评论 (*Wuhan University International Law Review*) 2020, no. 5: 106.
8 Ibid.
9 *Council Regulation (EC) No. 2271/96.*
10 Diane Bartz and Christian Shepherd, "U.S. Legislation Steps Up Pressure on Huawei and ZTE, China Calls it 'Hysteria.'" 17 January 2019, available at https://www.

reuters.com/article/us-usa-china-huawei-tech-idUSKCN1PA2LU, accessed 3 October 2022.

11 "商务部就《阻断外国法律与措施不当域外适用办法》答问（The Ministry of Commerce answers questions about the MOFCOM Order No. 1 of 2021 on Rules on Counteracting Unjustified Extra-Territorial Application of Foreign Legislation and Other Measures）," www.scio.gov.cn/xwfbh/gbwxwfbh/xwfbh/swb/Document/1696695/1696695.htm.

12 *International Criminal Judicial Assistance Law; MOFCOM Order No. 4 of 2020 on Provisions on the Unreliable Entity List.*

13 *MOFCOM Order No. 1 of 2021 on Rules on Counteracting Unjustified Extra-territorial Application of Foreign Legislation and Other Measures*, Article 4.

14 *Council Regulation (EC) No. 2271/96 and the subsequent updates.*

15 商舒，"中国域外规制体系的建构挑战与架构重点 – – 兼论《阻断外国法律与措施不当域外适用办法》（Carrie Shu Shang, Challenges and Keys to China's Extraterritorial Regulatory System: Also a Commentary on Rules on Counteracting Unjustified Extraterritorial Application of Foreign Legislation and Other Measures）," 68.

16 Tom Harris, "The Extraterritorial Application of U.S. Export Controls: A British Perspective," *New York University Journal of International Law and Politics* 19(4) (1987): 959.

17 Ibid.

18 Ann dePender Zeigler, "Siberian Pipeline Dispute and the Export Administration Act: What's Left of Extraterritorial Limits and the Act of State Doctrine," *Houston Journal of International Law* 6(1) (1983): 68.

19 Ibid.; Quentin Genard, "European Union Responses to Extraterritorial Claims by the United States: Lessons from Trade Control Cases," (January 2014), 7, Nonproliferation Paper No. 36, available at https://www.sipri.org/publications/2014/eu-non-proliferation-papers/european-union-responses-extraterritorial-claims-united-states-lessons-trade-control-cases, accessed 3 October 2022.

20 European Parliament, Directorate-General for External Policies of the Union, Christopher A. Hartwell, Henner Gött, Kateryna Karunska and et al., "Extraterritorial Sanctions on Trade and Investments and European Responses," (2020), 27, available at https://data.europa.eu/doi/10.2861/028506, accessed 3 October 2022.

21 "低调公布的商务部一号令，背后设计有何考量? (What underlies the low-key MOFCOM Order No.1?)".

22 *MOFCOM Order No. 1 of 2021 on Rules on Counteracting Unjustified Extra-territorial Application of Foreign Legislation and Other Measures*, Article 1.

23 Ibid., Article 7.

24 "China Opposes U.S. 'Long-Arm Jurisdiction': FM Spokesperson," www.xinhuanet.com/english/2020-02/17/c_138792742.htm.

25 *MOFCOM Order No. 1 of 2021 on Rules on Counteracting Unjustified Extra-territorial Application of Foreign Legislation and Other Measures*, Article 2.

26 Ibid.

27 Michael G. Faure and Xinzhu Zhang, "Towards an Extraterritorial Application of the Chinese Anti-Monopoly Law that Avoids Trade Conflicts," *George Washington International Law Review* 45(3) (2013): 502.

28 *Anti-Monopoly Law of the People's Republic of China*, Article 2.

29 John C. H. Wu, "The Problem of Extraterritoriality in China," (1921–1969) *American Society of International Law Proceedings* 24, no. Six Session (23–26 April 1930): 182–194.

30 *MOFCOM Order No. 1 of 2021 on Rules on Counteracting Unjustified Extra-territorial Application of Foreign Legislation and Other Measures*, Article 3.

31 商舒，"中国域外规制体系的建构挑战与架构重点 – – 兼论《阻断外国法律与措施不当域外适用办法》（Carrie Shu Shang, Challenges and Keys to China's Extraterritorial Regulatory System: Also a Commentary on Rules on Counteracting

Unjustified Extraterritorial Application of Foreign Legislation and Other Measures）," 64.

32 凌冰尧, "美国次级制裁的合法性分析（Ling Bingyao, Analysis of the Legality of US Secondary Sanctions）," 118.

33 *MOFCOM Order No. 1 of 2021 on Rules on Counteracting Unjustified Extra-territorial Application of Foreign Legislation and Other Measures*, Article 4.

34 Ibid.

35 *Council Regulation (EC) No. 2271/96*, Article 2.

36 *MOFCOM Order No. 1 of 2021 on Rules on Counteracting Unjustified Extra-territorial Application of Foreign Legislation and Other Measures*, Article 5.

37 *Council Regulation (EC) No. 2271/96*, Annex.

38 *Guidance Note: Questions and Answers: adoption of update of the Blocking Statute (2018/C 277 I/03)*.

39 Ibid.

40 *MOFCOM Order No. 1 of 2021 on Rules on Counteracting Unjustified Extra-territorial Application of Foreign Legislation and Other Measures*, Article 5.

41 Ibid., Articles 4–6.

42 Ibid., Article 6.

43 *Council Regulation (EC) No. 2271/96*, Article 11.

44 Gibson Dunn, "The 'New' Iran E.O. and the 'New' EU Blocking Statute – Navigating the Divide for International Business," 9 August 2018, available at www.gibsondunn.com/new-iran-e-o-and-new-eu-blocking-statute-navigating-the-divide-for-international-business/, accessed 3 October 2022.

45 *MOFCOM Order No. 1 of 2021 on Rules on Counteracting Unjustified Extra-territorial Application of Foreign Legislation and Other Measures*, Article 5.

46 Ibid.

47 *Council Regulation (EC) No. 2271/96*, Article 2.

48 Ibid.

49 *MOFCOM Order No. 1 of 2021 on Rules on Counteracting Unjustified Extra-territorial Application of Foreign Legislation and Other Measures*, Article 7.

50 *Council Regulation (EC) No. 2271/96*, Article 5.

51 Ibid., Article 4.

52 Ibid., Article 6.

53 "Guidance Note – Questions and Answers: adoption of update of the Blocking Statute C/2018/5344."

54 *MOFCOM Order No. 1 of 2021 on Rules on Counteracting Unjustified Extra-territorial Application of Foreign Legislation and Other Measures*, Article 11.

55 Jean De Ruyt, "European Policy Brief: American Sanctions and European Sovereignty" (2019), 2, European Policy Brief No. 54, available at https://www.egmontinstitute.be/american-sanctions-and-european-sovereignty/, accessed 3 October 2022.

56 European Parliament, "Extraterritorial Sanctions on Trade and Investments and European Responses," 67; De Ruyt, "European Policy Brief: American Sanctions and European Sovereignty" 2.

57 *International Criminal Judicial Assistance Law*; *MOFCOM Order No. 4 of 2020 on Provisions on the Unreliable Entity List*.

58 Shen Wei, "中美贸易摩擦中的法律战 – – 从不可靠实体清单低制度到阻断办法 (Shen Wei, Lawfare in the US-China Trade Friction: Understanding the Unreliable Entity List System and Blocking Regulations）," 比较法研究（*Journal of Comparative Law*）(2021).

59 Geranmayeh and Rapnouil, "Policy Brief: Meeting the Challenge of Secondary Sanctions".

60 European Parliament, "Extraterritorial Sanctions on Trade and Investments and European Responses," 31.

61 Kerstin Wilhelm to Lexology, 2020, www.lexology.com/library/detail.aspx?g=cf8569cb-f752-4938-8c86-d96f7a092150.

62 *Bank Melli Iran v Telekom Deutschland GmBH*, Case C-124/20.

63 Alexandra Hofer, "The Developed/Developing Divide on Unilateral Coercive Measures: Legitimate Enforcement or Illegitimate Intervention?," *Chinese Journal of International Law* 16 (2017).

64 Ibid., 208.

65 Manjiao Chi and Liang Qiao, "A Skeletal Review of the Sino-U.S. "Trade War": Contentious Issues, Trade Multilateralism and Policy Recommendations," *Canadian Foreign Policy Journal* 26(1) (2020): 99.

66 Deborah Senz and Hilary Charlesworth, "Building Blocks: Australia's Response to Foreign Extraterritorial Legislation," *Melbourne Journal of International Law* 2 (2001).

67 Ruys and Ryngaert, "Secondary Sanctions: A Weapon out of Control? The International Legality of, and European Responses to, US Secondary Sanctions," 8.

68 Hugh King, "The Extraterritorial Human Rights Obligations of States," *Human Rights Law Review* 9(4) (2009): 523.

69 Marko Milanovic to EJIL:Talk! (Blog of the European Journal of International Law), 2011, www.ejiltalk.org/european-court-decides-al-skeini-and-al-jedda/.

70 Idriss Jazairy, "Unilateral Economic Sanctions, International Law, and Human Rights," *Ethics & International Affairs* 33(3) (2019): 276.

71 Ibid., 298.

72 *Understanding on Rules and Procedures Governing the Settlement of Disputes*, Article 22.

73 Ruys and Ryngaert, "Secondary Sanctions: A Weapon out of Control? The International Legality of, and European Responses to, US Secondary Sanctions."

74 Colin Patch, "A Unilateral President vs. a Multilateral Trade Organization: Ethical Implications in the Ongoing Trade War," *Georgetown Journal of Legal Ethics* 32(4) (2019): 883.

75 "Report of the Panel: United States – Tariff Measures on Certain Goods from China (WT/DS543/R)." https://www.wto.org/english/tratop_e/dispu_e/cases_e/ds543_e.htm#bkmk543r.

76 WTO Dispute Settlement Body, "Dispute Settlement DS543 United States – Tariff Measures on Certain Goods from China" (2020). https://www.wto.org/english/tratop_e/dispu_e/cases_e/ds543_e.htm#bkmk543r.

77 "United States – Tariff Measures on certain Goods from China – Notification of an appeal by the United States under article 16 of the Understanding on Rules a[. . .] Settlement of Disputes ("DSU") (WT/DS543/10)."

78 WTO DSB, "WTO dispute settlement DS162: United States – Anti-Dumping Act of 1916."

79 Ibid.

80 Ibid.

81 Mitsuo Matsushita and Aya Iino, "The Blocking Legislation as a Countermeasure to the US Anti-Dumping Act of 1916: A Comparative Analysis of the EC and Japanese Damage Recovery Legislation," *Journal of World Trade* 40(4) (2006): 761.

82 Dai Yokomizo, "Japanese Blocking Statute against the U.S. Anti-Dumping Act of 1916," *Japanese Annual of International Law* 49 (2006): 36–37.

83 Ibid., 37.

84 Ibid., 38.

85 Ibid.

86 Matsushita and Iino, "The Blocking Legislation as a Countermeasure to the US Anti-Dumping Act of 1916: A Comparative Analysis of the EC and Japanese Damage Recovery Legislation," 767.

87 Ibid., 771.

88 Heather Drake, "The Impact of the Trade Wars between the United States and Japan on the Future Success of the World Trade Organization," *Tulsa Journal of Comparative & International Law* 3 (1996): 283.

89 *Xiaomi v US Department of Defense and US Department of Treasury* Case 1:21-cv-00280.

90 M. Moon, "US Adds Xiaomi to List of Alleged Chinese Military Companies," www.engadget.com/xiaomi-us-list-of-chinese-military-companies-082443043.html, accessed 3 October 2022.

91 Chimène I. Keitner, "Letter to the Journal – To Litigate a Pandemic: Cases in the United States Against China and the Chinese Communist Party and Foreign Sovereign Immunities," *Chinese Journal of International Law* 19(2) (2020): 229–236.
92 Ibid.
93 European Parliament, "Extraterritorial Sanctions on Trade and Investments and European Responses," 69.
94 Peter Harrell, Elizabeth Rosenberg, and Edoardo Saravalle, "China's Use of Coercive Economic Measures," (2018), https://www.cnas.org/publications/reports/chinas-use-of-coercive-economic-measures 19.

11

CHINA'S LAW ON COUNTERING FOREIGN SANCTIONS

1. Introduction

China's Anti-Foreign Sanctions Law (ASL) is another attempt by Beijing to counter foreign "discretionary and restrictive measures" that harm China's sovereignty and security as well as the Chinese people's lawful rights and interests.[1] Prior to this move, the Ministry of Commerce of the People's Republic of China (MOFCOM) implemented Order No. 1 of 2021 on Rules on Counteracting Unjustified Extra-territorial Application of Foreign Legislation and Other Measures (the Blocking Statute), which also has the effect of countering foreign sanctions.[2] The background against which the Blocking Statute entered into force is that the United States has sought to weaponize economic sanctions to push through its public policy agenda. It is said that the Blocking Statute is primarily targeting US secondary sanctions, namely those sanctions that seek to regulate the relations between the target states, and third countries and persons under their jurisdiction.[3] The Blocking Statute, by nature, is an administrative regulation issued by the competent governmental department, and its legality has to be upheld by law made by the National People's Congress and its standing committee. In addition to the Blocking Statute, in the year 2020, China issued the Provisions on the Unreliable Entity List, which provides procedures for designating non-Chinese operators, including any "enterprise, other organization, or individual of a foreign company," that broadly act contrary to China's national interests. At an earlier time, China enacted a criminal judicial assistance statute, the International Criminal Judicial Assistance Law, which regulates judicial assistance requests from other countries in criminal proceedings. Under this law, documents, assets, and testimonies relating to criminal matters have to undergo a mandatory preapproval process before they can be exported out of the People's Republic of China. It has been argued on the Chinese side that the aforementioned moves

DOI: 10.4324/9781003130499-11

represent positive changes since China is becoming a country that institutes and implements laws and then follows them. By the same line of argument, these laws, including the newly installed ASL, could provide more clarity for businesses operating in China or with Chinese people. The opposite view is that China's lawfare operations degrade the quality of the Chinese foreign policies and will not lead international law down the right path.

The ASL is so controversial that even its nature and title are in dispute. Some Chinese scholars have referred to this law as a type of blocking statute because it prevents foreign and Chinese persons and organizations from complying with "unlawful" anti-China sanctions.[4] Others argue that the ASL does not belong to the scope of blocking laws. The ASL focuses primarily on authorizing retaliatory measures against foreign sanctions, while the blocking laws and the related regulations serve the purpose of prohibiting the recognition and enforcement of specific foreign laws within the enacting country, and in some cases, entitle the citizens of the enacting country to sue over the damages in the domestic courts. Although China's new law is designed to counter foreign sanctions, the term "sanction" is not clearly defined in the ASL, and in fact, as a key legal term, it strangely disappears from the provisions of this law. Article 3 of the ASL seems to have been dedicated to the definition of "sanction," but the criteria being applied has many ambiguities, which will be discussed in detail later in this article. The relevant paragraphs reflect on both the content and the legislative process of Article 3. In theory, the competent Chinese authorities are authorized to take retaliatory actions against measures taken by foreign nations that China considers to be unfair or illegal. It is difficult to predict the gravity of the retaliation from the wording of the law.

As a methodological issue, this chapter must address the reason why China has been chosen for this article on the interaction between unilateral sanctions and international law. First of all, when facing foreign hostility or restrictions, China currently has both "the political will and the economic power" to act, as observed by Professor Wang Jiangyu.[5] The possibility of resorting to unilateral retaliatory countermeasures became real when China enacted the ASL. Furthermore, international law-making depends on the work of various legitimate actors, such as states, state-based international organizations,[6] and civil society actors. With regard to foreign sanctions and countermeasures, the role of the first actor is much more significant than that of the other two. China is a rising global power whose behaviours have a significant impact on others and whose patterns of behaviour towards others are increasingly likely to be followed by members of the international community. In the area of the use of unilateral sanctions, where research projects are generating different or even contradictory views, China's move to implement the ASL is an important source for the study of the behavioural roots of international law.

In the next section, this chapter introduces the legislative process of the ASL and explains the key components of the law. Then the chapter conducts a semantic study of "sanction" to understand what the ASL is designed for, and how this law may interact with international law and the domestic laws and policies of China. This is followed by the main inquiries of this work, namely whether China's ASL and other similar laws and regulations that fall within the same camp will lead international law down the right path, and how nations should proceed in identifying and dealing with unlawful or unfair foreign legal constraints on their citizens and businesses. These questions are approached by a careful examination of international law values and with consideration of China's role as a rising global power.

2. Key Components of the ASL

In China's recent moves to counter foreign aggression, its preference for legal mechanisms is apparent and has drawn much attention. It has long been a wish of the United States, as well as the international community, that China becomes a country with the rule of law. Now that China shows a great interest in employing legal mechanisms to deal with tensions between itself and other nations, new concerns arise. According to some commentators, this new law signals that China is attempting to build new standards in defining and using sanctions and retaliatory measures,[7] yet some of these standards may be vague or illegitimate. Other commentators consider that the measures authorized by this law are too wide-ranging and could be used pre-emptively by Chinese authorities for purposes that are not compatible with the collective interest of the international community. This section assumes the task of helping the readers to understand these new standards and how they might be applied by examining the details of the relevant provisions. It lays the ground for the study of this law from an international law perspective.

2.1 The Legislative Process

Under China's Law on Legislation, the bill of legislation on the agenda of the Standing Committee of the National People's Congress normally goes through three readings.[8] The bill of the ASL, however, went through only two readings due to the claimed fact that the level of urgency was high. According to Western commentators, the existence of an urgent situation is questionable. The "simplified" legislative process casts doubt on the compliance of the due process requirements and helps to enhance the view that the Chinese legislative process lacks transparency and consistency.[9] China's state media, Xinhua News, posed the opposite view: that the lack of a third reading of the bill has to be understood in a larger context. China has claimed that some foreign countries have imposed sanctions on Chinese individuals and organizations with the purpose of intervening in China's internal affairs, especially issues with regard to Xinjiang, Tibet, and Hong Kong, and therefore, expanding the legal tools of countering foreign sanctions is an urgent necessity.[10] In the Chinese understanding, although there is no survival risk, foreign interference is threatening China's core national interest, and this calls for a robust and swift response.

To understand the legislative process, the official explanation of the law issued by the head of the Legislative Affairs Commission of the Standing Committee of the National People's Congress is the most relevant material.[11] It is stated in the explanation that the ASL is designed to oppose hegemonism and power politics. It aims to safeguard China's "sovereignty, national security, and development interests" as well as to protect the "legitimate interests of Chinese citizens and organizations."1"[12] The legislators consider that the implementation of the ASL helps to improve China's rule of law since this law provides the legal basis for a wide range of countermeasures against foreign sanctions. However, the provisions of the law contain many ambiguities and are a mix of legal stipulations and political statements, which has obscured how the ASL could upgrade China's legal tool to address the risks from foreign sanctions and interference.

According to the official explanation of the law, it is the intent of the Chinese legislators to strengthen a sound and fair world order based on international law. But the discussion of how the ASL could interact with international law is absent. Discussions on this topic in academia are quite insufficient. The only view that the author could find is that the ASL has its legal basis in the Charter of the United Nations and the related international regulations and principles.[13] It is argued that some Western governments and politicians have been using various unjustified reasons to suppress Chinese individuals and to interfere in issues, from how China could govern its own territory to what technology Chinese businesses can import, which constitutes international law violations. China, therefore, is authorized to retaliate through measures that it sees fit. The aforementioned view faces challenges, mainly because the legal framework governing the legitimacy and the application of unilateral measures is incomplete at this moment. Unilateral measures taken by powerful nations against their rivals, on a pre-emptive or retaliatory basis, remain controversial. China's participation in the sanctions game, through the implementation of the ASL and other laws with the same character, is not instrumental in establishing the legal framework for the use of unilateral measures.

2.2 The Purpose of the ASL and the Underlying Principles

The content of the ASL could be roughly broken into three parts. The first part addresses some principles underlying the ASL and the purpose of the law. Article 1 has stated that the ASL serves China's goal "to safeguard its sovereignty, national security, and development interests," and "to protect the lawful rights and interests of Chinese citizens and organizations."[14] Article 2 of the law articulates some key foreign policies promoted by the Chinese government, such as the Five Principles of Peaceful Coexistence, China's policy to uphold a world order based on the global governance of the UN and international law, as well as China's vision to build "a community of shared future for mankind."[15] Article 3 goes further to explain China's foreign policy of non-interference, which is actually a reiteration of the previously mentioned "Five Principles." The same provision defines what China understands as "foreign discretionary and restrictive measures" or "foreign sanctions." It should be noted that "sanction" is a legal term from Western legal discourse. This term is used in the title of the ASL but disappears from the provisions of this law. One assumption is that this terminological feature is a so-called constructive ambiguity, which is a purposeful obstacle to the reflection on the language of the law. China always attempts to build its own discourse for the rule of law, and therefore, always tends to avoid the use of Western legal and political terms. But whatever differences may exist between China's "discretionary and restrictive measures" and the "sanction" in the Western sense, the implementation of the ASL signals China's determination to bring in "tit-for-tat" measures against foreign legal aggression.

Based on Article 3, there are three criteria for identifying a "foreign sanction" as the target of China's Anti-Sanction Law: first, such measures have violated international law and basic principles of international relations; second, the measures have the effect of containing and suppressing China or its citizens and organizations; third, the measures have interfered with China's internal affairs. From the wording of Article 3, it is clear that those criteria should be applied in combination. Many have argued that the law is currently the broadest legal tool that China has in dealing with foreign sanctions. But the author tends to argue that, because of the existence of the third criterion, the ASL is not as broad as it seems. For instance this law will not be able to relieve the pressure on high-tech companies, such as Huawei and ZTE, which are currently denied access to the market and to key technologies from some Western countries. Neither will the law help the case of Meng Wanzhou, who has been detained by the Canadian authorities and is accused of misleading HSBC about Huawei's business activities with Iran, which put the bank at the risk of violating US sanctions.[16] In the previously mentioned situations, economic sanctions and restrictions on Chinese persons could be imposed by the sanctioning state to force changes to the financial and political behaviours of China. But it could hardly be argued that the act of imposing the concerned measures is a direct interference into China's internal affairs and therefore violates international law and fundamental principles of international relations. Arguably, the principle of non-interference can never be complete. Its qualification as fundamental adds nothing to clarify to the current debate on what acts constitute a "foreign interference in China's internal affairs" that violates international law. The exact scope, meaning, and even the autonomous existence of the non-interference principle require further study.[17]

2.3 The Veiled Threats of Retaliation

China, through the ASL, threatens to take a series of actions to counter the foreign sanctions defined by Article 3 of this law. Article 4 of the ASL empowers the relevant departments of the State Council to add individuals or organizations, which are directly or indirectly involved in drafting, decision-making, or implementing restrictive measures against China, to a countermeasures list.[18]

The listed individuals and organizations face restrictions on their visa application, property, or commercial and other activities with persons within the Chinese territory.[19] The same restrictions could be imposed on a group of unlisted persons and entities: spouses and immediate family members of listed individuals, senior managers or actual controllers of listed organizations, organizations in which listed individuals serve as senior managers, organizations in which listed individuals are actual controllers of or which participate in entity's establishment or operations.[20]

Depending on how the State Council decides to interpret the term "Chinese territory," the geographic scope of the ASL could possibly be applied to Hong Kong, Macao, and theoretically Taiwan. For Hong Kong and Macao, the basic law provides the legal basis for the aforementioned possibility. For instance Article 18 of the Hong Kong Basic Law was drafted to allow national laws to be extended to Hong Kong Special Administrative Region (HKSPR) but confined such laws to foreign affairs, defence, and matters outside the autonomy of HKSPR.[21] Under this provision, Hong Kong is allowed to have its own legal regime, and national laws are not applicable in Hong Kong, except for those listed in Annex III of the Basic Law.[22] The laws listed in Annex 3 shall be applied locally by way of promulgation or legislation by HKSPR.[23] However, thus far, the motion has not been made to include the ASL in Annex III of the Hong Kong Basic Law. Due to the current trans-strait tensions, the real effect of the ASL in Taiwan can hardly be predicted.

Under Articles 7 and 8, decisions made by the relevant State Council departments on the target and the level of the restriction are final decisions. There is no provision regarding whether such decisions could be subject to judicial review, which concerns some foreign businesses and commentators.[24] It is found that the lack of the judicial review procedure likely creates an apparent imbalanced situation. Chinese persons affected by the alleged "discretionary and restrictive measures" are allowed to sue over these measures, but foreign persons affected by China's countermeasures do not have the legal basis on which a lawsuit could be brought. Questions could also arise from the use of the term "the relevant departments of the State Council" in some provisions. The term obscures how the retaliatory regime created by the ASL will actually work. Article 10 attempts to remedy the situation by stipulating that the State Council shall establish a mechanism for coordinating the work of countering foreign sanctions.[25] But it is, in the author's view, far from adequate.

Before the ASL was promulgated, the US and China had been restricting each other's individuals and businesses. The discussed law only formalizes some of the hostile practices. Previously, China was more reluctant and less frequent to resort to unilateral measures in solving the tensions in US–China relations, in comparison to the US. Earlier studies show that China used to have a preference for "informal coercive economic measures or sanctions," which was in contrast to US sanctions that had a highly formalized nature.[26] The introduction of the ASL and the recent blocking laws and regulations seems to be a turn in a direction that the author does not support, even though Articles 7–10 of the ASL display a level of self-constraint. It is hoped that the ASL is only used as a threat of retaliation, namely China will not strike out on its own, since it may not be in anyone's interest to escalate the lawfare by implementing new laws that could challenge the foundation of international law.

2.4 The Consequences for Violation

Articles 11–13 stipulate the legal consequences for violating the ASL, among which Article 12 is the most debated provision since it might significantly offset China's efforts to attract foreign investment. Article 11 is directed to punish "individuals and organizations within the Chinese territory" who fail to comply with the countermeasures. Article 12 seeks to reduce the effect of the discretionary and restrictive measures issued by foreign nations against Chinese individuals and organizations. The same provision provides a cause of action against those who assist or participate in the enforcement of the previously mentioned target measures. In other words, Chinese persons may bring a suit in a Chinese court for injunctive relief or damages.

Some Chinese scholars consider that Article 11 will not encounter problems of implementation, since it only concerns the authority of the State Council over individuals and organizations within the Chinese territory, namely that no foreign assistance is required. This might be true, but Article 11 increases the risks facing multinational companies and is likely to give pure domestic companies the leverage they need in competition with their foreign or foreign-invested counterparts. Therefore, the competent authorities will not want to increase the level of frequency of applying this provision. Article 12 advises multilateral companies to consider the elevation of the level of litigation risks. Some Chinese scholars have argued that such risks should not be overestimated, since the court will decide whether to accept the cause of action under the ASL in light of the Civil Procedure Law, as well as the state policies, and very likely, a negative decision will be made. The author considers this argument to have some validity since the Chinese court has the habit of deciding on their jurisdiction on politics-related issues after consulting the relevant governmental authorities. From Articles 7–10, it is clear that the relevant authorities have wide discretion in regulating and supervising the imposition of retaliatory measures. It can be anticipated that these authorities will instruct the court to refuse the cause of action when the negative impact is too large and extensive.

For outsiders, Article 15 may be confusing. This provision seems to be an extension of Article 3, serving the purpose of defining "foreign sanctions" with discretionary and restrictive nature. It is also possible that Article 15 serves the same purpose as Article 13. Namely both of them are constructed to be the catch-all clauses, based on which, if a foreign country or person commits an act that endangers China's sovereignty, security, or development interests, the relevant authorities may go beyond the ASL to take the necessary moves. Article 15 provides that for foreign countries, organizations, and individuals that implement, assist, or support acts that endanger China's sovereignty, security, or development interests, and where countermeasures are necessary to be taken, the competent authorities should refer to the relevant provisions of this law. The effect of Article 15 can hardly be predicted at this moment when both official explanation and empirical evidence about this provision are absent.

3. Sanctions in International Law

Sanctions can be a topic in both public and private international law. Public international law concerns about the legal status of sanctions and the interaction of sanctions with other key public international law norms such as human rights, sovereignty, and the right to non-interference. In the private law context, a sanction is often considered when the parties attempt to use it as a ground for exemption from liability for non-performance,[27] and the relevant discussions barely concern international law values. This section discusses sanctions and their countermeasure in the domain of public international law, mainly concerning whether international law warrants the use of sanctions and countermeasures, especially those being imposed unilaterally, in dealing with disputes between states, and how international law has evolved in defining these measures and setting up standards for their application.

Sanctions are the main concern of China in its lawfare with the US and have motivated the making of the ASL. Such sanctions may differ from one another in purpose and in content, which makes it harder to understand when and why certain types of sanctions are employed, how they are implemented, and what factors may influence their compatibility with international law. For instance the recent sanctions that the EU has imposed on China over the supposed human rights issues in Xinjiang include visa ban and asset freeze, which seek to limit the capacity for conducts of the relevant individuals and entities.[28] The EU considers that human rights concerns prevail over countries' right to non-interference and over the listed persons' rights to travel and to their property. However, the EU decisions will not be subject to a neutral international or multilateral legal institution that is able to investigate and to decide on whether the cited human rights concerns are real, and whether the gravity of the sanction is appropriate.

Some scholars distinguish "unilateral sanctions" from "countermeasures." They argue that countermeasures are allowed by international law, provided that some procedural and substantive requirements are met. In the literature, countermeasures are recognized as an established institution in international law, while proactive sanctions do not enjoy such automatic recognition.[29] However, this distinction has little significance in the context of the recent lawfare between China and some Western countries, since the group of requirements for legitimate countermeasures are not well defined. The author of this article, therefore, considers countermeasures to fall within the scope of unilateral sanctions. Countermeasures differ from proactive sanctions in purpose, but this does not change the fact that both are coercive measures that are not authorized by multilateral legal mechanisms and which seek to limit or deprive altogether the freedom that other countries or their persons enjoy under international law. In the following discussions, the measures issued under the ASL, and the foreign sanctions that this law aims to counter, are both referred to as "unilateral sanctions" or "unilateral measures."

The lawfulness of unilateral measures is contested in international law. In some areas where such measures are likely to be abused, international law prefers the centralization of the decision-making power on what sanctions can be imposed on the target nations and what actions these target nations can take to retaliate. The UN Security Council's authority to issue sanctions is a good illustration. This authority has its legal basis in Article 41 of the UN Charter, which provides that "the Security Council may decide what measures not involving the use of armed force are to be employed to give effect to its decisions."[30] The same provision empowers the Security Council to call upon the members of the UN to apply the previously mentioned measures.[31] The measures may take the form of complete or partial interruption of economic relations, and of rail, sea, air, postal, telegraphic, radio, and other means of communication, and the severance of diplomatic relations.[32] Compared to the sanctions mandated by the UN, non-UN sanctions, namely those imposed unilaterally by powerful states, are more likely to be subject to criticism, especially in the developing world.[33]

The ASL is mainly designed to enact unilateral sanctions. The effects of such sanctions have a mixed reputation, whether they are imposed through multilateral legal mechanisms or under domestic laws. On the one hand, unilateral sanctions are said to be an implication of public international law and help to safeguard the international legal order on some occasions. Judge Ronald F. Roxburgh reflected on this topic in his work in 1920. Therein, it is stated that, in the domestic context, there are authorities to enforce the law, but such authorities are absent in international law, and therefore, "external power supported by the consent of the family of nations" is always required for efficient enforcement.[34] That observation still makes good sense today. Pressure to compel a "refractory state" to obey international law may take different forms.[35] The war and military threat are the extremes. Unilateral sanctions represent a middle route that is more effective than mere denunciation, yet not violent, in contrast to military intervention.[36] Currently, international law does not prevent unilateral sanctions from being used as a means of retorsion. Therefore, China could argue that the ASL itself is not a violation of international law. On the other hand, sanctions likely cause human rights violations or other unintended negative outcomes and have been constantly used as a tool of hegemonism.[37] There is no unanimity on the content of rules regulating unilateral sanctions, and as such, a new surge of criticisms of unilateral sanctions, especially those imposed by the US on other countries to foster its foreign policy, has emerged since the 1980s.[38] Since then, the focus of academic study has been on formulating criteria for the effective and legitimate use of sanctions in achieving various goals. The idea of ending unilateral sanctions, unless they are part of a sanction programme of multilateral actions, seems to have been sidestepped.

China used to resent the use of sanctions, either as pro-active actions or as retaliatory measures. The reasons can be found in both the historical and current contexts. Due to its cultural and historical features, China believes that unilateral measures with extraterritorial effect, which can help to force one country's will on the other and are likely associated with imperialism, colonialism, and hegemonism, are illegal under international law. From a realistic perspective, in the past, China was likely to be the target state of sanction but would almost certainly not benefit from the sanctioning practice. Now that sanctions and the respective unilateral countermeasures are not the monopolies of Western powers, China's stand on the legitimacy of unilateral coercive measures may be altered. Currently, China is in a hurry to make laws that could warrant the issuance of unilateral measures, either in retaliation to real hostile action or to proactively identify and deal with hypothetical risks. The legislators, however, have not paid sufficient attention to the issue of how these laws interact with international law and what the possible consequences of the making of these laws are.

The question of whether to take retaliatory action against aggressive foreign sanctions mandated by the Western countries is often a thorny issue in practice. For one thing, sanctioning countries often has undeclared objectives. For another, the imposition of unilateral sanctions is a policy choice involving abundant non-legal considerations and is often a part of a large policy package. For instance the current EU sanctions against China have been issued for human rights reasons on the surface. But such sanctions belong to the wider relationships between the EU and China and can be attributed to not only political and legal reasons but also some profound historical and cultural factors. Therefore, judging whether it is the right move for China to issue the ASL is not a mere cost–benefit calculation. Policy makers and legislators are advised to note that the regulation of the sanctions relies largely on the current state practice, and therefore, they should develop a clear set of expectations about what the world's legal order should be before making policies and laws to counter foreign sanctions. The following section is tasked to contribute to the establishment of such expectations.

4. The Proposed Future for the Use of Unilateral Sanctions and Countermeasures

Countries continue to sway between easing sanctions and countermeasures and between stagnation and renewed intensification. Legislators pay most attention to the potential effect of the sanction, even though such an effect cannot be measured due to difficulties in establishing the link between the sanction and the policy changes in the target state. As a retaliatory move, China enacted the ASL but has not made clear the level and approach of the implementation. The practice of implementing the ASL contains no innovative elements. China is simply "taking a page from the playbooks of the United States and European Union."[39]

The legitimacy of the ASL under international law should be subject to further debate. This chapter, after revisiting China's vision of the global legal order and the international law values, establishes that the use of unilateral sanctions will achieve little success in forging valuable international law norms into useful legal principles or in helping China show that it is serious about its key foreign policies, especially the policy of building a community with a shared future for mankind. Moving forward, China should engage in establishing multilateral dispute settlement regimes and promoting centralized decision-making powers on the use of unilateral coercive measures.

4.1 Is the Imposition of Unilateral Coercive Measures Compatible With the Chinese Vision of the World's Legal Order?

A mantra of China's foreign policy is to build "a community with a shared future for all mankind."[40] The concept has important implications for the development of international law. China believes in peace and state equality. State equality further infers the right of the state to non-interference, which is at the centre of China's rebuttal to the foreign sanctions imposed by the US and the EU relating to China's governance in Xinjiang, Hong Kong, and several other areas. Inspired by the principle of non-interference, as has been claimed by China, the country intends to rise peacefully without intervening in the domestic affairs of other countries or compromising these countries' core interests. China expects the same "respect" from its follow countries. They should not block the rise of China and should allow it to have full discretion of addressing its specific needs and complex domestic issues in its efforts to revive the country.

China's understanding of non-interference has encountered challenges. One argument is that the effective implementation of the right to non-interference depends on the scope of internal affairs that are subject to the discretion of sovereign nations, yet such scope is arguably non-existent.[41] In the recent cases involving unilateral measures, China claimed that the governance of Xinjiang, Hong Kong, and other areas of Chinese territory is an internal affair that should be subject solely to the decisions of the government of the People's Republic. The counter view is that the scope of internal affairs should exclude those matters for which China has undertaken international commitment. Based on this view, the US and the EU have imposed sanctions on China and allege that China has reneged on its commitment to protecting human rights. The main problem of this allegation is that human rights represent an area of dispute. Generally speaking, human right is "the right one has because one is a human being."[42] But the question of what constitutes human rights can be translated into the question about the list of human rights. Unfortunately, there is little consensus on such a list. In the past few decades, defining human rights has fallen within the monopoly of a few Western countries. Many developing countries have not faithfully complied with the Western laws of human rights or the international treaties led by the West not only because they are not capable to do so, but also because they disagree on the connotations of human rights. China could argue against foreign sanctions imposed by the US and the EU for "human rights concerns" from at least three aspects: first, they are out of the UN Charter or any multilateral international treaties and do not necessarily serve the collective interests of the international community;[43] second, they likely have a negative impact on the human rights conditions in the target state, although obtaining evidence that certain negative consequences are a direct result of the sanction may prove difficult;[44] third, the sanctions likely constitute an erosion of the target state's sovereignty and encourages practices of interference which are resented by international law. It can be at least preliminarily concluded that China's vision of the world order is the one that excludes interference activities, which does not allow the Chinese government to remain unmoved when the US and the EU punish Chinese organizations and individuals for the Chinese way of governance.

There is another concept that has played an important role in shaping China's vision of the world order – multilateralism. On 25 January 2021, Xi Jinping has given a special address at the World Forum Virtual Event of the Davos Agenda, in which he explained why and how "the torch of multilateralism" lights up humanity's way forward.[45] He said that members of the international community should stay committed to openness and inclusiveness, and China remained objective to the idea of hegemony. Promoting the idea of "a community with the shared future for all mankind," China tries to circumvent the term "multipolarity" and "unipolarity," and instead, it advocates that multilateralism is the fundamental idea in shaping the world order, which is about "having international affairs addressed through consultation and the future of the world decided by everyone working together."[46] When disputes arise, multilateralism should guide states to the consultation table instead of war or conflict of whatever kind.[47] To uphold multilateralism, China suggests that countries should give up the outdated cold war and zero-sum game mentality and work with each other in building a new type of international relations.[48]

Multilateralism is a term with floating connotations in the Chinese discourse. In the 1970s, when China opened its door and started engaging with the world, it tended to hide behind the status of a developing country and to convince the rest of the world that it was willing but not fully prepared to play entirely by the international rules.[49] This tendency can be illustrated by Deng Xiaoping's famous proposal in the 1990s to "observe calmly, secure our position, cope with affairs calmly, hide our capacities and bide our time, be good at maintaining a low profile, and never claim leadership."[50] At that time, what multilateralism means to China was that the country can benefit from the world market economically and keep itself outside of the complex global affairs. Nevertheless, China under Xi Jinping's ruling portrays itself as a responsible global power which assumes a multilateral responsibility commensurate with the benefits that China has taken from the globalization and a peaceful world order based on the UN Charter. China realized that the US practices have contributed to the erosion of multilateralism, and it has to take a larger role in global governance in order to advance the Chinese interests and to secure a peaceful world order. In the world trade area, the US blocked the appointments of Appellate Body members which resulted in the paralysis of the WTO dispute settlement regime. In the US war against terror, the US foreign policies, without explicit statement, rejected multilateralism as a presumptive approach to security in favour of unilateralism. The US was pushing a global war on terror through the assertion of exceptionalism.[51] It seeks to justify the extraterritorial application of its laws against international crimes. But it has raised serious objections to foreign courts' extraterritorial reach to and the jurisdiction of international courts and tribunals over the US citizens.[52] In this situation where the international community feels that multilateralism has an uncertain future, China's opposition to the American provoking exercises appears very important. China is expected to not only embrace the idea of multilateralism but also help establish effective and efficient multilateral norms and institutions.

As far as Xi's speech at the World Forum Virtual Event of the Davos Agenda is inspiring, it has not explained the nature of multilateralism and the alternative options to inner-state negotiation in solving disputes, which brings obstacle to judging whether the ASL is compatible with China's vision of the world order. As previously discussed, the ASL is mainly designed to retaliate against foreign sanctions, but it could also be applied proactively and extraterritorially. Article 6 authorizes that relevant departments take a series of unilateral measures, from visa ban to asset freezing. Article 15 of the ASL demonstrates the extraterritorial effect of this law.[53] It states that countermeasures may be taken as necessary against any foreign country, organization, or individual that implements, assists in, or supports any act that jeopardizes China's national sovereignty, security, or development interests.[54] This provision goes against acts that endanger China's sovereignty, security, and development interests whose scope could be much larger than "discretionary and restrictive measures" as defined in Article 3. The ASL therefore may give the members of the international community the impression that China is implementing a law that is inconsistent with its foreign policies. One might question, as China rises, whether there will be a community with a shared future for all mankind or a community with a new global hegemony. The opposite view is that, although the making of the ASL is a unilateral move, it serves multilateral purposes since the ASL contributes to boycotting the US unilateralism. No matter which view will finally prevail, the uncertainty over the prohibition against unilateralism is clear. The ASL, if it has not undermined multilateralism, has posed questions about whether China truly believes in broader and more inclusive solutions to problems facing the international immunity. This chapter proposes that China should shift its focus from making domestic laws that could authorize countermeasures and retaliatory moves to layering new multilateral institutions and arrangements on top of old ones. It is argued that it is much easier for China to deal with US hegemony in a world with the legal order secured by multilateral institutions than in a world without rules or international institutions.

4.2 Will the ASL Lead the Development of International Law Down the Right Path?

We should not expect to witness an increase in unilateral sanctions and an escalation of lawfare between China and Western countries, partly because international law should be established as a set of value-based rules.[55] As a starting point, the literature on international law values usually distinguishes the concept of values in a moral sense from the same concept as applied in law. In this work, a value could be regarded as an enduring belief that reflects the nations' consensus on the nature of the global legal order. However, the content of international law is immense and ever-changing and, correspondingly, the values of international law are both long-lasting and continuously evolving at the same time. Currently, the debate on the following questions shows no signs of being resolved: how to define international law values and how should they be applied? The answers are too numerous to be included in this article. Due to the length limit, the author has simplified the discussion by choosing to analyze peace and justice as the key norms for international law as these play a vital role in shaping international law values.

International law should contribute to the establishment and maintenance of peace between nations. It has been argued that this partly explains why international law is not preventing unilateral sanctions, as these are viewed as kinder and gentler forms of coercion and, in some cases, help to enforce international law. Unilateral measures are a middle route, enabling countries to advance their foreign policies with little or no engagement of military force. The world's major powers share that view; however, China is using its legal weapon more diligently and systematically.[56] The ASL is only a proportion of a system of anti-foreign aggression laws. China has previously implemented other laws and regulations with similar characteristics and will eventually have a systematic toolkit to respond to foreign sanctions or other aggressive actions. A legal weapon, as a legal concept and a tool, is not a modern creation despite its increasing use in the present day. For instance the Dutch people invited Grotius to write about the freedom of the seas when they were excluded by the Portuguese from the Indian Ocean some 400 years ago.[57] In this case, and in other similar situations, the law could be regarded as a means of realizing military objectives. Modern lawfare has some unique features, one of which is its ambiguity. Scholars debate not only on whether lawfare is legitimate but also what constitutes lawfare.[58]

The fact that unilateral sanctions may help some conflicts to transfer from the kinetic battlefield to the so-called juris-combat does not ease the author's concern that the increasing use of such weapons signals a retreat from multi-lateralism and international institutions. Employing legal weapons represents a fundamental misunderstanding of the stand that the international rule of law is at the core of maintaining peace and solidarity among nations.[59] Unilateral coercive measures are the antagonistic use of international law and will not progress discussions on inter-state conflicts. Rather, the practice of using legal weapons has led some to draw the conclusion that a global legal order which relies on multilateralism and serves the whole international community rather than the interests of a few powerful nations does not exist.

If international law is regarded as a system of laws, it should serve the purpose of achieving justice. Sanctions, in some instances, force treacherous countries to comply with legal principles and obligations and therefore contribute to realizing the ethics of global justice. Nevertheless, unilateral sanctions create many questions about justice since they are not based on the collective will of most nations or the collective interest of the international community. Clear notions of justice, contrary to divine justice, have been evolving since the time of the Roman Empire or earlier.[60] At that time, justice was in two parts: the first was procedural justice, mainly involving a procedural standard for war; the second was nature law, which contained a set of rules applicable to all state members of the international community.[61] Since the 19th century, international law has mainly concerned interstate relations. Sovereignty, as one of the most important international law norms at that time and since then, indicates that a sovereign state should be granted the maximum possible freedom in determining its foreign policies and complete freedom in managing its internal affairs. There is, however, an enduring debate on whether the state has too much sovereignty or just about the right amount. Despite that, the sovereign rights of states still have important implications on the understanding of global justice, and therefore, are an important factor to consider when judging unilateral sanctions in the international law context. Particularly, sovereignty is at the centre of China's arguments for justice and the use of unilateral sanctions as a tool of defense, and thus bears great relevance to this chapter.

The most recent international law studies report various approaches to defining sovereignty and its scope. If sovereignty is defined in a narrow sense, one could argue that a state may be denied the sovereignty of a specific kind because of its conduct in dealing with foreign or domestic issues when it becomes "sufficiently dismal."[62] China, however, prefers to understand sovereignty in a different manner, namely that sovereignty gives rise to the right to non-interference, which allows a state to choose the best way to govern itself, meanwhile resisting manoeuvres of other states "tending to create disturbance . . . to foment discord, to corrupt its citizens, to alienate its allies, to raise enemies against it, to tarnish its glory, and to deprive it of its natural advantages."[63] In the recent disputes between China and some Western countries, the latter argue and the former attempts to defeat the view that China's governance in Xinjiang and Hong Kong generates valid reasons for concluding that the Chinese sovereignty may be overridden based on human rights issues. However, to determine the validity of this view and the extent to which it could justify the sanctions that the US and the EU have imposed on China, a major obstacle is the lack of appropriate international institutions that can define and protect the basic rights of individuals as well as the sovereign rights of states.

Among the most recent developments of international institutions, the best example is the creation of the International Criminal Court (ICC) and the

World Trade Organization (WTO). Disappointingly, the US has disregarded the functions of both entities. The US, although strongly opposing China's strict interpretation of sovereignty, has refused to join the ICC since it considers the jurisdiction of the ICC to be a violation of its sovereign rights[64] and argues that states should be responsible for justice in the institutional system.[65] In another sector of international law, the US has challenged the multilateral dispute settlement of the WTO since, in its view, the Appellate Body's judicial activism has adversely affected the sovereignty of WTO members.[66] This practice is regarded by some insiders as "an American assault on the rule of law in world trade."[67] It seems that a country's unilateral decisions on international law issues, especially those related to other countries, tend to be biased and inconsistent. The conflicts on whether a sanction is legitimate should thus be subject to international courts rather than domestic courts. One might rightfully have expected from China, as a rising global power, not only economic and military superiority but also effective leadership in promoting a sound and fair international legal order, resenting actions taken on a unilateral basis.

4.3 The Proposed Way Forward

China maintains in various diplomatic occasions that it advances multilateralism, which implies that, when disputes arise, countries should be guided to the consultation table and solve the disputes through peaceful means. But when consultation cannot solve the disputes, then what? Are unilateral measures the alternative option? If the making of the ASL constitutes a deviation from China's usual policy preferences and will not lead the development of international law down the right path, which direction does China go when foreign countries threaten to impose unilateral sanctions?

The realists' approach to unilateral sanctions shows no regard for the spirit of international law. They argue that no country could rule out the possibility of imposing unilateral sanctions on others when there are vital survival interests involved.[68] The increasing use of unilateral sanctions, however, occurs in situations in which the survival of a state is not at stake.[69] The most notorious example of such phenomenon in recent times is from the Iraq War and the various financial sanctions imposed on Iraq. Sanctions both against and employed by China could also illustrate the existence of the aforementioned phenomenon. The practices of superpowers inevitably shape international law. The powerful states' option of resorting to unilateralism has confused the international audience – is international law designed for justice or to ensure that the powerful state can manipulate the world for its own interests and avoid prosecution at the hands of international court judges? Thus far, unilateralism has not contributed to the resolution of disputes between states but, rather, it is responsible for the alienation of international law altogether.

Taking a value-based approach, the author has concluded that unilateral sanctions should have no place in international law, except in a few extreme and well-defined situations. Arguably, a self-proclaimed right to sanction other countries pre-emptively often violates the fundamentals of international law and possibly undermines the state's equality and the interests of weaker states. As previously stated, unilateral sanctions contribute to an increasingly dangerous warfighting environment and, meanwhile, generate double standards and selective actions which run counter to international law justice. The US is the most active nation in imposing unilateral sanctions on others. It punishes those states it has close ties with and has been criticized in the past few decades for this practice.[70] The criticism takes many forms including, but not limited to, political statements and blocking legislation, and comes from not only the target state but also its closest allies. For instance in the 1990s, the US forced embargoes and trade controls on Cuba based on its concern about the increasing communist threat it felt was posed by the Cuban authority at that time. This practice became a source of tension between the United States and its allies. The EU, for example introduced the 1996 Blocking Regulation (Council Regulation (EC) No. 2271/96 of 22 November 1996) to counter the effects of the relevant laws of the US. The resulting issues, such as whether the blocking and clawback measures adopted by other nations are permissible under international law, are still under debate. Overall, unilateral measures are not efficient in solving interstate disputes.

Although China's enthusiasm for "operation shock and awe" is not as strong as that of its Western counterparts at the present time, the retaliatory measures enabled by the ASL could also be dangerous if the severity of the measures implemented is inappropriate. This chapter presents an alternative for China that is built upon multilateralism and is expected to contribute to the international rules on the use of sanctions with the purpose of securing the world's peace and stability. China is a rising global power and has claimed to be a leader in building "a community with a shared future for mankind." Its foreign policies and law-making should accordingly not be completely of self-interest. Multilateral institutions benefit the smaller countries likely to suffer from foreign aggression and provide opportunities for China to partner with other nations to address unfair sanctions.

The approach of multilateralism could be justified in several aspects. First, multilateralism presumably works for issues surrounding sanctions because most states still believe that the UN and other well-established multilateral institutions are positive outcomes of international law and have contributed greatly to world peace and security. This is illustrated by the reality that sanctions based on the will of a single country, or a few countries, face stronger challenges than UN sanctions or measures based on multilateral international treaties.[71] Second, it could be assumed that multilateral institutions are more effective than domestic courts and administrative authorities in generating fair decisions on the legitimacy of sanctions and are more responsive to the claims of small countries. International courts and tribunals comprising competent legal experts could better account for the levels of intricacy of sanction-related issues than domestic courts and administrative bodies. Within the WTO regime, for instance the panel of arbitrators assumes the task of applying retaliation to wrongdoings. Although there are some instances where the parties challenged the penal decisions on the form and magnitude of retaliation, the consensus is still that the appointed panel members, who are usually eminent legal scholars and practitioners, should control the whole retaliatory process, from ex-ante authorization to ex-post evaluation. Third, multilateral actions usually have a greater impact on the target nation than unilateral measures since the former involves the participation of multiple members of the international community. In practice, the question could be how to efficiently implement the wider involvement of states in the decision-making and supervisory processes.

The author has noted that there is some scepticism regarding multilateral institutions. With the WTO again as an example, some member states have complained that the panel decisions on retaliation are often based on extreme positions.[72] Others expressed concerns over the inability of the WTO to prevent member states from taking unilateral actions beyond this multilateral regime.[73] The UN, as the most important multilateral institution established after World War II, should have assumed a key role in regulating the use of sanctions; however, the functions of the UN sanctions are often questioned or overridden by non-UN sanctions issued by powerful individual states.[74] The aforementioned realities point to the deficiencies in the legal designs of the existing multilateral regimes, but, in the author's view, have not denied multilateralism in general. Moving forward, the deficiencies should be fixed through well-structured procedural reforms in cases in which unilateral sanctions, like those employed by Western countries and China in the recent lawfare, must be imposed for urgent reasons. And the sanctioning state should be made obliged to report the relevant situation to the UN. The UN needs a special department with sufficient resources and staff to evaluate the reported sanction. Economic sanctions without many political elements could be regulated by other multilateral treaties.

China has already taken some positive steps in improving multilateral institutions. In facing the recent WTO crisis caused by the US blockage of the WTO Appellate Body members, China worked with other countries to establish an alternative appeal system based on the Multi-Party Interim Appeal Arrangement.[75] Despite this practice, China has not acted in a systematic and coordinated manner in implementing the ideas derived from the concept of "building a community with shared future for mankind" in solving disputes that it has with other countries. In some occasions, China has helped forge multilateral institutions and prevent the escalation of disputes between states. In others, however, it has resorted to unilateral measures without clear intent to limit their use. It is a key finding of this chapter that a distinctive feature of China's laws on countering foreign sanctions or blocking extraterritorial application of foreign laws and measures is that there is no description of the retaliation targets. This gives the impression that the previously mentioned laws are so wide-ranging and may be used for non-retaliatory purposes. In the next stage of constructing domestic laws with the purpose of fostering foreign policies and achieving international law justice, China's actions should be guided by the following notions: first, the use of sanctions remains at a minimum, to the extent of preventing wars and meeting the requirements of the UN policies; second, when sanctions are necessary, decisions on such sanctions should be subject to the jurisdiction of multilateral institutions. At the very least, China should at this stage help to ensure that the competent departments of the UN are provided with sufficient information and resources to conclude on whether the sanctions, loaded with political considerations, are legitimate and whether the sanctions are contrary to the international obligations of the sanctioning state(s). The relevant multilateral institutions should allow contradictory ideas to be exchanged in a free and open environment, even though the decisions of these institutions may not soon have significant impact on limiting the use of unilateral sanctions.

5. Conclusion: Possible Future for China to Counter Unlawful Foreign Sanctions

Globally, the increasing use of unilateral sanctions and countermeasures in dealing with interstate conflicts has become a phenomenon of our times and has been hotly debated in both law and politics. The promulgation of the ASL is a good illustration of this phenomenon. This law is in three parts. The first part contains both legal and political statements which articulate that the purpose of the law is to counter foreign sanctions as defined in Article 3. The goal of the ASL is "to safeguard its sovereignty, national security, and development interests," and "to protect the lawful rights and interests of Chinese citizens and organisations." The second part of the law provides details of foreign sanctions, what countermeasures could be taken, and how to implement the countermeasures. The third part describes the consequences of the violation. The measures that could be issued under the ASL are unilateral sanctions which constitute one of the most controversial topics of international law in modern times. In making the ASL, as the author has observed, Chinese scholars and legislators have paid too much attention to the efficiency of the sanctions in advancing financial and political goals, and far too little to their legitimacy under international law, which leads not only to criticism of the incompatibility of the Chinese law to Chinese foreign policies but also scepticism about what international law is designed for.

To bridge the understanding on how the ASL and other similar laws interact with international law, this chapter asks two questions: is the imposition of unilateral coercive measure compatible with the Chinese vision of the world's legal order, and will the ASL lead the development of international law down to the right path? Seeking answers to these questions, the author has revisited some key Chinese policy norms such as the community with a shared future for mankind, the peaceful rise of China, the equality of states, as well as two vital norms that are instrumental in shaping international law values and are applicable to cases involving sanctions – peace and justice.

Seemingly, the aggression of foreign sanctions warrants the implementation of the ASL by China. However, to employ legal weapons or weapons of any kind unilaterally in resolving international conflicts is a fundamental misunderstanding of the spirit of international law. It inevitably encourages some to draw the conclusion that a global legal order which relies on multilateralism and serves the whole international community rather than the interests of a few powerful nations does not exist. The use of sanctions may help the compliance of international law and therefore contributes to the realization of global justice. But when multilateral decision-making and supervision of these sanctions are absent, sanctions are likely to become a tool for powerful nations to advance their self-interests.

For China, there is an interest to minimize the use of laws like the ASL and turn to multilateral legal actions which benefit from a presumption of legitimacy drawn from a grant of power in the UN Charter and other multilateral treaties. This proposition fits more with China's foreign policies as well as international law values. When unilateral sanctions loaded with political considerations cannot be avoided for survival or urgent matters, the imposition of such sanctions contains the legal obligation of reporting the relevant information to the competent departments of the UN. If the sanctions occur in other areas such as trade and investment, the parties should also be required to work with multilateral institutions to ensure that sanctions are legitimate under international law. China, as a member of the UN Security Council, should help the institution obtain sufficient resources and staff to accomplish the task of regulating sanctions. The functions of the UN could be supplemented by other well-established multilateral regimes. Multilateralism is more than the idea that there are multiple powers existing in the world. It is the basis upon which the world operates and the method for resolving disputes and is believed by the author to be a guiding norm for the development of international law today and in the future. No matter how China will choose to act, it cannot prevent the modern ideas of multilateralism from challenging the conventional visions of unilateralism. The sooner that China understands the potential strength of multilateralism, the more likely it will be received by majority members of the international community as a responsible global leader. Lastly, it is important for China to accept that some areas of interstate interaction are, or must be, law-free or anarchic. Considering the circumstances, the decision-makers should address the following question: which option is more appropriate, dealing with the defined "foreign sanctions" through political strategies or through legal means?

Notes

1 *Law of the People's Republic of China on Countering Foreign Sanctions*, Article 3.
2 *MOFCOM Order No. 1 of 2021 on Rules on Counteracting Unjustified Extra-territorial Application of Foreign Legislation and Other Measures*.
3 "低调公布的商务部一号令，背后设计有何考量？ (What underlies the low-key MOF-COM Order No.1?)," https://news.sina.com.cn/c/2021-01-12/doc-iiznezxt2110178.shtml.
4 叶岩，"《反外国制裁法》第12条的问题、评析及建议（Ye Yan, Article 12 of the Anti-Sanction Law: Inquries, Comments and Suggestions),"https://mp.weixin.qq.com/s/-MpY3JL_3Nq9EOb30mb6aA.

5 Tian Yew Lun, "China Passes Law to Counter Foreign Sanctions," https://www.cityu. edu.hk/slw/rccl/20210610_news.html, accessed 3 October 2022.

6 José Luis Martí and Samantha Besson, "Legitimate Actors of International Law-making: Towards a Theory of International Democratic Representation," *Jurisprudence* 9(3) (2018): 504.

7 "China's New Anti-Foreign Sanctions Law Sends a Chill Through the Business Community," NPR, 11 June 2021, www.npr.org/2021/06/11/1005467033/chinas-new-anti-foreign-sanctions-law-sends-a-chill-through-the-business-communi

8 *Legislation Law of the People's Republic of China*, Article 29.

9 Reuters, "China Passes Law to Counter Foreign Sanctions," www.reuters.com/world/ china/china-passes-law-counter-foreign-sanctions-2021-06-10/.

10 Xinhua News, "Anti-foreign sanctions law necessary to fight hegemonism, power politics: official," www.xinhuanet.com/english/2021-06-11/c_1310001370.htm.

11 全国人大法工委 (Legislative Affairs Commission of the Standing Committee of the National People's Congress), "关于《中华人民共和国反外国制裁法（草案）》的说明 (An Explanation of the Anti-Sanction Law of the People's Republic of China (draft))," (2021).

12 Ibid.

13 "专家解读《中华人民共和国反外国制裁法》(Experts comment on the Anti-Sanction Law of the People's Republic of China)," www.legaldaily.com.cn/rdlf/content/ 2021-06/11/content_8528475.htm.

14 *Law of the People's Republic of China on Countering Foreign Sanctions*, Article 1.

15 Ibid., Article 2.

16 Sarah Berman and Moira Warburton, "In Huawei Extradition Case, Arguments Wrap Up About Alleged U.S. International Law Violation," www.reuters.com/article/us-usa-huawei-tech-canada-idUSKBN2BO6VI, accessed 3 October 2022.

17 Niki Aloupi, "The Right to Non-intervention and Non-interference," *Cambridge Journal of International and Comparative Law* 4(3) (2015): 566–567.

18 *Law of the People's Republic of China on Countering Foreign Sanctions*, Article 4.

19 Ibid., Article 6.

20 Ibid., Article 5.

21 *The Basic Law of the Hong Kong Special Administrative Region of the People's Republic of China*, Article 18.

22 Ibid.

23 Ibid.

24 Jeffrey Kessler et al., "China Enacts Anti-sanctions Law," www.jdsupra.com/legalnews/ china-enacts-anti-sanctions-law-3547911/.

25 *Law of the People's Republic of China on Countering Foreign Sanctions*, article 10.

26 Peter Harrell, Elizabeth Rosenberg, and Edoardo Saravalle, "China's Use of Coercive Economic Measures" (Center for a New American Security, 2018), 19. https://www.cnas.org/ publications/reports/chinas-use-of-coercive-economic-measures, accessed 3 October 2022.

27 Mercédeh Azeredo da Silveira, "Part III: Trade Sanction as a Ground for Exemption from Liability for Non-performance," in Mercédeh Azeredo da Silveira (ed), *Trade Sanctions and International Sales: An Inquiry into International Arbitration and Commercial Litigation* (The Hague: Kluwer Law International 2014), 197.

28 *Council Decision (CFSP) 2021/481 of 22 March 2021.*

29 Surya P. Subedi (ed), *Unilateral Sanctions in International Law* (Oxford: Oxford Univesity Press, 2021), 12.

30 *United Nations Charter*, Article 41.

31 Ibid.

32 Ibid.

33 Michael Brzoska, "International Sanctions Before and Beyond UN Sanctions," *International Affairs* 91(6) (2015): 1344–1345.

34 Ronald Roxburgh, "The Sanction of International Law," *American Journal of International Law* 14(1) (1920): 30.

35 Ibid.
36 Joy Gordon, "Reconsidering Economic Sanctions," in Michael L. Gross and Tamar Meisels (eds), *Soft War* (Cambridge University Press, 2017), 52.
37 Brzoska, "International Sanctions Before and Beyond UN Sanctions," *supra* note 33, 1346.
38 Gordon, "Reconsidering Economic Sanctions," *supra* note 36, 53.
39 Tian Yew Lun, "China Passes Law to Counter Foreign Sanctions," *supra* note 5.
40 Andrew J. Nathan and Boshu Zhang, "'A Shared Future for Mankind': Rhetoric and Reality in Chinese Foreign Policy under Xi Jinping," *Journal of Contemporary China* 31 (2021): 1.
41 Aloupi, "The Right to Non-intervention and Non-interference," 568.
42 Jack Donnelly, "Human Rights and Human Dignity: An Analytic Critique of Non-Western Conceptions of Human Rights," *American Political Science Review* 76(2) (2014): 304.
43 Subedi, *Unilateral Sanctions in International Law*, 234.
44 Ibid., 234–235.
45 Xi Jinping, "Let the Torch of Multilateralism Light up Humanity's Way Forward," www.fmprc.gov.cn/mfa_eng/zxxx_662805/t1848323.shtml.
46 Ibid.
47 Ibid.
48 Ibid.
49 Rafael Leal-Arcas, "China's Attitude to Multilateralism in International Economic Law and Governance: Challenges for the World Trading System," *Journal of World Investment & Trade* 11(2) (2010): 259.
50 Youyi Huang, "Context, Not History, Matters for Deng's Famous Phrase," www.globaltimes.cn/content/661734.shtml.
51 Fiona McKay, "U.S. Unilateralism and International Crimes: The International Criminal Court and Terrorism," *Cornell International Law Journal* 36(3) (2004): 469.
52 Ibid., 459.
53 *Law of the People's Republic of China on Countering Foreign Sanctions*, Article 15.
54 Ibid.
55 Andrea Liese and Nina Reiners, "The Eye of the Beholder? The Contestation of Values and International Law," in Heike Krieger, Georg Nolte, and Andreas Zimmermann (eds), *The International Rule of Law: Rise or Decline?* (Oxford Scholarship Online, 2019), 335.
56 Kittrie, *Lawfare: Law as a Weapon of War*, 3.
57 Ibid., 4.
58 Andrea Beck, "China's Strategy in the Arctic: A Case of Lawfare?," *The Polar Journal* 4(2) (2014).
59 Jielong Duan, "Statement on the Rule of Law at the National and International Levels," *Chinese Journal of International Law* 6(1) (2007): 185.
60 David Armstrong, "Evolving Conceptions of Justice in International Law," *Review of International Studies* 37 (2011): 2123.
61 Ibid.
62 Kristen Hessler, "State Sovereignty as an Obstacle to International Criminal Llaw," in Larry May (ed), *International Criminal Law and Philosophy* (Cambridge: Cambridge University Press, 2009), 39.
63 Armstrong, "Evolving Conceptions of Justice in International Law," 2125.
64 Marlene Wind, "Challenging Sovereignty? The USA and the Establishment of the International Criminal Court," *Ethics & Global Politics* 2(2) (2009): 83–84.
65 Ibid., 102.
66 Chang-fa Lo, Junji Nakagawa, and Tsai-fang Chen (eds), *The Appellate Body of the WTO and Its Reform* (Springer, 2020).
67 Ibid., 26.

68 Melvin L. M. Mbao, "Operation Shock and Awe: Its Implications for the Future of Multilateralism and International Law," *Comparative and International Law Journal of Southern Africa* 37(2) (2004): 255–256.
69 Ibid., 256.
70 William H. Kaempfer, "Unilateral Versus Multilateral International Sanctions: A Public Choice Perspective," *International Studies Quaterly* 43 (1999): 37.
71 Brzoska, "International Sanctions Before and Beyond UN Sanctions," 1344–1345.
72 Chad P. Bown and Joost Pauwelyn, eds., *The Law, Economics and Politics of Retaliation in WTO Dispute Settlement* (Cambridge: Cambridge University Press, 2010), 133.
73 Julia Ya Qin, "WTO reform: Multilateral control over unilateral retaliation – Lessons from the US-China Trade War (Wayne State University Law School Research Paper No. 2020–73)," (2021).
74 Larissa van den Herik, "Sidestepping the Security Council: The Use of Non-UN Sanctions for UN Purposes," *Revue Belge de Droit International* 50(2) (2017).
75 Geneva Trade Platform website, *Multi-party Interim Appeal Arbitration Arrangement*, https://wtoplurilaterals.info/plural_initiative/the-mpia/.

CONCLUSION

China's FDI and FIL: New Normal and Future

China now is the second-largest economy, the largest industrial manufacturer, merchandise trader, and holder of foreign exchange reserves. It is playing a much more important role in the global economy than it was four decades ago. However, China is still a developing country and is facing many challenges domestically and globally. Locally, its economic overcapacity, environmental unsustainability, income inequality, economic disparities, low efficiency, and lack of innovation hinder its long-term economic development, making it on the edge of the middle-income trap. Globally, its ongoing trade and economic conflicts with its major trading partners make its integration with the world harder. These trade conflicts may turn to the economic, technological, financial, and even cultural decoupling.

1. China's FDI and Economic Growth Model: Status Quo and New Normal

China enjoyed surging growth at an average annual GDP growth rate of 9.4% from 2000 to 2016.[1] China has experienced slower economic growth since 2014 and has transitioned from resource- and labour-intensive economic growth into a new normal of slower but more stable and sustainable development. The idea of rebalancing the economy and ensuring the quality of growth was introduced in the 13th Five-Year Plan in 2016.[2] The 13th Five-Year Plan also set the supply-side structural reform as the country's new thread of development with a focus on aggregate demand and new demands. In addition, the 13th Five-Year-Plan aimed at developing the service industry and addressing environmental and social imbalances. In line with these new policy goals, the GDP growth rate was lowered from 7% to 6.5%, reflecting the government's priority to ensure the quality of growth. While these ideals or slogans showed a new direction of economic development, they also witnessed the limitation of China's resource-, export-, and investment-driven economic growth model. IMF once attributed China's decelerated growth in trade volumes to China's ongoing significant structural changes. China's transition from an export-driven model to a consumption-driven one contributes to the slowdown of its exports.[3] For better or worse, China is no longer an export-dependent or export-driven economy. Prior to 2008, China's net exports had already accounted for a smaller share of Chinese GDP growth.[4] It was said that two-thirds of China's GDP actually had come from domestic demand in the 1990s.

Along China's outbound investment is China's gradual transformation of its economic growth model switching from an investment-driven one to a consumption-based one. The success of this transformation depends on a deepening economic linkage between China and overseas market and an increased commercial presence. This not only serves as a source of party legitimacy and political stability but also functions as a reform tool for further marketization.[5] Both the 12th and the 13th Five-Year Plans encourage overseas investments as a means to access supply chains, quality brand names, and advanced technology, which become a strong driving force for outbound investment into Europe and the US. In 2016, China's outbound investment in the high-tech sectors (24%) exceeds that in natural resources (20%).[6]

China's outbound FDI has been increasing significantly since the announcement of the Go Globally strategy, which aimed at relaxing outward capital flow control and encouraging Chinese entities to become global champions. This strategy not only promotes China's overseas investment but also upgrades Chinese entities' position in global value chains. The Belt and Road Initiative, launched by President Xi Jinping in 2013, has been a new route to deepen cooperation and expand the development among the countries along the Belt and Road. In 2015, the Plan of Global Cooperation on Production Capacity was put forward to increase output manufacturing capacity and facilitate domestic industrial upgrading. By 2016, China's net outbound FDI reached US$170 billion,[7] making it the second-largest investor in the world right after the US.[8] In 2020, outward FDI from China, despite a 3% decline, remained high at US$133 billion, making it the largest investor in the world.[9] China is committed to encouraging foreign investment and international trade through integrating itself more deeply into the global economy.

China's outward foreign direct investment (OFDI) generally goes to developing countries more than to developed countries. Africa is the major destination of China's overseas investment. China sees Africa as not only an important origin of crucial natural resources but also an expanding market for Chinese commodities. China's OFDI is beneficial to Africa as well by creating more jobs, improving public infrastructure, boosting trade, and facilitating human development. Europe is also a major destination of China's OFDI largely for M&A transactions targeting due to high-technology, brand names, and manufacturing chains.

China is still an active investor in other emerging economies such as Brazil.[10] China's outbound investment spurred great concerns to some countries such as Germany. Strong Chinese investment in strategic sectors presented a huge challenge and led to tightened rules on foreign takeovers. China Geely's acquisition of a stake in Daimler, the owner of Mercedes-Benz, caused concern over China's access to important automotive technology while China is in a pursuit of Made in China 2025.[11]

Chinese overseas investment differs from the usual norms and practices in various perspectives. Chinese investment is relatively concentrated in poor governance environment. China does not subscribe to global standards of environmental and social safeguards. Chinese firms' purchase of equity and assets overseas are somehow driven by China's unsustainable credit growth and overcapacity. In this sense, foreign markets are used to divert their overcapacity.[12] Chinese buyers' interest in high-tech sectors caused the concern that their investment could whittle away Europe's competitive advantage thereby weakening the EU's global economic positioning and standards of living. China has also been criticized in using the power or promise of expectation to obtain diplomatic concessions with few promises being kept.[13] China itself is closed to foreign investment in many sectors.[14]

The stock of FDI in the world mostly comes from the Western industrial economies. Much FDI is cross-investment among advanced economies. Of the ten largest recipients of FDI, eight are advanced economies – the US, the UK, France, Germany, Canada, Spain, the Netherlands, and Australia. China and Brazil are two emerging economies.[15] There is a strong correlation between FDI and better governance environments. This correlation is determined by the motivation of foreign investors to get close to markets so that investors understand demand trends and provide needed after-sale services. Another chunk of FDI is in search of natural resources. China's OFDI is somehow uncorrelated with the index of property rights and the rule of law though not statistically significant.[16] For instance China's main destinations in Africa and South America include Angola, DR Congo, Sudan, Ecuador, and Venezuela, which have worse governance indicators.[17] Slightly more than half of China's OFDI goes to the poorly governed countries. The pattern is similar for lending from the Export-Import Bank of China and China Development Bank. For instance, Venezuela is the largest recipient in Latin America for loan commitments from the Chinese banks.[18] China's indifference to the governance environment caused some suspects of its motivation for OFDI. There are some explanations for this pattern of investment. State-owned enterprises are major players for OFDI, and their investments in poor governance environments are part of the state-to-state deals. In other words, they have political motivations to execute deals in some poorly governed states.[19] Underestimation of political risks is another reason for Chinese enterprises which are newcomers to the global market. Globally, the concern is whether China's OFDI and overseas lending have an enhancing impact on poor governance in these recipient countries.[20] China's funding may support corrupt political elites and maintain their hold on power. Without such funding, Venezuela may have no choice but turn to the IMF and other traditional sources of finance in exchange for policy reforms to stabilize the economy and restore growth.[21] The other related concern is China's investment in mining and infrastructure projects involving significant environmental risks (let alone the involuntary resettlement of large population). China appears reluctant to subscribe to international standards for social and environment standards (under the rubric of the Equator Principles) rather than local regulations on the grounds that countries should not interfere in each other's internal or sovereign affairs. The Equator Principles (EPs) are a risk management framework adopted by financial institutions for determining, assessing, and managing environmental and social risk in projects. Eighty-three Equator Principles Financial Institutions in 36 countries have officially adopted the EP covering over 70% of international Project Finance debt in emerging markets.[22] Only one Chinese bank, the Industrial Bank, has joined the EP thus far.

The massive outflow of capital from China as the largest net creditor, capital exporter, and foreign aider is a new phenomenon that was not on the radar screen while the attitudes in the US towards China have been hardening. China's international influence is hampered by a lack of reliable data on Chinese foreign aid and by a lack of transparency on China's implementation of large and high-profile investment agreements. Many forms of China's foreign aid loans, debt forgiveness, the building of large public facilities, and trade and investment agreements – do not meet the traditional definition of "overseas development assistance" or ODA, which, however, is followed by most of the world's donor countries in foreign aid.[23] There is no clear policy in annual allotment. Rather, the funding schedule is determined by China's diplomatic priorities.[24]

China's economic rise is one of the factors that create strains in the international financial order. China became the largest net creditor and had an estimated US$2.4 trillion in net foreign assets by the end of 2015 through current account surpluses. China's reserves peaked at US$4 trillion at the end of 2014. Unlike Germany and Japan (in which private companies and households held most of the foreign assets), China's foreign assets have been international reserves accumulated by the central bank mostly invested in US Treasury bonds and similar instruments. This pattern has been in a shift. Both private and state-owned enterprises (instead of the public sector) started to purchase overseas assets. The commercial outflow of capital from China in the form of direct investment consisting of greenfield investments and mergers and acquisitions continued to grow owing to excess capacity and declining profitability.

In addition to direct investment, there has been significant overseas lending (as portfolio investment in the balance of payments) primarily through China EXIM Bank and China Development Bank. The top three destinations for China's overseas direct investment (apart from Hong Kong) are the United States, Australia, and the United Kingdom. Russia, Indonesia, and Kazakhstan are the only OBOR-involved countries among China's top ten investment destinations.[25]

There has been tension between developed countries which fund multilateral developmental banks and developing countries that borrow from multilateral development banks. The World Bank's safeguards are considered the most rigorous while safeguards of the AsDB, IADB, and AfDB have been tightened over the years. Amid some differences, safeguards on the hot-button issues of environment assessment and resettlement are largely similar. The World Bank's safeguards, though regarded as gold standards, supersede national laws in the borrowing country.[26] However, time-consuming, lengthy, complicated, and costly World Bank safeguards brought some side effects and drove some developing countries to other sources of funding. As a result, the World Bank's funding to infrastructure projects has declined from 70% of its lending in the 1950s and 1960s to 30% in the 2000s.[27] All the multilateral development banks together only provided around US$50 billion of infrastructure financing, which was a tiny fraction of lending. China's lending is viewed as an alternative source of funding and is welcomed by developing countries. China's lending has its own characteristics. Often, its lending is less bureaucratic, less complicated, and more efficient compared to other lenders. But China's approach not to attach any conditions to lending and to stick to the local laws is not risk free. As a matter of fact, China's lending and investment projects often go badly without resulting in any economic returns. World Bank and other Western development institutions often impose the neo-liberal package of reform under its "conditional provisions." Chinese aid by contrast comes without strings attached and is seen as supporting initiatives by African states to address development issues.[28]

The AIIB was born from China's frustration with the slow reform of existing institutions. The AIIB (along with the Brics New Development Bank) also provides a multilateral platform for China to use its excess savings. The US opposed the effort primarily out of concerns of governance, including the environmental and social safeguards. The AIIB promulgated its own environmental and social policies, which are quite similar to the principles embodied in the World Bank safeguards. Nevertheless, the AIIB approach differs from that of the World Bank in the sense that the AIIB does not provide for detailed descriptions for implementation and process. Between the AIIB and other traditional multilateral development institutions, the developing countries prefer "quicker" money and tend to avoid overtly complicated projects.

AIIB is the only multilateral bank in which developing countries have the majority of the shareholding. Naturally developing countries may lean more towards the AIIB for lending. China takes the AIIB as the opportunity to align its own interests with that of other developing countries. The AIIB may bring some positive changes to the ADB and World Bank and even the global system as a whole that emanated from China if they are pressured to streamline their procedures and practices for development finance. This can be an innovation China brings into the current global development finance practices.

The two-way FDI between China and the US in 2018 represented a 60% decline compared to 2017 and a 70% decline compared to the record US$60 billion in 2016.[29] In 2016 and 2017, China's FDI to the US surpassed the US counterparts to China. This was reversed in 2018.[30] While there was a chilling impact of Chinese politics on US FDI in the ICT sectors with a one-third drop in 2018,[31] US FDI in the consumer-related sectors (i.e. food) and other sectors with lowered equity shareholding restrictions (i.e. automotive, real estate, and financial services) continued to grow.

The COVID-19 pandemic caused a dramatic fall in FDI in 2020. Global FDI flows dropped by 35% to US$1 trillion (20% below the 2009 level), from US$1.5 trillion in 2019.[32] FDI flows to Asia's developing countries were resilient.

While there was a 25% decline in FDI inflows into South-East Asia, China actually attracted 6% more FDI than the previous year.[33] China and Hong Kong remained the second- and third-largest FDI importers.[34] FDI inflows into China and Hong Kong even made Asia an uptick in FDI. The continuous FDI growth in China reflects the success in containing the pandemic and the rapid recovery.[35]

2. China's Economic Reform and US–China Trade Confrontation

China's economic reform has been moving towards a rule-based and market-orientated economic system, converging with liberal market economy. It marketized its pricing system, lowered the tariffs and non-tariff barriers, and allowed more foreign investment presence, among others. These are ample evidence of China's genuine market-oriented economic reform and opening.

Although China experienced a wide range of reforms, it was not recognized as a country with market economy status when it joined the WTO in 2001. Twenty years after its joining the WTO, it still has not won the recognition of the market economy status by the US, the European Union, Japan, Canada, and Mexico.[36] The gap between China's self-recognition and the assessment made by the US and others is huge. In the ongoing US–China trade war, the US claimed China has been actually engaged in unfair and market-distorting trading practices from industrial subsidies to theft of intellectual property[37] and has been deviated away from the market economy.[38]

FDI is utilized by the government as a catalyst for innovation and economic structural transformation. China's official policy is to open up the economy, facilitate foreign investment and trade, reduce restrictions on market access, and bring in more foreign capital and technology. However, recent years witnessed the stalled foreign investment regime reform. On face, many measures have been taken to achieve these grand policy objectives. Deeper down, real value of these measures has been quite limited as the critical transformation is undergoing with old drivers of growth to be replaced by new ones.

Among others, China's FDI regime is the most restrictive one among all G20 economies.[39] According to OECD's index of FDI restrictiveness for OECD countries and major emerging markets, China is the most closed one with an index above 0.4 among BRICS states.[40] Mining, communications, and financial services are the most closed sectors among others. Meanwhile China investing abroad more in mining, infrastructure, and finance, which are closed at home.

Unlike other developed countries which are also key capital exporting states, China is less open to inbound foreign investment even though China welcomes FDI. The key of China's FDI policy is to steer FDI to particular sectors which are more needed by China in terms of technology. As a result, some sectors are more closed to foreign investment. In general, China is less open to foreign investment.

Prior to the US–China Trade War, there were some changes in the 2018 A.T. Kearney Foreign Direct Investment (FDI) Confidence Index.[41] China fell to the fifth position on the Index, its lowest-ever ranking in the Index,[42] even though it was the second-largest recipient of FDI, next to the US, which is more than US$150 billion greater than FDI to China.[43] This was the second year that China's rank has declined.[44] Although foreign investors remain relatively optimistic about China's economy, the general perception in the foreign investment community was China's business environment was becoming less favourable for foreign firms.[45] The souring US–China relationship and the possible trade war also affected foreign investors' confidence.[46] Relevant to this was a decline of investment intentions in emerging markets[47] with China and India being a draw for investors with the highest-ranking emerging markets on the index.[48]

Foreign investors' confidence on China's investment environment declined in mid-2010s given China's reduced transparency and increased regulatory burdens for investors. The US–China Business Council's annual survey indicated that 40% of companies are less optimistic about China's business climate. The Chinese government sent confusing regulatory signals to the market. It requires foreign companies to use Chinese-owned virtual private networks, creating costs and data security challenges. Meanwhile, the government tried to ease restrictions on foreign ownership and investment in the banking, transportation, securities, and insurance sectors. It made a move to phase out foreign ownership restrictions in the automotive sector by 2022.[49]

The lack of reciprocity creates an unlevel playing field for China's trading partners. In China, Chinese firms can grow unfettered by competition in restricted sectors while foreign investors are not allowed to hold majority shareholding in joint ventures. Consequently, Chinese firms can use their domestic financial strength to enhance their monopolistic positions at home and aboard. This is particularly the case for financial sectors. Foreign investors now only possess 1% of China's financial market while China's Big Four have already become top commercial lenders worldwide.

To further push China to open up its protected markets is on the top of the negotiation agenda with the Chinese government. This was the US and the EU's aim in the US-China Economic and Trade Agreement (Phase I) and the EU-China Comprehensive Agreement on Investment. Greater investment openness is part of China's own reform plan in its own best interests. CFIUS reform was said to be a policy response to China's slow progress in opening up more sectors to foreign investment.[50]

The question of reciprocity on trade and investment is a core concern for the EU and the US as this is related to a level playing field for Chinese companies and their counterparts in the EU and the US in each other's markets. Access to China's closed market gives Chinese parties more advantages in negotiating joint ventures with foreign parties as Chinese parties can obtain an unfair advantage in leveraging market access and outbidding foreign competitors. As China made no progress in reciprocity, there is a chance that the EU and the US may move towards negative reciprocity by restricting access to their own markets.

The US' and China's economies have been deeply intertwined since China's accession to the WTO. However, the close interconnection between two countries' economies also complicates the bilateral relationship. While the economic relationship brings mutual benefits, it also causes national security concerns over supply chains, technological exchange, and even economic competition. The COVID-19 outbreak worsened the soured economic and political relationship between the two largest economies and triggered heated debates over reshoring and resilience.

The concerns over China's trade practices, economic model, and its trade deficit's impact on the job losses[51] in the US come at a time of increasing anxiety over the national security risks China presents, in particular with respect to technology access and technology leakage.[52] The geopolitical concerns have driven the US government to control access to US technologies through foreign investment and export controls. The US addresses technology transfer issues with the enactment of the Foreign Investment Risk Review Modernization Act, which included the Export Control Reform Act of 2018. Consequently, Chinese investors encountered stepped-up investment screening by the CFIUS (in particular of information, communications and technology sectors) and uncertainty over the broader geopolitical relationship between the US and China. Chinese investors were said to have abandoned deals worth more than US$2.5 billion in the US in 2018 due to the CFIUS concerns.[53]

Chinese OFDI decreased also due partially to domestic crackdown on highly leveraged private investors. The Chinese government deliberately tightened the liquidity in China's financial system and blacklisted real estate and hospitality, which exacerbated headwinds and forced Chinese investors, especially private firms, to clean up their balance sheets instead of investing abroad. Some Chinese players not only stopped new investment but also divested most of their previously acquired assets.

Even worse is a multilateral approach taken by more developed economies to constrain China's OFDI with more foreign investment screening schemes. Some OECD or EU members are aligning with US views on China's OFDI. A new EU investment screening framework has been put in place since 2018.[54] Up to 2021's first quarter, 34 states in the world have adopted CFIUS's type of screening policies towards FDI.[55] These countries in total possesses the global FDI's 50% and the global FDI stock's 69%.[56] While some of these schemes are reflective of legitimate security concerns, others may be disguised protectionism. Moreover, the US administration embedded a poison pill clause in the USMCA disallowing Canada or Mexico to enter into negotiations for a free trade agreement with China or other non-market economies with the aim to ensure economic competition on a true market basis and to preserve fair market competition in North America.[57] The US also reached out to other major trading partners such as Japan and the EU which shared the same concerns with the US. They expressed the same view in joint statements.[58] The global economy would not benefit from a multilateral defensive approach to FDI from a major trading partner.

In a broader picture, the US is concerned about China's economic model and is pursuing a Make America Great Again (MAGA) or America First policy under the Trump administration, which makes the zero-sum machinations of the pre-Second World War world return to the global stage. The Biden administration, though no longer using these policy slogans, largely continues to constrain China through similar approaches. As a matter of fact, the Biden administration is trying to build up various coalitions involving its Western allies and other developing states to counter China's economic rise and technological growth.

Starting from 2006, the steady trend of displacing the state sector by private enterprises was reversed. This reversal became more obvious and blunter with the onset of the global financial crisis. However, this move was not a temporary policy adjustment. Rather, it appeared and now becomes a long-term divergence from market-oriented reforms. Regulatory state becomes a label which can be used to describe basically all major economies which are now relying on regulatory measures and tools for domestic economic governance.

From China's Indigenous Innovation initiatives in 2009, to Made in China 2025 in 2015, to state controls on data, the Chinese government has developed and deployed a mix of market access limits, industrial policies, and regulatory measures to support its self-reliance strategy, R&D and innovation ambition, competitive advantage, and domestic companies, thereby reducing dependence on foreign investment and technology. Made in China 2025, for example not only showed China's ambition in developing high technologies and lead the global technological competition but also intensified its state-led approach to expand global market shares and competitive advantage through both embracing the global economy and maintaining nonreciprocal restrictive policies at home.[59] Made in China 2025 involves China's multiple policies and regulatory tools such as licensing, standards, cybersecurity review, procurement, and market access. While the technological progress under the Made in China 2015 is hard to be assessed at this point, it has already separated China and the US on different paths.

In the 19th Party Congress, China described its economy as "socialism with Chinese characteristics for a new era."[60] In this economic model, the government sets economic goals and allocates resources to achieve them through industrial policy, incentives, and platforms for SOEs.[61] China seeks to tighten the dependence of international industrial chains on its economy to from a "powerful retaliatory and deterrent capability."[62] China's self-sufficiency[63] policy and dual circulation strategy with a clear emphasis on building resilience in domestic supply chains (e.g. import substitution) are not consistent with a trading system based on comparative advantage. The use and reliance upon the state-owned companies (together with a wide range of subsidies, preferences, supports, standards, and credits) as a tool of state economic policy undermines free competition, rule of law, and market economy as the operation and regulation of SOEs is not based on market forces or commercial standards. The strong state-owned sector crowds out private enterprises or even takes larger stakes in private enterprises.[64] As a result, the competitiveness, resources, and capability of foreign and private investors would be compromised. The state planning and industrial policy lead to excess production and dumping with negative externalities affecting global market and overseas markets.[65] Even the regulations and policies, if implemented or enforced unevenly, can be used a tool to benefit SOEs over private and foreign investors.

China has a long tradition to design, implement, and utilize industrial policy to achieve its broader economic, societal, political, and even security objectives.

Industrial policy has been used by other states in a wide range of areas. While the industrial policy may promote some industrial and economic development, it also has side effects of distorting the market, competitive conditions, and even rule of law. More emphasis and reliance on industrial policy in China justifies some mercantilist and discriminatory practices and strengthens state strategic interests. Domestically, voices supporting economic liberalism were almost silenced. The government is more confident about its functions and capability. Globally, the asymmetries in market access, commercial imbalances (such as no-risk financing and overcapacity), and the terms of global competition are less tolerable to other trading partners. Dumping and subsidies became the long-standing issues between China and its key Western trading partners, which are advocating some new norms and rules in the new-generation free trade agreements.

China is now pursuing an innovation-driven economy. To this end, China has been criticized by the US on two fronts. First, China has been using a variety of unfair and market-distorting tactics to take valuable technologies and intellectual property from the US.[66] As discussed in Chapters 4 and 6, China was accused of pressuring US investors, through joint venture requirement, shareholding cap, and market access, to surrender access to the intellectual property to their Chinese partners in the joint ventures. Other tactics include discriminatory regulations that barred US owners from receiving market rate returns for licensed technologies or claiming modified intellectual property rights.[67] Second, China's industrial policy is designed and applied for the purpose of lifting its creativity and innovation. The role of the state in the Chinese economy tilts the playing field in favour of Chinese businesses, in particular, state-owned enterprises through a suite of tools including regulatory measures, procurement policies, cybersecurity rules, and data regimes. However, these policies, at least claimed by the US side, may be inconsistent with the core value of market-based international trade norms and solutions such as non-discrimination, transparency, and rule of law. Rather, these policies are termed abusive market practices, state capitalism, economic statecraft, or market distortions.

The general consensus is that China has put the state and the ruling party, rather than market forces, back in the driver's seat even though the CCP continues to claim to promote deeper and broader opening-up. The overall policy is oriented towards increasing its own indigenous technological power and economic self-sufficiency. As early as in February 2006, the State Council issued the guiding document of the Indigenous Innovation Strategy – the National Medium- and Long-Term Program for the Development of Science and Technology (2006–2020),[68] which instructed Chinese companies to import foreign technology merely to assimilate, absorb, and re-innovate it. The guiding principle is to replace foreign technology in core areas with Chinese technology. A wide array of policy toolkit including technology standards, government procurement, antimonopoly law, approval regimes, patent rules, and product testing was put in place to achieve this mandate. Consequently, China's commitment to open-economy and market-based norms has flagged in key areas. China's intensifying illiberalism has made its dialogue with the Western countries more challenging. As a matter of fact, the indigenous innovation industrial policies, as expected, triggered contentious trade disputes with the US-led allies and inflamed political rhetoric between the two sides.[69] The US and perhaps other Western countries felt that China is more of a strategic competitor[70] than a partner. The US' decoupling policy are two-pronged. Driven by the security-related aims, the US tries to weed out economic interactions while forcing greater reciprocity and fairness. China's response to the US' decoupling effort is to publicly promote deeper engagement which, however, is sometimes dictated by state-led coercive terms instead of market-based norms. Insisting on these state-led terms itself may have a decoupling effect diverging from the liberal market economic norms.

China continues to lure foreign investment albeit selectively and on its own terms. These policy and regulatory moves make great sense along with other advanced economies' similar policy packages to cushion the effects of market liberalism for political, economic, or security concerns. These also are a natural response and even a must to counter the US-led coercion on China's technological growth. Meanwhile, these movements create de facto harsher or even more uncertain restrictions or hurdles to foreign investment let alone potential geopolitical tensions with and global playing field concerns to China's major trading partners.

3. National Security Concerns

The trend towards more regulations and restrictions related to national security intensified in recent years. Some regulatory measures are put in place to counter the pandemic while others are taken for geopolitical reasons.

In response to the US and EU sanctions, China quickly put in place the anti-sanctions laws, Unreliable Entity List rules, and blocking rules. The MOFCOM's blocking rules subject foreign companies that comply with US export controls and secondary sanctions to civil compensation claims in Chinese courts. These anti-sanctions rules, in the form of administrative regulations, were passed in contravention of China's formal legislative review process. Apart from vagueness, these rules do not possess practicality and specifics, leaving unlimited discretion to Chinese courts and government authorities. Meanwhile, China has been criticized by others for its economic coercion in the form of import bans and content censorship whenever it disapproves of others' political stances, policies, or behaviours. These altogether are the tools of China's buildup of a "powerful retaliatory and deterrent capability" sought by the Chinese ruling party and government.[71]

China's Regulation on the Unreliable Entity List establishes a framework of restrictions or penalties on foreign entities deemed to endanger China's national sovereignty, security, or development interests. China also tightened up its national security review of foreign investment by mandating pre-closing filings and authorizing the government authorities to review foreign investment in various sectors, including agriculture, energy, transportation, and information technology. In the field of data governance, the bunch of Chinese law, including the National Security Law, Cybersecurity Law, and the Data Security Law, have drawn great attention from the US and other countries as these laws implement the principle of localizing data storage and processing and supporting national data champions. Under these laws, both private companies and foreign companies are required to provide data to authorities and to cooperate on intelligence matters.

Anti-sanctions or retaliatory measures have been taken by China to assist its entities sanctioned by other states. The US administration made an executive order on 6 August 2020, that forces ByteDance to divest TikTok's US operations by 12 November 2020, with a possible 30-day extension.[72] ByteDance filed a lawsuit against the federal government on 24 August 2020, claiming that the executive order violates the firm's Fifth Amendment right to due process.[73] Meanwhile, ByteDance solicited the buyers for TikTok's US, Australian, and New Zealand operations with a valuation of $30 billion. Neither Oracle nor Microsoft and Walmart met the valuation.[74] China's National People's Congress quickly revised the Export Control Law to include artificial intelligence encompassing TikTok's video recommendation algorithm.[75] The amended Export Control Law allows TikTok to sell its brand, interface, and extensive user base without the code that has driven its wider adoption.[76] The algorithm is embedded in many of its application's features and the non-Chinese algorithm makes the deal lose its value.[77]

China certainly can easily justify its policy movements. However, its adoption of extraterritorial provisions in more laws (i.e. the data security law, the export control law, biosecurity law, and Hong Kong national security law) at an accelerating rate, while keeping its cross-border economic relationship with the rest of the world from being interrupted by other sanctions, may even speed up the decoupling Washington is now pursuing. The decoupling between these two economic powers will have tremendous impacts on the global economy. The disruption caused by decoupling will make any firm in the world hard to maintain the comparative advantage in the marketplace amid substantial costs involved (such as sunk costs, opportunity costs, and transaction costs). In addition, it can be an irony that the Chinese regulatory efforts to constrain the effect of the US or EU's extraterritorial laws and regulations ultimately help build out its own extraterritorial laws and regulations ranging from export controls to data security.

The US–China economic relationship has reached a critical juncture with a series of tit-for-tat tariff escalation. The domestic policies of the two largest economies determine the trajectory and dynamics of the bilateral and even multilateral investment and trade relationship. China's rise is the cause of the populism in the US[78] while the US assertive policy towards China is changing the geopolitical landscape between the two states. The consequence is slowing economic growth and roiled global financial markets. Trillions of dollars in wealth, assets, and commerce are at risk if the future relationship between the two countries is less engaged and more confrontational. Among others, targeted use of the foreign investment review process and export controls is the US key response to China's quest for US technology. The estimation is a loss of around US$25 billion per year in capital gains if decoupling leads to the sale of half of the US FDI stock in China.[79] Although the decoupling is expensive to both sides, the decoupling is likely to continue in one form or another. Further, the US' defensive and unilateral approach has a wide implication to and great influence on other Western allies. The polarizing approach risks a balkanizing of investment policy across the EU and the OECD. The policy concerns and questions would not be addressed effectively without multilateral cooperation.

While decoupling is beyond the key scope of this book, the importance of decoupling as related to FDI into and out of China should not be underestimated. Given the scale and depth of US–China economic interconnection and interdependence, decoupling seems unlikely at least in the short term. However, a complete rupture is a possible outcome as long as the decoupling continues even if it evolves in one form or another. Trade, investment, funding, tourism, and student exchanges are way down from the 2017 benchmark. The supply chains in telecommunications and semiconductors are being permanently cut by the US due to the national security concerns. Political distrust replaced the cooperative engagement policy that dominated the bilateral relationship between the two countries. China is pushing for de-decoupling by embracing more foreign investment and opening its door wider. For instance China relaxes regulatory restrictions on financial services, auto sector, and other sectors that have no strategic problem. Due to these new inducements, foreign investors may continue to invest into China regardless of the political rivalry between the US and China. The real concern, however, is China's attitudes towards the rule of law, open market, and free competition and its willingness to address Western complaints about distortions due to the heightened state role in the economy and its application of economic statecraft in economic planning.

4. Is the New Foreign Investment Law New in New Normal?

China's foreign investment law regime is based on a regulatory ethic that posits the state (both the government and the ruling party) as the primary designer, planner, operator, implementor, and regulatory agent for economic and social development. China's success in economic development and reform, that is in executing such policies as import substitution, export-led growth, and industrial transformation may suggest a positive role for the state in managing economic development.

Early proponents of dependency theory defined the state as a corporatist ally of foreign capital. Local elites serve as conduits for investment and act as local beneficiaries.[80] The corporatist state, however, is seen to use formalistic and authoritarian legal systems to retain power while pursuing national development goals through some reformist measures and tools.[81] In this regard, the corporatist state may not be in the same interest as foreign investors. This explains the mismatch and even confrontations between the state and foreign investment on some policy frontiers. For instance unregulated investment flows are seen to contribute to uneven distribution of economic growth and political instability.[82] The foreign investment regime in China is a strong and relevant indicator of dilemmas between the state, the market, and the rule of law.

In foreign investment law regime, state control over foreign investment activities was promoted and enhanced through financial controls (primarily in the areas of foreign exchange and taxation), the investment incentive system (by way of tax preferences), and the approval process for the establishment of foreign-invested enterprises, among others.

State control is also reflected in China's Catalogue approach to categorize sectors into permitted, encouraged, restricted, and prohibited groups so that foreign investment is steered into needed industrial sectors. However, the effect of this approach is hampered by the diverse effects of China's bureaucratic and non-transparent policy-making processes which are incremental and ad hoc responses to challenges in reality. As a result, national development goals are compromised by policy indeterminacy, regulatory inconsistency, and administrative discretion.

The tension between encouraging foreign business activities and maintaining state control over foreign investment was said to be a basic challenge to the ruling party. Although neo-classical and critical perspectives on the role of the state in economic development provide contexts in China's efforts to pursue economic growth,[83] the pursuit of an independent path[84] for developing indigenous technology and infrastructure is also a justifiable way of further development against the backdrop of the ongoing US–China trade war.

There have been many criticisms over China's legal system and regulatory system. Typical concerns include inconsistency of regulatory performance, lack of uniformity in interpreting and applying rules and regulations (more often based on parochial concerns rather than regulatory intent), conflicting goals of different bureaucracies, less functioning courts, local protectionism, among others. There has been a switch of government focus to macro-management, which departs from tight state control to more macro-level regulation of the market. However, there is no institutional permanence enhancing this regulatory or policy shift, which not only undermines state control but also lowers foreign investors' expectation.

The revival role of the state and the Party is also a concern to foreign investors. Even the private enterprises are called upon to "put country first" and to be patriotic.[85] The stronger state-owned sector has a strong implication for security, fair competition, and reciprocity. SOEs are entitled to preferential state financing and procurement contracts. The state is an appropriate focus of inquiry in understanding China's development effort.

Premier Wen Jiabao once warned that "the biggest problem with China's economy was still that growth was unstable, unbalanced, uncoordinated, and unsustainable."[86] Institutional economics confirms the positive results caused by reformist measures.[87] It was said that the removal of restrictions on investment helped sustain investment.[88] China's unorthodox policy making, adaptive governance, local experiments, and institutional innovation used to facilitate its rise.[89] Some obvious changes in China's policy process may change its policymaking and governance landscape.[90] Often overlooked is the much stricter regulation over market players and economic activities which may be also a factor driving down the economic growth as the stalled political reform (or in a more neutral term, local reform on its governance structure) may have hindered institutional development and technological innovation (evidenced by the decline in total factor productivity since the global financial crisis), thereby disincentivizing further economic reform but increasing transaction costs. Outsiders suspected China's economic reform seems to come to a critical juncture, if not an end, while the state strikes back.[91]

China is working on several upfronts. It is trying to form its own alliance. The signing of the Regional Comprehensive Economic Partnership Agreement in November 2020 involving ASEAN, China, Japan, South Korea, Australia, and New Zealand will boost FDI in the region. The RCEP including an investment chapter will promote investment, trade, and services. More importantly, the RCEP will help stabilize the supply chain despite the US–China trade tensions. This can be seen as a multilateral approach to the implications of the rise of more restrictive investment policies in the US–China context. The global economy and global FDI per se would benefit from a multilateral approach to re-configure investment policy.

The launch of free trade zones in Shanghai and other localities is another experiment to implement local autonomy with the hope that some new reformist measures can be tested and spread to the whole nation. The decline of the central state in economic reform and macro-management of socialist market economy also goes hand in hand with the emergence of local autonomy and local corporatism. In this process, local governments are able to ally themselves with capital to a greater extent, which weakens the centrality of state control. Local enterprises' efforts to forge close corporatist alliances with local officials further worsened local protectionism. There is a strong tendency to see the return of state centrality, which has changed the landscape of China's regulatory and governance framework in the past decade. The central government is in a great attempt to strengthen its policy autonomy and enforcement mechanism to achieve national development goals. More policy initiatives have been proposed by the central government which dominated the reform of foreign investment regime with the aim of freeing the market to foreign investment.[92] However, little policy space for local government may cause an unexpected effect seeing more control over foreign investment as the local government has no space and incentive to experiment any freer foreign investment policies. This dilemma is trapped in the central–local frame which is a unique feature in China's Party-state context.

The new FIL and its detailed implementation regulations emphasized the intention to provide equal treatment for domestic and foreign enterprises. Meanwhile, more measures including a shortened Negative List, wider market access policies, and more FDI facilitative measures are taken to open up more sectors to foreign investment. However, implementation of these measures remains uncertain. Moreover, these new steps do not address the fairness and reciprocity concerns. Taking into account a large geopolitical picture, FIL and its Implementation Regulations, assuming both are implemented well, are not grand solutions to the outstanding investment frictions[93] and to boost China's economy in a deglobalized and decoupled world. This may be a new normal both China and the world may have to face in the years to come.

Notes

1 United States Census Bureau, Historical Income Tables: Household, Table H-8. *Median Income by State – 2 Year Average*, www.census.gov/data/tables/time-series/demo/income-poverty/historical-income-households.html.

2 Energy Charter Secretariat, China Investment Report 2017, viii.

3 www.imf.org/external/pubs/ft/wp/2016/wp16106.pdf

4 Adam Tooze, *Crashed – How a Decade of Financial Crises Changed the World* (New York: Viking, 2018) Chapter 10.I.

5 John Seaman, Mikko Huotari, and Miguel Otero- Iglesias (eds), Chinese Investment in Europe: A Country-Level Approach (2017) A Report by the European Think-Tank Network on China (ETNC), 9–10.

6 "Chinese Investment in Europe." 10.

7 www.stats.gov.cn/tjsj/zxfb/201702/t20170228_1467424.html

8 http://unctad.org/en/PublicationsLibrary/wir2017_en.pdf

9 World Investment Report 2021, 7.

10 ATKearney Global Business Policy Council, Investing in a Localized World, 19.

11 Ibid., 21.

12 "Chinese Investment in Europe." 13.

13 Ibid., 13.

14 David Dollar, "China as a Global Investor, Foreign Policy at Brookings, ORDER from CHAOS Foreign Policy in a Troubled World," *Asia Working Group Paper 4*, May 2016, 4.

15 Ibid.

16 Ibid., 6.

17 Ibid., 6–7.

18 Ibid., 7.

19 Ibid., 8.

20 Ibid., 9.

21 Ibid., 9–10.

22 www.equator-principles.com/

23 Kerry Dumbaugh, "China's Foreign Policy: What Does It Mean for U.S. Global Interests? Congressional Research Service," *CRS Report for Congress*, Order Code 34588, July 2018, 4.

24 Ibid.

25 David Dollar, "China as a Global Investor," *Asia Working Group Paper 4*, May 2016, 3.

26 Chris Humphrey, "Infrastructure Finance in the Developing World," *Intergovernmental Group of Twenty Four*, 2015, p. 19.

27 David Dollar, 11.

28 B. Sautman and Y. Hairong, "Friends and Interests: China's Distinctive Links with Africa" (2007) 50(3) *African Studies Review* 75–114.

29 Thilo Hanemann, Daniel H. Rosen, Cassie Gao, and Adam Lysenko, "Two-Way Street: 2019 Update – US-China Investment Trends," *Rhodium Group and National Committee on US-China Relations*, May 2019, p. 11.

30 Id.

31 Thilo Hanemann, Daniel H. Rosen, Cassie Gao, and Adam Lysenko, "Two-Way Street: 2019 Update – US-China Investment Trends," *Rhodium Group and National Committee on US-China Relations*, May 2019, p. 19.

32 World Investment Report 2021, x.

33 Ibid.

34 Ibid., 5.

35 Ibid., 48.

36 Section 15 of China's Protocol of Accession obliges China's trading partners to recognize it as a market economy 15 years after China's joining the WTO. Nevertheless, major trading partners did not do so.

37 Office of the United States Trade Representative: 2019 Trade Policy Agenda and 2018 Annual Report of the President of the United States on the Trade Agreements Program, March 2019, p. 2.

38 James J. Nedumpara and Weihuan Zhou, *Non-market Economies in the Global Trading System – The Special Case of China* (Singapore: Springer, 2018).

39 U.S. Chamber of Commerce, "China's Approval Process for Inbound Foreign Direct Investment," 2012. www.uschamber.com/sites/default/files/documents/files/020021_China_InboundInvestment_Cvr.pdf

40 David Dollar, 13–14.

41 The A.T. Kearney Foreign Direct Investment (FDI) Confidence Index is an annual survey of global business executives that ranks markets that are likely to attract the most investment in the next three years. The FDI Confidence Index provides forward-looking analysis of the markets investors intend to target for FDI in the coming years. The 2018 FDI Confidence Index is constructed using primary data from a proprietary survey of more than 500 senior executives of the world's leading corporations. All participating companies have annual revenues of US$500 million or more. The companies are headquartered in 29 countries and span all sectors. The selection of these countries was based on UNCTAD data, with the 29 countries represented in the FDI Confidence Index originating more than 90% of the global flow of FDI in recent years. Service-sector firms account for about 46% of respondents, industrial firms for 35%, and IT firms for 17%.

42 ATKearney Global Business Policy Council, Investing in a Localized World, The 2018 A.T.Kearney Foreign Direct Investment Confidence Index. bit.ly/2018-FDICI, 1.

43 Ibid., 19.

44 Ibid., 30.

45 Ibid., 4.

46 Ibid., 14.

47 Ibid., 5.

48 Ibid., 29.

49 Ibid., 30.

50 David Dollar, 19.

51 It was once estimated that the direct effects of Chinese imports on job losses – such as a furniture factory closing down in North Carolina because the firm now imports from China – is only about 10% of US manufacturing job losses over the period 1999 to 2011. Daron Acemoglu, David Autor, David Dorn, Gordon H. Hanson, and Brendan Price, "Import Competition and the Great U.S. Employment Sag of the 2000s," (January 2016) 34(1) *Journal of Labor Economics* 141–198.

52 Joshua P. Meltzer and Neena Shenai, "The US-China Economic Relationship: A Comprehensive Approach," *Global Economy and Development at Brookings and American Enterprise Institute Policy Brief*, February 2019, p. 6.

53 Thilo Hanemann, Daniel H. Rosen, Cassie Gao, and Adam Lysenko, "Two-Way Street: 2019 Update – US-China Investment Trends," *Rhodium Group and National Committee on US-China Relations*, May 2019, p. 11.

54 Ibid., p. 13.

55 UNCTAD, World Investment Report 2021: Investing in Sustainable Recovery, 111.

56 Ibid.

57 The President's 2019 Trade Policy Agenda, p. 15.

58 Ibid., p. 20.

59 U.S. Chamber of Commerce, "Made in China 2025: Global Ambitions Built on Local Protections," 2017. www.uschamber.com/sites/default/files/final_made_in_china_2025_report_full.pdf

60 This is also said to be a euphemism for managed competition, with privileges carved out for the state. The Third Pillar.

61 Japan's keiretsu or South Korea's chaebols also share these features but with a less influential government in the marketplace.

62 Xinhua, "(Shouquan Fabu) Xi Jinping: Zai Jingji Shehui Lingyu Zhuanjia Zuotanhui Shang de Jianghua" [(Official Release) Xi Jinping: Remarks at the Symposium of Experts in Economic and Social Fields], 24 August 2020. www.xinhuanet.com/politics/leaders/2020-08/24/c_1126407772.htm

63 For instance the Made in China 2025 targets to 70% self-sufficiency in strategic technologies such as advanced information technology, robotics, aircraft, new energy vehicles, new material, and biotechnology.

64 *The Economist*, China's State Enterprises Are Not Retreating but Advancing, *The Economist*, 20 July 2017; *The Economist*, "China's Private Sector Faces an Advance by the State," *The Economist*, 8 December 2018.

65 OECD Directorate for Science, Technology and Innovation, *Excess Capacity in the Global Steel Industry: The Current Situation and Ways Forward* (Paris: OECD, 2015); David Lawder, "IMF's Lagarde Says China Needs to Do More to Cut Steel Capacity in the Global Steel Capacity" *Reuters News*, March 2018.

66 The President's 2019 Trade Policy Agenda, 7.

67 Ibid., p. 7.

68 State Council of the People's Republic of China, "Guidelines for the Implementation of the National Medium- and Long-Term Program for Science and Technology Development (2006–2020)," February 2006. Full translated text: www.itu.int/en/ITU-D/Cybersecurity/Documents/National_Strategies_Repository/China_2006.pdf

69 James McGregor, "China's Drive for Indigenous Innovation: A Web of Industrial Policies," *U.S. Chamber of Commerce*, 2010. www.uschamber.com/sites/default/files/legacy/international/asia/files/100728chinareport_0.pdf

70 White House, "Interim National Security Strategic Guidance," March 2021, p. 20. www.whitehouse.gov/wp-content/uploads/2021/03/NSC-1v2.pdf

71 Xinhua, "(Shouquan Fabu) Xi Jinping: Zai Jingji Shehui Lingyu Zhuanjia Zuotanhui Shang de Jianghua" [(Ofcial Release) Xi Jinping: Remarks at the Symposium of Experts in Economic and Social Fields], 24 August 2020. www.xinhuanet.com/politics/leaders/2020-08/24/c_1126407772.htm

72 U.S.-China Economic and Security Review Commission: Economic and Trade Bulletin, 8 September 2020, p. 5.

73 Rachel Lerman and Jay Greene, "TikTok Sale Slowed as Chinese Government May Get Involved," *Washington Post*, 3 September 2020. www.washingtonpost.com/technology/2020/09/03/tiktok-sale-slowed-chinese-government-may-get-involved/.

74 Katy Stech Ferek and Liza Lin, "TikTok Files Suit Challenging U.S. Ban," *Wall Street Journal*, 24 August 2020. www.wsj.com/articles/tiktok-to-file-suit-challenging-u-s-ban-11598281193.

75 Rachel Lerman and Jay Greene, "TikTok Sale Slowed as Chinese Government May Get Involved," *Washington Post*, 3 September 2020. www.washingtonpost.com/technology/2020/09/03/tiktok-sale-slowed-chinese-government-may-get-involved/; Sarah Nassauer et al., "Walmart Joins Microsoft's Pursuit of TikTok," *Wall Street Journal*, 27 August 2020. www.wsj.com/articles/walmart-joins-microsofts-pursuit-of-tiktok-11598544354.

76 Rachel Lerman and Jay Greene, "TikTok Sale Slowed as Chinese Government May Get Involved," *Washington Post*, 3 September 2020. www.washingtonpost.com/technology/2020/09/03/tiktok-sale-slowed-chinese-government-may-get-involved/.

77 Tom Daly et al., "China's New Tech Export Controls Could Give Beijing a Say in TikTok Sale," *Reuters*, 30 August 2020. www.reuters.com/article/us-usa-tiktok-china/chinas-new-tech-export-controls-could-give-beijing-a-say-in-tiktok-sale-idUSKBN25Q05Q.

78 Raghuram Rajan, *The Third Pillar: How Markets and the State Leave the Community Behind* (Penguin Press 2019) Preface.

79 US Chamber of Commerce China Centre, Understanding US-China Decoupling Macro Trends and Industry Impacts 2021, 3.

80 Charles K. Wilber and James H. Weaver, "Patterns of Dependency: Income Distribution and the History of Underdevelopment" in Charles K. Wilber (ed), *The Political Economy of Development and Underdevelopment* (2nd ed. New York: Random House, 1979) 114–129.

81 James A. Gardner, *Legal Imperialism: American Lawyers and Foreign Aid in Latin America* (Madison: University of Wisconsin Press 1980) 187ff.

82 Alexander Murphy, "Western Investment in East-Central Europe: Emerging Patterns and Implications for State Stability" (1992) 44(3) *The Professional Geographer* 249–259.

83 Stephan Haggard, *Pathways from the Periphery: The Politics of Growth in the Newly Industri-alizing Countries* (Ithaca and London: Cornell University Press, 1990); Anis Chowdhury and Iyanatul Islam, *The Newly Industrializing Economies of East Asia* (London and New York: Routledge, 1993).

84 Alexander Eckstein, *China's Economic Revolution* (Cambridge: Cambridge University Press, 1977), p. 123ff; Robert F. Dernberger, "The Chinese Search for the Path of Self-Sustained Growth in the 1980s" in *Joint Economic Committee of U.S. Congress, China Under the Four Modernizations* (Washington, DC: U.S, Government Printing Office, 1982) 19–76.

85 中共中央　国务院关于营造企业家健康成长环境弘扬优秀企业家精神更好发挥企业家作用的意见 [CPC Central Committee and State Council on Creating a Healthy Growth Environment for Entrepreneurs – Promoting an Outstanding Entrepreneurship for Better Playing the Role of Entrepreneurs], State Council of China, 8 September 2017, www.gov.cn, see also Jennifer Hughes, "China's Communist Party Writes Itself into Company Law," *Financial Times*, 14 August 2017, and Sebastian Heilmann, "How the CCP Embraces and Co-Opts China's Private Sector," *European Voices on China*, MERICS blog, 21 November 2017, http://blog.merics.org.

86 A. Wheatley, "Calculating the Coming Slowdown in China," *New York Times*, 23 May 2011.

87 www.stats.gov.cn/english/PressRelease/201610/t20161019_1411211.html

88 World Investment Report 2021, 48.

89 See generally, Sebastian Heilmann, *Red Swan: How Unorthodox Policy Making Facilitated China's Rise* (Hong Kong: Chinese University of Hong Kong Press, 2018).

90 Ibid., 197–220.

91 Nicholas R. Lardy, *The State Strikes Back: The End of Economic Reform in China?* (Washington, DC: Peterson Institute for International Economics January 2019).

92 It was once anticipated in the mid-1990s that the central government would be ineffective in managing foreign investment due to the combined effect of localism and corruption. Pitman B. Potter, "Foreign Investment Law in the People's Republic of China: Dilemmas of State Control" (1995) *The China Quarterly* 155, 184. However, the early proposition was made on the basis that China's move towards the market economy would not be reversed. The powerful central government in China's central-local structure, however, makes this proposition less valid. The reality has proved the inevitable dominant role of the central government in policy making.

93 Thilo Hanemann, Daniel H. Rosen, Cassie Gao and Adam Lysenko, "Two -Way Street: 2019 Update – US-China Investment Trends," *Rhodium Group and National Committee on US-China Relations*, May 2019, p. 13.

APPENDIX

Foreign Investment Law 2019

《中华人民共和国外商投资法》

Foreign Investment Law of the People's Republic of China

（2019年3月15日第十三届全国人民代表大会第二次会议通过）

(Adopted at the 2nd session of the 13th National People's Congress on March 15, 2019)

目 录 Table of Contents

第一章 总则 Chapter I General Provisions

第一条 为了进一步扩大对外开放，积极促进外商投资，保护外商投资合法权益，规范外商投资管理，推动形成全面开放新格局，促进社会主义市场经济健康发展，根据宪法，制定本法。

Article 1 In order to further expand opening up, actively promote foreign investment, protect the legitimate rights and interests of foreign investment, standardize foreign investment management, facilitate the formation of a comprehensive and new opening-up pattern, and promote the healthy development of the socialist market economy, this Law is enacted in accordance with the Constitution.

第二条 在中华人民共和国境内（以下简称中国境内）的外商投资，适用本法。

Article 2 This Law applies to foreign investment in the territory of the People's Republic of China (hereinafter referred to as "within the territory of China").

本法所称外商投资，是指外国的自然人、企业或者其他组织（以下称外国投资者）直接或者间接在中国境内进行的投资活动，包括下列情形：

Foreign investment mentioned in this Law refers to the investment activities of foreign natural persons, enterprises or other organizations (hereinafter referred to as foreign investors) directly or indirectly within the territory of China, including the following:

（一）外国投资者单独或者与其他投资者共同在中国境内设立外商投资企业；

(1) Foreign investors set up foreign-invested enterprises in China alone or jointly with other investors;

（二）外国投资者取得中国境内企业的股份、股权、财产份额或者其他类似权益；

(2) Foreign investors obtain shares, equities, property shares or other similar rights and interests of enterprises within the territory of China;

（三）外国投资者单独或者与其他投资者共同在中国境内投资新建项目；

(3) Foreign investors investing in new projects in China alone or jointly with other investors;

（四）法律、行政法规或者国务院规定的其他方式的投资。

(4) Other investment prescribed by laws, administrative regulations or specified by the State Council.

本法所称外商投资企业，是指全部或者部分由外国投资者投资，依照中国法律在中国境内经登记注册设立的企业。

Foreign-invested enterprises mentioned in this Law refer to enterprises that are wholly or partly invested by foreign investors and registered within the territory of China under the Chinese laws.

第三条 国家坚持对外开放的基本国策，鼓励外国投资者依法在中国境内投资。

Article 3 The State adheres to the basic State policy of opening to the outside world and encouraging foreign investors to invest within the territory of China.

国家实行高水平投资自由化便利化政策，建立和完善外商投资促进机制，营造稳定、透明、可预期和公平竞争的市场环境。

The State maintains a policy of high-level investment liberalization and facilitation, establishes and improves a mechanism for foreign investment promotion, and creates a stable, transparent, predictable and fair market environment.

第四条 国家对外商投资实行准入前国民待遇加负面清单管理制度。

Article 4 The State maintains a system of pre-entry national treatment plus a negative list management for foreign investment.

前款所称准入前国民待遇，是指在投资准入阶段给予外国投资者及其投资不低于本国投资者及其投资的待遇；所称负面清单，是指国家规定在特定领域对外商投资实施的准入特别管理措施。国家对负面清单之外的外商投资，给予国民待遇。

The pre-entry national treatment mentioned in the preceding paragraph refers to the treatment given to foreign investors and their investment at the stage of investment admission no less than that to domestic investors and their investments; the so-called negative list refers to the special management measures that are adopted for the admission of foreign investment in specific areas. The State gives national treatment to foreign investment outside the negative list.

负面清单由国务院发布或者批准发布。

The negative list is issued or approved by the State Council.

中华人民共和国缔结或者参加的国际条约、协定对外国投资者准入待遇有更优惠规定的，可以按照相关规定执行。

Where international treaties or agreements concluded or acceded to by the People's Republic of China provide for more preferential treatments for the admission of foreign investment, the relevant provisions may be applied.

第五条 国家依法保护外国投资者在中国境内的投资、收益和其他合法权益。

Article 5 The State protects the investment, income and other legitimate rights and interests of foreign investors in China in accordance with the law.

第六条 在中国境内进行投资活动的外国投资者、外商投资企业，应当遵守中国法律法规，不得危害中国国家安全、损害社会公共利益。

Article 6 Foreign investors and foreign-invested enterprises that conduct investment activities within China shall abide by Chinese laws and regulations and shall not endanger China's national security and harm the public interest.

第七条　国务院商务主管部门、投资主管部门按照职责分工，开展外商投资促进、保护和管理工作；国务院其他有关部门在各自职责范围内，负责外商投资促进、保护和管理的相关工作。

Article 7 The competent departments of the State Council responsible for commerce and investment shall, in accordance with the division of responsibilities, carry out the promotion, protection and management of foreign investment; other relevant departments of the State Council shall, within their respective responsibilities, be responsible for the affairs related to the promotion, protection and management of foreign investment.

县级以上地方人民政府有关部门依照法律法规和本级人民政府确定的职责分工，开展外商投资促进、保护和管理工作。

The relevant departments of the local people's governments at or above the county level shall, in accordance with laws and regulations and the division of responsibilities determined by the people's government at the same level, carry out the work relating to the promotion, protection and management of foreign investment.

第八条　外商投资企业职工依法建立工会组织，开展工会活动，维护职工的合法权益。外商投资企业应当为本企业工会提供必要的活动条件。

Article 8 Employees of foreign-invested enterprises may, in accordance with law, establish trade union organizations, carry out trade union activities, and safeguard their legitimate rights and interests. Foreign-invested enterprises shall provide necessary conditions for the trade unions thereof.

第二章 投资促进 Chapter II Investment Promotion

第九条 外商投资企业依法平等适用国家支持企业发展的各项政策。

Article 9 Foreign-invested enterprises may, in accordance with the law, equally enjoy the State policies concerning the support of enterprise development.

第十条 制定与外商投资有关的法律、法规、规章,应当采取适当方式征求外商投资企业的意见和建议。

Article 10 Before the formulation of laws, regulations and rules related to foreign investment, appropriate measures shall be taken to solicit opinions and suggestions from foreign-invested enterprises.

与外商投资有关的规范性文件、裁判文书等,应当依法及时公布。

Normative and adjudicative documents related to foreign investment shall, according to law, be made public in a timely manner.

第十一条 国家建立健全外商投资服务体系,为外国投资者和外商投资企业提供法律法规、政策措施、投资项目信息等方面的咨询和服务。

Article 11 The State establishes and improves a system serving foreign investment to provide consultation and services to foreign investors and foreign-invested enterprises on laws and regulations, policy measures, and investment project information.

第十二条 国家与其他国家和地区、国际组织建立多边、双边投资促进合作机制,加强投资领域的国际交流与合作。

Article 12 The State establishes multilateral and bilateral investment promotion cooperation mechanisms with other countries and regions and international organizations, and strengthens international exchanges and cooperation in the field of investment.

第十三条 国家根据需要,设立特殊经济区域,或者在部分地区实行外商投资试验性政策措施,促进外商投资,扩大对外开放。

Article 13 The State may establish special economic zones where needed, or adopt experimental policies and measures for foreign investment in selected regions with a view to promoting foreign investment and expanding opening-up.

第十四条 国家根据国民经济和社会发展需要,鼓励和引导外国投资者在特定行业、领域、地区投资。外国投资者、外商投资企业可以依照法律、行政法规或者国务院的规定享受优惠待遇。

Article 14 The State may, in accordance with the needs of national economic and social development, encourage and guide foreign investors to invest in specific industries, sectors and regions. Foreign investors and foreign-invested enterprises may enjoy preferential treatment in accordance with laws, administrative regulations or the provisions of the State Council.

第十五条 国家保障外商投资企业依法平等参与标准制定工作,强化标准制定的信息公开和社会监督。

Article 15 The State ensures that foreign-invested enterprises have equal access to the standard-setting work according to law, and strengthens information disclosure and social supervision regarding standard-setting.

国家制定的强制性标准平等适用于外商投资企业。

The mandatory standards set forth by the State are equally applicable to foreign-invested enterprises.

第十六条 国家保障外商投资企业依法通过公平竞争参与政府采购活动。政府采购依法对外商投资企业在中国境内生产的产品、提供的服务平等对待。

Article 16 The State ensures that foreign-invested enterprises have equal access to government procurement through fair competition in accordance with the law. Products and services provided by foreign-invested enterprises within the territory of China are equally treated in government procurement in accordance with law.

第十七条　外商投资企业可以依法通过公开发行股票、公司债券等证券和其他方式进行融资。

Article 17 Foreign-invested enterprises may, in accordance with the law, finance through public offering of stocks, corporate bonds and other securities.

第十八条　县级以上地方人民政府可以根据法律、行政法规、地方性法规的规定，在法定权限内制定外商投资促进和便利化政策措施。

Article 18 Local people's governments at or above the county level may, in accordance with the provisions of laws, administrative regulations and local regulations, formulate policies and measures for foreign investment promotion and facilitation within their statutory competence.

第十九条　各级人民政府及其有关部门应当按照便利、高效、透明的原则，简化办事程序，提高办事效率，优化政务服务，进一步提高外商投资服务水平。

Article 19 The people's governments at all levels and their relevant departments shall, in accordance with the principles of facilitation, efficiency and transparency, simplify procedures, improve efficiency, optimize government services, and further improve the level of foreign investment services.

有关主管部门应当编制和公布外商投资指引，为外国投资者和外商投资企业提供服务和便利。

The relevant competent authorities shall prepare and publish foreign investment guidelines to provide services and facilities to foreign investors and foreign-invested enterprises.

第三章 投资保护 Chapter III Investment Protection

第二十条 国家对外国投资者的投资不实行征收。

Article 20 The State does not expropriate foreign investment.

在特殊情况下，国家为了公共利益的需要，可以依照法律规定对外国投资者的投资实行征收或者征用。征收、征用应当依照法定程序进行，并及时给予公平、合理的补偿。

Under extraordinary circumstances, the State may expropriate and requisition the investment of foreign investors in accordance with the law and for the needs of the public interest. The expropriation and requisition shall be conducted in accordance with legal procedures and timely and reasonable compensation shall be given.

第二十一条　外国投资者在中国境内的出资、利润、资本收益、资产处置所得、知识产权许可使用费、依法获得的补偿或者赔偿、清算所得等，可以依法以人民币或者外汇自由汇入、汇出。

Article 21 Foreign investors' capital contribution, profits, capital gains, assets disposal income, intellectual property licence fees, legally obtained damages or compensation, liquidation proceeds, etc., may be freely remitted to overseas in RMB or foreign exchange according to law.

第二十二条　国家保护外国投资者和外商投资企业的知识产权，保护知识产权权利人和相关权利人的合法权益；对知识产权侵权行为，严格依法追究法律责任。

Article 22 The State protects the intellectual property rights of foreign investors and foreign-invested enterprises, protects the legitimate rights and interests of intellectual property rights holders and related rights holders, and holds intellectual property rights infringers legally accountable in strict accordance with the law.

国家鼓励在外商投资过程中基于自愿原则和商业规则开展技术合作。技术合作的条件由投资各方遵循公平原则平等协商确定。行政机关及其工作人员不得利用行政手段强制转让技术。

The State encourages technical cooperation based on the voluntariness principle and commercial rules in the process of foreign investment. The conditions for technical cooperation are determined by equal negotiation between the parties to the investment in accordance with the principle of fairness. Administrative agencies and their staff are prohibited to use administrative means to force any technology transfer.

第二十三条　行政机关及其工作人员对于履行职责过程中知悉的外国投资者、外商投资企业的商业秘密，应当依法予以保密，不得泄露或者非法向他人提供。

Article 23 The administrative organs and their staff shall keep confidential the business secrets known to them, of foreign investors and foreign-invested enterprises during the performance of their duties, and shall not disclose or illegally provide them to others.

第二十四条　各级人民政府及其有关部门制定涉及外商投资的规范性文件，应当符合法律法规的规定；没有法律、行政法规依据的，不得减损外商投资企业的合法权益或者增加其义务，不得设置市场准入和退出条件，不得干预外商投资企业的正常生产经营活动。

Article 24 The people's governments at all levels and their relevant departments shall be in compliance with the provisions of laws and regulations in formulating normative documents concerning foreign investment; unless authorized by laws and administrative regulations, they shall not derogate from the legitimate rights and interests of foreign-invested enterprises or increase their obligations, set forth conditions for market access and exit, and interfere with normal production and operation of foreign-invested enterprises.

第二十五条　地方各级人民政府及其有关部门应当履行向外国投资者、外商投资企业依法作出的政策承诺以及依法订立的各类合同。

Article 25 Local people's governments at all levels and their relevant departments shall honour their commitments on policies made available to foreign investors and foreign-invested enterprises under the law and various types of contracts concluded in accordance with the law.

因国家利益、社会公共利益需要改变政策承诺、合同约定的，应当依照法定权限和程序进行，并依法对外国投资者、外商投资企业因此受到的损失予以补偿。

If policy commitments or contractual agreements need to be changed for the State interests and public interests, they shall be conducted in accordance with the statutory authority and procedures, and foreign investors and foreign-invested enterprises shall be compensated for the losses they suffered accordingly.

第二十六条 国家建立外商投资企业投诉工作机制，及时处理外商投资企业或者其投资者反映的问题，协调完善相关政策措施。

Article 26 The State establishes a complaint and settlement mechanism for foreign-invested enterprises, with a view to promptly handling problems raised by foreign-invested enterprises or their investors, and coordinating and improving relevant policies and measures.

外商投资企业或者其投资者认为行政机关及其工作人员的行政行为侵犯其合法权益的，可以通过外商投资企业投诉工作机制申请协调解决。

If a foreign-invested enterprise or its investors believe that the administrative actions of the administrative organ and its staff infringe upon their legitimate rights and interests, they may apply for a coordinated solution through the complaint and settlement mechanism for the foreign-invested enterprise.

外商投资企业或者其投资者认为行政机关及其工作人员的行政行为侵犯其合法权益的，除依照前款规定通过外商投资企业投诉工作机制申请协调解决外，还可以依法申请行政复议、提起行政诉讼。

If a foreign-invested enterprise or its investors believe that the administrative actions of the administrative organ and its staff infringe upon their legitimate rights and interests, in addition to applying for a coordinated solution through the complaint and settlement mechanism for the foreign-invested enterprise in accordance with the provisions of the preceding paragraph, they may also apply for administrative reconsideration and file an administrative lawsuit according to law.

第二十七条 外商投资企业可以依法成立和自愿参加商会、协会。商会、协会依照法律法规和章程的规定开展相关活动，维护会员的合法权益。

Article 27 Foreign-invested enterprises may establish and voluntarily participate in chambers of commerce and associations according to law. The chamber of commerce and association shall carry out relevant activities in accordance with the laws, regulations and its articles of association to safeguard the legitimate rights and interests of its members.

第四章 投资管理 Chapter IV Investment Management

第二十八条 外商投资准入负面清单规定禁止投资的领域，外国投资者不得投资。

Article 28 Foreign investors shall not invest in the areas where investment is prohibited under the negative list for the admission of foreign investment.

外商投资准入负面清单规定限制投资的领域，外国投资者进行投资应当符合负面清单规定的条件。

Foreign investors shall meet the conditions set forth in the negative list for the admission of foreign investment to invest in the areas where investment is restricted under the negative list.

外商投资准入负面清单以外的领域，按照内外资一致的原则实施管理。

Management of foreign investment in the areas beyond the negative list shall be implemented in accordance with the principle of equality between domestic and foreign investment.

第二十九条 外商投资需要办理投资项目核准、备案的，按照国家有关规定执行。

Article 29 If foreign investment is required to go through the approval or investment project record procedure, it shall be implemented in accordance with relevant provisions.

第三十条 外国投资者在依法需要取得许可的行业、领域进行投资的，应当依法办理相关许可手续。

Article 30 If a foreign investor invests in an industry or sector where legal permission is required for investment, it shall go through relevant licensing procedures in accordance with the law.

有关主管部门应当按照与内资一致的条件和程序，审核外国投资者的许可申请，法律、行政法规另有规定的除外。

The relevant competent department shall, in accordance with the conditions and procedures equally applied to domestic investment, review the foreign investors' application for permission, except as otherwise provided by laws and administrative regulations.

第三十一条 外商投资企业的组织形式、组织机构及其活动准则，适用《中华人民共和国公司法》、《中华人民共和国合伙企业法》等法律的规定。

Article 31 Forms of organization, organization structures and activities of foreign-invested enterprises shall be governed by the provisions of the Company Law and the Law of the Partnership Enterprise of the People's Republic of China.

第三十二条 外商投资企业开展生产经营活动，应当遵守法律、行政法规有关劳动保护、社会保险的规定，依照法律、行政法规和国家有关规定办理税收、会计、外汇等事宜，并接受相关主管部门依法实施的监督检查。

Article 32 Foreign-invested enterprises that engage in production and business activities shall abide by the provisions of laws and administrative regulations concerning labour protection and social insurance, and handle matters such as taxation, accounting, foreign exchange, etc. in accordance with laws, administrative regulations and relevant provisions, and accept relevant supervision and inspection carried out by the relevant departments in accordance with the law.

第三十三条 外国投资者并购中国境内企业或者以其他方式参与经营者集中的，应当依照《中华人民共和国反垄断法》的规定接受经营者集中审查。

Article 33 If a foreign investor acquires a Chinese domestic enterprise or participates in the concentration of business operators in other ways, it shall go through the examination on the concentration of business operators in accordance with the Anti-Monopoly Law of the People's Republic of China.

第三十四条 国家建立外商投资信息报告制度。外国投资者或者外商投资企业应当通过企业登记系统以及企业信用信息公示系统向商务主管部门报送投资信息。

Article 34 The State establishes a system for foreign investment information reporting. Foreign investors or foreign-invested enterprises shall submit investment information to the competent commerce departments through the enterprise registration system and the enterprise credit information publicity system.

外商投资信息报告的内容和范围按照确有必要的原则确定；通过部门信息共享能够获得的投资信息，不得再行要求报送。

The content and scope of the foreign investment information report shall be determined in accordance with the principle of necessity; the investment information that can be obtained through the inter-department information sharing system shall not be required to be submitted again.

第三十五条　国家建立外商投资安全审查制度，对影响或者可能影响国家安全的外商投资进行安全审查。

Article 35 The State establishes a system of security review for foreign investment to review the foreign investment that affects or may affect national security.

依法作出的安全审查决定为最终决定。

The security review decision made in accordance with the law is final.

第五章 法律责任 Chapter V Legal Liability

第三十六条　外国投资者投资外商投资准入负面清单规定禁止投资的领域的，由有关主管部门责令停止投资活动，限期处分股份、资产或者采取其他必要措施，恢复到实施投资前的状态；有违法所得的，没收违法所得。

Article 36 Where a foreign investor invests in the areas, which are specified by the negative list for the admission of foreign-investment as prohibited areas, the relevant competent department shall order it to stop the investment activities, and dispose of the shares, assets or take other necessary measures within a specified time limit, and restitute to the status before the investment was made; if there is illegal income, it shall be confiscated.

外国投资者的投资活动违反外商投资准入负面清单规定的限制性准入特别管理措施的，由有关主管部门责令限期改正，采取必要措施满足准入特别管理措施的要求；逾期不改正的，依照前款规定处理。

Where the investment activities of a foreign investor violates the special management measures for the admission of foreign-investment regarding restricted areas in the negative list, the relevant competent department shall order the correction within a specified time limit and take necessary measures to meet the conditions set forth by the special management measures for the admission of foreign-investment; if no corrections have been made within the time limit, the provisions of the preceding paragraph shall be applied.

外国投资者的投资活动违反外商投资准入负面清单规定的，除依照前两款规定处理外，还应当依法承担相应的法律责任。

Where the investment activities of a foreign investor violates the special management measures for the admission of foreign-investment in the negative list, in addition to the provisions of the preceding two paragraphs, it shall also bear corresponding legal liabilities under the law.

第三十七条　外国投资者、外商投资企业违反本法规定，未按照外商投资信息报告制度的要求报送投资信息的，由商务主管部门责令限期改正；逾期不改正的，处十万元以上五十万元以下的罚款。

Article 37 If a foreign investor or a foreign-invested enterprise violates the provisions of this Law and fails to submit investment information in accordance with the requirements of the foreign investment information reporting system, the competent commerce department shall order it to make corrections within a specified time limit; if no corrections have been made within the time limit, a fine of more than 100,000 yuan and less than 500,000 yuan shall be imposed.

第三十八条　对外国投资者、外商投资企业违反法律、法规的行为，由有关部门依法查处，并按照国家有关规定纳入信用信息系统。

Article 38 Any violation of laws or regulations by foreign investors or foreign-invested enterprises shall be investigated and dealt with by relevant departments in accordance with the law and recorded into the credit information publicity system in accordance with relevant provisions.

第三十九条　行政机关工作人员在外商投资促进、保护和管理工作中滥用职权、玩忽职守、徇私舞弊的，或者泄露、非法向他人提供履行职责过程中知悉的商业秘密的，依法给予处分；构成犯罪的，依法追究刑事责任。

Article 39 If a staff of an administrative organ abuses his power, neglects his duties or engages in malpractices in the promotion, protection and management of foreign investment, or leaks or illegally provides others with trade secrets that he or she knows in the course of performing his duties, he shall be punished according to law; if he commits a crime, he shall be held criminally responsible.

第六章 附 则 Chapter VI Supplementary Provisions

第四十条　任何国家或者地区在投资方面对中华人民共和国采取歧视性的禁止、限制或者其他类似措施的，中华人民共和国可以根据实际情况对该国家或者该地区采取相应的措施。

Article 40 If any country or region adopts discriminatory prohibitions, restrictions or other similar measures on the People's Republic of China, the People's Republic of China may take corresponding measures against the country or the region according to actual conditions.

第四十一条　对外国投资者在中国境内投资银行业、证券业、保险业等金融行业，或者在证券市场、外汇市场等金融市场进行投资的管理，国家另有规定的，依照其规定。

Article 41 If the State provides other provisions for foreign investment in the banking, securities, insurance and other financial industries, or in the securities market, foreign exchange market and other financial markets within the territory of China, such provisions shall be applicable.

第四十二条　本法自2020年1月1日起施行。《中华人民共和国中外合资经营企业法》、《中华人民共和国外资企业法》、《中华人民共和国中外合作经营企业法》同时废止。

Article 42 This Law shall come into force on January 1, 2020. The Law of the People's Republic of China on Sino-Foreign Equity Joint Ventures, the Law of the People's Republic of China on Wholly Foreign-owned Enterprises, and the Law of the People's Republic on Sino-Foreign Contractual Joint Ventures shall be repealed simultaneously.

本法施行前依照《中华人民共和国中外合资经营企业法》、《中华人民共和国外资企业法》、《中华人民共和国中外合作经营企业法》设立的外商投资企业，在本法施行后五年内可以继续保留原企业组织形式等。具体实施办法由国务院规定。

Foreign-invested enterprises that have been established before the implementation of this Law in accordance with the Law of the People's Republic of China on Sino-Foreign Equity Joint Ventures, the Law of the People's Republic of China on Wholly Foreign-owned Enterprises, and the Law of the People's Republic of China on Sino-Foreign Contractual Joint Ventures may continue retaining their original forms of business organizations within five years after the implementation of this Law. The detailed implementation measures of this Law shall be prescribed by the State Council.

BIBLIOGRAPHY

Abbott, Frederick M., "The United States Response to Emerging Technological Powers" in Fredrick M. Abott (ed.), *Emerging Markets and the World Patent Order* (Edward Elgar, 2014).

Aglialoro, Matthew, "Defend and Protect: National Security Restrictions on Foreign Investment in the United States" (2015) 83 *University of Cincinnati Law Review* 1261.

Aloupi, Niki, "The Right to Non-Intervention and Non-Interference" (2015) 4(3) *Cambridge Journal of International and Comparative Law* 566–87.

Amerasinghe, Chittharanjan Felix, *Local Remedies in International Law* (Cambridge University Press, 1990).

Ann, Lee Soo, *Industrialization in Singapore* (Longman's, 1973);

Armstrong, David, "Evolving Conceptions of Justice in International Law" (2011) 37 *Review of International Studies* 2121–36.

Ayangbah, Shirley, and Liu Sun, "Comparative Study of Foreign Investment Law: The Case of China and Ghana" (2017) 3 *Cogent Social Sciences* 1–22.

Ayres, Ian, and John Braithwaite, *Responsive Regulation: Transcending the Deregulation Debate* (Oxford University Press, 1992).

Ayres, Ian, and Robert Gertner, "Filling Gaps in Incomplete Contracts: An Economic Theory of Default Rules" (1989) 99 *Yale Law Journal* 87, 91–93.

Azeredo da Silveira, Mercèdeh, "Part III: Trade Sanction as a Ground for Exemption from Liability for Non-Performance" in *Trade Sanctions and International Sales: An Inquiry into International Arbitration and Commercial Litigation* (Kluwer Law International, 2014).

Baldwin, Robert, "Why Rules Don't Work" (1990) 53 *Modern Law Review* 321.

Baran, Paul A., *The Political Economy of Growth* (Monthly Review Press, 1968).

Bauman, Richard W., "Liberalism and Canadian Corporate Law" in Richard F. Devlin (ed.), *Canadian Perspectives on Legal Theory* (Emond Mongomery, 1991).

Baumol, William J., and Janusz A. Ordover, "Use of Antitrust to Subvert Competition" (1985) 28 *The Journal of Law and Economics* 247, 250–51.

Beck, Andrea, "China's Strategy in the Arctic: A Case of Lawfare?" (2014) 4(2) *The Polar Journal* 306–18.

Behr, Volker, "Punitive Damages in American and German Law – Tendencies towards Approximation of Apparently Irreconcilable Concepts" (2003) 78 *Chicago Kent Law Review* 105, 106–7.

Bird, Robert, and Daniel R. Cohay, "The Impact of Compulsory Licensing on Foreign Direct Investment: A Collective Bargaining Approach" (2008) 45 *American Business Law Journal* 283 n1.

Black, Julia, "New Institutionalism and Naturalism in Socio-Legal Analysis: Institutionalist Approaches to Regulatory Decision Making" (1997) 19 *Law and Policy* 51.

Blomström, Magnus, et al., "The Determinants of Host Country Spillovers from Foreign Direct Investment: Review and Synthesis of the Literature" in Nigel Pain (ed.), *Inward Investment, Technological Change and Growth* 34 (London: Palgrave Macmillan 2001).

Bonnitcha, Jonathan, Lauge N. Skovgaard Poulsen, and Michael Waibel, *The Political Economy of the Investment Treaty Regime* (Oxford University Press, 2017) 57.

Bown, Chad P., and Joost Pauwelyn (eds.), *The Law, Economics and Politics of Retaliation in Wto Dispute Settlement* (Cambridge University Press, 2010).

Braithwaite, John, "Responsive Regulation and Developing Economies" (2006) 34 *World Development* 885.

Braithwaite, John, "Rewards and Regulation" (2002) 29(1) *Journal of Law and Society* 12, 21–22.

Broadman, Harry G., and Xiaolun Sun, "The Distribution of Foreign Direct Investment in China" (1997) 20 *The World Economy* 339, 355–59.

Brownlie, Ian, *Principles of Public International Law*, 7th edn. (Cambridge University Press, 2008).

Brummer, Chris, *Minilateralism: How Trade Alliances, Soft Law, and Financial Engineering Are Redefining Economic Statecraft* (Cambridge University Press, 2014).

Brzoska, Michael, "International Sanctions before and Beyond US Sanctions" (2015) 91(6) *International Affairs*.

Bu, Qingxiu, "Between a Rock and A Hard Place: Unreliable Entity List vis-à-vis the US Entity List" (2021) 1 *International Business Law Journal* 65–84.

Bu, Qingxiu, "China's Bocking Mechanism: The Unreliable Entity List" (2020) 19(3) *Journal of International Trade Law and Policy* 159.

Cai, Congyan, "Outward Foreign Direct Investment Protection and the Effectiveness of Chinese BIT Practice" (2006) 7(5) *Journal of World Investment & Trade* 621, 646.

Caprio, Gerard, et al., *Financial Liberalization: How Far, How Fast?* 4 (Cambridge University Press, 2001).

Casselman, Joshua W., "Note, China "Latest Threat" to the United States: The Failed CNOOC-UNOCAL Merger and Its Implications for Exon-Florio and CFIUS" (2007) 17 *Indiana International & Comparative Law Review* 155, 161–64.

Chai, Joseph C. H., and Kartik C. Roy, *Economic Reform in China and India: Development Experience in A Comparative Perspective* (Edward Elgar Publishing, 2006).

Chang, Ta-kuang, "The Making of the Chinese Bankruptcy Law: A Study in the Chinese Legislative Process" (1987) 28 *Harvard International Law Journal* 333, 336–54.

Chang-fa, Lo, Junji Nakagawa, and Tsai-fang Chen (eds.), *The Appellate Body of the Wto and Its Reform* (Springer, 2020).

Chayes, Abram, and Antonia Chayes, "Compliance without Enforcement: State Behavior Under Regulatory Treaties" (1991) 7 *Negotiation Journal* 311.

Chen, An, "Queries to the Recent ICSID Decision on Jurisdiction upon the Case of *Tza Yap Shum* v. *Republic of Peru*: Should China–Peru BIT 1994 be Applied to Hong Kong SAR under the "One Country Two Systems" Policy" (2009) 10(6) *Journal of World Investment and Trade* 829.

Chen, Chunlai, "The Liberalisation of FDI Policies and the Impacts of FDI on China's Economic Development" in Ross Garnaut, Ligang Song, and Cai Fang (eds.), *China's 40 Years of Reform and Development* (ANU Press, 2018) 612.

Chen, Huiping, "China's Innovative ISDS Mechanisms and Their Implications" (2018) 112 *American Journal of International Law* 207, 211.

Chen, Richard C., "Bilateral Investment Treaties and Domestic Institutional Reform" (2017) 55 *Columbia Journal of Transnational Law* 547, 554.

Chesney, Robert M., "National Security Fact Deference" (2009) 95 *Virginia Law Review* 1361, 1404–19, 1434.

Chi, Manjiao, and Liang Qiao, "A Skeletal Review of the Sino-U.S. 'Trade War': Contentious Issues, Trade Multilateralism and Policy Recommendations" (2020) 26(1) *Canadian Foreign Policy Journal* 99–107.

Chi, Manjiao, and Xi Wang, "The Evolution of ISA Clauses in Chinese IIAs and Its Practical Implications" (2015) 16 *Journal of World Investment and Trade* 869, 890–891.

Choudhury, Barnali, "Evolution or Devolution? Defining Fair and Equitable Treatment in International Investment Law" (2005) 6 *Journal of World Investment and Trade* 297.

Chow, Daniel C.K., "Why China Wants a Bilateral Investment Treaty with the United States" (2015) 33 *Boston University International Law Journal* 421.

Chowdhury, Anis, and Iyanatul Islam, *The Newly Industrializing Economies of East Asia* (Routledge, 1993).

Christie, George C., "What Constitutes a Taking of Property under International Law?" (1962) 28 *British Yearbook of International Law* 207.

Chu, Lynn, "The Chimera of the China Market" *The Atlantic Monthly*, October 1990, 56–78.

Cincinelli, Peter, and Domenico Piatti, "Non Performing Loans, Moral Hazard & Supervisory Authority: The Italian Banking System" in Gennaio–Giugno (2017) *Journal of Financial Management, Markets and Institutions* 5–6.

Clark, Harry L., and Jonathan W. Ware, "Limits on International Business in the Petroleum Sector: CFIUS Investment Screening, Economic Sanctions, Anti-Bribery Rules, and Other Measures" (2010) 6 *Texas Journal of Oil, Gas, and Energy Law* 75, 84–91.

Clarke, Donald C., "Economic Development and the Rights Hypothesis: The China Problem" (2003) 51 *American Journal of Comparative Law* 89.

Clarke, Donald C., "The Execution of Civil Judgments in China" in Stanley B. Lubman (ed.), *China's Legal Reforms* (Oxford University Press, 1996).

Clarke, Donald C., "Power and Politics in the Chinese Court System: The Enforcement of Civil Judgments" (1996) 10 *Columbia Journal of Asian Law* 43.

Connell, Paul, and Tian Huang, "Note, An Empirical Analysis of CFIUS: Examining Foreign Investment Regulation in the United States" (2014) 39 *Yale Journal of International Law* 131.

Corr, Christopher F., "A Survey of United States Controls on Foreign Investment and Operations: How Much is Enough?" (1993) 9 *American University Journal of International Law and Policy* 417, 456.

Correa, Carlos M., "Bilateralism in Intellectual Property: Defeating the WTO System for Access to Medicines" (2004) 36 *Case Western Reserve Journal of International Law* 79, 79–82.

Correa, Carlos M., "Investment Protection in Bilateral and Free Trade Agreements: Implications for the Granting of Compulsory Licenses" (2004) 26 *Michigan Journal of International Law* 346.

Crocker, Thomas E., "What Banks Need to Know About the Coming Debate over CFIUS, Foreign Direct Investment, and Sovereign Wealth Funds" (2008) 125 *Banking Law Journal* 457, 459–60.

Cui, Wei, Jie Cheng, and Dominika Wiesner, "Judicial Review of Government Actions in China" (2019) 1 *China Perspectives* 29–38.

Czarnecki, Łukasz, "The 2020 Foreign Investment Law of China: Confucianism and New Challenges for Social Development" (2019) 1 *Contemporary Central & East European Law* 94.

Davis, Kevin E., and Michael J. Trebilcock, "The Relationship between Law and Development: Optimists versus Skeptics" (2008) 56 *American Journal of Comparative Law* 895, at 899–901.

de Moraes Gavioli, Maira Goes, "National Security or Xenophobia: The Impact of the Foreign Investment and National Security Act ('FINSA') in Foreign Investment in the U.S." (2011) 2 *The William Mitchell Law Raza Journal* 1, 33–36.

Dernberger, Robert F., "The Chinese Search for the Path of Self-Sustained Growth in the 1980s" in *Joint Economic Committee of U.S. Congress, China Under the Four Modernizations* (U.S. Government Printing Office, 1982).

De Ruyt, Jean, "American Sanctions and European Sovereignty" (2019) 54 European Policy Brief 1–4.

Dicks, Anthony R., "Compartmentalized Law and Judicial Restraint: An Inductive View of Some Jurisdictional Barriers to Reform" in Stanley B. Lubman (ed.), *China's Legal Reform* (Oxford University Press, 1996).

Djankov, Simeon, "The Regulation of Entry" (2002) 117(1) *Quarterly Journal of Economics* 1–37.

Dodge, William, "Jurisdiction, State Immunity, and Judgments in the Restatement (Fourth) of U.S. Foreign Relations Law" (2020) 19(1) *Chinese Journal of International Law* 101, 115.

Dollar, David, and Aart Kraay, "Neither a Borrower Nor a Lender: Does China's Zero Net Foreign Asset Position Make Economic Sense?" (2006) 53(5) *Journal of Monetary Economics* 943–971.

Dolzer, Rudolf, "Fair and Equitable Treatment: A Key Standard in Investment Treaties" (2005) 39 *International Law* 87.

Dolzer, Rudolf, "Indirect Expropriation of Alien Property" (1986) 1 *ICSID Review – Foreign Investment Law Journal* 41.

Dolzer, Rudolf, and Margrete Stevens, *Bilateral Investment Treaties* (Martinus Nijhoff, The Hague, 1995).

Donnelly, Jack, "Human Rights and Human Dignity: An Analytic Critique of Non-Western Conceptions of Human Rights" (2014) 76(2) *American Political Science Review* 303–316.

Drake, Heather, "The Impact of the Trade Wars between the United States and Japan on the Future Success of the World Trade Organization" (1996) *Tulsa Journal of Comparative & International Law* 3.

Duan, Jielong, "Statement on the Rule of Law at the National and International Levels" (2007) 6(1) *Chinese Journal of International Law.*

Easterbrook, Frank H., "Detrebling Antitrust Damages" (1985) 28 *The Journal of Law and Economics* 445, 461 n.31.

Eckstein, Alexander, *China's Economic Revolution* (Cambridge University Press, 1977).

Enright, Michael J., "China's Inward Investment: Approach and Impact" in Julien Chaisse (ed.), *China's International Investment Strategy: Bilateral, Regional, and Global Law and Policy* (Oxford University Press, 2019).

Epstein, Richard A., and Amanda M. Rose, "The Regulation of Sovereign Wealth Funds: The Virtues of Going Slow" (2009) 76 *University of Chicago Law Review* 111.

Faure, Michael G., and Xinzhu Zhang, "Towards an Extraterritorial Application of the Chinese Anti-Monopoly Law that Avoids Trade Conflicts" (2013) 45(3) *George Washington International Law Review* 101–136.

Franck, Thomas M., "Legitimacy in the International System" (1998) 82 *American Journal of International Law* 705, 712.

Frankenberg, Gunter, "Critical Comparisons: Re-thinking Comparative Law" (1985) 26 *Harvard Journal of International Law* 434–440.

Freidman, David, *The Misunderstood Miracle: Industrial Development and Political Change in Japan* (Cornell University Press, 1988).

Friedman, Edward, "Theorizing the Democratization of China's Leninist State" in Arif Dirlik and Maurice Meisner (eds.), *Marxism and the Chinese Experience* (M.E. Sharpe, 1989).

Fukuyama, Francis, *Trust: The Social Virtues and the Creation of Prosperity 28* (The Free Press, 1995).

Furtado, Celso, *Development and Underdevelopment: A Structural View of the Problems of Developed and Underdeveloped Countries* (University of California Press, 1964).

Gantz, David A., "Challenges for the United States in Negotiating a BIT with China: Reconciling Reciprocal Investment Protection with Policy Concerns" (2014) 31 *Arizona Journal of International and Comparative Law* 203.

Gao, Simin, and Qianyu Wang, "The U.S. Reorganization Regime in the Chinese Mirror: Legal Transplantation and Obstructed Efficiency" (2017) 91 *American Bankruptcy Law Journal* 1.

Gardner, James A., *Legal Imperialism: American Lawyers and Foreign Aid in Latin America* (University of Wisconsin Press, 1980).

Genard, Quentin, *European Union Responses to Extraterritorial Claims by the United States: Lessons from Trade Control Cases* (Stockholm International Peace Research Institute, 2014).

Georgiev, George Stephanov, Comment, "The Reformed CFIUS Regulatory Framework: Mediating Between Continued Openness to Foreign Investment and National Security" (2008) 25 *Yale Journal on Regulation* 125.

Gilson, Ronald J., "Value Creation by Business Lawyers: Legal Skills and Asset Pricing" (1984) 94 *Yale Law Journal* 239, 243.

Ginsburg, Tom, and Gregory Shaffer, "How Does International Law Work? What Empirical Research Shows" in Peter Cane and Herbert Kritzer (eds.), *Oxford Handbook of Empirical Legal Studies* (Oxford University Press, 2010).

Gold, Thomas B., "Entrepreneurs, Multinationals and the State" in Edwin A. Winckler and Susan Greenhalgh (eds.), *Contending Approaches to the Political Economy of Taiwan* (M.E. Sharpe, 1990).

Goldstein, Judith, and Robert Gulotty, "The Globalization Crisis: Populism and the Rise of an Anti-Trade Coalition" (2019) 6(3) *European Review of International Studies* 57, 59–60.

Golumbic, Court E., and Robert Ruff III, "Leveraging the Three Core Competencies: How OFAC Licensing Optimizes Holistic Sanctions" (2013) 38 *North Carolina Journal of International Law & Competition Regulation* 729, 732–33.

Gordon, Joy, "Reconsidering Economic Sanctions" in Michael L. Gross and Tamar Meisels (eds.), *Soft War: The Ethics of Unarmed Conflict* (Cambridge University Press, 2017).

Gries, Peter Hays, *China's New Nationalism: Pride, Politics, and Diplomacy* (University of California Press, 2004).

Guan, Wenwei, "Beijing Consensus and Development Legitimacy: The Evolution of China's Foreign Direct Investment (FDI) Regime from a Law & Development Perspective" (2017) 12 *Asian Journal of Comparative Law* 115, 138, 139.

Haggard, Stephan, *Pathways from the Periphery: The Politics of Growth in the Newly Industrializing Countries* (Cornell University Press, 1990).

Harrell, Peter, Elizabeth Rosenberg, and Edoardo Saravalle "China's Use of Coercive Economic Measures" (Center for a New American Security 2018).

Harris, Tom, "The Extraterritorial Application of U.S. Export Controls: A British Perspective" (1987) 19(4) *New York University Journal of International Law and Politics* 959–72.

Hartge, Cathleen Hamel, Note, "China's National Security Review: Motivations and the Implications for Investors" (2013) 49 *Stanford Journal of International Law* 239.

He, Haibo, "How Much Progress Can Legislation Bring? The 2014 Amendment of the Administrative Litigation Law of PRC" (2018) 13(1) *University of Pennsylvania Asian Law Review* 137–190.

He, Wei Ping, "Why China's Banking Sector Remains Closed to Meaningful Foreign Competition" (2012) 27 *Journal of International Banking Law and Regulation* 186.

Heilmann, Sebastian, *Red Swan: How Unorthodox Policy Making Facilitated China's Rise* (Chinese University of Hong Kong Press, 2018).

Hessler, Kristen, "State Sovereignty as an Obstacle to International Criminal Law" in Larry May (ed.), *International Criminal Law and Philosophy* (Cambridge University Press, 2009).

Hofer, Alexandra, "The Developed/Developing Divide on Unilateral Coercive Measures: Legitimate Enforcement or Illegitimate Intervention?" (2017) 16 *Chinese Journal of International Law* 175–214.

Huang, Jie, "Challenges and Solutions for the China–US BIT Negotiations: Insights from the Recent Development of FTZs in China" (2015) 18 *Journal of International Economic Law* 307, 316.

Jadhav, Pravin, "Determinants of Foreign Direct Investment in BRICS Economies: Analysis of Economic, Institutional and Political Factor" (2012) 37 *Procedia-Social and Behavioral Sciences* 5, 12.

Jazairy, Idriss, "Unilateral Economic Sanctions, International Law, and Human Rights" (2019) 33(3) *Ethics & International Affairs* 291–302.

Jia, Shu-Xue, "On the Improvement of China's Legal System of Foreign Direct Investment" (2015) 8(4) *Journal of Politics and Law* 293.

Johnsons, Chalmers, *MITI and the Japanese Miracle: The Growth of Japanese Industrial Policy 1925–1975* (Stanford University Press, 1982).

Kaempfer, William H., "Unilateral Versus Multilateral International Sanctions: A Public Choice Perspective" (1999) 43 *International Studies Quaterly* 37–58.

Kaminski, Margot E., "The Capture of Intellectual Property Law Through the U.S. Trade Regime" (2014) 87(4) *Southern California Law Review* 979.

Karshtedt, Dmitry, "Enhancing Patent Damages" (2008) 51 *UC Davis Law Review* 1427.

Katzenberger, Paul, and Annette Kur, "TRIPs and Intellectual Property" in Friedrich Karl Beier and Gerhard Schricker (eds.), *From GATT to TRIPs: The Agreement on Trade-Related Aspects of Intellectual Property Rights* (Weinheim, 1996).

Keitner, Chimène I., "Letter to the Journal - to Litigate a Pandemic: Cases in the United States against China and the Chinese Communist Party and Foreign Sovereign Immunities" (2020) 9(2) *Chinese Journal of International Law* 229–236.

Kelman, Mark, *A Guide to Critical Legal Studies* (Harvard University Press, 1987).

Kent, Ann, *Between Freedom and Subsistence: China and Human Rights* (Oxford University Press, 1993).

King, Hugh, "The Extraterritorial Human Rights Obligations of States" (2009) 9(4) *Human Rights Law Review* 521–556.

Kittrie, Orde F., *Lawfare: Law as a Weapon of War* (Oxford Scholarship Online, 2016).

Kong, Qingjiang, "China's WTO Accession: Commitments and Implications" (2000) 3(4) *Journal of International Economic Law* 655, 675.

Kong, Qingjiang, "Towards WTO Compliance: China's Foreign Investment Regime in Transition" (2002) 3 *Journal of World Investment* 859–878.

Kriebaum, Ursula, "Illegal Investment" in Christian Klausegger et al. (eds.), *Austrian Yearbook on International Arbitration 2010* (Wien, 2010).

Krisch, Nico, "International Law in Times of Hegemony: Unequal Power and the Shaping of the International Legal Order" (2005) 16(3) *The European Journal of International Law* 369, 384.

Kueh, Y. Y., "Foreign Investment and Economic Change in China" (1992) 131 *China Quarterly* 637–690.

La Porta, Rafael, et al., "Law and Finance" (2002) 57 *Journal of Finance* 1147–1170.

La Porta, Rafael, et al., "Legal Determinants of External Finance" (1997) 52 *Journal of Finance* 1131–1150.

Lardy, Nicholas R., *The State Strikes Back: The End of Economic Reform in China?* (Peterson Institute for International Economics, January 2019).

Leal-Arcas, Rafael, "China's Attitude to Multilateralism in International Economic Law and Governance: Challenges for the World Trading System" (2010) 11(2) *Journal of World Investment & Trade* 259.

Lee, Jyh-An, "Shifting IP Battle Grounds in the U.S.-China Trade War" (2020) 43(2) *Columbia Journal of Law & Arts* 147, 158.

Lee, Y.S., "Bilateralism under the World Trade Organization" (2006) 26(2) *Northwestern Journal of International Law & Business* 357, 372.

Lee, Yong-Shik, "Weaponizing International Trade in Political Disputes: Issues Under International Economic Law and Systemic Risks" (2022) 56(3) *Journal of World Trade* 405–428, 405–407.

Lew, Julian D. M., Loukas Mistelis, and Stefan Kroll, *Comparative International Commercial Arbitration* (Kluwer Law International, 2003).

Lewis, Ian K., Mirror Zhou, and Elfie J.Y. Wang, "China Investment Policy – Ensuring the Mice Will Be Caught" (2021) 22 *Journal of Investment Compliance* 53.

Li, Xiaojun, "Durability of China's Lawmaking Process under Xi Jinping: A Tale of the Two Foreign Investment Laws" (2020) *Issues and Studies* 1.

Li, Yahong, "The Law-Making Law: A Solution to the Problems in the Chinese Legislative System" (2000) 30 *Hong Kong LJ* 120, 122.

Li, Yuwen, and Cheng Bian, "A New Dimension of Foreign Investment Law in China – Evolution and Impacts of the National Security Review System" (2016) 24 *Asia Pacific Law Review* 149, 161.

Lieberthal, Kenneth, and Michel Oksenberg, *Policy Making in China: Leaders, Structures, and Processes* (Princeton University Press, 1988).

Liese, Andrea, and Nina Reiners, "The Eye of the Beholder? The Contestation of Values and International Law" in Heike Krieger, Georg Nolte, and Andreas Zimmermann (eds.), *The International Rule of Law: Rise or Decline?* (Oxford Scholarship Online, 2019).

Lin, Tsai-Yu, "Compulsory Licenses for Access to Medicines, Expropriation and Investor-State Arbitration under Bilateral Investment Agreements: Are There Issues Beyond the TRIPS Agreement?" (2009) 40 *International Review of Intellectual Property Law* 152.

Liu, Meichen, "The New Chinese Foreign Investment Law and Its Implication on Foreign Investors" (2018) 38 *Northwestern Journal of International Law and Business* 285, 288–289.

Lubman, Stanley, "Introduction: The Future of Chinese Law" (1995) 141 *China Quarterly* 1, 3–4.

Lui, Gladie, "Shanghai Pilot Free Trade Zone: Shaping of China's Future Foreign Investment Environment" (2014) 40 *Journal of International Taxation* 31.

Luo, Danglun, K. C. Chen, and Lifan Wu, "Political Uncertainty and Firm Risk in China" (2017) 7(2) *Review of Development Finance* 85.

Mamounas, Joseph, "Controlling Foreign Ownership of U.S. Strategic Assets: The Challenge of Maintaining National Security in a Globalized and Oil Dependent World" (2007) 13 *Law and Business Review of the Americas* 381, 393.

Martí, José Luis, and Samantha Besson, "Legitimate Actors of International Law-Making: Towards a Theory of International Democratic Representation" (2018) 9(3) *Jurisprudence: An International Journal of Legal and Political Thought* 504–540.

Masseli, Markus, "The Application of Chinese Competition Law to Foreign Mergers: Lessons from the Draft New Guidelines" (2012) 3(1) *Journal of European Competition Law* 102.

Matsushita, Mitsuo, and Aya Iino, "The Blocking Legislation as a Countermeasure to the US Anti-Dumping Act of 1916: A Comparative Analysis of the EC and Japanese Damage Recovery Legislation" (2006) 40(4) *Journal of World Trade* 753–776.

Mbao, Melvin L. M., "Operation Shock and Awe: Its Implications for the Future of Multilateralism and International Law" (2004) 37(2) *Comparative and International Law Journal of Southern Africa* 253–266.

McKay, Fiona, "U.S. Unilateralism and International Crimes: The International Criminal Court and Terrorism" (2004) 36(3) *Cornell International Law Journal* 455–471.

McLachlan, Campbell, Laurence Shore, and Matthew Weiniger, *International Investment Arbitration: Substantive Principles* (Oxford University Press, 2007).

Meyer, Jeffrey A., "Second Thoughts on Secondary Sanctions" (2019) 30(3) *University of Pennsylvania Journal of International Law* 905–967.

Milanovic, Marko, "European Court Decides Al-Skeini and Al-Jedda" (2011) *EJIL:Talk! (Blog of the European Journal of International Law)*. https://www.ejiltalk.org/european-courtdecides-al-skeini-and-al-jedda/

Miller, Jonathan, "A Typology of Legal Transplants: Using Sociology, Legal History and Argentine Examples to Explain the Transplant Process" (2003) 51 *American Journal of Comparative Law* 839, 854.

Milner, Helen V., "Introduction: The Global Economy, FDI, and the Regime for Investment" (2014) 66 *World Politics* 1, 7.

Mnookin, Robert H., "Strategic Barriers to Dispute Resolution: A Comparison of Bilateral and Multilateral Negotiations" (2003) 8(1) *Harvard Negotiation Law Review* 15.

Murphy, Alexander, "Western Investment in East-Central Europe: Emerging Patterns and Implications for State Stability" (1992) 44(3) *The Professional Geographer* 249–259.

Nathan, Andrew J., and Boshu Zhang, ""A Shared Future for Mankind": Rhetoric and Reality in Chinese Foreign Policy under Xi Jinping" (2021) *Journal of Contemporary China*.

Naughton, Barry, *State Capitalism, Institutional Adaptation, and the Chinese Miracle* (Cambridge University Press, 2015).

Neagle, Anne-Marie, Andrew Fei, Richard Mazzochi, and Xiaoxue (Stella) Wang, *China's NPL Market: Implications of the China-U.S. Trade Deal* (2020). King & Wood Mallesons, https://www.kwm.com/global/en/insights/latest-thinking/chinas-npl-marketimplications-of-the-china-us-trade-deal.html.

Nedumpara, James J., and Weihuan Zhou, *Non-market Economies in the Global Trading System – The Special Case of China* (Springer, 2018).

Newcombe, Andrew, and Lluís Paradell, *Law and Practice of Investment Treaties: Standards of Treatment* (Kluwer Law International, 2009).

Newell, Ben R., Chris J. Mitchell, and Brett K. Hayes, "Getting Scarred and Winning Lotteries: Effects of Exemplar Cuing and Statistical Format on Imagining Low-Probability Events" (2008) 21 *Journal of Behavioral Decision Making* 317, 320.

North, Douglass C., *Institutions, Institutional Change and Economic Performance* (Cambridge University Press, 1990).

Packenham, Robert A., *The Dependency Movement: Scholarship and Politics in Development Studies* (Harvard University Press, 1992).

Pagnattaro, Marisa Anne, and Stephen Kim Park, "The Long Arm of Section 337: International Trade Law as A Global Business Remedy" (2015) 52 *American Business Law Journal* 4.

Patch, Colin, "A Unilateral President vs. a Multilateral Trade Organization: Ethical Implications in the Ongoing Trade War" (2019) 32(4) *Georgetown Journal of Legal Ethics* 883–902.

Peerenboom, Randall, *China's Long March Toward Rule of Law* (Cambridge University Press, 2002).

Perkams, Markus, "Piercing the Corporate Veil in International Investment Agreements" in August Reinisch and Christina Knahr (eds.), *International Investment Law in Context* (Eleven International Publishing, 2008).

Petersman, Ernst-Ulrich, "De-Fragmentation of International Economic Law through Constitutional Interpretation and Adjudication with Due Respect for Reasonable Disagreement" (2008) 6 *Loyola University of Chicago International Law Review* 209, 217.

Petsche, Markus A., "The Fork in the Road Revisited: An Attempt to Overcome the Clash between Formalistic and Pragmatic Approaches" (2019) 18 *Washington University Global Studies Law Review* 391.

Pinard, Laurie A., "United States Policy Regarding Nationalization of American Investments: the People's Republic of China's Nationalization Decree of 1950" (1984) 14 *California Western International Law Journal* 148.

Posner, Eric A., and Cass R. Sunstein, "Chevronizing *Foreign Relations Law*" (2007) 16 *Yale Law Journal* 1170.

Posner, Richard A., *Economic Analysis of Law*, 9th edn. (Wolters Kluwer, 2014).

Posner, Richard A., *Law, Pragmatism, and Democracy* (Harvard University Press, 2003).

Posner, Richard A., "Reply: The Institutional Dimension of Statutory and Constitutional Interpretation" (2003) 101 *Michigan Law Review* 952, 957.

Potter, Pitman B., *Foreign Business Law in China: Past, Progress and Future Challenges* (The 1990 Institute, 1995).

Potter, Pitman B., "Globalization and Economic Regulation in China: Selective Adaptation of Globalized Norms and Practices" (2003) 2 *Washington University Global Studies Law Review* 119, 119–150.

Puig, Sergio, "Can International Trade Law Recover? The United States-Mexico-Canada Agreement: A Glimpse into the Geoeconomic World Order" (2019) 113 *AJIL Unbound* 56, 56–7.

Purves, Bill, *Barefoot in the Boardroom: Venture and Misadventure in the People's Republic of China* (NC Press, 1991).

Pye, Lucian, *The Mandarin and the Cadre* (University of Michigan Press, 1988).

Rajan, Raghuram, *The Third Pillar: How Markets and the State Leave the Community Behind* (Penguin Press, 2019) Preface.

Ramaswamy, Muruga P., "The Impact of the New Chinese Foreign Investment Law 2019 on the Administrative Legal System Governing Foreign Investments and Implications for the Investment Relations with Lusophone Markets" (2019) 9(2) *Juridical Tribune* 330.

Reed, Lucy, Jan Paulsson, and Nigel Blackaby, *Guide to ICSID Arbitration* (Kluwer Law International, 2004).

Reich, Arie, "Bilateralism versus Multilateralism in International Economic Law: Applying the Principle of Subsidiarity" (2010) 60 *The University of Toronto Law Journal* 263–287, 265, 266.

Roberts, Anthea, Henrique Choer Moraes, and Victor Ferguson, "Towards A Geoeconomic Order in International Trade and Investment" (2019) 22(4) *Journal of International Economic Law* 655–676.

Rose, Paul, "Sovereigns as Shareholders" (2008) 87 *North Carolina Law Review* 83.

Rowe, Elizabeth A., and Daniel Mahfood, "Trade Secrets, Trade, and Extraterritoriality" (2014) 66 *Alabama Law Review* 63, 64, 66.

Roxburgh, Ronald, "The Sanction of International Law" (1920) 14(1) *American Journal of International Law* 26–37.

Ruys, Tom, and Cedric Ryngaert, "Secondary Sanctions: A Weapon out of Control? The International Legality of, and European Responses to, US Secondary Sanctions" (2020) *British Yearbook of International Law* 1–116, http://doi.org/10.1093/bybil/braa007.

Saha, Souvik, Comment, "CFIUS Now Made in China: Dueling National Security Review Frameworks as a Countermeasure to Economic Espionage in the Age of Globalization" (2012) 33 *Northwestern Journal of International Law and Business* 199.

Santoni, Giulio, "Foreign Capital in Chinese Telecommunication Companies: From the Variable Interest Entity Model to the Draft of the New Chinese Foreign Investment Law" (2018) 4 *Corporate and Financial Market Law* 589, 606–608.

Santoro, Michael A., *China 2020: How Western Business Can – and Should – Influence Social and Political Change in the Coming Debate* (Cornell University Press, 2009).

Sautman, Barry, and Yan Hairong, "Friends and Interests: China's Distinctive Links with Africa" (2007) 50(3) *African Studies Review* 75–114.

Sauvant, Karl P. (ed.), *Investing in the United States: Is the US Ready for FDI from China?* (Edward Elgar, 2010).

Sauvant, Karl P., and Huiping Chen, "A China-US Bilateral Investment Treaty: A Template for a Multilateral Framework for Investment?" (2013) 5 *Transnational Corporations Review* 1, 2.

Sauvant, Karl P., and Victor Zitian Chen, "China's Regulatory Framework for Outbound Foreign Direct Investment" (2014) 7(1) *China Economic Journal* 141–163.

Scalapino, Robert A., Seizaburo Sato and Jusuf Wanandi (eds.), *Asian Economic Development: Past and Future* (Institute of East Asian Studies, 1985).

Scalia, Antonin, "Judicial Deference to Administrative Interpretations of Law" (1989) *Duke Law Journal* 511, 511–12, 514.

Schreuer, Christoph H., "Fair and Equitable Treatment in Arbitral Practice" (2005) 6 *Journal of World Investment and Trade* 357.

Schreuer, Christoph H., *The ICSID Convention: A Commentary* (Cambridge University Press, 2001).

Schwarze, Torsten, and Jurgen Storjohann, "The Sale and Acquisition of Non-performing Loans under German Law" (2006) 21 *Journal of International Banking Law and Regulation* 77.

Seid, Sherif H., *Global Regulation of Foreign Direct Investment* (Routledge Taylor & Francis Group, 2017).

Senz, Deborah, and Hilary Charlesworth, "Building Blocks: Australia's Response to Foreign Extraterritorial Legislation" (2001) 2(1) *Melbourne Journal of International Law* 69–121.

Shackelford, Scott J., Eric L. Richards, Anjanette H. Raymond, and Amanda N. Craig, "Using BITs to Protect Bytes: Promoting Cyber Peace by Safeguarding Trade Secrets Through Bilateral Investment Treaties" (2015) 52(1) *American Business Law Journal* 1–74.

Shaffer, Gregory, and Henry Gao, "A New Chinese Economic Order" (2020) 23(3) *Journal of International Economic Law* 607, 612–13.

Shaffer, Gregory, and Terence Halliday, "With, Within and Beyond the State: The Promise and Limits of Transnational Legal Ordering" in Peer Zumbansen (ed.), *Oxford Handbook of Transnational Law* (Oxford University Press, 2017).

Shaw, Malcolm N., *International Law*, 5th edn. (Cambridge University Press, 2003) 751.

Shearer, W. Robert, "Comment, The Exon-Florio Amendment: Protectionist Legislation Susceptible to Abuse" (1993) 30 *Houston Law Review* 1729, 1732–35.

Shen, Wei, "Expropriation in Transition: Evolving Chinese Investment Treaty Practices in Local and Global Contexts" (2015) 28 *Leiden Journal of International Law* 579, 600–601.

Shen, Wei, "Is SAFE Safe Now? – Foreign Exchange Regulatory Control over Chinese Outbound and Inbound Investments and a Political Economy Analysis of Policies" (2010) 11 *The Journal of World Investment and Trade* 227, 245–250.

Shen, Wei, "Is This a Great Leap Forward? – A Comparative Review of the Investor-State Arbitration Clause in the ASEAN-China Investment Treaty: From BIT Jurisprudential and Practical Perspectives" (2010) 27 *Journal of International Arbitration* 379, 417–418.

Shen, Wei, *Shadow Banking in China: Risk, Regulation and Policy* (Edward Elgar, 2016).

Shen, Wei, "Three Paradoxes of Shadow Banking: A Political Economy Paradigm" in Shen Wei (ed.), *Conceptualizing the Regulatory Thicket: China's Financial Markets After the Global Financial Crisis* (Routledge, 2021).

Sherman, Steven J., et al., "Imagining Can Heighten or Lower the Perceived Likelihood of Contracting a Disease: The Mediating Effect of Ease of Imagery" (1985) 11 *Personality and Social Psychology Bulletin* 118.

Shi, Wei, "The Cat and Mouse Saga Continues: Understanding the US-China Trade War" (2020) 55 *Texas International Law Journal* 187, 214.

Shih, Victor, "Dealing with Non-Performing Loans: Political Constraints and Financial Policies in China" (2004) *The China Quarterly* 922.

Shirk, Susan L., *The Political Logic of Economic Reform in China* (University of California Press, 1993).

Shou, Huisheng, "Nationalism and State Legitimacy in Contemporary China" (2006) 1 *Journal of Washington Institute China Studies* 2.

Sicular, Terry, "Capital Flight and Foreign Investment: Two Tales from China and Russia" (1998) 21 *World Economy* 589–602.

Singer, Mark, *Weak States in a World of Power: The Dynamics of International Relationships* (Free Press, 1972).

Slovic, Paul, John Monahan, and Donald G. MacGregor, "Violence Risk Assessment and Risk Communication: The Effects of Using Actual Cases, Providing Instruction, and Employing Probability Versus Frequency Formats" (2000) 24 *Law and Human Behavior* 271.

Snyder, Francis G., "Law and Development in the Light of Dependency Theory" (1980) 14 *Law and Society Review* 722.

Sornarajah, M., *International Law on Foreign Investment*, 2nd edn. (Cambridge University Press, 2004).

Sparrow, Malcolm K., *The Regulatory Craft – Controlling Risks, Solving Problems, and Managing Compliance* (Brookings Institution Press, 2000).

Stapleton, Colin, Note, "The Global Colony: A Comparative Analysis of National Security-Based Foreign Investment Regimes in the Western Hemisphere" (2015) 92 *Washington University Law Review* 1647.

Stone, Alan, "The Place of Law in the Marxian Structure-Superstructure Archetype" (1985) 19(1) *Law & Society Review* 40–67.

Subedi, Surya P. (ed.), *Unilateral Sanctions in International Law* (Oxford Univesity Press, 2021).

Sunstein, Cass R., "Law and Administration After Chevron" (1990) 90 *Columbia Law Review* 2071, 2083–84.

Svensson, Jakob, "Investment, Property Rights and Political Instability: Theory and Evidence" (1998) 42 *European Economic Review* 1317–1341.

Sykes, Alan O., "Regulatory Protectionism and the Law of International Trade" (1999) 66 *University of Chicago Law Review* 1.

Tama, Jordan, "Forcing the President's Hand: How the US Congress Shapes Foreign Policy through Sanctions Legislation" (2020) *Foreign Policy Analysis* 16.

Tingley, Dustin H., et al., "The Political Economy of Inward FDI Flows: Opposition to Chinese Mergers & Acquisitions" (2015) 8 *Chinese Journal of International Law* 27.

Tipler, Christopher M., Note, "Defining 'National Security': Resolving Ambiguity in the CFIUS Regulations" (2014) 35 *University of Pennsylvania Journal of International Law* 1223.

van den Herik, Larissa, "Sidestepping the Security Council: The Use of Non-UN Sanctions for UN Purposes" (2017) 50(2) *Revue Belge de Droit International Belgian Review of International Law* 474–91.

Vandevelde, Kenneth J., *United States Investment Treaties: Policy and Practice* (Kluwer, Deventer, 1992) 143.

Wang, Bing, "Non-Performing Loan Resolution in the Context of China's Transitional Economy" in Y. Song and C. R. Ding (eds.), *Urbanization in China* (Lincoln Institute of Land Policy, 2007).

Wang, Guiguo, "China's Practice in International Investment Law: From Participation to Leadership in the World Economy" (2009) 34 *Yale Journal of International Law* 575, 577.

Wang, Heng, "The Differences Between China's Recent FTA and the TPP: A Case Study of the China-Korea FTA" in Julien Chaisse, Henry Gao, and Chang-fa Lo (eds.), *Paradigm Shift in International Economic Law Rule-Making* (Springer, 2017) 299.

Wang, Hui Yao, and Lu Miao, "China's Outbound Investment: Trends and Challenges in the Globalization of Chinese Enterprises" in Julien Chaisse (ed.), *China's International Investment Strategy: Bilateral, Regional, and Global Law and Policy* (Oxford University Press, 2019) 47.

Wanqiang, Li, "Chinese Foreign Investment Laws: A Review from the Perspective of Policy-oriented Jurisprudence" (2011) 19 *Asia Pacific Law Review* 35, 41.

Wang, Yong, "China's Domestic WTO Debate" (2000) 27 *China Business Review* 54, 56.

Werhan, Keith, "De-legalizing Administrative Law" (1996) 58 *University of Illinois Law Review* 423.

Weightman, William, "Is the Emperor Still Far Away? Centralization, Professionalization, and Uniformity in China's Intellectual Property Reforms" (2020) 19 *UIC Review of Intellectual Property* 145, 148–51.

Wei, Li, "Towards Economic Decoupling? Mapping Chinese Discourse on the China–US Trade War" (2019) 12 *The Chinese Journal of International Politics* 519, 532–533.

Weiler, T. J. Grierson (ed.), *Investment Treaty Arbitration and International Law*, Vol. 1 (JurisNet, LLC, 2008).

Wen, Yi, *The Making of an Economic Superpower: Unlocking China's Secret of Rapid Industrialization* (World Scientific Publishing, 2016).

Whyte, Martin King, "Urban China: A Civil Society in the Making?" in Arthur Lewis Rosenbaum (ed.), *State and Society in China: The Consequences of Reform* (Westview Press, 1992).

Wilber, Charles K. (ed.), *The Political Economy of Development and Underdevelopment*, 2nd edn. (Random House, 1979).

Wilber, Charles K., and James H. Weaver, "Patterns of Dependency: Income Distribution and the History of Underdevelopment" in Charles K. Wilber (ed.), *The Political Economy of Development and Underdevelopment*, 2nd edn. (Random House, 1979).

Williams, Mark, Competition Policy and Law in China, Hong Kong and Taiwan (Cambridge University Press, 2005).

Wind, Marlene, "Challenging Sovereignty? The USA and the Establishment of the International Criminal Court" (2009) 2(2) *Ethics & Global Politics* 83–108.

Woo, Jung-en, *Race to the Swift: State and Finance in Korean Industrialization* (Columbia University Press, 1991).

Woo, Margaret Y.K., "Law and Discretion in the Contemporary Chinese Courts" (1999) 8 *Pacific Rim Law & Policy Journal* 581, 584.

Wu, John C.H., "The Problem of Extraterritoriality in China" (1930) 6 *American Society of International Law Proceedings* 24.

Xiao, Jun, "How Can a Prospective China-EU BIT Contribute to Sustainable Investment: In Light of the UNCTAD Investment Policy Framework for Sustainable Development" (2015) 8 *Journal of World Energy Law and Business* 521, 525–528.

Xiao, Lin, *National Test: System Design of China (Shanghai) Pilot Free Trade Zone* (Springer, 2016).

Yah, Lim Chong, *Economic Restructuring in Singapore* (Federal Publication, 1984).

Yang, Songling, "China's Administrative Mode for Foreign Investment: From Positive List to Negative List" (2015) 33 *Singapore Law Review* 93, 96–97.

Yang, Weidong, "Can the Introduction of Administrative Reconsideration Committees Help Reform China's System of Administrative Reconsideration?" (2018) 13(1) *University of Pennsylvania Asian Law Review* 107–136.

Yeung, Karen, *Securing Compliance: A Principled Approach* (Hart Publishing, 2004).

Yin, Wei, "Challenges, Issues in China-EU Investment Agreement and the Implication on China's Domestic Reform" (2018) 26 *Asia Pacific Law Review* 170, 176–179.

Yokomizo, Dai, "Japanese Blocking Statute against the U.S. Anti-Dumping Act of 1916" (2006) 49 *Japanese Annual of International Law* 36–54.

Yoo, Christopher S., Thomas Fetzer, Shan Jiang, and Yong Huang, "Due Process in Antitrust Enforcement: Normative and Comparative Perspectives" (2021) 94 *Southern California Law Review* 843.

Yu, Danling, *Chinese Business Law* (Palgrave Macmillan, 2018).

Yu, Peter K., "The Transplant and Transformation of Intellectual Property Laws in China" in Nari Lee (ed.), *Governance of Intellectual Property Rights in China and Europe* (Edward Elgar Publishing, 2016).

Yu, Peter K., "TRIPS Enforcement and Developing Countries" (2011) 26(3) *American University International Law Review* 727, 781.

Zaring, David T., "CFIUS as a Congressional Notification Service" (2009) 83 *Southern California Law Review* 81.

Zeigler, Ann dePender, "Siberian Pipeline Dispute and the Export Administration Act: What's Left of Extraterritorial Limits and the Act of State Doctrine" (1983) 6(1) *Houston Journal of International Law* 63–92.

Zeiler, Gerold, "Jurisdiction, Competence, and Admissibility of Claims in ICSID Arbitration Proceeding" in Christina Binder et al. (eds.), *International Investment Law for the 21st Century* (Cambridge University Press, 2009) 76–91.

Zeitler, Helge Elisabeth, "The Guarantee of "Full Protection and Security" in Investment Treaties Regarding Harm Caused by Private Actors" (2005) 1 *Stockholm International Arbitration Review* 3.

Zhang, Jianhong, and He Xinming, "Economic Nationalism and Foreign Acquisition Completion: The Case of China" (2014) 23 *International Business Review* 212, 224–225.

Zhang, Mo, "Change of Regulatory Scheme: China's New Foreign Investment Law and Reshaped Legal Landscape" (2020) 37 *Pacific Basin Law Journal* 179, 181.

Zhang, Shu, "Developing China's Investor-State Arbitration Clause: Discussions in the Context of the 'Belt and Road' Initiative" in Wenhua Shan, Kimmo Nuotio, and Kangle Zhang (eds.), *Normative Readings of the Belt and Road Initiative – Road to New Paradigms* (Springer International Publishing AG, 2018).

Zhao, Min, "Analysis and Interpretation of the New Foreign Investment Law of the People's Republic of China" (2019) 2 *China and WTO Review* 351.

Zhao, Suisheng, "We Are Patriots First and Democrats Second: The Rise of Chinese Nationalism in the 1990s," in Edward Friedman, Edward McCormick, and Barrett McCormick (eds.), *What If China Doesn't Democratize? Implications for War and Peace* (ME Sharpe, 2000).

Zheng, Xinli, *China's 40 Years of Economic Reform and Development: How the Miracle Was Created* (The Commercial Press Ltd. and Springer Nature Singapore Pte Ltd., 2018).

Zheng, Yawen, "China's New Foreign Investment Law and Its Contribution Towards the Country's Development Goals" (2021) 22 *Journal of World Investment & Trade* 388, 410.

Zhou, Weihuan, Huiqin Jiang, and Qingjiang Kong, "Technology Transfer Under China's Foreign Investment Regime: Does the WTO Provide a Solution?" (2020) 54(3) *Journal of World Trade* 455, 457.

Zive, Joshua C., "Unreasonable Delays: CFIUS Reviews of Energy Transactions" (2013) 3 *Harvard Business Law Review* 169, 173–174.

Zou, Lixing, *China's Rise: Development-Oriented Finance and Sustainable Development* (World Scientific Publishing Pte. Ltd., 2014).

INDEX

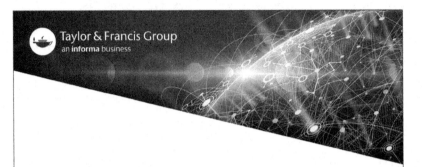